DATE DUE

THE STATE IN AFRICA:
THE POLITICS OF THE BELLY

First published in French as *L'État en Afrique.*
La politique du ventre
Translated from the French by Mary Harper,
Christopher and Elizabeth Harrison

THE STATE
IN AFRICA:
THE POLITICS
OF THE BELLY

Jean-François Bayart

Longman
London and New York

Longman Group UK Limited
Longman House, Burnt Mill,
Harlow, Essex CM20 2JE, England
and Associated Companies throughout the world.

Published in the United States of America
by Longman Publishing New York

French edition: *L'Etat en Afrique. La politique du ventre*, Librairie Arthème Fayard, 1989.

First published 1993
Second impression 1993

British Library Cataloguing-in-Publication Data

A catalogue record for this book is available from the British Library.

Library of Congress Cataloging in Publication Data

Bayart, Jean-François.
  [Etat en Afrique. English]
  The state in Africa : the politics of the belly/Jean-François Bayart.
    p. cm.
  Inclusive bibliographical references and index.
  ISBN 0-582-06422-8 (csd). – ISBN 0-582-06421-X (ppr)
  1. Africa. Sub-Saharan–Politics and government-1960- I. Title.
JQ1879.A15B3713 1993
967.03'28–dc20   92-28666
                                                                        CIP

Set by 13B in 10/12pt Bembo

Produced by Longman Singapore Publishers (Pte) Ltd.
Printed in Singapore

Contents

Foreword by Professor John Dunn   vi
Preface to the English edition   viii
Preface   xvi

Introduction   1

PART ONE: The Genesis of the State

1. The shadow Theatre of Ethnicity   41
2. The Unequal State: 'Little Men' and 'Big Men'   60
3. The Bourgeois Illusion   87
4. The Opportunity State   104

PART TWO: Scenarios in the Pursuit of Hegemony

5. Conservative Modernisation or Social Revolution? The
   Extreme Scenarios   119
6. The Reciprocal Assimilation of Elites: The Hypothesis of an
   Intermediate Scenario   150
7. The Formation of a Postcolonial Historic Bloc   180

PART THREE: Political Action

8. Entrepreneurs, Factions and Political Networks   207
9. The Politics of the Belly   228

Conclusion: Of *Terroirs* and Men   260
Notes   273
Index   360

Foreword

To write a book about the politics of half a continent is in many ways an extraordinarily ambitious undertaking. It is hard enough to understand what happens politically in a single country – at times, indeed, hard enough to understand what is happening in an individual town or a particular occupational community (a factory, a school, a university department). How can one sanely hope to comprehend such a treacherous and opaque subject matter on such a huge scale?

There is nothing about a modern professional training in the social sciences which gives even a modicum of trustworthy intellectual guidance on how to approach an undertaking of this extremity. Books that seek to comprehend politics on a continental scale (on Latin America, sub-Saharan Africa, Europe, perhaps on every genuinely continental unit except Australia: a continent which just happens to be a single state) certainly vary considerably in insight and intellectual force. But their ceiling of aspiration is understandably low and their analytical achievement and imaginative penetration for the most part correspondingly modest. University teaching requires textbooks; and textbooks are therefore produced. But, as for trying to capture the bemusing reality of the politics of the exotic in these massive dimensions, we look today not to the academy but to journalists, or novelists, or to the more imaginatively reckless and seductive of travel writers to do that for us.

Jean-François Bayart is a most unusual political scientist and *L'État en Afrique* is a most unusual book. Intensely alive to the challenge and exhilaration of any real attempt to understand somewhere so very different, he is also a thinker of great analytical power and determination. As much at home with the distanced *Annales* school vision of the starkly physical setting of human habitats over the *longue durée* as with the sundrenched immediacy and vividness of an African marketplace, he combines, in a way that no previous academic interpreter of African politics on a comparable scale has even tried to do, a feeling for the harsh material constraints within which the politics of Africa has always taken place with a wonderfully delicate ear for the rhetorical flamboyance and the scintillating social insight of the language through which it is so indefatigably expressed and carried onward. *L'État en Afrique* is an unsentimental, even at times a grim, book. But it crackles with the life of the continent it describes.

Like any serious scholar, Bayart began his work on African politics on a less overwhelming scale, with a study on *L'État au Cameroun* (Paris 1979), and has worked on Cameroon ever since. (An obvious comparison would be with the work of the distinguished English historian John Iliffe, from his two major works on what is now Tanzania to the development of capitalism in Africa or *The African Poor* on a far broader canvas.) But Bayart himself always saw the politics of Cameroon in a much wider perspective; and he has since set his mark, through the journal *Politique Africaine* which he helped to found and edited for some years, on a generation of younger French Africanists who have done much to revivify the study of African politics not merely in former francophone territories but across a much ampler terrain.

No one who reads *L'État en Afrique* with minimal attention could hope truly to understand the politics of Africa by reading a single book (or perhaps, for that matter, by living a single life). But they will be given the clearest guidance on how to begin to do so, and the most compelling sense of why doing so can be so intensely rewarding. To seek to understand the politics of anywhere is less a long journey than an endless quest. For anyone who wishes to understand the politics of Africa, there is no better book from which to start out.

John Dunn

Preface to the English edition

A brief presentation of the intellectual landscape from which *The State in Africa* derives may well be useful to the anglophone reader. Not that this book has tried to respond to particularly French preoccupations: on the contrary, insofar as it is possible, I have tried to relate my work to the totality of Africanist studies – or at least those to which my linguistic abilities gave me access – and I profited enormously from the English and American literature. Nevertheless, the problems encountered by the translating team, working with Professor Donal Cruise O'Brien, will have confirmed that my turn of mind is incurably French!

This characteristic will no doubt have been accentuated by my initial objective in writing the book. It was never my intention to attempt the impossible synthesis of everything to do with politics and the State in Africa south of the Sahara, to write a sort of 'Everything you always wanted to know about Africa but never dared to ask!' I have rather sought to construct a mode of analysis and interpretation in the hope of injecting new life into a theoretical debate which has tended to lose its way in recent years and perhaps above all to contribute to a revival of the so important empirical work without which no comparative discussion can have any sense.

I began my analysis on what is the central theme of the book, the historicity of the postcolonial State, in an earlier work *L'Etat au Cameroun,* Paris, 1979. There is now a wide consensus about this concept amongst anglophone Africanists, except naturally for those last of the radical Mohicans, neo-Marixists and neo-dependency theorists. The way in which I have explored this theme is also well known across the Channel and the Atlantic, since it is largely inspired by the historical sociology of the State dear to E. P. Thompson, Barrington Moore and Perry Anderson. In essence this means analysing the genesis of the

State, emphasising the strategies of the actors, the procedures of accumulation and the world of political make-believe which have all been vehicles for the production of social inequality. This brings us up against the big questions, which for the past twenty years have excercised the minds of Africanists, relating to the dominant class, 'straddling', factionalism and patrimonialism. Gramsci's work is sufficiently well known for readers not to be too troubled by my hypothesis that the genesis of the postcolonial State provides an example of 'passive revolution'.

The expression 'politics of the belly', which I have used to describe the politics of the postcolonial State, on the other hand needs some explanation if it is not to cause misunderstanding. First of all, I should stress that this expression (which I have borrowed from the Cameroonians) has absolutely no normative connotation: on the one hand, Africa does not of course have any monopoly on corruption and – however much the World Bank argues otherwise – I doubt that this is an explanatory factor in the economic crisis facing sub-Saharan Africa; on the other hand, not only can the expression 'politics of the belly' not be reduced to the sole aspect of corruption, but also it can just as well be used as a criticism of corruption. (This point has been explained to me by a number of connoisseurs of Cameroonian political language: to say 'The goat eats where it is tethered' also implies that it should not eat beyond this area.) Secondly, politics of the belly is not an overriding factor, similar to a more or less erratic 'political culture', for which it might be possible to substitute the idea of 'good governance'; rather it is a system of historic action whose origins must if possible be understood in the Braudelian *longue durée*. In order to conceptualise this arena – which we must emphasise is not the same as what newspapers describe trivially as 'tradition' or 'African culture' – I have made use of the notion of *gouvernementalité* which Michel Foucault began to develop towards the end of his life. This admittedly slightly complicated term should not cause undue alarm, because (at the risk of disappointing the American east coast universities!) I do not associate it with the postmodern fever sweeping through American anthropology. It seems to me to have above all the advantage of referring us to Foucault's extremely dynamic definition of power ('a set of actions upon other actions'). But as such it could be replaced without great loss by Norbert Elias' concept of 'figuration' with which the anglophone reader is perhaps more familiar and which allows us to bypass the sterile opposition between 'the individual' and 'society':

> If four people sit around a table and play cards together, they form a

figuration. Their actions are interdependent. In this case, it is still possible to bow to tradition, and to speak of the 'game' as if it had an existence of its own. It is possible to say, 'Isn't the game slow tonight?' But despite all the expressions which tend to objectify it, in this instance the course taken by the game will obviously be the outcome of the actions of a group of interdependent individuals. It has been shown that the course of the game is relatively autonomous for every single player, given that all the players are approximately equal in strength. But it does not have substance; it has no being, no existence independently of the players, as the word 'game' might suggest. Nor is the game an idea or an 'idea-type', constructed by a sociological observer through observing the separate behaviour of each individual player, abstracting the particular characteristics which several players might have in common, and deducing from them a regular pattern of individual behaviour. The 'game' is no more an abstraction than the 'players'. The same applies to the four players sitting around the table. If the term 'concrete' means anything at all, we can say that the figuration formed by the players is as concrete as the players themselves. By figuration we mean the changing pattern created by the players as a whole – not only by their intellects but by their whole selves, the totality of their dealings in their relationships with each other. It can be seen that this figuration forms a flexible lattice-work of tensions. The interdependence of the players, which is a prerequisite for their forming a figuration, may be an interdependence of allies or of opponents.[1]

In short, *The State in Africa* attempts to explore some of the pathways leading to the contemporary system of social inequality south of the Sahara, as a 'figuration' and the 'politics of the belly'. Published in French in May 1989, the book was soon tested against the real events of democracy and war. I leave it to the reader to decide how well my arguments stand up to the test. I should nonetheless very briefly like to sketch out my own views.

From 1989 most sub-Saharan African countries experienced an unprecedented wave of demands for democracy, which succeeded in bringing about the downfall of several authoritarian regimes and forced others to accept multiparty politics. Within the space of a few years the political map of the subcontinent was turned upside down. In retro-spect, the claim that "The mirages of revolution and democracy have disappeared" in Africa' (see below, p. 208) may well seem highly debatable. But less, perhaps, than it appears. We should note in the first instance, the 'external dynamics' played an essentially secondary role in the collapse of authoritarian regimes, however much a tenacious myth suggests otherwise. In particular the influence of the events of Eastern Europe on sub-Saharan Africa was more limited than is believed: for example, in Benin and in Gabon the political challenge was already strong before the fall of the Berlin wall. Moreover, opinion in the subcontinent was less influenced by this event than by the overthrow of the Ceaucescus – the most 'tropical' dictatorship of the Soviet block! – following one of the supposedly 'spontaneous' demonstrations of support for the regime which have become so familiar in Africa. In the same way, the French with their customary vanity, quickly persuaded themselves that the Franco-African conference at La Baule in June 1990 was a contributing factor in the move towards multi-party politics. The facts suggest otherwise: François Mitterrand's speech at La Baule was a tardy and ambiguous response to the unrest spreading through a growing number of countries (Benin, Gabon, Ivory coast, Zaire, Cameroon). Amongst the external factors contributing to a revival of democracy south of the Sahara, the specifically African dynamics were perhaps more decisive: the riots of October 1988 and the introduction of multi-party politics in Algeria, a country which, along with Bourguiba's Tunisia, had been one of the models of single party rule in black Africa; Nelson Mandela walking free in South Africa, a Nelson Mandela moreover who provided an alternative image of political modernity to that of a Mobutu, a Bongo or an Eyadéma (from any of whose prisons it should be said he would not have emerged alive after thirty years of being locked up); and, last but not least, the strong contagious effect of the Beninois prototype of National Conference.

However, these external events did no more than precipitate internal dynamics within sub-Saharan states, just as had happened in 1978 with the Carter doctrine in Zaire or in 1981 in Gabon with the election of François Mitterrand as President of the French Republic. The democratic fire had been smoldering for a long time and it had only been smothered by the combined efforts of the African actors of the 'passive revolution' together with their foreign partners, from the United States to the Soviet Union via France and Belgium. Demands for democracy in Africa are not exceptional and, just as with the logic of authoritarianism, they are grounded in their own historicity.

It remains to be seen if events turn out in democracy's favour. Unfortunately, I am not confident. The authoritarian regimes have managed to retain control over three precious attributes built up under more favourable circumstances: control over the security forces, which have enabled them to maintain a covert harassment of the opposition forces; control over economic rents, with which they have bought off dissident politicians and financed the creation of a multitude of small parties which have fragmented the opposition; and, finally, the support of western powers and the multilateral institutions of Bretton Woods and the Vatican who, despite having waved the flag of democratic conditionality and respect for human rights, have not dared to pursue such sentiments to their logical conclusion and have continued to think in terms of 'Mobutu or chaos' where Gorbachev had given up saying 'Ceaucescu or chaos'. Recent events in Zaire, Cameroon, Gabon and Togo, for example, all provide excellent illustrations of these three points.

The restoration of authoritarian rule has not been slow. It has been considerably helped by the weakness of the various opposition parties, prey to factional struggle and more given to fragment and allowing themselves to be bought off than to formulating governing programmes or responding to the expectations of the social outcasts of independence. This statement of course requires some qualification, and we should recognise the diversity of situations in Africa. In Zambia, a unified democratic movement led by a trade unionist and benefitting from the heritage of workers' struggles on the Copperbelt, succeeded in winning a clear majority in elections held under the watchful eyes of a determined team of international observers. In Benin, too, the transition to democracy has been relatively harmonious – the attempted poisoning of the favourite presidential candidate, Mr Soglo, notwithstanding – but the social base of the transition process has remained extremely narrow, and factional struggle has weighed even more heavily than in Zambia. In Mali, a popular uprising encouraged a military intervention which has probably denied the people its final victory: Bamako no doubt being closer to Bucharest than to Leipzig or Prague . . . In Gabon, the Ivory Coast and Cameroon election victories for the single parties have enabled heads of state to channel demands for democracy in such a way as to perpetuate their hold on power. In Zaire, a brutal scorched earth policy has up until the time of writing achieved the same result for president Mobutu. In Togo, the president who was expelled by the front door of the National Conference is biding his time before returning through the back door of universal suffrage or coup d'état.

The scenarios vary from country to country. However, it seems that on the whole the move to multiparty politics is a necessary but not sufficient condition for democracy. As we shall see in Chapter 8 of the book the most able African heads of state have for a long time understood the use they could make of competitive elections to maintain themselves in power. Today they are able to embrace multiparty politics as a way of weakening their opponents and reducing political pressure where formerly they would have consented to contested elections within the single party in order to undermine the position of the party 'barons' as in Tanzania, Kenya and – since 1980 – the Ivory Coast.

In Senegal, Senghor and then Diouf have been playing with this concept of pluralism for almost two decades, and in this sense there are no stronger advocates for multi-party politics than a Mobutu or a Biya, both of whom through the intermediary of willing placemen created several parties within the space of a few months! Understood in this way multi-party politics is nothing more than a fig leaf, covering up the continuation and even exacerbation of the politics of the belly from the prudish eye of the West. Democratic discourse can also be seen as a new type of economic rent: aid to help pay for democratisation is always good to have – witness the recent spectacle of Mobutu putting in a bid for it! – and the idiom of multi-party politics is like a pidgin language, which indigenous kings use to parley with the agents of the new world economy trade, that of structural adjustment. As institutional and ideological off-the-peg clothing, democracy may well be seen as an incarnation of the postcolonial 'passive revolution', becoming paradoxically a wheel in the 'anti-politics machine' described so well by James Ferguson[2]. In recruiting the best African intellectuals – and paying them salaries based on international pay scales whilst simultaneously enjoining African governments to pay their own civil servants less – the World Bank is pursuing this policy of cooption and contributing in a certain way to the multilateralisation of the 'passive revolution'. At bottom that is the significance of the Beninois model: a clone of the World Bank's headquarters at 1818 H Street, N W Washington DC, ruling on behalf of the holders of bureaucratic power and keeping the farmers and the urban youth at a respectable distance from the throne . . .

It cannot be assumed that the farmers and the youth will accept this situation for long. They could swell the ranks of the battalions of political entrepreneurs choosing to militarise the factional struggles. War's great advantage over simple delinquency is that it legitimises in the name of justice and the revolution the use of arms to get access to the resources of the State; it can mobilise the youth, where the single party has failed, and besides giving them bread it can provide them with an ideology, including an exaltation of martial values and recourse to witchcraft. This is how we must understand the armies of handsome young men in Liberia, Chad and Somalia with their Kalachnikovs, braided hair and amulets around their necks. The reduction of war to a mode of political production is all the more viable south of the Sahara since it is in itself a source of accumulation: it enables the collection of international aid – diplomatic, military or humanitarian; it enables the seizure of the resources of the modern economy; and it enables the adaptation to the growing criminalisation of the economy, as was proved by the financing of Unita by the smuggling of diamonds and ivory in a kind of joint venture with the South African secret services. The great achievement of Charles Taylor in Liberia was to have understood all this and to have exploited the territories he had 'liberated' before seizing hold of Monrovia, home to one of the world's biggest fleets of flags of convenience and a global centre for the laundering of drug money. The regional dimension was also exemplary: benefitting from the support of the Ivory Coast, Burkina Faso and Libya, enlisting the militant separatists of Casamance in Senegal, Gambians involved in the unsuccessful putsch of 1981 and members of the Guinean and Sierra Leonean opposition movements, his project was confronted by a regional coalition led by the Nigerian president, Babangida, whose business links with Sergeant Doe were well known. The Liberian war was thus the first example of the transfer to West Africa of the regional structures of conflict around which the Horn of Africa, Mozambique and Angola and Chad have been organised for several decades and which have now also come into play in the region of the Great Lakes. Our insistence in *The State of Africa* on the historicity of the State, on the role of political entrepreneurs and the capacity of African societies to construct their own dependency should help us to understand this evolution. I leave it to the reader to decide but I do not think that the tragic turn of events in Africa spoils my argument: war is not a negation of the State but rather, as Anthony Giddens reminds us[3], a constituent factor. I have not devoted sufficient space to this aspect of politics south of the Sahara, doubtless because at the time of writing I underestimated the potential ravages of war.

I should nonetheless like to raise one question. I have sometimes been criticised for having a very 'Cameroonian' understanding of the State in Africa and for paying undue attention to the intermediate scenario of the reciprocal assimilation of elites (Chapter 6). But this criticism ignores once again the fact that my aim was to come up with a paradigm, not a definitive description, of politics south of the Sahara. The dynamic of reciprocal assimilation is central only in its relationship to the quest for hegemony. In fact I have always attached as much plausibility to the paroxytic unravelling of factional struggle, the aggravation of hegemonic crisis, the institutional deregulation of the 'politics of the belly' and to what I have called the 'trajectories of divergence'. I have explicitly raised the hypothesis of an inversion of the scenario of reciprocal assimilation which, for example, threatens Cameroon and Kenya. I am vain enough to think that *The State in Africa* prepares the way for a comprehension of this trajectory insofar as it is intended to be a reflection on the *incompleteness* of politics, on this game of Fullness and the Space of which Chinese painters talk: 'Everywhere Fullness makes the structures visible, but the Vacuum structures the usage'. I can admit it now that in the end *The State of Africa* is less a book on Africa than an essay on the theme of Fullness and Vacuum in politics, a theoretical and comparative essay for which Africa is the pretext and provides the empirical material . . .

Paris, April 1992

Preface

One day in 1984 in the northern Cameroonian town of Garoua, Djoda, a worker in a large textile factory, woke to find his rent had been doubled. Driven by lack of money, he managed to get himself introduced to the local chief as a special representative of the President. The chief was taken in. He received Djoda with due ceremony and happily granted him a piece of land in a smart area, and then a furnished house. Following an imaginary trip to the capital, Yaoundé, and an equally imaginary conversation with the President, Djoda came back to his benefactor with the story that two members of his family had been nominated as mayor of Garoua and regional leader of the sole political party. Still fooled, the chief was unperturbed when Djoda asked him for one million CFA francs★ in order to support their nomination. Soon afterwards Djoda asked the chief to put in a good word for him with one of the rich traders to get him a free car. With success! And he even got himself a new wife before being found out.[1]

This story does not simply reveal the naivete of a barely literate chief, shaken by the year's political ups and downs. Around the same time a prisoner, who had escaped from Bafoussam prison in the west of the country, passed himself off as a member of the secret police on a special operation. He extracted large amounts of money from the town's richest businessmen with the promise of securing them high powered nominations. To convince them, he would give them telephone numbers which he claimed were those of the President's wife, and would at times have non-existent 'phone conversations with her or her aides. Ironically, he was arrested after telling the owner of the hotel *Le Président* that the President would be coming to stay there, and that the manager should hand over 100,000 CFA francs for a grand reception.

★20,000 French francs.

xvi

The bogus secret policeman undertook to see that the hotel owner was nominated for the vice-presidency of the National Assembly.

'The dignitary who believes in Father Christmas' commented the local newspapers.[2] We find ourselves here in the domain of what Michel de Certeau called 'make believe'.[3] Similar instances can be found in other African countries.[4] Such credulity, and the way in which the dignitaries concerned visualise themselves against all likelihood being promoted to responsible positions in reward for money, actually reveals a relatively astute understanding of politics. In Cameroon they talk of *la politique du ventre* – the politics of the belly. They know that 'the goat eats where it is tethered' and that those in power intend to 'eat'. When a presidential decree relieves a manager of his post, his close friends and family explain it to the villagers by saying 'They have taken his meal ticket.' A leader writer on the Cameroon Tribune observed disapprovingly, 'The most irritating thing is that the person concerned, when demoted or promoted, remains firmly convinced that his meal ticket has either been awarded or taken away.'[5] Still in Yaoundé, the word 'credit' – which is often granted by the banks on the basis of political considerations – has become '*kel di*', meaning 'go and eat'.[6] The terminology of the politics of the belly is not confined to Cameroon. Nigerians talk of 'sharing the national cake'. In East Africa, a faction is called 'kula' ('eating' in Swahili). When an observer was concerned by the 'appetite' of Guinea's ministers, the head of government replied, 'Let them get on with stuffing themselves. They'll have time to think about it afterwards'.[7]

Anyone seeking to dismiss this form of politics as no more than a symptom of corruption or of the decadence of the state is making a grave mistake. These representations can be institutional. The authors of Nigeria's draft constitution in 1976, for example, defined political power as 'the opportunity to acquire riches and prestige, to be in a position to hand out benefits in the form of jobs, contracts, gifts of money etc to relations and political allies'.[8] In general terms, 'the politics of the belly' can be applied more or less to any aspect of institutional mediation and to the 'situations' – in the Congolese sense of the term – that it engenders. It creates institutions itself in that it has directly contributed to excessive bureaucracy and bureaucratic structures. This is how an official of the Ivory Coast's single party explained the frantic attempts of the inhabitants of Kouto in the north of the country to have their town upgraded to a *sous-préfecture*:

> You know what really lies behind this business about the *sous-préfecture* are the ambitions of the local chiefs, both in Kouto and other villages. If

your village becomes a *sous-préfecture* you can be proud because everyone
looks at you and shows respect. You can do things for your village and
other villages in your area. More and more villages will vote for you in
elections since they will say that you have done much more for your area
than the other politicians, so you could become party secretary, or even a
deputy for the North, or sit in the National Assembly or get a post,
either here or in Abidjan if what you do locally gets noticed. Let's face it,
that's why we in Kouto put up a fight to become a *sous-préfecture*. When
you become a *sous-préfecture* you can relax, you can expect a much rosier
political future than someone who has no *sous-préfecture* and can't do
anything. When you become a *sous-préfecture* you can compete politically
with the other villages. It's like we say here in Kouto: better they look at
you than at others.[9]

This account might just as easily have been from Nigeria or Senegal
as from the Ivory Coast. Pressure to create new administrative districts
lies behind a good deal of social mobility south of the Sahara, and for the
men in power there is no easier way of increasing popularity than by
giving in to it.

We should be aware of the various shades of meaning in the phrase
'politics of the belly'. It refers chiefly to the food shortages which are
still so much a part of life in Africa. Getting food is often a problem, a
difficulty and a worry.[10] Yet, very often, the term 'eating' conveys
desires and practices far removed from gastronomy. Above all, it
applies to the idea of accumulation, opening up possibilities of social
mobility and enabling the holder of power to 'set himself up'. Women
are never very far from the scenario since in many ancient societies they
were the substance of wealth itself.[11] The politics of the belly are also the
politics of intimate liaisons, and mistresses are one of the cogs in the
wheel of the postcolonial State. 'Belly' also of course refers to corpulence – fashionable in men of power. It refers also to nepotism which is
still very much a social reality with considerable political consequences.
And, finally, in a rather more sinister way, it refers to the localisation of
forces of the invisible, control over which is essential for the conquest
and exercise of power: manducation can perhaps be seen as symbolic of
the dramatic, yet everyday, phenomenon of sorcery.

Finally, politics, as understood by Marcel Mauss, is a complete social
phenomenon. The condescending, sneering attitudes of the West
towards politics in Africa are fuelled by misconceptions. This book will
attempt to provide a more nuanced understanding of Africa's political
and State trajectory. Compared to the western or oriental experience of
power, Africa has its own specific trajectory, but of a strictly historically specific nature. I do not of course claim to provide an exhaustive

description of politics in sub-Saharan Africa, still less a definitive explanation: such a task, probably in any case impossible for a sub-continent
divided into thirty-six states (as against South America's thirteen or the
Far East's eighteen) would be beyond my ability. My more modest
intention is to put forward a means of reasoning and analysing and to
sketch out a model capable of helping future studies or comparisons and
to inject new life into a scientific debate which has abated somewhat
since the great theoretical discussions of the sixties and seventies.

The Method

Several of the themes developed in this book – beginning with the
theme of the true historicity of the postcolonial State and the rejection
of the dependantist articles of faith – stem directly from an earlier work,
L'État au Cameroun (Paris, Presses de la Fondation nationale des sciences
politiques, 1979). At that time I expressed my wish to conduct a more
general examination of the State in Africa. This is the result, enriched
by criticism and prepared in several intermediate articles which *Politique
africaine*, the *Revue française de science politique* and *Pouvoirs* were kind
enough to publish.[12] There is obviously no need for the reader to
consult these texts, apart perhaps from researchers taking care over
methodology. I have kept these considerations to a minimum, to avoid
exhausting the patience of the reader and in order to concentrate more
both on real political situations and on the accounts of the people
themselves. In the following pages, I shall alternate between empir-
icism and conceptualisation, albeit implicitly. This is how I have
approached my investigations throughout the last few years. On the
one hand, I have worked as often as possible in the field, in order to
collect original source material, to observe at first hand certain political
processes, and to talk to people – an indispensable source of material in
these oral cultures. However, I have also made a point of consulting the
available scientific literature, which is unfortunately too extensive to be
examined in its entirety, but which is, too, irreplaceable.

Out of gratitude for the work of my colleagues, without which this
book would not have been possible, and at the same time wishing to
allow the reader to confirm the validity of my investigations, I have
quoted my sources very comprehensively in the form of notes. However, they do not contain any other details and can be safely passed over.

In concentrating on the problematic of enunciation, and in coming to the conclusion that 'the politics of the belly' are an example of *gouverne-mentalité* ('governmentality'), a concept which interested Michel Foucault at the end of his life, I have to a certain extent highlighted the production of meanings as the production of social relationships. However, this book is a work of political science. Parting company here with Foucault,[13] I did not wish to be restricted to an analysis of régimes of statements which excluded the subject of enunciation. In line with the methodologically individualistic approach,[14] I have instead concentrated on the people involved, the social strategies and the material bases of this 'governmentality', with the aim of returning at a later date to a systematic study of the discursive genres of politics in the historical context of contemporary Africa. The problematic of the enunciation of politics , which I support,[15] is too often reduced to the presentation of stripped political discourse, whereas it should be something else entirely. One cannot separate the Word of society from the Flesh created by it. It is true that things sometimes happen in this way, and as we shall see in Chapter 9, the postcolonial State stems to a great extent from its own representation. But these two dimensions of reality are indissociable and should, as far as is possible, be seen together.

I have also avoided the distinction which is usually made between the internal political life of States and the international environment to which they belong. In contrast to a rather tedious tendency, the latter is not treated in a separate chapter, in the style of 'Africa and the world', which can be read (or not!) independently of the rest of the book. The 'external dynamics' are not really separable from the 'internal', and the postcolonial State has come about at the point where they meet. I have also preferred to refer to the international system whenever it seemed to serve my argument, in particular in the chapters dealing with extra-version (Introduction), to social stratification (Chapters 2,3 and 7) and to the hybridisation of politics (Chapter 9).

For reasons which will become clear later on, and not simply because of my ignorance, this book covers sub-Saharan Africa, but excludes some countries, mainly Sudan, Ethiopia, the islands of the Indian Ocean, the Republic of South Africa and its satellites. In practice I have concentrated more on some states than on others, either because they represent a particularly good example of a certain type of political structure or because they have been the subject of scientific study bearing on this work. These are : Senegal, Guinea, the Ivory Coast, Ghana, Nigeria, Cameroon, the Congo, Zaïre, Kenya and Tanzania, accounting for roughly 222 million people out of approximately 355 million in the whole of Africa. However the trajectory of other countries in the area does not weaken the argument, while Zimbabwe,

Zambia, Botswana, Malawi, Somalia, Liberia and, to a lesser extent, Angola and Mozambique would certainly have merited deeper examination.

As regards the spelling of proper names, I have kept, without excessive scholarship, to contemporary usage. The important thing to bear in mind is that the ethnic names are invariable.

THE PLAN

It would hardly be fair to leave the reader without a little *vade mecum*.

The introduction sets out the intellectual position of this work and defines its scope.

As soon as I became interested in the postcolonial State's own historicity, the first problem to be considered was that of its formation (Part One). Neither the concepts of ethnicity (Chapter 1) nor of social class stratification (chapters 2 and 3) seemed to me to be fruitful elements for analysis. Taking into account the historical background of the contemporary State, I decided to think rather in terms of the formation of the dominant class and the quest for hegemony (chapter 4).

In Part Two I identify the scenarios for this hegemonic quest. The two extremes of conservative modernisation and social revolution come together in a more or less pure way in situations of monarchical centralisation, lineage dispersal or in the domination of an alien minority (Chapter 5). The intermediate scenario of the reciprocal assimilation of sections of the elite appears, however, to be the most common (Chapter 6). It led us to see the postcolonial State as the matrix of a 'passive revolution' and a 'historical bloc' (Chapter 7).

However, there is the risk that one might form a conception of these processes which is too mechanistic and teleological. In reality, the strategies of the participants subject the production of the postcolonial State to various uncertainties (Part Three). These strategies are played out chiefly within the framework of personalised networks and factions, supervised by political entrepreneurs (Chapter 8). The stakes – apart from basic survival – are the accumulation of wealth and take on the form of the 'politics of the belly'; yet this can still go hand in hand with the institutionalisation of the State, albeit in a culturally hybrid way (Chapter 9).

To be specific, this kind of development is not without historical precedents. The model of 'governmentality', with its central practices of manducation and escape, leads to more generalised insights into comparative politics and on the incomplete nature of any system of power. The field is therefore open for further analysis of the discursive nature of the politics which make up the postcolonial State in Africa (Conclusion).

ACKNOWLEDGEMENTS

From its inception in 1984, this project has enjoyed financial support from the *Centre d'études et de recherches internationales de la Fondation nationale des sciences politiques*, and in addition, has benefited from the support, understanding and patience of its successive directors, Guy Hermet and Jean-Luc Domenach, and of the members of its *conseil de laboratoire*, and of Serge Hurtig, secretary-general of the FNSP. Sylvie Haas, Hélène Cohen and Nicole Percebois performed the enormous task of transforming my text from a messy manuscript to that of a typescript fit to present to the publishers Fayard. My thanks go firstly to those without whom this book would not have seen the light of day, as well as to Pierre Birnbaum and Eric Vigne, who asked me to write it.

I would also like to thank all those I cannot name, either because there are too many of them or because they have requested anonymity, who have helped with this work by discussing my theories, providing information, advising and welcoming me. It would, however, certainly not be right not to mention by name the members of the working group on popular modes of political action, the working group on political trajectories in Africa and Asia and the editorial panel of *Politique africaine* who have published and stimulated my thinking, as well as the *Centre d'études et de recherches internationales*; the staff at the *Centre de recherches, d'échanges et de documentation universitaires* (CREDU), who received me twice in Nairobi; M. Bérengier, cultural adviser to the French Embassy in Tanzania and his wife who provided me with the warmest hospitality during my stay in Dar-es-Salaam; Elizabeth and Olivier Karcher who extended me their friendship in Abidjan; the *Afrika-Studiecentrum* of the University of Leiden and the Centre of African Studies of the School of Oriental and African Studies in London, who were kind enough to discuss my approach; the governments of the Republic of Cameroon and the People's Republic of Congo who encouraged and greatly helped my research; the political and administrative staff in Senegal who united competence and liberalism in opening their archives to me; the *Centre d'étude et de documentation africaines* (CEDAF) in Brussels which granted me generous access to its library and press archives, and finally, at the risk of forgetting or embarrassing someone: Olivier Vallée, Gilles Duruflé, Pierre Meyer, Gérard Wolber, Denis Martin, Jean Bachelerie, Bernard du Chaffaut, François Gaulme, Zaki Laïdi, Comi Toulabor, Jean Coussy, Peter Geschiere, Jean-Claude Willame, Achille Mbembe, Richard Joseph, Yves-André Fauré, Jean-François Médard, Jean Copans, François Soudan, Jean-Pierre Chrétien, Donal Cruise O'Brien, John Dunn, Jean-Pierre Warnier, Anne Blancard, Christian Coulon, François Constantin and Jean-Luc Saucet, who have all, at one time or another and in one way or another, supported me.

I fear that the reader, now that he is aware of the extent of the help I have received, may expect too much. I ask for his indulgence. This work is simply an essay. I request that its imperfections and errors be seen as those of the author, and that any interest it might have be attributed to those on whom the author has leaned for help. I would feel acquitted of part of my debt towards them if my work has succeeded in contributing to a less simplistic perception of African societies.

INTRODUCTION

The Historicity of African Societies

Despite the mass of knowledge that has been accumulated over a whole century of African studies, there is still little understanding of African societies, little appreciation of the fact that they are ordinary, and (particularly) ordinary in their politics. The image of the continent which has emerged, although neither uniform nor entirely without foundation, turns out to be as ambiguous as the fantasy of the Orient denounced by Maxime Rodinson or Edward Saïd.[1]

As to the particularities of power and of the State, western public opinion is rife with stereotypes. Very often it is tainted with a racism which one might have hoped was now outdated, being slow to grasp the history of 'exotic' societies. This is the failing of those who portray the poverty of Africa and see it as the object rather than the subject of its future. Africa is variously seen as doomed, crippled, disenchanted, adrift, coveted, betrayed or strangled, always with someone to blame.[2] The French cartoonist Plantu with his usual skill conveyed this commonplace after a natural catastrophe in Cameroon, when he drew an African facing the lottery of death. The wheel turned between famine, civil war, drought, apartheid, the invasion of locusts, corruption and the AIDS epidemic. The same attitude tends to turn political science into pathology when it speaks of sub-Saharan societies as dependent, immature or morbid. This attitude also serves as a useful alibi for many Africans.

THE PARADIGM OF THE YOKE

There are some links between the reluctance to recognise African societies as historical and political entities in their own right and their subjugation by the west from the period of the slave trade to colonisation. Sir Harry H. Johnston , one of the theorists of British imperialism, doubted whether Africans had had a history before the coming of the Asian and European invaders.[3] Coloured with a sort of biblical or political mysticism, the study of migrations, or research into the origins of ethnic groups and the identification of dominant peoples dominated colonial historiography.[4]

The equation between the lack of historicity of African societies and the pathological nature of power within them nevertheless has its roots in an intellectual tradition which goes back at least as far as Aristotle. He concluded that Greeks had the right to rule over barbarians as a result of the latter's supposed servility, which was believed to help them to bear despotic power. This belief has persisted throughout the centuries and across continents. However, the key concept of despotism cannot be separated from the threat which Asia and, at one time, the Ottoman Empire posed towards the west.[5] This was not at all the case with Africa once the Europeans, who had always been a little shaky on geography, had ceased looking at the so-called 'Ethiopians' through the eyes of their imagined image of the Orient.[6] There is no doubt that as in Asia despotism was thought to be rampant: for example, in Montesquieu or Voltaire, history is seen as non-existent, time stands still. But there were no dangers other than those associated with diseases, wild animals, cannibals or the corruption of morals. Relations between Europe and black Africa were always unequal, always to the advantage of the former.

> Most of the people on the coast of Africa are savage or barbarian, they are lazy, they have no skills, they have an abundance of precious metals which they take straight from nature. All civilised peoples therefore are in a position to trade with them to their advantage. They can get them to value many things which are of no value, and get a very high price for them.[7]

The supposed excess of power in sub-Saharan societies continues to have a deep-rooted otherness in the eyes of western philosophers. These philosophers did not so much see a possible perversion of politics as a lack of politics, 'between imbecility and the beginnings of reason, that more than one nation has experienced'.[8] It was accepted that 'the race of negroes is a race that is as different from ours as the breed of Spaniels is from Greyhounds'.[a] Following in this repertoire, Hegel's

2

peremptory statement is literally paradigmatic:

> [Africa] is not interesting from the point of view of its own history, but because we see man in a state of barbarism and savagery which is preventing him from being an integral part of civilisation. Africa, as far back as history goes, has remained closed and without links with the rest of the world. It is the country of gold which is closed in on itself, the country of infancy, beyond the daylight of conscious history, wrapped in the blackness of night.[10]

The theme of the isolation of Africa from the rest of the world, and of African societies from one another, is a key one in the negation of their historicity. Montesquieu attributed their savagery and barbarism to the fact that 'countries which are almost uninhabitable dress themselves up as little countries which could be habitable [11].' This myth persisted into the nineteenth and twentieth centuries, and culminated in the motifs of the Jungle and the Desert. Captain Vallier wrote in 1900 from the depths of the Congo rainforest, 'We find here nothing but anarchy and ill-will, in other words, a society in its infancy, without any organisation, a scattering of humanity, who escape from contact with us and paralyse our most generous efforts with inertia.' Fifty years later, Governor Hubert Deschamps made a similar statement on the subject of South Cameroon:

> The jungle was once an obstacle to communications and a place of refuge to people driven back by the savanna. It seemed to be sparsely populated by tiny tribes, which were very different and which were isolated one from another by large expanses of vegetal desert. The tribes formed distinct political entities and lived by slash and burn and by shifting cultivation in the clearings, not rooted to any one place, ill-fed and, apart from a few coastal dwellers who had participated in trade, they led their traditional existence sheltered from the outside world, as if on another planet.[12]

The theme of isolation leads to a second and more basic one, that of the rape of a continent which had been closed in on itself, and is now forced to enter into general history. There was total agreement on this point between the practitioner of imperialism, Johnston, and the critics of imperialism, Hobson or Lenin. They all saw African peoples as 'the objects of outside manipulation'.[13] The historicity of sub-Saharan societies was identified with that of the western world which had made them dependent. In previous centuries Africa had only been waiting and preparing for colonisation, and, as Africans simply prostrated themselves before the colonial power, the slate of the past was wiped clean.[14] In this respect the post-war anti-colonialist intellectuals – for example, Fanon in his *Les Damnés de la terre* (The Wretched of the Earth), Sartre in his preface to Fanon or in his own *Critique de la raison dialectique* – did not distinguish themselves very much from their opponents: 'Not so long ago there were two billion inhabitants of the earth, that is 500 million men and one billion 500 million natives. The former possessed the Word and the others borrowed it. Between the former and the latter there were mercenary kingdoms, feudal barons, a false intermediary bourgeoisie.' And when the African took over his own destiny again it was seen that he rediscovered his own ahistorical innocence, 'his lost transparency'.[15] After decolonisation the image of the savage thus returned with a vengeance to the western philosophical imagination. In concentrating so fixedly on the rupture created by the formation of the State and the essential specificity of primitive societies, Marxist philosophers such as Althusser and Rancière assign these societies to metaphysics, removing them from history.[16] In doing this they become the bedfellows of writers who in other respects hold conflicting views, such as Turnbull, Jaulin, Clastres, Deleuze and Guattari, who, in a well-established literary genre, are primarily interested in the evocation of the savage as a critique of western civilisation. The salient feature of this approach is that 'history plays the role of priest for the dying' and that 'he is only called upon for the last rites, that of societies doomed to extinction by ethnocide, by westernisation or by capitalism'.[17]

In the field of political science, Africa has remained the country of gold, still in its infancy, living out its history in a tragic fashion. It is, incidentally, remarkably absent from the reasoning of the founding fathers, of the great theoreticians from Montesquieu to Hegel, from Marx to Weber, in contrast to the more or less informed attention these people gave to China, India, Japan or the Muslim powers. It wasn't until anthropology came of age that the sub-Saharan societies were fully integrated into political analysis. And there is no doubt that, thanks to the anthropologists, they have ever since held a prime position. For all that, some people remain unwilling to recognise their historicity. The tradition of atemporal ethnography, the influence of Durkheim (as opposed to Pareto and Weber) and of the structuralists were long opposed to this recognition until the diachronic dimension was rehabilitated by such scholars as Nadel, Evans-Pritchard, Leach, Balandier, Vansina or, more ambiguously, Gluckman and his colleagues in the Manchester School. In twenty years there has been immense progress in our knowledge of the past of African societies despite the prejudice met by Africanist historians from their colleagues specialising in other continents. However, it is still possible in France to

write excellent monographs on African kingdoms which completely
ignore the colonial or postcolonial State, to which such kingdoms have
belonged for a century.[18]

This is again significant because the study of African societies has yet
to be fully integrated into contemporary political studies. Following
the Second World War, political modernisation theorists attempted to
fill this gap and to free the analysis of political systems from the
prevailing spirit of parochialism.[19] They did this by a woolly uni-
versalism which quickly forgot the historical and cultural richness of
so-called Third World societies.[20] The school of dependency, to use the
questionable terminology which has entered academic parlance, originated in the observation of Latin American economic patterns. Its
application to Africa has given rise to an increase in dogma and hypocrisy
rather than to a careful study of political dynamics. Another very
important gap is in Weberian sociology of the state which, having
undergone something of a resurrection, has proudly ignored the
continent.[21]

The categories under which contemporary political thinking is organised, particularly those of democracy, authoritarianism and totalitarianism, have been drawn up, refined and discussed on the basis of
historical experiences which exclude Africa. The continent has
certainly never been at the centre of political science. The minor and
anecdotal role to which the founding fathers restricted it remains largely unchanged. It is therefore not surprising that political science is still
unable to embrace Africa's true historicity. This powerlessness arises
from several misunderstandings in the debates which have been going
on for three decades, all forming part of the paradigm of the yoke: the
yoke which western countries have imposed on African countries,
the yoke which Africa's own despots have inflicted on their people,
and the yoke which a hostile environment and obstinate tradition have
imposed on a lost continent.

Once the historicity of African societies was said to be bound up with
that of the western world, on which Africa had now become dependent, the history of African societies was easily divided with an external
periodisation. These are the only stages in the process of subjection
which are recognised as appropriate, giving some meaning to events.
The continuity of African formations over the long term has thus been
hidden, while the episodes of European penetration have taken on clear
outlines.[22] The identification of these events of course varies according
to the assumptions of individual authors. For liberal political scientists,
the colonial occupation and (more importantly) the introduction of

representative institutions provide useful dates which isolate the contemporary State from its social origins. The economists, sociologists and historians who wish to stress the integration of the continent into the world system emphasise different stages in this process by arguing that the vicissitudes of colonisation, and even of the 'false independences', are of secondary importance.

But these externally defined periodisations of the African past reflect a deeper misunderstanding, that of locating the determining dynamics of peripheral historicities. Such, almost by definition, is the major tenet of the dependency school.[23] *Almost* by definition because, as is often forgotten, the primary objective of the Latin American *dependentistas* was the understanding of the internal dynamics of the periphery.[24] Boubacar Barry defined his study of the kingdom of Senegambia in this way: 'Whatever is the importance of this external phenomenon, which constitutes a key experience for Africa, it should be regarded only as a partial explanation which can throw some light on the internal history of the Waalo.'

He quoted Nkrumah: 'We should write our history as the history of our society in all its fullness. Its history should be a reflection of its self, and contact with Europeans should only figure in it from the viewpoint of the African experience.'[25] The emphasis drifted towards the world economic system, so that the militant scion of this methodological view could see the evil hand of imperialism behind every political upheaval in the Third World. The degradation of the initial project of the dependency school was even more marked in Africa partly because it was introduced by foreign authors (Samir Amin and Walter Rodney in particular), partly because the singularly mechanistic and economistic book of André Gunder Frank was given prominence, partly also because historical research was not advanced enough at that time to counteract it. The importance which French economic anthropologists attached to indigenous modes of production articulating with the dominant capitalist mode of production, from which they deduced a theory of class alliance, served as a useful corrective. It did not, however, resist the 'dependency' tropism for long and, drawing on the totalicising thought of Althusser, it became a functionalist discussion on the scale of the international system.[26]

The rival approaches of modernisation and political development stemmed at root from a similar explicative logic. Contrary to what has sometimes been written,[27] they didn't make social change into an essentially immanent process, apart from in a very general and quasi-philosophical perspective. Far from denying external factors in Third

World societies, they discerned in their 'transitional' nature the consequences of colonial intrusion which had catapulted them onto the difficult road of modernity. National integration and the construction of the State relied on the reforming and mobilising activity of a limited number of elites, spreading the external values of universality. Almond and Powell wrote about 'the historical accident' of 'premobilised modern systems'. The existence of a 'modernised elite' and the differentiation of a 'political infrastructure' were, they argued, due to 'the impact of colonialism or to the spread of ideas and practices originating from the developed world a long time beforehand.'[28] Their view is not so different from that of David Apter, who defined 'modernisation' (as distinct from the vaguer notion of 'development') as the importation into traditional societies of new roles which stemmed from industrial society.[29]

Historicity on a world scale tends to confer exterior and recent origins on African political structures, laying the blame for their weakness on this distortion. According to the 'developmentalists', the State participated in the modern world and was opposed to the traditional world which it tried to 'penetrate' unless it was penetrated by it. Its indigenous roots were neglected or denied, and only appeared in the residual form of resistance to change. The dependency theorists went even further, to the point where they at times refused to admit that the State had any autonomy in relation to the world economic system. Citing 'the rapid growth of new local privileged classes, mainly administrative types, whose prosperity and power depend on external aid and who show no evidence of any economic dynamism', Samir Amin stated that: 'Ivoirian society has no real autonomy. It cannot be understood without reference to the European society which dominates it. The proletariat is African but the true bourgeoisie is absent, living in Europe, which provides capital and cadres.'[30] Apart from domestic predation, the puppets running the 'false independences', although occasionally granted some measure of national representation, could nourish no other ambition than letting sections of the local bourgeoisie have a nibble at the interests of the metropolitan bourgeoisie. The most powerful among them could even become regional 'outposts' of imperialism.

The debate which has grown up around the autonomy of the State in West Africa, particularly in the columns of the excellent *Review of African Political Economy*, has become more sophisticated thanks to the important fieldwork in support of the theoretical work inspired by Poulantzas and Alavi. Despite being trapped in its own economicism the debate takes as read the externality of the State while at the same time questioning the true extent of the influence of the colonial heritage.[31] For the same reasons, Marxist anthropologists have also abandoned their endogenous problematisation of contemporary political arenas, even though they have drawn attention to the repercussions within them of lineage dynamics, particularly in the case of Congo-Brazzaville.[32]

What is surprising is that, in the limited attention they have paid to Africa, historical sociologists have not diverged from this view. Transferring his interest in the analysis of postcolonial regimes to an analysis of the 'world system', Immanuel Wallerstein allied himself to the ideas of the dependency school in terms similar to those of Samir Amin: 'One of the characteristics of a peripheral zone is that the indigenous State is weak, moving from its non-existence (i.e. from its colonial existence) to a State with weak autonomy (i.e. a neo-colonial situation).'[33] Badie and Birnbaum more subtly argued that 'societies in the third world tackle the construction of the State by mimicry, by a more or less forced acceptance of exterior models originating in the industrial societies of the east or the west, artificially grafted on to economic, social and political structures which probably required a different type of organisation.' They then concluded that 'The State remains in Africa as in Asia a purely imported product, a pale imitation of the diametrically opposite European political and social systems, a foreign body, which is moreover overweight, inefficient and a source of violence.'[34]

For all concerned, the grafting of the State (the expression is widely used) has been a failure. Accounts of the different manifestations of instability and political coercion bear witness to this. The single party, the military regime, the presumed charismatic authority of the presumed 'African' chief, become the modern counterparts to the despotism of the 'bloodthirsty petty kings' against which the civilising mission of colonialism fought. The anthropologist, Murdock, attempted to construct a model of 'African despotism' drawing upon the well-known big brother of 'Oriental despotism'.[35] A consequence of the extraneity of the State, authoritarianism is seen to be unavoidable in view of the stage of development of African societies, or of their dependent entry into the world capitalist system. Bokassa and Amin Dada have come to symbolise a possible type of politics stalking the continent and threatening it at every turn. They are portrayed as being in opposition to the positive heroes, who, unless they are trying to build socialism, are attempting to construct a progressive secular city-state. The debility of political mediation reveals the disjunction of society itself. The theme runs through the work of the dependency school. The theoreticians of the articulation of modes of production have attenuated it, but they still see the peripheral social formations as a collection of bricks cemented together by the functional needs of capitalist dominance. In the eyes of the developmentalists the dichotomy between tradition and modernity led to to a series of gaps within the 'new State' which made it impossible to speak of 'political society' or 'civil society', as it was so 'profoundly heterogeneous, as much in itself as in its relationship to the State'.[36] Developmentalists were paradoxically criticised for overestimating the degree of integration of African political systems as soon as the first wave of *coups d'état* had shown the fragility of single parties and the risks of 'political decay'.[37] Anthropologists emphasised the plural nature of the societies upon which the State was built.[38] Aristide Zolberg suggested that we should distinguish between the 'modern' and 'residual' sectors within political sytems, while fortunately admitting that they were in no way mutually exclusive.[39] A few years later, Christian Coulon, substituting for these notions the ideas of a 'central political sector' and a 'peripheral political sector', rehearsed the essential premises: 'In Black Africa, total political phenomena exist only in the embryonic state [...] the new political system does not touch the entire political space of society. There is a lack of connection between political systems and social structures.'[40]

This was followed by a further cliché: that of the passivity or at least the powerlessness of subordinated social groups, 'inert' or 'indifferent', locked in tradition, illiteracy and particularism.[41] Focusing on trade rather than production (and showing themselves thereby to be closer to Ricardo and Smith than to Marx),[42] the dependency school transposed this idea onto a world scale. They thus opened the way to a sociology of domination which could see the process of assimilation as a form of brainwashing, describing it in terms more often associated with meta-anthropologists, bullying perpetrators of ethnocide and tearful poets bewailing the 'last Africans'. The representations and strategies of subordinated social groups that were analysed, often in detail, continued to refer to logical structures of power, as was argued in the course of a rich debate devoted to the practices of the invisible.[43] In any case, they seemed to be somewhat irrelevant with regard to that pitiless *deus ex machina*, the capitalist mode of production, so reluctant were they to resolve their contradictions in a revolutionary problematic conforming to the Marxist-Leninist canon.

The link between the classical philosophical allegories and the modern scientific images of an ahistorical Africa, bowed under the weight of oppression, has not come about merely by an identical reproduction of the fantasies of the eighteenth or nineteenth century. As a result of some very difficult, thankless and sometimes dangerous work our understanding of sub-Saharan societies has taken giant strides forward. Where would it be without the first ethnographic studies, often written by colonial administrators? Without the work of historians, sociologists and anthropologists who decade after decade applied themselves to understanding the changes the continent was undergoing? Without the written frescoes of the emerging political systems by structural functionalist authors? And without the Marxist analysis of the processes of domination and exploitation in social structures which had hitherto been represented as primitive and consensual? Without the sometimes modest chronicles (unfortunately too few and far between) kept by journalists and more or less illustrious political actors? In all their richness, the sources we rely on show that there is no one single paradigm of western discourse on Africa denying any acknowledgement of its historicity. 'It's easy to speak of superior races,' said Clemenceau at the end of the nineteenth century, when discussing the colonial lobby in metropolitan French politics (*parti colonial*). 'For my part, I particularly condemn it, since I saw German scientists scientifically proving that France should be conquered in the Franco-German war, because the Frenchman is of an inferior race to the German. Since that time I must admit that I think twice before I turn to a man or a civilisation and declare: "Here is an inferior man or race".'[44] A half century later the erudite Governor Deschamps regretted that French school curricula only represented the African peoples 'within the perspective of colonial conquest as an episode in our military history'.[45] There remains a recalcitrance in thinking about the historicity of African societies, whose influence should not be underestimated as it is found in the work of some of the most knowledgeable authors.

TOWARDS A HISTORICAL SOCIOLOGY OF ACTION

Thus this latent Africanist syntax does not stand up to the examination of facts. Not that the phenomena of dependence and domination, constant themes in the historicity of the continent, can be denied. The Cameroonian philosopher Eboussi Boulaga warned that, 'What is most important for the Muntu* is neither astonishment nor wonder but a stupor caused by total defeat'.[46] But it is important to see this 'total defeat' aside from the paradigm of the yoke. We could refute this point

---

**Muntu:* Human Being, Man (here, African)

by point. The easiest objection, if not the most honest intellectually, would be that none of the forecasts made by the developmentalists and the dependency theorists, however supported by scientific arguments, has actually come to pass. Africa has avoided both growth and revolution. Bearing the marks of teleological evolutionism, the two approaches taken by the academic world following independence were closely linked to the praxis of the postcolonial state as a 'well-policed state' (*policeystaat*), supreme architect of modernity, in this respect close in its philosophy to the monarchies of central Europe of the seventeenth and eighteenth centuries, more a direct descendant of the colonial administration and its dreams of planned economic exploitation (*mise en valeur*). The 1980s have witnessed the final failure of the 'socialist' and 'capitalist' reworkings of this voluntarist conception of 'development', along with their attempts to restructure the world economic system.

Apart from committing the injustice of condemning many interesting works for their initial premises, this polemical rejection misses the most important point. With the advantage of hindsight it is easy to make fun of the naiveties of the developmentalists: under the patronage of the 'non-communist manifesto' of W. W. Rostow they expressed the avowed hope of formulating 'strategies of political investment'; as criteria of modernity they identified structural differentiation and secularisation associated with the historical trajectories of western countries and, undaunted, concluded that Anglo-American societies were the nearest to the model of political democracy.[47] But it is more useful to ask how they arrived at such aberrations when they wished explicitly to escape from the normative definitions of authoritarianism and totalitarianism which were in vogue between the two world wars.[48] The many errors of economic reasoning in dependantist economicism, which it is now unnecessary to criticise in detail, similarly should not conceal a more deep-rooted error of method.

Both groups, led astray by their structuralist precepts, invoked explanatory categories which, thanks to their lack of historical consideration, shared a fictional coherence. This is also the case with the idea of 'tradition', which we now know to have been largely invented first by the coloniser and then by local social groups who hoped to gain some advantage from domination.[49] Philosophers have demonstrated how making the continent dependent involved attributing to 'African culture' and to 'ethnic cultures' this fictive unity which led to their subordination, folklorisation and reification. Such representations express an attempt on the part of the foreign invader to confiscate social change and modernity, before possibly instituting a crititical and mobilising Utopia.[50]

11

In fact, tradition was neither monolithic, immobile nor closed. These ideas in all illiterate societies are linked to the contextual circumstances of their enunciation more than to a programme of beliefs which were impossible to depict graphically; they are, therefore, subject to constant variation.[51] Also, contemporary social actors constantly straddled the arbitrarily circumscribed sectors of tradition and modernity. It is doubtful that they have a clear awareness of their limits: the attachment that the city dweller retains with his original rural background leads one to think the opposite. The urban Bamileke participates in the life of his chiefdom with all that that implies in terms of his physical presence at meetings and in financial expenditure. His social success is not complete if it is not accompanied by holding a title in one of the societies of notables. He contributes to the development work in his area, which he frequently initiates, and in the course of constant travel and trade, he spreads models of new ways of eating, living and dressing. In the cocoa-producing south of Cameroon, the habit of returning to the villages on retirement suggests that the move towards city dwelling is not irreversible, contrary to what we might infer from the dramatic concept of rural exodus. As a corollary, there is more and more talk of 'ruralisation' in the cities as the intermediate situations of urbanisation in the Kikuyu district of Kenya or the Yoruba country of Nigeria make it increasingly difficult to identify a geographical sphere of tradition.[52] In such circumstances the members of African societies pursue family, therapeutic, economic or political strategies which transcend the usual divisions to which we try to assign them. Someone who is ill will consult, one after another, the doctor in an Abidjan hospital, the faith healer in the suburbs and the witch doctor in his village because he simultaneously inhabits these different worlds. Similar 'itineraries' in the social sphere, to employ an expression used by medical sociologists, reveal a level of cultural integration and flexibility which contradict the dichotomic categories of which the developmentalists are so fond.

The capitalist world system never had the cohesion that the dependency interpretations gave it. As a structure it has not been intangible, for example, from the slave period to the 'legitimate commerce', at the beginning of the nineteenth century or to the depression of the 1870s and then the military expansion of Europe. Although brief, colonisation went through substantial changes, as, for example, during the 'second occupation' with an intensification of the harnessing of the local productive forces, in response to the great economic crisis of the 1930s and to its threat to the tax revenue of the European possesions.[53] And since they were clearly a result of history, the forms of subjection and exploitation on the African continent were riddled with fractures which cannot be blamed upon the overarching nature of the capitalist system. As early as the aftermath of the Second World War, one French employers' newspaper supported the thesis of a planned and fake decolonisation in the interests of the capitalist mode of production: 'It is better to change the name and keep the thing as it is.'[54] The paper was displaying both cynicism and economic far-sightedness: the figures bear it out forty years later, when French capitalism is suffering more from the remnants of its empire than from that empire's disappearance.[55] But whatever the reader of *Tricontinental* might have thought, it still did not provide proof of a conspiracy between the business community and the metropolitian political power – a conspiracy, moreover, whose existence has never been demonstrated. In the case of France, cooperation between the two spheres was, on the contrary, difficult. There was a 'divorce' from the 1930s onwards which made the process of decolonisation particularly laborious. As for the steps to be taken, the business community was divided along shifting lines, and the most committed overseas companies did not constitute in the business world a 'colonial party' in the sense in which Ageron identifies it in the political class.[56] The 'third empire' of Portugal was no better at responding to the functional demands of lusophone capitalism; the gulf between its growing insertion in the west European economy and the authoritarian stiffening of the Salazar regime prevented it even from keeping the neo-colonial influence it had managed to achieve in Brazil in the nineteenth century.[57]

The contradictions between the key players of colonialism were even more acute within African societies. Kenya is a prime example. From the First World War to the declaration of independence, the British administration and the settlers, who disagreed over economic issues and the political status of the blacks and Asians, were also in dispute over control of the territory. The administration, furthermore, had little time for the zeal with which the Protestant missionaries were combating the practice of female circumcision. But the settlers, for their part, did not make up a homogeneous community. Those who lived on the coast or in the towns were politically more moderate than the farmers in the Highlands, and the businessmen and the biggest planters understood in the 1950s the need to compromise with the nationalist movement.[58] The institutionalisation of racial segregation in the Republic of South Africa and the unilateral declaration of independence in Rhodesia give an indication of the stakes involved with such cleavages. The evidence points to their being traceable back to diverse, indeed diverging, economic interests. In trying to understand how the political trajectories differed from one territory to another, it is significant, for example, that the dominant group of whites installed in Kenya were from a social class which was higher than that of the whites in South Africa, and that they had kept firmer links with British society. In other words, a political sociology (indeed, a straightforward sociology) of the actors in colonisation, which has been neglected for too long, would add a much-needed nuance to the theses of economicist functionalism.[59]

Dependency is much more a process than a structure. Its chronology, geography, demographic and institutional modalities, together with the bitter inter-European rivalries punctuating it, have all had their effect. It is particularly important in trying to understand the present to bear in mind how old certain European presences are, the complex layers of their successive influences, in contrast to areas which were occupied and culturalised more recently. Senegambia, the Gold Coast, the Niger delta, the Zaïre delta, and the Mombasa coast had all been visited over a period of three or four centuries by Europeans by the time the Germans penetrated the South Cameroon rainforest and began their move up to Grassfields between 1880 and 1890. Huge areas of the continent (including the Angolan hinterland, allegedly colonised a very long time ago) experienced no more than five or six decades of European presence, whereas elsewhere European communities of *lançados, pombeiros* and *prazeiros* survived the dismantling of the first Portuguese Empire, in common with many mixed-race areas including the Dutch colony in the Cape, founded in 1652, whose subsequent history is well known. These diachronic disparities have a great deal of influence on attitudes towards the west, as F. Gaulme points out so well in connection with the Mpongwé of Gabon.[60] The vicissitudes of the conquest and the modalities of colonial economic exploitation make up the genes of the contemporary state. The variations in the different types of administration (British, French, Portuguese, German or Belgian, and also Italian and Spanish) have been much discussed – and exaggerated. In fact, an imperial power such as France applied varying forms of government, including the notorious indirect rule which it favoured much more than mythology allows. In its colonies in Equatorial Africa it inflicted the trauma of company rule (which Gide made infamous) but spared this on its West African possessions. The variation in the colonial impact is therefore more complex than is often thought. A notable example of this is the singular nature of the Cameroonian nationalist movement, and the specificity of the country's juridical status resulting from the variety of colonial experiences (German, then French and English).[61] Quite apart from those countries which which escaped colonisation altogether, such as Liberia and Ethiopia,

African countries progressed to modern international sovereignty from a heterogeneous institutional and administrative past, which should have dissuaded people from treating them as an undifferentiated periphery of the capitalist centre.

Structural determinants of recent political evolution in Africa have been mediated by situations and strategies which must be taken into account. The error of the 1960s and 1970s was to ignore both the lessons of history and also the precepts of an indispensable 'theory of action'.[62] This consisted, first, of being unaware that the 'traditional' nature of African societies stemmed from an optical illusion supported by ethnology:

> African social and cultural 'fabric' has never been inert: it has constantly been producing black societies and cultures, with internal dynamics as well as those resulting from their relations with the 'environment', [...] it becomes impossible to ignore the fact that all African societies have stood up to the tests of history.'[63]

As such, they were debating societies in the sense in which Moses Finley speaks of the Greek city to which, at least in certain respects, they were roughly comparable.[64] They were far from being all either 'despotisms' or indeed 'democracies'. They displayed subtle interactions between the circles of domination and subjection which, to begin with at least, encourage us to reject the facile idea of archaic totalitarianisms, whether structural, symbolic or ideological. In his study of one of the twenty Mossi kingdoms, Izard uses the felicitous phrase 'metabolism of predation', and says: 'It is a strange universe where the respect due to the chief coexists with the firm – and often humorous – intention of escaping as far as possible from an onerous authority whilst knowing just how far it is possible to go'.[65] Deliberation (more or less institutionalised according to the degree of structural differentiation of power, and designed to promote the union of the group rather than expose rifts) was inherent in the exercise of authority. We have some arresting descriptions of the conclaves of the 'excellents' in the holy monarchy of the Moundang which are counterbalanced by a second college stemming from the royal power. The two courts which assist the monarch do not strictly speaking hold power but they express the division of sovereignty within the clan itself 'between the king as a "being outside the clan" and the clans as "masters of the land"'.[66]

The interplay of debates, compromises and resistances within ancient societies refer to their 'engenderment', as Georges Balandier vigorously emphasised. The split between stateless and state societies, magnified by the classic work of Fortes and Evans-Pritchard, has thus now been relativised and freed of its possible evolutionist connotations. The passage to the State is neither in any way inevitable (the Igbo in the east of Nigeria have adopted another type of political organisation, in spite of their degree of economic development and their entry into a prosperous commercial space), nor irreversible (the Kongo kingdoms and the Mandingo Empire in Mali have given way to segmentary societies). These oscillations are cumulative and belong to the *longue durée*. The Bamoum kingdom in Cameroon thus developed within a lineage coextensive to the society, and continues to make use of its political procedures. The Kotokoli at the centre of Togo moved in two centuries from being an 'acephalous' kingdom to a chiefdom then to a kingdom: at each stage the lineage organisation was maintained within the framework of the new political construction by fulfilling other functions. Nor, on the other hand, did the dissolution of the Mandingo empire and its political contraction around the traditional *kafu* lead to the disappearance of imperial representations, which continued to play a role in the reorganisation of substitute local political structures and in the perpetuation of expansionist projects up to the rise of Samori in the nineteenth century.[67] Neither lineage nor statist concepts seem to correspond to uniform political configurations. In their discussion of Africa the French Marxist anthropologists paradoxically advanced the hypothesis of a lineage mode of production, at the time when the notion of lineage was attracting growing scepticism; the monographs of segmentary societies* provide evidence of the great diversity of situations covered by this category.[68] Furthermore, the idea of the State, which is highly debatable as a term for most of the monarchies of the continent, has many forms which have changed with time. The successive changes in the Asanti are illustrative here, from the model of the holy Akan monarchy to the 'bureaucratic revolution' undertaken by Osei Kwadwo at the end of the eighteenth century, then to the institutionalisation of constitutional and quasi-republican monarchy during the nineteenth century.[69]

Centralised societies did not (and do not) have any monopoly on political innovation. They were indeed the ones which elaborated the most global and perhaps the most noticeable projects for social renewal.

---

*Following a section of the ethnographic literature, throughout this work we shall use the term 'segmentary society' as a synonym of lineage society in order to designate the ensemble of acephalous societies which are characterised by a diffused rather than centralised or statist power. In reality we ought also to distinguish within acephalous societies true segmentary societies in the strict sense of the concept, of which the Tiv and the Nuer afford the classic examples.

The most consistent attempts at 'authoritarian modernisation' – if that semi-anachronism can be forgiven – seem to have been those of the Imerina, Ethiopian and Bamoum monarchies in the nineteenth century.[*] In their principles and motivations such modernising experiences seem to be similar to those undertaken, under the pressure of western European imperialism, by Russia, Japan, Siam, the Ottoman Empire and Egypt. But they should not obscure the powerlessness of the biggest African States, such as the Sokoto caliphate, Buganda, Bunyoro, Asanti or Benin, to rise to the challenge in productive terms. And in any case, when it came to territorial conflict, the invention of the repeater rifle, steam power, quinine and the telegraph helped to ensure that Europe's military superiority was decisive.[70] Lineage societies were equally open to the winds of change, and profited by their flexibility. On the Mouyondzi plateau in the Congo, the peacekeeping efforts of a Mwa Bukulu, in the second half of the nineteenth century, began the political construction of the Beembe country and the birth of a society which was beginning to discover markets and was noted for its strong agriculture.[71] In the Sahelian belt, the hill-dwelling people (frequently classified as paleo-nigritic) were able to respond to demographic pressure by introducing intensive agriculture and by 'active conservatism'.[72] Lineage societies (and particularly segmentary societies in the strict sense of the phrase) consequently retained in colonial and postcolonial times this ability to accommodate the demands of the State, in a unitary and dynamic way, as they had done within the precolonial monarchies.[73]

In spite of Africa's unequal relationship not only with the west, but also in a much earlier period with the Arab and Asian worlds – a point which the dependantists generally ignore – the production of African societies did not respond, in a peripheral way, to external determinations. Africa certainly felt the changes in the European world economy, in particular the shifting of its axis from the Mediterranean to the Atlantic.[74] These changes did not, however, have the influence attributed to them, and in so far as the influence was real it was not simple. The slave trade, which seems to have encouraged political centralisation on the coast of West Africa, appears to have had the opposite effect further south, on the coast of Central Africa. The effect of the European presence in the structuring of the city states in the Niger delta has

---

[*]Some earlier examples should, however, not be ignored. These include the notorious precedent of the Kongo in the fifteenth and sixteenth centuries, the 'bureaucratic revolutions' of Oba Ewuare in Benin in the fifteenth century and of the Kwadwoa in Ashante in the eighteenth century as well as the essentially military reforms of Samori, Shaka, Rabeh, Behanzin and Mirambo.

probably been overestimated, and in any case does not explain the formation of a monarchy in the Nkomi of Gabon, prior to the arrival of the Portuguese. The Yoruba wars which were the final blow to the regional supremacy of Oyo, the *jihad* which sealed the hegemony of the Fulani in the north of Nigeria and Cameroon, or the Mfecane which led to the creation of a series of states in East Africa, similarly were not caused by growing European pressure. Between the 1860s and 1880s, the Samori episode had more to do with the contingencies of Malinke internal rivalries, than with the tightening of the Franco-British vice. Many economic areas did not participate in trade with the west, such as the east of Nigeria, or, especially in the central Sudan, where the salt market was not really affected by capitalist expansion before the final years of the century.[75]

Relations with the external environment were, however, inseparable from the production of politics. After Edmund Leach had shown this to be true in the case of the Kachin of Burma and Georges Balandier had confirmed it with the help of African sources, many anthropological studies have facilitated a closer understanding of the overlapping between the internal and external dynamics.[76] They prevent us from presenting ancient societies as monoliths withdrawn into themselves, in line with the old myths of their isolation. Africa has always been open to trade with the rest of the world, particularly as an exporter of gold, slaves and ivory. The survival of Christianity in Ethiopia; the spreading of Islam on the coast; the installation of Indonesian colonies in Madagascar; regular trade with India, the Persian Gulf and the Mediterranean, all revealed the centuries-old integration of West and East Africa into the pre-modern world economies. It was, after all, in East African ports at the end of the fifteenth century that the Portuguese found pilots who were to help them to cross the Indian Ocean and establish alternatives to the ancient trade routes between Asia and Europe.[77] The Sahara was not that 'ocean of sand and desolation' to which James Coleman attributed the so-called 'isolation' of black Africa.[78] Criss-crossed with caravan routes and a patchwork of tribal and brotherhood networks, a vehicle for Islam and link between the gold-producing Akan States and the Mediterranean markets, it was the geographical axis for political areas which were sufficiently vigorous to enjoy a resurgence after the colonial period. As early as the fifteenth century the Portuguese aimed to double the trans-Saharan trade which was controlled by their Arab rivals, using the west Atlantic coast. They also established bases for regular maritime trade before being supplanted by the Dutch, the British and the French. Both the transatlantic slave trade and 'legitimate trade' increased, and tragically diversified the entry of black Africa into the world system. An African-Atlantic arena was created helped by progress in navigation, with the creole communities as the regional axes. The annexation of sub-Saharan societies to the western world economy was thus more complex than is at first suggested by their colonial involvement with the metropoles which later conquered them. Angola was, of course, an exception: its racial mix reflected the multi-continental lusophone empire, in the nineteenth century it traded more with Brazil than with Portugal, and it attracted international capital on a scale unknown elsewhere before the Second World War.[79] But this only heightened the multi-lateral character that black Africa's dependence always had and which was to be further complicated by Asian and Syrian-Lebanese immigration. The later penetration of Japan or the United States, which worried the European powers from the inter-war years on, can thus be seen as being no more than a phase in the old mercantilist rivalries of the sixteenth and seventeenth centuries, or the imperialist clashes of the nineteenth. As such it confirms Africa as a continent within the world.

On the other hand, the interior of the countries was in no way compartmentalised. It was structured into economic areas – commercial, monetary and productive – into political or military areas and into cultural, linguistic and religious areas. It was irrigated by permanent currents of which long distance trade and demographic movements – too often dismissed as 'migrations' – were the most visible signs.[80] One should have no illusions about the network of perfectly maintained highways which radiated around Kumasi and formed the spine of the Asante confederation.[81] Communications were most of the time difficult and hazardous. But whatever difficulties it posed to the circulation of men and goods, the equatorial forest did not prevent all movement, nor did the dispersion of its population inhibit trade. Amongst the Beti of south Cameroon, the *nkul*, the tam-tam telephone, which had a range of 3 or 4 kilometres, sometimes more, 'spoke' continuously and relayed the most important information over dozens of kilometres. (In September 1945, it transmitted the news of the riots in Douala from village to village as far as Yaoundé in a matter of hours).[82] The attraction of fabulous wealth which the peoples of the interior knew could be traded for 'further to the west', led not just to considerable political upsets in these regions (which the colonial administrative divisions attempted to control with limited success) but also to an 'extraordinary mingling of clans', so characteristic of the human geography of south Cameroon.[83] The intensity of inter-societal linkages across the continent and their organic relationship to the internal configuration of ancient political formations lead anthropologists and historians to emphasise the existence of a truly 'international area', of 'chains of societies' and 'symplectic relations'.[84] Within these regional aggregates there were inequalities, favouring the statist and warrior societies, which were themselves very hierarchical and which sometimes included peasant societies, forcing them back into the mountainous areas. The kingdoms of Oyo and Dahomey, Bornou and the caliphate of Sokoto, the Asante and the sultanate of Zanzibar are well-known examples of such dominating States. Their changing fortunes show that the formation of these regional complexes was not fixed in time, although they became well-established in the *longue durée* of landscapes and the localisation of productive activities.[85]

HISTORICITY WITHIN EXTRAVERSION

The vitality of these regional areas and the depths of their historical roots – two phenomena which have been obscured by the exogenous periodisation of the past – leads to an observation of great significance to our argument. These societies have never been and, even after their military defeat, could never have been the passive objects of a process of dependency. Colonisation did not radically weaken their ability to pursue their own strategies to produce their own modernity. As with any other historical process, it could lead to the destruction or the reduction of certain of them. Africa did not, however, have to wait for the arrival of the Europeans before it witnessed the disappearance or weakening of its communities through conquest, economic decline, cultural assimilation, demographic weakening or ecological disaster. Some societies were naturally better than others at exploiting foreign occupation, and their comparison from this point of view has become a favourite approach of anthropology since Balandier's classic study . In his *Sociologie actuelle de l'Afrique noire*, whilst insisting on the ability of the Fang of Gabon to 'retake the initiative' through the *alar ayôg* movement for clan reconstruction, Balandier emphasised the more efficient resistance within the baKongo group as a whole, which he tried to explain by, amongst other factors, the long history of trade with the west and by its urban traditions.[86] In the same vein, G. Dupré recently drew a parallel between the acclimatisation of the Beembe region to the contemporary economy and the destruction of the Nzabi order under the colonial shock.[87] Pregnant with physical and, perhaps even more, symbolic violence, the colonial situation did not suspend the historicity of African societies. Rather, it was a new development, albeit one in which the cards had been energetically reshuffled. Beneath the totalitarian universe that it tended towards (and that in Southern Africa it approached) one finds social strategies, with a logic of their own which belong squarely to the indigenous timescale.[88] The best historians now believe that these dynamics have had more effect on the development of colonisation than the functional necessities of the cap-italist mode of production.[89] And with the exception of the Republic of South Africa, the salient feature of the last three centuries is not the growing integration of Africa into the western world economy but, on the contrary, the latter's inability to pull the continent into its magnetic field.[90]

Agricultural revolutions, accompanying the stages of the process of dependency, certainly occurred. They were, however, the result of African innovations rather than a response to the external factors stressed by the dependency and development theorists. In their study of the Ivory Coast, Chauveau and Dozon have confirmed what numerous studies of the cocoa planters of the Gold Coast and Nigeria have also shown, that 'the development of the plantation economy stems from largely independent socio-economic processes' and that it exceeded, even subverted, the colonial plan for economic development.[91] In his analysis of Kenya, Cowen reached a similar conclusion, that the multi-faceted State intervention in Kenyan agriculture probably held back the accumulation of agrarian capital in a context of otherwise remarkable expansion.[92] It is significant that the European planters thought it necessary to obtain from the colonial authorities a quasi-monopoly over the cultivation of the most profitable crops: indeed, the repeal of these discriminatory and Malthusian provisions – a natural demand of the burgeoning nationalist movements in the inter-war years – resulted in an explosion in production.[93] But in spite of the agricultural booms which made some areas into great exporters, the African peasantry resisted the 'second colonial occupation' promoted by the metropoles in the forties and fifties.[94] It did not allow itself to be 'captured', to use Hyden's attractive phrase, in the same way as in the past it had demon-strated its historical ability to resist the extraction of a surplus from its productive activities.[95]

We have put a finger on the major problem that black Africa poses to conceptual apparatuses constructed from western historical experi-ences. The leading actors in sub-Saharan societies have tended to com-pensate for their difficulties in the autonomisation of their power and in intensifying the exploitation of their dependants by deliberate recourse to the strategies of extraversion, mobilising resources derived from their (possibly unequal) relationship with the external environment.[96] This recurring phenomenon in the history of the continent results not just from the weak development of its productive forces, comparative to Asia and Europe, but also – and the two factors are probably inextricably linked – from the bitterness of its internal social struggles. Subordinate groups contributed to the production of ancient societies, notwithstanding the harshness of the machinery of subjection. They had first of all the weapon of mobility, made possible by the availability of land and the simplicity of agrarian technologies, and which the powerful feared wherever their influence was calculated by the number of people under their authority. Hirschman very astutely noted how much the 'exit option', which prevailed in acephalous societies, in the form of the institutionalised secession of clans and lineages, held back the emergence of centralised States.[97] It also strengthened the negotiating hand of subordinate groups, including those within State societies. It offered a perilous but realistic escape from the excessive demands of the dominating class. 'Emigration will always be a fact of life,' the editors of *Histoire et coutumes des Bamoum* admitted philosophically.[98] Anthropologists and historians are unanimous in recognising the widespread nature of escape routes in ancient and colonial Africa. These, however, did not exclude other modes of political action, in the registers of conflictual participation, ideological enunciation or of symbolic struggle. The domain of the invisible and its associated sorcery, together with the manipulations of genealogies, have always been major areas of social antagonism. The dependants were not without a voice within either lineage or centralised societies. They were (more or less) represented in a range of councils, associations and societies in which they often had important functions. One author estimates that over a third of the monarchies and the chiefdoms he investigated included councils of commoners who were involved in political decision-making and that more than three-quarters of the chiefdoms, and the quasi-totality of the monarchies, had created lay courts of justice.[99] These figures provide some indication of the limitations which the subordinate actors were able to impose upon the leaders. A monarchy as powerful as that of Yatenga, for example, was obliged to respect them, and 'did not make use of force in order to make a population accept a chief '. Nevertheless, if an unfortunate choice was made, a subtle challenge invited the authority to reverse its decision:

> A man named by the king will never leave his assigned village in the unenviable situation of a chief whom nobody wanted and nobody liked. He won't have had to face obvious hostility; he will have been greeted respectfully but by a silent population; the master of the land will not

have said anything but the local replay of the royal nomination ceremony which takes place at the village shrine will have been constantly postponed and each time the chief summons the elder of the village the latter, protesting his great age or an illness, will send one of his deputies, etc. Everything will be done in such a way that one fine day the chief will 'discover' that the village does not suit him, because he does not understand the local language [...], because the shrine is too powerful or, simply, because there are too many termites or he doesn't like the taste of the water, etc. And in the king's entourage a new assignment will be found for the unfortunate chief.[100]

It was also common for the subordinate actors to revolt. The farmers' and slave revolts, regional dissidence and banditry do not amount to a mere ritual of rebellion (in which Gluckman discerned integrationist virtues).[101] Nor were they expressions of authentic ruptures, as in – an extreme example – the Asante revolution of 1883, provoked by the exasperation of the youth (*nkankwaa*) with the costs of war.[102] The colonial power also came up against armed resistance, particularly in the case of segmentary societies. Contrary to the well-known thesis of Lanternari, precolonial elites were involved in these insurrections, which thus cannot be properly labelled 'popular'.[103] They nevertheless bear witness to the fierce desire of Stateless peoples to defend their autonomy against any outside power which threatened to subject and exploit them.

Whether it took the form of true class antagonism (as in Ethiopia, Rwanda or the caliphate of Sokoto) or whether it aimed to prevent the emergence of classes (as in the lineage societies of the south of Angola),[104] the social struggle was such that it turned Africa into an under-exploited continent where the power to inflict violence did not match the power to force people to work. In these conditions, although the correlation between the formation of the State, the slave trade and long-distance commerce no longer appears to be as simple as was thought a few years ago, the relationship with the external environment became a major resource in the process of political centralisation and economic accumulation. The origin myths often record this genetic autonomy of power in relation to the indigenous community and the decisive role played by 'people with neither fire nor hearth', or by 'drunken kings' in conquest and consolidation.[105] The economic opening up of the continent naturally accentuated political extraversion by multiplying opportunities for trade mediation, making the intensification of internal exploitation even less necessary. In their alliance with the outside world in the areas of trade and ideological legitimation, the Malagasy monarchies are almost a caricature of this type of historic trajectory.[106] In the same way the Omani sultanate of Zanzibar largely built its regional hegemony in the eighteenth and nineteenth centuries on its intermediary position in the trade in slaves and then in ivory. In the Central African kingdoms of the savanna, rival factions were always trying to persuade either the Portuguese or the Arabs to fight. In the Sahelian belt, adherence to Islam, with its northern origins, became almost essential in the conquest of power. One could think of other examples of this sort. None would be as eloquent as that of the Yoruba kingdom of Ilesha, as analysed by J.D.Y. Peel in its regional context. Indeed, the concept of *Olaju*, which put such a value on social change that it can be translated as 'enlightenment', and which today still means 'development', referred explicitly to control of external resources by the monarch.[107]

Africans here have been active agents in the *mise en dépendance* of their societies, sometimes opposing it and at other times joining in it. It would be naïve to indulge in an anachronistic interpretation of these indigenous strategies in terms of 'nationalism' or 'collaboration' where in fact considerations of local interest came into play, in a world which was indifferent to the national idea but which was subject to serious intra- and inter-societal tensions. The factions and groups which squabbled over power and access to wealth called on foreign support to overcome rival parties and to ward off the threats of internal revolution. Political formations made use of European occupation in order to safeguard or perfect regional hegemonies, or indeed to be fore-armed against a military threat. There is hardly any period in African history in the last century which cannot be understood in the light of one of these ideas. Cooperation between the coloniser and the African actors was by its very nature ambivalent. It operated through 'working misunderstandings' of which the Yauri Day Book, kept in a north Nigerian emirate from 1928 to 1931, is a marvellous example.[108] Even the case of a character such as the 'friend of France', King Denis on the coast of Gabon, was not as clear cut as his contemporary nationalist detractors claimed. Virtually all African societies alternated between resistance and collaboration according to circumstance. This oscillation is personified in the biography of Martin Paul Samba, a devoted and gifted agent of the German army in Kamerun before heading the Bulu revolt.[109]

As a system of 'syncretic articulation' sensitive to indigenous social contradictions,[110] colonisation perpetuated the political strategies of extraversion, by providing through the monetary economy unheard of possibilities for domestic accumulation of wealth by the dominant classes. The production of African societies could no longer be distanced from the technological civilisation of the west. But all the evidence shows that the extraverted, even centrifugal, nature of the political process that this implies does not in any way diminish the role of indigenous participants. This is demonstrated by the political constructions born of decolonisation. Félix Houphouët-Boigny in the Ivory Coast played the card of structural alliance with the old colonial power, and he was quickly joined by the same peers who had sharply reproached him for this. The endogenous routes to wealth and development, upon which the sub-Saharan variants of socialism laid so much store, proved to be abortive. The dominant groups who hold power in black Africa continue to live chiefly off the income they derive from their position as intermediaries *vis-à-vis* the international system. Revenue from agricultural surpluses seems – with some exceptions of which the Ivory Coast ironically (given its history) is one – to be less great than those derived from levies on mining exports, miscellaneous imports, foreign investment or even on development aid. Niger is a typical example: the chronic stagnation of the rural world dissuaded President Kountché from demanding from the peasantry what it could no longer give, and the principal source of accumulation, for the dominant actors of the country, lies in the more or less legal trade with Nigeria and the embezzlement of international aid.[111] In addition, it is very common to look for foreign protectors in internal political or military combat. It was the main driving force of the Chadian civil war. The MPLA in Angola, deprived of its rural base, obtained an advantage from its alliance with sections of the Portuguese army following the 'revolution of the carnations', and then with the Cuban-Soviet intervention. Its opponents, UNITA, strengthened by South African and American support, managed to reproduce the historic scheme of the old inter-monarchic wars in which the Portuguese meddled so keenly.

And yet it is not merely a matter of the inconsistency of the indigenous political arenas and the external nature of their resources. Not that foreign interference was non-existent. Leaving aside spectacular, but quite commonplace, military operations, it is in fact an everyday occurrence. Inasmuch as it is quite open, the interference does not involve any conspiracy. A former French ambassador in Libreville, for example, quite calmly told the story of how in 1966 the vice-president of the Gabonese government, who was 'almost illiterate', asked him 'whether or not he could sign some documents' in the absence of the head of state who was ill, how he himself 'regularly took instructions from Jacques Foccart who was following the situation very closely' and how, in the end, he obtained from the dying Léon Mba a draft constitutional reform in favour of Bongo.[112] But it would be insulting to infer from these admissions that political power in Gabon was mere puppetry, masking a false independence. Far from being the victims of their very real vulnerability, African governments exploit, occasionally skilfully, the resources of a dependence which is, it cannot ever be sufficiently stressed, astutely fabricated as much as predetermined. Both on their political stage and within the world system, they pursue their own objectives, within the margins of failure and success that the implementation of any strategy entails.

This is true in the economic sphere: the astonishing backwardness of Ghana during the 1970s was the result of erratic choices, not an inevitable necessity of the capitalist mode of production.[113] It is even more obvious in international relations where, despite their fragility, African countries are not forced into any old diplomatic alignment. The alliance of some of them with the Soviet Union is not a product of the 'satellisation' dreamed up by a stubborn mythology, it is pragmatic even if it also involves the structuring of internal political arenas.[114] The relations that other regimes have initiated with the west are not signs of their subordination. Thus 'Kenya's foreign policy is decided in Kenya in keeping with the interests of the dominant class and the tribulations of local politics', whatever may be its 'manifest penchant' for the west.[115] Relations between France and its former possessions, surprisingly 'neo-colonial' in the eyes of anglophone observers, also support this observation. During the Nigerian civil war, Cameroon and Niger both refused to support Biafran secession in spite of the Élysée, and the Ivory Coast maintained its loyalty to the Biafran cause even after General de Gaulle had withdrawn his support. In just a few years the francophone African capitals renegotiated the cooperation agreements which linked them to Paris, engaged in a more distant diplomacy and diversified their economic relations. As a result, quarrelling and shows of force have become the norm in Franco-African relations. The leaders who appeared to be most dependent upon the Élysée – for example, Field-Marshal Bokassa in the Central African Republic or General Eyadéma in Togo – have not been the most reluctant to resort to such actions. And the blackmail diplomacy practised from 1981 to 1986 at the expense of a French left-wing entrenched in its dependantist preconceptions was another reminder that occasionally the puppets pull the strings.[116] The development of Zaïro-Belgian relations since Mobutu's accession to power in 1965 also follows this pattern quite closely.[117] Thus the multi-lateralisation of the continent's dependence, heightened in the 1970s by African governments' search for new economic partners, by the internationalisation of conflicts in Angola and the Horn of Africa and by the outbreak of the world crisis, gave the sub-Saharan states more room for manoeuvre, not only by increasing the amount of aid at their disposal, but also by allowing them to stir up competition amongst the aid donors themselves. Striking in their scale and the severity of the conditions they impose, the interventions of the World Bank and the IMF are imposed by the harsh laws of economics and are viewed, not without justification, by most African leaders as an attack upon their sovereignty. However, inasmuch as loans granted following long negotiations and ostensibly binding agreements seem to a significant degree to have been used for different purposes from what was intended, even these interventions do not undermine our argument.[118]

Everything points in the end to the fact that unequal entry into the international systems has been for several centuries a major and dynamic mode of the historicity of African societies, not the magical suspension of it. Their internal structure itself stems from this relationship with the world economy. Of course the concept of dependence still keeps its meaning, but it should not be dissociated from the concept of autonomy, as Anthony Giddens invites us to do when he speaks of the 'dialectic of control':[119] all subjections are in themselves actions. This is better understood when one examines the relationship between African societies and external cultures introduced through trade and colonisation. Penetrable, and one might even say greedy, they constantly borrowed from abroad to the extent that their clumsy mimicry, and eagerness for baubles and trinkets have long been sources of amusement. The colonial episode gave this appetite the suspect connotation of alienation against which militant discourse could find no words harsh enough. If we look again at Sartre's preface to *The Wretched of the Earth*, we see 'The European elite attempted to fabricate an indigenous elite: they selected adolescents, branded them with the principles of western culture, stuffed their mouths with grandiose words which stick to the teeth; and, after a short stay in the metropole, sent them back home, as fakes. There living lies no longer had anything to say to their brothers'.[120] However, all borrowings are also acts of reappropriation and reinvention. Perhaps it would be useful here to introduce an example which is more of a parable than an anecdote. Depending on one's sources of information, the word '*fula-fula*', which from Kinshasa to Brazzaville refers to lorries that have been customised to carry passengers, comes either from Lingala (in which case it would mean 'who goes fast'), from the English 'full' (the meaning speaks for itself!), from the imitation of the noise of a steam locomotive on the Congo – Océan railway, or from an Angolan language (expressing the action of blowing on a fire, which itself suggests the speed of these vehicles).[121] The transfer of representations, attitudes and cultural models – particularly, as far as we are concerned, in a political dimension – follows similar patterns of creative derivation. Mingling with the idea of dependence, the phenomenon of creolisation is inherent in the historicity of African societies. A child of 'total defeat', it derives precisely from the playful repertoire of the conquered and is thus not unrelated to Egyptian and Italian cultures of derision. The *zwam* who come from the old slave quarters and the royal servants of Tananarive speak a Malagasy language (*vary amin' anana*) larded with French words; the young speakers of *Sheng* and *Nouchi*, the syncretic languages of Nairobi and Abidjan, lay claim in their humorous and provocative way to the exteriority on which the dominant class rests its power.[122] These practices denote a projection of the social struggle into this area of relations with the outside world, which was historically so crucial, more than the 'Europeanisation' which offends contemporary ruling elites (as it did missionaries and colonial administrators) and is a source of chagrin for disappointed culturalists. Today, as at the time of the slave trade, what is really at stake is not the safeguarding of a problematical cultural veracity, but controlling the ideological and material resources resulting from integration into the world economy. And in fact it has implications for the contradictory definition of modernity of which such social conflicts are the matrix. Far from suggesting the withering of African societies, their marriage to overseas cultural influences shows their vigorous temperament. Drawing on western military music and dress, the craze for the *beni* dance, which caught on throughout East Africa at the beginning of the century, was an expression not of the hegemonic power of colonialism, but of the 'extraordinary flexibility' of the people in its grasp. In a more overtly challenging way the Kenyan students in a technical school in Kabete in 1929 were not averse to taking a Swahili chant, the *Mselego*, and adding elements of the fox-trot to protest against the missions' condemnation of clitoridectomy. Twenty years later, Mau Mau sympathisers set the words of the main demands of the revolution to the tune of Christian hymns, going so far as to hijack the sacrosanct 'God save the King'.[123] These mixes were more than the instrumental utilisation of heterogeneous registers intended to ridicule the colonial police or to recapture for similar purposes the cultural badges of the occupier. The fusion of Akan rhythms and European harmonies within Ghanaian highlife, as a 'creative response to the modern world', showed as early as the 1920s that these were true cultural innovations, comparable in this respect to jazz, the tango or the rebetiko.[124] The development of other new genres, such as Nigerian *juju* and *Afro-beat* music, or so-called 'Congolese' music have shown that this response is still very much alive. In this sense it is not sufficient to see dependence as an idiosyncrasy. It includes productions full of irreductive modernities.

It is a serious mistake then to imprison Africa in a *tête-à-tête* with a mythical tradition. As far back as we can go, the continent has revealed its desire to enter the universal world of wealth and values. The idea of progress was always important to it and autochthonous ideologies of development – among the Yoruba, the Asante or the Beembe, for example – emphasised the advantages of social change, of well-being and prosperity.[125] In technology, the inventive abilities of ancient societies were considerable, no matter how big the gap with western civilisation, which was to prove such a fatal military handicap. Africans were thus often keen to take on the practices and cultural expressions which accompanied (and which seemed to them, with some justification, to be a necessary prerequisite for) the formidable material power of the occupier. To an emissary sent to convince him of the British Crown's altruistic desire to bring his kingdom the benefits of civilisation, the Asantehene replied, in so many words:

> That cannot be your motive. As regards industry and the arts, you are superior to us. But we have relations with another people, the Kong, who are as little civilised in relation to us as we are to you. Yet there is not a single one of my subjects, even amongst the poorest, who would be willing to leave his home to civilise the Kong. So how do you hope to convince me that you have left the prosperity of England for such an absurd motive?[126]

The Myènè on the Gabonese coast who called themselves the *ayogo*, the 'civilised', in contrast to the people of the interior, or the hunter who protested furiously to the Marquis of Compiègne, 'Me speak French, trade and hunt. Me born Mpongwé: Mpongwé know everything like white man. Mpongwé not black'; or the *évolués* at the Brazzaville conference who declared their support 'for the extension into Africa of western civilisation' were seemingly as clear-sighted as the Asante king.[127] Relations with the west were a crucial factor in local power struggles, with survival much more than 'authenticity' being at stake. Schools, the dispensers of European knowledge, also benefited from an extraordinary infatuation, setting aside the initial reluctance of certain dominant groups to send their offspring there, or the inevitable animosity of the 'elders' towards the spread of insolent morals. Education is still a very important social issue and gives rise to considerable financial mobilisation, of which the *harambee* movement in Kenya is merely the best-known example. An important item of 'legitimate trade' in the nineteenth century, European clothing suddenly became a coveted adornment by means of which one's rank was displayed as much on the domestic social scene – where nudity often symbolised dependent status – as in relations with a foreign master. Western travellers have given extravagant descriptions of the value that the Mpongwé social elite, for example, attached to their clothing.[128] And in the 1930s the pupils at Chidya in Tanganyika threatened to riot in the passion aroused by the suspicion of the missionaries towards the *beni* dance, to secure the right to wear shorts instead of the *shuka*.[129] The large portion of the family budget set aside for clothing – about 25 per cent in Brazzaville in 1951[130] – the splendour with which the young city-dwellers dress and which the Congolese *'sapeurs'** take to extremes, following a tradition already apparant in the 1950s, and the sense of decorum displayed by the leading elites contradict the sub-limation of the past so beloved of dependantist culturalism. And when we come to religion, the role of westernisation in the conflictual rela-tionship between Africa and Europe is clearly illuminated. Christian-ity, like Islam imported by the whites, penetrated hearts to the extent that people saw in it a particularly pernicious brew of colonisation. But can one seriously accept such a view in the light of the explosion of syncretic churches which it brought, and the research carried out by churches which have stayed within the bosom of western religious institutions into the areas of the liturgy and therapy in particular? The Sartrian notion of alienation seems very inadequate, and it is concisely challenged by the Ivoirian singer Alpha Blondy, speaking as 'a total idiot':

> We are a cultural melting pot, cultural mutants created by the West. They came to us and said: 'We are going to colonise you. Throw away your loincloths and your leaves. Put on terylene and blue jeans, Ray Ban style.' And then, half way through they change their minds: 'Look, this is getting too expensive – you are independent!' That would be too easy. We don't want that sort of independence. We would like the cooperation which has got off to such a good start to continue. You know that you have no choice but to recognise me, you cannot call me bastard: I am the fruit of your culture. I am now a projection of you [...]. The whites should not throw in the towel. Those who have conquered me and put their words onto my tongue should make no mistake. I cannot allow them.[131]

This is the way Africa is going, and it is astonishing that it is so little acknowledged as part of the total historicity. For the extraverted trajec-tory of sub-Saharan societies is, after all, quite ordinary. As a result of its unequal relationship with the international environment, it exagger-ates an old academic problem, that of the influence of 'external' factors on

---

*Young people from the Bacongo district of Brazzaville, the 'sapeurs' – who become 'Parisian' following their return from their 'adventure' in Paris – call themselves members of the *Société des ambianceurs et des personnes élégantes* otherwise known as the 'Sape'. [Translator's note: in colloquial French 'sape' means 'dress'.]

the internal political order.[132] The question was posed initially by Lowie, Hintze and Weber, and the disciplines of anthropology, history, international relations and sociology of the State have constantly returned to it.[133] It is now widely accepted that the structure of political arenas cannot be isolated from their articulation with related arenas, and that 'internal and external explanations are inextricably linked', as Braudel put it so simply.[134] The dependent entry of African societies into the world system is not especially unique and should be *scientifically* de-dramatised. Inequality has existed throughout time, and – it should be stressed *ad nauseam* – does not negate historicity. Extraversion and the cultural schisms it causes have been common currency in the past. They constitute viable modalities of politics. In his work on Rome, Veyne remarked: 'a people with as its culture that of another people, Greece'.[135] Japan, medieval Europe and the Ottoman Empire were also formed around external representations, but did not become any the less Japanese, European or Ottoman – no less 'authentic', as they would say in Africa. But, did Africa have the good fortune of these powerful civilisations? The fallacious objection only manages to prove that a society can be extraverted *and* take part in the hit-parade of history, and that miserabilism appears within the paradigm of the yoke almost as a catechism.

We do not intend, against all the evidence, to embellish the history and fate of a continent murdered in its flesh and in its conscience. Nor do we wish to present as a model the 'skilfulness', rightly challenged by the nationalist demand for 'dignity', to use the words of one of the leaders of the *Parti de la fédération africaine* before independence.[136] Nor finally do we wish to disqualify any claim to an identity which is other than western. The constituent hybridisation of cultural invention in the colonial or postcolonial situation is always a wrench. Like the hero of Cheikh Hamadou Kane's novel, *Ambiguous Adventure*, the actor is always 'anguishing because there are not two of him'.[137] And the demand of Mudimbe is too widely shared south of the Sahara for it to be conceivable that we should not listen:

> For Africa, really escaping from the west entails appreciating exactly what it costs to detach oneself from it; it means knowing to what extent the west has, perhaps insidiously, drawn nearer to us; it means knowing what is still western in what we reproach the west for, and to measure how much our claim on it is perhaps a ruse, at the end of which it is waiting, immobile and elsewhere.[138]

But since this epistemic dependence which bothered the Zaïrean philosopher does not entirely interrupt the production of political societies, there is an urgent need to trace a paradigm which takes greater account of their trajectories.

AN AFRICAN POLITICAL ARENA

We should perhaps ask the question one last time: is this still a useful exercise? After all, the problematisation of African societies in terms of historicity, recently controversial, has now become a scientific commonplace. A growing number of political scientists, anthropologists and historians acknowledge it, now that the great debates about the future of Kenya, Tanzania and the Ivory Coast have not turned out to the advantage of the dependency theorists, some of whom – including some of the most eminent – have revised their position.[139] Purely economic answers will no longer do, the autonomy of politics or of the 'national bourgeoisies' has been proved and the role of the subordinate participants in the structuring of societies is beginning to receive the treatment it deserves.[140]

Yet the western media are now more than ever saturated with clichés, and it was still possible in the 1980s for a serious author to write, and for a serious publisher to publish, this sort of nonsense:

> The neo-colonial state, particularly in the case of France's African colonies, is not a political subject and can never be one: it is simply an element of the structuring of African space by French imperialism. As such it can fall under the rule of another imperialism, in the course of the periodic redistribution of the cards by the imperial powers. But it could not be said to have anything approaching a true ideology.[141]

The hypertrophy of the State is easily explained by its 'artificial' construction on colonial foundations, as opposed to an 'organic' growth from the entrails of civil society.[142] And one of the books which has dominated Africanist discussion in the last few years still talks of a 'State without structural roots in society, like a balloon floating in the air'.[143]

More fundamentally, the protestation of historicity is imprecise. It is clear that political constructions in contemporary Africa are made with a cross-fertilisation whose extraordinary vitality we have already had occasion to mention, and at the meeting point between several traditions of conceptualisation: on the one hand, the tradition of the State stems from the differentiation of an economic field and the growth of a politically informed public in Europe from the eighteenth century onwards, a tradition which has been presented as a technological universal of government and which was spread throughout Africa by the colonisation/de-colonisation binomial; on the other hand, the same is true of African traditions of power, sometimes also related to the State or at least monarchical. The difficulty in this analysis stems from its numerous intersections. As early as 1959, Georges Balandier set the preconditions by reminding us that the present situation of African societies was the result of a triple history which has 'drawn together its constituent parts' – precolonial, colonial and postcolonial history.[144] No one thinks any longer that decolonisation has 'simply been the replacement of one "type" of man by another "type" of man', as Fanon predicted, that it can be defined by this 'sort of *tabula rasa*'.[145] The continuity of political movements from the beginning of the century to those of the 1950s or 1960s is widely acknowledged. The participants themselves were aware of it at the time of national liberation struggles, especially in Mali, Guinea, Tanganyika, Zimbabwe or the Belgian Congo.[146] One of the foremost analysts of Nigeria described the culturally admirable but politically catastrophic way in which the Yoruba live with their past and continue to be divided along lines drawn up during the inter-monarchic Yoruba wars of the nineteenth century.[147] The Malian griot from the Sikaso region saw no significant change in power from the time of Saba, the founder of the chiefdom, to that of the *commandants de cercle* of the colonial and postcolonial era.[148] The contemporary State is moving closer and closer in the way it functions to ancient societies.[149] Yet it is not enough to call this the 'autonomy' of the State towards the world economic system, or the 'revenge of societies' or even its 're-patrimonialisation' in relation to the colonial bureaucratic phase.[150] These are specific lines of continuity and discontinuity, precise procedures for the invention of politics, distinct situations which it would be useful to understand if one is to avoid substituting another incantation for the fairy tale concept of dependency. The 'historicity' of Maradi in Niger, where the homogeneity of the Hausa culture contains social polarisation, is not, for example, the same thing as 'historicity' in Abidjan, created by the coloniser and where the monetary economy dominates. It is wise to take such differences into account.

This leads to a second uncertainty: is it possible to present as a paradigm the political historicity of a continent so heterogeneous as to be termed an abstraction dreamed up by geographers and imperialist historians? The States which make up that continent naturally have some common characteristics, but as Richard Hodder-Williams jokingly remarked, elephants and tables both have feet.[151] From the shores of the Indian Ocean to the Atlantic, there is diversity: climatic, physical, human, political, economic, historical. The things listed as being African often only have the commonality given to them by our ignorance. With Islam's rejection of figurative genres using three dimensions, 'African' art is characterised by the extreme diversity of styles in the absence of a universalist religion which could take on a similar homogenising role to that of Christianity in Europe.[152] There have been many attempts to identify an 'African mode of production', all of them unsuccessful.[153] The multiplicity of ancient monarchic forms has discouraged attempts to forge a regional type of 'traditional State' and one is reminded that the notion of lineage society has stood up no better to the test of time.[154] 'African Islam' is not as distinct from Muslim orthodoxy as has been thought but, on the other hand, it spread throughout the continent in a variable way, according to regions, periods and social groups.[155] One could find many other examples of cultural and political compartmentalisation. The idea of an 'African culture' governing the specific organisation of society and conception of power has been thoroughly discredited, although it is all too evident in contemporary humour. Of course, Africa does exist in our heads. Universities have set up centres for 'African' studies, businesses and banks have 'African' departments, careers are made (more often than they are ruined) in 'Africa', and, last but not least, Africans declare themselves to be 'Africans'. But in spite of all these conflicting claims, the keener observers agree on the individuality of the political development of each sub-Saharan country. In saying this, are we not in danger of negating the object of our study?

Not entirely, since geographical proximity has none the less brought about a relative commonality of historical destiny, of which the colonial interlude is only of secondary importance. It allows us to construct a scientific object, to circumscribe a political area in a comparative perspective, even to talk of an 'African' civilisation in the sense intended by Braudel as a reality of 'great, inexhaustible length'.[156] In comparison with Asia and Europe, its principal particularity lay in its extensive and itinerant agriculture which knew neither plough nor wheel, with all that that implied in terms of harnessing the energy of animals, water or wind, or of productivity and of creating surpluses. In the context of the spatial mobility of societies and weak demographic pressure, the appropriation of land was scarcely formalised and, above all, scarcely individualised. The index of power was less the control of land than the control of people. There was little scope for social and cultural polarisation or for the technological possibilities of political centralisation, and one can find evidence of this in the absence of a 'great cuisine' and more generally in the cohesion of models of consumption.[157] In short, it could be said that 'the most distinctive contribution of Africa to the history of humanity has in fact been the civilised art of living in a reasonably peaceful way without a State.'[158]

Although the last century has changed several of these circumstances, black Africa still has a profound originality with regard to the principal parameters of the comparative analysis of politics. In common with Asia and the Arab countries, and in contrast to Latin America, it does not belong to the west. But the dynamics of the hybridisation of politics unfold in Africa's case in a particular way bearing in mind the absence of a 'great' historical tradition of power. The development of productive forces has prevented the emergence within it of three groups to which political sociology attributes a cardinal role. Because of a lack of stable land tenure, the category of landowners was either non-existent or marginal before the colonial juridical revolution. The peasantry was (and still is) less monolithic and less obviously formed a social class than is generally the case in Asia. As industrialisation was long in coming and limited in scope, the working class was only a recent creation, limited in size. Politics was also long conceptualised without 'graphic reasoning', in spite of the spread of writing by Islam in the Sahelian belt and on the Swahili coast; and even today political conceptualisation largely derives from the oral tradition.

Apart from the fact that they demand their own problematisation, these facts make it impossible for us to include in our study, if not the intermediate historical configurations of the politically centralised, socially hierarchical and culturally polarised complexes of the north of Nigeria, of the Swahili coast or the area of the Great Lakes, then at least some of the clearly atypical situations such as the Maghreb, Libya, Egypt and the north of the Sudan (since the uncontested dominance of Islam has integrated them into the Arab world),* the Republic of South Africa (since it underwent a true industrial revolution in the space of a century), Ethiopia and Madagascar (since these centralised monarchies, having little to do with the kingdoms of the rest of the continent, rested on different agrarian structures). In the vast area which extends from Lake Turkana in the east and the Limpopo in the south to the edges of the Sahara in the north and the Atlantic Ocean in the west, the production of contemporary political societies has taken place in a definable area of historical congruence.

*I shall nevertheless mention the case of Mauritania, which was at one time integrated into French West Africa and was consequently in a close synergetic relationship with sub-Saharan political dynamics.

It remains to be seen if this process has an influence on the formation of States or merely on the constitution of centres of power. Some people question the pertinence of the first notion, inasmuch as the functioning of what are conveniently called African 'States' (where the mechanisms of de-differentiation seem to have dominated) is manifestly different from their western counterparts.[159] The objection, epistemologically valid, as Lacroix firmly reminds us,[160] and empirically corroborated in some situations on the continent, nevertheless betrays a superficial grasp of the facts and belongs too closely to the paradigm of the yoke to enable us to apply it a priori to all African political societies. Moreover, each one of the considerations which support it (pre-eminence of the community organisations in contrast to the individualisation of social relationships, absence of civil societies, presence of anti-State cultures, slight differentiation of power in relation to ethnicity or to a dominant political movement) is subject to discussion in the cases that concern us. The adherence of a group of African social actors to western (or 'northern') representations is not so insignificant that it should not be taken into account. It would be prejudging our analysis to try to settle the debate straight away. Let us agree for the sake of convenience, subject to an inventory which we forecast will be complex, to speak of States in Africa with precisely the aim of being better able to identify their particular trajectories and their schemes of *gouvernementalité.*[161]

In this respect, the true problem facing the analyst is less terminological than methodological. There is indeed now a widespread consensus about the argument of the invention, or production, of politics within an Hegelian or Marxist perspective.[162] It is not enough in itself to enter into the situations of political hybridation found in African societies, such as their equivocal participation in the international system and the permanent interaction within them between internal dynamics and external factors. In their petitions of theoretical principles, the structural-functionalists were aware that a structure is multi-functional, that political systems are by definition culturally mixed, and that the monist models are unable to explain them. Their sociology called itself 'dynamist' (as it was known at the time), and Georges Balandier for one did not conceal the hopes he invested in it.[163] We have seen what became of it. Throughout the 1960s and 1970s, the radical heterogeneity of African societies (which we do not deny) has tended to be conceptualised in terms of territorialities: those of tradition and modernity, of two sectors of political systems, of the centre and the periphery of world capitalism, of modes of production articulated between them, or indeed of society and the State. However much the authors wished to transcend it, the tendency to binary divisions has always in the end been too strong. Rather, apart from the fact that, as Bakhtine prophesied, it is inherent in any historical area, the heterogeneity of African societies refers to a multiplicity of enunciative procedures put into practice concurrently by the actors.[164] Balandier was close to this conceptualisation when he quoted linguistic studies and wrote in *Sens et puissance*, 'the relationship of social agents to society reveals the continuous creation to which society is subjected'.[165] The theme of society as an 'approximate' and 'plural' order dominates his work. However, the trail seems to have been abandoned in favour of a sociology of contestation and modernity. In any case, it has not led to a study of contemporary political societies in black Africa. The structuring of these in the historical context of hybridisation is not separable from the production of meanings as a product of social relations.[166] The political systems, whose dynamics are equivocal and reversible, do not have any value outside their heterogeneous actualisation from one actor to another and from one context to another, in the same way that a text is created by the way in which it is read. Our job is thus to identify, in historical situations, within a clearly defined social arena, procedures (differentiated between one actor and another or, if the actors are the same, between one context and another) of enunciation of a same institution, a same practice or a same discourse. The incompleteness and ambivalence of African political societies will then be better understood: an apparatus of control and domination or a line of dependence are not just what the government or imperialism want them to be, they are also what the actors, even if they are subordinate, make of them.

In arguing thus we do not want to appear affected. These remarks reflect the factual evidence very closely, in that the relationship of African societies to their environment goes hand in hand with their own production and that their historical impetus bows to a logic of incompleteness.[167] Amongst the Marakwet of Kenya, the social area is constantly being redefined by the contradictory enunciation that the actors make of it.[168] It is exactly the same with the postcolonial State. It is this element of vacuum or, as others would put it, the role of 'disorder', of the 'magma' in the dialogue that Africa has with its past, and also with the international system that is encountered by any attempt to comprehend contemporary political production.[169] On one side the work of unification and totalisation which belongs to the hegemonic enterprise of governments, and on the other (but indissolubly linked) the deconstruction assured by the scattering of statements: a subtle play of the Full and the Empty, of governmentality itself.

The Genesis of the State

CHAPTER ONE
The Shadow Theatre of Ethnicity

Our generative conception of African political societies might imply that we study their genesis according to a classic problematic of the historical sociology of the State. However, this truth should not conceal the principal risk of such an enterprise, which Perry Anderson's panoramic study of European absolutism did not entirely avoid, the holistic representation of societies as totalities and a rather teleological reconstitution of their trajectories.[1] As I am not aiming to be a historian and my concern is rather with the intelligibility of contemporary political arenas, I will offer an 'interpretative analysis'[2] of the various, ambivalent and fatally contradictory relationships of intertextuality they have with the past. Seen in this light, the problem lies more in identifying the dynamics of the State's genealogy than in identifying the historical entities which are thought to make up the hypothetical starting point of the construction of the State and which give it its finality. It is, however, complicated by the colonial deal which radically reshuffled the cards: apart from a few exceptions – Lesotho, Swaziland, Rwanda, Burundi – contemporary political structures do not coincide territorially with those of the past.

The developmentalists of the 1960s particularly used to stress the idea of ethnicity and its journalistic equivalent, tribalism. They constructed the State out of the horizontal integration of heterogeneous communities that the European powers, sitting around the conference table in Berlin, had regrouped, between two glasses of sherry, within arbitrary territorial boundaries.

For their part, Marxist anthropologists did not escape the attraction of the ethnic idea.[3] Both sides formalised a double political discourse –

that of the coloniser, holding forth about Africa's transition from primitivism to the situation of modern State, and those of the indigenous representatives of the independent regimes who wished to transform their plans for domestic domination into 'national integration', whatever the legitimacy they may have derived from the 'liberation struggles'. Time may have passed and many academic or ideological reveries may have been consumed in the heat of the 'suns of independence',[4] but still the decoding of the sub-Saharan State trajectories in terms of tribalism persists, describing incontestable realities while making them practically incomprehensible.

CONSCIOUSNESS WITHOUT STRUCTURE

The existence, even the irreducibility, of ethnic consciousness cannot be denied. It is not the expression of an elementary stage of development to be condemned by modernisation. Neither is it simply the result of manipulations by colonists, imperialists or even the incumbents of the contemporary State. Marxist political scientists now recognise this. As the analysis of concrete historical situations inevitably comes up against this point, one simply bows to the evidence. There are examples of nationalist leaders who, despite being eager to transcend 'tribalism', were forced to make ethnic gestures in order to prove their credentials: Lumumba, for example, chose to lodge in Bukavu 'with someone from another tribe' to convince his supporters he was a 'non-tribalist'.[5] *Les Cahiers de Gamboma*, seized during the repression of the Mulelist rebellions in 1965, demonstrate that the Congolese revolutionary militants had a clear opinion of this 'tribalism': 'a bad train of thought and action, which consists of putting the interests of the egoists of one's own tribe and clan before everything else'.

> Tribalists think, more or less consciously, that the men and women of their tribe and clan are superior to others, and that as a result the others should serve and obey them. The tribalist tries to impose the hegemony, the predominance of his tribe and his clan. In practice, tribalist ideas and feelings are used most often to create a clientele who can help them to satisfy their selfish interests and ambitions. Tribalism is expressed in different forms, of which the following the main ones:
> 1 The tribalist constantly exaggerates and boasts about the qualities, merits and good deeds of the people of its tribe and its clan; on the other hand he refuses to recognise their faults, and even tries systematically to hide them. With respect to other tribes, exactly the opposite attitude prevails [...].
> 2 The tribalist indulges freely in liberalism and favouritism towards the

people of his tribe and his clan [...]. By contrast, he is in general very sectarian towards people of other tribes and other clans [...].

3 The tribalist tries to grant all the privileges and posts of responsibility to the people of his tribe and his clan [...].

4 Conversely, the tribalist seeks to exempt his own people from their duties and obligations, from any difficult work, or from the most dangerous, difficult or humiliating missions [...].

5 The tribalist practises this favouritism in the division of material benefits and the distribution of services [...].

6 Occasionally, the tribalist even believes that those who are not of his tribe and his clan are too rich and fortunate to deserve his help [...]

7 Some extend tribalism as far as preferring marriage between black women and white men to marriage between tribes [...].

8 In politics, the supreme expression of tribalism consists of demanding the formation of so-called independent republics which in fact have a tribal basis; failing this, tribalists demand 'federation with regional autonomy' with the distribution of political and administrative power following tribalist lines.[6]

A few years previously Um Nyobé, the leader of the *Union des Populations du Cameroun* (hereafter UPC), also bemoaned the 'concerns of "fraternity" and "clan"' which caused problems for the smooth running of the central committees of his party. In a letter to the Prime Minister, André-Marie Mbida, who had blamed 'the Bassa' for nationalist mobilisation and had threatened them with reprisals, he was reassuring:

> We are not detribalisers as some allege ... We recognise the historical value of the ethnic groups among our people which we believe is a source of modernisation in our national culture. But we do not have the right to use the existence of ethnic groups as an excuse for political struggles or personality clashes.[7]

And today, in a very different context, a Gabonese opposition movement, said to favour the Fang, believes that 'when nature is chased out, it comes back at a gallop'. It suggests that the political system should recognise 'ethnic reality' by creating a 'Community Council' elected proportionally by 'each ethnic group'.[8] In some places – Senegal and Tanzania particularly – the influence of 'tribalism' in political life is not so strong as a result of the long history of inter-mixing of populations, or the dominance of an indigenous lingua franca. Thus throughout Africa as a whole, ethnic discourse seems unavoidable.

This discourse concerns singularly fluid social phenomena, and it is also occasionally objected to by Africans with the same vehemence with which they espouse its representations. Cameroon in the 1980s is a good example of this contradiction. If we can believe the accounts, as far back as 1975 the question of the successor to the President of the Republic, Ahidjo, took on a regionalist aspect as he wished to retire in favour of his Minister of Defence, Sadou Daoudou, a fellow native of 'the North'. He came up against the opposition of the 'Southerners' in the Political Bureau.[9] Thereafter, his *dauphin* appeared to be Youssoufa Daouda. During this period the government appeared to give encouragement to the growth of Muslim business interests (showing little concern for the means by which they grew rich) whom public opinion gave both religious and regional names: *aladji* and *haoussa*. Ahidjo's surprise resignation in November 1982 threw these interests into confusion by raising a question mark over their illicit accumulation of wealth. The particularist flavour of this crisis was even more unavoidable since it was seen to rest on the suspicion, not without foundation,[10] that the constitutional succession organised in favour of Biya was a decoy which only temporarily pacified the politicians from the South; it did not prevent a 'second ballot', which saw the arrival in the Supreme Magistrature of Ahidjo's new 'Northern' protégé, Bello Bouba Maigari. Suddenly, the transfer of power took on an ethnic-regionalist flavour. The former President of the Republic, who had remained leader of the single party, heightened this perception when his calculations seemed to misfire: in June 1983 he tried to regain his advantage by demanding the resignation of the ministers from the 'North', using the same tactic that had worked for him twenty years earlier in a manoeuvre against André-Marie Mbida, and despite the fact that he had no shortage of supporters in the rest of the country. The move failed and opened the door to a military confrontation less than a year later. Since Biya had refrained from restructuring his predecessor's presidential guard, so as not to be accused of 'tribalism', the list of people harassed following the uprising in April 1984 was very suggestive, with a large proportion from the Northern departments. In drawing attention to this fact ('All the rebels were from the North') some political and military leaders talked in terms of a rope being left in the house of a hanged man, and were sharply rebuffed.[11] Wasn't it also being said that the Muslim traders in the Briqueterie quarter of Yaoundé had warned their customers about the coming drama the day before it broke out, and were accomplices?

The Southern ethnic groups, or at least the 'elites' who spoke for them, constantly affirmed their identity and interpreted the political changes accordingly. The Beti and the Bulu, in particular, strengthened by their prosperity and the mass schooling of their children, were aiming at a share in the government of Cameroon, and, despite their reservations about him, had felt the ousting of André-Marie Mbida in 1958 as a usurpation. One of Biya's first actions as President of the Republic was to show the door to a Bulu delegation which had come to congratulate him. And he was making a definite point when he visited the province of *Centre-Sud* after the other provinces in the country, to show them that they should not expect too much from his accession to the Presidency. The local leader of the party, speaking in support of the region's Oath of Allegiance, said, 'Mr President, we of the *Centre-Sud* are men of our word. We have only one word. We give you our word. You have our word.' In his reply, Biya reminded him of the precepts of national unity:

> It would be a dangerous illusion if some of our compatriots claimed particular rights and privileges, particularly in the process of nomination to important posts, beyond their abilities, their loyalty and fidelity towards institutions, as well as the example of their professional awareness and of respect for republican legality.[12]

Beti and Bulu groups were no less uncompromising in challenging what they saw as Bamiléké interests at work in the corridors of the Ministry of Finance, the banks and the university, until, one after another, first an intellectual felt himself drawn to condemn the 'ethnofascism' of the westerners, and then priests denounced a plan for the 'Bamilekisation' of the Catholic hierarchy.[13] In this atmosphere the indignation of Cameroonian opinion towards the French media in 1983–84, which had stressed the regionalist dimension of the succession crisis, seems slightly surreal. But the conflict between Biya and Ahidjo was also constitutional, political and economic. Cameroonians thus did not want to obscure what was truly at stake.[14] In their fury they rightly exposed the woolliness of entities which regionalist or tribalist interpretations presented as explanatory factors.

The 'North' in particular is riven with societal divisions, which Biya cleverly exploited. It is far too simplistic to reduce them to a contradiction between a dominant Peul minority, uniformly Muslim, and the dominated *Haabé* or *Kirdi* pagan majority.* No Peul would call himself non-Muslim, but the faithfulness of some of them – the Mbororo shepherds, for example – to the faith of the Prophet seems superficial. There are also some Muslims, like the Choa Arabs from the far North, who have been marginalised and do not hold a privileged

---

*Here it is necessary to clarify some terminology. One speaks of Peul in the singular, of Foulba (or Fulani in English speaking countries) in the plural, particularly for the settled population of this 'ethnic group' of nomadic origin. The Mbororo have remained nomadic shepherds within the Peul framework. Lastly, the Foulba/Fulani are completely distinct from Hausa, whom they conquered in the nineteenth century. But the Southern Cameroonians use the term 'Haoussa' to mean anyone who originates from the North, wears the boubou and follows the Prophet.

socio-political position. The Kirdi are a human mosaic, socially hetero-geneous, whose integration into the regional system of inequality varies from one group to another.

The historic equation of the North can be expressed in the hegemony of a block in power, cemented culturally by the Islamic way of life, but ethnically heterogeneous, since it is made up, in addition to the great Foulbé notables, of Hausa traders and converted 'elites' of Kirdi origin. In its time, the German colonial regime relied on this scaffolding, as did the French, albeit more subtly. Although Ahidjo achieved his rise against the wishes of the *lamibé*,★ having imposed on them the creation of a western-style political party and restricted their prerogatives, he pursued this strategy right up to the time of his dismissal, perhaps towards the end abandoning a little of the ground gained from the chiefdoms at the beginning of the sixties. His intentions were clear. Elected to power in 1958 because he seemed the best able to deal with the secessionist whims of the Peul aristocracy, he opposed the divided 'South' by the arbitrary construction of an immense unitary 'North', ruled over by an immovable Governor. This base guaranteed the permanence of his position. Biya set about dismantling this false mono-lith in 1983, bringing to a head the frustrations he initiated: frustration in Maroua and Ngaoundéré, where the *lamibé* had had their knuckles sharply rapped in 1958 and 1963 for having stood against Ahidjo and had seen Garoua systematically preferred; suppressed rage from the mass of Christianised or pagan farmers, under pressure from an Islam-icised canton chiefdom, integrated into the dominant social group of the region; irritation from the Catholic missions, surreptitiously perse-cuted by this chiefdom for having taken too great an interest in the peasant condition; and, finally, frustration from a considerable group in the Muslim elite who deplored the politically suicidal Malthusianism of the regional social hierarchy.[15]

The southern half of Cameroon was no simpler, and the dichotomic presentation of a confrontation between North and South, so common in news commentaries, cannot reasonably be sustained. The very notion of ethnic group, at least in the form in which it is usually imagined, that of a given entity, going back over centuries and corre-sponding to a limited geographical area does not square with fact. Anthropologists are now interestingly abandoning this aim.[16] The mistake of tribalist interpretations of politics stems largely from the fact that they confuse two perspectives: social structures, on the one hand,

---

★*lamido* (singnal), *lamibé* (plural), Peul ruler of a *lamidat*.

and participants' awareness, on the other. There may even be such a thing as an ethnic awareness without an ethnic group. Ethnicity is a complex and relative phenomenon, not a stable combination of invariables, a static and atemporal structure. A product of history, it also must have a generative definition. One could easily apply the same description to it as historians of ancient Greece for the *genos, phratry,* or tribe: 'Far from representing the basic constitutional framework of pre-civic society, these institutions, *as far as we know*, matured only within an already formed *polis* and so were not the vestiges of an age long gone but the indispensable arena for the expression of cohesion, of the *philia* which united the citizens'.[17]

Thus contemporary ethnic groups, far from being the links between the postcolonial Cameroonian State (for example) and its historical background, are often of recent creation, and do not seem to have existed for much longer than the State itself. Thus the archetypal Northern pagan ethnic group is 'a collection of heterogeneous groups which have come together in the same territory as a result of their migrations'; it is not completely uniform, and the awareness its members have of it is 'due more often ... to an opposition to the outside world than to the recognition of organic links between individuals of the same group'. The Kirdi identify themselves more by their mountain range or, on the plain, their village than by their ethnicity. Its structure and even its ethnonym are frequently given from the outsider's viewpoint.[18] The name of Mofu, for example, goes back sixty years and 'is only just being accepted by the Mofu themselves'. What is more, it refers to 'two totally different ethnic groups'.[19] In that particular area, only the Islamicised Kotoko have been settled in their present area for a very long time, but they also come from an old fusion of disparate elements. Despite their dominance, the Foulbé are no exception. Most specialists avoid the concept of ethnic group and prefer to speak of a 'population of Peul culture – more or less homogeneous – made up of heterogeneous groups'.[20]

This genetic complexity of human groups is also found to the south of Adamaoua. The origins of the Bamiléké group lie not so much in driving back the Sudanese people of the north, as was thought for a long time, as in the convergence of immigrants of various backgrounds on the basalt plateau of Grassfields and their commercial, cultural and political integration.[21] Although more far-reaching than on the neighbouring plateau of Bamenda, this process of unification has not erased chieftaincy particularities inherited from the wars of the nineteenth century, whose memory may be invoked with the implantation of a UPC maquis, or the building up of business networks, or during a football match. The term 'Beti', broadly meaning 'gentlemen', 'masters' or 'the civilised', is in the same way basically naturalising. It refers to cultural and assimilatory preponderancies, 'absorbing ethnic groups', being the product of amalgamations. From this point of view the Beti can be seen as a warlike minority coming from the north, imposing their authority and protection on people bearing their name, but from whom they took many features of civilisation, beginning with language. In the Minlaaba area the ethnologist can identify six levels of population where the natural process of osmosis has not succeeded in erasing all tension. The cultural unity of the Pahouin group, to which Beti identity and political coherence within the contemporary State belonged, seems to have been exaggerated.[22]

The ethnonyms used to describe a modern political situation in fact are usually applied to pluri-ethnic power constructions. Can one find Peul domination in the North of Cameroon in the powerful *lamidat* of Rey Bouba? Certainly. It must, however, also be pointed out that this State, effectively founded in the nineteenth century by Foulbé warriors, very quickly came to terms with the local populations, some elements of which have attained prominent positions in its institutions.[23] The conflict which opposed the cultivators to the *baba*★ in 1984 was neither ethnic nor religious, but social. It threatened production relationships and expressed the exasperation of an exploited peasantry towards a *lamidat* and predatory canton chiefs. The protest letters written by faithful Catholics were unambiguous in this respect, having recourse to ethnic identifications only to describe the lines of economic extortion.[24] Will one also speak of the key role of the 'Bamoum' in the consolidation of Ahidjo's regime, in the reunification of the English and French Cameroons in 1961 or in the victory of Biya during the constitutional crisis of June 1983? It would not be groundless as far as the action of the Bamoum royalty is concerned. This was historically constructed from composite groups drawn together through links of consanguinity or mystical alliance and by means of military or political submission.[25] Such truisms have regrettably been systematically neglected: from sultan to ex-slave, not everyone is a 'Bamoum' in the same way.

The extent of politicisation of the ethnic heterogeneity of ancient or contemporary State structures is variable: weak in the North of Nigeria, more intense in Burundi and above all in Rwanda.[26] On the other hand, the social heterogeneity which lies behind ethnic identity entails cultural and, therefore, political differences, which the 'ethno-philosophical' view, so rightly criticised a few years ago, does not take

★*baba*: sovereign of the *lamidat* of Rey Bouba

account of.[27] S.F. Nadel found amongst the Nupe the various cultures of riverside dweller, hunter, peasant, an urban and a rural culture, a culture of the ruling class and a culture of the people. The Peul conquest complicated the situation still further, since it ended up with the assimilation, particularly linguistic, of the victorious minority, and by its social perpetuation as an elite.[28] The frequently overlapping contradictions without which one cannot conceive of the historicity of African societies – economic divisions caused by production relationships; biological divisions between men and women and between young and old; historical divisions between victors and vanquished – tend to be projected as so many cultural repertoires, even conflicts of power. Within a social or ethnic group there will be different languages for the old and the young, for the men and the women and for the conquerors and the subjected, albeit some more silent or secret than others.[29]

It is possible that these registers result, as Marc Augé has argued, in 'an overall logic in which not only the institutional variants of society but also its intellectual, moral and metaphysical variants are related to each other in a multiple and varied way' in contrast with the 'virtual totality' by which 'power' is generally perceived.[30] It has not, however, been proven, and an 'ideo-logic' of this nature has more to do with social relationships than with an ethnic quintessence. It would, furthermore, be an external contribution, whose importance in the definition of ancient and contemporary societies we have already noted. As with almost all political systems of the past, the great cultural movements which swept across the continent before colonisation – in particular Islam, prophetisms and millenarianisms – were trans-ethnic.

Ethnicity cannot provide a basic reference point for postcolonial political areas, because it is itself constantly being formed and is largely mingled within the phenomenon of the State, for which it is supposed to provide the explanatory key. It is just one example of the production of African societies that the anthropologist finds, for instance, in the mechanism of 'clanification' in the sacred royalty of Léré in Chad. Clans are 'constituent elements of the Moundang population considered overall as an ethnic group independently of its territorial divisions':

What we are dealing with here is not a division of the Moundang population into clans stemming from an original unity from far back in the past, but integration of different groups into a clan, into a group territorially defined by the sovereignty of the King of Léré. Although some of them have a common geographical or ethnic origin, all the Moundang clans have a distinct origin which can seldom be located with precision but which are sufficiently defined in relation to the North–South and East–West axes.... In the history of the population, the clans obviously predate the ethnic group, but this anteriority hardly has any meaning for us since we know nothing about the clan group itself, apart from what precisely makes it a Moundang clan.

By means of this dynamic of 'clanification' the captives incorporate themselves into the village communities, as well as the 'great mass of those agents of royal blood', who pose a constant threat to the stability of the kingdom.[31]

If we bear in mind this generative character of African societies and its organic relationship to their external environment, it is easy to understand the flexible nature of ethnicity which the Manchester School was keen to stress back in the 1950s.[32] As a scheme of identification, it is contextual.

The Swahili are perhaps too good an example. The word 'Swahili' was introduced by Arab travellers, to distinguish the inhabitants of the East coast, the Kiswahili speakers, from the Zanj (Bantu). Today, 'swahilitude' depends on the circumstances of its enunciation:

> For an Arab from Arabia or for someone from a tribe in the interior, the Mswahili is someone who speaks Kiswahili as his mother tongue, who lives on the coast and is a Muslim. On the other hand, locally, in Lamu, Zanzibar or Mombasa, people use the word Waswahili freely to denote a community, thus conferring a great sociological importance to the term. But, except for the descendants of slaves or the detribalised Africans, 'Mswahili' is never used as the only term of identification by the Waswahili themselves. In this way it is still true that someone is Mswahili and also something else: for example, one person can be Mswahili, but also Mngwana, Hadrami or Sharifu; another could be a true Mswahili but also the son of Pokomo parents (a tribe in the north-east of Kenya), Islamicised and living in Lamu.[33]

Yet the same is true of kinship in a lineage society.[34] Ethnic identity does not furthermore exclude other lines of identification; biological, religious or economic. Being Bamoum makes a person no less a man or a woman, planter, labourer or trader, Muslim or Christian, scholar or illiterate. Far from the problematical intangibility of tradition, ethnic consciousness reveals social change, of which it is a matrix. It cannot be divorced from the changes of this century: urbanisation, the construction of a new communication network, the introduction of new relationships of production, and the increase in migratory and commercial movements.[35] If this extreme diachronic flexibility of ethnic identities were recognised historically, one would see that pre-colonial black Africa was not, strictly speaking, made up of a mosaic of ethnic groups.[36]

THE PRODUCTION OF ETHNICITY

Most situations where the structuring of the contemporary political arena seems to be enunciated in terms of ethnicity relate to identities which did not exist a century ago or, at least, were then not as clearly defined. This is true in the cases of the presidential succession in the Ivory Coast, apparently blocked by the irritating Bété question; of the Kenyan regime of Daniel arap Moi which appeared to ensure the revenge of the Kalenjin over the long predominance of the Kikuyu; of the 1964 revolution which is said to have reversed Arab domination in Zanzibar; of the attempted secession by the Igbo in Biafra; the civil wars between Tutsi and Hutu in Rwanda and particularly in Burundi; or even the proneness to tribal struggle in the first Republic of Congo-Léopoldville.[37] Although it would be too much to maintain that all contemporary ethnic groups are the products of the colonial period,[38] the precipitation of ethnic identities becomes incomprehensible if it is divorced from colonial rule. It admirably illustrates Marcel Mauss's view that language is 'essentially always an instrument of action' which 'acts in expressing ideas and feelings, that are then translated and substantiated by words.'[39]

The colonisers conceptualised indistinct human landscapes which they had occupied as specific entities, constructed in their imagination on the model of a bargain basement Nation-State. With its Jacobin and prefectoral origins, the French administration had an avowedly territorial concept of the State, British indirect rule, by contrast, being much more culturalist. Aside from such nuances, it was along these lines that the colonial regime was organised and that it aimed to order reality. To achieve this it used coercion, by an authoritarian policy of forced settlement, by controlling migratory movements, by more or less artificially fixing ethnic details through birth certificates and identity cards. But the contemporary force of ethnic consciousness comes much more from its reappropriation by local people, circumscribing the allocation of the State's resources. Thus the function of chief in the Belgian Congo was swiftly taken up by the elders of the lineage, who then drew an administrative salary and became entitled to levy a so-called customary 'tribute'. These payments, proportional to the number of people and sub-chiefs which the chiefdom could boast, led the title-bearers to appeal to ethnicity in order to invent historical and genealogical arguments in their own support.[40] Interactions of identity became tied between, on the one hand, the important structures of power and of allocation of resources and, on the other, the populations over whom power was exercised. The colonies which were subjected to indirect rule were obviously typical in this respect. Nelson Kasfir has shown how this was true in the case of Uganda, where Lord Lugard first experimented with indirect rule.[41] And it was mainly around the Western Region of Nigeria that Yoruba consciousness was founded, on the ashes of the inter-monarchic wars of the nineteenth century, or from the institutions of local government that took on more restrained community functions.[42]

The French prefectoral model, however, had very similar consequences. The Aïzi, a small group of about 9,000 living on the lagoons of the Ivory Coast, are a case in point. Judged by any criteria – language, patterns of filiation and residence or traditions of origin – each of the thirteen constituent villages has an original configuration. 'Aïzitude' does not refer to a pre-colonial phenomenon but to a reaction (in the chemical sense of the word); the ethnic 'precipitate' being 'radically different from the elements of which it is composed'. Since the notion of ethnic group was one of the ideological premises of the colonial administration it has become 'the means of affirming one's own existence' and, hence 'the language of relationships between the subject peoples themselves'. The colonial power quickly lost its grip on the process it had unleashed:

> It becomes a system and literally produces particularities (tribe/ethnic group). The progressive refinement of the administrative structure is less the effect of a deliberate will than catching up with a dynamic fuelled by all possible conflicts, whether economic or political. The Ivoirian State is no exception in its attempts, at any rate in the lagoon region, to make each sub-prefecture correspond to an ethnic group regardless of their large number and small size.

The fishing rivalries between, on the one hand, the Adiou-Krou and Alladian (who enjoyed the status of privileged interlocutors in the colonial administration) and, on the other, the 'Aïzi', who were losing their prerogatives as 'masters of the lagoon', helped to make it necessary to designate them as an ethnic group before the Second World War. The scramble for land and the formation of land reserves in the forest area later made this change even more necessary.[43]

Thus there came about a process of retroaction between the indigenous social strategies underlying colonisation and the construction of the apparatus of state. Ethnicity is one of the results where the stakes are totally material: access to the factors of economic production, and hence accumulation, the construction of hospitals, roads and schools, and communication with the decision-making centres and the markets. These representations were none the less crucial in the way this flow of goods and services was established. The functionaries of the colonial bureaucracy, half administrators and half ethnologists, gave a decisive stimulus to ethnic consciousness. They were soon supported by the missionaries, particularly the Protestants, who helped in the standardisation and extension of regional languages through education, the translation of the Scriptures and the training of an indigenous learned elite, of which the figures of the Reverend Johnson in Yorubaland , or the Abbé Kagame in Rwanda, are notable examples.[44] Ethnology itself, in producing ethnic monographs, took part in the invention of this fiction and became in its turn a sought-after resource: the Nkoya, whose ethnic unification was no exception to the rule, emerging as it did from their incorporation into a 'North Rhodesian' and then 'Zambian' area, welcomed with great interest the anthropological study that a Dutch researcher intended to make of them, hoping that it would enhance their status against Lozi hegemony.[45]

The ethnic idea currently enjoys a wide consensus. It was an African head of state, not a western journalist or retired colonial administrator, who saw 'the tribes, before the arrival of the Europeans [as] something similar to small nations where there was a shared language, culture and destiny ... where one felt safe ... and which saw themselves as separate entities'.[46] Although this view is inaccurate in the strict historical sense, it now has its place in the political landscape of the continent. Ethnic pluralism may not provide the cultural infrastructure underlying the genesis of the contemporary state. The interplay of actors in this process does not amount to a confrontation of ethnic forces, like the clash of billiard balls (to borrow the metaphor used by Aristide Zolberg in his critique of the classic theory of international relations.)[47] In this respect there is nothing particularly complex about the Cameroonian crisis of 1982–84. None of the contemporary political phenomena which some have attempted to reduce to an ethnic dimension can be limited to this single explanation.

Nigerian tripartism of the 1950s has often been linked to the significance of the tribal vote, on the grounds that each of the dominant formations drew its basic support from one of the three administrative regions. Closer study, however, reveals how Ilesha, for example, in its rivalries with the other Yoruba cities, voted mainly for the National Council of Nigerian Citizens, reputed to be dominated by the Igbo, although in some areas there was support for Chief Awolowo's Action Group, the governmental party of the Western Region.[48] The great Hausa cattle-dealers in Ibadan voted for the Action Group and not for the Northern People's Congress, as would have been expected. They hoped thus to prevent the Yoruba butchers from obtaining a ruling from the regional government which would be unfavourable to them.

They carried with them virtually the whole of the Hausa community in the town, of which 93 per cent voted for the Action Group in the 1961 elections.[49] In 1978–9, the elections which led to the return of a civilian regime to a large extent saw the resurgence of the regionally divided political sociology of the 1950s. The candidates saw themselves as 'trapped by the ethnic perceptions of their supporters and their opponents' in spite of strict constitutional rules designed to prevent this happening. In the words of an alert observer, however, one cannot 'conclude that the parties, the electoral campaign and the results were dominated and determined by tribalism'.[50]

Contrary to commonly held beliefs, Kenyan political life since 1963 has not been limited to a confrontation between Kikuyu and Luo. It is true that the Kikuyu were a driving force in the growth of the nationalist movement, because they were faced more directly with the inconveniences of British colonialism, particularly over land. Although aware of their common origin, they nevertheless identify first and foremost with their sub-clan and its corresponding territory, and secondly with their district.[51] This certainly helps us to recognise the growing influence of Kikuyu leaders in public life or indeed the drying up of investment in the Luo area once Mr Odinga Oginga had gone into opposition.[52] However, the most obvious splits of the last twenty years have not come about because of such macro-ethnic boundaries. It was an intra-Kikuyu rivalry which decided the outcome of the succession to Jomo Kenyatta, himself a Kikuyu from Kiambu. Mr Njonjo, a native of this District, who was Attorney-General at the time, scotched the 'Change the Constitution' movement inspired by the family of the old President, thus allowing the transition to the Vice-President, of Daniel arap Moi, a Tugen from the Kalenjin group. Political life in Kenya since then has been dominated by Moi's struggle against the Gikuyu, Embu, Meru Association (GEMA), a holding company which had promoted these ethnic communities since 1971, and some of whose leaders had been involved in the 'Change the Constitution' movement. The President here had the support of Mr Njonjo and the more guarded support of his Vice-President, Mr Kibaki, also a Kikuyu. The competition which set the latter two against each other should not be forgotten. At the time of decolonisation the Luo also were split between Mr Odinga Oginga and Tom Mboya, and then, after the latter's assassination in 1969, between the Odingists and the anti-Odingists, particularly during the elections of 1974 and 1979.[53] A strictly ethnic interpretation of an event such as the attempted coup in August 1982 thus becomes an extremist caricature.[54]

The sociology of rural rebellions, which tends to tribalist interpretations, also draws on factors other than those of ethnicity, even if the
armed uprisings kept to geographical and cultural boundaries for military reasons. In Cameroon, the struggle between UPC supporters
painfully divided the societies it embraced, and does not break down (as
has been claimed) into a 'Bassa' and a 'Bamiléké' phase.[55] Commonly
presented as the archetypal tribal conflict, the Congolese rebellions of
1964–65 do not entirely follow this pattern either: the BaPende of
Kwilu fought *en masse*, but not those from Kasai: in Kwilu itself other
groups, such as the BaDinga and the BaLori divided over the call of the
Mulelists.[56] And much the same may be said of the Chadian and
Angolan civil wars, in spite of the myths surrounding them.[57]

There is an infinite number of similar examples. They all lead to a
double conclusion: in Africa ethnicity is almost never absent from
politics, yet at the same time it does not provide its basic fabric. Put this
way, the dilemma is naturally absurd. Manifestations of ethnicity
inevitably involve other social dimensions, as anthropologists have
long demonstrated. And in the context of the contemporary State,
ethnicity exists mainly as an agent of accumulation, both of wealth and
of political power. Tribalism is thus perceived less as a political force in
itself than as a channel through which competition for the acquisition of
wealth, power or status is expressed. There are many examples of this.
The tensions between Igbo and non-Igbo in Port Harcourt, and between Yoruba and Hausa in Ibadan, reveal not so much disembodied
linguistic or cultural oppositions as a struggle for the control of the
town and its resources in the first case, or for the trade in kola and cattle
in the second.[58] The bitterness of the Luo and Kalenjin towards the
Kikuyu is directly linked to the distribution of spoils of power, and to
the difficulties of unequal economic development from one region to
another.[59] In Uganda, the outbreak of a paroxystic crisis, from the
1960s onwards, demonstrates the anger of other ethnic groups at the
rewards the BaGanda had gained from their early alliance with the
British under indirect rule.[60] In Zanzibar, the ethnic unification of the
'Africans', to use the expression current in the 1950s, expressed their
rejection of the economic structure dominated by a group more easily
defined as a social coalition of planters and merchant money lenders
grouped around the State, than as a homogenous 'Arab group'.[61] Lastly, in Mauritania in 1966 the *Manifeste des dix-neuf* condemned the
Moors' monopoly of all sectors of national life; more recently the
Manifeste du négro-mauritanien opprimé bitterly criticised the confiscation
by the tenants of the 'Beydan (i.e. Arab) State' of bank loans and 'fertile
alluvial lands on the Senegal river', calling on the black community to

Boycott, banish or kill if necessary all those who encourage the sale of land. Destroy and burn the property of any foreigners who come and move in on your land. The land belongs to the village. The only land reform acceptable is one which redistributes land proportionally (*sic*) according to the needs of the whole population of the village.[62]

The most striking examples of ethnic strategies are those connected with the resources of the modern economy, for example, in gaining employment, education or loans. If we absolutely have to find a definition of ethnicity, we could resort to the extreme, provocative and of course reductive one proposed by Robert Bates. 'Put briefly, ethnic groups are a kind of winning coalition with a wide enough margin to guarantee profits in the struggle for the division of spoils but also sufficiently restructured to maximise the per capita return on these profits'.[63]

But the problem remains. On the one hand it is important to identify the processes by which such coalitions are formed, the historical materials they use and the cultural resources they draw upon. Ethnicity also relates to what Pierre Bourdieu calls *habitus,* which can give rise to reactions of sympathy or, conversely, suspicion, even revulsion (the 'X' eat monkeys, the 'Y' smell bad, the 'Z' have ghastly scarifications, or are cannibals). It also implies a history of wars, razzias and economic competition, what some historians call 'traumatic events', which play a role in moulding contemporary political interactions.

On the other hand, the question of the relationship of ethnicity to social stratification and the State, posed so openly by Bates, needs to be clarified. Ethnicity is of course a process of culture and identity, rather than a given structure. It is inseparable from the political process structuring the State. Unless it results in an irredentist or separatist plan – something surprisingly rare in postcolonial Africa – ethnic allegiances by definition form part of a 'universe of shared meanings', that of the State.[64] These generative dynamics are themselves facets of a wider process, the emergence of a new system of inequality and domination.

It is thus insufficient to say, with Immanuel Wallerstein, that ethnicity can be functional for national integration or the construction of the State.[65] It is plainly false to maintain, as did Richard Sklar, in an article whose popularity is difficult with hindsight to understand, that tribalism masks class privileges.[66] And it would certainly be naïve to see in ethnic groups, which have within themselves an economic hierarchy, the seeds of future classes, as Mr Lissouba, a former Prime Minister of Congo-Brazzaville, suggested in 1967 in speaking of 'class-tribes'.

A relative and not a substantial notion, ethnicity is just one among many areas of social and political struggle. It is thus ambivalent with regard to lines of inequality and domination. It is created by the contradictory action of social categories, even when they are sub-ordinated. One could even say that the role of these categories in the enunciation of ethnicity is probably determinant, as the ethnic commu-nity is a channel through which redistribution is demanded, as well as being a means of accumulation.[67] When Mr Libock was appointed head of the President of Cameroon's private office, he immediately became the focus for the hopes of his 'country'. One of the village leaders exclaimed:

> For the first time in its history Nyong-et-Kéllé has the honour of having two of its sons as members of the government. Until now there was only one. There is a Basa proverb which says that you don't attack a wild beast with a single spear. We therefore give our heartfelt thanks to the President of the Republic, His Excellence Paul Biya who has done us such an honour.

The new Minister rightly interpreted the sub-text of this sort of talk, and issued a reminder that he was after all a servant of the State, in the service of the whole nation, in the same way as the President of the Republic:

> Himself a native of Mvomeka'a, if he only had regard for the interests of his village, he would not have appointed me. Following our proverb which says that the goat eats the same grass as its mother,* I am determined to follow in its footsteps. Your fervent wish should not be for Libock to become a permanent fixture in the government, rather for the President's confidence in our department to be maintained.

The application of 'charity begins at home' should be qualified: the 'grievances of the people' would only cut ice with him if they had an economic justification.[68]

One year previously, at the time of a reshuffle, President Biya thought it appropriate to stress that ministers 'are not and should not be the representatives of a tribe, a department or a province'. According to the leader writer of the *Cameroon Tribune*, this declaration came as 'a

---

*The metaphor is in fact quite ambivalent, since there is also a popular saying in Cameroon that 'the goat feeds where it is tethered' in order to poke fun at political and administrative corruption.

timely bucket of cold water over those weekend revellers who had only seen the recent ministerial reshuffle as possible titbits for their tribe'.

> Ridiculous and improper calculations have built up around these promotions, with the beneficiaries now held as prey. The tribe has in fact sometimes gone to dance around a particular minister, who may be embarrassed by so much ostentatious effusiveness, as our ancestors used to do around a huge piece of game. The best part – the ivory, skins and attributes of strength – would soon be divided within the clan, ... There is the greedy expectation that the promoted person will distinguish himself by promoting his own people, as if he were indebted to them for his promotion and thus under obligation to them with a debt of gratitude ... that he should recruit and give jobs to his brothers in the village – regardless of their qualities, their merits or their morality – that he will get new roads built in the village and get existing ones tarmacked; that he should get his village upgraded to the administrative centre of the department, or even of the province, since, once in government, doesn't one have complete power, and shouldn't it be one's native village which primarily profits from it? ... And then that he should not succumb to that bad habit of his predecessors, who also came from the village, who had made themselves unpopular by giving business to all comers, as this should be reserved for their brothers in the village. Thanks to him, they would immediately become entrepreneurs, businessmen presenting the best guarantees etc. etc.[69]

We could not have put it better. A product of history (or of what Pierre Bourdieu calls *habitus*) and the race for accumulation, created 'from the bottom' as much as by the 'national bourgeoisie' or 'imperialism', ethnicity criss-crosses the lines of social stratification and those of integration within the State. None of these three orders of meaning can be separated from the other. Whatever its local extent, prosperity cannot be imagined outside the national, or even world, arena; and it has to come about through trans-ethnic networks. In these circumstances, to speak of 'Bamiléké' business circles has hardly any meaning, as is demonstrated by the composition of the principal shareholders of the *Crédit mutuel du Cameroun*, founded on the initiative of the President of the Chamber of Commerce and Industry, Mr Tchanque.

It is also fairly meaningless to draw distinctions between attributes of ethnicity and social class in educational investment:[70] the two aspects are indivisible. And the exacerbation of inter-regional competition in trade, light industry or banking is in line with Cameroonian economic nationalism towards French interests. The development of such interdependence between social categories born from relationships of production and the particular communities inherited from history and the sphere of the State, these permanent processes of interweaving (so well analysed in John Peel's remarkable study of Ilesha)[71] should dissuade us for ever from seeking the key to contemporary politics in ethnicity. They also leave us with the feeling that the postcolonial State also lacks a precise class structure.

CHAPTER TWO
The Unequal State: 'Little Men' and 'Big Men'

In Africa as elsewhere, the State is a major manufacturer of inequality. The 'development' which it boastfully claims to promote, and in whose name it attempts to ban political competition and social protest, plays its part in this process. Better than any international expert, a pupil at an agricultural school showed his awareness of this fact in the following replies he gave to a questionnaire:

Question: In what areas has the village made progress?

Answer: These villages have made most progress in work on the fields of 'Baba'. By this I mean: work in the fields of the chief of Rey Bouba only. The village people don't even have the right to work in their own fields. At the start of the rainy season, the *dourgourous* (guards, militia) of the chief fetch them from the villages to go and work first of all in the chief's fields before they come back late to work on their own fields. This is why I say that they have made progress in the fields of the chief of Rey Bouba.

Q: Have all peasants contributed to this progress? Or only some? Why?

A: I tell you that all peasants have contributed to this progress because the region or *lamidat* of Rey Bouba includes the tribes of [there follows a list of names of tribes]. They are all slaves of the chief of Rey Bouba. None of the tribes whose names I have just given you have individual rights.

Q: Does this progress cause any problems? Please specify.

A: This progress causes a lot of problems if the village of such and such a tribe does not present itself straightaway in the fields. When this happens the chief of the village is locked up in the house of the chief of Rey Bouba for two or three months. He leaves with a fine for himself and for the rest of the village, who also get soundly whipped. Whilst their chief is in prison the peasants have to finish their allotted cultivation.

Q: What do you wish for in order to develop the villages where you work?

A: For the villages where I work to be better developed in all things, I wish that the *arrondissement* of Rey Bouba had a southern *sous-préfecture* and a police brigade, so that the episode which I have just told you about would no longer be possible and the peasants really could have their independence, and be better developed in agriculture and we teachers could help them with new techniques of ploughing and drilling with ox-drawn drills with two spouts in parallel line, treating the fields with weedkillers, mechanical weeding, mechanical and manual threshing.[1]

It is impossible to abstract the ideology or technology of 'development' from the exploitation of which it is the vector. The voluntarist conception of 'modernisation', from which the postcolonial State acquires a large part of its legitimacy, derives initially from an intellectual tradition: that of the Enlightenment, in the very particular sense of the enlightened despots of the eighteenth century, and that, too, of progress in the proud and 'civilising' nineteenth century. Marx identified completely with this philosophy when he evoked 'the natural laws of capitalist production' and 'their inevitable results', and when he declared that 'the most industrially developed country merely shows the least developed the image of its own future'. These notions, born of the French Revolution and the British Industrial Revolution, have inspired ideas of 'backwardness' in certain societies and of 'short cuts' which will enable them 'to catch up': in short, all the detestable discourse of 'under-development'.[2]

From the *chef de région* Briaud, who forced the Maka into a programme of 'obedience and work'; to the *administrateur* Pernet, who in 1938 made plans to organise them into 'teams' who would be made to work in the fields from 7 a.m. until 4 p.m. and to sell them soap from Marseille; to the *sous-préfet* of Loum, who in 1968 was horrified that the people whom he administered should 'shamelessly expose their nudity to any passer-by' and inveighed against the use of marijuana and *arki* (an illicit, home-made spirit) and who called for human investment, the continuity is obvious.[3] The same disillusion with the natives' 'laziness' and the 'backwardness' of their customs, the same exhortations and, also, the same temptations. 'The only remedy is to force them to work,' grumbled the French district officers [*chefs de cercle*]. 'The amount of cotton produced in Upper Volta is in direct proportion to the amount of pressure put on the natives by the Administration,' growled the renowned industrialist Robert Boussac. A lecturer in the Colonial School of Angers did not hide his belief that 'the whip is essential'.[4]

These lessons were not lost. In Oubangui-Chari the 1958 laws on vagrancy maintained the principle of forced labour. Barthélemy Boganda did not think there was anything odd about this: 'Everyone knows that work, call it what you will, has always been and remains obligatory.' The same causes often produced the same effects, as the use of the lash on reluctant farmers, for example, continued, and perhaps became even more widespread.[5] The example of the Central African Republic is not merely an exception, explained by the cruel heritage of the charter companies. Immediately after independence in Tanganyika the District Council of Handeni ruled that 'anybody who does not take part in development projects will receive a punishment of six lashes of the whip'. Several years later a civil servant in Tanga warned a group of women 'to wear the *kiboko*', which evoked sinister memories of the German occupation. 'I am not a benevolent and civil man. I am cruel! If I see that government orders are not being carried out, I shall know where to find you and punish you!' declared another official in Rungwe at the same time.[6] The Mozambican authorities also thought that the construction of socialism would be facilitated by bringing back the lash.[7] Farmers in Senegal who did not repay their loans were at one time flogged and sprayed with fertiliser or insecticide.[8] Finally, in Ghana, one of the ministers in the redeeming government of Jerry Rawlings warned cocoa-planters who disobeyed the rules that in future not only would they be prevented from growing anything at all, but also they would have their farms confiscated and would be hauled before the tribunals on charges of 'economic sabotage'.[9]

This 'setting to work'[10] supervised by the State, which is confused with 'development', takes us back to the installation of a system of inequality and domination. Colonisation, independence and national integration are moments in this process of social stratification. The hero of A. Kourouma's novel understood this well when he wrote about the 'little marsh rat' who 'dug a hole for the rat-swallowing snake'. The son of a princely family that has fallen from grace and a former nationalist activist, he has not received the 'two fattest and meatiest titbits of Independence', that is to say the posts of either secretary-general of a sub-section of a single party or of cooperative director. All that decolonisation has given him are cards – one for national identity and the other for the single party: 'They are scraps in the carve up, as dry and as tough as old bull's meat. You can bite them with the teeth of a famished mastiff, but you won't get anywhere, there's nothing to suck.'[11] The race for goods and privileges is by no means a new phenomenon in Africa's history. On the contrary, even in lineage societies its roots go far back.[12] However, the relationship of power to social stratification is clearly somewhat different, now that the governing circles of the continent are more or less integrated to the world capitalist economy and that 'personal wealth has become fully autonomous, not only in itself but also as a superior form of wealth'.[13] For our purposes, it is less important to set about looking for the underlying structure of relations of production which make up African social formations, than it is to identify the lines of social stratification that will contribute to our understanding of the postcolonial State.[14]

THE 'LITTLE MARSH RATS'

The State in Africa – no matter what the political experience – has diverted the surplus and the rent of agricultural exports into its own pockets. The principal agencies of this diversion have been marketing boards, overvalued national currencies, and the allocation of public expenditure.[15] The extent of these processes, their institutional modalities and the social groups who benefit from them may all have differed from one country to another. Very few regimes, however, have been exceptions to the rule. In those rare exceptions – above all, in Zimbabwe as a result of the importance of the 'peasant option' that the indigenous farmers tenaciously used to oppose their integration into the regional labour market, and to a lesser extent in Burkina Faso, Niger and even perhaps in Mali[16] – the evidence has, moreover, been ambiguous rather than conclusive. We can therefore take it for granted that the political revolution of independence was not a peasant revolution. Indeed, it frequently led to a worsening of conditions for farmers, as shown by the changes in prices paid to producers, rural revenues or the distribution of public expenditure.

The Senegalese example is illuminating, as after the Second World War the political rise of Léopold Senghor was based on the rural vote. Between 1960 and 1967 the farmgate price of groundnuts paid to producers remained more or less the same at current prices, equivalent to a decrease of about 20 per cent in real terms, which was compensated for by an increase in production. In 1967 the abolition of the French subsidy for Senegalese groundnut exports was passed on to the peasants who saw the price of groundnuts fall from 21.5 francs CFA/kg to 18 francs CFA/kg. In comparison to the average for the years 1960–66, the fall in agricultural average per capita real cash incomes in the agricultural sector ranged, depending on the harvests, between 25 per cent and 65 per cent over the period 1968–74. Thanks to more favourable conditions, the groundnut price was increased by 30 per cent in 1974 and again by 38 per cent in 1975, and within a few years real incomes had more than quadrupled. The remission did not, however, last long. From 1978 onwards the Senegalese economy began to sink. Agricultural average per capita cash incomes started to decline again, and in 1978 and 1980 had fallen to the levels of the bad years at the beginning of the decade. Responsibility for this decline was shared by bad harvests and the freezing of the groundnut farmgate prices paid to producers which, deflated by the consumer price index, were lower than during the period 1969–73. In contrast, average urban per capita real income, which had clearly declined between 1968 and 1975, increased by 16.3 per cent between 1975 and 1980. The structural adjustment attempt, begun in 1980 under the auspices of the International Monetary Fund and the World Bank, has accentuated this contrast:

> The measures which have been most fully implemented have had the most direct effect on agricultural incomes, urban consumers, particularly consumers of staples, whereas the salaried groups of the modern sector (civil service, parastatals) and both the legal and illegal intermediaries involved in agriculture were more protected, and non-salaried incomes (land, property and commercial rents) escaped altogether.
>
> From the point of view of social justice, the bias against the rural areas which has developed since the end of the 1960s has become considerably more acute since 1980. As a result of a combination of factors, including the saturation of land, unfavourable climate and a fall in real producer prices, agricultural cash real income fell between 1981 and 1984 to its lowest level since independence despite a 30 per cent increase in the population. Even in a year of good rains like 1983, the total real cash income in the rural area was lower than it was at the beginning of the 1960s. In the town, the bias is accentuated to the disadvantage of those on low incomes and to the advantage of salaried employees of the modern sector and, above all, of high non-salary revenues.[17]

Figures available for other countries, such as Ghana, Nigeria, Cameroon and Zaïre, all show a similar pattern of urban groups benefiting from the pauperisation of farmers.[18] The distribution of public expenditure does not favour the rural areas, which have often been said – and not without exaggeration – to have subsidised the growth of towns or agro-industrial investments which provide little benefit for the peasants. In Cameroon between 1960 and 1980, for example, 60–75 per cent of all levies made on the agricultural sector were used to finance other activities, and during the fourth Five Year Plan, 60 per cent of national investments were allocated to agro-industrial complexes. Similarly in Congo-Brazzaville in 1984, peasants farmed 68 per cent of the cultivated land, were responsible for 98 per cent of agricultural production, but received less than 10 per cent of agricultural investments, equivalent to 1 per cent of national investment.[19] However eloquent these figures

Table 2.1 Senegal, 1960–1984: changes in groundnut prices paid to producer

Year	Net purchase price paid to producer	Price index (1971=100)	Purchase price in francs at 1971 value
1960	20.8	68.2	30.5
1961	22.0	71.6	20.7
1962	22.0	76.1	28.9
1963	21.5	79.7	27.0
1964	21.5	82.7	26.0
1965	21.5	85.9	25.0
1966	21.5	87.8	24.5
1967	21.5	90.0	23.9
1968	18.0	90.0	20.0
1969	18.0	93.6	19.2
1970	18.5	96.3	19.2
1971	19.5	100.0	19.5
1972	23.7	105.8	22.4
1973	23.0	118.2	19.5
1974	29.8	137.8	21.6
1975	41.0	181.5	22.6
1976	41.5	183.4	22.6
1977	41.5	204.1	20.3
1978	41.5	211.2	19.7
1979	41.5	231.6	17.9
1980	41.5	251.4	18.1
1981	46.0	266.2	17.3
1982	60.0	312.3	19.2
1983	60.0	348.7	17.2
1984	50.0	386.0	13.0

Source: République française, ministère des Relations extérieures, Coopération et Développement, *Déséquilibres structurels et programmes d'ajustement au Sénégal*, Paris 1985, multigr., p.79

may be, they still give little indication of the often dramatic deterioration in rural living conditions. Shortages of basic necessities or medicines are commonplace. Venality abounds in overcrowded hospitals and schools. The deterioration of the road network has in places been quite terrifying. In Zaïre, for example, the network was reduced from 140,000 km in 1959 to a mere 20,000 km at the beginning of the 1970s, and the Roads Department is now better known as the Potholes Department. Transport costs in the countryside are 40–50 per cent higher than they were before independence, and the life expectancy of a lorry is no more than 80,000 km.[20] To the horrors of repression and civil war can be added the daily exactions of local and central authorities.

Table 2.2 Zaïre, 1960–1974: changes in official prices paid to producer for selected range of products

	1960	1970	1974
Maize (Shaba, Kasai)	114.9	126.7	96.0
Manioc (Ouest)	157.9	75.6	36.4
Rice	157.9	109.2	104.0
Haricot Beans	137.9	90.7	43.2
Cotton (top quality)	172.4	85.0	67.5
Palm oil	241.4	79.3	64.8
Coffee Robusta	195.4	90.7	64.8
Coffee Arabica	202.0	93.9	52.4
[(June 1967 = 100)]			

Source: G. Gran ed, *The Political Economy of Underdevelopment* New York, Praeger, 1979, p.5, according to IMF figures (cited by C. Young, T. Turner, *The Rise and Decline of the Zaïrian State*, Madison, University of Wisconsin, Press, 1985, p. 94)

As for the peasantry, the states which have been credited with a different 'class nature' have fallen a long way short of their promises. The lusophone regimes which emerged from 'armed national liberation struggles' are prime examples. The MPLA in Angola did not take root in the countryside and represents above all urban creole interests. FRELIMO in Mozambique, showing its lack of understanding of a peasantry which it claimed had 'been destroyed by colonisation', launched itself into an extreme programme of collectivisation and succeeded in plunging the provinces into chaos following the forcible resettlement of thousands of town dwellers in 1983. The agricultural policy of Guinea-Bissau was almost as erratic, if less aggressive, at least to begin with, and the quarrel between the PAIGC and the Balante peasantry which supplied it with its soldiers seems set to last.[21] Tanzanian socialism, which for a long time enjoyed considerable prestige, seems to have served its farmers no better. The Tanganyika African National Union (TANU) initially reproduced certain aspects of the colonial model of authoritarian development. Following the Arusha Declaration in 1967, the policy of *Ujamaa* increased State and Party pressure: the independent farmers' movements – especially the Ruvuma Development Association – were broken up, for a time cooperatives were outlawed, the marketing of harvests was nationalised and homes were forcibly regrouped. At the same time State levies on agricultural revenues were raised, regularly amounting to as much as 60 per cent after 1971–72, reaching a peak of 84 per cent in the period 1972–75.[22]

At the other end of the political spectrum, the relationship of the State to the peasantry is similar. The Kenyan agricultural success story up until the mid-1970s in reality disguised the transfer of the inegalitarian agrarian structure of the White Highlands to the hands of the major national landowners. Approximately 80 per cent of the land in the Highlands was sold intact and untouched by agrarian reform. At the beginning of the 1990s 5 per cent of the landowners owned 70 per cent of the farmland, and this trend is continuing. It has been estimated that as many as 90 per cent of the farms of more than 3ha. have absentee landlords. The government's decision to pursue a protectionist policy to help its industry has penalised agriculture, whose terms of trade – the ratio between agricultural income and agricultural expenditure – fell from 100 in 1976 to 81.1 in 1981.[23]

Despite the mythology of the 'planter', which Houphouët-Boigny has encouraged, the trend has been broadly comparable in the Ivory Coast.[24] From 1960 to 1968 the urban sector gradually used up more and more of the national wealth, to the detriment of the rural sector. Although less marked than elsewhere at the same time, this change in the situation of agricultural producers was none the less real enough, and was perhaps responsible for the decline in output by the end of the first decade of independence. From 1969 to 1973 real per capita income in the agricultural sector stagnated, whereas urban per capita incomes increased slightly. The trend was reversed in 1973, when the increase of prices paid to producers for cocoa, coffee, rice, cotton and palm produce allowed them to make up the ground they had lost at the end of the 1960s. From 1974 to 1978 average per capita agricultural cash incomes grew at a rate of 7 per cent per year, in contrast to a growth rate of only 2.9 per cent in non-agricultural incomes from 1975 to 1978. Then, as a result of the very severe measures of structural adjustment imposed from 1980 onwards, agricultural incomes at constant prices stabilised until 1985, equivalent to a reduction of approximately 10 per cent in per capita income if it is assumed that the agricultural population was growing at a rate of 1.8 per cent. It is true that this halt is scarcely comparable with the brutal decline in Senegalese agricultural incomes, especially as the urban salaried workers – including employees of the administration and public enterprises – were also hard hit.[25] Furthermore, the Ivoirian *Caisse de stabilisation*, unlike its Cameroonian equivalent, redistributed funds in the form of subsidies and equalisations in favour of the countryside. Its primary function, however, was to institutionalise the intersectoral transfers of resources from the primary to the secondary and tertiary sectors, and to tap into agricultural wealth. Despite a common belief, a 'bourgeoisie of planters' does not form the dominant class in the country. The main village planters from Moronou and Ketté, for example, are worlds apart from the 'entrepreneurial planters', the absentee landowners who belong to the political and administrative elite of the towns and whose control over the resources of the State enables them to control the countryside.[26]

These cases might suggest to us that the peasantry is, in the Fanon perspective, the dominated postcolonial class.[27] However, it is not so straightforward. To start with, the peasantry is clearly not homogeneous. Quite apart from the extraordinary diversity of regional and local situations, within the peasantry there are considerable disparities in terms of landownership, capitalisation and technology. Positions are furthermore not mutually exclusive, and an individual can be simultaneously a salaried worker and an independent producer, depending on the farming calender or the time of the week. On the Kenyan coast, the agriculture of the squatters and the agriculture of the plantation are intimately linked.[28] Secondly, the very notion of the peasantry is, as we know, problematic in Africa for historical reasons. The metamorphosis of farmers into a 'social class' is generally associated with the colonial period, at least in Central, eastern and southern Africa – it is more debatable in the case of West Africa – and consequently some authors prefer to speak of 'peasantisation', a peasantry in the process of creating itself.[29] Despite the Zimbabwean precedent, it cannot be taken for granted that this process will reach maturity. The hypothesis has been advanced of a 'bureaucratisation' of Senegalese groundnut producers and thus of their disappearance as peasants.[30] In most parts of Africa the development of agro-industrial complexes or concentrations of agriculture has resulted in the growth of a rural proletariat. Cash-crop agriculture does not always reproduce itself: Yoruba cocoa-planters, in particular, have invested in other sectors, and the highest earners have left their land or sent their children to town.[31]

Subordinate urban social groups – workers, those employed in the 'informal' sector and the 'poor' – can no longer be disregarded, as almost one-third of the population of the continent now live in towns, but are no less exploited for that.[32] With regard to the range of its historical incarnations, the myth of a coherent and special 'working class' does not stand up any better to examination than the myth of the 'peasantry'.[33] The sphere of dominated social actors thus appears to be both singularly volatile and relatively unified, if only because of the recurrence of exchanges between town and countryside.[34] Popular representations introduce many different nuances to the construction of inequality: Ivoirians speak of the 'bottom of the top', the 'top of the top' and the 'top of the bottom'; the Yoruba distinguish between, on the one side, *mekunnu* (a man without money), *talaka* (a very poor man), *otosi* (a lazy man), *alagbe* (a beggar), and, on the other, *olowo* (a rich man), *omowe* (an educated man), *oloola* (a notable), *oloye pataki* (a man of honour and prestige) and *alagbara* (a powerful man).[35] But the increasing polarisation within African societies is also designated in a straightforward manner and is structured as a dichotomy along the lines of the old theme of 'us' and 'them'. The Ghanaian 'big man–small boy' syndrome, so felicitously described by R. Price,[36] is found in most other African societies. The 'small men' also do not lack for epithets to identify 'the big types' (in the Ivory Coast), the 'decree men' (in Cameroon), the 'acquirers' (in Zaïre) the *wabenzi* (in eastern Africa, referring to Mercedes Benz cars), the *nizers* (in Tanzania, referring to those who have profited from Africanization) and the *mafutamingi* (the 'dripping with oil' in Uganda).

There is little doubt that the social mobility which some claimed to perceive two decades ago, no doubt overhastily, has already slowed down. Hierarchies close up, and tend to the reproduction of the governing classes, particularly in schooling.[37] The early results of the policies of structural adjustment, pursued since the end of the 1970s under the aegis of the financial institutions of Washington, show this freezing of social stratification, particularly in Senegal and the Ivory Coast.[38]

We need now to understand by what economic activities this stratification crystallised, within the cover of the genesis of the State. Most studies agree that neither the 'informal' sector (except where, as in Uganda, Angola, Zaïre and Sierra Leone, the formal sector has fallen apart)[39] nor agricultural activity have in the past been sufficient bases in themselves for accumulation, which has been associated rather in a parallel way with the revenue of the tertiary sector – the profits, for example, of trade or of a transport business or even a salary. Taking up the pioneering work of M.P. Cowen, G. Kitching has shown precisely in the case of Kenya how a minority of households were able to save and invest throughout the 'years of opportunity', the 1920s and 1930s. This transformation of relations of production shaped the following decades. Far from changing these relations, the much vaunted 'agrarian revolution' of independence followed the existing lines of differentiation.[40] S. Berry reached similar conclusions in her study of Western Nigeria: salaries were a major source of initial agricultural investments; later on, the principal road to riches no longer lay in cocoa but in the tertiary sector, which explains why Yoruba farmers did not reproduce themselves as a peasantry.[41] These dynamics of 'straddling', to borrow again M.P. Cowen's expression, seem to have been crucial across the

continent. We have already seen how the big village planters of Moronou and Ketté in the Ivory Coast were not capable of true accumulation, in contrast to the absentee 'commercial planters' of the political
class and the bureaucracy.[42] In Tanzania, the autonomisation of a purely
agricultural wealth was even more unthinkable, since the cooption of
the 'modernist' farmers by the colonial power was late and limited (at
independence there were scarcely a hundred of them) and was then held
up and eroded even by *Ujamaa*. Here again the investment behind the
growth of certain farms was derived either from salaries, small-scale
production or commerce.[43] In Zimbabwe the seizure of the best land by
the European settlers means that even the Zimbabwean 'peasant' trajectory follows the general rule.[44] We need therefore to look elsewhere.

POWER AND ACCUMULATION

Many people have repeated G. Balandier's assertions that 'participation
in power [...] provides a hold over the economy, much more than the
opposite' and, related to this point, that 'the young national State is thus
comparable to the traditional State since one's position in relation to the
apparatus of the State also determines one's social status, the nature of
one's relationship to the economy and one's material power.'[45] Although accurate in general terms, these affirmations none the less need
to be treated with caution because they have led prematurely to the
identification as a dominant class of a 'bureaucratic or State bourgeoisie', or of an 'aristocracy' or a 'political class' or an 'organisational or
managerial bourgeoisie', all of whose definitions raise more problems
than they solve.[46]

We must make one point clear. The major role of the government in
the moulding of social stratification does not, or at least does not only,
reveal a cultural resurgence of ancient political forms. It cannot be
separated from the colonial episode. The Europeans mixed up the
genres more frequently than the authentically bureaucratic phases of
British and French colonisation might lead one to think. Extortion and
the confusion over the exercise of public authority were inherent in the
company regimes whose extraordinary greed shocked many travellers.
In the former Belgian Congo it has largely survived the bizarre patrimonial formula of the 'Free State' which King Léopold brazenly proposed, and today the symbiosis between the worlds of administration
and business remains more obvious than elsewhere.[47] But equally in
Angola the rapacity of the agents of the Portuguese Crown was legendary, whilst in Kenya the 'straddling' between official duties and lucrative activities was not unknown.[48]

The indigenous intermediaries of the colonial State furthermore made free use of their privileges as auxiliaries of the administration to enrich themselves. In this sense 'corruption', as it is called today, was an organic part of the system of 'indirect rule', especially in Northern Nigeria.[49] The chiefs and their aides appointed by the administration competed with one another in finding new opportunities for extortion, as the following account from the Cameroonian archives clearly demonstrates:

> The *Office du Travail* said to the head chief: 'You must give me forty men.' His eyes shining, he called to his village chiefs to pass on the message; 'They want sixty men from me. Give them to me, quick.' The village chiefs decide amongst themselves how many each should give to supply the sixty men. 'I can give ten.' Then he calls his messengers and tells them in secret, 'Give me fifteen men.' Then the messengers, armed with their trusty whips, set upon the villages and seize anybody they meet by day or night. In huts and in fields, they hunt men. Showing no pity, they hit and wound, but so much the better. 'You want to be freed? Then give me a chicken. Give me five francs. You haven't got any? Hard luck.' They take as many as they can in order to free as many as possible in exchange for remunerative presents. How they enjoy the recruiting season! They quickly return to the village chief with those who have not been able to buy their freedom, often without even letting them go back to their huts or take leave of their wives. These men are locked up to be taken the next day to the next level. The chief has got the twenty men he asked for. But then he in turn intervenes: 'Those who want to be freed should give me presents. Who wants to buy himself out?' One man promises two chickens, two others club together to give him a goat, a fourth will bring ten measures of maize, a fifth a big calabash full of oil. How easy it is to understand each other! Five will be freed, and the other fifteen will be sent as requested to the head chief. But can the five freed men return to their homes? That would be too simple. 'If you really want to be freed, let your wife bring me the present you promised but first of all you will do a week's work for me.' He has no option but to accept without arguing, and with scarcely any food these five men will be put to all kinds of work before finally they are able to return home.
>
> During this time their fifteen friends are taken to the head chief. Within a few days the sixty men are found and assembled in front of him. Then the same business of buying yourself out starts all over again: 'Who would like to give me a present? Anybody who gives me a goat will be free to return home.' Even if the sacrifice is enormous, people prefer it to the certain ruin of going to work in a plantation. 'Me, I'll give you a goat,' says one man. 'I don't want your goat,' replies the chief, who for a long time has had his eye on the wife of the wretched man. He knows from the start which ones will go whatever the cost, and they have to go, they can't appeal to anybody if the head chief has made his mind up. One or other of them might want to plead his case at the subdivision, but he can't for fear of the terrible persecution he would face from the head chief, his village chief and his messengers.

   Whilst the recruits are processed by the administration, the twenty
freed men go to work for the chief. They spend between a fortnight and a
month working in his own coffee plantations where they are locked up at
night, are very poorly fed and are given a daily fee of 0.30 francs. They
are kept until the payment of their price of freedom.

   Now, let's consider our recruits taken to the sub-division. They go for
their medical inspection. The doctor, if he is unscrupulous, sees all these
terrified men arrive and says to himself: 'The nurse can do this lot.' What
an opportunity for the nurses! For they too can say: 'I'll pass you unfit if
you give me a chicken.' Another will be visited by a concubine who says:
'This one's my brother. Don't take him. You can replace him with one of
the sick men you have rejected.'

   In all the contingents there are some who fail their medical. One has
got rickets, another a hernia, a third is too old. The more unfit there are
the more pleased is the head chief because they will be 'picked' after the
medical, and instead of going home the men with rickets and hernia and
the old man will go and work with the others who have bought back
their freedom. As a result the head chief has been able to recruit his
workforce as if it were a European plantation.

   Finally, the contingent is complete and they can go off to work in the
plantations, under the watchful eye of the policemen. 'And we wouldn't
be so daft as not to take our own little profit, would we? If you give me
two francs I'll replace you this evening with another.'[50]

The yawning gap between the reality and the administrative theory of
forced labour can be explained by the moral laziness of the Europeans in
charge, who did not always try and find out more about their chiefs'
ways of operating – which they were in any case inclined to file under
'Negro problems' as long as they did not upset public order. It also
indicates a degree of ignorance and naïvety. Thirty years on, M. Delauney, a former administrator in Cameroon, had still not understood that
'the very kind present' he received from the Bamiléké chiefs, a splendid
American car, had above all enabled the chiefs to levy a supplementary
tax which they presented to their subjects as a demand from the whites,
out of which they retained a sizeable percentage.[51]

Whatever the situation, habits were formed and patrimonies built up,
especially since chiefs were legally entitled to retain a percentage of the
taxes they collected, and also benefited from various other payments.
The colonial auxiliaries, moreover, took full advantage of the new
economic order, particularly through their limited access to bank credit
and, above all, to the cadastral register of land. Even today, the origins
of some of the biggest fortunes in Cameroon lie in the inter-war years in
the former officers of the JEUCAFRA, the association which the
French administration dreamed up in 1938 to challenge the pro-German
sympathies which it thought it could discern in certain sectors of the

indigenous population. In Nigeria the representative institutions created in 1951 soon provided the politicians with the bulk of their resources.[52] The Kenyan Local Native Councils (LNC), created in 1925, similarly provided many of the chiefs and the 'educated' former pupils of the mission schools with the opportunity to accumulate their initial capital during the notorious 'years of opportunity'. Whatever the limits of their budgets or of their abilities, they soon became major suppliers of credit, subsidies and contracts for entrepreneurs and planters of the African reserves. Their role was further enhanced with the introduction in 1942 of the Agricultural Betterment Funds.[53]

Kitching's analysis of the Councils has clearly revealed the inadequacy of the usual nationalist historiography. The members of the LNC did constitute a privileged group (particularly from the point of view of landownership) who prepared the way for the division of the anti-colonial movement, in the aftermath of the Second World War, into a moderate and a radical wing. To begin with there was nevertheless no obvious contradiction between the promotion of the personal interests of a class of African entrepreneurs and the desire for progress in the community which they claimed to represent. To found a transport business or a school, buy some land, increase one's maize harvest or send a child to a mission school – all had the side effect of undermining the colonial myth of the 'backwardness of the natives'. The resources of the LNC furthermore helped to contain the commercial expansion of the Asians.

The ambivalence of the nationalist programme thus becomes more apparent. It simultaneously expressed aspirations to wealth and to dignity. There is thus nothing in the least unusual about the history of the Kikuyu Central Association: the same economic frustrations and the same ambitions were evident in the *Union des populations du Cameroun*, the *Syndicat agricole africain* in the Ivory Coast and the Convention People's Party in Ghana.[54] These anti-colonial movements sheltered schemes for individual enrichment which anticipated the later pillage the independent administrations. In Cameroon in 1954, Um Nyobé issued 'a warning to all collectors of subs and other funds of the Movement' and declared his intention to 'show no mercy to any Comrade found guilty of embezzlement'.[55] In Senegal, the political secretary of the UPS declared soon after independence that 'underhand manoeuvres, venality, the pursuit of private profit and nepotism all belong to the colonial era': 'For some citizens politics means cheating, lying and making a fortune.'[56] In Congo-Léopoldville, the sale of the party cards of the MNC/L gave rise to litigation and constant abuse. The low-ranking party members quickly identified the higher-level cadres as profiteers, who were confiscating all the fruits of independence:

> We deserving members of the MNC are like dogs with their master: early in the morning the dog and his master go into the forest to hunt for game; the dog is always willing to go and fetch the game for his master. In the evening, the two of them return to the village to eat the game. They get home and prepare the game. When the meat is cooked it is put on a plate and the first thing the master does before he starts eating is to kick out the dog, despite the fact that it was the dog who caught the meat. In the same way we fought for independence along with today's government agents, and none of them has helped us. They continually conspired with the colonialists to stop the MNC activists. Right up until now they still have all the seats and they are still arresting us to make us stop our activities.

This complaint by the vice-president of the MNC/L to Kalima was, however, not as straightforward as it seemed, since it also contained a request for work within the government of Kivu. At the same time, in April 1961, the activists of the town of Kasongo demanded 'top jobs as recompense for the political parties' from the Provincial Assembly.[57] In 1964–65, the Mulelist *simba* (the lions, revolutionary fighters) were similarly conspicuous in their predatory behaviour.

One of the decisive breaks with the past at independence lay in the ability of indigenous elites, previously restrained by the coloniser's tutelage, to have access to State resources. The end of the colonial occupation lifted a number of constraints, political, economic and administrative, which had frustrated the aspirations of African accumulators. It allowed them to take control of land registration, credit, taxation, marketing boards, public investment, and negotiations with private capital and imports.

Once we have specified the historical background, we need to identify the contemporary procedures in the relationship between power and accumulation in order to avoid mixing different practices under the generic denomination of a given class or of the ideal type of Weberian patrimonialism.

Firstly, positions of power give priority, even monopolistic access to *resources of extraversion*. These resources are of various kinds, including diplomatic and military resources which can be mobilised in order to alter the domestic power relationship, as happened in Nigeria during the Biafran war, or in Congo-Léopoldville/Zaïre under the First Republic or at the time of the invasion of Shaba by dissident armed forces, or in Angola or Mozambique since 1974, and, perhaps more than anywhere else, in the sphere of French influence, where there was always the possibility of a show of arms to counter a rebellion, riot or putsch.

The resources of extraversion also include cultural resources, which have assumed a decisive role now that the mastery of western knowledge also conditions mastery of the State and the economy. Since the first days of colonisation schools have been powerful contributing factors in the shaping of social stratification, and have been an integral part of the process of 'straddling'.[58] The truth of this observation is seen in the value attached to education in individual, social or ethnic strategies. In Nigeria, Chief Awolowo was well aware of this when he consistently made education a major issue of his electoral campaigns.[59] Families and villages made great sacrifices in their investment in education, supplementing public funding.[60] Because of the shortage of equipment, teachers and books, school places are rare and expensive: in Cameroon in 1985 head teachers sold school places for between 5,000 and 15,000 francs CFA in the primary sector and between 50,000 and 200,000 francs CFA in the secondary sector.[61] One indicator of the importance attached to educational success, for example, is the fact that the Ivoirian daily newspaper *Fraternité-Matin*, devotes entire pages to detailed lists of names of young Ivoirians who have been given places in secondary schools. In keeping with almost all other societies, the distribution of educational establishments or, more precisely, their qualitative ranking, accurately reflects socio-economic divisions.[62] Both because social prerogatives are attached to power and because educational instruments are managed in a highly politicised way by governments, membership of the ruling classes is one of the salient criteria of this unequal access to knowledge. The establishment of colleges and faculties, the distribution of grants, enrolment in the prestigious western universities, even the regional quotas for exams all tended to reflect the essential structure of power.

Secondly, a job in the public service carries with it a *salary*. In a situation of massive underemployment a salary, even if it is modest, paid late and irregularly, is no trivial thing: Cowen, for example, has argued that it is more important than illicit income.[63] Salaries are sometimes generous – a member of the Political Bureau in Zaïre, for example, earned $6,000 in 1974[64] – and are supplemented by the attendance fees to which participants of board meetings are entitled. For the most part, however, they are, at least to western eyes, relatively modest and are eroded by inflation. But they also carry numerous perks such as accommodation, cars, bursaries for children, health care and overseas travel, which are sometimes very big (as in the Ivory Coast) and which are always highly valued because of their rarity. The scandal linked to the Communauté économique de l'Afrique de l'Ouest in 1984 demonstrated that travel expenses could run to millions of francs CFA per annum.[65] Above all, the holding of a public position makes it easier to obtain bank or political credits. Until recently Ivoirian ministries budgeted for this, and in the course of a memorable speech Houphouët-Boigny revealed from on high what is probably the attitude of all presidents deep down:

> The budget of the President of the Republic is two billion francs CFA (for personal expenses and political funds). I am not selfish. For me, money only counts for the good use that can be made of it. Money gets its value from good use. I asked three representatives, one of whom is in this room, to manage some of the political funds. The fourth man, who distributes the most, is the Secretary General of the Government: not being from the country, he shows no favour. There are some people who go as far as to demand a year's advance. I accept this. For example, some people ask me to give them one million two hundred thousand francs when they are entitled to one hundred thousand francs a month.[66]

Such interconnections between the networks of power and credit operate at all levels of the institutional pyramid. The vigour of the attendant struggles, and the frequency of financial scandals, are evidence that opportunities for securing finance are among the most precious of the privileges usually associated with public-sector employment. The following extract from the *Manifesto of the Oppressed Negro-Mauritanian* (from which we have already quoted) argues, for example, that:

> [Bank loans] are decisive in the enrichment of the Beydan [literally 'white', i.e. Arab] comprador bourgeoisie (BCB). Such loans enable members of this bourgeoisie to invest in commerce, industry and property. Racial discrimination in bank loans helps the BCB to stifle any attempt at economic development by the Negro-Mauritanian bourgeoisie (NMB). [...] In Mauritania there are two racial bourgeoisies: the black one and the Beydan. The former is handicapped by the fact that it has never enjoyed political support, unlike its Beydan rival. [...] Within the Beydan bourgeoisie there are various lobbies. Each is linked to a political lobby which grants it financial and commercial priveleges.[67]

Thirdly, as has always been the case, positions of power can also be *positions of predation*. Holders of power use their monopoly of legitimate force to demand goods, cash and labour. In the countryside at least, most of the administrative and political cadres act in this way. Villagers from the north of the Ivory Coast told this story:

> The family of the canton chief are also bosses within the PDCI, and you know that the PDCI is the government which rules the world. The canton chief and his family take advantage of this to take your money when they come to take cattle, chicken and sheep – for independence. Here, in Zanguinasso and in other villages [...] they say that it is for the PDCI but we know that it all goes to their homes in Kouto.

Other voices confirm this view:

> The time of the whites isn't completely over yet because the canton chief, the village chief of Kouto and the Party secretary of Kouto give us as much bother as the whites used to. With their traditional and their modern powers, they come and help themselves to whatever they want – chickens, cattle – on independence day.[68]

If one believes the accounts from northern Cameroon, the exercise of customary justice and police functions, together with the register of births, deaths and marriages and the collection of taxes, are the most common opportunities for extortion. In Alantika-Faro in October 1984 two villages received fines of 60 and 40 naira for the theft of a bicycle bell, worth about 5 naira, at a time when 1 naira bought an adult daily food ration. It goes without saying that the canton chief simply pocketed the fines.[69] At the same time the policemen of Koza freely admitted that the district was 'a good patch': 'You arrive without so much as a bicycle and you leave with a big motorbike.' The following tale of woe is commonplace:

> Both in 1980–81 and in 1981–82 I paid my taxes but did not get a receipt. During the 1982 dry season I went to look for seasonal work at Sanda-Wadjiri. The policemen asked me for my tax receipts. I explained that I wasn't given any. They arrested me. Just then K.C.,the *sous-préfet* of Koza, and the president of the Koza section of the Party, were passing. They asked me: 'Where do you come from?' – 'From Guedjélé in the *canton* of Koza.' 'Why have you come here?' – 'To look for work.' – 'We're not bothered if you don't have tax receipts. It concerns your local chief.' They took me to the Mora detachment. I spent a week in prison. It was the time of great heat and they only gave me one cup of water a day. Someone from outside took pity on me and gave me a little bit of food. At the end of a week I sold the two articles of clothing I was wearing to pay 3,500 francs. The commandant of the detachment took 3,000 and the warders 500. But they still didn't give me a receipt.

It was commonly believed before 1983 that the *sous-préfets* were implicated by the canton chiefs in these tax embezzlements. In the same region the obligatory identity card could only be obtained by paying a backhander of between 1,500 and 2,500 francs CFA to the commissariat at Kerawa and between 2,000 and 3,000 to the commissariat at Mora. The amount of money taken in this way, by threat of physical force, clearly added up to millions of francs CFA.[70]

Another less visible form of predation lies in the links between the holders of power and criminal circles. It is hard to imagine that the police in Douala or Lagos don't have tributary relations with the best-placed gangs. And if they don't, the prison warders certainly do. In Kenya a wave of hold-ups in 1964–66 was attributed to the activities of unscrupulous politicians. The governing classes have also at times been implicated in various kinds of smuggling, including that of drugs.[71]

Fourthly, positions of power provide pretexts for prebends without recourse to violence. Nowhere has this been more thoroughly documented than in Zaïre, where there are almost as many words to describe it as Eskimos have for snow. *Matabiche*, *pot-de-vin*, corruption, beans for the children, a little something, an encouragement, an envelope, something to tie the two ends with, to deal, to come to an understanding, to take care of me, to pay the beer, to short-circuit, to see clearly, to be lenient or comprehensive, to put things in place, to find a Zaïrian solution: so many expressions (not without a sense of poetry and humour) to describe a flourishing informal State economy.[72] Once again, one must understand that at the base of the administrative pyramid this is above all a survival economy. From 1973 to 1977 Zaïrian civil servants lost 60 per cent of their salary in real terms. At the end of the decade their top salaries represented no more than ten cartons of milk or 24 kg of meat or eight chickens; a bailiff earned the equivalent of one carton of milk or one chicken.[73] In such conditions, a servant of the State makes his living from the people he administers rather than from his official salary. True enrichment or authentic accumulation can, however, also be achieved through the prebends that go with office. The gulf between the official salary and the accompanying benefits is staggering: in 1974 the regional commissar of Shaba received $100,000 a month in prebends, and a salary of $2,000.[74]

Any official decision affords an opportunity for gain, from a fiscal control to a technical verification, from the signature of a nomination form or a concessionary market to an industrial agreement or an import licence. Civil service departments and public enterprises constitute virtually bottomless financial reservoirs for those who manage them, and for the political authorities which head them. This has been the case in particular of the Marketing Boards and the *Caisses de stabilisation* in West Africa and of the cooperatives in East Africa, and from the 1960s the numerous State companies and other parastatals whose 'nizers' have burdened their economies. It is difficult if not impossible by definition to put a figure to the sums involved, though several press reports suggest that they are considerable. In Senegal between 1966 and 1980, embezzlement and fraud within the *Office national de coopération et d'assistance au développement* (ONCAD) were thought to amount to as much as 5–10 per cent of the total revenue of producers, representing tens of billions of CFA francs.[75] In the Ivory Coast the clear-up of the

State companies, instigated in the context of a drastic policy of structural adjustment, uncovered the extent to which they had been pillaged during the 1970s.[76] The *Direction et contrôle des grands travaux* (DCGTX), created in 1977 to manage the major construction projects, controlling prices and ensuring that the financial conditions were adhered to – in short, to limit so far as possible the abuse of public funds in the name of infrastructural investments – was said to have achieved savings of more than 800 billion francs CFA in approximately ten years. In 1987 the cost of constructing one kilometre of road was 70 million francs CFA, but would have cost as much as 120 millions had the trend of 1971–77 been allowed to continue.[77] These differences cannot, of course, be explained solely by closer surveillance of fraud, or by a reduction in commissions, as they also reflect a rationalisation of public policy. The jealous care which Houphouët-Boigny lavished upon the DCGTX demonstrated that it was in his interests to dry up the financial resources of the factions which disputed his succession.

If further proof is necessary, numerous revelations of administrative commissions and of the Nigerian press corroborate the importance of sinecures attached to the major investments in public works. In 1980, an enquiry conducted under the auspices of the Ministry of Finance established that the cost of contracts signed by the Federal government was 200 per cent higher than in Kenya, and 130 per cent higher than in Algeria. In 1983 a commission headed by one of the presidential advisers again pointed out that construction was three times dearer in Nigeria than in East or North Africa and four times dearer than in Asia. Such discrepancies can in part be explained by purely economic factors, but one cannot ignore the role of a French civil engineering company (to take one example from many) which was accused of paying 10·79 million naira into the accounts of the National Party of Nigeria within the country itself, and a further 13·5 million naira into the party's foreign accounts, for contracts worth 746 million naira.[78]

In the world of sinecures, foreign links are crucial, because they are the main conduits for the circulation of wealth. International trade is in itself a major source of accumulation for the State, which derives a large part of its revenue from customs duties. African governments pursue a fiercely protectionist policy, to the point of cynicism. President Hissène Habré of Chad, for example, imposed duties on the French armaments which he had begged them to supply, and the Mozambican authorities did the same with the coffins that Zimbabwe had kindly supplied at the time of the funerals of President Samora Machel and his ill-fated companions when they perished in an air crash, whilst Uganda, Malawi and Rwanda all subjected emergency food aid to the usual import tariffs.[79] One of the points of this impudent protectionism is that it requires authorisations and also dispensations. The distribution of highly marketable import licences (whose high costs are soon recouped as licence holders pass them on to consumers by organising artificial shortages) and contraband (which it would be naïve to equate with a marginal and popular practice) are both among the principal sources of revenue of the continent's political classes, to the point that they threaten entire sectors of national economies with bankruptcy.[80] Many factories have been built which have had no other function than to exist, and which will quite clearly never produce anything.[81] Incompetence plays a part, but is much less widespread than racist stereotypes suggest, and much less a factor than the pursuit of wealth. We are faced with one of the most vigorous contemporary manifestations of the strategies of extraversion whose crucial historical role we are trying to quantify. In Nigeria in the 1970s, General Obasanjo popularised the term 'gatekeeper' to describe the senior civil servants' intermediary role between the international environment and the national market. This functions either in a triangular mode, bringing together an indigenous middleman with a foreign operator and a political or bureaucratic decision-maker; or in a binary mode, from which the middleman is excluded.[82] Thus democracy, which seemed to be bequeathed to the country by the soldiers on their return to barracks in 1978–79, was transformed into a 'Contractocracy', 'a government of contractors, for contractors and by contractors'.[83] None the less, we should not allow the Nigerian tree – however lush its foliage – to obscure our view of the African forest, as throughout the continent the 'commission' is an essential part of investment and commerce.

Finally, food aid (much more than public development aid, which is quite tightly controlled by the donors) is to a very considerable degree piped through private interests.* It is well known that between 1979 and 1984 the Commissariat in charge of food aid in Mauritania sold considerable amounts of foreign gifts on the market, with the profits going to certain members of the *Comité militaire de redressement national*. In Bamako people joke about the Avenue and Palace 'of the drought'.[84]

Richard Joseph is quite right to characterise this intimate relationship between positions of power and enrichment in terms of prebendalism, rather than patrimonialism.[85] However, fifth and last, in so far as

---

* Angry spirits are wrong to get too alarmed, because even so it remains humanitarian aid. In Niger it was precisely its diversion which enabled the State to relax its fiscal pressure upon the peasantry.

they are sinecurists, the agents of the State also find the doors of *appropriation* opening up before them, less because the public sector holds the greater part of the means of production and trade (as has frequently and laboriously been affirmed) than because the exercise of administrative and political responsibilities does not at all preclude the possibility of accumulating and managing a personal patrimony.

Thanks to their salaries and perks, civil servants have been able to invest heavily in agriculture, transport, property and, more rarely, industry as in the model of 'straddling' which Cowen has applied to Kenya. In Kenya, however, regulations inherited from the colonial era relating to the incompatibility of belonging to a public service and the acquisition of a personal patrimony for a while restricted the higher levels of the bureaucracy to the property and agricultural sectors. The regulations were not changed until 1971 when the Ndegwa Commission, finding itself unable to recommend an increase in salaries, instead successfully proposed the lifting of these restrictions. The civil servants then launched themselves into business with a level of enthusiasm that soon alarmed the Chamber of Commerce, and scandalised the populist MPs. President arap Moi reinstated a number of the safeguards at the beginning of the 1980s, as much to assure his own economic preeminence and control over the administration as to calm others' fears. It is none the less unlikely that these safeguards will upset the existing symbiosis between public office and private interests.[86]

In Tanzania the leaders' code of conduct, supported by the personal integrity of Julius Nyerere, contained even stricter limitations which were incorporated into the Civil Service regulations. Moreover, by confiscating all houses not occupied by their owners, or worth more than 100,000 Tanzanian shillings, the Buildings Acquisitions Act of 1971 removed one of the few remaining possibilities for enrichment after the Arusha Declaration. However, the growing number of regulations and anti-corruption and anti-saboteur campaigns throughout the 1970s suggest that the reality did not match the theory. It was not until 1981 that the 'President's broom' (*ufagio wa Nyerere*) began to affect the principal leaders. Since then economic liberalisation may have created a few more bridges between positions of power and positions of accumulation.[87]

The Tanzanian experience is quite unique south of the Sahara. Everywhere else the 'straddling' phenomenon sprawls insolently across society. As early as 1963 Philippe Yacé, the Secretary General of the *Parti démocratique de Côte d'Ivoire*, complained that 'The truth is sad but it is there for all to see: ministerial departments are neglected in favour of the pursuit of personal businesses'.[88] These were crocodile's tears as the head of State had personally watched over this fusion of public and private spheres, in order at least to retain his political control. Thanks to their levies on the revenues of the State and its various industries, and their realisation of an agricultural surplus and export earnings, the members of the bureaucracy have accumulated massively without, however, being able to act as capitalist entrepreneurs: in the Ivory Coast, there is scarcely any indigenous wealth conceivable outside the vigilant tutelage of the 'Old Man' and not consisting of a controlled recycling of delegated political influence.[89] The lines of 'straddling' are even more marked in countries such as Liberia, Sierra Leone, Nigeria or Zaïre.

Because these appropriation mechanisms primarily involve land and property, we can reintroduce the notion of patrimonialism in its narrow sense. This form of ownership constitutes wealth *par excellence*, all the more valued because it was introduced to favour agrarian settlement, representing a qualitative mutation in autochthonous accumulation.[90] Its profit yields were of course vastly increased by the extension of State leases, as a consequence of the expansion of the public sector, and by the dizzying increase in rents, often payable several years in advance, which the economic booms encouraged in the 1970s, particularly in the petro-economies. Ownership of property and land furthermore determines access to credit. Ownership is most readily available to agents of the State who are in the best position to know the administrative procedures, to anticipate the plans for urban growth, to profit from their influence and to overcome the 'long obstacle race' – the expression is widely used – associated with any acquisition. The first specialists in land appropriation in the colonial era were the surveyors. Given the task of the allotment of land for new parts of town, they know how to keep some of the best land for themselves, enabling their families to profit. They are thus able to cash in on their interventions while inventing taxes for those seeking land.

The surveyors are now being challenged by senior civil servants and the politicians on whom they depend. Thus one of the most sought-after plots ('facing Sobraga') in Libreville was reserved by the principal surveyor before being claimed by a minister. Of the ninety five land registration files examined by a researcher in this district, fifty relate to lots assigned to senior civil servants, almost all of which can be traced to landowners chosen by the Minister in charge of the State Budget. In another zone close to the airport, a 1968 decree awarded eighteen plots of land, with a total area of 18 ha., to ... eighteen serving ministers, ranked according to protocol, without any charge. In the Central African Republic in 1976, 200 houses belonging to the State were

apparently sold at low prices, the principal beneficiaries of this profitable transaction being members of the government: the Finance Minister, for example, paid 3,690,000 francs CFA for a villa which he rented
out to an expatriate business for 400,000 francs CFA a month.[91] Such
operations are common in capital cities throughout the continent, and
help to explain why urgently needed official housing policies come up
against insuperable problems. Naturally they do not exclude similar
practices for buying up agrarian capital, particularly under the cover of
nationalisation of unregistered land or major development projects. In
Mauritania or Senegal nobody doubts that this is what is really at stake
in the development of the Senegal River Valley. The bureaucracy in
Mali, since the time of Modibo Keita transformed into an 'agrarian
bourgeoisie' 'under the pretext of "return to the land" and faithfulness
to the traditions of Sudano-Sahelian civilisations', employs a salaried
workforce to exploit the large plantations on the peripheries of the
towns.[92] In the Ivory Coast and in Kenya the agents of the State were by
no means the last to benefit respectively from the downgrading of
forest reserves and the transfer of the 'white lands'. The pattern is the
same in Cameroon, even though the President of the Republic did not
encourage civil servants to create 'farms' before the mid-1980s.[93]

THE ZAIRIAN MODEL: THE 'MEASURES OF 30 NOVEMBER'

If one wants to understand the organic relationship between positions
of power and private appropriation of the means of production and
trade, one should return to the case of Zaïre, where the regime introduced a short-cut between power and the accumulation of wealth. On
30 November 1973 Mobutu announced the 'recovery' of economic
goods held by foreigners, whose exact definition was left unclear. At
the same time he encouraged his 'collaborators' to undertake 'lucrative
activities' outside of their official functions. The sense of the presidential speech became clear to everyone. The only problem, as the
students on the campus of Kinshasa wondered as early as December,
was 'who is going to share in the loot', whilst the leader of the *Union des
travailleurs zaïrois* described the parliamentarians as 'racketeers' (*margou-
lins*). The Minister of Information quickly let it be known, to anybody
who wanted to listen, that the aim of the 'measures of 30 November'
was not to build up a bourgeoisie 'at the expense of the labouring
masses' but, on the contrary, to improve the condition of all Zaïrian

citizens. None the less, the question of the selection of the 'acquirers', as they began to be called in a way which was not yet pejorative, remained unanswered. A summit meeting on 26 December of the head of State, the political bureau of the *Mouvement populaire de la révolution*, the Council of ministers and the deputies – some 300 people in all – provided a preliminary answer. Plantations and 'strategic' companies were to be transferred to the public sector. The large farms or estates and the principal traders were to be reserved for the members of these three political organs. Small shops were to be allocated to local notables 'who have the means and the vocation'. The members of the governing elite who were not present at the meeting were excluded from the share-out, as well as the officers, magistrates, ambassadors, civil servants, local government officials and traditional chiefs. The list of beneficiaries was to be published on 31 December.

The 'tripartite decision' was met with indignation: no Zaïrian believed in the official slogan, 'To serve and not to be served'. At the end of one his solitary river cruises of which he is so fond Mobutu returned to the principle, or rather the modalities, of this rush for the spoils. The State would take possession of the goods destined for 'Zaïrianisation', and reallocate them later on. Only the small shops were to be sold direct to nationals. In reality, the Zaïrianised property was given away according to the criteria established initially at the time of the 'tripartite decision', and 'the triumph of the politico-commercial class was complete'.[94] Applications to take on the businesses were to be submitted to the relevant ministries and local authorities. Competition was so fierce that one civil servant from Lubumbashi pocketed $25,000 by selling the questionnaires designed for this purpose. In such furious competition, success depended upon the applicants' political influence. Members of the Political Bureau, parliament and government did not have to bother with the formalities, and were served first. They grabbed most of the large farms and the most profitable businesses: in the region of Equateur alone, the Minister of the Interior, Baanga Engulu, was granted 35,727 ha. of plantation (see Table 2.3). Civil servants denied a share in the spoils managed to participate through the intermediaries of relations and proxies. The procedures were much more complicated for ordinary applicants, who needed to know how to mobilise political support, particularly at the regional level.[95] Enquiries made in different towns across the country confirmed that people in positions of power obtained a large proportion of the 'Zaïrianised' goods. In Lubumbashi, 35.4 per cent of such goods ended up with politicians, 4.6 per cent with civil servants, 34.4 per cent with businessmen and the remaining 25.6 per cent with various other social

Table 2.3 "Zaïrianisation" and positions of power in Equateur region (1974): acquisitions of Mobutu and Engulu (in hectares and percentages)

	Coffee	*Cocoa*	*Rubber*	*Palm*
M. Mobutu, Head of State	3,049	3,395	6,804	20,114
M. Engulu, State Commissioner	2,132	887	20,026	12,682
TOTAL	5,181	4,282	26,830	32,796
Total Équateur	79,749	27,489	81,964	114,826
Land belonging to Mobutu and Engulu as a percentage of total for Equateur region	6%	16%	33%	29%

Source: Région de l'Équateur, Division régionale de l'agriculture, *Rapport annuel 1974*, pp. 84–89, 132–138, cited by M. G. Schatzberg, *Politics and Class in Zaïre, Bureaucracy, Business and Beer in Lisala*, New York, Africana Publishing Company, 1980, p.138.

categories.[96] This pattern is even more marked in M.G. Schatzberg's investigations in Bumba and Lisala.[97]

'30 November' was thus indeed a 'class action'. It was intended to sweep the patrimony of foreigners into the pockets of the politicians, whilst keeping popular appetites at a distance. It plunged the country into chaos. Nevertheless, its fundamental effects on social stratification were not undone, either by the 'radicalisation' of 1975 or by the 'clarifications' (for which read, backtracking) of 1977. In the eyes of the political scientist at least, the brutality of 'Zaïrianisation' has the advantage of illustrating in a cruel, but not stereotypical way, the nature of the nationalist wave which swept across the continent in the early 1970s. From the pinpricking measures against alien commercial minorities, enacted almost everywhere, to the 'economic war' waged by Amin Dada against Uganda's 'Asians', from the Nigerian 'indigenisation' decrees to the Togolese nationalisations, and from the swelling of the public sector to the renegotiation of international agreements and the move towards multi-lateral borrowing, it was as if there was an attempt at a 'second independence', echoing John Lonsdale's and David Low's notion of the 'second colonial occupation'.[98] In the manner of what Nkrumah called the independence of the flag, the stakes involved were both political and material. '30 November' represented one of the high points in the production of inequality. Furthermore, we should not be too impressed by the apparent questioning of such policies under the pressure of structural adjustment, which in no way undermines the capacity of the social groups who profited from these '*nizations*' (to borrow the very accurate expression of ordinary Tanzanians) to bounce back. Privatisation – the remedy favoured by the western doctors for all the economic ills of the continent – does not represent as big a break with the previous dynamic of the postcolonial State as people like to think.

CHAPTER THREE
The Bourgeois Illusion

We can now take it for granted that it is their relationship to the State which largely enables actors to get rich and dominate the social scene. If this is true on a local level, in the villages,[1] it is even more true on the regional and national scale. In the typical case of Nigeria, there is less exploitation from the labour market than from that of contracts, licences and public jobs provided by the 'entrepôt state'.[2] The oil boom has thus perhaps been less significant in itself than for the import trade it facilitated, whatever may have been the percentage of oil revenue diverted by successive holders of political power. In other countries, various export rents (from agriculture, mining or oil) have contributed both directly or indirectly to social polarisation along similar lines.

The link between holding positions of power within the State apparatus and the acquisition of wealth is also clearly related to the political hierarchy. The exercise of supreme authority in particular generally goes hand in hand with a proportional increase in wealth. The political scientist has been mistaken in leaving this phenomenon to the pamphleteer or moralist, for it should not be dismissed as mere anecdote. It introduces a qualitative rupture within the systems of inequality and domination of the continent, and it will no doubt spread widely. The postcolonial State thus represents an historical mutation of African societies, taken over the long term: never before, it seems, has the dominant class managed to acquire such marked economic supremacy over its subjects.

The figure of Mobutu springs readily to mind. He was said to control between 17 and 22 per cent of the national budget for his personal use. The budget of the presidency of the Republic was estimated in 1981 at 1.48 billion Belgian francs, on top of which came 600 million FB in 'endowments'. Mobutu also seems to have amassed most of his fortune from exporting (in his own personal right) copper, ivory and, above all, diamonds, thanks to his friendship with Maurice Tempelsman. In 1982 his foreign assets were estimated at $4 billion. His wealth within the country is also immense. The head of State was one of the first beneficiaries of Zaïrianisation, and he grouped his acquisitions into a conglomerate, *Cultures et Élevages du Zaïre* (CELZA), which, in 1977, employed 25,000 people (including 140 European managers). To this one should add the wealth of his immediate family, particularly that of Mr Litho Maboti.[3] Confusion between public property and that of Mobutu runs through the regime and, in the words of a previous director of the Central Bank, Mr Blumenthal, it is as fruitless to wait for reform as 'to convince oneself that a cat can one day stop being interested in mice'.[4] The scandal of the fortune of the 'founding President' of Zaïre should not, however, divert attention from the frequency of these extreme situations, where political institutions function like trading companies and exploit national resources. General Acheampong in Ghana, Siaka Stevens and his successor, General Momoh, in Sierra Leone, Moussa Traoré in Mali, Sékou Touré in Guinea, His Majesty Jean-Bedel Bokassa in the Central African Republic, the dictator Macias Nguema in Equatorial Guinea, the 'Great Helmsman' Gnassingbe Eyadema in Togo, Mr Abdallah in the Comores – all these characters, straight out of a novel by the Congolese writer Sony Labou Tansi, whose departure 'would seem more like filing a bankruptcy', are, or were, either personally or via their entourages, perfect incarnations of what can without exaggeration be called 'kleptocracies'.[5]

Does this mean to say that systems whose rulers are better regulated, or which at least enjoy a more flourishing economy, have a completely different logic? It is doubtful, even if the tragedy is not quite so surreal.

In Kenya, the flourishing businesses of the 'Family' of Jomo Kenyatta, appeared at the end of the 1960s 'as the most powerful and most efficient groups of private interests in East Africa'.[6] Daniel arap Moi has followed in the footsteps of his predecessor, fully living up to his new political philosophy, *nyayo* (footsteps). Within a year or two he had become involved with the main Asian and coastal business affairs of the country, and had investments in all sectors of the economy. According to *Africa Confidential* his wealth includes, apart from his land, assets in transport, oil distribution, films and food, banking, the tyre industry and civil engineering. The unavoidable intermediaries of foreign investors and exporters, a handful of operators who follow the progress of paperwork through the maze of the highly secret Kenyan bureaucracy, do not forget in the end to reward the State House's endorsement.[7]

President Omar Bongo in Gabon, who in 1967 owned one single piece of land in Libreville, today owns thirty-nine in the most fashionable quarters and has an interest in manganese and oil exports, as well as a share in foreign investments.[8] Houphouët-Boigny in the Ivory Coast availed himself of his 'billions', which he emphasised 'do not come from the budget'.

> These are the fruit of my labours. One of the banks manages my profits from pineapple production. I have 4 billion in turnover from pineapples. I pay some 50m francs a month for boxes for pineapples. Boats and 'planes come to 150m francs a month. I had two sharp falls two years ago when I had reached 3,000 tonnes of pineapples a month, producing a third of the national total. And I asked a bank to manage all this. I have stopped producing coffee. At one time it brought in very little, perhaps 100 million francs, but that 100 million is today worth billions. I put all this money into my bank accounts in Switzerland, and that produced a lot of interest. My deposits account for a quarter of the deposits in one of the banks in Abidjan. Would I keep all this money here if I didn't have confidence in my country? I have confidence in the Ivory Coast. There is even a bank which manages my profits in avocados, of which, I think, I am the main producer in the Ivory Coast. There is another bank which modestly manages my profits from poultry farming. But these billions, because this all amounts to billions, are in this country.[9]

The austere President Kountché in Niger is said to have been involved in the cigarette business. His wife furthermore had a monopoly on the importation of the highly prized Malian indigo and traded with the Malian President's wife, Madame Moussa Traoré, whose brother Moumini Kountché is one of the biggest businessmen in the country.[10]

It would be a grave error to see all these dealings simply as the corruption of the State. They are, conversely, the State's fabric, and the struggle for power is perhaps chiefly a struggle for wealth. Was it in all innocence that General Amin Dada dubbed the expulsion of the Asians 'Operation *Mafutamingi*' in Swahili, 'Operation Grease My Palm'? Is it out of pure derision that the Tanzanians sometimes refer to the CCM party as '*Chukua Chake Mapema*', 'Dig In and Help Yourself'? Is it just a coincidence that we hear the same hunting metaphor from the lips of a cadre in Congo-Léopoldville as from an Idoma politician – a minority group of the State of the Benue: the retriever (in this case, the minority ethnic group) is supposed to bring back to the National Party of Nigeria (the hunter) the prey he has missed (the votes) but he waits in vain for the hunter to leave him the scraps from a feast he doesn't want to share?[11] At the same period, one party called itself 'I chop, you chop' ('I eat, you eat'), and in this calm admission is echoed the scepticism of a

Cameroonian citizen towards the 'moralisation' called for by President Biya, 'Yesterday the goats were tethered and grazed. Today, the goats are tethered and graze. Tomorrow, the goats will be tethered and will graze!'

We will have to return to the ethos of this 'politics of the belly', as they say in Yaoundé, and the representations that the leader writer of the *Cameroon Tribune* evocatively sketched for us at the end of a previous chapter. Georges Balandier's assertion, on the eve of decolonisation, has been borne out. The apparatus of the State is in itself a slice of the 'national cake' (to use an expression current in Nigeria) so that any actor worthy of the name tries to get a good mouthful. This partly explains the apparently excessive value attached south of the Sahara to the creation of new administrative structures: offices and public works, *préfectures* and *sous-préfectures*, and even, in Nigeria, Federal states. These institutions are in themselves providers of riches and wealth, and the struggle to control them is only one of the aspects which we call, in the west, the 'class struggle'.

THE 'BUREAUCRATIC' AND THE 'BUSINESS' BOURGEOISIE

Yet we should not draw too hasty conclusions about this privileged relationship between power and wealth. On the one hand – and this will be noticed in succeeding chapters – the patrimonial tag, which is only too readily attached to the postcolonial State, cheapens a whole series of dynamics which cannot be reduced to the Weberian model of 'sultanism'.[12] And on the other hand the positions of power never absorb all the channels of wealth, in the sense that they tended to in the Soviet Union, eastern Europe or the People's Republic of China. The extent of State appropriation of the means of production and trade should not be exaggerated. It is not of the same nature as in a socialist or mixed economy, although the mediation of the State is clearly stronger and more specific in Tanzania than in Kenya, Nigeria or, *a fortiori*, in Uganda, and although the activity of private firms still depends closely on power in that it relies on administrative authorisations (such as import licences, industrial grants and standardised pricing) and on violations of the law (in the form of customs and tax frauds). It is, rather, a revival of ancestral claims of sovereigns and elders to monopolise trade.[13] From the Asantahene to the Osagyefo★ there is a worrying continuity, as Ivor Wilks has remarked.[14] The regimes describing themselves as socialist – 'African' or 'scientific' – have tried to prevent the emergence of a local private sector, and even to eradicate or weaken existing trading networks. Yet the strategy of Houphouët-Boigny, in looking after the investments of those in power and countering the emergence of an independent business sector, is not so different.[15] His aim was essentially the same as an Nkrumah, a Sékou Touré, or a Modibo Keita. It was a question of preventing the crystallisation of forces which might provide political or economic competition. Others pursued a similar aim, playing off the commercial networks against one another: for example, in Cameroon Ahidjo counterbalanced Bamiléké predominance by supporting Northerners, then Biya by supporting Bafia operators and, less successfully, outsiders from the South.

Only the political gangsterism of a Touré family in Guinea, or an Nguema family in Equatorial Guinea, approaches a *de facto* confiscation of the means to wealth, and even these examples were only partially successful. A 'private bourgeoisie' thus survived in Guinea, and regained much of the ground lost after the economic upturn of 1977.[16] In contrast to the continental picture, a class of national entrepreneurs seems to have emerged in Kenya, distinct from both the power holders of the State and what is called for convenience the 'petty bourgeoisie'.[17] Even in an intermediary regime, such as that of Mobutu, for all its patrimonial and prebendary centralisation, there emerged a group of entrepreneurs independent of power, and even suspect in its eyes, such as the Nande traders of North Kivu, according to interesting research by MacGaffey in Kisangani.[18] And in the Ivory Coast, where a new generation of operators aspires to an exclusively economic status, such a change is no longer unimaginable.[19]

More than the intentions of the authorities, which in the end are quite similar, the effects of scale contribute to the formation (or not) of a true local private sector. Demographic or geographic scale, first of all: giants such as Nigeria or Zaïre cannot be as easily controlled as micro-States of one or five million inhabitants. Economic scale, secondly: solid financial circles separate from the banks can provide large entrepreneurs with the capacity they need, particularly in West Africa and Cameroon. Out of total savings in the Ivory Coast estimated at 2,000 billion CFA in 1986,

---

★*Asantahene*: Sovereign of Asante; *Osagyefo*: the redeemer (Kwame Nkrumah's surname).

the amounts entrusted to the *tontines*★ were estimated at 200 billion and capital 'submerged' in the 'deep' country at 1,000 billion (against a budget for the functioning of the State of 433 billion in 1986 and a debt servicing requirement of 350 billion in 1985).[20] In the same way the Nigerian and Zimbabwean industries are strong enough to stand up to the *dirigisme* of the State. Tycoons on the scale of a Chief Alhaji Yinka Folawiyo and the Dantatas in Nigeria, Njenga Karume in Kenya or Soppo Priso in Cameroon become almost untouchable, enjoying economic independence and prestige. Finally, there are the effects of historical scale: some commercial networks are older than the postcolonial State, and this limits the State's capacity to disrupt them. The great families of 'Savanna merchants' were thus traditionally granted greater autonomy than in the forest areas.[21] This is the case also with the Bamiléké traders in the west of Cameroon, or 'Arab' traders on the Swahili coast.[22] But even the trading communities of more recent origin – such as the Mourides in Senegal, or the *'nana-benz'* in Togo – also benefit from having existed before the contemporary political regime.[23]

Without for the moment going as far as to question whether these configurations reveal the differentiation of an economic arena of the Polanyian type, or a Marxian civil society,[24] one cannot avoid the problem they pose regarding the identification of the 'dominant class', supposedly associated with the postcolonial State. Since Mamdani's well-known book (*Politics and Class Formation in Uganda*, 1976), it has become commonplace to postulate a contrast between a 'bureaucratic bourgeoisie' and a 'business bourgeoisie', manifested in political institutions in conflict or alliance.[25]

This is, for example, how Amselle has interpreted Malian society. In 1946 'when politics began' (as the people of Bamako say), 'the different social classes and political forces which ran deep within colonial Soudan were suddenly able to express themselves'. On the one hand, the *Parti soudanais du Progrès* (PSP) defended the interests of local notables and rural aristocrats, while receiving the support of the French administration. On the other, the *Union soudanaise du Rassemblement démocratique africain* (USRDA) 'represented those who later made up the State bourgeoisie' and managed to forge 'a tactical alliance' with the traders and to increase membership for the 'main party of the peasantry'. The elections of 1959 helped:

★Informal and rotative procedures for savings and credit which owe their name to Tonti, an Italian banker of the Seventeenth century.

When Mali obtained independence in 1960, the petty bourgeoisie of teachers, clerks and trades unionists, who made up the workers' aristocracy of the USRDA took power. ... This petty bourgeoisie, now having access to supreme responsibilities, immediately took the form of a '*nomenklatura*', ... a new privileged class whose political power does not stem from their control of the means of production and trade, but whose means of accumulation are rather a result of the place they occupy in the State apparatus. When it came to power, this 'nomenklatura' succeeded in totally eliminating its rival class, the landed aristocracy, thanks to the suppression of the political party representing it: the PSP. Its tactics revolved around getting rid of the merchant bourgeoisie and pressurising the peasantry into forming a class. To do this, the 'nomenklatura' dresses itself in socialist clothes.

The expansion of the public sector undermines the economic and political foundations of the traders at the same time as providing the burgeoning nomenklatura with a 'bureaucratic rent', raised through 'human investment' and the enforced commercialisation of cereals. The creation of a non-convertible Malian franc in 1962 provoked the decisive confrontation, resulting in the defeat of the 'merchant class' which then 'ceased to exist as an organised political force'; 'Having thus beaten the landed aristocracy and the merchant bourgeoisie, the nascent bourgeoisie could fulfil its historical destiny, and form itself as a class'. The rupture caused by the overthrow of Modibo Keita in 1968 was thus only relative. President Moussa Traoré continued to rely on the nomenklatura, and to look after its interests, at least until 1981. A partial liberalisation of the economy, particularly the privatisation of cereals and groundnuts, were responses to the traders' expectations. Repeated stop–starts serve, so the argument runs, as a reminder that the contradiction between 'bureaucrats' and 'traders' is 'the eternal lot of Malian politics'.[26]

More subtly, Dauch and Martin believe that political conflicts in Kenya during the years 1975–77 had less to do with Kenyatta's imminent succession than with 'the economic direction of the country'. It might facilitate the formation of a true national bourgeoisie, with a decisive influence both on the apparatus of production in the country, including the most modern sectors, and on the State apparatus.' The political strength of the entrepreneurial class which has developed over the previous few years did not match their new economic power, and through the factional confrontations of the time can be glimpsed the demands of this 'aspiring national bourgeoisie': 'These [factional] teams appear to represent the transmission into the political arena of conflicts of economic interests. ... Elections in the party were the occasion when new political alliances appeared, looking for power to pursue or modify the present economic policy. To put it simply, we see a struggle between "nationalists" and "multi-nationalists".' At one time Daniel arap Moi gave the impression of wanting to satisfy some of the hopes of this 'aspiring national bourgeoisie', by presenting to Parliament his *Sessional Paper No. 4* of 1980 in a spirit of determined economic nationalism. The dilemma of 'the relationships to be established between the entrepreneurial bourgeois (in the true sense of the term) and the men in power' remains open.[27]

However it seems that the economic rise of the Kenyan President and his reluctance to allow Asians or indeed Kikuyu the control of the parastatals, which the World Bank recommended should be privatised, place the theme of 'national bourgeoisie' under a slightly different light. In Cameroon too the liberalisation undertaken by Biya from 1983 onwards gave the impression that a strongly bureaucratic regime was becoming open to the representation of national business circles. At the Bamenda Conference in 1985, eminent business leaders – such as Kondo, Tchanque, Sack and Onobiono – joined the Central Committee of the party, and willingness to diversify external economic partners, revealed in the diplomacy of the new President, seems to have underpinned this rebalancing. On closer examination the situation is more complex, and the radical otherness which clearly distinguishes the 'business bourgeoisie' from the 'politico-administrative bourgeoisie', making them 'two distinct entities' whose 'conflict' is 'potential but ... still hidden',[28] has been very elusive. Certainly the career of a Monkam, a Kadji or a Kondo is different from that of a minister or senior civil servant, although this is less true of a Tchanque, Secretary General of the *Union douanière et économique d'Afrique centrale*, before starting up a brewery. In addition, the big businessmen, particularly the industrialists, have their own concerns which cause them to criticise the administration's grip on business, the direction of the government's economic policy or the proliferation of competing imports of national products. Last but not least, the billionaire, Paul Soppo Priso, from Douala, had an authentically liberal political philosophy, at the other end of the scale from the Statist authoritarianism of Ahidjo, before he was beaten by him in the Presidential elections of 1960 and withdrew from the struggle for power. But in the end 'bourgeois' and 'bureaucrats' drive the same Mercedes, drink the same champagne, smoke the same cigars and meet up in the same VIP lounges at airports. The divisions between the two activities, economic and politico-administrative, do exist and are partly expressed in the form of personal rivalries. None the less, they express antagonisms between roles rather than status groups or classes. They are not necessarily any more bitter than the factional struggles which divide the political class, the conflicts of responsibility paralysing administration, or the contradictions which set major businessmen against one another.

The private and State paths to accumulation share, broadly speaking, the same ethos of personal enrichment and munificence. And conversely, there is nothing to suggest that their articulation rests upon a relationship of exteriority. It matters little in the end that the fortunes of Ahidjo and Moussa Yaya were amassed under cover of their political responsibilities, or those of Soppo Priso, Kuoh Tobie or the late André Fouda dated back to the colonial period, or that that of Mr Kondo came from industry. Nor is it of vital importance that Mr Kadji long benefited from the deliberate short-sightedness of a regime anxious to set up Bamiléké businessmen against the UPC sympathisers' rebellion, that great traders of the North took advantage of a similar calculation, nor that Mr Monkam worked for a foreign brewery and that Mr Fotso entrusted the management of his companies to expatriates when others dream of freeing themselves from French investments, nor, finally, that some have opted for capitalist management when others think that 'getting by is no crime'. The maelstrom of ever-shifting disagreements and alliances sweeping them along is traced back to a network of closely meshed interests running back through time, through contracts, loans, acquisitions and marriages. In this mêlée, State and private operators act complementarily when they are not just confused, changing hats to fit the circumstances. The falsely naïve characters of the *Messager* give a good description of this osmosis between the two spheres:

Takala:	How many categories of businessmen would you say there were in Cameroon?
Muyenga:	I would say there must be several: there are the true businessmen who make money from the sweat of their brow, and there are those who become businessmen through circumstance.
T.:	What does that mean?
M.:	I mean those accidental businessmen and women who get converted to business once their brother, cousin or husband has been appointed to a post of responsibility.
T.:	So what is the connection?
M.:	The connection is that this brother, cousin or husband will now shower them with all sorts of business opportunities. Mainly in construction, public works, stationery or office equipment, interior decorating, etc.
T.:	Can this all happen overnight?
M.:	As long as it is the father, cousin or husband who is there and decides on suppliers. There are some people who become businessmen because they have got themselves a good job

within the party, and they then use their political cover to get
a good position in the business jungle.

T.:   And the others?

M.:   The others are the ones who are used to clean up and launder
stolen money.

T.:   I don't really understand.

M.:   You know that in this country there was at one time a
generation of thieves and swindlers who amassed a lot of
money, too much money for them to invest themselves.

T.:   I see.

M.:   With the *Renouveau* they found cousins, uncles and nephews
whom they used as a cover for their business. If you ask one
of them today he will say that he was selling empty bottles
on the streets of Douala or was an illicit street trader ... to get
where he is today.

T.:   I see.[29]

It is true that the specificity of a 'business bourgeoisie' occasionally
has its own ethos, as, for example, with the 'Wahabists' in Mali or the
Mourides of Senegal.[30] Nor is it a question of denying that entrepreneurs are personally independent of power. This, however, in no way
negates the central place of mechanisms of 'straddling' between salaried
jobs – particularly in the civil service – and private investment, which,
as we have already seen, conditioned what one might call true accumulation. There is here once again an undeniable continuity between the
colonial and the postcolonial periods, although it covers a change in
salaried positions from which there was a transfer and enrichment (the
post of schoolteacher, very advantageous in the twenties, is now
worthless in comparison to posts related to the State's control over the
economy).[31] If one looks at the symbolic example of Kenya, a study of
the top fifty company directors by numbers of firms managed in
1974–75 confirmed the continuation of this interpenetration of management, of the ownership of the means of production (agriculture included) and of politico-bureaucratic decision-making.[32]

John Iliffe suggests that the lines of 'straddling' are much more visible
and systematic in East than in West Africa, where the pre-colonial
capitalist sectors gave traders independent opportunities for accumulation.[33] This is by no means certain. In Ilesha there has been a similar
convergence between trade and bureaucracy since the inter-war years,
and in the fifties Chief Awolowo's Action Group as well as Dr Azikiwe's National Council of Nigeria and the Cameroons were also good
examples of 'straddling'.[34] In spite of the long-standing traditions and
commercial networks in the west of Cameroon, the history of the
contemporary Bamiléké traders shows that for them too a salaried job
was the 'necessary gateway' for the establishment of their capital. Out

of thirty-six businessmen interviewed by Champaud, thirteen started out as commercial employees of a relation or of a foreign company, six worked for a while in teaching, generally private, and three in public services, nine were in various odd jobs (three were waiters, two labourers), others were a photographer, a baker, a chauffeur and a manual worker. Only four of those interviewed had gone directly into commerce either as market stall-holders or as street traders, and one was a planter.[35] To such indices of 'straddling' we should add other interrelations between public and private channels of accumulation. We have already mentioned that most Bamiléké entrepreneurs, like their Muslim colleagues, at one time or another enjoyed government patronage. Some of them were, moreover, undoubtedly direct associates of members of the political class with whom they collaborated in the recycling of prebends, as Muyenga shrewdly suggested to his friend.

Commercial and political circles support each other in the same way in Senegal, Togo, Burkina and Niger, and, as in Cameroon, the co-option of certain businessmen (or women) into the higher echelons of the party sometimes completes this collaboration.[36] In the light of structural adjustment programmes applied since 1980, the case of Senegal is particularly instructive. Although in theory a public-sector body, ONCAD (*Office national de coopération et d'assistance au développement*) was in reality a creature of certain rural interest groups – traders, transporters, money-lenders, large producers and great *marabouts* – upon whom rested the political patronage of the *Parti socialiste*. These commercial, financial and religious intermediaries immediately hijacked the structures established to replace ONCAD and diverted the economic measures intended to reduce the excessive surcharges imposed on the groundnut industry. The 'private sector', in which the International Monetary Fund and the World Bank held such Messianic hopes, was identical with such interest groups and was, in a certain sense, part of the 'bureaucracy' upon which the disaster of the two preceding decades was blamed. The various parts added up to a complete system, brilliantly described by Donal Cruise O'Brien.[37]

Even where the 'State bourgeoisie' seems to predominate, the 'straddling' process is still clearly seen. It has been seen at work, personally supervised by the President of the Republic, in the Ivory Coast; one commentator on the Angolan economy has reported 'the beginning of a fusion, between the politico-syndical pseudo-bourgeoisie and the business class, which derives its income from parallel activities';[38] and Amselle's description of the '4 Vs' (*Voitures, Vergers, Villas, Virements*) so dear to Malians is an excellent example of 'straddling':

The collection of a bureaucratic income, stemming from the extra-salarial income of the 'nomenklatura', creates a process of accumulation and consumption which unfolds in a particular way. The process begins in private transport firms which prospered particularly in Bamako following the dismantling of the *Compagnie publique des transports urbains* (TUB). Their profits then finance, either wholly or in part, housing or market gardening. Apart from the costs of maintaining a large social clientele, the rest goes on the 'V' luxuries – Vacation abroad and Video cassettes which are valued highly in Bamako despite the lack of a television network – not to mention the costs of entertaining a large social circle.[39]

The dichotomy between a 'business bourgeoisie' and a 'bureaucratic bourgeoisie' (which refuses to go away despite Saul's immediate criticism of it in the work of Mamdani) is thus misleading.[40] An obscure analysis of the political economy of Sékou Touré's regime unwittingly provides one further proof:

The 'collective' modes of realising a surplus, which are institutionalised (and demanded by the existence of budgets, plans, and so on) are constantly threatened by individual initiatives. The State bourgeoisie tends automatically to become a 'private' bourgeoisie and to reinforce the latter which, incidentally, is always present alongside the former. This process is, however, impeded by the State's need to survive and to maintain the domination of the State bourgeoisie, which ensures that State power prevails.[41]

Apart from the fact that it complicates unnecessarily something which is after all quite simple, this sort of argument prevents one from understanding that there is a relationship of complementarity and hybridisation between private and public capital, rather than a relationship of exclusion and competition. Cowen even argues that nationalisation is a condition of private accumulation: the dominant class centralises capital through the State sector, by 'straddling' or by any other means.[42] The 'privatisation of the State' in Zaïre[43] can also be seen in this light. Private investment in Nigeria was fuelled by the extraordinary growth in Federal government and parastatal expenditure in the 1970s; the triangular pattern linking the foreign operator to the bureaucrat and to his courtier operated against this background.[44] In the Ivory Coast one also comes across the same 'ubiquity of a group of managers both of the State and private investor'.[45] Similarly, in Niger the merchants increased their savings in relation to the expenditure of the public and parapublic sectors within which they constantly moved.[46]

To this extent, access to the State – as a form of merchant capital, as the Marxists would put it[47] – is truly vital for the social groups who aspire to domination. It must nevertheless be borne in mind that the practice of 'straddling' weakens the specifically bureaucratic tenor of the State: like ONCAD in Senegal, the 'State industries' and the parastatals are 'state' only in name: the Ivoirian example shows that their privatisation, in the form imagined by the World Bank, necessitates in advance their rebureaucratisation.[48] More generally, the statist stage in African economies seems to be confined to a certain point in time. Its origins have been traced to the 'second colonial occupation', following the Great Depression. But, aside from the precedents of Ghana, Mali, Guinea and Congo-Brazzaville, it was during the 1970s that it became a reality both in self-proclaimed 'socialist' countries such as Tanzania, Angola, Mozambique and Guinea-Bissau and in 'capitalist' states (in particular Nigeria, where federal expenditure rose from 12 per cent of GDP in 1966 to 36 per cent in 1977, and the Ivory Coast, where public expenditure rose to 32.6 per cent of GDP in 1976 and to 42.7 per cent in 1978).[49] The preeminence of the public sectors has now been eroded by structural adjustment plans. Members of the governing classes within the State are also by no means the least active participants in the 'informal' sector, whose involvement in the official economy is too often underestimated: even in socialist countries they tolerate it politically as a safety valve, they cover it administratively, obtaining a sinecure, and above all they fuel it with their own investments and other dealings.[50]

THE MYTH OF THE 'NATIONAL BOURGEOISIE'

We must therefore conceptualise this straddling class, this 'mixed bourgeoisie' in its unity, as much as in its plasticity.[51] Some experts on Zaïre suggest specifying it as a 'politico-commercial class', an appealing expression suggestive of the interdependence of two major sectors of the process of accumulation at the top of the social scale.[52] On the one hand, the distribution of 'Zaïrianised' goods in 1973 was determined by affiliation to the government. But on the other hand, property qualifications made wealth one of the criteria for the selection of candidates for the legislative elections in 1970 and 1975, thereby advantaging the traders. It can now be seen that Georges Balandier's initial assertion is a little reductive. The privileged relationship of power to wealth is neither exhaustive (salaried positions in businesses or education were a classic starting point for social improvement; the public sector is indissociable from private business and the 'informal' economy), nor unequivocal (more and more, economic wealth opens the doors to power).

It merely denotes a point in the emergence of a dominant class, of which the state is less a constitutive part than the incubator.

However, the characterisation of this class is still problematic. The idea of a 'national bourgeoisie', which dominates as soon as one challenges that of the 'bureaucratic bourgeoisie', as for example do Richard Joseph or Michael Schatzberg, is itself 'contestable'.[53] The epithet 'national' is singularly ill-conceived. Not that this 'bourgeoisie' is divided along ethnic lines, as is often asserted: on the contrary, we have seen that networks of accumulation almost necessarily transcend regional particularities. But the term 'national' supposes a latent and irreducible contradiction between the African business environment and foreign capital, where in fact there are frequently relationships of association and overlapping. Historically, European businesses supported the development of African trade increasingly from the Second World War onwards. Even before then their struggle against local traders, which was in any case less widespread than has sometimes been noted, chiefly targeted the powerful compradors of the coast.[54] On the other hand, in Nigeria the Dantata who specialised in the kola trade, or the Abu Lafiyas who dealt in trans-Saharan trade became the agents of Raphaello Hassan and Co., then of the United Africa Company. Having introduced these firms into the brotherhood and family networks of the North, they received in return lines of credit, regular supplies and an opening into a wider market.[55] In Kenya the British companies, more than the programmes of the colonial administration, contributed to the expansion of 'native' shops and transporters, who faced stiff competition from the 'Asians'.[56] This collaboration between the African business community and foreign firms continued and expanded after independence. It became institutionalised as private joint ventures, or in the shape of State participation in the principal foreign investments. It also gave rise to transnational mobility, with African entrepreneurs daily operating in collaboration with western, Indo-Pakistani, Lebano-Syrian, Israeli, Korean, Japanese or South African entrepreneurs. The best-known example of this phenomenon is undoubtedly that of Lonrho.[57] Spectacular as it may be, it is still the rule rather than the exception, as Swainson's study of three multi-nationals operating in Kenya (Brooke Bond, Bata and Lonrho) confirms.[58] As economic magnates, heads of State from Mobutu to Houphouët-Boigny, from Bongo to Daniel arap Moi, from Siaka Stevens to Major-General Joseph Momoh, his successor, have incidentally not been slow to assure themselves of foreign cooperation.

These lines of interdependence do not of course exclude inherent conflicts of interest. However, there are no grounds for interpreting them teleologically, as populist Kenyan deputies have done. Such conflicts may lead to a greater integration of local and foreign capital, the result not of a defeat but of a conscious choice on the part of the 'national bourgeoisie'. From this point of view there is no distinction between a 'national' bourgeoisie and its treacherous comprador sister. Gavin Kitching rightly remarks that any businessman or bureaucrat belongs sometimes in one of these categories, sometimes in another, depending on the activity, the motivation and the particular alliance in which he finds himself at the time.[59] It will perhaps be remembered that we have similarly given up classifying ancient African societies as either 'resisters' or 'collaborators'. This is the fundamental logic of extraversion. One could, after all, wonder at the historical aberration presented by this form of 'national bourgeoisie' in Europe – the bourgeoisie was not always national, nor did it always remain so – and question whether it could be reproduced in a situation and a century where accumulation was taking place on a world scale, on a transnational basis. In the light of the past we may suppose that the historical trajectory of the African continent leads social groups who dominate it politically to become involved in extraversion. The facts are consistent enough to suggest that this is deep rooted.

Africa firstly remains partly 'without frontiers' a whole century after the Congress of Berlin.[60] This is obviously an exaggerated proposition, above all since the disappearance of the great colonial federations. But at least it has the merit of drawing attention to the intensity of the transcontinental flow of accumulation. Regional economic integration is more developed than is commonly supposed, as is evidenced by Malian and Senegalese branches of the Zambian emerald industry, Zaïrian investments in West Africa, the regional spending of Nigerian business and the continental network of Muslim traders and Cameroonian placements in Dakar and Abidjan – let alone the flourishing smuggling industry which is by no means confined to the 'small boys', accounting as it does for 30 per cent of Central Africa's diamond production, and 80 per cent of Sierre Leone's.[61] Finally and most importantly, presidents' billions which amass interest in western bank accounts – 'Who in the world would not deposit part of his goods in Switzerland?' asks Houphouët-Boigny[62] – should not obscure a much more general exodus of African capital. From a point in the 1960s where it already accounted for 4 per cent of GDP, private transfer of capital out of the Ivory Coast expanded in the 1970s, particularly after 1976 with the opulence of State industries, reaching 7 per cent of GDP in 1980, amounting to 150 billion francs CFA. Expatriates of European origin were responsible for just under half, with the Syro-Lebanese community, together with national 'high earners' whose opportunities for enrichment increased throughout the decade, being responsible for the remainder.[63] This additional indicator of the extraverted orientation of the Ivory Coast model reflects a wider continental reality. It is borne out by the amounts of foreign deposits from the non-banking sector originating from Africa which, taking demographic differences into account, are disproportionate compared with those from Asia (in the third quarter of 1986 they stood at $17.8 billion and $38.14 billion respectively).[64] And the former Director-General of the *Caisse Centrale de Coopération Économique*, Monsieur Postel-Vinay, commented, 'Experts are well aware that a large proportion of bank loans granted to underdeveloped countries to allow them to meet indispensable external payments, in fact go to finance the flow of capital into Switzerland or other countries of refuge'.[65]

On the whole, the term 'comprador class' would be preferable to that of 'national bourgeoisie' if it were not tainted with infamy and misconception: the compradors served their own rather than foreign interests, and the coloniser, who understood this well, made it his priority to break them. The phenomenon we are faced with, and which we cannot examine in more depth here, is the crystallisation of social stratification astride the international system. Dependency theorists tried to take account of it by stressing the 'transnationalisation of capital' or by arguing that the dominant class of peripheral societies was 'absent' and that its place was taken by the bourgeoisie of the capitalist centre.[66] This specious reasoning nevertheless succeeds in drawing our attention to the structuring of an area which Domenach and Laïdi suggest we call 'cardinal', within which there is a criss-crossing of pluri-continental dynamics, an integral element of the historical production of African societies.[67] The groups which dominate them are formed in a dimension which extends beyond the State boundaries. Almost one after the other in 1983–84, first the Njonjo affair and then the Diawara scandal threw the spotlight on the 'jet-set societies' of West and East Africa, unifying true regional areas and operating in step with the great financial markets of the world economy. One has only to see the air-conditioned lounges of African airports, to fly the never-ending coastal route stopping at all airports between Libreville and Dakar, or to wonder at the ramifications which lead Mouride pedlars to the markets of the South of France or to Chicago, to get a feeling of the vitality of these transnational flows.[68] Even more now than in ancient times, Africa is the continent of mobility, and now as then inequality largely stems therefrom.

One of the reasons is that trade, more than production, is still the major economic activity south of the Sahara. In this respect the dependency theorists were not entirely wrong when, without actually admitting it, they preferred Ricardo to Marx. This suggests a new footnote which warns us against the notion of 'bourgeoisie' in a historical context, which, apart from a few exceptions, seems to include neither class exploitation in the Marxian sense, nor a productive economy. This is clearly shown in the best research on social stratification in Africa – in particular, that of Gavin Kitching on Kenya and Sara Berry's studies of Yorubaland.[69] The remarkable studies of the Ivory Coast and Senegalese economies completed under the auspices of the *Bureau des Evaluations* of the French Ministry of Cooperation, on which we have previously relied on several occasions, also agree on the crucial role of rents in the process of domestic accumulation.[70] The sub-Saharan agricultural and industrial sectors are thus fragile and not very competitive.[71] However little one accepts Max Weber's view that 'the major problem of the expansion of modern capitalism is that of the development of the mind of capitalism', and that the bureaucratic State is the necessary institutional vector, it must still be admitted that Africa's affiliation to the bourgeois ethos remains uncertain and varies enormously from one area to another.[72]

To this we shall add a final objection. Historically, the bourgeoisie in Europe was formed in relation to an established class, the aristocracy. It is not at all certain that the concept holds great meaning if one abstracts from this pluri-secular experience of cohabitation, collaboration and confrontation. The theme of a 'national bourgeoisie' sheds no light at all on the ancient classes in relation to which this bourgeoisie is defined in Africa. The yardstick remains that of the international capitalist system. It is high time that we acknowledge the depth of experience of African social groups, attempt to illuminate their trajectories and identify the changes and continuities in their development.

CHAPTER FOUR
The Opportunity State

The linking and telescoping within the *longue durée* of systems of inequality and domination can be seen in a historical trajectory. According to Perry Anderson, for example, the concatenation of 'Antiquity and feudalism' made the transition to capitalism in Europe 'a unique fact'.[1] French theoreticians of the articulation of modes of production have attempted to establish some of these lines of concatenation in Africa, in the familiar Althusserian manner, confusing structures, processes and actors.[2] This is an unsatisfactory position for us, in that we are not concerned with the 'profound' relationships of production but with the relationships of the postcolonial State to social stratification. For our purposes, we simply put the question of the linking of historical lines of inequality and domination, of their repercussion within contemporary political arenas, and the social strategies they engender.

THE ABSENCE OF HEGEMONY

It would be a mistake to organise our study around the fundamental break represented by the colonial interlude, the antecedent of trade or the capitalisation of production. Because it reflects an essential heterogeneity of any society, whose importance is clearly shown in Marx's *Critique of Political Economy*, the multi-dimensional nature of social stratification systems south of the Sahara is original. It bears witness to the intensity of Africa's historical exchanges, whether warlike or peaceful. Ancient Africa cannot be reduced to easily identifiable classes – the aristocracy against the peasantry or slaves, or 'elders' over 'juniors'.[3] It harboured tangled social divisions which historians and anthropologists are less and less willing to conceptualise through the usual notions of State, lineage society, social class or feudalism. This complexity should not in itself trouble western readers so long as they are not unduly influenced by tribalist measure; it recalls the configuration of Europe at a time when 'every territorial division was ... a social division'.[4]

So the question of concatenation is very much a precolonial one. With the Wolof in Senegal, two systems – castes and orders – were superimposed. The first, probably preceding the emergence of the State, divided a society which probably included a limited number of slaves. The second was born out of the institution of a centralised power, a great trader of slaves, whose ranks were constantly being swelled by internal and external wars. The order of slaves had, however, also formed into a 'pseudo-caste' in response to 'the caste system's criterion of totality', and these captives belonged 'like all members of society to two social systems at once'.[5]

J. P. Olivier Sardan's account of the Songhay-Zarma societies of Niger is even more subtle. These were divided by 'a very marked ideological dichotomy between free men and slaves'. But slavery just before the colonial conquest was really the product of two systems, corresponding to two distinct historical phases:

> (1) an ancient lineage system, which had disappeared by the time of the Songhay empire ... with a 'soft' system of captivity, where slaves were fewer in number, where occasional prisoners were seen as dependants and were gradually integrated into the lineage. (2) A new system of slavery from the Arab world which developed with Islam, the strengthening of the Songhay of the Askias and the production of slaves for trans-Saharan trade.

The particular category of the *horso*, dependants who escaped many aspects of the servile condition, cannot, however, be assimilated either to the first phase or to the second phase of so-called trade slaves, who experienced much harsher conditions. The *horso* seemed to be 'stuck between two ideological matrices':

> One matrix, leading to an absolute division of society between nobles and slaves, stemmed from the slave trade, assimilated slaves who had been seized or bought in exchange for cattle ... and systematised the ban on polygamy for male slaves, referring to the source of production of the slaves as a social category, kidnapping. The other matrix, stemming from a transformation of lineage slavery within heterogeneous village communities, takes on the contours of the patriarchal family: younger members, women and *horso* have the same dependency towards the patriarch, a dependence which takes the form and language of kinship.

The free man–slave dichotomy was also linked to other contradictions – between warriors and peasants, chiefs and subjects, patriarch and dependants, men and women, elders and juniors – each with its own dynamic, reciprocally influencing each other. These linkages can only be explained by history, particularly the establishment of aristocratic chiefdoms whose members continued to draw on the ideological repertoire of ancient lineage or village societies:

> The frequency of these permutations, the large amount of reciprocal borrowings between kinship and political terminology, the frequent absence of singular clearly defined categories does not, of course, point to the absence of a specific political arena, nor the social predominance of kinship relationships, nor indeed the existence of a general confusion of social relations.

The idea of 'dependence' could be a matrix common to these 'multiple and occasionally changing representations', allowing participants to pass from one dimension to another according to contexts and strategic demands. Against this moving background, which did not correspond to any precise ethnic identity and whose vast range of political forms was an obvious indication of heterogeneity, there was however clearly a Songhay–Zarma social space, unified by language, culture, ecological background and the similarity of social relationships and economic practices.[6]

The lines of concatenation, from the precolonial to the colonial and postcolonial phases, have been added to previous linkages. In the daily lives of its actors, at least, the contemporary repercussions of these ancient cleavages are obvious. In Songhay–Zarma country, for example, the ban on marriage between slaves and nobles still persists, even in prosperous urban districts, and it is perpetuated by the continuation of cultural stereotypes attached to each of these two conditions. So a descendant of a slave is still the 'sponger' (*naarekwo*), always trying to extract money from the nobleman through trickery, flattery or mendacity. He does not experience the aristocrat's shame (*haawi*) of curses and foul language.[7] Soninke slaves likewise 'can do anything, apart from forget that they are slaves'.[8] And amongst the Fulbe of northern Cameroon, the descendant of *maccuBe* who converts to Islam (*o nasti fulBe*, 'he who becomes a Fulbe') may wear the boubou and learn a few surahs of the Koran, up to the surah *Al Baqara*. If he goes beyond that and himself attempts to teach, he will be mocked: 'He is only a *maccu-Do*'.[9] Caste identities are also maintained in the societies of the Sahel. Even when they no longer determine the professional and functional specialisation of the people concerned, they limit matrimonial relations and prescribe a status which is almost impossible to escape.[10] In Mali and Senegal, certain political leaders are seen as 'casted' and only a few years ago in Dakar, it used to be said that you were going 'to the forge' when the Prime Minister granted you an audience.

Of course, such 'ideological relics' are not found everywhere, or may be in a much weakened form.[11] Yet it has to be acknowledged that the cleavages of the past preserve a contemporary validity more systematically than was for a long time thought. They are particularly likely to be reproduced with capitalist or para-capitalist relationships of production, as shown by the continuity of the economic exploitation of women and the maintaining of old social categories in the organisation of manual labour.[12] This observation does not assume any permanence of the social groups, *an sich*. It does not mean that historical lines of stratification are assimilable today to what they were yesterday, and does not allow artificial description of contemporary social relationships in terms of ancestral qualifications. It simply acknowledges the need for a genealogical approach which reveals the strategies by which social actors managed the rise of the State over the long term.

Upheaval is thus, paradoxically, the salient feature of the last century. Where continuity seems to have prevailed, and where the historically dominant groups were able to channel changes to their advantage, the rupture is in fact just as deep since 'a whole world has changed' – in the North of Nigeria, for example: 'The emirs still rule, and the peasants are still tilling the soil with their hoes'.[13] African societies have been catapulted into a spatial scale magnified tenfold by the fact of their 'incorporation' into the coloniser's territorial frameworks.[14] They have been more or less confronted by the demands of the capitalist world economy, demands of conquerors more foreign than any conqueror had ever been. Ancient societies had certainly known occupations, and violent defeats: it was their common lot. Conquerors had not, however, made such exorbitant demands as the exclusive use of the land, as the white invaders suddenly did in their settler colonies.[15] They had not introduced such significant innovations as cadastral surveys, railways, lorries, aeroplanes, the telegraph, banks, salaries, or machines.* In whatever way one conceptualises it, the colonial change had an effect both on the enlargement of social space and on the mode of production.

Contemporary actors are keenly aware of the resulting conversion of social relationships. The remark of a Yoruba planter, from which Sara Berry took the title of one of her books, is revealing: 'At one time, sons

*On the other hand, anthropologists and historians now tend to relativise the colonial 'monetarisation' of African economies, arguing that the use of coinage was widespread in ancient societies, and that the African continent can be divided into true 'monetary zones'.

worked for their fathers but today we have schools and civilisation, and fathers now work for their children.' This echoes the complaint of a Voltaique living in a suburb of Abidjan, who regretted that 'it is no longer possible, as it used to be, to ask a son to hand over most of his salary to his father', or even the words of a villager in Niger: 'Once it was the elder who profited from everyone's work, today it's the opposite as it's the children who benefit from the work of the elders.'[16]

Discontinuity is even more apparent during the colonial episode since no established class of landowners could act as pivot and backbone in the process of State formation as happened in Europe, Asia and Latin America. The coloniser failed to transform dominant African groups into a landed aristocracy where the social structures seemed best suited to this thaumaturgy – in Buganda, Zanzibar and the north of Nigeria.[17] Conversely, the suppression of some of the essential resources of domination (starting with slavery), competition from European commercial companies or foreign minorities, multiplication of new opportunities for prosperity through trade or salaried jobs, institutionalisation of new political hierarchies (described as 'traditional'), the spread of western knowledge by schools the bulk of which preached the gospel of the Christian God: all these developments linked to a real economic and cultural revolution could not fail to have social consequences. At the very least they made a wholesale redistribution of the cards possible, if not inevitable.

Region by region, village by village there have been many detailed studies of the new deal.[18] They enable us to formulate the hypothesis of an 'hegemonic crisis' in relation to the postcolonial State.[19] Once the necessity of locating its social foundations in an historical framework is accepted, the Gramscian concept nevertheless still raises more questions than it answers. It is in some ways reductive: the spread of the tsetse fly at the end of the nineteenth century, the influenza epidemic of 1919, the demographic curves and caprices of the climate have had as much influence on Africa's development as social relations, from which they cannot after all be completely separated. (Marx reminds us of this when he speaks of man's struggle against nature.)[20] The concept of hegemonic crisis, moreover, flattens the irregularities of trajectories of inequality and power. It also presupposes a degree of integration of social systems which is not borne out by orality, spatial mobility, recurrent feuds, peasant struggles and inter-monarchic wars, organic incompleteness and economic underexploitation. This was the case, naturally, with lineage societies whose destinies were controlled by the logic of segmentation and the exit option. But the idea of hegemony, while it may be applied to the kingdom of Rwanda, seems excessive when applied to another centralised and highly stratified monarchy such as Burundi, or, *a fortiori*, to Yoruba towns.[21]

Only perhaps the quasi-bureaucratic and constitutional Asante of the 1880s justifies the use of the concept of an organic crisis, since the *nkwankwaa's*★ overthrow of the monarchy was truly revolutionary. The later restoration of the monarchy in no way suspended the central contradiction between royal mercantilism and the quasi-bourgeois aspirations of the *asikafo*★★, anxious to escape from an economic regime which hampered their prosperity. These other oppositions did not coalesce politically with the dissatisfaction of the merchants, the *ahiafo*† rejected the obligations of conscription and the *amanhene* ‡ refused the reconstitution of an excessively vigorous central authority which would have undermined the authority they had regained. In line with the Gramscian model, two basic groups confronted each other over the economic organisation of society; the old was about to die, but the new could not yet be born.[22] The conflict of the 1880s thus provides a perspective for the subsequent evolution of Ghana. Under colonisation, the *asikafo* became involved in cocoa production, successfully as we know, and benefited from the suppression of the succession rights which so obstructed their attempts at making money, before Kwame Nkrumah's regime submitted them once again to the Republican mercantilism of the Marketing Board.[23]

Although it was not absolutely without parallels in West Africa – John Lonsdale talks similarly of a 'crisis of monarchies' in Dahomey, the Yoruba towns and the Senegambian kingdoms[24] – the Asante trajectory, in its relative purity, does not have a general continental significance. It is obviously possible, perhaps even probable, that the dynamics of divergence and predation south of the Sahara were a consequence of the swing of the western world economy from its Mediterranean axis to an Atlantic one in the sixteenth century, and beyond that to have witnessed, as Braudel notes, the failure of Africa in its connection with the ancient world, the Arab and the Indian world.[25] Yet for all its credibility, this diagnosis of a long-term lack of hegemony, does not make it any easier to apply the concept of an organic crisis to the analysis of postcolonial political configurations.

★*nkwankwaa*: young men
★★*asikafo*: the rich
†*ahiafo*: the poor
‡*amanhene*: chiefs of an *oman* (political and administrative district)

THE PURSUIT OF HEGEMONY

The concept of organic crisis does, however, emphasise the importance of the pursuit of hegemony for social groups caught up in the whirlwind of the last century:

> Such a 'hegemonic quest' aims at the creation and crystallisation of a relatively stable balance of forces between different dominant groups, both old and new, and their regional or ethnic parts, in the national framework fixed by the coloniser; at the arrangement of relationships between this formative dominant class and mass of the population; at the ordering of relationships between this dominant class and western economic and political power; at the elaboration of an ethnic or a common feeling which gives its coherence to the whole and which cements the new system of inequality and domination, while camouflaging it at the same time.[26]

This is far too mechanistic a definition. Its only merit is to point out the triple game of the hegemonic quest. First of all, one has to draw the boundaries, ideological as well as territorial, of the new area of domination, brought about by the colonial change of scale, in which the dominated were enclosed. Here, in another guise, is the central dynamic of ethnicity: that of the structure of the area of the State as a double area of identity and inequality. The chains of ancient societies which ignored linear frontiers, and recognised each other through a right over persons, have been replaced by the wider dimension of the State, the right over space.[27] This change, whose importance has often been stressed, opened the way to the appropriation of land, which henceforward was the consequence of power. The reconstruction of the social space seems then indissociable from the second stake: the opportunity, not just for enrichment but for real primitive accumulation, arising from the monopolisation of the means of production by dominant groups.[28] The State's close involvement in this development reveals the third and clearest element of the hegemonic quest: holding political power; that is to say, the use of legitimate force which controls the 'putting to work' of subordinate groups and the control of the economy. Here, too, the colonial period was innovative. It separated the participants from the ancestral symbolic representations which contributed to limiting social polarisation, it introduced the technology of the bureaucratic centralised State which gives the dominant groups the means – from writing to modern communication via massive armament – to achieve their ends.[29]

Within the space of a few decades the production of inequality has made a qualitative leap in relation to previous centuries. Indigenous dominant groups have never had at their disposal so many resources, political, economic and military, with which to enforce their domination and assure the autonomy of their own power. Social stratification has never been as wide. Thus it is not simply the reproduction of ancient hierarchies which the last century has brought into question, but rather their widened reproduction in previously unsuspected and inaccessible ways.

It will be remembered that Gavin Kitching refers to the inter-war years in Kenya as 'the years of opportunity'. All African actors tried to seize the 'opportunity' introduced by the coloniser, missionary or trader. This was true, first of all, of societies divided by military or commercial rivalries. They tried to exploit the new economic and territorial framework, sometimes to maximise an existing advantage, sometimes to improve on a weak position. The race for resources of extraversion continued throughout colonisation. Let us go back to the Cameroonian example. In the nineteenth century, the 'rush to the West',[30] across the great forest of the South in search of the mysterious ocean of untold wealth, continued through locally differentiated alliances upon which successive European occupations rested. Deprived of their profitable middleman role by the German advance, the Bassa tried to resist militarily, and were crushed. This drove them into a cycle of economic decline and proletarisation, which led many of them in the 1950s to rally behind the most radical nationalist organisation.[31] The Beti, on the other hand, looked favourably on the arrival of the whites, who short-circuited costly Bassa mediation and protected them from the pressure of other peoples. They later rebelled when they realised the true nature and scale of the German domination implied: State centralisation, which was intolerable to an acephalous society.[32] But having checked the revolt of their lineage chiefs, the Beti chose to play the card of conflictual alliance with the coloniser, in the avowed hope (at one time realised) of taking control of the country upon its accession to independence. The approach of the Duala was somewhat more circuitous. After calling first on Britain, then on Germany to bring about the emancipation of their dependants and keep commercial control of the hinterland, the great families of the *Ngondo*★, came into confrontation with the colonial power which seized their land, only to seek a *rapprochement* in order to challenge Bamiléké and Bassa immigration.[33] The regional tensions which haunt the Cameroonian political scene followed from these strategies, which, it can never be sufficiently stressed, were led not by faceless 'ethnic groups', but by identifiable

★*Ngondo:* Duala assembly

historical actors. We could easily substitute for these examples that of the contentious warriors and merchants of the Yoruba towns, or that of the Foulbé suzerains of populations conquered in the Fouta Djalon or Adamawa.[34] They too would confirm that in Africa, as elsewhere, 'the organisation of space itself creates inequality and hierarchy'.[35] In this respect it was and still is one of the dimensions of social struggle.

Nevertheless, the persistence of this type of intersocietal cleavage or, more precisely, their permanent actualisation in the new context of the State and of a para-capitalist mode of production, is inseparable from another aspect of the hegemonic quest. Within each of these old societies, historical actors competed with one another to seize the colonial opportunity. To simplify matters, we shall first discuss those who made up the two subordinate categories *par excellence* in the old systems: 'youth' and 'women'. The quotation marks are necessary, as these categories were social constructs as much as biological differentiations linked to gender and age. They originate from relationships of economic production, legal relations and, of course, cultural particularities. To this extent they did not entirely match biological criteria. Amongst the Bamiléké, for example, certain women participated in the system of power and enjoyed its privileges, such as the granting of land, servants and matrimonial rights. The highest status was that of the *ma-fo* (mother-chiefs), originally 'from a sort of feminine aristocracy', who authorised the transfer of the title:

> The *ma-fo* was a woman, and feminine society organised around her through numerous neighbourhood and group hierarchies; but she is recognised as a man in order to give a foundation to her participation in the system of power and administration. Woman-chief, she is also woman-man so that social relations of 'male-sign' and 'female-sign' are expressed by her.[36]

The definition of 'youth' departed even more clearly from the simple criterion of age. As in Ancient Greece and Rome, or in France under the Ancien Régime, one could be a minor up to the age of 36 or older, or, more rarely, one could attain majority with adolescence if death had prematurely decimated the ranks of the elders. (Even today political parties retain this social acceptance of 'youth', and in Senegal a circular of the Socialist Party explains, for example, that 'between 27 and 35 years the young boy can choose to struggle with the adults or to stay with the young socialists.')[37] In the unequal relationship that the ancient lineage societies instituted between a minority of elders and a majority of 'juniors', only a few reached positions of social control when their elders disappeared. It was not a question of temporary inequality that generational succession would have obliterated. Anthropologists have thus come to distinguish between 'open' or 'relative' seniority (the father/son relationship which supposes that the younger generation will eventually be promoted to a position of seniority) and a 'closed' or 'absolute' seniority (the relationship elder/minor in which the younger generation is permanently denied superiority except through individual achievement, secession or manipulation of genealogy). Recent studies have shown that this 'absolute seniority', underpinning inequality and the social definition of 'youth', was not limited to West Africa, as used to be thought, but was found also in the societies of East Africa.[38]

If the social positions of feminity and youth tended to represent a universal feature of dependence, one still cannot take their subordination literally. In reality there is enormous variation between situations.[39] Neither 'women' nor 'minors' submitted passively to the law of the elders. Some relied on institutions which guaranteed them an autonomy feared by men.[40] It was not unusual for others to compensate, however sporadically and partially, for their economic and political inferiority by displaying their warlike qualities, like the young Fang and Bete men.[41] In the same way, subtle inversions in the invisible world added nuance to domination: women were feared for the efficiency of their sorcery, and therapeutic art often allowed the minor to escape his allotted role.[42]

There is nothing surprising in the fact that 'women' and 'minors' should have turned the colonial change of scale to their advantage in order to further their ancestral struggle against social elders. We should beware of any teleological or populist *faux pas*.[43] Their actions were not 'revolutionary', and they were as often individual as collective. Prostitution may be related to attempts at female emancipation, in the same way as may the nationalist mobilisation in the 1940s and 1950s, the cultivation and retailing of new agricultural products, conversion to Christianity, entry into the business world or political denunciation on behalf of some of the continent's most repressive regimes.[44] It is difficult to construct a general model here: during the Congolese rebellions of 1964–65, for example, women supported the 'Mulelists' in Kwilu, Kindu and Stanleyville, but not in South-Maniema.[45] What is important, for the moment, is that they burst upon the scene of Africa's modernity, putting down their mark, as so memorably described in the case of a Yoruba town by Wole Soyinka.[46]

In order to achieve autonomy, young men similarly used Christianity, salaried work, military service, skilled work, even mass migration. Their acceptance onto the colonial scene led to conflicts between elders and minors. The period of the whites became one of insolence, where 'children' 'with fire in their belly'[47] broke their silence and, most scandalous of all, appropriated the art of dressing. Schooling, new media and salaried work gave them control over resources of extraversion which were increasingly beyond the ken of the elders. Thus Ba-Kongo society was shaken by various youth protest movements, from the 'Gaullists' of the 1940s to the '*Swankers*' and '*Existos*' of the 1950s or to the 'Parisians' of the 1980s.[48] The pop group most in touch with the feelings of the Brazzaville youth a while ago was called '*Les Très Fâchés*' ('The Furious') ...

Beyond the anecdotal and colourful, the antagonism of seniority dominated political life throughout the colonial period – particularly between the two world wars – in the form of conflict, whether masked or declared, between 'chiefs' and 'scholars' (or *évolués*).[49] Social change and political demands in the mode of youth consequently became a theme in their own right: thus the considerable number of African organisations identifying themselves as youth movements. The Nigerian Youth Movement, the Zikist movement (in honour of the Igbo leader Nnamdi Azikiwe, whose name could mean 'youth is full of indignation' or 'the New Age is heavy with revenge'),[50] the Youth Social Circle of Sokoto, the Young African Union (in Zanzibar) and the Zanzibar African Youth Movement, the *Jeunesse camerounaise française*, *Juvento* (in Togo), the *Association de la Jeunesse Mauritanienne*: the passionate resonance of these names cannot be underestimated. The heroes of the new politics were indeed young, at least in terms of relative seniority. Out of thirty-two African representatives elected to French assemblies in 1946, for example, six were aged between 25 and 30, nineteen between 30 and 40, and seven between 40 and 46.[51] They were also often young in terms of absolute seniority and, like Bikounou-le-Vespasien in a novel by F. Bebey,[52] the leaders of the nationalist movement, the holders of positions of power, in other words the 'nizers', were often perceived as juniors. 'Bear in mind that the youth of today, who are supposed to be irresponsible, will become the famous chiefs, and the great rich men of tomorrow,' exclaimed the Secretary of the Ijeshaland Welfare Party in 1947.[53] Independence thus undoubtedly accentuated a veritable inversion of inequality in African societies, which the myth of the 'Revolution' subsequently tried to amplify. In 1964 the youth (in the biological sense) seemed to have made up the majority of the first 'Mulelist' recruits in Congo-Léopoldville. But it is even more remarkable that the word 'youth' should later have been applied without distinction to adults, young people and children in order to signify the 'advanced', as in Kwilu terminology current even before the beginning of the rebellion, the progressives, the partisans of the revolution.[54] On the other side of the river in Congo-Brazzaville, in the same period from 1963 to 1965, the *Jeunesse du Mouvement national de la révolution* (JMNR), which P. Bonnafé perceptively described as 'a political age group' rejecting an unbearable tutelage attracted 'almost all the young population between about 14 and 30, with the unmarried seeming to take a more active part'. Here too the use of the decription 'youth' was ideological, since amongst the leaders of the JMNR there were men of 40 or more, such as the 45-year-old official who had seen it 'as an opportunity to break into the circles of authority from which he had been excluded as a descendant of slaves'.[55]

The rediscovery of youth and women claimed by independence and revolution is of course largely idealistic and symbolic. It can at best only be partial, whatever the concrete improvements they might bring. Their demographic mass alone – females make up half of the population, and the under-30s of both sexes make up 70 per cent – is not sufficient for these two social categories to represent the nucleus of State domination. 'Youth' and 'women' can easily integrate themselves into power blocs, the wives of heads of States can preside over women's organisations, and the Republic can celebrate a 'Festival of Youth' or a 'Women's Year', but the real extent of dependence is not affected. One needs indeed to ask whether the State is not in the process of installing an 'absolute seniority' to the detriment of the 'small men', the 'voiceless', the 'lowest of the low', as the system of social stratification closes in on itself. We should remember that ancient lines of inequality may be grafted onto, and, as Marxist anthropologists have emphasised, may reinforce, contemporary procedures of accumulation. These processes of accumulation and hybridisation relate to the structuring of the State. We may retain the hypothesis of the diachronic reproduction of dependence, by which 'the dominated of yesterday make up the mass of the dominated of today.'[56]

Yet the origins and history of the dominant groups within the postcolonial State still need to be established, without forgetting that groups that had been dominated in the past have been capable of overthrowing the established hierarchy through the colonial economic revolution. The fascination of history lies in the fact that the favourites at the start are not necessarily the winners at the end. The continuity of old systems of inequality and domination of the contemporary State, which we assume methodologically, is in reality shot through with discontinuities.

PART TWO
Scenarios in the Pursuit of Hegemony

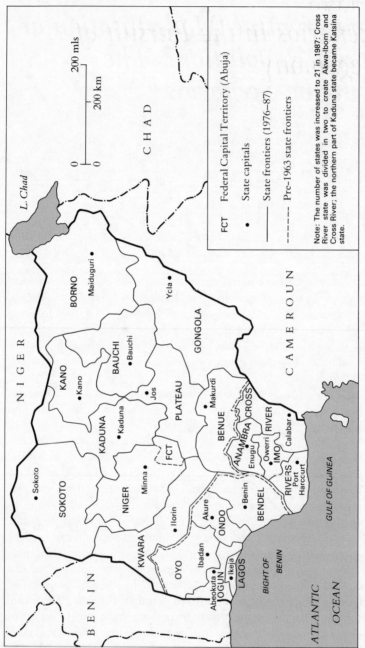

Nigeria's 19 states (1976–87)

CHAPTER FIVE

Conservative Modernisation or Social Revolution? The Extreme Scenarios

The 'pursuit of hegemony' should be defined between two ideal types: firstly, that of conservative modernisation whereby the already established dominant groups maintain their power – as Tancrède wrote in *The Cheetah*, 'Everything changes so that everything stays the same' – and secondly, that of social revolution, which brings about the downfall of the dominant groups and the rise of at least a section of the subordinate groups.

Due to the rapid changes during the past century, the social foundations of the State can be seen to vary according to region, time and place.[1] This characteristic, first described by Braudel in his analysis of France where it no longer pertains, remains as strong as ever in the case of Africa where it is just as fanciful to hold forth about the 'class nature' of political configurations which have been abstracted from their different historical and geographical backgrounds. Apart from the rare exceptions where the postcolonial State coincides territorially with its precolonial predecessor, such as in Zanzibar, Burundi, Rwanda, Lesotho and Swaziland, the ideal types under discussion can only be found regionally, most often within social groups amongst complex societies, as they are defined in contemporary anthropology, and not within the imaginary boundaries of ethnicity. In Senegal, for example, the *Tooroodo* oligarchy has continued to dominate the Fouta Toro from the eighteenth century to the present by maintaining control over major social innovations such as western education, party politics and rural development. One of the reasons behind the dam-building in the Fleuve region in the Fouta Toro must be an attempt to weaken the Tooroodo's dominance of the fertile *Waalo* area★ On the other hand, the Mouride brotherhood in Senegal was a vehicle of economic emancipation and relative mobility for the slaves and members of the artisan castes in traditional Wolof society; it is not an exaggeration to say that these groups experienced a 'veiled social revolution'.[2] Similarly, in Cameroon, both the colonial powers and the Ahidjo regime allied themselves with the already dominant groups in the northern and western regions, which often led to the reinforcement of the existing local systems. However, they also had to deal with widescale social changes in the acephalous societies of the south.[3] *In fine*, it is by the conjunction or the disjunction of these regionally defined trajectories that one can understand the meaning of the 'nation-state' in terms of social stratification.

Although it is significant, the importance of the different regional systems of colonial administration must not override that of the ability, or inability, of social actors to pursue strategies adjusted to the new circumstances. 'Western education is the new form of war used against us by the colonisers,' declares a *Tooroodo* aristocrat in Cheikh Hamidou Kane's famous novel, *Ambiguous Adventure*; 'and we should send our elite to these schools before sending the general public. As usual, it is right that the elite should go first for if there is any risk, they are the group best prepared to cope with it as they have the most to lose. And if there are any benefits, they must be the first ones to have them'.[4] The Fulani aristocracy of Northern Cameroon lacked such political shrewdness, for they sent underprivileged children to the French schools, thus condemning themselves to losing control to a new elite at the time of decolonisation. In sum, during this period, there were princes so enlightened as to become a threat, and revolutionary commoners no less so. Their skilfullness and audacity would take them a long way, and they cannot be ignored or treated as negligible factors.

KINGDOMS AND CHIEFDOMS

The analysis of the ideal types of conservative modernisation and social revolution is made more difficult by the heterogeneity of traditional

★The *Waalo* area is fed by the Fleuve.

systems of inequality and domination. Apart from the false dichotomy between 'state' and 'lineage', which has now been abandoned by anthropologists, the distinction between 'kingdom' and 'chiefdom' is no more enlightening.[5] According these categories nothing but didactic value, this analysis shall proceed from the most simple to the most complex societies, starting with those monarchies whose precolonial territorial make-up coincides with that of the modern State. However, these examples are not true models of conservative modernisation. The influence of the *Ngwenyama*★ Sobhusa II on political life in Swaziland after 1967 was too dependent upon the regional dominance of the Republic of South Africa to be of much significance in Africa as a whole.[6] The case of Lesotho, which is completely surrounded by the apartheid state, is even more aberrant; and that of Botswana, where the first President of the Republic, Seretse Khama, was the paramount chief of the most influential Tswana group, is also ambiguous.

The case of Burundi would fit most closely with the model of conservative modernisation if it could be claimed that the crushing of the Hutu putsch and of the peasant revolts from 1965 to 1972 was a true aristocratic counter revolution which involved the overthrowing of the monarchy in 1966. It is true that the ensuing regimes, which laid claim to the title of the Parti de l'unité et du progrès national (UPRONA), maintained Tutsi supremacy by exterminating part of the Hutu elite in 1972. But this general cleavage between Hutu and Tutsi cannot disguise other divisions which played a more determinant role in the historical context of a monarchical system in which the *Mwami*† was simply the *primus inter pares* and the feuds between royal princes (the *ganwa*), especially those between the Bezi and Batare branches of the royal family, have shaped Burundi's history, including the competition between western-style political parties. Between 1966 and 1976 a series of intra-Tutsi transformations were brought about by the regime of Colonel Micombero, but these cannot be termed 'conservative modernisation' although the brilliant prince Rwagasore, who was assassinated at the dawn of independence, seemed to be a prime exampler. These transformations included the dictatorship of the 'Bururi group' faction which brought about a regional transfer of power from the Central to the South-Western region; the partial revenge of the Tutsi-Hima against the Tutsi-Banyaruguru primacy; and finally the rise to power of the western-educated Tutsi cadres which worked to the detriment not only of the traditional aristocracy but also of the Hutu *and* Tutsi peasant

---

★*Ngwenyama*: sovereign
†*Mmami*: sovereign

masses. Successors to the Micombero dictatorship – Colonel Bagaza from 1976 to 1987, and Major Buyoya – involved themselves in similar but less extreme activities.[7]

In contrast, the case of Rwanda offers an indisputable example of social revolution. This stratified and highly centralised kingdom was much more impervious to any kind of mobility than Burundi. Moreover, the inegalitarian system of the allocation of power, riches and status corresponded almost exactly with, and helped to reinforce, ethnic identity. In short, the Tutsi aristocracy (who made up 15 per cent of the population) monopolised the political and economic resources of the monarchy whilst using its privilege and hegemony to control the Hutu cultivators and the small Twa minority (who made up 84 per cent and under 1 per cent of the population, respectively). As often happened, the colonial period made this historical situation more explosive by increasing injustice and rigidity. Indirect rule, Christian education, and the loan system imposed by the Belgians, as well as the chiefs' misappropriation of 'customary benefits' which were codified in a more or less arbitrary way by the colonialists, ended up in over-exploiting the peasantry. The *Mwami*'s suppression of the clientelist system (*buhake*) in 1952 put the finishing touches to this exploitation. Although this measure appeared to be progressive, in reality it deprived the peasants of their traditional system of support, which had guaranteed them a minimum of reciprocity from their patrons, and also broke the links of solidarity which had united the majority and the minority, albeit on unequal terms. The Tutsi aristocracy, who were still benefiting from Belgian support, took advantage of colonial liberalisation: in 1959, 94 per cent of the members of the Supreme Council, 98 per cent of the chiefs and 95.5 per cent of the sub-chiefs in the country were Tutsi.

Strengthened by their continuing dominance and, if one agrees with René Lemarchand, blinded by their own 'hegemony', the dominant oligarchy could not see when it was time to compromise. No prince Rwagasore emerged, and until 1958 no courtier could even go as far as contemplating the existence of a 'fraternity' between Hutus and Tutsis without the *Mwami* feeling it necessary to deny openly such a threat. However, in the Catholic mission system, a Hutu counter-elite was formed although it was too small to be compared in any useful way with the *évolué* of West Africa. Eventually this group was to benefit from the help of the Belgian 'Resident', which allowed them to transform the 1959 millenarian movements in the north and the legitimist *Jacquerie* in the centre of the kingdom into social revolution. Within a few months, twenty-two out of forty-three chiefdoms and 297 out of

559 sub-chiefdoms passed into the hands of Hutu 'provisional authorities'. In June–July 1960 the local elections accelerated this transfer of power from the elite to the counter-elite: out of 229 communes, 210 were won by Hutu burgomasters. In October, the president of the Hutu liberation movement was made head of the provisional government, which proclaimed the abolition of the monarchy from the beginning of the following year. But this institutional turn-around heralded more radical developments in the heart of the country by Hutu salaried workers and the Hutu '*moniteurs*': from November 1959 to January 1964, horrific massacres decimated the Tutsi community, first of all with the aim of removing them from power, then to prevent them from reconquering from the outside. The ensuing regimes of Gregoire Kayibanda and of Major-General Habyarimana have, since independence in 1962, ratified and consolidated this drastically altered situation.[8]

The case of Burundi may be too simple and straightforward. Social upheavals were often caused by the incorporation of traditional political structures into the broader colonial state, and, to an even greater degree, by the changes that occurred when the '*évolués*', '*diplômés*' and other educated people took over from the indigenous elite during the independence period. It was probably during efforts to stop this process that the generational conflict, related to the notion of 'absolute seniority', became more apparent. The classic confrontation between 'chiefs' and '*évolués*', which became a general phenomenon between the two world wars, did not in itself take on the dimensions of a social revolution. As in the case of Buganda, this tension resulted in a strictly political contradiction between the state at the 'centre' and the monarchy at the 'periphery'.[9]

However, the formidable process of 'incorporation' was often accompanied by an exacerbation of social contradictions. The ideology of nationalism and the ideas of 'civilisation', 'development' and even 'revolution' helped to mediate and synthesise these two kinds of process. In Zambia, the Litunga hoped for the secession of Barotseland in the years preceding independence, but this idea was opposed by the educated Lozi. The educated Lozi collaborated with the United National Independence Party and stood firmly against any *rapprochement* with the Republic of South Africa, Moïse Tshombe's Katanga, or Ian Smith's Rhodesia. After this, Barotseland, like Buganda, lost its autonomous status.[10]

The example of Guinea is even more revealing. The French administration restored the Fulani aristocracy to power in the Fouta Djalon (albeit to a lesser extent than in Cameroon) where the *Tenda*★ people took this as an opportunity to free themselves from the *Almamy's*† authority. The nobility in Guinea initially succeeded in taking advantage of the liberalisation brought about by the colonialists. The *Amicale Gilbert Vieillard* (AGV), the first proto-political organisation in the country, was set up in 1943 by Fulani graduates of the William Ponty School in Dakar. This association, which had both aristocratic and non-aristocratic members, campaigned for reform in the Fouta Djalon. The antipathy between the two social orders in the AGV, which had already been complicated by a dynastic dispute, became more evident in 1945 when a candidate had to be chosen for the French Constituent Assembly. The chiefs thought that the president of the AGV, Diawadou Barry, was too radical, although he was a descendant of the Fouta's principal royal lineages. They therefore elected a commoner, Yacine Diallo, in his place. Diallo became an affiliate of the SFIO and, with the open support of the French administration, dominated the political scene until 1954.

This alliance soon attracted the hostility of the *Parti démocratique de Guinée* (PDG), the territorial branch of the *Rassemblement démocratique africain*. This PDG became increasingly popular from 1952 onwards, and won the elections in 1956. The divergence between the aristocracy and the Fulani intellectuals intensified under the influence of nationalism, whose main target was the chiefs, and this culminated in the death of Yacine Diallo in April 1954. After this, the chiefs renounced their previous prejudices and put forward the name of Diawadou Barry to succeed Yacine Diallo, but by this time Barry had been discredited by his old allies and could no longer win their support. The most extreme militants of the old AGV founded a new party, the *Démocratie socialiste de Guinée* (DSG), led by the reformist nobleman, Ibrahima Barry, and attacked the very institution of chieftaincy. Diawadou Barry became leader of the *Bloc africain de Guinée* (BAG), which was backed by the French administration and leaders of various ethnic groups, who were becoming increasingly disturbed by the rise of populism in the country.

During the territorial elections of 1957 the BAG lost badly, and the PDG, led by Ahmed Sékou Touré, rose to power supported by most of the electoral constituencies of Fouta Djalon (occasionally with the support of the local chief, as in Dalaba). The DSG, having refused an

★*Tenda:* non-Fulani
†*Almamy:* sovereign

alliance with the PDG, managed to return only three deputies from its home base. During this period, a widespread popular movement grew up alongside the PDG campaign, progressively paralysing the institution of chieftaincy. The movement was particularly pointed in the Fouta Djalon, where it was initially confined to the *cantons* which had historically resisted the Fulani conquests (Youkounkoun, Gaoual and Mali), before moving into the very heart of the *Almamy*'s sphere of influence. In this climate of latent violence, Sékou Touré's government, newly constituted in line with the *loi cadre* of 1956★, convinced the French administration to abolish *canton* chiefs in 1957. For the first time since the *jihad* of the eighteenth century, the Fulani aristocracy saw themselves relegated to village-level positions of power, losing their judicial prerogatives and the direct and indirect revenue they received as administrative assistants. They also lost their political influence: the BAG distanced itself by allying with the DSG to form the *Union progressiste guinéene* in May 1958. The triumphant 'No' vote to the referendum of France's Fifth Republic a few months later, Guinea's break-away from the metropolitan power, the transformation of the PDG into a state party, and the violence of Sékou Touré's regime – up to the denunciation of a 'Fulani plot' in 1976 – all brought the social revolution in the Fouta Djalon to an end, thereby causing a huge exodus from the country.[11]

In contrast to the case of Guinea, the chiefs of the Sierra Leonean hinterland resisted the populist movements of the 1950s. The critical moment in this movement of conservative modernisation was between 1946 and 1949, when the new 'educated' elite from the interior formed the Sierra Leone Organisation Society. They declared that they were no longer satisfied with the compromises made between the two wars, especially the insufficient number of seats – they had only two – reserved for them in the Protectorate Assembly. Following the advice of the Governor, Sir George Beresford-Stoocke, and his successor, R.O. Ramage, and under pressure from various upheavals in Mende country, the chiefs finally increased the number of seats to six in 1950. Dr Milton Margai, who headed the group of intellectuals, set up the Sierra Leone People's Party (SLPP) in collaboration with the more progressive chiefs. The SLPP won the elections and stayed in power until 1967. It was this alliance that confronted the populist riots against chiefly abuses in 1955–56. The SLPP also led the country to independence. The

★*Translator's note:* The *loi cadre* of 1956 gave a measure of autonomy to each of the constituent territories of France's African empire but retained overall French executive control within the framework of the Union française.

downfall of the SLPP and the rise of the All People's Congress under Siaka Stevens at the end of the 1960s did not bring an end to this structural balance of political society. However, as elsewhere in Africa, the central power tightened its control over local authorities. Today, Sierra Leone is the West African country where the chieftaincy, as an apparatus of social inequality, has best retained its place within the postcolonial state.[12]

The example of Sierra Leone is, however, eclipsed by that of northern Nigeria. This case is exceptional due to its demographic density (the population of northern Nigeria is about 44 million), and the extreme turbulence of the last forty years. Despite military defeat and dependence upon slavery, the Fulani aristocracy were able to become intermediaries in the colonial administration by putting down the Mahdist revolt of Satiru (1906) which the British troops were no longer able to control. Northern Nigeria became the testing ground for the policy of indirect rule, which had been started by Lord Lugard in Buganda. Existing rulers were retitled 'Native Authorities', and, although always subject to the superior power of the administration, they added the western economy and the bureaucratic State to their traditional sources of power, even though they never constituted a landowning class despite the hopes of certain theoreticians of British imperialism. Meanwhile, the Fulani enlarged their sphere of influence by extending their supremacy throughout the Northern Region and by dominating the previously autonomous non-Muslims, especially those in what were to become Plateau and Benue states.

However, when the Northern Region was united with the rest of Nigeria in 1914, and when constitutional talks began after the Second World War with the object of leading the country to self-government and then to independence, the Fulani aristocracy became worried that they would be dominated by the Southern elites who were better versed in western culture and opposed to societies they considered 'feudal' and 'backward'. The nomination of colonial administrators from the Western and Eastern Regions in the north of the country, and the penetration of Igbo commercial interests, rapidly confirmed their fears about decolonisation. The primary aim of the northern leaders, particularly the emirs, was to protect the autonomy of their region from Southern imperialism. Secession was consequently widely believed to be a risk. But the northerners' preoccupation with protecting themselves was clearly in order to preserve a social order so strongly stratified that the notion of the 'dominant class' – namely, of 'hegemony', is of relevance (as it is in the case of Rwanda). This proposition is supported by the demographic concentration in the north, the ideological glue of Islam, the polarisation of cultural models of consumption, the diffusion of the written word, the extent of political centralisation, and the existence of capitalist relations of production and exchange.[13] Based upon the moral authority of the Muslim clerics the leadership (the *sarakuna*) was completely differentiated from the masses (the *talakawa*). From 1950 onwards, the *sarakuna* ensured their dominance of the Northern Peoples' Congress (NPC) by purging it of its radical elements. Up until the first years of independence, the hierarchy of the NPC faithfully reflected the hierarchy of the various emirates. In 1958, for example, four of the most prestigious local leaders – the Sultan of Sokoto, the emirs of Kano and Katsina, and the *Aka Uka* of Wukari – were also ministers without portfolio in the Northern Region Executive Council.[14] Ahmadu Bello, president of the NPC, a gifted policy maker (and, moreover, a descendent of Usman dan Fodio, the founder of the Sokoto caliphate) wanted to become sultan of Sokoto (his title of *Sardauna*, master of war, was given to him as compensation when he failed in his ambition) and, as was well known, he continued to cherish hopes of succeeding the man who had been preferred to him as sultan in 1938.

This was not, however, an exact reproduction of the dominant class of the *sarakuna*. Having been well versed in western culture and bureaucratic methods, Ahmadu Bello was perfectly aware of the need to keep up with the times. He paid particular attention to training a new elite capable of competing on equal terms with the southern elite in its command of western bureaucratic principles. Bello continued to reform the Native Authorities until 1963, when the deposition of Emir Sanusi of Kano brought the silent political revolution into the open: the NPC was no longer the preserve of the emirs as it had been in the past, but of a large and complex power bloc. The Sardauna's main achievement was to build up a political community in the North (*jama'ar Arewa*) around Kaduna, the administrative capital of the region. This did away with the particularisms of the past and conformed to the party slogan, 'One North: One People, Irrespective of Religion, Rank or Tribe'.[15] It was with good reason that Ahmadu Bello compared the electoral success of the Tories in Great Britain to that of the 'Tories' of Northern Nigeria when he spoke to Harold Macmillan in 1959. Bello also predicted the longevity of the *sarakuna*, which he considered to be similar to the English aristocracy, under the system of parliamentary democracy.[16]

This is not to suggest that the *sarakuna* were free from all revolutionary pressure. The radicals who seceded from the Northern People's Congress in 1950 created the Northern Elements Progressive Union (NEPU), even before they left the NPC. NEPU was the first political

---

Table 5.1 The structure of traditional social stratification in Northern Nigeria

---

1 *Sarakuna (rulers):*

reigning emirs
sons of reigning emirs
sons of former and late emirs
grandsons of reigning, former or late emirs
other members of royal dynasties
emir's councillors
hereditary district head
client district royal slaves officials
free courtiers *(fadawa)*
village heads
other employers of Native Administration

2 *Koranic malamai (teachers), imami (Islamic 'priests'), alkali (judges)*

3 *Talakawa (commoners)*
wealthy merchant-traders *(attajirai)*
lesser traders and contractors
small traders
farmers
weavers
blacksmiths
mat-makers
woodworkers
dyers
barber-doctors
house servants
musicians
butchers

Source: C.S. Whitaker, Jr., *The Politics of Tradition: Continuity and Change in Northern Nigeria 1946–1966*, Princeton, NJ: Princeton University Press, 1970, p.315.

party to be officially created in the region. The radicals were reacting to the existence of 'a class struggle between the members of the vicious circle of the Native Administrations [...] and the ordinary *talakawa*', and they announced their determination to work for the 'emancipation' of the *talakawa* by reforming 'autocratic political institutions'.[17] The social make-up of both the base and the leadership of NEPU suggests a popular counter-elite unlike the NPC, where the Establishment was over-represented. But the '*talaka*' (also known as '*sawaba*', freedom) remained a minority in parliament except in Ilorin Division, which was composed mainly of Muslim or Christian Yoruba, where a Talaka Parapo (party for the masses) succeeded in momentarily taking over from the *sarakuna* in 1957.[18] Aminu Kano, the leader of NEPU, admitted himself that if a revolutionary government that chose its civil servants according to their qualifications emerged, it would find itself at the head of a bureaucracy made up of the social class it intended to destroy.[19]

A far more serious challenge arose in January 1966, when the assassination of the Sardauna and of Abubakar Tafawa Balewa (Prime Minister of the Federation and member of the NPC) was immediately followed by the seizure of power by an army faction hostile to the Northern political class.[20] The formation of a unitary state in Nigeria brought into reality the *sarakuna*'s haunting fear of the physical liquidation of the Northern elites, following a similar pattern to that of Rwanda. However, the July counter-coup wiped out their fears. The new head of the military government, Lieutenant-Colonel Yakubu Gowon, was a Christian from the Anga tribe, a minority from the Middle Belt, and was a member of the Sardauna's political entourage, having been his favourite officer.[21] Gowon rapidly re-established federalism, but also announced that the constitution was to be reformed. This proposed reform was enacted the following year, although the Biafran secession and civil war could no longer be avoided. The country was divided into twelve federal states, six of which were in what had previously been the Northern Region. Lieutenant-Colonel Gowon hoped to prevent the ethnic minorities of the Eastern Region from becoming involved in Igbo separatism. He also hoped to appease those Middle-Belt minorities who had previously been integrated into the Northern Region, but who had not been well disposed towards the policies of the Sardauna.[22]

The renunciation of this strategy was felt to be a necessary sacrifice for the stable future of Nigeria, but such self-denial was always more fiction than fact. Northern identity (*danArewa*) remained strong and continued to be linked to Islam, although it started to identify more closely with a national ideal, rather than being a defensive reaction against Yoruba and Igbo expansionism. Throughout this tumultuous period of military governments, the capacity of the Northern Establishment to maintain its dominance was remarkable, but there was no one person with sufficient legitimacy or breadth of vision to occupy the position of the Sardauna. The dissolution of the Native Authorities in 1970 should not be misinterpreted, for they were immediately replaced by Local Government Authorities, and the reform carried out was simply a continuation of the transfer of power initiated by Ahmadu Bello and Abubakar Tafawa Balewa during the 1950s. On the other hand, the Northern leadership which was as 'traditional' as it was administrative, and as political as it was economic, was associated with the exercise of power by numerous 'consultative' procedures. They continued to dominate the groups which succeeded Yakubu Gowon after he was overthrown in 1975. Murtala Mohammed was from the aristocratic establishment of Kano, and those who organised his succession in Febuary 1976 – Joseph Garba, a Christian, and Shehu Yar'Adua, a Fulani from Katsina – also originated from the North. Murtala Mohammed was replaced by a Yoruba, Olusegun Obasanjo, but he was overshadowed by Yar'Adua, who did his best to ensure the continued supremacy of the dominant Northern political class.[23] This class reaped the new institutional and economic benefits simultaneously. Several members of the Northern Region Civil Service, which had been dissolved in 1967, left the administration to join the private sector, thus bringing new blood into the old Hausa merchant communities.[24] However, the political and bureaucratic opportunities of accumulation were multiplied by the systems of 'straddling' within the military regime, the drastic 'federalisation' of public resources (especially the revenues from the Marketing Boards which had previously been managed on a regional basis, as well as the rapidly rising petrol revenues), and the creation of new states in 1975. The Northern establishment's field of operation was therefore widened, even though the crumbling of regional institutions gave the impression that the political system was becoming increasingly divided.

This process was consolidated during the transition to civilian rule from 1977 to 1979, although the ascent of the younger generation of the Northern elite was somewhat restricted. This generation was informally grouped together within the Committee of Concerned Citizens, commonly known as the 'Kaduna mafia', even by its members, since the troubled days of 1966. This clique was made up of high-level civil servants, businessmen, army officers and academics who were solidly westernised as well as being fiercely attached to the historical specificity of the North and to the promotion of the region. A significant proportion of this group came from aristocratic families, although they were not dependent upon the emirs. They were generally closely associated with the prestigious Barewa College, and many were involved in certain organisations such as the Northern Region Civil Service and the *New Nigerian* press group. In other words, this group had been shaped by the Sardauna's system, of which they were the ultimate product. But they were distinguished from the 'Old Brigade' of politicians from the

Northern Peoples' Congress in terms of generation and professionalism. During the 1970s, the 'Kaduna mafia' was a powerful pressure group for the promotion of Northern interests. It ensured that the constitutional reform of 1967, the internal promotions in the army, the application of the decrees to 'indigenise' the economy and the distribution of credit from banks worked to their advantage. However, in 1978, the 'Kaduna mafia' did not succeed in taking control of the National Party of Nigeria (NPN) which was, in many ways, a continuation of the Northern Peoples' Congress and was intended through the process of elections, to ratify the primacy of the North, whilst giving an appearance of being a multi-regional coalition of political clienteles. The informal Northern Caucus which controlled the party remained in the hands of the 'Old Brigade', and the 'Kaduna mafia' was unable to secure the adoption of Mallam Adamu Ciroma, their proposed candidate for the presidential elections. Alhaji Shagari, who had more supporters in the South and whose image had not been tarnished by the scandals of the past decade, was preferred instead. Shagari brought the party to victory in 1979, and again in 1983 under highly questionable circumstances. The plasticity of the *sarakuna* Establishment was revealed even more clearly in the fact that the leader of the Great Nigerian People's Party (one of the parties which competed with the NPN for the control of the Northern states in 1979) was Waziri Ibrahim, an old member of the Northern Peoples' Congress and member of the Hausa-Fulani aristocracy, who benefited from the active complicity of several emirs.[25]

Despite the vitality of the populists and revolutionaries, they did not pose a serious threat to the strength of the *sarakuna's* hegemony. Aminu Kano was the only political figure in the region who could rival the late Sardauna's prestige, and, as such, he represented a threat. However, his reputation as a radical was steadily diminished. Lieutenant-Colonel Gowon's military regime was backed by Aminu Kano in the North, and in 1977–78 the possibility of a reconciliation between the founder of NEPU and members of the NPC became real. However, the persisting resentment of the emirs and the 'Old Brigade' of the National Party of Nigeria against the '*talaka* line' ensured that any attempt at reconciliation was stillborn. Aminu Kano was so upset by the modest post he was offered in the government that he left the NPN and took control of the People's Redemption Party (PRP), that had been formed by a handful of ex-trade unionists and Marxist-Leninist intellectuals. As well as injecting this party with his appeal, he also brought in many supporters of what had been NEPU. The PRP only won 10 per cent of the vote in the 1979 elections due to competition from Chief Awolowo's socialist Unity Party of Nigeria, and from the Great Nigerian People's Party standing for historical specificities of the now defunct Northern Region. PRP supporters were concentrated in the vital states of Kano and Kaduna, and they faithfully espoused the traditional divisions between the *talakawa* and the *sarakuna*. Abubakar Rimi, who had been elected governor of Kano, took it upon himself to break down the remaining privileges of the emir which favoured the NPN. But in the contest for power, the PRP soon split into a radical wing, made up of the governors of Kano and Kaduna, and a faction that remained faithful to the old *malilam*. In the 1980s, this division flourished and then degenerated into juridical foolishness. Aminu Kano died in 1983, never realising his ideal of *Sawaba* (liberty) which had made the aristocracy so suspicious of him.[26] However spectacular and disturbing, the millenarist uprisings which caused so much trouble in Kano, Maiduguri, Kaduna and Yola during this period were more a part of the social disintegration brought about by the economic crisis in these towns, caused by the great enrichment of a few and the pauperisation of many people, especially the floating population of Koranic students (the *gardawa*), than the crystallisation of a viable revolutionary movement.[27] These uprisings were bloodily put down.

Further south in the Middle Belt, some politicians, most of whom were Christians, also tried to shake off the *sarakuna*'s hegemony by founding the Council for Understanding and Solidarity (CUS) in 1977, with the aim of making their opinions known in the Constituent Assembly. They fiercely struggled against the imposition of *Sharia* law, which was supported by the 'Kaduna mafia' despite the reservations of the 'Old Brigade'. However, this attempt to form a 'majority of minorities' was not successful and soon collapsed in the miasma which occurred when the 'national cake' was shared out.[28]

In reality, the dangers faced by the Northern Establishment during the early 1980s were due to the growing weakness and illegitimacy of the Shagari government. The NPN's wild racketeering and bad economic decisions led the country into bankruptcy and threatened the industrial interests of some members of the 'Kaduna mafia'.[29] In other words, the 'mafia's' influence on the state apparatus had never been so dramatically diminished. Therefore this group split away from the NPN, and tried, without success, to take control of the People's Redemption Party. In the end it signed a secret agreement with the Unity Party of Nigeria (UPN). However, the UPN did not win the rigged elections of 1983. Without going as far as saying that General Buhari's rise to power on 31 December 1983 was orchestrated by the 'Kaduna mafia', it certainly did have links with the new regime, and Dr

Mahmud Tukur, who was one of its leading members, received the strategic Commerce and Industry portfolio. Buhari chose chiefs, mainly emirs, as his favoured allies – his political style was so brutal that he alienated the other forces in the country – and the Supreme Military Council that he presided over did not disguise its Northern bias. The most excessive privileges granted to the Northerners were removed by General Babangida when he replaced General Buhari in August 1985.[30] Due to the series of events described above, the transformation of the Hausa-Fulani aristocracy into a modern dominant class seems now to be complete. The main danger it faces today is that it will be blinded by its own strength, and force its Southern allies into religious secession by encouraging the rise of Islamic law, which has been an issue since the constitutional debate of 1977–78.

LINEAGE TRAJECTORIES

Although the models of conservative modernisation and social revolution fit relatively well into the contexts of intense social stratification and political centralisation, they fit rather awkwardly into certain other historical situations, such as those of segmentary, acephalous or lineage societies* and those of societies where a non-native minority tends to dominate economically, and sometimes politically.

The case of lineage societies is particularly complex, and their relationship with the pre-colonial or contemporary state has been a favourite theme for analysis by anthropologists.[31] We have already mentioned the contribution the French school of economic anthropology has made to this discussion. However, even the definition of the appropriate category for these societies poses problems.[32] As I cannot prove to the contrary, I will, for the time being, go along with the opinions of P. Geschiere, J-C. Barbier and R. Joseph when they insist upon the inadequacy of the notions of aristocracy or generational superiority to explain how the lineages of acephalous societies insert themselves into the postcolonial State.[33] This particularity of lineage trajectories is revealed in violent or veiled responses to the State. Most of the massive upheavals after the colonial conquest were caused by lineage societies. In addition just after independence, the African political authorites also had their share of difficulties in creating the intermediary power structures necessary for a government bureaucracy to

*See note on p.16 above

function in these societies. For example, the Sardauna failed to do so in the Nigerian Middle Belt, and the administrative reforms carried out in Tiv country in 1964 led to bloodshed. In a similar way, Dakar Jacobinism is weakened by the autonomist movements of the Diola in Casamance in southern Senegal, and the PAIGC's Marxist-Leninism in Guinea-Bissau is threatened by the Balant.

In lineage societies, conceptualisation of the dominant group considered likely to reproduce itself in the modern state had been problematic. However, the notion of aristocracy is possibly not as irrelevant as J-C. Barbier has suggested. An aristocratic ethos is compatible with lineage organisation due to the powerful mythology of ascendance. It is with this in mind that one ethnologist refers to the 'lords of the forest' in his work on the Beti in Cameroon.[34] And the glory attached to good breeding was of great significance in the condescending attitude that important families had in 1958 towards the Prime Minister, André-Marie Mbida, whom they knew to be of lowly origin. Acephalous societies thus have social differentiations which continue to be reproduced today. Amongst the Kukuya of the Teke ethnic group in Congo, a distinction arose between the richer and poorer lineages at the end of the slave trade in the eighteenth and nineteenth centuries, and this was linked to the emergence of a 'small lineage aristocracy'.[35] In a similar way, the continuous and cumulative fissions amongst the Beembe which generated the struggle between prosperous and weak lineages ended up, in the second half of the nineteenth century, in the regional assertion of the most powerful villages, before colonisation forced them to retract.[36] Everybody recognises the existence of more or less stable relations of authority within acephalous societies, and Evans-Pritchard defined the main clans of the Nuer as 'aristocratic', even though the egalitarianism of their segmentary system is not disputed.[37] From this point of view, the Bassa, whom J-C. Barbier uses as an example, do not really constitute an exception even if the *mba-mbombok*, the elders of the clan, are not in fact chosen 'from the dynastic lineage'.[38]

But it is clear why these 'aristocracies' cannot be defined as a solid and self-perpetuating social category, and why our criticisms are essentially well founded. In a lineage situation the primacy of the elders depends more on individual performance than it does on birth. It involves 'a circumstantial preeminence acquired during a person's lifetime'.[39] The example of the Bete of the Ivory Coast throws much light on this argument. The elders do not all come from a dominant lineage which is reproduced through time by a system of accumulation, starting from an 'inaugural pole'. To reach the position of 'elder', it is necessary to emancipate oneself 'from a relationship in which one was previously in a dependent position and to produce or focalise asymmetrical relationships' which constitute lineage domination, without relying entirely upon chance, or on individual strategies. Although being the elder is an advantage, this is not automatic. An elder must know how to take advantage of his position, for war and 'the invisible' – the 'indeterminate areas within the lineage' – can help the social junior to free himself from his lowly status, despite the handicapped position of his birth:

> In general, the elders of the *grigbe* (patrilineage) do not reproduce the conditions of access to their position via their family ties; in other words, there are not given elder or junior positions or minority lineages, created by the recruitment of the dominant or subordinate members within the lineage institution. This is not to say that the lineages, the minor lineages, and the *grigbe* are one and the same. In this context one can speak of an unequal development: some segments rapidly become autonomous by forming groups which, via the elders, accumulate more matrimonial goods, women, captives, etc. than other groups. On the contrary, some segments may become isolated and place their members under the control of a lineage segment that happens to be dominant at that point in time. Although there are certainly inequalities in the lineage situation, these cannot be referred to as class relations. Without denying the disadvantages which accompany the membership of certain lineages, for example, no possibilities of inheritance, the process of dependency is not irreversible, and can be changed by individual strategies or by any circumstance which causes a reversal in the asymmetrical relations.

Even captives can see their servile positions coming to an end one day. Their descendants form minor lineages, even though other lineage segments are always aware of their origins. In the end, they are able to turn the asymmetrical relations of the lineage to their advantage.[40]

Lineage societies, which are characterised by the absence of a dominant social class, are a qualitative leap away from political centralisation and incorporation into the modern state. It is therefore not surprising that during the nineteenth century the 'rupture' scenario prevailed in acephalous societies, as has been shown in P. Geschiere's excellent history of the Maka in Cameroon. In this case, the elders' authority was related to their performance: their authority consisted of a 'repertory' of roles acted out with more or less goodwill depending on the circumstances. As with the Tiv in Nigeria, the temporary autonomy of leadership was largely effective in the external environment, mainly as a response to a threat, and it had limited domestic effect. In particular, the elders did not have control of the agricultural surplus. Due to failure to institutionalise the social hierarchy, the recruitment of administrative auxiliaries by the German and French colonialists intro-duced a radically new function into village life and experienced serious difficulties. In general, the first 'chiefs' were people who had served or entered into other relationships with the European authorities. Howev-er, the precolonial authorities often sent a poor dependant such as a captive or an adopted escapee (*loua*) to the foreign powers. This hap-pened in Atok, the most important chiefdom in Maka country. This case is particularly significant because the first incumbent there suc-ceeded in making his post hereditary, and the same family held this position of power from the period of German colonisation to the postcolonial period, in complete contradiction with the norms of Maka society. However, Doumé, the other major chiefdom in the region, was the scene of unending struggles for power which, conforming with the old ideal, prevented it from ever having a monopoly. In the 1930s, the head chief of Atok tried to extend his power into the rival Doumé district. By manipulating his family genealogy, he claimed that his ancestors had held sovereignty over Maka country well before the arrival of the Germans. Such fabrications did not disguise the fact that the 'boys', the soldiers, porters, cooks and 'orderlies' from among whom the French authorities selected their collaborators, did not come from the 'good' families of the past. These people were young adven-turers anxious to explore the new 'indeterminate area of the lineage', which was salaried employment. As one such adventurer admitted in 1971, chiefs were truly 'born in the hands of the white man'.

Some members of this 'new breed' also benefited from the growth of cash-crop farming after 1945, and the social inequality which resulted corresponded neither to differences in age nor to the differing ranks of certain patrilineages. Other *homines novi* in Maka country were the 'évolués' who had acquired western education, played successful roles in the decolonisation process, and become brokers of the modern State. Contrary to what one might have expected, these men did not come from the chiefly classes.

On the one hand, the power of lineage elders has been eroded in the villages, as the new elites are better equipped to discuss modern political and economic problems, and deal with the local authorities, the rural development organisations, and the ministries in Yaoundé. On the other hand, these new elites, especially the 'évolués', have not achieved the status of being part of the national dominant class, if such a thing exists. The 'intellectuals' who gain their superiority at the village level by participating in the State system are caught between the fluctuations of political life in Yaoundé and lineage egalitarianism which plays an important role in the 'invisible world'. It is not clear how long the local

dominance of these new elites will last. As they are still encouraged to
be polygamous by the lineage ethos, since this adds to the legitimacy of
their descendants, they cannot for financial reasons send all their numerous children to school. Moreover, secondary school, which is the
only route to increasing one's social status, is not entirely closed to the
children of villagers. The influence one may have in Maka country
cannot be taken as a measure of one's success at the national level since
this area does not have a great deal of political and economic significance in the capital city. In conclusion, the elite of Maka country is not
rooted in the distant past and it cannot yet be termed hereditary.[41]

For the Beti of the Ivory Coast, the introduction of the plantation
economy brought to an end the assymetrical relationships which
allowed a minority of individuals to control the circulation of women
and the ranking order of the lineage. As the most lowly families became
more autonomous, so the relationship between elders and juniors
disintegrated, due to numerous individual experiences. This relationship does not explain the fundamental differences between the farmers
of the village:

> Some people who were 'elders' in genealogical terms were relatively
> poor, while the descendants of captives, for example, had more decent
> revenues. In the end, the development of the plantation economy showed
> how the preceding system had been fairly indeterminate; in more precise
> terms, the development of private appropriation revealed how the social
> relationship between elders and juniors in the precolonial period had not
> crystallised and how this relationship reinforced and diversified the
> process of individualisation. These processes are made more significant
> by the fact that they do not only take place in the villages, for the rural
> exodus and education created new opportunities. The position reached by
> an individual, or the professions he or she enters into (from manual
> worker to high-ranking civil servant), cannot be explained by the status
> of one's forefathers and ancestors – and nor can one's successes or failures
> in towns be explained by this. These are the results of individual
> strategies or are due to reasons outside the lineage context.[42]

In conclusion, the changes that took place during the colonial period,
as well as the dynamics of incorporation, had more deleterious consequences for acephalous societies than for centralised societies. The
lineage society alone is not sufficient for the individual success of even
the most promising of its children. The status of elderhood conferred
by the lineage only allows one to control a demographic unity which
has been steadily marginalised by the development of the modern State,
and the lineage in itself does not have any influence in the State context.
Worse still, the lineage saw itself replaced by the 'indeterminate zone' –

that of school, salaried employment, national politics and the business world – which incorporate and transcend the lineage society and seem to reduce its value more and more every day.

Despite this, it is important not to underestimate the capacity of the lineage to reappropriate the preserves of the contemporary state.[43] However violent they may be, the 'tremors' caused by incorporation should not permit the exclusion, a priori, of the hypothesis that there is a fundamental continuity from past to present which is analogous, *mutatis mutandis*, to conservative modernisation, and that has allowed certain aristocrats to remain in positions of centralised power. (Let us leave aside the special cases of Somalia and Mauritania.) In Mauritania, the 'well-bred' Moors were the almost exclusive beneficiaries of colonialism. Disturbances during the independence period reflected the divisions, especially the generational ones, which existed in the main lineages, and the politics of 'Arabisation' accentuated Beydane ('white') supremacy.[44] Moktar Ould Dadah's regime and the military governments which followed it after 1978 delayed the structural changes which had been hoped for by the black minority from the Fleuve region, and, to a lesser extent, by the theoretically freed slaves.[45] This situation is dependant upon, though not entirely typical of, the situation in the Maghreb, with certain elements being reflected in the conflicts in Sudan and Chad, and is not representative of sub-Saharan lineage trajectories.

The continuities that can be discerned in the sub-Saharan lineages are less obvious. However, when comparing the Maka course to that of the neighbouring Mvang, P. Geschiere admits the possibility that such continuities do exist. In Mvang society, most of the indigenous chiefs in the colonial period, and some postcolonial political figures and civil servants as well, came from the extended family of Nkal Selek which had forcefully attained a certain dominance before the German conquest. Some examples from Congo-Brazzaville are even more revealing, as the State is directly involved. In the nineteenth century, the *nkanyi* (eminent personages) of Beembe country detached themselves by recourse to 'the invisible world', by the use of force, and also through the novel institution of markets. During the colonial conquest, the *nkanyi* tried to complete the political unification of the Mouyondzi plateau, sometimes collaborating with the French and sometimes fighting against them.[47] Despite its extreme brutality, the military occupation did not disrupt Beembe country's geopolitical system, and the preeminence of the Mimsunda, anticipated several decades earlier by the nineteenth-century hero, Mwa Bukulu, was confirmed. Several *nkanyi* became chiefs in the service of the colonial powers, and traded in their magical powers for the authority conferred upon them by the French administration. The plateau population's unflinching refusal to engage in forced labour during the 1920s and 1930s was met with severely repressive measures. The *nkanyi* sided with the occupying forces, but could not entirely dissociate themselves from their subjects and were made to pay a price for their resistance. Due to this political situation, Beembe country escaped from being a labour reserve, and became specialised in agricultural production instead. The *nkanyi* who had been promoted in the colonial hierarchy adapted to the changes once again. Most of them 'used their positions to reduce as many people as possible to slavery', despite the avowedly anti-slavery nature of French policy.[48] In the contemporary State, positions of lineage authority continued to be the core of village autonomy, and it is revealing that urban dwellers are *de facto* excluded from positions of power in the lineage.

The existence of such a system leads us to believe that in Congo, 'the elders, especially lineage or clan chiefs, did not lose their power, but have adapted to the new situation of the complete domination of capital and market relations.'[49] Without going as far as discussing 'lineage capitalism', and the 'alliance between the bureaucratic bourgeoisie and lineage chiefs', nor systematically arguing in terms of the articulation of modes of production,[50] one cannot avoid discussing the projection of these lines of historical continuity into the heart of the state apparatus. It is generally agreed that the 'northern' members of the central committee of the *Parti congolais du travail*, which was in power from 1968 to 1991, united together as a caucus and dominated political decision making. But within this informal group of 'northerners', the voice of those traditional holders of power is still heard by the leaders of the party and the army.[51] There was an analogous situation on the Kukuya plateau during the nineteenth century, when the violent and active chiefs of the sky coexisted with the chiefs of the earth, who exercised 'a hidden power'. The two types of power are different:

> lineage chiefs head the chiefs of the earth, whilst chiefs who create a territorial, juridical and political power head the chiefs of the sky. But the frontier of conflict between these two powers always verged towards compromise. The chiefs of the sky succeeded in controlling both external trade and the arts and craft industry; but it is debatable whether they could have done this without the collaboration of the other aristocracy. In opposition, the chiefs of the earth hoped to limit the development of the *yulu* aristocracy, and to benefit from this [...] all prestations and gains were in fact divided between the chiefs of the earth and the sky.[52]

It is probably with such systems in mind that P-P. Rey, a real expert on Congolese society, asserts that

The relations of hostility or of alliance between regional or ethnic groups within or outside the state are explained above all by the relations of power within each ethnic group. In 1959, Youlou, who was leader of the South, and Opangault, who was leader of the North, agreed in Brazzaville to bring an end to the confrontations between northerners and southerners. They were able to do this because each held a traditional position of power that allowed him to make such decisions for his ethnic group and for his region. Like the confrontation, the agreement only served to reinforce precolonial positions of authority. On the contrary, [...] the attempt to reach an agreement between Ngouabi (from the North) and Massemba-Debat (from the South) in 1977 ended in the death of both of them because this agreement would have allowed Ngouabi to transform the precolonial hierarchy of his ethnic group. [...]. The traditional political system, especially the 'non-state' one, entered the state system and prevented it from following its own logic.[53]

In his discussion of the pre-revolutionary parliamentary regime, the same author confirmed that 'the real source of power remains the lineage chief':

Until 1963, the system of ethnic supporters of parties ensured the total fusion of political power inherited from colonisation and lineage political power. In each ethnic group, all chiefs, whether lineage chiefs or colonial chiefs, who succeeded in maintaining power in their chiefdoms, chose the political orientation of their ethnic group and also chose their political representative; the deputies and the ministers chosen in this way, whatever they seemed to be to a French observer saturated in 'political science', remained totally dependent on the traditional chiefs. Their principal mission was to promote the interests of the ethnic group, in other words, to find as many lucrative positions as possible in the administration for members of the ethnic group.[54]

Similar things have happened in other political societies in Africa – for example, in Cameroon, the Ivory Coast, Gabon, and in Central Africa or in Kenya. To symbolise this coexistence of two forms of government within the contemporary State, one institutional and apparent, the other informal and secret, an anthropologist has evoked the duality of the 'air conditioner' and the 'verandah'.[55] The coexistence of these two systems is particularly profound in lineage societies, and the 'verandah' plays a conspicuous role. Acephalous societies are often distinguished by the double roles of people: they will engage in open deliberations and will be part of the official hierarchies 'parachuted' in by the colonisers, but the real exercise of power will be concentrated in occult conclaves.[56] We must avoid going as far as reducing the contemporary state to being a conspiracy of old people. However, if they really take place as we imagine, such processes seem to be elements of social stability which have been neglected or not known.

THE QUESTION OF NON-NATIVE DOMINANT MINORITIES

The grafting of non-native minorities onto African societies – the result of their growing integration into the western economy and that of the Indian Ocean – has become one of the elements in their stratification. Some of these foreign communities, such as the Chinese and Indo-Chinese, have not reached a dominant position or have not left a trace. Others, however, have installed themselves, and their presence has been one of the crucial factors in the hegemonic quest.

This was certainly the case for the European colonialists who started to establish themselves along the coastlines during the sixteenth century, and who inter-bred extensively with the local communities until at least the end of the last century. The imperialist ideology, which led to an increasingly extreme form of racism, and the military conquest of the continent, changed the nature of Europe's involvement in African societies. Colonial conquest gave rise initially to new arrivals, especially in the territories which became 'settler colonies': Kenya, the two Rhodesias, Angola and Mozambique. Later on, colonisation led to the white communities being in a dominant position, to such an extent that these communities expressed themselves in terms of racial superiority. It sometimes led to the confiscation of the means of production and monopolisation of the best land. Where it was most extreme – for example, in Kikuyu land in Kenya, in the north-west of Angola, in the Belgian Congo and Southern Rhodesia – this transformation of the type of European presence made decolonisation in the years after the Second World War more dramatic. In most of these places, including even Mozambique and Angola, an indigenous political revolution prevented the colonialists from monopolising power after the withdrawal of the metropolitan administration. Since the fall of Ian Smith's Unilateral Declaration of Independence in Zimbabwe, the sole but significant exception to this development is the South African *laager*, which is a belated example of conservative modernisation. In contrast to South Africa, decolonisation led to a social rupture and an exodus of the white communities in Angola, Mozambique, the Belgian Congo and, to a lesser extent, Guinea-Bissau, Equatorial Guinea, Guinea and Kenya. However, in a greater number of cases, including Zimbabwe, independence did not seriously threaten European economic interests, which adapted to the new conditions and often extended beyond their previous limits.

This fact is well known even if it is not always well understood. However, it must not override the importance of other, equally important, foreign influences. In these cases, the main consequence of the nationalist movements was that of revolutionary 'rupture', as it was for the Europeans. This was certainly the case in Zanzibar, where the Arab aristocracy were, in terms of proportion of foreigners to the indigenous population, the second largest foreign minority in Africa, following the white communities in South Africa (in Zanzibar there were about 50,000 Arabs in a population of slightly more than 300,000). In a similar way to that in Rwanda, the 1964 revolution in Zanzibar involved the 'crystallisation' of an ethnic identity – in this case 'African' – as the means of unification and mobilisation of socially subordinate groups. However, the case of Zanzibar was different from Rwanda in that it did not involve the breaking down of an initially hegemonic situation. Committing a classic error of a protectorate regime, the Omani aristocracy which controlled the sultanate became the exclusive intermediaries of the British colonialists. The aristocracy intensified its political monopoly and made Britain recognise the 'Arab' nature of the state. It was not until the Second World War that representatives of the 'African' majority, historically and culturally heterogeneous, joined the 'Legco', the Legislative Council, and it was only in 1957 that they gained a majority. However, despite British efforts the Omani aristocracy were not transformed into a Prussian-style landed class, because it did not succeed in removing the ex-slaves from their agrarian base and transforming them into a salaried force to work exclusively for the plantation economy:

> By the 1920s, the state had not succeeded in creating an agricultural proletariat the Arab landowners had failed to keep ex-slaves as personal dependants tied to their estates; and the ex-slaves had not acquired the security they desired. All the compromises led to a structure that was neither equitable nor harshly exploitative, but it was above all brittle and unadaptable.[57]

Moreover, the Arabs' traditional financial dependence on Indian markets worsened rapidly and threatened their monopoly of clove production. A serious commercial conflict followed between Arab landowners and Indian tradesmen. This did not end until 1938, when an agreement was signed under the protection of the British administration. From 1951 onwards, the stagnation of the world clove market diminished the Omani's economic base. The worsening of social tensions in the plantations and in *Ngambo*, the African quarter of Zanzibar city, became inevitable. Simultaneously, the aristocracy's efforts to achieve cultural hegemony met its limits, and contributed to the precipation of ethnic conflicts. Only the ex-slaves who had a relatively stable status recognised themselves as 'Swahili' Muslims, and then as 'Arabs'.

142

Those at the bottom of the social ladder increasingly saw their sub-ordination to the plantation economy and to the State in terms of their 'African' identity, even if the division between the 'continentals' (about 60,000 people, mainly non-Muslims from Tanzania, Kenya and Uganda, the Great Lakes and Maniema) and the indigenous 'Shirazi' (about 200,000 people claiming to be of Persian descent present before the arrival of the Omani) continued to be felt and contributed to political demobilisation, especially on Pemba island.

Faced with this difficult situation, the Omani aristocracy engaged in a daring project of conservative modernisation. The 1938 agreement had put the 'Asiatics' off the constitutional debate, and the political life of the protectorate ended up as an Arabo-African tête-à-tête. In contrast to the European colonialists in Southern Africa, the Omani aristocracy supported the idea of a multi-racial society, and in 1954 it started a nationalist movement against Great Britain. This was a shrewd and elegant calculation, but it was also risky. For the African majority would one day claim Zanzibar's independence as their own, even though they did not immediately benefit from this due to their lack of an 'educated' elite. From this point of view, Ahmed Lemke, who was born into a prosperous Arab family and who was a dynamic force in the nationalist movement, was not unlike Prince Rwagasore or the Sardauna. In 1955, the Omani aristocracy, who started the 'Zanzibari' movement, took control of a rural league of Swahili militants (known as the National Party of the Subjects of the Sultan of Zanzibar) and changed it into the Zanzibar Nationalist Party and brought it to town. Honorary posts were given to these 'African' militants, but the Arabs maintained real control of the organisation.

When faced with this situation, the African majority could do nothing but adopt a conservative strategy. Its meagre elite was employed mainly in the protectorate administration, and, in 1953, a government circular forbade civil servants from becoming involved in politics. Therefore most African members of the first nationalist organisations had to resign. Once again the Arab oligarchy gained exclusive control of political life, but in this way the Arabs were prevented from forming the multi-racial coalition they had been hoping for. In spite of Julius Nyerere's entreaties (he was at the time the nationalist leader of Tanganyika), the Africans failed to establish a relative unity of action between the 'continentals' and the 'Shirazi' until 1957, and then only in the island of Zanzibar. In Pemba, the Shirazi, whose economic situation and landed status had not suffered so much from Arab domination, became involved in the problematic of multi-racialism and grew suspicious of the 'continental' immigrants. They scorned the newly formed Afro-

Shirazi Union and its offshoot the Afro-Shirazi Party, and eventually created the Zanzibar and Pemba People's Party (ZPPP) in 1959.

The failure of the Zanzibar Nationalist Party to win the first legislative elections in 1957 might have given the impression that the Omani aristocracy had come to an end. However this defeat did not signal the true victory of the Afro-Shirazi Union, which was forced to oppose the nationalist movement for fear that it would serve the interests of the oligarchy. After the 1961 and 1963 elections, the ZNP and the ZPPP formed a coalition government, although the ASP won 54 per cent of the votes. In the end it seemed as though the introduction of a representative regime, and the withdrawal of a supervisory power, did not necessarily interrupt the rule of the aristocracy. The ZNP imposed itself in nearly half of the electoral districts, attracted the African vote, and divided its adversaries by allying with the ZPPP.

However, this continuation of aristocratic power was a short-term illusion. The ZNP lost its best organiser, Abdul Rahman Mohammed, known as 'Babu', as well as its radical Marxist wing, which seceded and formed a new party called the Umma. The ZNP pushed its luck too far by adopting a series of repressive measures, thereby increasing the resentment of an African majority whose victory had been frustrated by the way the electoral boundaries had been defined. By sacking some policemen of continental origin, without repatriating them, the ZNP started off the very process that would eventually destroy it. On 12 January 1964, just one month after independence was declared, a handful of Africans, who had come from Uganda a few years beforehand led by an obscure chief, John Okello, overthrew the government and founded a revolutionary council led by members of the ASP and the Umma. The sultan was banished and fled the country; thousands of Arabs were arrested or killed, and their goods destroyed or confiscated; the ZNP and ZPPP were banned. From April 1964, the resolution to reunite Zanzibar with Tanganyika to create a Republic of Tanzania protected the new African leadership from the Arab aristocracy.[58] At the same time, the Arab aristocracy in Kenya failed to organise the secession (*mwambao*) of the coastal strip and could therefore not avoid the rise of nationalists from the highlands.[59]

Sierra Leone and Liberia provide two other meaningful examples.[60] The ransomed or freed slaves, and those repatriated from the Americas in the eighteenth and nineteenth centuries, became Creole minorities and dominated the indigenous hinterland populations. In Sierra Leone the administrative reunification of the 'colony' of Freetown with the hinterland 'protectorate' in 1951 confirmed that the British colonialists were hesitant to favour the interests of the Creole elite as opposed to the indigenous majority. Due to the demographic disequilibrium the defeat of the Creole party, the National Council, and the rise of the Sierra Leone People's Party were inevitable. But the Creoles maintained some influence which they invested with a certain flexibility in the administration, the law, the liberal professions and business.

In Liberia the advantages of international sovereignty and the fragmentation of the inland populations worked for a long time to the benefit of the American-Liberian colonisers. As in Sierra Leone, they were not interested in the hinterland until the end of the nineteenth century, when they were threatened by European imperialist expansion. After the Second World War at the instigation of President Tubman, the True Whig Party, which had been in power since 1877, launched a double political strategy – the open door policy and the unification policy – in order to guarantee American-Liberian hegemony and to enlarge this group by co-opting 'tribal' elites. In April 1980 the coup led by Sergeant Doe interrupted this process of conservative modernisation by representing the aspirations of the indigenous majority.[61] However, the reality was more complicated, and it is telling that the bloody protests in Monrovia in 1979 – a shock from which the regime never fully recovered – were caused primarily by raising the price of rice, which should theoretically have favoured the rural producers, although it was also convenient for the Whigs who had a big hand in agricultural production. The radicalism of Doe's Council of Redemption was rapidly diluted when it lost the support of its first political allies, the Movement for Justice in Africa (MOJA) and the Progressive Alliance of Liberians (PAL). It did not take long until Doe's regime was seen as a brutal, predatory and personalised power, with a very small social base. However, the unification policy was not without effect, and historical-ethnic criteria were not enough to shape the divisions within the dominant power once the True Whig Party was overthrown.[62] Also, the continuing monopolisation by large American-Liberian families and their supporters is undoubtedly more significant than the sinister execution posts set up on Monrovia beach. These families were not allowed to compete in the 1985 elections – all candidates were natives of the interior – but until the civil war in 1990 they still managed to obtain a place in the state apparatus in a way that was at least equal to the Creoles in Sierra Leone.[63]

The existence of a 'rupture' scenario cannot be denied in Sierra Leone and Liberia. This reflects the more general process of the erosion of the power of coastal elites following the colonial conquest, as in Ghana, Ivory Coast, Cameroon and Gabon. Elsewhere, it was not until the period of liberalisation after the Second World War that this happened.

In Senegal, the electoral victory of Senghor's *Bloc démocratique sénégalais* over Lamine Gueye's SFIO in 1951 was largely a victory of the '*broussards*', or the 'subjects', over the elite from the Four Communes.* Thirty-five years later, a Dakarois journalist affirmed that this was what saved Senegal from having troubles similar to those in Liberia, and also those in Benin and Togo where independence had given rise to a certain preeminence of 'Amaro', 'Afro-Brazilians'.[64]

There are clear parallels between events in Sierra Leone and Liberia and the erosion of the power of the Asians in East Africa (whose ancestors had long been financially dominant in the region and whose position had been favoured by more recent British attempts to install a multi-racial government at the expense of the black populations). The regional hegemony of the Zanzibar sultanate, and later that of British colonisation, had increased Indian immigration from 35,000 people in 1900 to 190,000 in 1948. Their advance into the interior was often encouraged by Africans because of the economic services they could provide.[65] The black nationalist leaders quickly took an interest in Asian designs, and suspected the colonial powers of assisting them. The political status of Tanganyika, which had been conquered from the Germans during the First World War, soon became the centre of regional tension. Had there not been a plan to create an Indian colony in 1918, an idea supported by some members of the Indian National Congress? African resentment grew in the 1930s and 1940s as their Indian rivals advanced in the administration and the economy. Since 1924 the official policy of the Colonial Office was to set Uganda aside for the Africans, Kenya for the Europeans, with Tanganyika having an intermediary status. From 1955 it became increasingly clear that Governor Twining's mission was to start up, in Tanganyika, a sort of multi-racial regime that might also be appropriate for the Central African colonies and in Kenya, which was now troubled by the Mau-Mau insurrection. A United Tanganyika Party adopted the idea of a 'non racial' nation in order to defeat Nyerere's Tanganyika African National Union (TANU) which campaigned for African rights in the leadership of the country. This turned to TANU's advantage during the 1958 elections, and contributed decisively to the destruction of the 'multi-racial' perspective in the region.[66] The fact that the Asians' economic position was not affected by the inter-party conflict, and their

---

*Translator's note: In 1848 the Four Communes – the Senegalese towns of St Louis, Dakar, Rufisque and the island of Gorée – had been accorded a status comparable to a metropolitan *département* and its citizens, regardless of race or religion, had full voting rights.

concern that they could be taken over by Africans, may have played a major role in the socialist orientation that the party persuaded the government to adopt after independence.[67] Although after the Arusha Declaration Nyerere stressed that 'socialism is not racialism', the 1971 Acquisition of Buildings Act and the nationalisation of small-scale trade (known as Operation Maduka) in 1976 directly affected the Indians and Pakistanis. Between 10,000 and 20,000 left after buildings were nationalised in 1971.[68] At the begining of the 1980s the Asians who had decided to remain in the new socialist Tanzania, despite the danger of doing so, were often the first to suffer from Prime Minister Sokoine's campaign against 'economic sabotage'. Tanzanian *Ujamaa* brought about a social 'rupture', although it was less brutal than the 'economic war' launched by Amin Dada in 1972, in which Asians were expelled and their goods confiscated, and truly less effective than the Kenyan methods. Although some Asian businessmen who had been chased out by nationalisation have returned after the liberalisation of trade in Tanzania or the *magendo*★ in Uganda, their golden days in the region seem to have come to an end.[69]

Paradoxically, the real exception to this scenario of the reversal of expatriate domination comes from ex-Portuguese regimes. To varying degrees, the Marxist-Leninist regimes in Angola, Mozambique and Guinea-Bissau imposed a 'creole' dominance over the 'African negro' masses. The most extreme case is Angola, where the MPLA recruited many people from the 'assimilated' mixed-blood elite. Even after the rural rebellions of 1961, the MPLA was not able to mobilise the rural areas, even though it had paid a great deal of attention to them. Just before the 'marigold' revolution which opened up the capital to the MPLA, its hold on the country was weak and its attempt to organise an 'eastern front' from bases in Zambia did not succeed.[70] The 'Nitiste' populist faction (named after its leader, Nito Alves) which benefited from the resentment of the Mbundu cadres (many of whom were Methodists) towards the mixed-blood minority from Luanda, failed to take power by a *coup d'état* on 27 May 1977, and were totally wiped out in the process.[71] Since the fall of the FNLA, it has been the armed resistance of UNITA, assisted by South Africa and the United States, which has been the vehicle of the specifically 'African negro' ambitions under the form of Ovimbundu ethno-nationalism.

★*magendo:* black market

147

THE NUANCES OF COMPROMISE

Significant compromises are, it seems, often made both in instances of conservative modernisation and social revolution, however extreme these scenarios may have been in the historical situations we have identified.

Notwithstanding the rupture involved when an acephalous system becomes incorporated into the State context, the Maka trajectory, for example, is characterised above all by the interlinking process of continuity and change.[72] This seems to be the case for most lineage societies and represents the true meaning of the co-existence of the 'verandah' and the 'air-conditioner', neither of which two systems of power and authority could be considered as negligible, whatever the tendencies may have been over the last few decades. Foreign concatenation is not affected by this dichotomy. Historically, the links established between Asians and Africans were largely complementary and collaborative, despite the elements of rivalry and conflict. In the 1950s, many Indo-Pakistani merchants realised that now was the time for Africans to become involved in business, and one of them even opened a business school for Africans in Kampala;[73] and some Asians even supported the nationalist parties. Similarly, it has been noted that President Tubman's so-called unification and open-door policies involved the co-optation of a 'tribal' elite after the Second World War and that the 1980 *coup d'état* did not eliminate the power of the True Whig oligarchy. This political style was taken so far that Sergeant Doe even sacked one of his ministers for calling the politics of William Tubman a 'failure'. Doe said that, in reality, Tubman had brought about a 'significant social-economic development (...) to the nation and all Liberians'.[74]

The force of unavoidable compromises can be seen within the most homogeneous examples of conservative modernisation. Kilson has already stressed that the dominant class in Sierra Leone did not only consist of an alliance and amalgam of the traditional chiefs and the higher levels of the new 'educated' elite. The 1951 agreement and the creation of the Sierra Leone People's Party, under the leadership of Dr Milton Margai and the Paramount Chief Julius Gulama, opened the way to a fusion of these two categories by marriage, school and the exercise of power.[75] In the same way, political life in Fouta Toro in Senegal consisted of 'the alliance of the modern and the traditional elites'.[76] In Nigeria, Ahmadu Bello's strategy of 'Northernisation' also consisted of a double process of integration.[77] Firstly, there was the horizontal integration of leaders of different groups in the region, which often divided solid historical alliances (in particular, the alliance between the Hausa-Fulani aristocrats and those of Kanuri, and between these two groups and representatives of Middle-Belt minorities). Secondly, there was the process of vertical integration whereby the *talakawa* were recruited into the Northern Peoples' Congress and the Councils of emirs; these were the commoner civil servants from the Northern Region Civil Service, and above all the rich merchants (*attajirai*) who were involved in the international markets, starting with the recruitment of the wealthy Alhassan Dantata in Kano. The 'united front' in the North, which has been symbolised first by the collaboration between the Sardauna and Abubabakar Tafawa Balewa (a *haabe talaka** from the emirate of Bauchi); then by the Emir of Kano joining the Tijaniyya brotherhood which was controlled by merchants; and finally by young aristocrats who entered high level state bureaucracy side by side with young commoners, is an example of the molecular process of reciprocal assimilation referred to by Gramsci.[78]

This gives us an idea of the intermediate scenario of the quest for hegemony. Such a scenario may perhaps provide the decisive analytic key, because when considering the changing scale of colonial control and the regional differentiations in the social foundations of the State, this intermediary course of events becomes almost inevitable.

**Haabe:* non Fulani

CHAPTER SIX

The Reciprocal Assimilation of Elites: The Hypothesis of an Intermediate Scenario

Ahidjo's regime in Cameroon from February 1958 to November 1982 gives the best illustration of the molecular process of reciprocal assimilation. These two decades witnessed 'the progressive emergence of a widespread alliance of different regional, political, economic and cultural segments of the social elite'. The postcolonial State in its totality – and not just particular institutions, whatever role the party and bureaucracy played in this process – served as the matrix of this new union.[1] As in Northern Nigeria, this process had a double dimension. Not only were spokespersons from most parts of the country also members of the representative institutions of the regime (the Central Committee of the Union nationale camerounaise, the National Assembly and the government) but also Ahidjo, an ex-member of parliament in France's Fourth Republic who enjoyed discussing *canton* elections in France, was as a result a past master in the subtle art of ethnic politics. Political power presided over continual local arbitrations between diachronic strata of inequality – for example, between the holders of traditional legitimacy, the colonial chiefs and the educated 'elites'.

The real capacity of these mechanisms of reciprocal assimilation, and their degree of realisation, are by definition subject to questioning and must be treated with caution.[2] However, the presidential succession crisis from 1982 to 1984 and the early years of Biya's government have shown that the means of reproducing and completing the hegemonic alliance are in place. The patrimonialist recuperation of the State, which had been attempted by Ahidjo between January and June 1983 in his desire to assure the supremacy of the party over the Presidency of the Republic, had failed. In spite of isolated sedition by individuals, and the divergence of interests, the political class remained remarkably united around the new head of State until 1987. It is even more significant that the President renounced the idea of forced change and brought back individuals into the regime who had been adversely affected by the upheavals of transition, although many of the President's supporters hoped that he would break away from the 'barons' and create his own party.[3] According to a Douala newspaper,

> Biya does not reject anybody. Accept your auto-mutation, your renaissance and you could embark on the process of renewal. We see a way shaped by the desire for national reconciliation. Biya does not want to divide Cameroon into two camps, with the good people on one side and the bad people on the other. It is a way that gives everybody the possibility of pardon, of repentance.

The newspaper added, not without reason, that 'It would be true to say that there is something religious about the President's policy'.[4] When the situation is analysed fully it becomes clear that the uncertainties weighing upon the hegemonic alliance are as heavy as they were at the end of the 1970s. One could even believe that the unprecedented degradation of the economy, the inherent contradictions in attempts to liberalise the authoritarian regime, the growing struggles for power, the increasing 'appetites' which exacerbated ethnic problems, and the functional paralysis of the executive, could subject this alliance to previously unknown tensions and make the hypothesis of a political rupture more credible. Apart from the fact that this 'political rupture' would not necessarily endanger the process of reciprocal assimilation, it would also not nullify the developments of the previous decades.

From the example of Cameroon, it is possible to identify a 'middle path' whereby the geographical diversity of the social foundations of the State, and the *rapprochement* of the historical remains of the elite, are organised around a political pole. The Cameroonian case is an important one because it represents a situation similar to that of most countries in Africa. R. Sklar has shown how, from 1963 onwards, the Nigerian party system contributed to the 'fusion of the elites', a process from which Sklar tended, unfortunately, to exclude the traditional hierarchies in the west and east of the country.[5] Twenty-five years later, the National Party of Nigeria defined itself as a 'mixed-breed party of young and old, men and women, rich and poor', and claimed that it was now trans-regional, thus conforming with the constitution. This coalition, which was controlled mainly by Northern leaders, governed the country through the zoning system whereby responsibilities were granted on the basis of regional mixing. All military regimes which succeeded Shagari were backed by similar amalgams of different groups with varying degrees of success. From the cases of Nigeria and Cameroon one can generalise the hypothesis of the 'fusion of elites' in the State matrix and their establishment as a dominant national class.[7] The trajectories of Senegal, Ivory Coast, Kenya, Tanzania and Niger seem to conform most closely with this intermediary model.[8] These cases contrast with the more type–cast examples of social revolution and conservative modernisation previously described. They also differ from some other trajectories which involve bloodshed due to paroxytic repression, or the recurring lack of hegemony, as in Uganda, Mozambique, Angola, Equatorial Guinea, Chad and Guinea.

It is pointless to attempt to squeeze the complex historical reality of a social formation into a simplistic scenario. We have seen how the process of conservative modernisation and social revolution resemble each other, due to the substantial compromises they had to make with the groups they wanted to destroy. The two dynamics of divergence and reciprocal assimilation may always coexist. The tragic case of Nigeria shows how these dynamics can intervene alternately. They can also occur simultaneously, even if it is in two different regions. In this way, those which seem to be the most highly developed instances of the fusion of elites tend, in reality, to have left out some segments of the elite. Although they were Muslims, the Choa Arabs of Cameroon were not part of Ahidjo's power bloc in the north, and they had to wait until Biya's rise to supreme power before they gained political recognition. The anglophone Cameroonians, particularly those in the North-West Province, felt alienated by the 'Reunification' since it destroyed their hopes for autonomy.[9]

Conversely, even the most asymmetrical political configurations rarely exclude all mechanisms of reciprocal assimilation. In Zaïre, some leaders of the First Republic were reinserted into Mobutu's regime.[10] On the other side of the river, the Congolese, who are good at playing with words, mockingly adapt the name 'NATO', the 'North-Atlantic Treaty', to denounce the disequilibrium which has worked to the advantage of the *vili* (coastal, i.e. Atlantic, people), *mbochi* and *kuyu* (natives of the north) cadres. The Comité Militaire du parti (CMP), set up in 1977, is known as 'La Cuvette Monte au Pouvoir' (meaning the Northerners, from the region of La Cuvette rise to power). This has not prevented the spoils of the State, the 'situations' and all that they can give rise to, from being dispersed in a circular movement since independence. Without doubt the 'situationist

tontine'★ was one of unequal opportunities. All the regions were however more or less associated with this 'situationist tontine', and we have
already noted that the lineage elders were not banished after the 1963
revolution.[11] Finally, in Ghana, the Provisional National Defence
Council, having virulently attacked members of the liberal professions,
market women, farmers and chiefs in 1982–83, ended up by admitting
them into the People's Defence Committees.[12]

   This is the reason why there is no standard correlation between
political stability and the process of reciprocal assimilation of elites.
Without doubt, the longevity of the dominant or single party regimes
in Senegal, Ivory Coast, Cameroon, Kenya and Tanzania is explained
by this correlation. On the other hand, it does not take much to realise
that if the dynamics of divergence and exclusion prevail, the result is
civil war and repression: for example, in Chad, the political marginalisation of arabophones educated in Egypt and Sudan caused them to
join the secessionist Frolinat in the 1960s.[13] However, all historical
'trajectories' based on reciprocal assimilation are reversible; no 'hegemonic alliance', however vast, is completely safe. In Kenya and Cameroon, the transition from the founding president to his successor, and
the degradation of the economic and financial equilibrium, suggest that
the passage from the dynamic of fusion to that of disintegration, from a
centripetal force to a centrifugal force, can be a swift one. In other
words, these societies lack the historical depth to allow a precise differentiation between scenarios. It is also difficult to link the relationship
each sub-Saharan State has to the social hierarchy. It is only in time that
it will be possible to show whether the structure of inequality is
becoming deeply ingrained in society, and whether this structure is
likely to reproduce itself in the future. A functional equivalence can be
established between the most stable regimes and this latent process of
accumulation and unification by dominant groups. But is it not also
possible to envisage a similar process taking place in contexts of recurring crisis such as in Uganda?[14]

   We should therefore dissociate the analysis of political forms from
social stratification more systematically than neo-Marxists do. Not that
the State is neutral in this respect. Numerous upheavals in the political
world do not match the hidden development of inequality; they do not

---

★In 1976 President Ngouabi explained that, 'The situationists are those who look out
for situations'. 'tontine' is a credit association in which participants make a monthly
contribution, and each in turn has access to the total sum contributed. The delicious
expression of 'the situationist tontine' comes from D. Desjeux. The 'situationists' of
course were a far-left anarchist group active in France during the 1960s and early 1970s.

coincide exactly with the contours of the search for hegemony. First, there is the important fact that colonisation and its abolition – the major events of the past century – must be put into proper perspective for they do not constitute the major divisions in time that they are thought to do. Secondly, the different scenarios, or, more precisely, the diverse dynamics that we have isolated, are made up of heterogeneous institutions and do not necessarily involve the same power structures. For convenience sake, let us say that Senegal, Ivory Coast, Nigeria, Cameroon, Tanzania and Kenya are characterised above all by the process of reciprocal assimilation. In Senegal, and in Nigeria during certain periods, this takes place via the multi-party system. In other cases it occurs through the single party system. And what political, ideological and sociological variation there is in single party situations! In almost every case where a multi-party system has been followed by a single-party system, the dynamics of these two systems have reinforced rather than contradicted each other; single-party systems have achieved at the national level what multi-party systems started at the regional or local level. The military and civil phases which have ordered political life in so many sub-Saharan countries are similarly linked. The eruption of praetorians has occasionally enabled the conciliation of the elites, endangered by the erring ways of civilian governments. The equivocal roles of institutions, political instability, coercion and war in relation to the production of inequality are verified in this way: in Guinea, the 'State-party' engendered divergence where other territorial sections of the RDA favoured political cohesion; in Burundi, the *coup d'état* occurred in order to maintain social order, and in Nigeria, the military regime brought back Igbo elites, who had been intrigued by the illusion of secession, into the Federation; in Zaïre, Mobutu's predatory regime prevented the country from disintegrating into rival and weakened 'provincettes'.

If the attempt to create a typology of the social foundations of the State in Africa is renounced as unrealistic, and solidly differentiated scenarios are defined as illusory, what remains is the analysis of the dynamics of social aggregation in the political field and the formation of a dominant class.

BASES AND PROCEDURES OF RECIPROCAL ASSIMILATION: CIVIL SOCIETY

Initially, the fusion of elites took place within the boundaries of 'civil society'. 'Civil society' is to be understood in terms of Marx's definition as 'the true foyer, the true scene of all history': 'The forms of exchange, which condition and are conditioned by the forces of production existing in all historical stages preceding our own, amount to civil society which [...] has as its prerequisite and fundamental basis the simple family and the complex family (also known as the clan).'[15] This primary definition, which is loose and verges on the ahistorical, pinpoints one of the particular features of African societies: that the lines of inequality match, perhaps more than elsewhere, those of the family. The lineage basis of the continent could help one to understand this process because, in lineage societies, power is primarily presented in terms of the family. However, this is a dangerous way of proceeding because, as it coincides so closely with the culturalist phantasmagoria of the eternal Africa, it could be easily adopted without being properly analysed. Let us examine some of the evidence. With some exceptions (notably Nigeria, Zaïre, Tanzania, Kenya, Uganda, Mozambique and Ghana), the population of sub-Saharan States are small; sometimes very small with populations of less than one million. Moreover, they have extremely young populations, with the majority being under 20 years old and possessing only a mediocre education. We can thus understand the reasons for restricted size of the dominant class. A socio-political study of Cameroon estimated that the dominant class numbered about 950 people at the end of the 1970s.[16] In the Ivory Coast, the orators during the 1969 'Dialogue', who represented the dominant force of the nation, numbered 1,500.[17] In January 1966, just before it took power, the Nigerian army was led by only 511 officers.[18]

During the important decades between the two wars, these numbers were even lower. J. Spencer estimated the number of militants in the Kikuyu Association/EAA to be about 300 in the 1920s; however, the major 'excision' crisis resulted in strong political mobilisation – Jomo Kenyatta claimed that the Kikuyu Central Association had 10,000 members from 1929 to 1931 – but these numbers quickly sank again.[19] Similarly, the Ivory Coast's Syndicat agricole africain (African Agriculture Union) had 8,548 members at the end of 1944, half of whom lived in Bouaké and Dimbokro districts.[20] In every country, the hard core of the nationalist movements only had a handful of cadres, and the colonial years offered opportunities to a very limited number of people or groups. But just after independence the numbers of people capable of

Table 6.1 Population of African States (in millions)

Micro States less than 2 mn.		Small States 2-4 mn.		Medium States 5-11 mn.		Populated States more than 11 mn.	
São Tomé & Principe	0.11	Liberia	2.22	Chad	5.14	Ghana	14.04
Cape-Verte	0.34	CAR	2.67	Guinea	6.21	Mozambique	14.36
Equatorial Guinea	0.40	Togo	3.05	Rwanda	6.27	Uganda	16.00
Gambia	0.65	Sierra Leone	3.66	Niger	6.28	Kenya	21.16
Guinea-Bisson	0.91	Benin	4.04	Senegal	6.60	Tanzania	22.46
Botswana	1.13	Somalia	4.79	Faso	6.75	Zaire	31.24
Gabon	1.17	Burundi	4.86	Zambia	6.85	Nigeria	98.40
Congo	1.79			Malawi	7.28		
Mauritania	1.95			Zimbabwe	8.41		
				Mali	8.44		
				Angola	8.97		
				Ivory Coast	10.18		
				Cameroon	10.45		

Source: L'État du monde, 1987–1988, Paris, La Découverte, 1987

assuming power in a western-style State was even smaller. Even without mentioning the cases in which the colonialists shamelessly adopted a Malthusian educational policy (the Belgian Congo, Rwanda, Burundi, Angola, Mozambique and Guinea-Bissau), a country such as Zambia had only 109 university graduates and 1,200 secondary school leavers in 1964.[21] Members of wealthy and powerful circles had known one another on an intimate basis and often for a very long time, by having grown up in the same village or the same area of town, by sharing a dormitory in a boarding school or a military academy, and by philosophising all night long in the halls of residence of British or French universities.

There is therefore an intimate character to the dynamics of the reciprocal assimilation of segments of the social elite. Assimilation often takes place in private life, and this is one reason why in francophone society the informal 'tu' is so common at the top of the social hierarchy, despite the fact that this group attaches more importance to etiquette. One of the main areas where the fusion of the dominant Ivoirian elites takes place is during funerals:

> High society models its funeral practices according to the status of the deceased. If he was linked, by his past and status, to the State apparatus, his funeral becomes a pretext for political liturgy. The President or a presidential envoy give a funeral oration, State dignitaries participate in various activities, and the media widely reports the event. Ceremonies last for several days and the series of rituals transpose the supremacy of the State into all things, at the ethnic, regional, religious and village levels. The speeches commemorate the foundation of the State and the anti-colonial struggle; they repeat the epics of Houphouët-Boigny, and unite into a single legitimacy the dead militants and the powerful men present at the celebrations. One can ask whether the symbols of the ceremony are really modern after all [...].
>
> If the deceased's only merit was that he was closely related to a powerful person, the funeral would not extend beyond the private domain; however, these ceremonies would go beyond the family boundaries, not due to political institutionalisation as it would for the 'traditional' nobility, but because of social links, some of which renew traditional symbols while others come from the present situation. Vast gatherings attend these funerals, which are often extremely costly events requiring ostentatious investments. However, funerals are different from the other official demonstrations carried out to affirm the single-party system, since these bring together heterogeneous, even opposing social groups. In this respect, it would seem that in the whole Ivorian liturgy, funerals are the most symbolically integrated occasions.[22]

However, funeral ostentation, with its rigorous protocol, leads one to think of other instances in civil society where a more effective alchemy occurs. Matrimony, for example. It would be an exaggeration to suggest that the circulation of women continues to make or break political and economic alliances as it did in the past. Today, endogamy is social rather than 'ethnic'. New ties are created which transcend the old geographical and family divisions; and they play a role in the creation of the State and of unequal relations. Félix Houphouët-Boigny, who is a Baule, is an archetypical example of this phenomenon. From the 1930s onwards, he developed one of the critical alliances upon which his political ascension would depend by taking as his first wife a woman coming from the Agni royal lineage on her mother's side, and from the 'foreign' Senegalese community on her father's side.[23] In 1944, Houphouët-Boigny persuaded Governor Latrille to depose the chief of Indenie and to replace him with his own brother-in-law. Through the intermediary of his relative, he then became involved in the succession to the throne of the great Agni kingdom.[24] Houphouët-Boigny continued to organise such unions and to manipulate his relations in order to increase his authority not only in the Ivory Coast, but also in the rest of the region, going as far as Guinea, Liberia, Burkina Faso and Senegal. To take one example from among many, one of the 'barons' of his regime, Amadou Thiam, is related to his first wife and is therefore of Senegalese origin. Houphouët-Boigny gave Amadou Thiam his cousin, Amoin, as a wife, and has publicly recognised their children as his heirs 'according to custom'.[25] In 1985 he attended the wedding of Yamousso, the daughter of Amadou and Amoin Thiam, and René Ekra, the son of the Minister of State, Mathieu Ekra. The presence at the wedding of Yacé and Konan Bedie, whose names have most often been cited as presidential successors, can only be seen as symbolic.[26]

Although it is so extreme, the Ivoirian example is not altogether absurd. We already know that in Kenya, Jomo Kenyatta's 'Family' plays an important role in economic accumulation. In Nigeria, the Sardauna consolidated the 'Northern community' (*Jama'ar Arewa*) by uniting the relatives of various people from Kano, and by encouraging similar links between traditionally rival areas in the region.[27] And in Congo, the 'North Atlantic Treaty' found its supreme conjugal expression in the marriage of Denis and Marie-Antoinette Sassou Nguesso, who were Mbochi and Vili respectively.[28] During the 1985 presidential elections in Sierra Leone, Major-General Momoh's family background was an important factor because it was seen as the incarnation of national unity: Momoh could boast, like his predecessor Siaka Stevens, of his Limba roots, but also of a Temne mother, a Mende wife... and a childhood in Wilberforce, a Creole village in the Freetown area.[29] Such marriages at the high levels of society represent wider-scale unions within the class of the 'en haut d'en haut' (as the establishment are known in the Ivory Coast), which leads to its progressive homogenisation. More prosaically, the mistresses of powerful men – who are known as the 'second', 'third' or 'fourth' 'offices' – weave the fabric of social integration by night and day, from embrace to rupture, from malicious gossip to caresses.

Other places where the reciprocal assimilation of the elite occurs are educational channels (Makerere College in East Africa, Fort-Hare in Southern Africa, the William Ponty School in West Africa, Barewa College in Northern Nigeria), student associations (of which the well-known *Fedération des étudiants d'Afrique noire en France* (FEANF) was an early example), Christian churches, Islamic brotherhoods, and the pilgrimage to Mecca. It is possible that some of these have now been supplanted by mystic channels whose intervention may not be entirely new. Most of the large religious gatherings of the century were trans-ethnic, and the composition of such groups foreshadowed those of the nationalist period. In Gabon during the 1950s, Léon Mba justified his involvement in the Bwiti cult in the name of unity: 'We have sub-stituted this movement for the old ancestor cults which did not succeed in uniting us from Libreville to the frontier with Cameroon. We need to unite ourselves; we can only progress in this way'.[30] But the expansion of secret brotherhoods and sects today is quite extraordinary. They give a quasi-Messianic aspect to social mobility; when people get to know about the 'President's' membership of a particular sect, they all try to join it, in the same way as others join the party: they do this when the doctrines give value to 'individual success' and, as in the case of the *Rose-Croix* or the Manikari cults, they assure success.[31]

In reality, however, the boom of esotericism turned out to be a mechanism of selection and exclusion which has reinforced the dom-inant circles. Freemasonry exercised this function in Blaise Diagne's Senegal, for the Creoles in Sierra Leone and the Whig oligarchy in Liberia, and in Ghana and the Ivory Coast. Today, it is in Gabon that Freemasonry plays its biggest role, together with the *njobi* rite: Bongo himself is master of one of the lodges, and membership of the fraternity is obligatory *de facto* for every member of the country's political elite.[32] Other mystic societies have been established in Africa, and they have received a significant audience from the higher strata of society. Al-though it initially appealed to the masses, celestial Christianity has become the preserve of civil servants and middle- to high-level cadres in the Gulf of Guinea since the end of the 1960s; and it is probably not by chance alone that the only official political execution in Gabon was of a seditious soldier who claimed to be a member of this movement.[33] To put it more precisely, the *Rose-Croix* in Cameroon is one of the havens in which Biya's closest entourage takes communion.[34]

The transactions taking place in this mystic 'abyss' are an extreme example. Their importance cannot, however, be quantified easily because they are the visible tip of more general and silent activities taking place in the different realms of social life of the elites. In France, the court, the salon, the mystic society, the cafés of the literati the theatre, the concert, and certain restaurants had an important role in the formation of the dominant class. One of the most urgent tasks facing analysts of African politics is the listing and study of the occasions during which members of the dominant class mix with one another. Apart from the 'courtesy visits' that are paid to the office or home – these signify the hierarchical relationship between the visitor and his host – such a list would probably contain a restricted number of places: a few high-class restaurants and clubs, some nightclubs in Paris, London and on the continent, the major international hotels of which Africa is so full, executive lounges in airports, first-class cabins on the regular flights of national airlines, private mosques in Islamic territories, and the endless celebrations which mark the passage of time south of the Sahara.

Aside from the brilliance and splendour assumed by the *en haut du haut*, the social group below them in the social hierarchy are involved in a similar system. A study carried out in Léopoldville in 1964–65 revealed the existence of many 'weekend' groups which united the 'elites' in a 'relatively intimate way' regardless of their ethnic origin: the groups of 'Friends of Primus', or 'Friends of Polar' (who only drink these particular brands of beer), the May Gul group (which meets on Saturdays to drink beer in shirt-sleeves, without ties, and with bare feet), the 'elegance' groups, the groups of people sharing the same name, or groups of 'Friends of VW' (they help one another to acquire Volkswagen spare parts from a central garage which imports them)… In these groups, 'opinions, attitudes, mentalities and different values are shared, confront one another, and then mix together, dissolve or disappear'.[35] Phenomena similar to this example occur in every town on the continent, and there is an enormous sociological literature on this subject. In cultures in which expression is mainly oral or gestural, everyday life and the interactive rituals – to use the ideas of E. Goffman[36] – participate directly in the structuration of the dominant class. Above all, and for all the reasons we have given, this is a fabric of personal relations, and in this way the private order is not separate from that of the state.[37]

Once we accept this, Marx's more precise definition of 'civil society' – 'civil society only develops with a bourgeoisie'[38] – imposes itself. The fusion of elites also occurs in the business world, and events in the 'private' world, marriage for example, often guarantee unions of a financial nature. From one perspective, the contemporary economy reproduces the 'multi-functional alliances' of ancient long-distance trade, which linked together politically and culturally heterogeneous regions.[39] The example of *Crédit mutuél du Cameroun* is significant in this respect. Despite the predominance of the Bamiléké, the credit group is made up of businessmen from all regions (except the Eastern province which is economically marginal), and the 'tontine' (informal credit unions) meetings take place sequentially in every major town in the country.[40] This experiment may appear to be recent and still uncertain; it may seem naïve or, on the contrary, a crafty way of dealing with power. However, the significance of this example is corroborated by the important case of the 'Kaduna mafia' in Nigeria. In spite of their 'Northern' sensibilities, members of this group were not opposed to forming an '*entente*' with Southern businessmen, especially the Yoruba, among whom figured Chief S. Sowemino, a reputable lawyer, Chief J. Udoji, president of the Stock Exchange, and Chief M.K.O. Abiola, head of ITT in Africa. *In fine*, these economic contacts led to the signing of a secret electoral pact between the 'mafia' and Chief Awolowo's Unity Party of Nigeria in June 1983.[41] In the same way, the Gikuyu, Embu, Meru Association (GEMA) in Kenya, whose ethnic connotation was undeniable from the start – P. Anyang' Nyong'o defined it as 'an organisation of Kikuyu capitalists' – was also significant in terms of alliance on the national level. This was particularly true in 1977 when, as the succession to Jomo Kenyatta was approaching, it tried to reconstruct the historical coalition between Luo and Kikuyu elites on which the Kenya African Union, and then the Kenya African National Union, had been founded, and which was broken up by the dissidence of Oginga Odinga.[42]

All these links are not sufficient to constitute a relation of exchange, according to the strict sense of the word. However, they do form a relatively homogeneous social bloc, and a system for the interaction of groups or trade networks which were previously disparate and competitive. They constitute a determining, unifying factor as much as do the multiple lines of 'straddling', although there is no need to discuss these again. The 'material relations between individuals,'[43] are increasingly being organised in specific ways. The existence of 'ethnic' associations, which are the integrating factors within a region and between town and country, must not be allowed to disguise the proliferation of other forms of association which articulate economic or professional interests on a trans-ethnic or trans-geographical basis: directors' unions, lawyers' or architects' associations, and so on.[44] The way into all these types of organisation is similar. In Congo, the *ngwala*, or mutual aid associations, are set up in order that the dead may be buried in the proper way. These Beembe organisations are also tied to socio-professional or socio-biological categories (*ngwala* for workmen, parents of schoolchildren, youth and so forth). They also function as systems of accumulation, due to the practice of multiple membership which allows for the maximisation of investments.[45]

One can therefore see the beginning of the crystallisation of 'civil societies', including their autonomy and therefore their conflict with the State. The most complete example of this is the case of Nigeria where in 1984 General Buhari gave the proof a *contrario* that it was not at all possible to govern the country without the consensus of a 'civil society' which was much less 'primitive and gelatinous' than elsewhere.[46] This contradiction between the two domains exists in every country, although to a varying extent. In Cameroon, for example, it took the form of a rebellion by lawyers and architects in 1986; in Congo, where the apparatus of the state is being steadily overtaken by the energetic associative movement; in Zaïre, the Catholic church rose up against the extremes of the politics of 'authenticity' in 1972, and the local councillors elected in June 1982 fought against the prerogatives of the territorial administration; in Senegal, the Islamic brotherhoods have resisted the reformist policies of Abdou Diouf; and in the Ivory Coast, entrepreneurs have tried to free themselves from political clientelism.

A double advantage is gained by progressing from the Marxian definitions of 'civil society' to Gramsci's distinction between this category and 'political society'.[47] On the one hand, the crucial weight of societal dynamics on the formation of a dominant class should be emphasised for one last time, as well as the irreducibility of this 'war for positions' through which the lines of inequality have been linked throughout history. On the other hand, there is the role that 'political society' itself plays in the general process of reciprocal assimilation. 'Civil society' plays a part that is as great as the indigenous associative tradition on the Gulf of Guinea, for example, is ancient and rich.[48] The impact of the State is so strong that, since the inter-war years, it has absorbed the procedures of accumulation and has assumed the monopoly of modernity by defining itself against society, becoming instead a *Policeystaat*.[49] In a way the 1970s and 1980s were the years of the 'revenge of African societies' against the distortion caused by the State since colonisation, according to G. Hyden, the years of the 'economy of affection'.[50] As Abdou Diouf said, they pose the problem of the 'redefinition of the relationships between state and civil society'.[51] Speaking in economic terms, the solutions proposed by the World Bank and International Monetary Fund during this period were not that different.

Apart from the fact that it is hampered by serious theoretical and methodological objections,[52] the systematisation of this dichotomy between 'civil society' and 'political society' obscures the relations which link these two categories. These relations do not involve exteriority and antagonism, but plurality and impetus. First, institutions such as parliaments, parties, trade unions and the several consultative commissions, 'represent', in one way, civil society within political society.[53] Secondly, despite their autonomy, structures of power do not escape the infiltrations of civil society, as has been shown by the dissolution of the specifically military character of the armies in Dahomey, Upper Volta, Sierra Leone, and Nigeria in situations of heightened political competition.[54] These examples only portray the radical ambivalence of the state, and are sufficient to bring back to centre stage the mechanisms of 'straddling' in the process of accumulation. From now on, it will be more convenient to analyse this particular vocation of power structures, the reciprocal assimilation of elites, in terms of the equivocal interpenetration and mutual reinforcement of political society and civil society, rather than in terms of two separate structures.

BASES AND PROCEDURES OF RECIPROCAL ASSIMILATION: POLITICAL SOCIETY

Five political practices seem to be particularly conducive to the unification of the elites and the creation of the dominant class: ideology, chieftaincy, the bureaucracy, elections and the party. Their function in this respect is neither univocal nor exclusive. But, for the time being, the important thing is to understand the mechanisms of production of a relatively homogeneous social group.

R.L. Sklar was one of the first to demonstrate how this works in political parties.[55] The compromise between the two generations, aspiring to the leadership of the postcolonial State was organised under the party's direction and within its apparatus. Instead of returning to the examples of conservative modernisation which confirm this rule – the SLPP in Sierra Leone and the NPC in Nigeria – we shall discuss, as a supplementary example, the case of the territorial sections of the RDA (*Rassemblement démocratique africain*), with the exception of Guinea where the chiefs were openly attacked. In Niger the PPN was made up of 'captives' and 'masters' who happened to have gone to the colonial schools together, and this prevented any possible politicisation of this major fracture within Songhai-Zarma society.[56] Since the mid-1950s the *Parti démocratique de la Côte d'Ivoire* (PDCI) in the Ivory Coast has been an imposing coalition of heterogeneous roles and statuses.[57] To the south in Gabon, Léon Mba, who was one of the founders of the *Bloc démocratique gabonais*, shone out due to his 'ability to attract the less "educated" as well as the "modernist" elements', and gave his political action *stricto sensu* 'an ambivalent character which allowed him to control the Old Fang as well as the Young Fang'.[58]

Even nowadays, chiefs willingly associate themselves with the local party organs, either by being elected to them or by joining as members.[59] It is almost impossible to hold a meeting in town, or even more so in a village, without the consent of the chief or even his assistance in sending out the invitations. The local and national level party organs offer many sinecures to the ex-commoners of the 'political era', which secure them a place in the power structure. Western-style political formations are thus true microcosms where the lines of concatenation can be found. They have been one of the main vectors of the horizontal integration of regional elites, which the changes brought about by colonialism have made so necessary. Even the so-called tribal parties quickly understood the necessity of expanding their activities, and forming trans-ethnic alliances. Reciprocally, the nationalist movements which dominated the decolonisation period often started as simple particularist organisations, before developing and diversifying the geographical sources of their recruits.[60]

From this double perspective of vertical and horizontal integration the single party is placed in continuity with the multi-party system, rather than being separate from it. The single-party system systematises, and transposes into a national dimension, the compromises and amalgams developed by the local parties, which had been either supported or opposed by the colonial power.[61] The single party institutionalises the 'situationist *tontine*', and the regional distribution of the spoils of the state, through the intermediary of delegates from all over the country, which assures a minimal representation of the 'periphery' in the presidential 'centre'.[62] The single party is thus a site of arbitration or of conflict, which its apparent monolithic nature must not disguise.[63] The governing structures of single parties allow some space for the country's forces: the army, unions, business world and Christian churches.

When considering the reciprocal assimilation of segments of the social elite, even the process of the construction of the single party itself is of significance. The term 'unified' which has so often been favoured by ideologues to describe the single party, and the ideas of 'movement' or 'rally' which are so commonly used, are not mere euphemisms, in spite of the widespread use of coercion and intimidation used by those in power, anxious to achieve their goals. Negotiations with the dominant party have not always been formalities, and the pledges given to the ex-opposition have not been merely symbolic. For example, Jomo Kenyatta's position went to Daniel arap Moi, an ex-member of the Kenya African Democratic Union, which had allied with the Kenya African National Union in December 1964. In opposition to the Leninist ideology favoured by *Spark* in Ghana, and by the inner ranks of TANU in Tanzania, the creators of the 'unified' parties in Africa intended to apply the logic of inclusion rather than exclusion, with the opposition being 'amalgamated' and not 'eliminated'.[64] The solidity of the alliance cementing the single party tends of course to be proportional to the equity of those at its head: in Cameroon, the anglophone elite tried to reintroduce political plurality in 1972, once it was certain it had been swindled by the UNC, and in Kenya it could be said that Oginga Odinga had the same intention in 1982.[65] However, the centripetal force of the party is so strong that it has a significant influence over the distribution of the nation's riches. The 'ethic of unity'[66] which this force claims to represent, and the redundant theme of 'union' (versus 'division') which it uses *ad nauseam*, should be taken seriously, despite the inexpressible boredom it invokes.

R.L. Sklar's reference to the famous essay of R. Michels is neither completely irrelevant, nor anachronistic.[67] In Africa, too, it is rare that 'the struggle between the old chiefs and the youth ends up in the total victory of the former', and the functioning of parties 'ends up less in the circulation than in the fusion of the elites, in other words an amalgam of the two elements'.[68] The agreement of well-known analysts should not lead us astray. It is the character of the coalition of clienteles and leaders, more than the bureaucratic nature of the parties, however problematic that may be, that keeps the process of reciprocal assimilation going. Single parties in Africa, according to most observers, do not abandon their state of lethargy except on certain occasions, especially during elections. This lethargy is taken to such a degree that they have been referred to as 'no party states'.[69] In spite of their imposing organisational structures, they do not have much in common with the North

European social democracy which is the subject of R. Michels' analysis. In the sub-Saharan situation, his remarks apply above all to the personalised mechanisms of political recruitment.

According to tradition, the very idea of elections in Africa is laughable. However, these are more often of a competitive nature than is thought.[70] From the perspective of the reciprocal assimilation of elites, it is of little importance whether this competition operates from above, in the highest institutions of the regime, or from below, in the secret corners of the polling booths. The main thing is that the contented victors come from all the geographical, sociological and historical sections of the social elite; that they reflect this plurality and simultaneously go beyond it. During elections, the resurgence of the remainder of the political class, who were removed from power during troublesome periods, is of particular significance. In Zaïre, the legislative elections of 1970 resulted in the reinsertion of an appreciable number of politicians from the First Republic into the state system, and at the same time highlighted the osmotic relationship between commerce and the bureaucracy. Subsequent elections, especially the local ones of June 1982, have confirmed this development.[71] In the same way, the 'democratisation' of the single-party regime in the Ivory Coast was expressed by the reintegration of the radical nationalist generations who were victims of the purges in the National Assembly in 1963-64 and above all, in the municipal councils in 1985.[72]

In Cameroon, finally, renewal of the local organs of the party in 1986 allowed for the victory of people previously opposed to Ahidjo, many of whom did not hide their sympathy for the UPC. This episode helped to eliminate the schism that had torn the country apart during the nationalist movement. It also helped to put an end to the conflict which was brewing between reformers and conservatives. The official commentary on the results issuing from the State House was clear:

> We can see that a certain global equilibrium exists between the newly elected and the re-elected, although the former are slightly more numerous [...] this equilibrium constitutes a political plebiscite which allows the head of state to know all Cameroonians, without a priori discrimination between the 'old' and the 'new'.[73]

Le Messager, usually keen to call for change, admitted that it was 'a period when waiting was essential' if the regime was to avoid 'finding itself faced with an uncontrollable army of crazed adversaries'.[74] As during the period of political pluralism in the 1950s, the highly conflictual system of universal suffrage was paradoxically revealed to be a vector of political compromise. We have even seen unsuccessful candidates for the presidency of a departmental section being elected to the post of vice-president or of councillor, in order to appease them and to conform with the 'ethic of unity'.[75] The offices were paralysed, but the morale of reciprocal assimilation was saved.

The aggregation of electoral procedures owes more to bitter 'struggles for influence', which often involve the trauma of witchcraft, than to factors which merit a positive social value. Furthermore, this aggregation is not universal. Not only are the 'little people' excluded from the race because of the requirements of wealth and generational superiority, or frankly because of their lack of property, but some members of the social elite see themselves disqualified due to the vigilance of the security services, the will of the prince, the selective historical memory of the regime, or diverse legal procedures and rules.[76] The elected bodies, parliamentary assemblies and party organs are therefore nothing but representatives of the dominant order. Despite everything, they serve as the privileged zone of unification for those engaged in the quest for hegemony, and one can choose not to agree with J. Samoff when he affirms that the 'institutionalisation of the elections [in Tanzania] slowed down the consolidation of power by a governing bureaucratic class and an aspiring bourgeoisie':

> By their adhesion to at least some of the elements of liberal democracy, the elections have simultaneously disturbed such a consolidation and helped to legitimate it. The elections have supported the initiatives of Nyerere and his allies in the centre to counter the formation of an elite. They have allowed certain members of the elite to maintain local bases of support and have simultaneously permitted the elite in general to clothe themselves in populism.[77]

The contradiction between these two mechanisms does not really exist. In reality, they are both involved in the same unsteady process of social production, which has been of great significance in the *longue durée*. Jomo Kenyatta understood perfectly well that it was not necessary to have control over the minor details of local political life in order to establish an inegalitarian system at the state level. On the contrary, electoral contests in rural districts could add to the plasticity of the system, providing that they remain on the infra-political level of 'development'. *A contrario*, Daniel arap Moi's propensity to become involved in the local districts is connected with the general aggravation of the dynamics of dissent during the 1980s.[78] The case of Senegal validates this theory. What L.S. Senghor called *la politique politicienne* (and which is by definition a ruthless struggle between 'clans' – in the Dakarois or Saint Louisien sense of the word) is indissociable from a tradition of compromise, accommodation and incorporation that has been optimistically termed by Donal Cruise O'Brien a 'success story'.[79] In other words, the unification of dominant groups is caused as much by political conflict and personal confrontation as it is by the 'voluntarist' process of consensus and institutionalisation.

It is, however, the true bureaucracies which seem to work towards the fusion of the elites: the administration and the army (which R. Michels emphasised have affinities with the party). These two institutions bring together people of diverse social and geographical origins, ordering them around a common pole which is far away from the previous divisions and particularities of society: there are a restricted number of places for training and socialisation (there are a mere handful of large establishments such as Sandhurst, Saint-Cyr, Fréjus, l'École nationale de la France d'outre-mer), the adoption of universal technologies of government and modern armaments, and the innumerable social rituals (for example, the officers' mess), the specific modes of consumption, and the adhesion to a more or less internalised professional ethos.[80]

The civil and military bureaucracies have historically brought about revolutionary inversions of the lines of inequality. It has often been suggested that the colonialists modified the unequal relationships between indigenous societies by recruiting their assistant officers and soldiers from underprivileged regions, such as the northern areas of Uganda, Congo, Dahomey and Togo. These military counter-elites rapidly tried to compensate for the distortions of the economy by carrying out one coup after another. But, with the exception of Uganda (even though it had a complex political economy under the dictatorship of Field-Marshal Amin Dada) these coups ended up in trans-regional amalgams or alliances which ensured that the regimes of Gnassingbe Eyadema, Mathieu Kerekou, Marien Ngouabi and their successors were not reduced to the 'northerners'' domination.[81] Political ruptures sometimes open up the way to recompositions and associations of new interests which upset the status quo. Military regimes generally operate in this way. By reinforcing the high levels of the civil service, they brought back politicians who had been ostracised, and rehabilitated the role of chief, to fill the political void which they had created by coming to power.[82]

We therefore need to relativise the revolutionary opportunities created not just by changes in regional inequalities but also by the introduction of new 'zones of indeterminate lineage' and new channels of social mobility. It is in exceptional cases that only the juniors, common people and members of castes benefited from the opportunities of colonialism, whatever the initial reluctance of powerful members of the traditional order to send their offspring to colonial schools. In practice, the bureaucracies served as the spaces for mediation and collaboration between social positions inherited from the past, even if the ideological prejudices to which we have already referred remained, especially in the matrimonial domain. Once again, the Nigerian example of the Northern Civil Service serves as the continental model. The sons of *talakawa* and *sarakuna* coexisted in this institution, and the dominant contemporary intelligentsia comes from this group.[83] Similarly, a noble or wealthy background has never been indispensable for an honorable career in the Nigerian army. For every Hassan Katsina, son of the emir of Katsina, or Ojukwu, son of a millionaire businessman, one can count several children of railway workers (Ironsi, Adebayo), catechists (Gowon), low-level civil servants (Shodeinde), or artisans and farmers (Ademulegun, Fajuyi), whose names have been at the forefront of the politico-military scene during the last two decades.[84]

The social mixing upon which the bureaucracies are founded occurs deep within the state apparatus. The eminence of bureaucratic power that was instituted during the colonial years has in no way been eroded by independence. The competition between the party and the administration turned to the disadvantage of the former, apart perhaps from Julius Nyerere's Tanzania and Sékou Touré's Guinea.[85] Military regimes have put the finishing touches to this development, even in Congo where Marxist-Leninist terminology disguised the pre-eminence of the CMP, the *Comité militaire du parti* created in 1977. In the provinces, the active forces (the 'elites' of the district) generally meet with the administrator for work sessions and discussions. Today, this procedure is one of the most effective methods of reciprocal assimilation, even if only because of the extent of the political and economic arbitrations over which it presides. The political class is regulated by the higher echelons of the civil service, for it is here that deputies, ministers and presidents are recruited. This part of the civil service is also the 'shock absorber' which softens the blows of fluctuations in individual careers; it is the provider of ambassadorial posts, and also the posts of managing directors of national companies, of high-level administrators and of delegates. It prevents disgraced people from leaving the system, for they are always likely to stir up a dissident counter-elite.

Strangely enough, the chiefs contributed to the integration of dominant groups. This assertion could invite criticism because there are so many glaring exceptions. These exceptions are the ones which are generally used to explain the more or less precipitate disappearance of the institution of chieftaincy. In fact, the social and political revolutions in Fouta Djalon, Rwanda, Burundi, Buganda and Barotseland signalled a more general erosion which could not even be escaped by the *sarakau-na* of Northern Nigeria, foreshadowed by conflict between chiefs and educated people since before the Second World War. However, the phenomenon must not be exaggerated. A period of recovery, or at least a revival of legitimacy, has followed the classic confrontation between the 'centre' and the 'periphery' of the political system, as well as the social upheavals of the 1950s and 1960s. Such a recovery is clear in Bamiléké country in Cameroon where there is a true 'recuperation of modern institutions being proposed by the developing state'. This took place within the single party, the cooperative movement and the municipalities.[86] Many of the chieftaincies destroyed in the uprisings were rebuilt. Although it is spectacular, this is not a unique example, as can be seen from the common practice of prostration in Yorubaland and in the high reputation of the Asantehene in Ghana.

The very idea of 'chieftaincy' leads to confusion. It can refer to a precise sector of the social hierarchy in certain strongly polarised historical situations – that is, to the aristocracy. But it is, in most cases, only a position of power to which one accedes through individual political or economic performance. This is not only the case for colonial chieftaincy created entirely in an integral lineage context, but also for older chieftaincy such as those in Bamiléké country.[87] Although the rotation of these chiefs comes about through conflict, in the end it links together dominant categories that were previously heterogeneous. It is not uncommon, for example, that an elected chief is also a civil servant or a member of a liberal profession with an array of western qualifications.

In Bandjoun, the most prestigious chiefdom in Bamiléké country, with a population of 10,000, Ngrie Kamga, the *fo* enthroned with great ceremony in 1984, was a civil administrator and head of the department of Mefou in the central province when he was elected to the post of *fo* by the council of nine notables. He succeeded his own brother, to whom he was the *nkwipo* (the assistant or palatine). His predecessor was not an old greybeard selected by tradition, but rather an agricultural engineer who was reproached with having a 'foreigner' as his favourite wife (she came from a different region). Could one imagine a better illustration of the process of reciprocal assimilation than the controversial circumstances of his death? – nothing is more suspicious than a motor accident. When he died, he was travelling in 'a Mercedes which belonged to Fotso Victor, a very rich businessman also from Bandjoun'. His funeral oration was given by Nkuete, another native of Bamiléké country and the assistant general secretary to the Presidency of the Republic. This did not happen by chance, for 'one of the first important people to make

make an act of allegiance to the new chief' was Wabo Fadouop, 'a dignitary of the Bandjoun chiefdom and an important businessman in Douala'. He was followed by Messrs Fotso, Koloko, Kadji Defosso, Sohaing and Tchanque – entrepreneurs whom we have already met in preceding chapters.[88] And this is not an isolated case: in Bali, V.S. Gelega II, who reigned as *fo* for forty-five years, who presided over the local section of the party, and who left 'a human inheritance of 37 wives and 417 children', was succeeded by 'a seasoned intellectual' who had studied at the American University in Cairo, and then in West Germany; in Limbe a journalist was elected chief of the Kom and Bum in the towns; and in Foumbam, the municipal magistrate who had, according to the state, 'the qualities of a good manager and administrator', was none other than the sultan of Bamoum, the 'mayor-sultan' as the *Cameroon Tribune* wrote with a touch of humour.[89]

The oldest chieftaincies, which existed in the precolonial days, certainly had stronger integrating characteristics than those created by the colonialists. However, the latter had significant abilities, and their use of the invention of tradition gave them coagulating properties. Mayi Matip, who was criticised for allying with Ahidjo after the death of Ruben Um Nyobé and for his ambition to be the dominant member of the fiercely acephalous Bassa society, used and abused the benefits of a reinvented tradition, and implored the chiefs to be the 'ultimate forces which bring and hold together all the elements, all the active and useful energies'.[90] His request was not in vain: he dominated Nyong-et-Kellé for thirty years, and it is possible that his failure to win the legislative elections in 1988 was a fatal blow.

Almost everywhere, those who held 'modern' political and economic roles hastened to obtain noble titles in their chieftaincies or native kingdoms, while in turn, those who held traditional authority and legitimacy entered political parties and businesses. As in Western Cameroon, the example of Yorubaland shows this pattern of movement extremely well. The lines of 'straddling' between chiefs and traders seem to have intensified during the period between the two wars.[91] The compromise between chiefs and educated people was less easy, but it was made in the end. In reality, the conflict between these groups was of a political nature, and did not reflect the absolute social contradiction which R.L. Sklar suggested when he mentioned the 'new and rising class' in reference to the 'educated people'.[92] With the introduction of western-style representative institutions, the extension of local government and the mutations of the economy, the chiefs could not co-opt the 'educated' sector as they had co-opted the traders some years previously. Helped by the dominance of the party, the Yoruba leadership changed hands without the sovereigns and chiefs being removed from the Establishment, even though they had to accept the new rules of the game. The cooperation between Obafemi Awolowo, the founder of the Action Group, and Sir Adesoji Aderemi II, the *oni* of Ife, closely resembled a pact signed between Dr Milton Margai and the Paramount Chief Julius Gulama in Sierra Leone during the same period. Better still, the 'educated' group consecrated their social ascendancy by buying noble titles, even though the price of these had risen sharply, and did not correspond with the effective prerogative they granted. Obafemi Awolowo became Chief Awolowo in October 1954, and, since 1950, Bode Thomas has occupied the honorary position of *Balogun* of Oyo. Thomas was installed in this position by the *alafin* (king) of the city, who was later deposed because he did not recognise the superiority of the party. Tension between the intellectuals and the monarchs diminished progressively as the rules of the social game were changed at the end of the 1950s and during the 1960s. Royalty ended up by recovering much of the prestige it had lost, although the successive reforms of traditional authorities had progressively weakened its powers.

The collapse of political parties, the explosion of civil wars and the repeated installation of military regimes have done much to influence this reorientation, this reconciliation of 'tradition' and 'modernity', to maintain these execrable terms. However, this pattern of movement and fusion of roles is not specific to Yoruba and Bamiléké countries. There have been similar but less dramatic developments throughout the continent. In the Ivory Coast, for example, the *Association confraternelle des chef coutumiers*, set up in 1945 by Houphouët-Boigny, did not take long to break away from its founder and take sides with the French administration against the PDCI. Its president, Prince Kwame Adingra, head chief of the Abron, set up the Progressive Party with the help of the colonial authorities. This party ended up by opposing the RDA, and in 1951, the Association, whose members included 100 out of the 104 main chiefs, openly condemned the RDA. It was only in Baoulé country that the nobles cooperated with the nationalist movement, and this was because Houphouët-Boigny was one of them. Divisions between the chiefs and the party did not, however, degenerate into total divorce, as they had done in Guinea. On 12 August 1956, Houphouët-Boigny promulgated a 'large-scale national reconciliation' which led to the rallying of chiefly support and to maintaining most of them in their auxiliary roles in the administration. Prince Adingra benefited from these measures, as the Association was transformed into a union of professionals to which Houphouët-Boigny was elected honorary president.[93]

There has been a similar intermediary scenario in Cameroon, although this has been made more complicated by Ahidjo's modest background, the Fulani aristocracy's attachment to the past, and the 'UPC' insurrection. The chiefs continue to play a significant role, although this varies from one region to another.[94] In 1977, a statute institutionalising their functions declared 'the restoration of their dignity' as an objective.[95] During the latter years, Biya has treated customary authorities in a prodigal way, which cannot be entirely explained by the tactical necessities during a troubled period. It is true that the *lamibe* of the north, the *fo* of the west and north-west, and, to an even greater extent, the sultan of Bamoum represented the main points of equilibrium in the 'hegemonic alliance' which resisted Ahidjo's adventurist intrigues in 1983–84. But perhaps more profound agreements were forced between the state and customary authority when the President of the Republic received the benedictions of the Duala ancestors at the sacred Mbanya river, and when he was enthroned as *fo* of Bamenda.[96]

The absorption of the chiefs by the dominant national group does not actually modify political decision-making, however much influence the nobles have on the distribution of prebends. The dominance of the central state established by the colonial regime cannot be reversed. Nevertheless, the inability of Field-Marshal Mobutu's absolutism to impose itself on at least the most ancient chiefs, if not those grafted onto acephalous societies, is significant. To distinguish between these two types of chieftaincy, T.M. Callaghy borrows the terminology of the French *ancien régime*, and opposes the 'country of election' to the 'country of the state'.[97] This impotence demonstrates that the precolonial and colonial positions of local power remain integral parts of the global economy of inequality, on which the reciprocal assimilation of elites remains partially dependent.

The formulation of solid political ideologies, finally, brings a lingua franca to the dominant group which allows it to subsume its heterogeneity in a solid way. This represents a 'grammar of production' of the dominant class.[98] Far from being absurd, its frequently outrageous characteristics, often bearing no relation to the most elementary indigenous social realities, facilitate the integration of a composite elite which is stuck in its particularisms. From this perspective, the language of power may be all the more effective for its lack of elegance. It is of little importance that it is indigestible – the humour of the 'little men' remedies this – provided that it is useful and that it has an answer for everything. As a universal discourse, Marxist-Leninism, especially if it was 'scientific', satisfied this requirement perfectly.[99] One could almost be tempted to say that its adoption as the unifying code of the political class usually happened when this class was highly divided, as in Congo, Benin and Angola. One could not accept this as a specific theory, for it does not apply to the case of Mozambique, and it could not be treated as a general law (how does it apply to Senegal and Kenya?). Other ideologies, imported or created – it scarcely matters if one considers that all cultural conversion is in fact recreation – fill this mission of synthesis with the same lack of joy, and even more plasticity. Witness, for example, Julius Nyerere's and Kenneth Kaunda's Christianising socialism, Ahmadou Ahidjo's colourless, odourless and flavourless 'planned liberalism', or, finally, Félix Houphouët-Boigny's bland paternalism, when, with a touch of pity, he described the 1963 'plotters' imprisoned at Yamoussoukro as his 'little perverts'. During an audience Houphouët-Boigny's gave to a delegation from Sanwi, the kingdom which had attempted to secede in 1962, he declared:

> I am certainly the happiest person amongst those gathered here this evening, as I find myself amongst all my brothers and sisters of Aboisso. I would like to reassure the whole population of Aboisso, and above all the cadres. You must get rid of your guilty consciences. You have not betrayed the country. [...] There are problems in even the most united of families. You must understand what I am about to say: those who have left Côte d'Ivoire to struggle for their own successes, slamming the door of the communal house behind them, must know that I have never shut that door to them. I am waiting for them inside the house. And they need make no effort in order to be accepted back inside'.[100]

The use of parental terms is a true reflection of the system of reciprocal assimilation. But the use of such terms does not mean that reciprocal assimilation has really taken place. His Majesty Jean-Bedel Bokassa, who liked to present himself as the 'good father' of the Central African Republic, governed more by confiscation than by conciliation.[101] But the family idiom is used most convincingly by Bongo, Mobutu and even Biya: 'I am the father of the nation, I take care of everybody, of all my children'.[102] The use of this idiom reflects their preferred mode of political unification, the 'return of the prodigal son' which simultaneously signifies the dominance of the presidency. 'I recognise my mistake in not wanting to punish those who have acted wrongly for their family, and I also hope that they will ask to be pardoned' confessed Houphouët-Boigny, who could go on talking forever in this way. He continued in a threatening manner – 'But to demand pardon repetitively is a weakness and a fault against the community which I would never commit' – and then immediately followed with more gentle words –

'Wickedness has deep roots. All of us have wickedness in us, and there is no miracle cure that can help anybody to remove this unless everybody works together'.[103] Throughout the continent, rallying support for the party, which is the central act in the quest for hegemony, is expressed in the effusive style of filial reconcilation and pardon, even if the president is a violent father:

> The voice of the people who are your children rings out to implore your help and pardon.
> Breathless, ashamed and confused, we must confess our use of demagoguery truthfully.
> We have to depend on you because the forces of heaven and earth recognise your power.
> It is in this way that you should counsel a father who is amongst his prodigal sons.
> Above all, you should not counsel us according to the extent of our abusive transgressions'.[104]

The language of power is not only ideological. It also has a properly linguistic dimension. In this context, independent Africa chose simply to step into the shoes of the departing European colonial powers, but the 'national language' debate suggests that they probably had little choice in this given the change of scale associated with colonialism. P. Anderson has stressed how much language in itself can serve as an instrument of inclusion which is indispensable to the formation of all 'imagined communities'.[105] This can be seen in the project of the dominant class south of the Sahara; a class which forges itself in the language of the State, transcending the particularisms of the past. There are very few regimes, however anti-imperialist they may be, which have given up the administrative language left behind by the colonialists. Congo and Benin have retained the French language, Angola and Mozambique still use Portuguese, and Tanzania's originality is more apparent than real as the Germans governed through the medium of Swahili.[106] The two glaring exceptions of Mauritania and Somalia do not weaken the argument. In the former case, the politics of Arabisation have been a powerful factor in the division of the elite, which is now split between 'beydanes' and 'black-Mauritanians'. In Somalia, the cultural homogeneity of the country has made the promulgation of Somali as the national language possible. This has led to the fanciful pursuit of irredentism, and has not weakened the damaging intensity of factional struggles. There are also the less extreme cases of Burundi and Rwanda, where French is not the language used by the political class but continues to be the key to social promotion. There is also the case of Zaïre, where the presidential coterie, which originates from the Equatorial province, encourages the expansion of Lingala, especially in the army and the party, and therefore confirms its 'Sudanic' identity in the eyes of other ethnic groups. In these less extreme cases, language is also not an obstacle to factional struggles.[107] It is therefore possible that the extraneous character of the idiom used by the governing groups favoured their precipitation into a dominant class, while weakening their hegemonic capacity. This hypothesis is neither original nor provocative. Throughout history, inequality has been structured by 'diglossy' – by the coexistence of a scholarly language and a popular language. Whatever the case, the essential thing is to recognise the progressive emergence of a *Weltanschauung* within which powerful people can communicate, and whose language is an irreplaceable resource.

THE SEARCH FOR A 'DOMINANT CLASS'

It is now possible to draw some conclusions about the interaction of elements from 'political' and 'civil' society which play a role in the fusion of an homogeneous dominant group. It is also possible to introduce some theoretical perspectives, although there are still many unclear areas in my argument.

In one way, it is possible to see how the superlative relation of the State to accumulation, the interlinking of systems of 'straddling' with those of concatenation, and the active inter-penetration of 'civil society' and 'political society', *could* be resolved in many cumulative 'spirals'. These processes work towards the production of a dominant class based on the reciprocal assimilation of the social elite. The extent of this molecular process of assimilation, and its degree of realisation vary considerably from one historical situation to another. It is important to continue to argue against the abundant literature and to refuse to relate the postcolonial State to an existing dominant class, which is its tenant (*Träger*). As Georges Balandier has already put it, 'contemporary political life does not seem to manifest a structure of constituted classes, but rather acts as an instrument of a class in formation'.[108] Balandier's warning has not been heeded and most analysts continue to address the themes of the national, bureaucratic and 'comprador' bourgeoisie, in spite of the evidence against their existence: due to the lack of historical depth, it is too early to define the contours of this dominant class and its economic character, and to evaluate how it affects the social situation and its ability to reproduce itself. In order to explain the quest for hegemony, we emphasise its developmental pattern and also what is referred to by M. Kilson as a 'model of reciprocity'.[109] The 'little people' themselves seem to think of this trajectory in terms of its historical continuity; in Zaïre, for example, there is a genealogical line which links a contemporary 'dominant class' to the 'citizens', 'intellectuals' and '*évolués*' of the past.[110]

Reciprocal assimilation is not a recent phenomenon. In Ilesha, there has never been a complete divorce between the educated people in the colonial administration and the more or less illiterate traders; the ideological predominance of Christianity, the prestige attached to western schooling and the education of children, and the practice of 'straddling' by salaried workers in the tertiary sector served to link the two categories.[111] This pattern of alliance and fusion preceded the satellisation of African societies by the west. Trans-regional religious movements, especially of Islam, were powerful means of 'social rapprochement'.[112] From this point of view, the 'united front' of the Sardauna took on its 'hegemonic function'[113] which had been developed during the bloody *jihad* period. The nineteenth-century dynastic upheavals were swiftly ended by agreements between the competing aristocracies. In these agreements, merchants were not excluded on account of their low status. Moreover, there is the fact that economic exchange and political contract, both sealed by the circulation of women, were inherent to the lineage world in the deep forest. Once again, we must challenge the classical image of an atomised continent, condemned to being dispersed.

From another perspective, we cannot ignore the dynamics of divergence which hinder the contemporary quest for hegemony and fill it with uncertainty. The zones of indetermination and the vacuums within society seem to be part of the production of a dominant class rather than preventing its emergence. According to John Saul, this idea of a 'class in the making' poses problems because it leads to teleology.[114] Admittedly, historical sociology has fortunately qualified the determinism of structuralist Marxism, and the role of action in the 'making' of social classes has been rehabilitated.[115] But it would be a mistake to imagine that the 'dominant class in the making' is settling in and flirting with projects and dreaming of its coming unity. The moment has not yet arrived when it 'attains its own fulfillment' in the sense of Henry's Marxian analysis:

> The complete concept of class, which implies that the class has become aware of itself as a class, becomes a political concept when the adoption of this consciousness is complete, when the class thinks of itself and sees itself as a unity, and when it thinks and acts as such.[116]

Weber speaks of 'communities', capable of realising the collective pursuit of their interests, in the same way.[117]

The uncertain process of the fusion of African elites takes place progressively, almost mechanically, from funerals to marriages, from *tontine* meetings to electoral campaigns. It is true that the actors only retain the froth from this process, and this means that severe and costly conflicts are sometimes so harrowing that the 'invisible' dimension comes into play. The development of productive forces, the crystallisation of markets, and, last but not least, the development of a common external danger – such as the Soviet-Cuban intervention in Angola, the Libyan involvement in Chad, the incubation of popular anger, and ever present 'juvenile delinquency' – can contribute to the development of a unitary and obsessive mentality amongst the 'elite'. In a general way, African societies do not correspond to the configurations that would make them real class societies, if one adopts a rigorous definition.[118] From this point of view, and contrary to current opinion, it is not even clear that the concretisation of the dominant class is any more advanced than that of the subordinate classes.[119] The sociology of the 'making' of a working class, or even of the peasantry, seems simpler and is often more convincing than the rarer sociology of the 'making' of a dominant class.[120]

If the researcher relies on scientific analysis alone, he will be forced to agree with A. Morice's comment on Angola: 'The class which controls monetary fluctuations and the circulation of goods is not a single unity: it is defined, above all, as the sum of individual strategies; it does not have any perspective of accumulation.' Is this a situation belonging only to a socialist State, whose economic problems confirm 'the centrifugal tendencies of all of its dependants'?[121] We have seen that the situation is not so different in Nigeria, Kenya, the Ivory Coast and Cameroon. Also, some choose the concept of 'alliance' to substitute for the dominant class, 'In Tanzania, power is held by a heterogeneous alliance of groups who are defined by their positions in the party, the government, the high levels of the administration and State enterprises, and these men are always circulating between these positions,' writes D.C. Martin.[122] And to advance the hypothesis according to which, in Tanzania, '[the] powerful people find themselves in a position where they are unable to become a bourgeoisie', unlike the case of Kenya. Although Yves Fauré and Jean-François Medard mechanically identify the Ivoirian regime with the pre-eminence of a 'State bourgeoisie', in the end they are not too far away from this suggestion when they refer to the 'remarkable fluidity' of the 'dominant class' and admit their 'difficulties in distinguishing between the different sections of the elite, leading categories, and segments of the class which interact with each other, because these elements generally interpenetrate without their roles being confused'.[123]

It is at this point that Giddens' 'structuration theory' becomes useful. He insists upon a contextual definition of social stratification, and gives as much value to the mechanisms of the dissolution of social groups as to the mechanisms of their creation.[124] In opposition to the various scholarly or political definitions of the bourgeoisie, we must define the State in relation to a social structure which is built on several dimensions due to the existence of the complex procedures of 'straddling' and 'concatenation'. The heterogeneity of the points of departure is of fundamental importance. Participating in ancient systems of inequality and of domination, of State power, and of the western world economy, these procedures are combined or contradicted within every individual. The interlinking of these relations varies according to the historical situation. The positions do not of course have an equal value. The particular trajectory of each State highlights the importance of some of these. Village by village, region by region, the conflicts between these positions bring about a different system of inequality. The political realm is in some ways the matrix of this system, because it creates the relations of power between these positions. The probable result of this process, which is the transformation of dominant segments into one homogeneous social class, remains subordinated to this radical heterogeneity because the social foundations of the contemporary State are geographically differentiated.[125]

CHAPTER SEVEN
The Formation of a Postcolonial Historic Bloc

There is a conceptual difficulty in the fact that we have simultaneously to analyse the unity of the developing system of inequality and its composite character; the dynamics of integration and divergence; and the problematic of the fusion of elites and their alliance. This problem can be resolved in two ways. First, we must hold to our generative conception of the State. The State must not be seen as a static class structure, even if it may become one in the future, but as a historical process, a trajectory. Secondly, the conclusion of the quest for hegemony – if this expression is to have any meaning – must be restored to its multi-dimensional essence, to its organic incompleteness. The work of Gramsci (which has been largely ignored by Africanists who have favoured Marx and, more recently, Weber) provides two concepts that are interesting in this respect: those of the 'passive revolution' and the 'historic bloc'.

THE 'PASSIVE REVOLUTIONS' OF THE SUB-SAHARAN REGION

The notion of 'passive revolution', which Gramsci borrowed from V. Cuoco, a historian of the 1733 Neapolitan revolution, is not absolutely clear and has been the subject of numerous theoretical debates, some of which are extremely polemical. Part of the confusion comes from the fact that this expression is used in Gramsci's, *Prison Notebooks* to describe the Risorgimento period, the factors that brought about the unification of Italy and the development of the fascist State, and to outline the parallels between the fascist State in Italy and Taylorism in America.[1] The term was used again in western Europe after the Second World War in debates on the 'transition to socialism' and the strategies of communist parties, to strictly political and ideological ends. To repeat Gramsci's enigmatic phrase once again, the 'passive revolution' is a 'revolution without a revolution' different therefore from the French Jacobin revolution. The divergences of interpretation about the exact meaning of this concept remain. Does it exclude socially subordinate actors from having any role whatsoever? Is it incompatible with the concept of hegemony? Is it meant to refer to the creation of a 'bastard state' or can it on the contrary refer to the construction of an 'integral state'? This term is surrounded by numerous controversial uncertainties, but these are not of major concern to a historical sociology of African politics.

The other connotations of the concept of 'passive revolution' are of a more direct use in this context. First, Gramsci explicitly associated it with the Marxian problematic of concatenation. In his *Notes on Machiavelli*, he deduced the 'passive revolution' of the articulation of diverse modes of production at the heart of a social formation. In this way, this term refers to the historical 'telescoping' between feudal Mezzogiorno and industrialised Piedmont, and the essential heterogeneity of the Italian State which ensued. There is no need to labour the analogy of this configuration with those of sub-Saharan Africa. It is therefore also unnecessary to postulate the 'passivity' of the subordinate classes during the Risorgimento period – to affirm this would be historically erroneous[2] – but one must stress their inability to prevent a decisive compromise having been made between the industrial bourgeoisie of the north and the 'old feudal classes' of the south, which ensured that their positions were preserved, agrarian reform avoided, and all Jacobin-style revolutionary experience averted.

When it is understood in this way and applied to the case of Africa, the concept of 'passive revolution' is extremely useful for it synthesises the 'educated' people's rise to power, their seizure of State resources, and their refusal to enhance and radicalise the popular movements against colonialism. And even better, Gramsci's concept explains the process whereby the 'educated' group reached an understanding with those who held power previously, and how this process was reproduced on a larger scale. It is only recently that analysts have become aware of this arrangement between these two groups and have devoted an increasing number of studies to it.[3] It has been very significant. First, it has qualified the theory, popularised by Georges Balandier and Richard Sklar, that contemporary inequality has arisen from the postcolonial State. Secondly, it enables comparisons to be made with the general theory of authoritarianism in Europe, Latin-America and Asia, which has also pointed to similar compromises between groups, and has termed these compromises as being genetic factors in the construction of the State by the intermediary path.[4]

According to Gramsci, the concept of 'passive revolution' is a more precise method of analysing the way in which the bourgeoisie exercises its supremacy over the forces of the *Ancien Régime*, or how one part of the bourgeoisie gathers the rest of this class around itself.[5] It applies in particular to the fusion, via reciprocal assimilation, of the bourgeosie and the aristocracy which has characterised not only Italy after the Risorgimento but also most countries in western Europe during the nineteenth century.[6] 'Passive revolution' is especially equivalent to what the Italian philosopher called '*trasformismo*' ('transformism'), the absorbtion of the 'intellectuals' by the dominant class, who are politically and ideologically capable of leading the subordinate classes. A similar process of harnessing was seen during the anti-colonial struggle and during the 'honeymoon of independence'. Amilcar Cabral, who led the liberation war in Guinea-Bissau, and who was Africa's main Marxist theoretician, anticipated the 'suicide' of what he called the 'petite bourgeoisie'.[7] However, precisely the opposite happened. Instead of identifying themselves with categories at the bottom of the social hierarchy, the '*évolués*', the 'educated' people and the 'intellectuals', happily jumped onto the bandwagon of accumulative power. * It is in this context that the scornful maxim of Roberto Michels should be understood: 'The fact is that the revolutionaries of today are the reactionaries of tomorrow.' It is also in this light that his remarks on the contribution of the party and the army to the fusion of elites should be interpreted: 'By the actions of the organs which assist it, the class struggle provokes social modifications and metamorphoses in the party, which is itself meant to organise and direct the class struggle. In this struggle, certain groups of individuals, who are numerically insignificant but of great qualitative importance, find themselves taken from low positions in the proletarian class and raised to the dignity of the bourgeois level'.[8] From this point of view, the unified party of sub-Saharan Africa functioned in the same way as German social democracy,

---

*We should emphasise the convergence between the acceptance of the '*évolué*', the 'educated' person and the 'intellectual' in Africa, and Gramsci's concept of the 'intellectual' as a 'civil servant of the superstructure' (*Gli intelletuali e l'organizzazione della cultura*, Turin, 1966, p.9): 'I have greatly widened the definition of the intellectual and I will not limit myself to the current definition which refers to the "great intellectuals"'(*Lettere del carcere*, Turin, 1968, p.481).

or the Prussian army. Using either the stick or the carrot, it continued to co-opt into its ranks counter-elites which were likely to take on the 'little people's' cause.

Listening to his speeches, one would have thought that the uncontested master of 'transformism' was Félix Houphouët-Boigny, who professed in 1945 that 'I come from all milieux and all corporations. I am chief of the *canton*, ex-civil servant, farmer, transporter, the "uncle" of traders or employees of traders. [...] I will conscientiously and courageously serve in everybody's interest, in the general interest'.[9] In 1952 he created, with limited success, a *Union pour le développement économique de la Côte d'Ivoire* (UDECI) with the aim of winning over the leaders of the competing parties of the PDCI-RDA, and getting them to work for his own ends. His alliance with the French administrative and commercial sectors, together with the strength of his electoral machine, gave Houphouët-Boigny a quasi-monopoly of the distribution of positions of power and enrichment. He was nevertheless careful not to abuse this advantage, as Ahmed Sékou Touré did.[10] The system of compromise and amalgamation continued to dictate the composition of electoral lists and the distribution of prebends. This was to such an extent that most of the opposition, whether they were traditionalists or radical nationalists, ended up by joining the PDCI-RDA after the success of the 'Yes' vote to the referendum of 1958. A similar thing happened with Usher Assouan, the sole man in charge of the nationalist youth organisation, who won a seat in the 1957 elections (and later became the municipal magistrate of Cocody, the richest part of the capital city).[11]

One of Houphouët-Boigny's main worries seems to have been how to maintain his guardianship of the intellectuals, in order to avoid the development of a 'learned neo-bourgeoisie'[12] and to prevent them from questioning the post-war preeminence of his faction, which had been gained since the Second World War. The division between the 'Ram of Yamoussoukro' and the radicals opposed to a *rapprochement* with the French authorities (generally ex-militants from the communist study groups) became apparent as early as the end of the 1940s. 'De-linking' from the Communist Party in 1950–51 naturally exacerbated this tension.[13] The conflict emerged again in 1959, when the president of the Association of Ivoirian Students in France, which was affiliated to the FEANF, was arrested in Abidjan and when members of this organisation were deprived of their scholarships. At the same time, Houphouët-Boigny set up the *Union nationale des étudiants de Côte d'Ivoire* (UNECI) with the aim of recruiting the youth who were ready to 'eat from its hands', as is said in West Africa. The PDCI now thought it necessary to use the stick: the UNECI were experiencing great difficulties in establishing themselves; the radicals won over to the regime (who in 1959 had founded an organisation called the *Jeunesse RDA de Côte d'Ivoire* (JRDACI), were more vocal and were suspected of 'entryism'; the struggle for the distribution of spoils intensified; all in all, the social base of power in the Ivory Coast was fragile, if one looked beyond the misleading unanimity of the elections.[14] Elsewhere in the region, the environment was threatening: Sylvanus Olympio, who did not enjoy good relations with France, was assassinated in Togo; General de Gaulle did not intervene to prevent the overthrow of the President of Congo, Abbé Fulbert Youlou; and the Ivory Coast was involved in a cold war with Guinea and Ghana.[15] The story of the 'plotters' who were denounced in Abidjan in 1963 and in 1964 remains to be written. The personal role of Houphouët-Boigny in starting off the crisis, in its repression, and in its possible international ramifications, have not yet been elucidated. Whatever the case, this event ended up by 'wiping out the first generation of intellectuals'.[16] Many of the JRDACI's leaders, whose financial resources had dried up after independence, were removed from the government, tried and received heavy sentences. One of them, Ernest Boka, was mysteriously found dead in his prison cell.

It did not take long, however, for those who had been purged to be liberated, and then rehabilitated with grand ceremony in 1970–71, after accepting various material compensations.[17] From being persecuted by the regime, the intelligentsia became its new ally and were given back their places in the political bureau. In 1980, 'transformism' received an additional impulse which benefited the 'democratisation' of the regime. Konan Banny, an 'ex-prisoner' and Minister of Defence and Civic Services, became a member of the Executive Committee, replacing the General Secretary of the PDCI, Philippe Yacé, who had been the man behind the repression of the 'plotters' in 1963–64, and was therefore held in contempt by the intelligentsia. Moreover, the head of State reiterated his desire to give 'the youth' a role in the exercise of power. The leaders of the *Mouvement des étudiants et élèves de Côte d'Ivoire* (MEECI, which had replaced UNECI in 1969 and which had succeeded in camouflaging student grudges), reached the highest levels in the party.[18] In the following years, the application of a strict policy of economic austerity, the prospect of presidential succession, and the recurring social unrest, have not put an end to the co-optation system, although relations have worsened in recent years between the government and the teachers, who have been deprived of numerous privileges. The spectacular return to fortune of Emmanuel Dioulo, mayor of

Abidjan; the restoration to grace of Yacé and his cohabitation with Konan Bedié as possible successor; the insertion of a new political generation into the municipal circuit, and the relative isolation of the exiled dissidents, Gbagbo and Amondji, have all confirmed Houphouët-Boigny's talent for absorbing counter-elites and decapitating social movements.

Although it is impressive, there is nothing exceptional about this performance. Ahidjo attracted a significant proportion of ex UPC students, and proceeded to 'juvenise' (as the Cameroonians used to say) his governmental staff.[19] Léopold Senghor also succeeded in attracting past opponents such as those of the *Parti du regroupement africain*, and some of his competitors from the end of the 1960s, into the *Union progressiste sénégalaise* (UPS) and two of its offshoots, the *Club Nation et développement* and the *Centre d'études, de recherches et d'éducation*. When the decay of the economy cruelly accentuated the limits to such practices, a tripartite system was set up, and the rules of co-optation were made more complicated. The UPS, now called the *Parti socialiste* (PS), benefited from Senghor's decision to set up a tripartite system, whilst the existence of competing parties meant that intellectuals of both left and right no longer offered a radical challenge to the legitimacy of the State. Joining the new parties was often a political tactic, and did not signal a true fracturing of the political system. Similarly, in the district of Sine-Saloum, 'many leaders of "clans" [...] only joined the PDS (Wade's Senegalese Democratic Party) so that they could rejoin the UPS in force'.[20] After Senghor resigned, Abdou Diouf continued this '*ouverture*' (opening up) by legalising an integral multi-party system and thereby offering the extreme left a 'rope with which to hang itself'.[21] The new system he wished to introduce alienated the sympathies of the 'barons' of the PS. However, he succeeded in calming down the teachers, by urging them to join a government conference on education and training in January 1981.[22] Risking the loss of the bird in the hand bequeathed him by Senghor, Abdou Diouf tried to woo the intellectuals by setting up several 'support associations', principally the *Comité de soutien à l'action du président Abdou Diouf* (COSAPAD) and the *Groupe de rencontres et d'échanges pour un Sénégal nouveau* (GRESEN) led by Iba Der Thiam, an ex-trade unionist who flirted with Islamism and was promoted to the position of Minister of National Education.

Jomo Kenyatta for his part managed to 'politically emasculate'[23] the rural areas by setting up about thirty 'secretaries of state', chosen from amongst his members of parliament:

> Making up nearly a quarter of the deputies, this group was essentially composed of young and energetic men who had set up the district

systems and had been elected with a considerable majority, or easily re-elected. Most of these secretaries of state occupied a slightly ambiguous position, as they were often neither clients of ministers, nor really close to the President. As they had organised the districts so well, they were considered as future local leaders (that is to say, ethnic leaders), and also as constituting a possible source of opposition to the centre. Their nomination to these posts by the President may thus represent a compensatory promotion, for the services they had rendered, as much as it represents an effort to include them in the clientelist system, in order to smother any initiatives they may make to defy presidential authority.[24]

The success with which Field Marshal Mobutu used promotions to decimate his opposition, from 'revolutionaries' of the First Republic to the parliamentary members of the *Union pour la démocratie et le progrès social* (UDPS), has become legendary, and Zaïrian exiles have gained a strong reputation for being hypocrites. According to rumour, Mobutu received Kamitatu and Karl i Bond in his office whilst satirical pamphlets that both of these men had previously written about him were lying on his desk...[25]

Although intellectuals and the political class joining the single party may remind us of the Italian *Risorgimento* and the annexation of the Action Group by the Moderates of Cavour, this should not relegate the two other aspects of 'transformism', which correspond closely with Gramsci's ideas, to second place: the rise and integration of elites who represent regions which had been ignored by, and excluded from, the State, as in President Tubman's 'politics of unification' model; and above all, the capturing of the leadership from the major popular organisations. It was extremely naïve to anticipate the 'suicide' of social categories which had already shown their ability to benefit from the opportunities presented by colonialism. The destruction of the autonomy of workers' and peasants movements, and their osmosis into the regime's apparatus of domination, were perhaps more unexpected, and the repercussions of these are still being felt. Abdou Diouf was insincere when he claimed he was aware of the need to reverse the system of allocation in urban and rural areas, saying: 'But I am not backed by the necessary rural political forces to allow such a reversal of action'.[26] In Senegal, everything is done to deny peasants the right of association, and to 'bureaucratise' the process of agricultural production.[27] In the same way, cooperatives have been confiscated by the State in most African countries.[28] Even in Tanzania, one of the first repercussions of *Ujamaa* was to take control of the villages which were most likely to improve. The Ruvuma Development Association, which grouped together the most dynamic villages, was banned by presidential decree in 1969, and from 1968 the government dissuaded other communities in the Tanga region from following this example. Prior to this, local heads of the party and the administration could not bear the idea that *Ujamaa* could succeed without them, and therefore ostracised villages which showed an independence of spirit, such as those in Matendo in Kigoma region, Maren in Arusha, and Kabuku Ndani in Tanga.[29] 'Villagisation' policy in the 1970s, the entry of rich peasants into the party and local collectives, and the mediation of clientelism allowed rural elites to penetrate the organs of the central State, even though it has not hampered the peasants' ability to escape 'capture'.[30]

Trade unions experienced a similar developmental pattern, except those in Nigeria, Zambia and Upper Volta. The most populist workers' tribunes – which included colourful personalities such as Pobee Biney in Ghana – were ousted, the central organisations were 'unified', and their leaders accepted by those in power and swallowed by the party machinery, where they often sat as honorary members.[31] The domestication of workers' organisations was peculiar neither to the first generation of postcolonial regimes nor to the 'bourgeois' concept of the State which some have accused them of articulating. In Mozambique, the workers' commissions were suppressed in 1975 because they were seen as agents of the 'dissolution of authority in the firm', and the government preferred to nationalise the goods of the Portuguese *petits blancs* in spite of encouraging the development of self-governed cooperatives.[32] Similarly, in Angola the repression of Nito Alves' putsch attempt in May 1977 helped the MPLA to break the autonomy of the workforce.[33]

The postcolonial State has generally been less tolerant of the forms of organisation specific to subordinate social groups in populated urban areas, and the political revolutions which dreamed of '*poder popular*' (popular power) in Mozambique, Angola, Ghana and Burkina Faso were quickly put down.[34] From this point of view, the operations of 'population removal' which are regularly carried out in areas of so-called 'spontaneous' housing under the pretext of urban renewal or the struggle against delinquency, are the counterparts of the regrouping of hamlets in Tanzania, Burundi and Mozambique. At the same time as they facilitate the fruitful manipulation of land rights, they destroy the potential leadership of movements of the 'little people', who exist on the margins of the State. The dominant party can also adopt an alternative strategy, by making some form of agreement with the social movements which bring nothing to the state, but which it would be very costly, even dangerous, to get rid of. The cadres from these organizations are then recognised by the authorities as valuable intermediaries, and are brought under the party,' as has been done in

Dakar-Pikine, Nairobi-Mathare Valley, and Douala-Nylon.[35]

The many restrictions to the freedom of association introduced by the single party, and ratified by law, are not simply an expression of brutal domination by the State, or of the insane jealousy of those in power. They are also part of the social dynamic of 'transformism', for they dissuade the intellectuals from allying with the interests of subordinate rural or urban social groups. Simultaneously, and without excessive finesse, they incite and urge the intellectuals to make a compromise with or to be compromised by, the State. As they say in Cameroon: 'The mouth which eats does not speak.' This shrewd method has been largely successful, and international recognition of figures such as the Kenyan Ngugi Wa Thiongo, the Nigerian Wole Soyinka or the Cameroonian, Mongo Beti should not disguise the fact that intellectual dissidence has not been the rule in sub-Saharan Africa.[36] Before becoming indignant, one should recognise the critical works quietly produced by authors like Fabien Eboussi Boulaga or Sony Labou Tansi. One also needs to understand the powers available to the State: the difficulties faced by Africa's universities, publishers and media; Daniel arap Moi's harshness towards the university campus in Nairobi; and the corrupting patronage of Félix Houphouët-Boigny all bear witness to the strength of State resources.

In further mitigation of Africa's intellectuals we should remember that religious groups do not offer, contrary to what one might believe, any stiffer resistance to the logic of cooption. These are, in effect the 'intellectuals' of the people:[37] the men of the church, the prophets, the healers, the *malamai* and other marabouts have been involved in all the upheavals of the past century, they have been heroes of the struggle against colonialism, and ancestral leaders of the rural areas. Nevertheless, the complexity and ambiguity of their roles are now known so well that anthropologists and historians have now stopped assimilating them mechanically to a pre-nationalist spirit of resistance or, on the contrary, to a simple collaboration.[38] In preceding chapters, we have seen how Islam, Christianity and independent religious movements have contributed to the production of inequality. The ambivalent nature of their contribution reflects the intermediary social position of their agents. Some analysts have even been tempted to draw a parallel between religious innovation and the articulation of modes of production.[39] It was inevitable that the State should attempt to absorb religious personalities who are suspected of having the ability to control the youth, and to instil them with an alternative model of society.

Rwanda offers an extreme example. It was only in 1985 that the Catholic archbishop of Kigali resigned from the central committee of the single party. This withdrawal, which had been requested by the Vatican for several years, did not by any means initiate a separation between the church and a regime which is, to a large extent, an extension of the church.[40] However, in reality, the cases of the Ivory Coast and Togo are not at all different from the case of Rwanda. And throughout Africa, the central powers bestowing gifts to the church hope to integrate religious cadres into their structures. Houphouët-Boigny, Mobutu and arap Moi are experts at this game, and every Sunday, the latter attends (depending upon the week) Catholic, Baptist, Presbyterian and Methodist services.[41] Rivalling one another in extravagance, all three are simply following the norm: State construction of mosques and churches, and the (more or less) disguised presidential offerings through public allocations, are all a part of the necessary paraphernalia of political action, and represent a diplomatic procedure of primary importance. Conflicts between God and Caesar are of course legion. They can become venomous as in the case of Kenya today, and they can even be dramatic, as in Guinea, Congo, Equatorial Guinea and Uganda. These conflicts rarely, however, prevent the process of cooption of religious elites into the State. This is shown by the period immediately following the overthrow of Bagaza in Burundi in 1987; the ending of the quarrel between the Catholic church of Zaïre and Mobutu in 1972–74; and the gradual disappearance of the Ndongmo affair in Cameroon in 1970-71.[42] Characteristically caustic, M.G. Schatzberg counted three Mercedes Benz cars at Lisala during his stay there: one belonged to an official in the administration, one to a rich merchant, and one to a Catholic bishop.[43] It could not be more clearly shown that the church hierarchy constitutes, together with bureaucratic power and the practice of trade, one of the foundations of the State, and that it played a role in shaping the nature of the regime.

The pattern is similar in Islamic territories. The alliance between the 'marabout and the prince' is consubstantial with Senegalese society. Legendary amongst Africanists, the Senegalese example is to political science what the Rift Valley is to geomorphology.[44] But we have also seen how the *malamaï*, the *imami* and the *alkali*, the traditional pivots between the *sarakuna* and the *talakawa*, contributed to the new dominant class in Northern Nigeria.[45] Also very revealing of the strategies of 'transformism' in the religious world is the way in which certain regimes have channelled the faith of the Prophet into specific organisations (*l'Association islamique du Niger, l'Union musulmane du Togo*, the Uganda Muslim Supreme Council, *la Fédération des associations islamiques du Sénégal*, and *l'Union pour le progrès islamique du Sénégal*) and the way in which they have integrated the counter-elite of 'Arabisant' reformists into the State.[46]

This is by no means limited to the two monotheistic religions, which have a long experience of accommodation with the State. It is also true of local so-called 'syncretic' movements, which have long been felt to have the potential to compete with other forms of power. In reality, analysis of 'independent' churches is indissociable from that of accumulation and inequality; it is no different from the study of official Christian churches, as has been shown in McCracken's remarkable study of the Watch Tower in Malawi.[47] The two types of religious organisation have similar relationships with the social hierarchy. Consequently, the State has adopted the same annexing procedure towards the 'independent' church, severely repressing the movements which have fought against it or, worse still, have ignored it. The state generously rewarded those who obeyed it and therefore regulated the burgeoning world of indigenous healing. Zaïrian Kimbanguism is a supreme example of this, from the struggle against colonialism, to its 'systemisation' and its institutionalisation in the quasi-gallican model of 'authenticity'.[48] In the Ivory Coast, similarly, Albert Atcho one of the most eminent of the 'Harris' prophets* and a traditional *canton* chief, rejoiced until his death in the ostensible solicitude of the regime, which never missed taking part in the annual celebrations of 1 November. He developed an ideological theme which converged with that of the President, for whom he had previously been an electoral agent in the coastal region. Symbolically, he received the title of the Ivoirian National Order, from the hand of Augustin Denise, Minister of State and also a medical doctor. The following is an extract from Denise's speech on 1 November 1968:

> Monsieur the Prophet, Messrs pastors,
>   I cannot find words powerful enough to express the joy I feel to be amongst you this morning, on the occasion of this annual celebration. I would like to begin, first of all, by thanking you for the reception you have given me [...], the warm reception from which, once again, I feel the warmth of your special friendship – not only yours Monsieur Prophet, but also that of all the Harris prophets – a friendship which you all know is reciprocal. This friendship [...] has its roots in, and also originates from, two sources, if I can express myself in this way. The first, I would say, is the community of believers [...], and the second source of our friendship is our common membership of the same political movement, the *Rassemblement démocratique africain*, [...] I would like, my dear Atcho – forgive me for this familiar appellation – to thank you for

---

*Translator's note: William Wade Harris: a Liberian Christian preacher who attracted a large following in Liberia and the Ivory Coast at the time of the First World War.

the help that you and all the Harrisists continue to give our government, the government that the Ivoirian people have freely voted for. The government tells me to thank you for the constant support which is equal to its own [...]. On the religious plane, you have tried to heal the spirits [...] and to teach belief in God, faith in God, and fear of God. You preach good morals, excellent moral principles, to be short, and your teaching is done in such a way that you incite your fellows to have the fear of God within them every day and every night. In this way, you are making your contribution to the training of Ivoirian people who remain on the moral path and flee from criminality. In other words you are contributing to the training of honest Ivoirian citizens [...]. In one word, you are working towards the formation of complete Ivoirians, who are mentally and physically balanced, and rejoice in excellent health. At present, I can affirm that you are one of the great workers of the national confession; from which, my dear Atcho, I must thank and congratulate you. And about the list of grievances, lengthy list from which our friend gave us a reading just now, the friend who made the brilliant intervention just now, I would simply like to say that I am aware of the different problems you have underlined and I will take it upon myself as a duty to inform my government in such a way that they will be investigated [...] Long live Pastor Atcho, long live the Harris pastors, long live the Harrisists'.[49]

We should be wary of investing this long quote with meanings it does not have. It is possible that Albert Atcho had, in one way or another, served the process of individualisation, and that this was advantageous for the mode of capitalist production, and that putting the blame on Bregbo's sick people was 'a rampart against criticism of the regime', as has been debated by A. Zempleni and M. Augé.[50] For the time being, however, this is not the crucial point. This speech, which is a dignified example of the French cantonal tradition, shows how the State daily invests in material and symbolic exchanges with the masses, and how its privileged intermediaries are often religious agents. Far from float-ing in the air like a balloon, the State derives much of its substance from this kind of transaction, and from its ability to adjoin the spiritual grass roots practitioners.[51] In this way, the political life of sub-Saharan Africa is parochial in the ecumenical sense of the word, applying as much to the presbyterian pastor as to the Bwiti initiate, to the *malam* as much as to the prophet.

The incorporation of religious intellectuals into the State apparatus is perhaps more difficult and conflictual than the incorporation of politic-ians, members of cooperatives and teachers. On the one hand, the political and economic resources of the leaders are not infinite. On the other hand, the sacred market is particularly volatile, and sensitive to the strategies of the 'little people' or the counter-elites who are frustrat-ed by the established order.[52] In spite of the enormous symbolic and material investments which it makes, the State never succeeds in controlling it. If one believes that certain regimes such as Congo and Angola, were truly Marxist-Leninist, one should not be surprised that they had to confront Messianic eruptions such as the Zéphyrins of Pointe-Noire or the Tokoistes of Luanda.[53] But the performance of powers which shamelessly flaunt their religiosity is not much more convincing: in Kenya and in Zambia, there is a recurrent spiritual dissidence, and the assimilation of the independent churches by the centre comes up against some improbable factional struggles, involving, in some extreme cases, the sodomisation of disciples or the crucifixion of young girls.[54] The cooption of the 'invisible', the statist arrangement of illness, madness and death, and the 'enslavement' of the marginal and poor, who take on suffering with a vast humanity and great art in the villages and towns, in roles other than police informants, are chimerical.[55] In the underworld of society, the State loses its integral nature and reveals its radical heterogeneity. However, this does not affect the vigour of its attempts of seduction.

THE HISTORIC POSTCOLONIAL BLOC

How, then, can the conclusion of this process of 'transformism', which remains highly hypothetical, be conceptualised? Another of Gramsci's ideas may be helpful. Fortunately, it replaces the terms currently in use, as it allows the two instances that we have separated to be linked together: that of the relationship of the State to social stratification, and that of the articulation of modes of production.

In itself, the concept of the 'historic bloc' is no clearer than the idea of 'passive revolution'. According to Gramsci, this concept brings about the organic unity of the superstructure and the infrastructure, and also of civil society and political society; in itself, it cannot be separated from the study of hegemony. It also refers to some concrete historical phenomena – especially the development of France and Italy in the nineteenth century – in order to analyse the inegalitarian development of social classes and the capacity or incapacity of the 'founding class' to conserve or build up its hegemony. Due to the fact that the 'historic bloc' is indissociable from this last idea, it cannot be reduced to a simple 'class alliance' (although it does not exclude this type of articulation, between the 'founding class' and 'auxiliary classes'), and it attributes a determinant mission to the intellectuals, who are defined as the 'civil servants of the superstructure'.

It could be argued that in contemporary African societies there is probably neither any constituted historic bloc, in the strict sense of the term, nor an established dominant class, except perhaps at the regional level in the form of what Gramsci called 'local historic blocs'. Northern Nigeria would provide the best example. It must also be pointed out that this concept is not being used in an orthodox way, as I have already revealed my doubt about the period of the formation of social classes in contemporary Africa. Nevertheless, I would argue that the trajectory of the 'quest for hegemony' entails the edification of a postcolonial historic bloc, usually in the 'bastard' mode of the 'passive revolution'. By understanding the concept in this way, it can have a triple use, as long as the role of indeterminacy and autonomy presupposed by Gramsci in this concept is kept in mind.[56] The notion of 'historic bloc' allows one to go beyond the semantic dichotomy between the 'alliance' and the 'fusion' of dominant social groups engaged in the quest for hegemony. It recognises the central action of the 'évolués', the 'educated people', and the 'intellectuals' throughout the last century. Above all, it creates a new synthesis out of the false contradictions in which studies of African societies have been trapped for thirty years by balancing ethnic explanations, dependency theory and class analysis. The concept of the 'historic bloc',with its axiom that the regional asymmetry of power within a society, and the involvement of this society in the world economy, constitute one and the same reality, allows one to think simultaneously of the international, national and local dimensions of the development of the postcolonial State.[57]

Most observers seem to polarise this state around the regional or ethnic dimension which is, in itself, historically meaningless, and this has given rise to a great deal of poor literature on Africa. All social stratification is initially incarnated in space and then in time, in regionally differentiated social formations which are also hierarchically divided from one another.[58] 'All national unity is superstructure; it is a net thrown over dissimilar regions. The net returns to the hand that threw it, to a privileged centre. Inequality is created. I ask myself if there has ever in the world been a single nation which is not assymetrical', wrote Braudel, having in mind the 'almost catastrophic distortion' that the preeminence of the north of the country (*Langue d'oeil*) inflicted on the rest of France. He added: 'We still need to know whether it has ever been possible (which I don't believe it was) to do without the Unitary State, to live on a regional level only. Regions which had once been autonomous and dominant, then logically ceased being so. I believe in a certain logic of nations'.[59] In this respect, the concentration of power and wealth in the hands of geographically labelled factions (for example, the 'untouchables' of Field Marshal Mobutu, who tend to originate from the Equator and who speak Lingala; the 'Bururi group' of Burundi; the *watoto wa nyumbani*, the 'children of the country', of J.K. Nyere rein Tanzania), and the structuring of the State by regional or ethnic factors (for example, the Zarma of Niger, the Baoulé of the Ivory Coast, and the 'united front' of Northern Nigeria) are not necessarily of a different nature from the unification of Italy by Piedmont or the unification of Germany by Prussia.[60] At least this kind of comparison, or more precisely this putting into perspective, could teach us more about African society than the ritualised invocation of 'tribalism', however little we remember about the dialectic link between the ethnicity argument and the exploitation of colonial opportunities.

However, all instances of geographical asymmetry are not the same. Sometimes the construction of the State takes place due to an economically significant regional factor. This was the case in Félix Houphouët Boigny's Ivory Coast with the Baoulé plantation economy, and Jomo Kenyatta's Kenya with the agricultural dynamism of the Kikuyu. This correspondence between the political and the economic order could favour the crystallisation and unification of a true 'civil society', under the cloak of 'ethnic' advancement. It also runs the risk of provoking frustrations in other regions, which are under a double system of domination, when they are actually 'colonised' in the territorial sense.[61] One should not, however, exaggerate the African exoticism of this unbalanced situation. It is in Italy that they say 'Christ stopped at Eboli'!

Sometimes no link can be found between the implementation of the principal economic dynamics and the regional concentration of power; the latter works as a corrective of, and a compensation for, the former, and this causes rancour. Such was the case in Cameroon under Ahidjo, and in Togo, Congo and Benin when the army's rise to power diminished the economic handicaps of the northern regions.[62]

There are several intermediate situations in between these ideal scenarios. One such intermediary case is Senegal, where the cultural 'Wolofisation' of society was not accompanied by a corresponding economic development of the Wolof, despite the activity of the Mourides. The Wolof therefore had to make links with the Toucouleur, who have formidable economic power. Moreover, the factor of inequality in space is not defined forever in time. In the Ivory Coast, the Baoulé only supplanted the dominance of the Agni during the 1930s; according to some people, the surname Boigny, Bo-agni, means 'conquerer of the Agni'.[63] In Cameroon, even if the elites of the central-southern region allowed a northerner to take power in 1958, they recovered it with obvious satisfaction in 1982 through the intermediary of Biya. These changes through time can also be found in Gabon in 1967, in Congo in 1968, and in Kenya in 1978. The possibility of change dominates periods of presidential succession as we see, for example, in present-day Ivory Coast, and, in a more hidden way, in Tanzania. These spatial and temporal instabilities (which western commentators inspired by the paradigm of the yoke have portrayed as being particularly serious) should neither be exaggerated nor be viewed as being outside the classic conceptualisation of politics. Apart from describing much instabilities for what they are – namely, the quest for the accumulation of power and wealth – and for what they do not exclude – that is, a more general process of the reciprocal assimilation of leading groups – the concept of the 'historic bloc' links such mutations to the 'external dynamics' from which they derive. Respecting the orthodox view, I can almost agree with Samir Amin when he describes the domination of the bourgeoisie of the 'centre' – the 'absent class' – over the 'periphery'. In the European bourgeoisie, Gramsci discerns the 'founding class' from which the Italian national historic bloc was formed. In a way, he presented this idea like a Russian doll, with the international, national and local levels successively contained within one another. But at a deeper level of analysis, this overly mechanical idea of a 'founding class', of a 'leading class', is not of much use to us. Let us be done once and for all with the common theory according to which Africa holds a relationship of exteriority with the west. It is, rather, a Western-African field, cemented by the postcolonial historic bloc.[64] We know now that dependency theory does not help us to understand this field. However, the opposite theory, of the 'autonomy' of the 'national bourgeoisie' in relation to the 'bourgeoisie of the centre', is no better.[65] It conceals the process of reciprocal assimilation between these two 'bourgeoisies', and it says nothing about the trans-continental fusion of dominant groups which are too hastily termed as 'national'.

In other words, we do not wish to suggest that, country by country, Africa represents a collection of historic blocs, each one articulated with the west, and each one having a different degree of actualisation. On the contrary, we argue that Africa should be seen as being engaged in the edification of *one* postcolonial historic bloc whose degree of actualisation varies from country to country and region to region, and which integrates sub-Saharan States in diverse ways.

The proposition will upset those who falsely associate the concept of hegemony or the historic bloc with a single totality. But according to

Gramsci, 'every application of a model of integration calls for a model of disintegration'.[66] His aim was to comprehend 'the historical base of the State' as the result of a relationship of contradictory forces, to see it as an 'unstable equilibrium'.[67] Gramsci claimed that this includes the essential heterogeneity and incompleteness even if the State is 'integral' rather than 'bastard', being closer to the model of the French Third Republic than the counter-example of the Risorgimento. He insisted upon the 'disaggregated and discontinuous [function] of the history of States or groups of States'.[68]

The strategies of extraversion favoured by Africans are presented in a new light. They naturally have differing orientations and scales according to the situation. For the dominant actors, they can be forged by mere alliances, excluding cultural absorption and matrimonial exchange. Collaboration between the Kenyan political class and the British, 'Asian' or 'Arab' business worlds is an example here, as is the reconciliation between the Zimbabwe African National Union and the white farmers and industrialists.

In other countries, the process of fusion has started, and has been explicitly accepted. In 1959, a faction of Senegalese *marabouts* claimed that their country was 'united with the people of France, for better or for worse' on the basis of 'a symbiosis of Islamic values with universal values and the rich French culture'.[69] Was this a Malthusian response, from a social category which had been granted many favours by the colonial State, and which was afraid that these privileges would be removed by radical nationalists? Without doubt it was, since numerous traditional chiefs – for example, the Fulani aristocracy in Guinea and Cameroon, or the traditional chiefs in the Ivory Coast – have done the same thing since the end of the Second World War. Nevertheless, the genuine anti-colonial leaders, such as Houphouët-Boigny and Léon Mba, also opted for 'Françafrique', and they only renounced it unhappily when they were forced to by the Gaullists. Houphouët-Boigny refuted 'this spirit of vengeance which was expressed at Bandung against the colonialists', and on Independence Day in the Ivory Coast, he used the same words to describe his breaking away from France as he did to talk about the reciprocal assimilation of indigenous elites: 'When we become mature, we are going to leave the family house, where we have so often been spoiled, and also sometimes reprimanded [...] to found our own house, our own hearth. I would like to tell you that in leaving the French family, we do not intend to forget all that we have received from it. We would like, instead, to develop and to enrich the large patrimony which it has left us, to the benefit of our people'.[70] Twenty-five years later, Mitterrand praised the 'relationships and the friendships which ensure that the Ivoirians and the French are not strangers, but feel as if they were brothers', this 'family atmosphere which we have never abandoned'.[71]

One should not of course attribute too much to the power of the word. However, this is demonstrated through the human, economic and financial flux. Although it failed to find its institutional and communal expression from 1958–60, 'Françafrique' maintained its own form of organisation. Its 'familial' atmosphere – almost 'incestuous' according to one journalist[72] – which gives it its particular tone, and which irritates Anglo-Saxon observers so much, is due less to the manipulation of the secret services than to the production of an intercontinental cultural sociability. Most of the factors responsible for the reciprocal assimilation of sub-Saharan elites also work towards the creation of this sociability. The 'intimacy' that French publicists claim is a result of more than just fine words as it has been forged by fifteen years of shared parliamentary life. It is fed by incessant exchange, the intensity of which can be evaluated in the departure lounges of Paris's international airports of Orly and of Roissy-Charles de Gaulle. One can find numerous other examples. Houphouët-Boigny, for example, sent 150 scholars to France in 1946. Thérèse Brou, who later became his wife, was in the first group. She studied at school in Villeneuve-sur-Lot, a town whose mayor, Raphaël-Leygues was later appointed French ambassador to the Ivory Coast.[73] He remained in this post for fifteen years... In the same way, one of the managers of the 'disaffiliation' process in 1950, Raphaël Saller, who had been a senator in Guinea and had close links with René Pleven, became Minister of the Economy, Finance and Planning in independent Ivory Coast. And in the 1980s, some of Houphouët-Boigny's direct collaborators are still French citizens or of French origin. A similar osmosis is also found in Senegal, Niger, Chad, the Central African Republic, and in Gabon where the American ambassador was surprised one day to meet his own secretary – who had French nationality – in Léon Mba's waiting room: she had come to ask the President to help stop her husband, a butcher – who also had French nationality – from trying to divorce her![74]

Franco-African links are reproduced by the social relations formed in universities, the military, brotherhoods and also in matrimonial exchanges, the importance of which must not be disregarded. This reproduction also occurs in political life: from the daily flow of information, visits, telephone conversations, and requests that make sub-Saharan diplomacy in the Elysée, the Quai d'Orsay and the Rue Monsieur resemble a clientelist system. It is symbolically strengthened by the Franco-African summits, started by Georges Pompidou. The dominant members of the francophone group are always angry to see new participants attending this event. It is clear that the privileged axis from Paris to a handful of African capitals will not exist forever. It could be said that France does not provide the means to ensure its domination, and cannot adapt, or does not want to adapt, to the multi-lateralisation of the continent's dependency, which will eventually threaten its interests.[75] Before this occurs, the extent of its power, however small it may be, is an integral part of the quest for hegemony in the colonies. And this exists, at least in the model of development left by France, and in the contributions made by 'cooperation' and the franc zone.[76]

In these cases, the notion of an alliance between dominant indigenous groups and the metropolitan bourgeoisie puts too much emphasis on the relationship of 'otherness' which was intended to unite these two groups. Moreover, it does not clearly express the spatial asymmetries upon which the francophone group rests, for longer or shorter periods of time. Such distortions can be seen in each State. The Paris–Abidjan axis, for example, initially favoured the Agni 'évolués' in the 1920s and 1930s, before turning to the Baoulé plantation economy. It is possible that this axis will focus on yet another area during the period of succession to Félix Houphouët-Boigny.[77] But these distortions go beyond the frontiers established during the colonial era; they also give structure to 'spaces' on the sub-continental level. The 'Baoulisation' of the Ivory Coast has been extended into an 'Ivoirisation' of part of West Africa. Houphouët-Boigny's skill in ensuring his pre-eminence as the 'old sage' amongst his peers in the *Conseil de l'Entente*, and his expertise in building Abidjan as a key economic centre, have been as significant as his decapitation of internal opposition.[78] In the same way, the 'Gabonese clan' described by P. Péan might equally well be called the 'Central African clan' or the 'Chadian clan'. The same French 'aid' workers and businessmen meet up in Libreville, Bangui and Ndjaména. The new Paris–Franceville axis, which is the result of Bongo's *savoir faire* and oil wealth, is now dominant. This is shown by Gabon's interventions in Chad and the Central African Republic, or its involvement in Batéké country in Congo and Zaïre.

The zones of powerful French influence in Africa, with their Senegalese, Ivoirian and Gabonese spies, and their expansionism into the hinterlands represent the most culturally complete instances of the 'postcolonial historic bloc'. In these cases, the process of fusion is so advanced that no political or social force can escape, apart perhaps from the Islamists in Senegal. Opposition movements to existing regimes do not so much demand French disengagement from the continent as the suspension of French political, military and financial assistance to the regimes in power. A document of the *Mouvement de redressement national* (MORENA) appealed to the French ambassador in Gabon:

> We are asking France to help us in the search for an effective solution. We need to change the leadership in order to change the regime. That is why we are coming to you, Mr Ambassador, to help us find solutions to rectify the catastrophic situation into which Bongo and his men have plunged Gabon. You cannot ignore this disaster, and you cannot stand back, because *you, France, like us, Gabon, have true and important stakes in this country*. Together we can and must find solutions, and we will be pleased when we come up with one.[79]

This adhesion to francophone culture which is so characteristic of the elites in these countries, reflects more that just powerful personalities of Senghor and Houphouët-Boigny; it corresponds closely to the Gramscian definition of hegemony, for it is often freely accepted and even acclaimed.

The idea of 'cultural extraversion' is not only applicable to the francophone countries. In Kenya, Charles Njonjo affected an entirely British persona – he could not imagine having a secretary who was not white, and he imported his eggs from England.[80] In the same way, his friend President Banda of Malawi has always refused to speak in anything but English, ordering that his speeches be translated into Chichewa, the lingua franca of Malawi, which one may well ask whether he still understands. Nevertheless, the identification with the west is certainly more advanced in most of the old French colonies, despite the progress of Wolof in Senegal, the creolisation of French in the Ivory Coast, the vitality of indigenous cults in Gabon, and the general decline of education. It would, however, be a mistake to deduce from this a unitary conception of the postcolonial historic bloc, reducing it to an inculcation of western culture through alienation or aggression, and emphasising colonial relations of force. The Franco-African domain in particular is not in the least bit uniform. Due to their nationalist histories, countries like Guinea, Mali and Cameroon cannot be seen in the same light as Senegal, Ivory Coast and Gabon.

The geographical bases of the postcolonial historic bloc are in general as heterogeneous as those within each state. First, the integration of this bloc with the western world economy does not necessitate any corresponding ideological or cultural alignment. This is shown by the examples of Kenya, Zimbabwe, and especially that of Northern Nigeria, whose industrial metropolis, Kano, is one of Africa's main centres of the capitalist mode of production, despite the fact that it is under Islamic hegemony.[81] Secondly, some social formations in Africa stand at the periphery of the postcolonial historic bloc. Some of them have been slowly marginalised by stagnation: for example, Uganda, Ghana, and Liberia.[82] Others, which have deliberately chosen the 'exit option', have been forced to enter the western world economy because of a crisis in their productive system or because of war: Angola financed its military activities with the duties it received from petrol companies, whose presence is encouraged by a light taxation system. And Mozambique had to liberalise its economy under guidance from the International Monetary Fund in order to regain the confidence of its creditors – because it has not withdrawn from the South African sphere of influence: but will this ever be possible?[83] Finally, entire regions remained outside the capitalist sphere of influence during the colonial era, and remain in splendid isolation except when they barter for modern-day 'glass beads' such as firearms, hi-fi systems and Mercedes in markets in the no man's land which links southern Sudan with eastern Zaïre, the east of the Central African Republic, and northern Uganda.[84]

The old links of colonialism were weakened by the arrival (or return) of North Africans, North Americans and Asians in sub-Saharan Africa.[85] The economic 'decompartmentalisation' of Africa, which has dissuaded me from accepting the existence of a 'national bourgeoisie'; has occurred alongside a growing political and cultural integration. The community of social interests that serves as a guarantee for the State and its 'Holy Alliance' is exemplified by major problems which have been widely covered by the media, such as the ECOWAS scandal and the para-judiciary hearing of the case against Charles Njonjo in 1983–84, the relative frequency of mutual exchanges of the services of the military and the police between governments; and the varying brutality and duration of regional ostracism of populist troublemakers such as John Okello in Zanzibar in 1964, Flight Lieutenant Rawlings in Ghana in 1979, Sergeant-Major Doe in Liberia in 1980, and Captain Sankara in Burkina Faso in 1983.[86] Although the performance of African multinational organisations is usually derided as pitiful, the institutional dimension of continental integration is significant and decisive. This is because the economic communities and customs agreements, the central banks of the franc zone, the Air Afrique travel company, and the deliberations of the 'front-line' states, have more value as systems of sociability and creators of a real political domain than in their economic efficiency.

Instead of providing a complete list of the systems of cultural unification of dominant African groups, their progressive religious fusion
will be taken as an example. The fact that W.R. Tolbert was able to
become President of Liberia by using the international contacts he had
formed through his activities in the Baptist church, of which he was a
faithful member, shows that in social reality religion is not a secondary
activity. Even without the help of institutionalised religious exchange,
sectarian and esoteric transactions have abounded. In the same way, it is
rare that reputable *marabouts* in the service of heads of State work for
only one president, or remain in their country of origin. According to
Africa Confidential, President Kerekou's *marabout*, the Malian Mamadou
Cissé, had previously served Mobutu. Omar Bongo was also advised
by Malians – Baba Cissoko and Thierno Hady – and the President of
Mauritania, Ould Salek, recommended the Mauritanian *marabout*,
Mohamedou Ould Cheichkna, to Moussa Traoré. Oumarou Amadou
Bonkano, the untrustworthy mentor of President Kountché – he made
a coup attempt against his master in October 1983, and rumour has it
that he was responsible for the President's illness in 1987 – also worked
for the Ivoirian minister, Aoussou Koffi, who was Houphouët-
Boigny's nephew.[87] This circulation of religious men and the 'invisible
domain' in West Africa, which has been accelerated by the aeroplane,
but has its roots in a centuries-old tradition, takes place with the help of
Islamic brotherhoods, especially the Qadiriyya and the Tijaniyya, but
also the Mourides. This is not only a spiritual enterprise. Consulted by
Presidents Abdou Diouf and Houphouët-Boigny, the Mouride *marabout* from Louga, Djily M'baye, is one of the most powerful men in
Senegal. He is involved in the cocoa and coffee trade in the Ivory Coast,
in the kola-nut trade in Sierra Leone, and the peanut trade in Senegal.
The Wahhabiyya, the Tijaniyya, and its Niassene branch – the *baraka* of
Ibrahima Niass, the famous *marabout* of Kaolack, stretches as far as the
North of Nigeria – are also involved in market activities.[88] This fusion
of religious elites strengthens links between certain political personalities that were not entirely destroyed by the dismembering of large
colonial federations. Houphouët-Boigny, who had several Senegalese
acquaintances, has sometimes revived old RDA friendships. He did this
in 1983–84, in order to rally support for Hissène Habré in the south of
Chad. One of Sassou Nguesso's diplomatic advisers was a Malian, and
ex-minister of Modibo Keita, who used to spend his time between
Dakar and Brazzaville.[89]

The horizontal structuring of space in Africa takes place around
certain poles – Nigeria, South Africa and, to a lesser extent, Algeria,
Zaïre and the Ivory Coast – due to their demographic significance, their

economic strength or their military capacity. All these dynamics are interlinked and, at the continental level, should be referred to in terms of the 'model of reciprocity' which Martin Kilson applied to political society in Sierra Leone.[90] It is in this way that they constrain political action. Abidjan and Accra are engaged in a serious and silent struggle for influence in Togo and Burkina Faso; Mobutu pulls his weight in the Central African Republic, Chad, Angola, Rwanda and Burundi; and the fear of French sub-Saharan diplomacy is that it will facilitate the installation of a leader in Niamey who is under the influence of the Hausa majority in Nigeria. In East Africa the regional and international agreements which form the triangular set of relations between Tanzania, Uganda and Kenya continue to play a role.[91] And the brutal role played by South Africa in Southern Africa is even more dramatic. These fluctuations lead to a new continental structure. It will inevitably be cruelly hierarchical and will have a role in determining the structure of inequality within each country. However, it is better to imagine it as a burgeoning totality which is polycephalous and constantly changing in form, rather than as a pyramid headed by a 'founding class' or as an indistinct domain where the 'central' bourgeoisie extends its vast hegemony.

The postcolonial historic bloc in Africa is not a completely original configuration, as the structure of inequality in Africa is relatively unified due to the congruence of its political and economic repertoires, and to the use of a restricted range of cultural idioms. This bloc has its counterparts in the international communist system, the structuring of States in the Americas and in the Arabo-Islamic world. This analysis does not make comparisons with a view to evaluating the respective degrees of multi-national integration. It is sufficient, lastly, to emphasise how the production of inequality in the African postcolonial State cannot be dissociated from its exterior environment. The old preoccupation of anthropologists still remains – the interlinking of 'interior dynamics' with 'exterior dynamics'. But the analysis of these international systems of social stratification cannot be resolved synchronically despite the fact that one school of economics believes it can be. This analysis must not obliterate the coexistence of pluralities of space and time. It must restore the *longue durée* which not only applies to the constituent elements, but also to the whole international order. In the same way as Franco-Russian, Russo-Polish, Greco-Turk, or Sino-Vietnamese relations, Africa's relations with the west, the Arab world, and the 'Asiatic' diaspora have a history; with the passage of time, these relations have crystallised into specific *répertoires*, which take us back to what Vovelle has called 'traumatic upheavals'.[92]

The inanity of the distinction between internal and external causality is especially clear in representations of 'the invisible', hypothetical manifestions of the indigenous culture. G. Dupré provides a captivating illustration of this – he recounts how a Frenchman who was in charge of a forested area in Congo agreed to a village chief's request to save him from the workers' union, and how he became involved in an ordeal of the *njobi* rite, which was performed in order to reveal the 'authors' of a series of accidents at work. This ceremony was relatively violent, and arbitrated a conflict that was connected with capitalist relations of production in a foreign enterprise, at the same time as it offered the village authorities the opportunity of extorting a significant amount of money.[93] In this example, the alliance between the European and the chief was sealed, or at least was reflected, in the invisible domain. Nevertheless, a relationship of exteriority persists in the register of instrumentality.

This is no longer the case for *ekong* witchcraft, which is particularly virulent on the Cameroonian coast, but also takes place throughout the region. If one wants to become a member of this evil organisation, it is good to start off by 'selling' a member of one's family to work in the *ndimsi** on the infamous plantations of Mount Kupe. The Europeans are accomplices in these crimes, and people are always suspicious of their presence in an isolated part of town or a village, as Father Eric de Rosny discovered when he was conducting research on the healers of Wouri. The origin of this alleged collusion is clear:

> A white man who acts as the intermediary between the *nganga*† and the chief reminds everybody of a system that is unfortunately already well known. There is a relationship between the period of slavery, which is an historical event, and the *ekong*, which is a belief. The white man came to buy slaves to work for him in faraway countries. They would never be seen again. According to modern belief, a white man can still find men to work for him. And they always disappear forever, apart from some rare exceptions. The witches send them to another world which is far from that familiar to them.[94]

To dream that one is sent, hands tied, towards the river or the ocean, is a well-known sign that one must visit an *nganga*. The *ekong* exists, above all, to bring about economic success and monetary accumulation, which are shady by definition. The ideal culprit is an 'honorary white', as they say in South Africa, a 'white' in the sense that Zaïrean children shout '*mundele, mundele*' when wealthy people pass by, and in the sense that the city is commonly described in Africa as the 'white man's

---

ndimsi: the invisible.
†*nganga:* healer.

country', and salaried work is described as 'white man's work'.[95] The social power of becoming rich, or at least the fantasy of becoming so, is the true meaning of the *ekong*. Within this true meaning, one can easily see the emergence of major opportunities inherent in the State, the possibilities of accumulation and exploitation opened up by colonialism, the triumph of wealth, and the acquisition of land and educational knowledge: one can thus see the difficult route of the search for hegemony.

PART THREE
Political Action

CHAPTER EIGHT
Entrepreneurs, Factions and Political Networks

Having set out looking for a paradigm capable of restoring the historicity of the postcolonial State in Africa, we can now see the outline of a preliminary sketch. It seems to us that for the past thirty years analyses have lost their way in two blind alleys. One set of analyses dealt with the western-African arena while remaining incapable of grasping the historical irreducibility of political trajectories south of the Sahara. The other set, insisting on the singularity of States and their dominant categories, had difficulty in conceiving the coherence of the ensemble. This dilemma, it seems to us, can be resolved by our hypothesis of the formation of an historic bloc on the western-African scale: a participant of this system, the postcolonial State is likely to construct itself through the agency of a 'passive revolution', instead of registering the domination of a national class.

It goes without saying that this canvas, which may inspire analyses of particular historical situations, makes no claim to portray the reality of the continent, but only to put it in perspective. We have already insisted sufficiently upon the particularities of the divergent trajectories in relation to this paradigm for us to hope to be understood on this crucial point. By contrast, the hypothesis of the hegemonic quest, whatever the theoretical reminders with which one surrounds the use of Gramscian concepts, tends towards teleology.

There are good reasons to doubt that the process of the quest for hegemony could reach maturity. The first of these is of a theoretical, if not theological, nature, and for this reason there is no need to dwell on it unduly. In the eyes of Gramsci, the 'passive revolution' is not the royal road to hegemony, although it does not necessarily exclude it.[1] Rather, it would lead to the 'bastard' State and 'Caesarism'. This aborted pathway is all the more imaginable south of the Sahara because it already appears to have started: the mirages of revolution and democracy have disappeared; political predation has become systematised, the economic viability of the borrowed historic trajectory is in doubt, and the African continent is being erased from the map of world capitalism.

The second reason to doubt relates to the 'intellectual' dimension of this process. This alone invests the dominant groups with the hegemonic capacity of 'directing' society, which the concept of the 'historic bloc' supposes. Following the seminal work of E.P. Thompson,[2] historians of social classes have demonstrated the full importance of this fact. However, we can scarcely hope to go further along this path because its exploration would in itself justify a second book.

Finally, and above all, the process of the quest for hegemony is not a determining principle, the *deus ex machina* of the postcolonial State. It is an action and goes back to the social struggles for primitive accumulation, the delimitation of the space of domination, the control of the political system and its insertion into the world economies. To admit this amounts to no more than repeating that the State, born of the colonial occupation, has been the object of multiple practices of reappropriation which each day distance it more and more from its original model and which make it an arena of relative indetermination. The same is true of the towns geometrically designed by colonials at the opening of the twentieth century which have since been refashioned by multiple 'ways of doing'.[3] These enunciative procedures are the very texture of the historicity of African societies. They do not belong exclusively to the dominant groups, contrary to the long-held views of the believers in the paradigm of the yoke. In Africa, as elsewhere, politics is produced 'from the bottom up'.[4] Revolts, non-compliance or underproductivity by certain cultures, strikes, electoral abstentionism, migrations, recourse to sacred rites, contraband, the blossoming of what is frequently called the informal economic sector, improvised housing, intensive circulation of news not controlled by the official media, delinquency, disqualification of government by a corrosive humour or through reference to a movement of a religious or Messianic nature, participating in but at the same time challenging the apparatus of political control: there is a long list of 'popular modes of political action' which directly or indirectly influence the statist arena.[5]

If one borrows Michel de Certeau's distinction, these practices are closer to mobile and changeable 'tactics' than to counter-hegemonic 'strategies', capable of acting in an historically significant fashion upon the whole system.[6] From this point of view the success of 'trans-formism' is undeniable. The salient feature of the last few decades south of the Sahara has been the absence of any collective agent capable or desirous of taking the lead in a social movement aspiring to a revolutionary alternative to the current grinding of the postcolonial State. Urban and rural uprisings have certainly been able to bring the 'wretched of the earth' into the centre stage. These have sometimes shaken the authorities, devastated the capitals and even extracted political changes. In one or two cases they have briefly brought about situations of 'catastrophic equilibrium', such as the conflagration of Congo-Léopoldville in 1964–65.[7] Nevertheless, the general redistribution of power, which these movements were expected to bring about, has not taken place, with the exception of some social revolutions already mentioned which, in truth, owed much to the action of counter-elites. Not only have subordinate social groups been progressively dispossessed of their investment in the nationalist or agrarian struggle – including countries such as Mozambique, Guinea-Bissau, Zimbabwe and Angola, where there has been a war of liberation – but also the only organisation with revolutionary pretensions which has ever taken power *after* the proclamation of independence – FROLINAT in Chad – imploded and quickly betrayed the ideals which it had claimed.[8]★ In any case, the impoverishment of the 'little men' does not necessarily provoke any radicalisation of their political consciousness, nor does it erode the prestige of the State brokers, the 'big men' on whom they depend.[9]

Another type of binary analysis which we need to challenge consists of freezing the practices of historical reappropriation of the State in the form of a dichotomy between the 'high' and the 'low', or between civil society and the State. In this respect the vivid expression of the 'revenge of African societies' which we have occasionally used, or even the hypothesis advanced by Goran Hyden of a State plagued by the 'economy of affection', should not be interpreted too literally, as they may lead to error. We should not attempt in an academic and artificial balancing act, to oppose the statist 'totalising' work with the divergent tactics of 'detotalising', even if the latter more than any others do lead directly to the erosion or dilution of the State.[10] In reality, the logic of deconstruction in the statist arena is not so easily separated from the logic of its construction. The matrices of disorder are frequently the

---

★It is still too early to say whether the government of Yoweri Museveni, who seized power in Uganda in January 1986 at the head of the National Resistance army, will prove an exception to this rule.

same as those of order, as is evident during elections. There is certainly no need to invest these conflicts with integrationist properties and to identify them as 'the rituals of rebellion' so dear to M. Gluckman. It is more simply that the State is the fruit of its contradictory enunciation by the various actors with which it is engaged. One cannot usefully think about it outside of the necessarily unfinished game of these procedures.

In repeating with the ancient Chinese that the vacuum structures the usage, we would like, one last time, to borrow the warning of J.S. Saul, rejecting any linear or finalist conception of the quest for hegemony, and highlighting the equivalence between the production of the State and the unpredictable unfolding of social struggles. Even if it is a bit vague, this last concept is a priori preferable to that of the 'class struggle'. In the few established cases of social classes, or formation of social classes, the concept of their confrontation is not absurd. It does not betray the historic tenor of the great workers' movements of the continent – those, for example, of the so-called Adebo strikes in Nigeria in 1970, of the railwaymen's strike in Sekondi-Takoradi in 1961, the fights of the dockers of Dar-es-Salaam and Mombasa, of the miners of Zambia or the proletariat of Kano.[11] T. Ranger, a shrewd historian, has given us a picture of a Zimbabwean peasantry determinedly following a class strategy.[12] The exceptions, however, should not be taken for the rule. Once again we must stress that as soon as one adopts a rigorous definition of class societies, one in effect disqualifies African societies from the definition. For, south of the Sahara, class relations are in no way the primary source of conflict, despite the acuteness of social inequality.[13] In Ghana, for example, it has been remarked that factional or local struggles have dominated over 'class politics' in the decades following the proclamation of independence.[14] This remark can be applied to the continent as a whole.

THE INSTITUTIONAL TREE AND THE FACTIONAL FOREST

The unloosing of the highly personalised antagonisms, within the institutions of the postcolonial State, appears increasingly to be one of its primary modalities. Certain authors, former followers of a Marxist methodology, are becoming aware of this and have fallen back upon the old neo-Weberian stereotypes of 'personal power', and risk throwing out the baby (the analysis of the material foundations of 'govern-mentality') with the bathwater (their interpretation in exclusive ide-ological terms).[15] This is a superfluous dilemma since the class struggle should not be seen 'Just as the struggle of classes, but as a struggle about class'.[16] By contrast, the tenacious efforts of 'developmentalist' and 'structural-functionalist' authors to differentiate the different types of regime according to their ideological orientations or their institutions, has been a pure waste of time. Whether of 'socialist' or 'capitalist' persuasion, dominated by a party or by the army, pluralist or mono-lithic, all these constitutional formulae – whose attributes are further-more uncertain and changeable – rest upon one common denominator: at bottom, the actors organise themselves in factions in order to win or conserve power at the various echelons of the social pyramid, and this competition is the very stuff of political life.

Léopold Senghor stigmatised this state of affairs (from which he benefitted and in which he showed an unrivalled talent) by speaking of 'politicking' (*politique politicienne*) and 'Senegalitis'. An eloquent neol-ogism. In Senegal, factional struggles, known as 'clan' struggles, have beset the institutions.[17] Political debate, at the national level, has always opposed two personalities, conforming to the bipolar configuration which is characteristic of all factional arenas. The duel between Blaise Diagne and Galandou Diouf during the inter-war years was succeeded by Senghor's battles first against Lamine Gueye (1951–57), then against his Prime Minister, Mamadou Dia (1962–63) and finally against Abdoulaye Wade (at the end of the 1970s). The latter then became Abdou Diouf's challenger. Nevertheless, these combats between lead-ers reflected a more general reality. Even though Abdou Diouf straight-away announced his intention of putting an end to the 'clan politics', and Moustapha Kâ, the coordinator of the *Groupe d'études et de recherches* of the *Parti Socialiste* (PS), felt able to mention in 1984 that there had been 'a reduction of the phenomenon at the regional level' thanks to the policy of rotating the post of secretary-general of the regional unions between the different secretaries-general of coordination,[18] all the evi-dence shows that the factional dimension has continued to predom-inate. Speaking to the PS Congress in 1986, Abdou Diouf himself admitted that the 'renewals of the basic party units [...] have again been characterised by struggles between tendencies in many of the *coor-dinations*': 'If the desire to democratise the internal life of the Party is slowly making some progress, there is no doubt that the factional struggle, as well as questions of individuals and money, are always reflected in the normal functioning of our structures.' And he expressed the almost ritual wish that the 'party spirit' should take the place of 'the clan spirit'.[19] The fact that the sixteen opposition parties all made similar noises provided some small consolation.

In truth, the recurrence of factionalism can only be explained by its deep-rootedness in Senegambian history. Donal Cruise O'Brien discerns in it a 'bizarre but effective' synthesis between the Islamic culture of the *zawiya* and the electoral experience of the 'Four Communes' under the Third Republic.[20] Far from being the result of obscure manipulations of dominant groups or of foreign imperialism, as was long believed, the permanence of factionalism is an expression of a consensus on the part of the social actors. Moustapha Kâ did not disguise the fact:

> However regrettable the behaviour of tendencies, it cannot be denied that they arouse [...] a certain animation at the base of the *Parti Socialiste*. An observer has remarked that a certain moroseness prevailed in places where the tendencies had disappeared. In effect, the tendencies have their own logic, from which it is difficult to escape. They have their own life, in which the sale of cards and renewals are exciting times. They have their own well-defined space in the districts, villages, *arrondissements* and the *coordinations*. They have their general staff and their headquarters. The men in charge, who are often absent because of their professional obligations, delegate their powers to their right-hand men. These men occupy the terrain and are in permanent contact with the activists whom they train. They are entrusted with the practical tasks. The tendencies animate the life of the Party. It is a colourful, throbbing and noisy life which unfortunately is often subjected to tensions, conflict and violence. They even awaken artistic creativity. I am thinking, for example, of the songs, *baks* and *tassous* composed by the artists of the various tendencies to the glory of their leaders.[21]

The Senghorian distinction between a 'tendency' and a 'clan' (the former supposedly having similarities with divergences of ideas within the same party, the latter with personal rivalries revealed as divergences in the application of the statutes of the party) is specious: 'At the base, and this is a characteristic of our political sociology, political life revolves around individuals, families, religious, socio-cultural and economic groups [...] the tendency can easily substitute for the clan and the clan for the tendency'.[22] The current saying, 'do politics' (*faire de la politique*), is simply a translation of the Wolof *ngurgi* or the Pular *laamunga*, which both mean to be a devotee of a leader or a faction, and work actively in their interests. 'It means that a whole body of relationships, which are not obviously political, are located in the parties,' quickly adds an anthropologist, emphasising that politics in Senegal are not to be situated in the two-dimensional arena of political representations.[23] On the one hand, all institutions in society – the Islamic brotherhoods or the trade unions, for example – are subjected to the same type of action, and the development planners start to take stock of the integrationist force of the factional networks, resigning themselves to making their peace with them rather than trying to bypass or confront them.[24] On the other hand, the 'clan' struggles are a reflection of the contradictions of the segmentary order of the family, and more particularly of competition between agnatic brothers, in relation to which the differentiation of political and religious arenas may be debatable.[25]

The Senegalese example – a textbook case – is not unique. On the other side of the continent, the Kenyan party regime is little different. Within KANU, branches and sub-branches 'function as political machines and frequently constitute the official clothing of clientelist relations'.[26] There too, the factional contradictions which disturb every constituency spread to all sectors of society: the churches, as we have already seen, the cooperatives, the unions, the football clubs, the technical institutes.[27] At the summit, the national scene is traditionally dominated by the contest between two personalities who aspire to the second place, after the president of the Republic, in the secret hope of one day succeeding him.

In Zambia, Sierra Leone, Ghana and Somalia, keen personal rivalries suck the life out of the State.[28] Does this mean that this model is distinct from another, better organised, type of political organisation? Not at all. In countries such as Tanzania and Cameroon, where the mediation of the party, administration and ideology seems undeniable and autonomous, the power of networks, the acuteness of 'struggles for influence' are more hidden and inhibited than truly exorcised.[29] In the same way, in the Ivory Coast, the preeminence of Félix Houphouët-Boigny presides over the unending conflicts which destabilise the PDCI and which necessitate the regular convocation of meetings of 'reconciliation', sometimes in the provinces, under the wing of special delegations sent by the Political Bureau to the four corners of the country, sometimes even in Yamoussoukro itself, the regime's home base. The return to competitive elections in 1980 was marked by a proliferation of settling of scores between candidates, both successful and unsuccessful. At the time of the 'Yamoussoukro days' of May 1982, Mr Alliali, the Keeper of the Seals, explained in a speech, which could be anthologised as part of the discourse of the reciprocal assimilation of elites:

> The head of the Party's wager to put the train of democracy back on the rails has been won, but for the train to progress it is necessary for the wagons of all the activists of the PDCI, winners and losers, to be coupled to it. Fed by tenacious opposition, unsoothed rancours, unhealed wounds and above all by a thirst for revenge, divisions can only hinder the

progress of the train and delay its arrival. This is why the Political Bureau, on the instructions of the president of the Party, busied itself in searching everywhere for the reconciliation of divided cadres and activists. It did not, however, succeed in dissipating all incomprehension and misunderstandings. Here and there islands of resistance held out, necessitating a meeting under the authority of the president of our Party.

After several days of 'dialogue' there followed one of those deceptively good-natured exhortations of which Houphouët-Boigny is the master. It is such a good example of the true texture of political action south of the Sahara that it, too, deserves to be quoted at length. Once the customary congratulations had been offered ('Comrade activists, I should like once again to offer you my thanks and congratulations. You have come to Yamoussoukro where the accommodation is not as good as in our capital, Abidjan.* You have kept your seats for five continuous days. Etc.'), and after the audience had been reminded of the institutional generalities, the head of State proceeded to review the six regions where factional struggles still prevented 'divided comrade militants from working together, as reconciled brothers'. Thus, for example, speaking about Korhogo in the north of the country:

We do not agree with those who propose the separation of family problems from political problems. If it was only a question of families we would not be here. In the traditional family, hierarchy is a golden rule which no one would dream of transgressing. There are the father, the brothers, the nephews. The purely family problems should be sorted out by family members and by nobody else. But because of the influence which the Gon family still exercises in Senoufo country, arguments between the members of this family on political matters have always had unfortunate consequences throughout the region. The traditional chiefdoms have been abolished in several African countries, including Upper Volta and Guinea. In the Ivory Coast we have retained certain chiefdoms, including that of Korhogo. The children of this family are in the process of destroying it by their behaviour. These arguments, these fratricidal struggles, prejudice the peace necessary for the development of this region, which is so full of human and material potential. The trusty Senoufo peasants, and the numerous cadres of the region deserve better than this. I should like to remind the Gon family, whom I consider as my own, that, as with nobility, honour is in our blood. A nobleman neither insults nor is insulted. We should put an end to this sad state of affairs by forcing uncle Gon and nephew Gon to bury their differences, which have lasted too long already. The prefect of the *département* of Korhogo is delegated by the government to guarantee public order. Anything which might disturb the public order should be rooted out. I solemnly call upon these two political officers to inform their followers publicly that they

---

*A typical manifestation of courtesy. The transfer of the capital dates back only to 1984.

have once and for all buried their fratricidal struggles which, I repeat, do no service to the cause of peace in Senoufo country. This country which is so dear to me.[30]

One should not have any illusions about the capacity of the centre to pacify the periphery of the political system. One of the regional officers of the PDCI in 1985 did not disguise the fact that 'reconciliation missions [...] sent to put out the fires at the time of the various election campaigns of 1980' had frequently been no more than 'free opportunities to play act whilst sealing a fictitious reconciliation': 'the many embraces in front of the television and photographers' cameras were mere camouflages, to put the Party officials off their guard. As soon as the missions returned to Abidjan, the protagonists lost no time in unearthing the hatchet and returning with renewed bitterness to their internecine struggles.'[31]

Better than any abstruse academic lecture on development, these long extracts illustrate the daily reality of politics in Africa: the bad-tempered froth of factional conflicts and their uneasy resolution within the framework of the State according to the logic of the reciprocal assimilation of elites. In the end, no institution, however 'massive' or 'bureaucratic' it might be, escapes from the pernicious miasmas of personal rivalries. The phenomenon has been apparent since the time of the nationalist struggles. In 1957–58, a cadre of the *Parti démocratique de Guinée* was already remarking that his colleagues 'were killing each other in an implacable struggle for places'.[32] The observation could just as easily have been made of the Kenya African Union, the Kikuyu Central Association, the Convention People's Party or of the *Union des populations du Cameroun*.[33] Indeed, in neutralising the common appeal of the anti-colonial ideal, the achievement of independence left the way wide open for the exacerbation of factional cleavages. Today, the party, the administration, the revolutionary movement, the opposition in exile, are all prey to the demons of division.[34] Ideology has nothing to do with it: the personal attacks in avowedly Marxist-Leninist systems simply clothe themselves in the finery of respect for dogma, the vulgate of the 'party line' revealing itself to be singularly well-adapted to the task of setting individuals apart.[35]

Furthermore, the insertion of African societies in the international system (or, if one prefers, their articulation within the historical postcolonial bloc) is also filtered through this factional dimension. The 'Gabonese clan' is not a curiosity, uniquely typical of the favourite sphere of French influence south of the Sahara.[36] The pivotal role of a Bruce Mackenzie or a 'Tiny' Rowland in Eastern and Southern Africa, or of a Maurice Tempelsman in Zaïre or of a Jamil Said Mohammed in Sierra

Leone, have been or still are similar.[37] The para-judicial investigation of the Njonjo case in Kenya, in 1983–84, showed how a 'machine', controlling a good part of the wheels of the State and the national economy, firmly established in a Kikuyu constituency, making remarkably good use of electoral and parliamentary divisions, was able to benefit from tapping into the 'Asiatic', Arab, British and South African networks.[38] Daniel arap Moi did not overlook this tradition for long.[39]

There is nothing innately surprising in this supremacy of the factional dimension. The legal rational model beloved of Max Weber is an historical aberration which, moreover, has been modified by various detours and practices of sociability.[40] Outside the narrow time-space – the western industrial societies – of Weber's model the logic of factional struggles is predominant. One is entitled to wonder about the heuristic utility of a concept which is applied to historical contexts in societies as varied as those of the Melanesia of the 'big men', of the Iran of the *dowré*, of the Mexico of the *caciques* and the Thailand of cliques, of the China of the great campaigns of political rectification or of the Japan of the *habatsu*.[41] It is clearly not enough just to cite the evidence of factions. It is important to restore the specific historical background against which the factional struggle is played out. Without prejudging either the unity of the phenomenon across the continent, or on the contrary its particularity from one sub-Saharan society to another, we will simply observe that the structuring of African political societies around factional networks derives from historical continuities and recurrent sociological realities. In former times, the circulation of power and wealth followed similar modalities, so much so that long-distance commerce or the intrigues of the old kingdoms are in the eyes of the political scientist not without similarities to more contemporary facts. In particular, what we today, in a somewhat confusing way, call ethnicity, implying the intervention of interregional chains of political and economic transactions, is equivalent to this 'articulation of internal and external networks of exchange' through which the integration of the continent and its docking to various world economies was undertaken.[42]

Here is a constant, or rather a line of concatenation, which deserves further thought. Implicit in it we find the social processes which we have already encountered: conflicts appearing to feed off 'tribalism'; 'straddling' procedures between the private and public sector and the personal accumulation of capital; the frequent recourse to proxies in the world of business; subtle and ambivalent coupling of official political hierarchies and discrete local hierarchies; the vigorous support of 'civil society' for the architecture of the State; the jumbling up of varied positions underlying the project of the dominant class or of the historical postcolonial bloc; and, finally, the attribution of status depending upon context along an axis of elders–juniors, and big men–small boys. To a greater or lesser extent all these mechanisms derive from the universe of networks. They all echo a global organisation of African societies to which a growing number of studies devoted to trade, the salaried class, migrations and family relations all bear witness. And as such they suppose that political entrepreneurs exercise their talent, weaving the web of constant wheeling and dealing, capable of rationally managing their material and symbolic resources in their own best interests and in the interests of the community which has given them fame and influence, able to mobilise the forces of the Word, of passion and anxiety, even in the nocturnal world of the invisible, and, finally, educated in the knowledge of the white man to which the contemporary State claims kinship. In the absence of a true structuring of social classes, the predominance of the big men at the head of networks continues to be circumstantial and in large measure dependent upon the accomplishment of individual performances.

An immediate paradox emerges, therefore, from the fact that one of the most visible continuities between former polities and the postcolonial State is ensured by such volatile procedures and agencies. The networks are not invariables which provide us with the thread of continuity. They are constructed and as such are very flexible. In the contemporary world they reflect the inherent fissiparity of lineage societies. In no sense do they rest upon fixed identities which can, without too much alteration, be simply translated across time and space. In particular, family bonds and ethnicity, which appear to be consubstantial with networks, are above all instrumental arguments, idioms at the service of actors. This is not a new phenomenon, and its existence in the past has been demonstrated.[43] But the change of scale associated with the colonial era, the intensification of trade and the creation of new communities in urban areas, has systematised this cobbling together of identities.

Thus, in the new town of Pikine on the outskirts of Dakar, the struggle for control over the health committees certainly takes on an ethnic dimension which results in 'disguising individual power conflicts with more noble and motivating appearances'. One report revealed that in January 1982 in the medical centre of D., 'racism divided the Toucouleur and Wolof' and that 'lots of wrangling prevented the correct execution of the tasks assigned to each member of the office'. The account of the head of the centre bears this view out: 'It is the Toucouleur who gave us problems.' However, analysis of the vote, which brought about the eviction of the Wolof president in favour of his Toucouleur opponent, contradicts this explanation. On his own admission, the outgoing president won five Toucouleur votes (56 per cent of his supporters), three Wolof votes (33 per cent) and one Serer vote (11 per cent). The new president claimed a different pattern of voting with eight delegates from the Toucouleur quarter (54 per cent), five Wolof (33 per cent) and two Serer (13 per cent) voting for him, and two Toucouleur (67 per cent) and one Wolof (33 per cent) for his unfortunate adversary. In both calculations, the Wolof loser did not receive more Wolof votes, and the Toucouleur winner did not collect more Toucouleur votes. Each one of them only invoked the ethnic factor in their analysis of the vote because it was advantageous for 'clan politics'.

> For the elected president, there are obvious advantages in ethnicising his rivalry with his predecessor in quarters with a majority of his own ethnic group, the Toucouleur, to increase the number of those who support him. For the outgoing president, blaming his personal defeat on collective, even demographic factors, softens the blow of his own fall.[44]

Whatever echo they may find and whatever the passions they arouse around their respective *habitus,* these identities constructed from family relations, ethnicity, religion or locality are unable to hide the extreme social heterogeneity of the networks. The task of the big men amounts precisely to the achievement of a synthesis of composite influence, whilst assuming multiple roles in various functions.[45] Never-ending work of Sisyphus! A second paradox now becomes apparent: the political integration of contemporary African societies follows in the first instance from the segmentary and compartmentalised nature of this network.

THE RHIZOME STATE: NETWORKS AND POLITICAL INTEGRATION

The illusion of the disarticulation of African societies, implicit in the paradigm of the yoke, is thus seen in all its vacuity. The central dynamic of the reciprocal assimilation of elites rests on a more common incorporation of subordinate social groups in the mesh of networks. B. Joinet has estimated, for example, that 80 per cent of the Tanzanian population and 99 per cent of its leaders belong to one or more of the horizontal chains of solidarity which emerged in response to the economic crises and poverty of the 1970s.[46] Similar estimates have been made for West Africa.[47] But networks are also stretched along a vertical axis within the framework of the unequal exchange of goods and services. They transcend, without nullifying them, the divisions of status, income and power. They link the 'lowest of the low' with the 'highest of the high' through the agencies of continuous news, requests, gifts and far from disinterested symbolic celebrations. The integration of African societies is all the more effective because, as we know, their populations are small. Freely described in terms of family relationships, the personal knowledge that individuals have of one another is the rule rather than the exception. The practice of 'dash' is a consequence of this personalisation of institutional relationships, particularly in the civil service.[48] The force and speed of social communication which results is sometimes disconcerting.

What can be observed in matters of daily sociability can be verified in the strictly political sphere. Even though one cannot, of course, accept without questioning the news bulletins on the 'Pavement Radio' (*Radio Trottoir*), the 'small men' are frequently up-to-date with the stratagems of the 'big men'. They follow these with sceptical attention, and demonstrate an undeniable civic knowledge which contrasts strongly with the poverty of the media.[49] Family celebrations, village reunions, the circulation of women and mistresses and the tangle of bars and popular eating places are sources of much of this knowledge. Furthermore, access to the 'boss', even if he is a minister, is much easier than in western industrial societies. With representations of witchcraft a factor, a notable cannot evade with impunity the 'courtesy visits' of his clients and his 'country' and deny them access to his verandah.[50]

In these conditions, as A. Cohen has shown in his work on the Creoles of Sierra Leone, the extreme personalisation of power relationships is not necessarily diametrically opposed to political institutionalisation.[51] In Senegal and in Kenya the vitality of the party (or parties) system has tended to be in proportion to that of the factional struggles which it shelters. In Tanzania, the integrationist potency of networks coincides with the crystallisation of a political society strongly welded around a far from insignificant socialist ideology.[52] It is even necessary to accept the hypothesis, advanced long ago by Ibn Khaldun, that factional struggle is a mode of political production, not of disintegration. At the price of a clearly alarming human cost, the rotation which makes competing entrepreneurs and political cliques succeed each other in power legitimises the statist framework inherited from the colonial era, in the image of a bloody alternation. In doing so, it contributes towards its reproduction. The fact that no Chadian or Ugandan thought seriously about secession, in ten or fifteen years of appalling civil war, speaks volumes. In its cruelty, the contradiction is only superficial because this model has the weight of the *longue durée*. In the past, power was distributed in this way, often to the advantage of 'men with neither fire nor hearth'.[53] Jan Vansina's notes on the former kingdom of San Salvador take on a decidedly modern significance:

> The kingdom was reduced to nothing and royalty was no more than a symbol. Nevertheless, the possession of the title of knight and other titles of nobility retained a fascinating prestige, and the infantes who had broken the kingdom continued to act as if this was still the imposing State that it had been in the 16th century. [...] Clearly, the processes of fragmentation which around 1900 were seen in a two hundred-year-old structure cannot simply be thought of as a 'decadence' but as a way of life, a structural socio-political system.[54]

In less extreme cases, political centralisation in the form of the progressive 'presidentialisation' of the regimes has been effected through the agency of liege men or locally influential personalities who have negotiated and presided over the incorporation of regions into the bosom of the State. In Nigeria, for example, the Sardauna, in order to federate the composite North in a 'united front', relied upon representatives whom he had delegated to the various emirates and minorities of the Middle Belt, and who acted as gatekeepers to these groups; he also made use of family ties, age classes and school friendships, and excelled in the ritual joking relationships which traditionally united members of the diverse communities of the region.[55] Other leaders, such as Kwame Nkrumah, Félix Houphouët-Boigny, Ahmadou Ahidjo and Field-Marshal Mobutu ruled in the same way.[56] Spurred on by the politico-military factions of the party, President Sassou Nguesso made use of his family in order to secure the Congolese system: in 1984, the ambassador in Paris was an uncle, the head of the cabinet and several other ministers were also relatives and, last but not least, the political commissar of Hydro-Congo, the national oil company, was his brother.[57]

In short, the postcolonial State operates as a rhizome rather than a root system. Although it is endowed with its own historicity, it is not one-dimensional, formed around a single genetic trunk, like a majestic oak tree whose roots are spread deep into the soil of history. It is rather an infinitely variable multiplicity of networks whose underground branches join together the scattered points of society. In order to understand it, we must do more than examine the institutional buds above ground and look instead at its adventitious roots in order to analyse the bulbs and tubers from which it secretly extracts its nourishment and its vivacity. We are also 'tired of the tree', of this arboreal metaphor of the State which, in truth, has exhausted the theoreticians. Our time would be better spent trying to understand the mysteries of the rhizome.[58]

It is indeed through the medium of these rhizomatic networks that the retroactive belt linking African societies to postcolonial institutions is formed. Although this belt belongs to the concept of political systems, its existence in the context of the Third World was doubted by R. Kothari.[59] However, there is certainly symmetry and interpenetration between, on the one hand, the hurly-burly of struggles for influence at the base of the regimes and, on the other hand, the soft-shoe intrigues at their summit. It is quite true that in the absence of almost any revolutionary threat south of the Sahara these factional struggles represent the principal agencies of change in government.[60] But, whatever the Africanist orthodoxy tells us, the precariousness of national political equilibria is not a manifestation of the organic inadequacy of the State, nor even a supplementary proof of its extraneity. On the contrary, it reveals its narrow symbiosis with the grassroots that sustain it.

In other words, factional struggle does not belong to the periphery of political systems; it is not the opposite of the centralising and presidentialist principle which has come to dominate under the cover of the single party or military regimes. It is the mainspring of this evolution and reverberates at the heart of the State of which it is the true dynamic. In many cases conflicts for influence within the nationalist movements before independence prepared the way for the construction of the postcolonial political order, in such a way that it consisted of the autonomisation of a presidential network among the competing factions.

In a few cases, the holder of supreme power acquired an absolute preponderance by politically and physically eliminating his rivals and turning his back on the logic of the reciprocal assimilation of elites. With massive recourse to coercion, the presidential network – one is tempted to say, mob – appropriated all the resources of the State and absorbed the political arena for its own profit, even with a veneer of sometimes delinquent ideological logomania. Ahmed Sékou Touré was the person who came most quickly and closely to this model. From 'plot' to 'plot', his 'family clan', which formed 'the narrow circle of primary beneficiaries of the regime', brutally rid him of any of the inclinations of restraint which were still held by the other segments of the political class, the former members of the *Parti démocratique de Guinée*, or more recent converts who had been caught up in the fever of the 'No' vote delivered to General de Gaulle at the time of the constitutional referendum of 1958. This network was flanked by two half-brothers of the head of State, Amara and Ismaël Touré, by his half-sister Fatima Touré, his paternal cousin Mamourou Touré, another cousin (or, on some days, nephew) Siaka Touré, and by a whole line-up of other personalities more or less closely related to him.[61]

Nevertheless, the mob's monopoly is not always perfect. When its monopoly does become closer to perfection the mob soon becomes divided. In Guinea, for example, the trauma of the Portuguese raid on Conakry in November 1970 encouraged the wife of Sékou Touré, Andrée, née Keita, to throw her lot in with her family: her half-brothers Seydou and Mamadi Keita, the husband of her younger half-sister Moussa Diakité, and Nfanly Sangaré, the husband of another half-sister.[62] Moreover, some other influential networks survived, including that of the Prime Minister, Louis Lansana Beavogui. As all opposition to the inner circle of the regime had disappeared, political life was restricted to a 'struggle to the death fought out between clans who ripped power out of each others' hands' and who 'fought their battles through proxies, directors, deputy directors, women of high and low estate [*de grand et petit milieu*]'.[63] The sinister character of the Guinean case lay in the fact that this pitiless rivalry, knowingly regulated by the head of State, extended to the precincts of the Boiro detention centre through obtaining, under torture, crazy confessions designed to 'take' one or the other of these enemy groups.[64] After the death of the old dictator in 1984, the incapacity of the factional components of the regime to overcome their animosities and to agree on the succession finally opened the way to the intervention of the army. The saga of the Tourés and Keitas came to an end several months later with their massacre in prison.

By contrast, the toppling of Macias Nguema by his relation Obiang Nguema in Equatorial Guinea was above all an act of self-defence by a related clan (the Mtumu, based in Mongomo) who had served the tyrant during the first years of independence but suddenly found themselves out of favour.[65] 'The Mongomo clan remains the real structure of power,' said a western diplomat in 1986, a few months before a new coup attempt, which was also inspired by natives of this region.[66] In this sense the initial (or supposed) calculation of Macias Nguema triumphed at the price, it is true, of the life of its author. The extermination of the country's elite – 103 intellectuals were shot in public in a single day on Ngolayop Square in Bata, many others died in prison or under torture – was intended to 'settle the regime and assure its duration': one prisoner prophesied,

Nobody with eyes on winning power, capable of seeing clearly or raising their voice or even so much as a finger. In this human desert it is necessary constantly to extend the power which is kept within the family of the president for life. Thus will reign for ever the single family of the 'Miracle of Equatorial Guinea' and thus will be perpetuated this blood-stained regime whose thirst for blood is never sated.[67]

However, for most of the time political competition has, despite appearances, remained relatively open, and the autonomisation of the presidential faction has been relative. Even the most prestigious leaders have seen their primacy, which had been dearly bought, being permanently threatened by the manoeuvres of competing networks, possible rivals or dauphins in a hurry. Aristide Zolberg has rightly emphasised that the vigour of the single parties has too frequently been perceived through the distorting prism of the nationalist mobilisation or of the heady days of congresses and elections.[68] Even in the Ivory Coast at the end of the 1950s, when the PDCI prided itself on achieving phenomenal levels of support, the reality was always more nuanced and precarious. Like Jomo Kenyatta or Ahmadou Ahidjo, Félix Houphouët-Boigny has always been aware of the fragility of his power. From the very beginning, the postcolonial regimes have been haunted by the problem of succession. M. Yacé declared (not in 1985 as one might have thought, nor even in 1980 nor 1975 but in … 1963 at the time of *les complots* [the 'conspiracies']).[70]

One of the most serious remaining problems, which is one of the causes of these subversive activities, is the problem of the succession of President Houphouët-Boigny, which people have done their utmost to exploit to the full. President Houphouët-Boigny is still alive and displays such physical splendour that it is curious to note that the preoccupations of certain sections of our youth, and of a good many foreign countries irritated by the development of the Ivory Coast, are focused on the search for a 'dauphin' to succeed President Houphouët-Boigny on the presidential chair.

In Kenya, Tom Mboya, who was killed in 1969, a little less than ten years before the eventual demise of the *Mzee*, was probably also a victim of this same obsession.[71] This explains the important role of coercion and political intelligence in the maintenance of regimes: any relaxation in the vigilance of the head of State could be fatal. The power market is all the more competitive in Africa because the average age of mortality is much lower than in Europe, and assassinations can drastically reduce it still further.

As with elders in lineage societies, or heads of networks in a suburban district, presidential preeminence is also circumstantial and depends upon the individual performance of the holder. It is earned week after week in this hard world of intrigue and 'court politics'.[72] There is consequently an important distinction to be made between the founder presidents and the successor presidents. The former achieved their primacy during the nationalist combat, generally extracting some additional legitimacy (which we should not exaggerate) and above all benefiting from the advantages of endurance which provided them with knowledge of the political networks and financial gains. The latter had to impose themselves upon a jealous and obstinate political class, and perhaps upon their former boss if he had installed a dyarchy favouring transition. In some fifteen years, the experiences of Kenya, Senegal, Cameroon, Tanzania, Sierra Leone, Guinea-Bissau, Congo and Niger enable us to begin to establish a model.[73] Firstly, as we have seen, the succession problem begins a long time before (and continues a long time after) the fateful day when the head of State either resigns, dies or is overthrown. For many years beforehand, pretenders to the throne have to jostle for favourable positions. They come up against a deafening silence, in the tutelary shadow of the Prince. It is this which makes the study of the 'Number Twos' of the different regimes so useful, of these 'patrimonial officials' (as Weber might say) who covet the place of the master or – what amounts to the same thing – are suspected of doing so.[74]

As soon as he has acceded to the highest office, having escaped the traps set by his adversaries, the lucky successor must in as comradely a way as possible attempt to weaken his opponents in order to prevent them from attempting to take their revenge. But he must also take care not to demoralise them too much, and offer them remunerative sine-cures, thereby compromising the credibility of his plans for renewal, liberalisation and moralisation of political life. Above all the successor has to confront the designs of the patrimonial officials who, having helped him to power, lose no time in starting to talk about his replace-ment. Furthermore, these people frequently enjoy the scarcely con-cealed support of the former president who may have deliberately snared the way for the 'first round' of the new president: either because the former head of State intends to keep control of the political system through the intermediary of the party of which he remains the presi-dent; or because, in order to satisfy an impatient political class, he threw a decoy alternative into the arena favouring a region or a man who had some reason to claim it, whilst all the time intending a more durable transfer of power to one of his own faction at the time of a 'second round'.

In any case, the president attempts to limit the possibilities for political and economic accumulation open to competing networks and diverse other political forces and institutions. Certainly, the constitutional and administrative evolution since independence – which is too well known for us to need to rehearse it here – has gradually responded to this demand by ensuring the presidentialisation and centralisation of regimes. But other, perhaps more decisive, procedures have also contributed towards the necessary autonomisation of the head of State. Firstly, factional and ethnic conflicts have proved themselves useful in this respect, even if they have been constantly criticised by the official ideologues. They have confirmed the presidents of the Republics in their role of 'Elder' or *Mzee* – to borrow the surnames of, respectively, Félix Houphouët-Boigny and Jomo Kenyatta – lifted above the political scrum and assuming the function of supreme arbiter. To this extent, struggles for influence have frequently been a necessary ingredient for political stability, and not the reverse. Draped in the noble cloth of conflicts about 'principles' ('liberalism' versus 'statism' or 'nationalism', 'continuity' versus 'change', and so on) they have acted as points of equilibrium for the regimes by safeguarding the autonomy of the presidential power, however able the holder might be at playing off one 'clan' against another.[75] More or less manipulated either before or after elections, universal suffrage – or, as one high-ranking municipal administrator in Cameroon confused it in a phrase which was more accurate than he knew, *chiffrage universel* ('universal counting') – is in this sense a priceless instrument for eroding the positions occupied by the 'barons', in other words (and sticking to our botanical metaphor), a first-class rhizome-killer. Furthermore, it is not the case that the freer the elections the worse they are at this particular job. The 'democratisation' of the Ivoirian systems and of Cameroon's single party have given the base of the system the task of carrying out purges, which would have been difficult to undertake from the top.[76]

Secondly, the economic austerity programmes made inescapable in the 1980s by worsening balances of payments and pressure from creditors have also in their turn been used to advantage. Many commentators have failed to understand this. The dismantling of the public sector which the international financial institutions demanded need not condemn the regimes in power. By drying up the principal channels of autonomous accumulation without creating a true market, it suits the hand of the president who finds himself restored to his position of principal distributor of sinecures. Abdou Diouf (in closing down ONCAD, the unofficial cashbox of the 'barons' of the *Parti socialiste*), Sassou Nguesso (in launching a 'structural adjustment plan') and Houphouët-Boigny (in dissolving the State companies, in abolishing the posts of directors-general, in accepting the demand of the World Bank for separating the functions of management and accounting in the civil service and in attaching the Department of Public Works to the Presidency of the Republic) have all three recovered their freedom of action with regard to a political class and a bureaucracy which had cut loose financially from the centre, and they have regained their control over a patrimonial machine which had run out of hand at the expense of a wild and runaway foreign debt.[77] The policies of structural adjustment are thus not so very different from the policies of nationalisation during the two previous decades. By different means they both pursued the same ends. The 'Congolisation' of the Mining Union of Upper Katanga in 1966–67 deprived both a possible attempt at secession and the opposition activities of Moïse Tshombe of their natural resources for obtaining finance whilst at the same time enlarging the fiscal plate and Mobutu's patrimonial potential. The *maduka* operation launched in 1976 in Tanzania to suppress private commerce suffocated the local notables and made it possible to allocate stores on clientelist principles.[78]

Thirdly, 'moralisation' campaigns which were launched from the very first days of independence were aimed much less at the general level of corruption than at restraining the growing power of the groups of 'nizers' which had a hold on the apparatus of the State. They indicate the desire of a network to confiscate prebendal currents for its own purpose or the wish of a president to gain control over the process of exploiting public institutions in order to regulate them. The denunciation of embezzlement is never innocent. It chooses its targets in much the same way as did the old Gabonese radio programme Désinvolture ('At ease'), or the 'Dossiers of Gabonese television' or the 'Makaya' columnn of the daily *L'Union*. In targeting only the 'Mamadous', these unscrupulous ministers and senior civil servants , in assuming the right to speak for the man in the street, the *makaya*, the denunciation *de facto* spares the 'great friend the honorary Makaya' who 'does a good job!' but who is betrayed by the 'big shots' (*gros pontes*).[79] This is the old tale of the good prince surrounded by evil advisers, which has also been interpreted, not without talent, on Ivoirian airwaves by 'the little story of Nalewe Kpingbin Tiecoroba' and in the *Times of Zambia* by the chronicle of 'Kapelwa Musonda' ...

If one takes this argument to extremes, one has to admit that the copious thefts from State funds by competing networks makes it all the more important for the president of the Republic to enrich himself if he is to affirm his own authority over the other networks. Thus there is no real paradox in seeing all new presidents start off their terms of office with a severe critique of corruption, only to allow their own factions to help themselves to wealth before even their first term is up. Faced with the manoeuvres of the 'Royal Family' of Jomo Kenyatta or of the partisans of Ahidjo, did Messrs arap Moi and Biya have any choice? Will things be any different for Houphouët-Boigny's successor? The example of Captain Thomas Sankara, who had discredited the Voltaic political class by dragging them before the popular tribunals but who failed to bring his own companions in arms to heel, the case of the honest and heeling Nigerian President, Murtala Mohammed, who was also assassinated, and the condemnation of the Beninois Captain Janvier Assogba, who in 1975 had publicly accused President Kerekou of embezzlement, are all evidence of the limits on good intentions, whether faked and tactical or sincere.

Fourthly, and to repeat, the diplomatic, financial, military and logistical resources of the international ramifications of indigenous networks are crucial for the conquest and retention of presidential power. Very much part of the *longue durée*, 'court politics' accord an important role to strategies of extraversion. The regional environment was thus a factor in several of the post-Kenyatta episodes, whilst the difficult contest between Messrs Ahidjo and Biya in 1983–84 included a decisive but as yet little-known inter-African dimension. But perhaps Sierra Leone has provided the clearest example, so much so that the various Lebanese, South African, Israeli, Iranian and European interests which overtly involved themselves in the succession question ended up becoming major players in the contest.[80]

The analysis of the phases of presidential succession in postcolonial regimes destroys the usual image of personal leaders who had succeeded in breaking free from their respective societies. Two or three decades no doubt witnessed the autonomisation of the presidential role. But in general this was never so marked that it ruled out all possibility of censure by the other factions taking part in the political struggle. Furthermore, the concepts of 'Caesarism' or 'Bonapartism' which have sometimes been advanced in this context[81] should be used in their fullest possible sense. It is not just the (hypothetically 'catastrophic') disposition of social groups which is in question here. It is also the emergence of a handful of individual actors faced with a certain kind of the 'parliamentary cretinism' of which Marx spoke in his *Eighteenth Brumaire;* the resistible rise of a man, even if he was a 'bastard', and his band of adventurers whose coarseness is very much on a par with that of those 'people with neither fire nor hearth' of old.[82] This consideration ought finally to rid us of any overly etherial conception of the rhizomatic integration of African societies.

CHAPTER NINE
The Politics of the Belly

The networks are founded upon inequality but are themselves producers of inequality. There is consequently no contradiction between the interpretation of the State in terms of social stratification and the analysis of the internal logic of political entrepreneurs.[1] Not that this second dimension wholly lacks specific coherence: the attempts to reduce factional cleavages to no more than social relationships of production are always found wanting and are not very convincing.[2] However, the strategies of heads of networks resemble the capture, accumulation and partial redistribution of wealth. As such they are difficult to distinguish from the quest for hegemony.

NETWORKS, DOMINATION, INEQUALITY

The creation of a clan in the anthropological sense of the term in the context of a lineage society is, in Georges Balandier's words, 'a global political enterprise which challenges kinship, rights over women, wealth and genealogical conventions'.[3] *Mutatis mutandis*, the same could be said of the 'politicking' within the postcolonial State. Furthermore, the mechanisms which govern it are arranged in a way which is similar to the unfolding of lineage competition:

> Phase 1. – capitalisation of goods and matrimonial powers
> Phase 2. – capitalisation of relations and dependants
> Phase 3. – capitalisation of prestige and influence
> Phase 4. – secession and legitimisation of secession through manipulation of genealogies.[4]

This helps us to understand the comment of Sally Ndongo, the president of *Union générale des travailleurs sénégalais en France* that, 'In

Senegal when there are three of you, you form a party and when there are five of you you split into factions'.[5] To understand this problem better let us return to Pikine in the suburbs of Dakar. A local committee of the *Parti Socialiste* normally has at least 150 members; the political entrepreneur who intends to form a committee thus has to sell 150 party cards. There are two ways for him to do this: either he forces them on people during some local assembly, or he sells them to a handful of faithful supporters who then sign up names from the neighbourhood. As a result, the local committee of the PS is managed by a bureau of a dozen individuals under the directorship of a secretary-general. Everybody is elected in the course of an assembly which brings together the entourage of the political entrepreneur and his followers who took the initiative in forming the committee. Voting, by a show of hands, simply confirms the rise of a boss and his team.

The second stage consists of taking control of the function of the local delegate. This function is both one of a dependable broker for the administration and representative of the inhabitants who are supposed to have chosen him freely and in whose name he expresses himself. Once he has become the local delegate, the secretary-general of the local committee of the PS can either combine the two positions of secretary-general and local representative or abandon his first mandate in favour of his deputy. Whatever he chooses, from now on he exercises a strict control over the social life of the district. He channels its conflicts and legal actions, resolves matrimonial and property disputes, intervenes with the public powers on behalf of an individual or to obtain the installation of a standpipe, takes control of socio-economic structures such as the health committee, which has been described as one of 'the favourite arenas for political rivalry':

> On the one hand election to a key post, particularly in the presidency or in the treasury, constitutes a demonstration of power over quite a large area since a committee can draw together as many as twenty districts allowing those elected to become superdelegates of the district if not in their official powers at least in their symbolic powers – which amounts to giving them real powers. On the other hand, the size of the sums controlled by the committee confers considerable importance on those entrusted with financial management. This importance stems as much from both the legitimate and the illegitimate possibilities of using the money (including denying opponents the use of the money) as from the actual use of the money (purchase of medicines, paying the wages of volunteers, payment of running expenses for clinics which account for most of the budget allowing little room for manoeuvre).

As soon as positions of power within the dominant party command access to social and economic resources, the logic of schism becomes irrepressible, and political fragmentation spreads. The districts of Medina-Gounasse in Pikine, for example, were initially designated with numbers, but as the districts multiplied they had eventually to be identified with a combination of numbers and letters.[6] Anyone who has used the very rich archives of the *Parti socialiste du Sénégal* can confirm that 'one buys a party card to affirm one's affiliation to a tendency rather than to a party, or more seriously to proclaim one's devotion to a man'.[7] Given these conditions, recruiting members represents a decisive moment pregnant with conflict in the strategies of the political entrepreneur.[8] Party headquarters in Dakar are inundated with petitions of activists complaining that 'the commission which sells party cards has refused to sell us any'.[9] Besides rationing these precious documents to the disadvantage of certain candidates, it is common to see in other circumstances more cards being issued than there are in fact real members. For example, in Kolda in 1963 the member of parliament, Yoro Kandé, revealed that 4,500 cards for a total of 3,280 registered voters amongst a population of 6,050 inhabitants, 'including foreigners' had been sold for 'higher and higher amounts'. He accused the commission in charge of issuing the cards of being in collusion with his principal rival, Demba Koita:

From the very first day the cards went on sale I was in a clear lead over the opposing tendency with majorities in all the sub-sections of the three wards. Once they returned to base in the evening, having seen which way people were voting in the country the delegations changed their approach as they had at all costs to ensure I did not win a majority. Those were their orders. But from whom? They won't say. [Yoro Kandé was in reality hinting that Mamadou Dia, the Prime Minister in conflict with President Senghor, was responsible.] The following morning, the second day of the distribution of cards, they sent us on the wrong route saying they were going to Medina El Hadji where we followed them to meet up with the activists. In fact they went to Sare-Yoba, 35 km in the opposite direction to where they said they were going. It took my followers a good half day of searching to find the commission at Talto, a village a further 15 km away. Having been tipped off, Koita's followers had spent the night there with the agreement of the commission.

Some of our local activists told us that cards were being distributed clandestinely in the huts, and this information was quickly confirmed when out of the 60-odd cards sold in the presence of our delegates there were more than 100 voters afterwards. The commission refused to go to the neighbouring villages, saying that it couldn't spend more than an hour and a half selling cards even though this sector comprising more than twenty villages could easily have taken 700 cards.

Sometimes refusing to sell cards to activists, sometimes refusing people the right to vote, the commissions sowed doubt in everybody's mind and caused trouble throughout the country. From that moment onwards they worked haphazardly, not bothering to follow the correct order of seccos*, bypassing some and arriving without warning at others. Not even the *commandant de cercle* in charge of the commission's safety knew where it was going. In short, the commission contrived to create sub-sections with the few individuals that Koita had with great difficulty managed to attract in the country.

The stakes involved in these rivalries and these frauds are without doubt sufficiently high for violence to be common. Yoro Kandé's testimony, for example, continued:

> One of our women's committees in the 2nd District of Kolda was literally stoned during a meeting in a private house by members of Koita's action committee. Several women were wounded. At Tankanton, two of my friends were beaten up and seriously wounded whilst selling cards; one of them, Diallo Hady, was kept in hospital in a coma for three days. In the market at Kolda one of our female activists, Bouya Balde a milk seller, was insulted, kicked and beaten before having a lot of her possessions stolen.[10]

Even today it is thought necessary to issue reminders that one should not come armed to meetings of the *Parti socialiste*. Not that the Senegalese are especially hot-blooded: throughout the continent election campaigns are frequently interrupted by brawling. At first sight the ferocity of the factional struggles south of the Sahara seems out of all proportion to the real powers invested in the posts for which the political entrepreneurs are allowed to compete. Was it reasonable, for example, in the Ivory Coast in 1985 to resort to poison and the forces of the invisible or to buy up the entire petrol reserves of a constituency in order to deprive one's rival, all for the sake of the simple hope of winning a seat in an Assembly crushed by the preeminence of the President? Apparently yes; and in the middle of a period of economic crisis the Ivoirian political class, taken in its totality, did not flinch from sacrificing huge sums of money to the electoral rite, equivalent, according to some estimates, to the revenue of exporting 40,000 tonnes of cocoa.[11] ... In cultures which attach value to the 'wealth of men' and which submit to this objective 'fortune in money' (in Hausa *arzikin mutane* and *arzikin kud'i*) the constitution of what Malinowski called 'resources of power' is valorised in itself. The Congolese 'partisans' offered this explanation in 1964–65:

> The struggle for influence consists essentially in making use of all means available to build up one's prestige and authority at the expense of others and in contempt of truth and justice. In political organisations, the administration, etc. one pursues the struggle for influence in order either

*Translator's note: *secco:* agricultural cooperative.

to achieve or maintain oneself in positions of responsibility or to install or consolidate one's personal power.[12]

Positions won in combat, even if relatively subordinate, permit a minimal accumulation of wealth which can then be redistributed according to the dictates of 'strategies of offering' in order to satisfy and increase one's clientele'.[13]

In any case, one should not make too much of the principle of reciprocity – whether symbolic or concrete – institutionalised by the personalisation of social and political relations within networks. Malinowski went so far as to argue that 'the primitive state is not tyrannical for its own subjects' since 'everyone is linked, in reality or in fiction, to everybody else' through kinship, clan membership or through age groups.[14] We cannot allow ourselves such an idealised conclusion as far as African societies are concerned. Their intimate character is in no sense the opposite to, nor even necessarily a reduction of, domination and inequality. If a powerful cousin can indeed get you a job, a passport or off a criminal charge, if he can soften a prison sentence or at least give you information about the fate of a prisoner, if he feels obliged to help you get your child into secondary school for fear of 'spoiling his name',[15] an Ahmed Sékou Touré can just as easily chat on the telephone with prisoners of the Boiro detention centre whom his own half-brother had sent to be tortured. These conversations which sometimes took place immediately after the victim had been let out of the so-called 'technical cabin' resonate with an appalling surrealism:

> 'Alata, I wanted to tell you myself how pleased I am with your latest statements. You have helped the cause and you know you can count on me.'
> 'President? (...) Tenin and my child?'
> 'What?' my interlocutor exclaimed. 'Haven't they told you that you have had a boy?'
> 'What has he been called?'
> 'Your wife said that you would have liked him to have my name.'
> I agreed to be his godfather. Everything has been done.
> 'After everything that was written, after my statements? Mr President, how could my child have your name?'
> 'That doesn't change my feelings. You were misled. As long as you are where you are I promise to take good care of your family. Perhaps you'd like to see them? (...) I'll arrange a visit by your wife and child. Calm down, Alata, and have confidence in me.'[16]

It was certainly not through any generosity of spirit that Léon Mba ruled Gabon 'in the manner of a village chief', giving up an impressive amount of his time to sort out himself the many 'small personal problems', such as the notorious divorce between the butcher and the secretary.[17] In this respect the small population of most African States is a major advantage. It enables a leader in power for one or two decades to acquire direct knowledge of every individual with money or influence. Sékou Touré took surveillance of the social elite to extremes. He made a point of personally receiving not just students returning to Guinea after studying abroad but also political prisoners released from detention who were obliged to pay him 'wholehearted homage' at the risk of appearing 'to bear a grudge'. He also decided on 'the distribution of the income from bauxite exports and from the thirty-four factories which he pompously called his 'heavy industry' and on the allocation of foreign exchange from the Central Bank: 'Nothing is done without his order. No operation is undertaken unless he has ordained it. The President of Guinea has become the Papa Bondieu giving out thousands of francs CFA here, sheets of metal, a sack of cement, a motorbike or a bag of sugar there.'[18] In some ways, far from being a threat to the regime, economic stagnation and hardship have made this method of regulating political society easier.

Redistribution of sinecures and other benefits of power must be treated carefully. It is certainly not unheard of for a 'big man', influenced by the ethos of munificence, to make a point of honour of doing so.[19] However, it is more common for it to be imposed upon him by meetings of collective savings societies in his home town or village and by the continuous stream of beggars, masters either of the language of kinship and flattery or, more disturbingly, of the accusation of witchcraft: a man who manages 'to make good' without ensuring that his network shares in his prosperity brings 'shame' upon himself and acquires the reputation of 'eating' others in the invisible world: social disapproval and ostracism and, in extreme cases, a death sentence may in time be his reward. This is not enough to ensure that the redistribution of wealth always takes place: far from it. The personal relationship on which redistribution is supposed to depend is by definition highly inegalitarian and hierarchical.[20] The personal nature of the system makes the communication of grievances increasingly difficult as social stratifications become petrified and as the *habitus* (to borrow Pierre Bourdieu's concept for the world and culture of the dominant class) become more detached from society and as the dominant actors start to reproduce . As a railway worker from Sekondi-Takoradi told Richard Jeffries: 'Have you ever seen a wealthy man stop his Mercedes to get out and dash [give money to] a poor man? Not at all. It is we workers who have to look after our jobless brothers and friends.'[21]

The object of factional struggles is equally not just the distribution of status and power. They also resemble the distribution of wealth, or more accurately, the distribution of the possibilities of realising a primitive accumulation, in the strict sense of the concept, by the confiscation of the means of production and of trade.[22] And because they take place against a double backdrop of material scarcity and political precariousness, the combats are ruthless.[23] When the GNP is low and when the conservation of a position of power depends solely upon the good humour of the Prince, the temptation to exploit 'the situation' as quickly and as fully as possible is enormous: hence the unbridled predatoriness and violence of political entrepreneurs. It is not always an exaggeration to discern in the confrontations of the seraglio the settling of scores amongst mafiosi. In Kenya the populist member of parliament Josiah Mwangi Kariuki, who campaigned for the restitution of land to Kenyans, preached an economic nationalism and vilified corruption and social inequalities, was assassinated in 1975 with the evident complicity of the political police, if not of the State House, shortly after embarking on a virulent offensive against Lonrho which was closely connected with the so-called 'Royal Family'. Coming from a man who was not only rich but also adored by the public, who had been a personal secretary to Jomo Kenyatta and later one of his ministers before becoming a dissident voice in parliament, this attack was undoubtedly considered as treason as it took place at a decisive time in the division of the spoils of the colonial era. At the beginning of the 1970s the recovery of the 'white lands' by a small number of large Kenyan landowners was coming to an end, the system of social stratification engendered and guaranteed by the State was consolidating, and as a result the opportunities for upward social mobility grew fewer by the day.[24]

Political life in Benin since 1972 has also been a bloody affair, with the murder of several of Kerekou's economic competitors following various so-called 'conspiracies' or 'adulteries'.[25] In Guinea Alpha-Abdoulaye Diallo described the members of the 'revolutionary committee' responsible for judging him – if one can use such a word – as thugs who were capable of all kinds of violence:

> Louceny Condé, a policeman and former administrator at the presidential residence where his indelicacies were notorious (...) had an old Mercedes which seemed to be calling for its last rites with each turn of the engine. Jacques Demarchelier owned a brand new Mercedes. Demarchelier was arrested. He was taken to Boiro camp. Condé was watching out. One of the cars took the place of the other.'[26]

Lies, provoked by an unjust detention? It would be naïve to minimise the importance of such accounts, often related in a tellingly matter-of-fact tone. In reality, many regimes on the continent operate as *kleptoc-racies*.[27] With the material stakes so high no holds are barred in the competition between the chiefs of the network, however violent they may be: homicides, arbitrary imprisonment, forced displacement of whole communities or (simply) burning down buildings which contain evidence of malpractice.

'GOATS EAT WHERE THEY ARE TETHERED'

We are now able to think of 'corruption' as well as conflicts inaccurately dubbed as 'ethnic' as being no more than the simple manifestation of the 'politics of the belly'. In other words, the social struggles which make up the quest for hegemony and the production of the State bear the hallmarks of the rush for spoils in which all actors – rich and poor – participate in the world of networks. 'I chop, you chop' was the promise of a Nigerian party. Whilst one cannot deny this, one has to stress that not everybody 'eats' equally. We recall the Cameroonian proverb 'Goats eat where they are tethered'. The interest (and probably the key to the success) of A. Kourouma's novels lies in his ability to bring to life the intensity of these appetites and the social desperation caused by their frustration.[28] Reality is often stranger than fiction. According to the testimony of one of its own junior officers, Zaïre's Air Force (FAZA) was actually cleared out as a result of the looting of its personnel. The pilots and other air crew first of all transformed it into an air transport company, undercutting the rates of the official national airways Air Zaïre by more than a half: 'With the money they got from this they bought produce in the interior of the country which they sold at three times the price on their return to Kinshasa where the cost of living was much higher. With this new system of commerce the crews hit upon a goldmine.' However, the ground-based maintenance staff took a dim view of these profits from which they were excluded, and took less and less care of the aircraft, 'which caused numerous accidents and deaths amongst the military flight staff':

> Finally, in view of so much uncertainty and the fear of flying on board such perilous machines, some air captains took stock of the seriousness of the situation which was deteriorating all the time, and began to offer the ground staff the possibility of finding passengers of their own to enable them to earn a modest daily income. Consequently, several flights a day took off from Kinshasa with clandestine passengers on board (approximately two out of five!). Indeed, to alleviate the poverty which

affected all levels of society it was necessary for everybody to find a solution by exploiting their profession or their workplace and thereby inadvertently bringing about the ruin of the nation. Those who had a right to fly on board the military planes were no longer sure of finding a place or, if they did, they were obliged, like civilians, to pay a fee, albeit smaller than usual in recognition of their military status. (...) This new life for the air force had one important side-effect: a dramatic reduction in the number of accidents, thanks to the solidarity between ground and air staff cemented by their mutual search for an improvement in the harsh conditions of life imposed on them by the ruling minority.

Alas! This 'solid solidarity between ground and air' aroused the jealousy of the fighter pilots, *de facto* excluded from 'the alliance which existed between the transporters'. Out of spite, the fighter pilots, swiftly followed by the rest of FAZA, began to sell the spare parts of the planes. Only the C-130 of the 'Guide' was spared. As a result of this 'thoroughgoing campaign of pillage' the entire fleet was soon grounded. Chaos ensued within FAZA as it was deprived so suddenly of its supplementary income. The 'discovery of another system of compensation' became a priority.

This was quickly done. Every morning pilots and mechanics arrived at the base and towed two planes to the fuel pump of Air Zaïre for a complete refuelling. As soon as they had been filled up they were towed back to the hangars where their fuel tanks were emptied. The first clients of this little operation were the wives of the soldiers based at the CETA training camp, who bought the petrol at half price, then proceeded to resell it in Masina, Kimbaseke and especially Kisangani. It was not long before the sale of air-force fuel became semi-official, as no attempt was made to hide what was happening: every day a flood of empty barrels, big oil drums and all kinds of receptacles passed though the main entry gate to Ndjili airbase under the watchful eye of guards who, had they been above corruption, would never have allowed so many customers to pass through, let alone help them carry their barrels to and from the hangar.

This account is interesting for reasons other than its humorous detail. It is a good illustration of how 'corruption' is a method of social struggle, in the full sense of the term, and how much it rests squarely upon a lively political consciousness of inequality:

Whilst all these operations were going on there was always plenty of gossip, directed principally against the dishonesty of the established authority which stubbornly refused to treat its subjects decently. Everybody mumbled: 'It isn't possible to live with that great jackal, he must go and give way to somebody who might do a better job'; 'It's not possible for us soldiers to live in our own country. Our families are so badly treated even though the rest of the country thinks we are the right-hand men of Mobutu.' These sentiments were heard in military circles throughout the country, even amongst the most illiterate of the soldiers who were sick of the Guide, but above all by veterans of the colonial army who were nostalgic for the colonial period and by those who had started off in the ranks of the ANC until that unfortunate day of 24 November 1965 when Mobutu became the guide of our nation. Under Monsieur Joseph Kasa-Vubu, our first President of the Republic, everybody in the army was treated fairly, as they were in other sectors, both public and private, whilst now the child of Mademoiselle Yemo has the lion's share and holds the rest of his people hostage.[29]

The picture painted by A. Morice in Guinea in 1985 – after the death of Sékou Touré, and before the arrival on the scene of the International Monetary Fund – corroborates these hypotheses. The principal result of the irruption of the soldiers, soon after the funeral of the old leader, was the ending of the mafia-like monopoly of the gang that had been in power for twenty-five years. The soldiers' revolt ended in the liberalisation (one might even say, the deregulation) of the looting of the State. A political revolution, if ever there was! Not that the beneficiaries of the former regime have lost all their wealth. If the leading figures of the Touré clan were secretly exterminated after several months of prison, the majority of the senior civil servants stayed in place and, despite being 'cut off from their former trafficking and positions of influence', were able to inject into the economy their considerable wealth accumulated during the seventies by dealing in the black market and smuggling diamonds. President Lansané Conté was nevertheless obliged to uphold 'the demand of all groups who had been victimised in the past to share in the distribution of wealth and jobs'. This extravagant and 'potentially explosive' promise 'widened the rifts between the public and private sector, the civilians and the military, the inhabitants of the capital and the regions, residents and exiles as well as the ethnic groups'. Within these various groups and networks one could see the appearance 'of an ensemble of ambivalent and dialectical relations where social forces are constantly required to define their relationships with one another as both accomplices and adversaries'.[30]

Onto the corruption of civil servants and the massive embezzlements of goods and equipment in businesses, ports and the administration is grafted what the Guinean national daily paper calls the 'indescribable ballet' of trade.[31] As in Zaïre, activity within the informal economy is closely tied to official State practice: the two spheres are indivisible. Furthermore, the strategies adopted by the great majority of the population for survival are identical to the ones adopted by the leaders to accumulate wealth and power. The line dividing these two categories of actors is a thin one. The hazards of the economic climate or the dealings of competing networks under the pretext of cleaning up politics or respect of the law which everybody ignores, can bring ruin at any time – as, for example, Malinké traders in Guinea discovered in 1985 when their shops were sacked following an unsuccessful coup attempt.[32]

Contrary to the popular image of the innocent masses, corruption and predatoriness are not found exclusively amongst the powerful.[33] Rather, they are modes of social and political behaviour shared by a plurality of actors on more or less a great scale. The longest overhead power line in the world joining the dams at Inga and Shaba serves as a perfect symbol of this truth: the corner irons of the pylons have been appropriated by villagers living underneath to make beds, shovels and other tools. The daily cannibalisation of the line is a modest and popular counterpoint to the huge profits made by foreign civil engineers and Zaïrois decision-makers as a result of the construction of this grandiose and useless project.[34] The celebration of the 'cargo cult' of the postcolonial State, which is by definition inegalitarian, affords the dominant actors the means of vociferously defending their material interests whilst at the same time laying claim to the highest ideals of development and public order. In this sense the 'politics of the belly' is truly a matter of life and death. Life – if one succeeds in taking one's part of the 'national cake' without being taken oneself. Death – if one is forced to make do with a hypothetical salary that will only feed the family for the first three days of the month; if one doesn't take one's chances; if one is ambushed and beaten by opponents no matter that they are dressed up in the tawdry finery of legitimacy and coercion. Such was the sad fate in Zaïre in July 1979 of the diamond miners of Katekelayi and Luamuela who were fired upon by soldiers under direct orders from central government and MIBA, the Bakwanga Mining Company. The majority of the miners were already paying fees to the traditional authorities as well as the local police force, and thought they were doing things by the book:

> When the soldiers arrived they placed themselves with their backs to the hills in such a way as to allow us only one possible escape route – across the river Mbuji-Mayi. Then they ordered us to give ourselves up one by one and hand in to the commandants the stones we had dug. We didn't move. We were forced to react by the very same soldiers who dug for diamonds for the colonel, the commandant of the regional gendarmerie who made us pay for mining permits, who claimed they were there to protect us and took diamonds from us in return. We didn't move. As time passed the order was given to fire into the crowd. The order was carried out and some were killed. In the ensuing panic the survivors divided into two groups: one lot flung themselves into the river and attempted to swim across, whilst the others tried to make their way through the line of soldiers. That's when the shooting increased. Men fell

like flies. Policemen stripped the bodies to steal the precious stones. [...] In eastern Kasaï it has become the norm for policemen to shoot clandestine diggers and in a cowardly fashion massacre the young and the unemployed who have no other means of supporting themselves in a town where the only industry is MIBA. [...] The situation was all the more serious because we genuinely believed that we were digging legitimately for diamonds. In fact, the Zaïrois army was receiving a duty of 5 Z from the clandestine diggers and 20 Z from the smugglers. On top of that the soldiers took turns on the mines and demanded diamonds from us to allow us to continue. Then to our great surprise as we thought that all the soldiers were following orders from the same boss, when the relief teams arrived they came into conflict with the departing teams of soldiers. Imagine our surprise when, with the arrival of the shock forces (soldiers plus MIBA agents), the soldiers who were surrounding us and who were digging in the mines belonging to the commandant of the gendarmerie began to hide or run away or pack up.[35]

The significance of this account can only be fully appreciated if one remembers that Mobutu, along with his family and the politico-military hierarchy of the regime, were all personally involved in the diamond trade.[36] Within these sorts of contexts social struggle is a zero sum game where the only prize is the accumulation of power. It is a truism that it is easier to get rich from a position of power than from a position of dependency and penury, but it is a truism that in Africa one may not easily survive. It would be something of an exaggeration to apply this theory too rigidly to the whole of the continent. The division of spoils is less cruel in, for example, Senegal, Ivory Coast, Gabon or especially Tanzania. Neverthless in the latter country we find a case which is curiously reminiscent of eastern Kasaï except – crucially – that the result was not a tragic one. In the districts of Kahama and Nzega in 1988 gold prospectors asked the government to punish senior managers within the State Mining Corporation (STAMICO) and the local administration whom they accused of being involved in the illegal export of the precious metal. They admitted that they themselves worked illegally, but they accused the leaders of STAMICO of doing the same in their attempt 'to assure themselves of the monopoly of exploitation rights in the region for their own personal gain': 'Experts in charge of mining affairs were said to have been implicated in "trafficking" and "rackets" and were said to have employed policemen on the illegal mines to prevent local miners getting access to the sites.'[37] The conversion within the space of a few years of a country such as Kenya or Cameroon to a predatory economy suggests how easy it is to cross from one side to the other of the 'politics of the belly'.

Delinquency plays a role as well as corruption. Notwithstanding the discourse of the powerful or the exasperation of the townships, it is important to understand delinquency for what it is: namely, the brutal conquest by an active and desperate minority of the riches of the State. Such a political definition of theft and crime may cause some surprise and may even shock some people. But how can one think otherwise, bearing in mind the criminal instincts of the authorities themselves? Recurrent underemployment prevents those without money from acquiring fashionable imported goods or from being able to choose a spouse – the *sine qua non* of social recognition. The social frustrations caused by the economy of survival force many 'little men' to make radical choices: either allow oneself to sink into dementia, like the unemployed man in Douala who cut off his penis because he 'never had enough money to merit a woman',[38] or to seize by force that which society denies them.

The 'highest of the high' are very much aware of this and increasingly live in a siege mentality, protected by their personal guards. They perceive banditry as a political threat to their absolute seniority, a threat which derives in the main from the 'youth', the 'juniors' and the 'little men'. The president of the Wouri section of the *Union nationale camerounaise*, for example, alluding to the UPC rebellion of the 1950s, wrote in 1972 that 'The memory of the beginnings of terrorism in the department were still fresh in our minds. The terrorism was the work of the youth.'[39] In the 1950s the white settlers in Douala were already convinced of the connection between nationalist agitation and criminality.[40] More generally, the European bureaucracy, in keeping with its projects for a 'second occupation' and unnerved by the first large-scale strikes on the continent, often reacted from the 1930s onwards by attempting to co-opt a stable, well-disciplined and relatively well-paid working class, isolating it from the lumpenproletariat of temporary workers who were seen as constituting the major social danger. The Kenyan trade unionist Tom Mboya rehearsed this thesis when he became Minister of Labour.[41] At the end of the 1980s in the north of Nigeria the *sarakuna* likewise associated the millenarist uprisings of the *'yan tatsini* with the growth of the urban class of *gardawa*, the students of Koranic schools who used to live off charity and seasonal work.[42]

In many ways the juvenile underworld has succeeded where the peasant revolts and trade-union marches have failed. In many of the metropolitan areas of the continent, it has installed a veritable balance of terror and has left the rich with little choice but to resort to the systematic use of violence. Hunted by a merciless police force – if the police are not their accomplices – and subject to the harsh law of the lynch mob, the young thieves have no choice but 'to kill or be killed'.[43] Their numbers are nevertheless on the increase. Statistics show that banditry has become one of the principal 'popular modes of political action' south of the Sahara if one accepts that the enunciative procedures of the State are primarily related to distribution of wealth. As one of the elder statesmen of the Cameroonian regime admitted in 1971: 'We could mobilise the entire army under our command but we still couldn't arrest all the young criminals ... because criminals outnumber our forces of law and order.'[44]

In reality the problem is not quite as simple as this. The space of legality cannot be neatly differentiated from that of misdemeanour and crime. A good many respectable actors are regularly forced to stray beyond its boundaries as a result of an urgent bill to pay, a family celebration to subsidise or to satisfy a long-held desire. As they are unlikely to be caught out on such occasions they are able to return to the bosom of the law – until their next transgression. At the time of the riots in Banjul in 1981, in Nairobi in 1982 or in Dakar in 1988, upstanding family men joined in with the lumpenproletariat to loot the shops. As for economic crime, it is common currency in all companies. By contrast, members of urban gangs have often come to crime by a roundabout route, and their participation in criminal activity is not a sign of their definitive marginalisation in society.[45] Given its temporary nature, contemporary deviancy has certain parallels with the diets of milk, meat and violence by means of which young warriors used to acquire their adult status in the social hierarchy. Whether irrevocable or durable, it prolongs the tradition of rural banditry.[46]

The 'politics of the belly' is firmly located in the continuity of the conflicts of the past. Today as yesterday, what is being fought for is the exclusive right to the riches claimed by the holders of 'absolute seniority'. The young challenge this claim. What is perhaps more revealing is that women are no more willing to accept the claim than the youth and that they are waging an authentic 'sex war' against the men.[47] Once again morality is not necessarily the victor: in order to achieve emancipation and economic advancement, young women are forced to sell their bodies as well as engage in other commercial activities or work in industry or on the land.[48] With the spread of sexually transmissible disease – and the tragic consequences of one of these diseases in particular – we see further proof of our proposition that south of the Sahara 'to eat' is a matter of life and death. All the same, we need to verify that in the end it is still a political question, albeit in a somewhat less than rigorous use of the epithet.

THE EMERGENCE OF A POLITICAL SPACE

We do not intend to succumb – as too often happens – to the temptation of reducing African social actors to no more than glutinous enzymes, motivated by the sole desire of stuffing themselves as quickly as possible with the fruits of western modernism. The expression 'politics of the belly' must be understood in the totality of its meaning. It refers not just to the 'belly' but also to 'politics'. This 'African way of politics' furthermore suggests an ethic which is more complicated than that of lucre. A man of power who is able to amass and redistribute wealth becomes a 'man of honour' (*samba linguer* in Wolof).[49] In this context, material prosperity is one of the chief political virtues rather than being an object of disapproval. President Houphouët-Boigny, for example, once attempted to discredit a political opponent by describing him as a man who 'didn't own anything, not even a bicycle'.[50] The Ivoirian President was proud of having been the first person to import a Cadillac into the country, to the great annoyance of Governor Péchoux. He brought the full weight of his wealth to bear in a speech of epic proportions delivered to striking students: 'People are sometimes surprised that I like gold. It's because I was born in it.'[51] Such boasts are well understood in Kenya. Doubtless Mr Oloitipitip, one of Daniel arap Moi's ministers, was exaggerating a little when with his usual truculence he declared: 'I am a Maasai. I've got money. I don't sell chickens. [...] I am able to spend 150 million shillings from my own pocket for the marriage of my son. [...] I have six cars, two big houses, twelve wives and sixty-seven children.' Talking about his opponents, he said: 'These men are not small men; they are men with big bellies like Oloitipitip.'[52] Jomo Kenyatta upbraided a radical nationalist opponent in a similar way: 'Look at Kungu Karumba. He has invested in buses and has earned money, but what have you done for yourself since independence?' Kenyatta cashed in his nomination to the post of permanent secretary of the Kikuyu Central Association for a salary equivalent to what he earned from the municipality of Nairobi, a supplementary allowance for his expenses as a representative and a motor bike. One of his contemporaries recalled that 'Kenyatta was a braggart, a drinker and a womanizer but he was very good at his job. He liked tidiness and was always very well dressed. He was fond of spending but he also knew how to walk with courage.' Finally, forty years later the populist deputy J.M. Kariuki had absolutely no need to disguise his wealth in order to win credibility with the citizens – the *wananchi*.[53]

Other politicians – Nnamdi Azikiwe in Nigeria or Major-General Mobutu in Zaïre, for example – confirm that fortune is an attribute of a true chief, sometimes because it helps presumably to discourage the abuse of power.[54] It may be a good thing that physical corpulence is a sign of a true chief, and from this point of view as well the expression 'politics of the belly' carries a much richer symbolic meaning than its polemical connotation might at first suggest. In short, wealth is a potential sign of being at one with the forces of the cosmos.[55] This is, of course, an equivocal manifestation, as apparently undeserved enrichment or wealth that does not benefit others can be denounced as being the result of witchcraft. Politicians can appeal to another set of values and capitalise on popular resentment of the 'enrichers', as Jerry Rawlings or Thomas Sankara did, or indeed as did Bernard Fonlon in Cameroon who used to drive a Volkswagen Beetle until President Ahidjo suggested that it would be more in keeping with the ministerial car park if he had a Mercedes.

Social phenomena which western common sense interprets as 'corruption' of the State or 'political decay' lie right at the heart of our understanding of the State. They shed light on its social struggles, its relative indetermination and, finally, its moral culture, which condemns (and sometimes prevents) the monopolising of power, nourishes a certain idea of liberty and, at the same time, makes some forms of social injustice illegitimate. In other words, they flesh out the generic concepts of democracy, authoritarianism, totalitarianism or the State with a single truth which can be applied south of the Sahara – namely, that which is produced by history and which is drawn by the long-term trajectory.

Not that Africans haven't simultaneously adopted other representations imported from Europe, America or Asia. Certainly, they adhere to liberalism, Marxism-Leninism, Christianity, and are willing to mix them with other ingredients from the indigenous political repertoires. The range of languages and knowledge systems in which Africans deal is quite remarkable. One thinks of Bertille, a 13-year old girl from Brazzaville who speaks Lari with her parents, can express herself perfectly in French, is quite at ease with Munukutuba, knows English from school and thinks in Lingala! This flexibility is reproduced at the level of the State.

It is this flexibility which allowed Charles Njonjo, dressed in his usual three-piece suit in the manner of a London City banker, to dance without embarrassment with an old Kikuyu peasant woman of his constituency when he decided to give up his post of Attorney General and contest a parliamentary seat. Similarly, it allowed Alhaji Sir Ahmadu Bello to combine aristocratic influence, bureaucratic reformism and Muslim piety. Actors are thus able to draw upon a range of tightly interwoven 'discursive genres' of politics – defined by Mikhail Bakhtine as relatively stable types of statements which combine time and space in a specific fashion.[56] The daily processes of creolisation, far from reflecting an inherent cultural alienation to the supposed extraneity of the State, suggest instead a real ideological interiority which is capable of inspiring institutional or administrative innovations in the pure constitutional and bureaucratic register of power.[57]

This situation of cultural pluralism and range of knowledge systems is not ideal. It is a source of contradictions, of rifts and of suffering which, for example, the Christian Kikuyu forced to take the Mau-Mau oath in the 1950s experienced in the flesh.[58] Political cross-breeding can, however, lead to the invention of particular State modernities which circumscribe the sharing out of the 'national cake' and limit an idea of power based on the principles of the hunt. Indeed, the postcolonial share-out of the spoils of independence has not been without any regulation, dependent solely upon the force of violence. It is at least partially subjected to political mediation, both institutional and ideological, which Marxist authors have generally ignored but whose significance is quite clear. In Kenya the so-called 'Royal Family' and its allies tried to block Mr arap Moi by inaugurating the campaign of 'Change the Constitution'. It is quite possible (as the partisans of the new President claimed) that they also envisaged using more direct methods, but they none the less felt that it was important to invoke this institutional dimension.[59] Likewise in Cameroon, the theme of 'Republican legality' was a powerful means of mobilising opinion against the designs of Mr Ahidjo when he made his attempted coup – first constitutionally, then militarily – on 18 and 19 June 1983. In Senegal and the Ivory Coast the revision of the constitution has likewise been a useful mechanism for regulating the presidential succession. It would be as foolish to pretend that such actions counted for nothing as it would be to dress them up into something too grand. Such evidence reveals the emergence of true political societies endowed with relatively stable ruling personnel and a limited number of accepted forms of action. Contrary to the arguments of R.H. Jackson and C.G. Rosberg, the evolution of these societies has become increasingly predictable.[60]

In less than a century political spaces have thus formed themselves around the State, thereby consolidating the change of scale introduced in the colonial era. One should neither exaggerate nor underestimate their strength, which, in any case, varies a lot from case to case depending on several types of process.

First of all, territorial unification has been made possible by western technology with its roads, planes, telephones, computers and its weaponry. Having said that, in the manner of K. Deutsch,[61] one has not said very much. It is more important to specify the political use to which this technology is put: how, for example, Mr Ahidjo put the completion of the road between Douala and Yaoundé to one side in order to slow down the advance of the Bamiléké and maintain the human division of the south; or how Major-General Mobutu liked the idea of constructing the 'longest overhead power line in the world' in order to have control over 'the switch which controls the energy supply of Shaba', a region suspected of secessionist inclinations.[62]

Secondly, the space of the State is fabricated with recourse to coercion, which the postcolonial authorities are no less reluctant to use than their predecessors. Domination is exerted without disguise, especially as it is facilitated by all the technological innovations at the State's disposal. Forced labour under the pretext of human investment, police raids and other so-called 'thorough searches' for the purpose of tax verification, the authoritarian repatriation of unemployed town dwellers into the countryside, the struggle against 'human litter' and 'undesirables' in the centre of towns, the grouping together of villages and the military 'slum clearances' from urban areas, obligatory participation at endless demonstrations of 'solidarity' and other rallies, the administration of neo-traditional rituals of political submission, *de jure* or *de facto* obligatory adhesion to the single or dominant party, the imposition of discriminatory symbolic codes – particularly related to clothing and gestures – floggings and massacres, tortures, denunciations, public executions, extra-judiciary imprisonments: through the armed forces and a network of informers the men of power exercise robust control over the populations they want to subject, to the extent of appearing to be an occupying military power.[63] The State is thus imposed in the most basic sense of the word. 'We are like women. If someone comes to the village to tell us what to do, we can only say yes,' confessed one group of villagers.[64] The Nigerian singer Fela Ransome Kuti declaims in his vituperative style: 'Soldiers whip people in the street. Yes, soldiers lashing backsides with their whips! Tell me where else in the world do you see such shit! In South Africa? Not even there!'[65] Once again it is important not to cover our eyes. This political integration which is admired by American structural functionalists above all sanctions constant police activity. M.G. Schatzberg has shown how the Zaïrois National Documentation Centre, which is independent of the politico-administrative hierarchy, taking its orders instead direct from Major-General Mobutu, is a crucial element of the

Zaïrois regime, Not only is it an effective instrument of surveillance and intimidation but it is also a very real channel of political feedback between the top and bottom of society inasmuch as it provides the authorities with the provincial information it requires, even if its innumerable reports conclude with the laconic comment 'The situation is calm.'[66] Mr Vunduawe Te Pamako, a commissar of the State in the territorial administration, declared in 1982: 'If, in spite of the economic crisis, there is one thing which works well in Zaïre it is our intelligence services!'[67] In Cameroon during the 1970s the National Police took on a similar role, actively participating in the selection of candidates chosen by the party for various elections, observing association meetings or religious celebrations with sufficient ostentation for their officers to be frequently regarded as the official representatives of the legal establishment. The task of investigating individuals suspected of opposition was swiftly handed over to the formidable General Directorate of Studies and Documentation whose mobile Mixed Brigade had acquired a sinister reputation for torture.[68] According to Wole Soyinka's account, the Nigerian security services are just as powerful despite a more correct relationship between the State and civil society.[69] The Njonjo affair has likewise revealed the omnipresence of the security forces in Kenya.[70]

These forms of social oppression cannot be effective unless they are complemented by other procedures of State totalitarianising. Some of these are economic and financial: the State, in Africa, if not quite a 'market' in the liberal sense of the word is at least an 'entrepôt' governed by a minimal degree of interconnection. Others are political and are of more explicit concern to us. For better or worse, the highly personalised regulation of the State rhizome by the president of the Republic relies on the intervention of the administration, which almost everywhere has supplanted the party as the means of government. The administration, it should be said, has remained faithful at least to the letter, if not to the spirit, of a bureaucratic model of government whose origins are foreign. Its formalism is proverbial. Patrimonial officials, in direct contact with the Prince for whom, as we have seen, they often serve as 'gateways', keeping a watch over the regions on his behalf, the staff of the territorial administration none the less follow a code and a rationality which aspires towards universality. First-class spokesmen for the Weberian idiom, they practise bureaucracy with a zeal for the good of a government which frequently depends upon a different sort of legitimacy.[71]

We now come to the central dynamic of the genesis of the space of the State. In a century of European or Creole domination, of anti-colonial struggle and postcolonial management, 'legitimate problematics' have arisen which delimit the 'field of what is politically thinkable'.[72] Schemes of action have become stabilised, political repertoires have established themselves and discursive genres have become fixed; not only have they become intimately linked with the production of societies but also it has become less and less conceivable that social actors can act outside their boundaries. This explains why the tenor of political life varies so much from one sub-Saharan country to another. It is the result of a particular chain of historical events from which political actors cannot escape, even if their relationship to the events is sometimes contradictory. We have often written of these as 'traumatisms' following our reading of M. Vovelle.[73] The inter-ethnic clashes of 1959 and the revolution of 1963 in Congo, the armed struggle in Kenya, Cameroon, Zimbabwe and the former Portuguese colonies and, in Zaïre, the historical chain of events which linked the rebellions of 1964–65 with the riots in the inter-war years and the prophecies of the past, the 'plots' of 1963 and 1964 in the Ivory Coast, the great millenarian peasant movements and the larger mobilisations of the workers – all these are archetypal examples of such events.

But there is also a less dramatic chain of events which has shaped the contemporary 'legitimate problematics'. The endless administrative reforms of the colonial governments and their successors, the local confabulations, the chance events of economic conjuncture; the oral tradition of local societies belong to the historical memory inherited by social actors. Above all the application of ideological meta-languages has had to a certain extent some foreseeable effects. 'In the beginning was the Word,' wrote Zolberg somewhat sceptically just after the proclamations of independence. 'The African leaders hope that these words will create life, that the one-party concept will be transformed into national unity, into effective authority, into an orderly State. They hope that some day the Word will be made Flesh.'[74] Well, it has to be said that these theoreticians of the single party were not entirely wrong. The perpetuation of the bureaucratic *Weltanschauung* and the victory of 'republican legality' over Ahidjo's attempt to reclaim Cameroon between 1982 and 1984, the maintenance of Marxism-Leninism as the lingua franca of Congo, the triumph of the rhetoric of the 'dialogue' in the Ivory Coast, the difficulties in Guinea of detoxifying itself from the poisonous legacy of the Touré years or the appropriation of the redeeming vein by Flight-Lieutenant Rawlings in Ghana – all suggest that some thirty years after the end of colonial rule the Word has indeed become Flesh. A good portion of social practices are described by words taken from this vocabulary and validate the space of the Nation State. With its huge following south of the Sahara, football is a case in point: if point: if championship matches attract local loyalties, matches in the Africa or World Cup provide the opportunity for the exuberant expression of national sentiments, sometimes to the extremes of pogroms, riots and expulsions.[75] Fashions and symbols peculiar to each country are grown and replicated within administrations, businesses, national airlines: interior decorating uses the national colours; the picture of the president hangs from the walls; trains, buildings and aeroplanes are named after the country's rivers and mountains; commercial or bureaucratic acronyms have the same sound ...

It is important, however, not to invest the 'legitimate problematics' with the monist definition to which the concepts of Bourdieu may lead.[76] In reality, these 'fields of the politically thinkable' are composite and at least partially reversible. They consist of ensembles, relatively integrated but nevertheless incomplete, disparate genres of discourse which the competing social actors mix enthusiastically. The baroque style of contemporary political constructions is the result of many different formative processes and borrowings from political repertoires, made possible by cultural heterogeneity and extraversion. A common fault of analysis lies in the overemphasis of one particular type of discourse and the unwarranted reduction of the political identification of a society. A good many observers have, for example, typified the Congolese or Beninois political systems solely by their Marxist-Leninist statements without understanding that the repertoire of the invisible which is also very active in these countries fragments these statements according to location and specific times in the struggle for power.[77] It is just as erroneous to ignore one of these aspects of the State as the other. Linked to this habit is another common error, which is underestimating the attachment of Africans to western judicial representations, parliamentarianism, the philosophy of the rights of man or the bureaucratic technology of government in order to extrapolate upon Africans' allegiance to the mysteries of 'tradition'. This is, moreover, a mistake which was often made by the same observers who were quick to denounce Soviet penetration but who expressed no surprise at the cultural influence of Europe ...

A second misapprehension is the belief that these discursive genres represent a coherent stock of values whose political impact will always be the same. On the contrary, they are also composites and ambivalent; their heterogeneity being a consequence of the fundamental social diversity.[78] Witchcraft, for example, far from being an ideological tool of lineage in the hands of the elders, as Althusserian anthropologists used to argue, is equally manipulated by the 'small men' who are anxious to defend their interests and to make sure (with varying degrees of success!) that the rich honour their obligations to redistribute wealth. It is as much a sign of the incompleteness of power as of the inaccessible totality of power.[79] In the same way, Islam is not monolithic. *Talakawa* and *sarakuna* do not share the same perception, and the Sufi, Mahdist and militant strands of Islam all add to the number of divergent social strategies.

In order to understand 'governmentality' in Africa we need to understand the concrete procedures by which social actors simultaneously borrow from a range of discursive genres, intermix them and, as a result, are able to invent original cultures of the State. We can then see that the production of a political space is on the one hand the work of an ensemble of actors, dominant and dominated, and that on the other hand it is in turn subjected to a double logic of totalitarianising and detotalitarianising. Too often the creation of the postcolonial State has been portrayed as the Titanesque achievement of enlightened Princes, combating the dark forces of tribalism, tradition and imperialism. Despite the interest and comfort in such imagery it does not do justice to the complexity of the facts. The 'small men' also work hard at political innovation and their contribution does not necessarily contradict that of the 'big men'.[80]

N. Kasfir's claim (which is often heard) that the decrease in political participation is the salient feature of postcolonial politics is in this respect debatable.[81] First of all, because the degree of nationalist mobilisation to which subsequent political activity is compared has for a long time been overestimated and it is only recently that people have begun to be more realistic about it. Secondly, because political participation – whether for or against the government – remains considerable, despite appearances. It retains the ambivalence which marked the tributes and forced labour of former times: the Bamoum *pamfie*, for example, which in theory 'offered the population the chance to renew their support for the king whilst at the same time letting him know about their grievances' was, however, imposed by force.[82] Independence has certainly been a source of disappointment, and the coercion employed by the postcolonial state or the illicit enrichment which it guaranteed to its rentiers are bitterly resented. Such facts do not entirely prevent legitimacy or popular assent. At least the demand for self-respect, which foreign occupation made impossible and which is still intact today, has been partially satisfied – in spite of the cynical sentiments one hears across the continent which some people like to report. The wisdom of the 'small people' – particularly women – draws upon an almost mystical acceptance of the miseries of the human condition in order to come to terms with the power and its wrongdoing. For example, a Cameroonian woman, whose husband had been the victim of some machination, wrote:

> My benefactor, the abbot Etienne, is dead. My husband, Jean N., is in prison. I am unhappy and lost: my life is in a bad way. I am at the end of my tether. What must I do: fly like a bird? bring my benefactor back to life? give my husband his freedom? Oh, my Father, I don't know what to do. I spend days and nights holding my head, staring at the banana trees, tears streaming down my face as I think about my future life. I believe that the goodness of God the Father, his Son Jesus Christ and the Holy Spirit will help me to get through these endless days; man proposes and God disposes.[83]

However, it should not be assumed that this resignation is universal, for it can easily give way to anger. In 1977 the extraordinarily courageous protests of the market women of Guinea forced the Touré regime to vacillate and go on the defensive.[84] Street demonstrations are common throughout Africa. In thirty years of independence they have been seen in most of the continent's capitals and have sometimes brought about a trail of destruction. If one adds to these urban outbursts the rural revolts, land occupations, boycotts, strikes and school riots, one is forced to admit that Africa, contrary to a tenacious myth, is not a continent of political apathy.

In the intervals between these rushes of fever – which, until we have proof to the contrary, are no less frequent than elsewhere in the world – the capacity of regimes to institutionalise fundamental social conflicts is real, even if it does vary from one situation to another. Faced with the all-powerfulness of the administration, the single party does allow the 'little man' to express some of his grievances. This relationship is of course distorted by the effects of 'false identification' and 'closedness' induced by the dominance of a 'legitimate problematic' in politics.[85] Popular demands are necessarily expressed in the 'borrowed language' of development, nationality and the fashionable statist idiom. Nevertheless, as long as they respect the norms of 'political politeness', villagers can hope to have their voices heard, if not by the president of the Republic and his ministers, at least by their local representatives. They benefit in this respect from the traditional rivalry between the civil servants and the party cadres which encourages those who are subject to election to listen to them attentively every now and then and exercise a role of tribune *vis-à-vis* the bureaucracy.[86] The party also provides a good conciliating service for the resolution of local, interethnic or professional conflicts.[87] Finally, through the agency of its sub-organisations, it has communicated the social demands of women, and, at the price of frequent violent abuses it has enabled the youth to take its share of the loot through its militias, always ready to erect police barricades when they feel in need of a drink or to take advantage from its assigned tasks of repression.[88]

It is revealing that some of the most repressive regimes of the continent have been precisely the ones lacking a true single party either because the party had been emasculated by the faction in power or because its emergence dated from after the anti-colonial struggle and it had become too dependent upon the State for it to claim even a minimal degree of representivity. By contrast, where the single party has been most firmly established and where it brings together the most important members of the political class, following the logic of reciprocal assimilation of elites, the single party can paradoxically act as a check, counteracting the growing autonomy of presidential power and the preeminence of the bureaucracy, thereby contributing in a real way to the differentiation of the political arena. The examples of the Ivory Coast, Cameroon, Congo, Tanzania and, until the late 1980s, Kenya, follow this model. Furthermore, the increasing use of competitive ballots within the single party, along the lines of the Tanzanian or Kenyan system, favours the electoral expression of political refusal.[89] The representativeness of governments is not necessarily increased as a result, but at least political communication is improved.

One cannot conclude from this, as its praise singers have done, that the single-party system is in itself better adapted to African societies than the multi-party system. When it is authorised or tolerated, competition between parties very quickly latches onto divisions and conflicts which cannot be reduced to simple factional antagonisms, nor even ethnic ones. In Northern Nigeria, for example, first NEPU, then the People's Redemption Party, articulated the aspirations of the *talakawa* as opposed to the *sarakuna*. In Senegal, the *Parti démocratique sénégalais* (PDS) of Master Wade was a vehicle for peasant *malaise* in the 1970s before becoming in the 1980s the party which held out the hope of *sopi* (change) in the eyes of the youth. In Zaïre the *Union pour la démocratie et le progrès social* has been the voice of the middle classes who have lived on the margins of the regime and who have been impoverished by twenty years of erratic economic policy. The memory of banned parties, moreover, lives on in the collective historical memory, as was shown by the resurgence of the symbolic capital of the *Union des populations du Cameroun* after two decades of strict police censure.[90] Finally, the judges, barristers, press and parliaments attempt to balance the absolute primacy of the executive, and even if (as we know) their endeavours are only partially successful their conviction is sufficient to ensure that

251

from time to time – as, for example, in Tanzania, Kenya, Zambia or Zaïre – we see the outbreak of true political dissent.[91] These are all institutions, even if they are of foreign origin, which contribute towards the emergence of political mediation, once they have been 'appropriating reinterpretations'.[92]

It would doubtless be foolish to accord this phenomenon more significance than it deserves and to forget how often the single party is an evanescent apparatus caught between the hammer of presidential supremacy and the anvil of popular scepticism, incapable of defending a civilian regime against a military coup or of preventing the outbreak of wildcat strikes on the fringes of its trade-union monopoly. None the less, the concretisation of political societies has progressed sufficiently for the contestation or abandonment of these institutions to take on a sense other than that of the under-politicisation of the masses. Acts such as electoral abstention or the non-purchase of party cards are considered acts which betray either a social or a local political dissatisfaction which prove *a contrario* the solidification of a representative tissue.[93] Distancing themselves on this precise point from the paradigm of the yoke, analyses today take full account of popular participation in the configuration of the postcolonial State.[94] In doing so they acknowledge the more or less complete break between the contemporary political space and other arenas, such as precolonial institutions, religion, economy, ethnicity, family, social relations of production or of foreign influence. This is an important and undeniable conclusion which we must now make more precise and complete.

THE ROLE OF ESCAPE

Inasmuch as it is a plural space of interaction and enunciation, the State does not exist beyond the uses made of it by all social groups, including the most subordinate. The State buzzes with their constant murmur: the murmur of social practices which tirelessly fashion, deform and undermine the institutions and ideologies created by the highest of the high; the murmur, above all, of *Radio-Trottoir* ('pavement radio') or its white-collar counterpart, *Radio-Couloir* ('corridor radio'), which insolently ignore the embargoes of the censors and obstruct the totalitarian designs of the government and its 'legitimate problematic' with their black humour. There is no official policy which is not immediately deciphered in the back streets, no slogan which is not straightaway parodied, no speech which is not subjected to an acid bath of derision, no rally which does not resound with hollow laughter.[95] Despite the Latin sympathy one feels towards this phenomenon, the political impact of this popular parasitism of the splendours of the State is limited. The research of C.M. Toulabor on the attitudes of young Loméans shows that it has little potential for opposition or revolution.[96] It can only add nuance to domination and seems essentially to be an indication of an amusing, but fatalist, culture of impotence exemplified in this Mando-Negro song from the banks of the River Congo around 1970:

> I have been dead for a long time
> Drinking is my work
> Big centre-forward of red wine
> Give us the bottle!
> Give us the bottle!
> Ah, what can we do about it?
> My eyes become red with wine
> As I await the day of my death.[97]

This culture of juvenile derision is also a rapidly expanding culture of alcohol and drugs. Its favourite haunt is the bar where one can dance, boast and drink beers until dawn. Authoritarian governments either pretend to ignore them or profit from them directly. The resistance movements which directly challenged the colonial and then the postcolonial State drew upon other repertoires, such as the sacred, the ancient art of war, the tradition of women's associations and of trade-union militancy.

Nevertheless, just as carnival used to do in sixteenth-century Europe,[98] the culture of derision relativises the concept of the political arena and complicates it by adding a supplementary dimension. By showing that social actors cannot define themselves exclusively in relation to the scene, this culture resembles a box of secrets which, when searched, reveals a more general characteristic essential for our understanding of the State. From this point of view the Marxist imagery of struggle is as naïve as the liberal one of participation. Social groups do not necessarily act on the same level. South of the Sahara the key problem for the dominators is to find the dominated and then force them to settle down in a domestic social space where they can be further dominated and exploited.[99] Whilst waiting for this hegemony, some of the process of historical production evolves elsewhere in a remarkable burst of activity. The modernity of popular layers of society is largely independent of that of the 'decree men', as the people of Yaoundé call the men of power. The inadequacy of political tools is a measure of this independence.

To underline this fact, G. Hyden has developed the idea of 'an uncaptured peasantry'. This is a suggestive but none the less unfortunate expression.[100] Actors are found neither in nor outside the State. Rather, all actors, depending on circumstance, sometimes participate within a statist dimension and sometimes turn away from it. It is difficult to see how any problematic other than that of enunciation enables us to come to terms with these permanent movements. Our inability to see a dichotomy between the categories of 'bourgeoisie' or between the 'sectors' of the economy and our insistence upon the overlapping between the various social positions and the root-like functioning of the networks are reinforced by the observation of a final ambivalence. Exchanges within the sub-Saharan political systems have a double base.[101] Actors advance in an indirect way, 'by chameleon's footsteps', to use the picturesque metaphor of a young Malian.[102] Africans are past masters in the techniques of evasion and pretence which the colonials used to deplore so much: 'Depriving us of the possibility of defeating them in open battle, these scattered peoples have recourse to the best system of defence against us'.[103] State injunctions are ignored or subverted and met with an obstinate silence or, worse still, an impavid *ndiyo bwana* [Yes, sir, in Swahili] which one can be sure means a definitive refusal.[104] As ever, the small men take refuge in the 'things which cannot be stolen in order to escape from the incessant thefts' of the authorities.[105] As before, they prefer such tactics of evasion and silent reproach which characterise the 'predatory metabolism' which Izard described so well in the case of Yatenga.[106] They never pay more than lip-service to their adhesion to the State; sometimes, as in the case of the Tanzanian and Zaïrian 'show villages', which local farmers created in order to obey the land collectivisation measures but which they deserted as soon as the official inspections were finished, obedience to the State was no more than a decoy.[107]

Political action south of the Sahara contains many other examples of such 'creative dissimulation'[108] and is stamped with ambiguity responsible for its subtle but sombre appearance. Perfidy and denunciation are common currency. The uprising of the Nzambi-Mpungu sect in Kwilu in 1978, for example, enjoyed the active complicity of a faction of the territorial administration and of the Popular Youth Movement of the Revolution before being repressed in an horrific way. The leader of the sect, Kasongo, was protected by the local commissar, who took a share from the profits of his healing activities. He was accused of subversion and imprisoned several times, but was freed each time as a result of the personal interventions of the official. In the end the commissar, fearing that he was being compromised, betrayed Kasongo.

He supervised the extermination of the rebels with exceptional zeal and cruelty, and witnessed the public execution of his former associate who cursed him before he died with the words, 'My spirit will follow you all your life!' This sordid episode symbolised the entanglements of the revolt. Kasongo was a faith-healer by trade who had entered the Idiofa zone during the 1960s and had become a recruiting agent for the Nzambi-Mpungu sect, which, in all probability, had grown out of Kimbanguism. He won over some 'intellectuals' – a pastor and a clerk who had fallen on the wrong side of the administration – who introduced into his prophetic speech the more explicitly political heritage of the Mulelist and anti-colonial Messianic movements. Along with his correligionists he was not above profiting from embezzlements and other swindles at the same time as he practised his healing. In the course of the uprising in December 1977 and January 1978 the repertoire of the invisible and of magic combined with pillage, economic critique of the regime and the millenarian announcements of the return of Patrice Lumumba and Pierre Mulele.[109] This social and discursive cocktail is typical of sub-Saharan rebellions.[110] It is no more than the extreme symptom of this daily reality to which we have already referred; namely, that instead of being dressed in a single or predominant 'ideo-logic' or 'cultural scheme' (in the words respectively of Augé and Sahlins),[111] the political arena draws upon a plurality of 'time-spaces' to which all political actors subscribe.

Several of the principal dynamics of political identification are furthermore located on the margins of the State and owe more to the world environment or the continental expansion of a handful of peoples. The national space has no real claim on food, clothing or music. The progression of some common languages – such as Swahili, Lingala, Mandingo, Hausa and Fula – gradually modifies feelings of social identification and could in the future engender 'special solidarities' forming the basis of new 'imagined communities'.[112] The same can be said of the contemporary boom of religious cults from which will emerge a redefinition of social cohesion, of civic space even, following the model of the birth of the Greek *polis*.[113] The Islamic *umma* is already creating problems for the western model of the State, and Ivoirian commentators are openly worried about the hold of 'Yoruba cultural imperialism' over heavenly Christianity.[114] It is by no means impossible that these reconstructions of identity will one day become systematic, especially if they are combined with economic and military reordering around two or three regional axes of power. They demonstrate that the contours of the postcolonial State are not fully stabilised and that the idea that sometime in the future the colonial boundaries may be either altered or abolished is not absurd, notwithstanding the solid vested interests which would resist such a move. In truth, history – not just Africa's but Europe's and Asia's as well – is full of such examples of territorial adjustments. One should remember that empires and kingdoms more majestic than those of the Ivory Coast, Zaïre or Senegal now exist only in our memory.

In these circumstances it is hardly surprising that the spatial hold of the State is incomplete. There are some capitals which enjoy an effective domination of the national territory. The authorities of Yaoundé, Libreville, Abidjan and Dar-es-Salaam, for example, are in a position to impose taxes, the party system, vaccination and the currency on the whole of the population. However, the progressive incorporation of northern Cameroon into the Nigerian economy, for example, proves that their hold is fragile. Furthermore, some of the States which are generally thought of as stable do not meet these criteria: Somali bandits in the north-east districts of Kenya, and Diola separatism in the Casamance region of Senegal, for example, both expose the vulnerability of the State. Above all the list of provinces south of the Sahara which have detached themselves from all central authority grows inexorably longer: Angola, Mozambique and, with some qualifications, Chad and Uganda are *de facto* partitioned into several sovereign zones even if the fiction of their judicial integrity is piously upheld. The Central African Republic has effectively abandoned its eastern departments. From 1964 until 1986 Zaïre was unable to reduce the 'liberated zones' held by the *Parti de la révolution populaire* in the north of Shaba and the south of Kivu. In Zimbabwe, following the liberation struggle, the government experienced great difficulties in Matabeleland. And finally, some parts of Lagos or Douala are effectively no-go areas for the police.

The 'exit option' continues to be a viable strategy whose persistence is evident in the political arena which, when taken to extremes, leads to territorial sanctuaries.[115] It is nevertheless more common at the micro level of cohabitation with the State and is generally of a religious character. The coexistence is not completely peaceful because the State cannot officially agree to the existence of movements which refuse all civic obligations, such as respect for the national colours, censuses, electoral participation, incantation of party slogans, purchase of party cards, payment of taxes or of health care. However, the failure of the Zambian or the Cameroonian authorities to eject the bad apple left by the Jehovah's Witnesses is evidence of the futility of official policy. In Mobutu's words, 'churches, temples and mosques have sprung up like mushrooms'.[116] If all these places of worship do not set out to subvert the space of the State, very few of them commend themselves to the authorities, payment of taxes or the expectations of the ideology of development and national unity. In their actions they double up the statist root system with their own networks and provide logistical support to the 'exit option', all the more appreciated as the stagnation of the official economy forces the 'little men' to fall back on other social solidarities. Like the prophetic movements of the colonial period, contemporary sects ignore rather than contest the State. Their rivalry is all the more formidable because it makes conflict inevitable. Even when it becomes routine and aligns itself with *raison d'état* taking on a Gallican profile along the lines of Zaïrois Kimbanguism,[117] the so-called independent church fragments on the periphery and feeds social dissidence. In 1970 it was estimated that some 15,000 Kitawalists of the Zaïrian province of Equateur had retreated into the forest and lived an independent existence based upon farming and hunting. According to the very rare accounts available, they refused to use Zaïrian money except the 20-makuta note which bore a portrait of Lumumba, and they used coins from the First Republic. Their primary motive seems to have been rejection of taxes, a principle for which they declared themselves ready to fight.[118] Similarly, in Zambia, the Lumpa church, having made a pact with the United National Independence Party, set itself up as a peasant counter-society and effectively removed the region of Sioni from the authority of Lusaka: land was occupied without the agreement of local chiefs, and special shops were opened to insulate the faithful from all impious contact with the exterior. There, too, the entire process of incorporation into the state was being challenged, and persecution was not long in following.[119]

In cases of extreme dilapidation of the State – Zaïre, for example – the machinery of the Catholic and Reformed missions substituted for the failing organisational capacity of the public authorities, and in so doing provided avenues of political escape.[120] In Islamic societies, finally, the cultural model of *hegira* seems to legitimise the abandonment of the turbulence and turpitude of the City. Once more we see that disengagement from the area of the State can be a mental one consisting for the most part of a religious practice transcending the State. However, it is equally likely to give birth to other social spaces of a theocratic nature. A notorious example is the holy town of Touba in Senegal, which is also the headquarters of contraband with the Gambia. When President Senghor, visiting the town in 1972, asked the Mouride peasantry 'no longer to confine their activity to the framework of their religious community but to work also within the national framework', the Khalife Abdou Lahat M'Backé replied one year later: 'We Mourides live within an enclosure. Our lives are governed by the teachings of Amadou

Bamba.; beyond this we see barriers, we see Satan and all his work'.[121] Christian Coulon also records the even clearer example of the Tijani village of Medina-Gounass in Casamance whose population of several thousand live for a stretch of 3km along either side of the road to Guinea. Its founder, a personality endowed with a strong charisma, forbad all *bida* (innovations), made the wearing of the veil and prayer compulsory and banned dancing, wrestling and western schools. The community's only points of contact with the State are the sale of groundnuts and the payment of taxes with a tax base which assumes a tax-paying population of 5,000.[122]

These cases of collective dissidence, whether inspired by politics or religion, simply bring together the multiple individual practices of social escape within the hollowness of the State. The frontiers of the State are transgressed, the informal sector is a canker on the official economy, taxes are not collected, poaching and undisciplined exploitation of mineral resources become endemic, weapons circulate, resettled villages split up, the people appropriate the legitimate use of force to themselves and deliver summary justice, delinquency spreads, businesses suffer from languor induced by under-productivity, delays and absences.

The geographical mobility of Africans remains enormous. It is clear that the diversity of its expressions and motivations do not allow us to reduce it to a simple tactic of resistance or escape, to what certain Marxist authors have pejoratively described as 'a substitute for the class struggle'.[123] The search for a little bit of money – enough to enable one 'to stand up straight' and particularly to take a wife – the attraction of the town and all its riches, the curiosity of travel and boredom with life in the bush, drought or, if one is to believe the theoreticians of the articulation of modes of production, the structural necessity of a capitalist economy, all to a very large extent explain why migration is such a widespread and regular phenomenon. This is not to say that other factors such as the domination of elders and fear of their witchcraft, the underpayment of agricultural labour and the brutality of territorial administrations and the armed bands who patrol the countryside could also be significant, and perhaps even sufficient, reasons which explain why people leave their home.[124] Desertion is sometimes the only suitable response to the arbitrariness and the slovenliness of the State. Desertion from its institutions: for example, in 1982–83 the desertion rate amongst Cameroonian subjects in the *Service civique* was as high as 45 per cent.[125] Desertiom, too, from its space: hundreds of thousands of citizens of Guinea, Equatorial Guinea, Chad, Zaïre, Mozambique,

Rwanda, Burundi and Uganda have emigrated to escape from dictatorship or war. This reality translates into the continent's sad world record in the number of refugees. In comparison to the spectacle of unfortunate crowds hurrying towards frontiers and vegetating in reception camps, the brain drain seems unimportant. Nevertheless, the productive and innovative capabilities of African societies are hard hit by the loss of what is sometimes a large proportion of the few professionals who have received western training – Ghana, for example, lost between 50 per cent and 75 per cent of its graduates during the black years of the *kalabule* (black market).[126]

Escape, in the old sense of the word – the action of escaping from a place – is still one of the constituent strategies of the production of politics and social relations. The authors of *Histoire et coutumes des Bamoum* were correct in their assessment; 'running away' has by no means disappeared, it has remained as a major mode of historicity south of the Sahara, it persists in eroding the civic space, constraining the processes of accumulation of power and wealth and in making predacity easier than exploitation.

CONCLUSION
Of Terroirs* *and Men*

Take a look at the photograph opposite: Ahmed Sékou Touré, radiant, still young and dressed in a western suit, is crossing the rope footbridge of N'Zérékoré. We know what was waiting for Guinea, on the other side. Nevertheless, how can one be indifferent to the joyous forces which leap out of this snapshot, to the certainty that the film has indeed captured history in the making?

Throughout these pages we have seen societies, that is men and women, forge their own destiny, painting the fresco of their political modernity in broad brush-strokes. From one country to another the designs and the dominant colours differ so much that it might seem inappropriate thus to express oneself. But inasmuch as our objective was to construct a mode of reasoning and analysis, we do not feel obliged to impose a typology at the end of this book. It is more important in the short term to consider the sub-continental arena one last time. One lesson emerges from our subject which is difficult to refute, even if it does call into question the cherished thesis of the yoke. The State in Africa rests upon autochthonous foundations and a process of reappropriation of institutions of colonial origin which give it its own historicity; it can no longer be taken as a purely exogenous structure.

This affirmation is, however, immediately complicated by a second conclusion: the social foundations of any State are socially, geographically and culturally heterogeneous. The most spectacular manifestation of this characteristic is the extreme complexity of political identifications from one context to another south of the Sahara. Coexisting within the heart of any given power are several time-spaces,

---

*Translator's note: 'Terroir' is a term taken from French historiography – specifically Paul Bois *Paysans de l'Ouest* (Paris, 1960) and much used by Fernand Braudel, *L'Identité de la France: espace et histoire* (Paris, 1986).

whose adjustment is problematic and always precarious. Consequently the State in Africa is not an 'integral State' but a State of 'variable polarisation' to use an expression of Guy Nicolas.[1] Its structure is fundamentally indirect, as studies of Nigerian or Zaïrian society have shown.[2] Some of its architects – Ahmadu Bello, for example – have moreover sometimes thought of it in this way.[3] The majority of African politicians have, however, yearned for a total, 'well-policed' State, not so very different from the absolutist dreams of Campanella during the Renaissance.[4] In doing so they have shown themselves closer to the authoritarian reformers of the Middle East than to the Indian fathers of independence.[5] It should be said that up until now they have failed to achieve this ideal; the development of an 'integral State' from a 'soft State', which at one time it was tempting to predict,[6] has not taken place despite advances in the technology of social control. Seen from this angle the postcolonial State is not dissimilar from its colonial and precolonial predecessors. It obeys a law of incompletion.[7] It functions as a rhizome of personal networks and assures the centralisation of power through the agencies of family, alliance and friendship, in the manner of ancient kingdoms, which possessed the principal attributes of a State within a lineage matrix, thereby reconciling two types of political organisation wrongly thought to be incompatible.[8]

From a scientific perspective, such a form of power should not be labelled as pathological. It is one political affirmation amongst others, which does not lack for historical equivalents and whose mark we now know is to be found in the most powerful centralised state structures of the west. Recalling 'the chequered history of the origins and formation of the state in western Europe', Georges Lavau observes that, '"the new monarchies" which became established from the sixteenth century were not formed outside of (or *in opposition to*) feudalism but rather were established *in the heart of* feudalism and made use of many of its elements'.[9] The French Third Republic – the Gramscian prototype of hegemony – did not achieve its cultural integralism until late in its life, according to some historians.[10] In the same way, the concentric and unitary interpretation of the birth of the Greek city-state has now been thoroughly discredited. It seems that, far from establishing itself as the result of 'the erosion of clan and tribal distinctions', the city-state depended heavily upon the full development of genos, phraty and tribe as 'indispensable expressions of the cohesion of the *philia* which united the citizens'.[11] The emergence of the great Hellenic monarchies or the Roman Empire were in no sense synonymous with political and cultural homogenisation:

> Rather than imagining a reduction or a cessation of political activities through the effects of a centralised imperialism, one should think in terms of the organisation of a complex space. Much vaster, much more discontinuous, much less closed than must have been the case for the small city-states, it was also more flexible, more differentiated, less rigidly hierarchised than would be the authoritarian and bureaucratic Empire that people would attempt to organise after the great crisis of the third century. It was a space in which the centres of power were multiple; in which the activities, the tensions, the conflicts were numerous; in which they developed in several dimensions; and in which the equilibria were obtained through a variety of transactions. It is a fact, at any rate, that the Hellenistic monarchies sought much less to suppress, curb, or even completely reorganise the local powers than to lean on them and use them as intermediaries and relays for the levy of regular tributes, for the collection of extraordinary taxes, and for supplying what was necessary to the armies. It is a fact as well that by and large Roman imperialism tended to prefer solutions of this kind to the exercise of a direct administration. The policy of municipalisation was a rather constant line, whose effect was to stimulate the political life of the cities within the larger framework of the Empire.[12]

The question of the singularity of the trajectory of the State in Africa in relationship to the west European source in any case remains intact. The fundamental problem, so often discussed and in the end somewhat academic, is to know to what extent the adequacy (or inadequacy) of sub-Saharan political configurations, based on the Weberian model, allow (or more probably do not allow) us to speak of them as 'States'. Max Weber himself would have had his doubts. He believed that 'only in the west did one find the complete range of characteristics which describe "the state" (defined as a political *institution* with a written "constitution", a rationally established legal system and an adminis- tration based upon rational rules or "laws" and competent civil servants)'.[13]

Amongst these 'possible similarities', the classification of sub-Sah- aran powers with their complete lack of national 'ideo-logic'[14] in the category of 'authoritarianism' rather than 'totalitarianism' seems self- evident, if one perceives their generally collegial character. It seems clear that we are discussing 'powers of the state concentrated in the hands of individuals or groups who are above all preoccupied with separating their political fate from the hazards of a competitive game over which they are unable to exercise total control'.[15] However, the question remains. Are we talking about 'powers of the State' or, as many writers have argued, simply 'powers' of a patrimonial or neo- patrimonial type? The differences between the sub-Saharan postcolo- nial State and the bureaucratic ideal beloved of Weber are obvious. At one extreme one only talks of the State out of diplomatic convention: during the years of civil war and *kalabule*, Uganda, Chad and Ghana were able to uphold their claim to the status of the State only in the eyes of the international system.[16] The denial of State status, however, frequently occurs through a rather basic methodological error. Deter- mination to avoid the traps of evolutionism and teleology can lead to another simplification: the comparison of an institutional transplant scarcely a hundred years old in Africa with the institutional maturity achieved in the west after a process of many centuries.[17]

The contemporary orbit of politics south of the Sahara, inasmuch as it refers to the past trajectory of the continent, is capable of change one day. Seen in this light, the long-term prison sentence is more like probation. It is, of course, never a mere mechanical reproduction of forms taken from the past but rather a theme on which the actors can improvise. Beyond this one may also wonder whether black Africa isn't on the point of changing register and entering one of those periods of upheaval around which history is woven from millennium to millen- nium. The preeminence of strategies of extraversion and escape, lack

of overexpoitation, the mediocrity of accumulation, under-productivity in the economy, wealth valued in men rather than goods and
land, extensive representation of space in terms of mobility, a plural
conception of time: all these characteristics probably owe much to weak
demographic pressure.[18] We are encouraged to wonder about the future
in the light of rapid demographic change and the social changes which it
either accompanies or provokes – accelerated urbanisation, economic
and financial destabilisation, spoiling of the ecological environment,
modifications in the relationship between the individual and time and
space. There is no reason why we should not imagine that one day these
forces could lead to an intensification of economic exploitation and
political domination resulting in an institutionalisation of processes
closer to the Weberian ideal of the bureaucratic State. Bertrand Badie
and Pierre Birnbaum argue that 'the State has had to impose itself at the
heart of societies which, as a result of extreme resistance of their
traditional structures or of particular technological or political circumstances, have had the greatest difficulty in proceeding to the new
distribution of tasks, implied first of all by the crisis of their own social
formation and then by the arrival of a market economy'. Citing the
examples of the Netherlands and England, they found it 'significant
that the development of State structures has been much less distinct in
societies which were able to profit fully and without resistance from the
new facts of the world economy than in the societies found on their
immediate periphery'.[19] In the case of Africa, economic dependency
and the persistent strength of the old dominant groups could eventually
favour this scenario.

There is, on the other hand, nothing to stop us thinking that the
disintegration of the family and the financial collapse of the western-
inspired school system will prevent the state from ensuring the minimal
political socialisation of youth. The gangs of children who depend upon
their street wisdom and theft for their survival, and whose only contact
with the government is through police raids and the truncheons of the
commissariat, perhaps presage a mass dissidence which is already in
evidence in the form of banditry but which for the moment at least is
kept in check by the strength of the networks.[20] Economic pauperisation and the proliferation of syncretic cults likewise tend to increase
the share of the 'Vacuum' at the expense of the hegemonic 'Full'.
Urbanisation thus does not constitute any guarantee for the State: the
Kenyan political system, firmly entrenched in the rural constituencies,
is experiencing some difficulty in integrating the *wananchi* of the town,
as was evidenced by the widespread looting in Nairobi in 1982 or
respective percentages of abstention during the last elections.[21]

The future of the State will depend not so much upon some over-arching factor as upon the unpredictable development of social struggles. The historicity of politics in Africa is here, very classically, a historicity of *terroirs*. Conflicts wrongly labelled ethnic, rural revolts and interfactional rivalry can all be traced back to this.[22] The systematic identification of cleavages related to *terroirs* should consequently be a priority in which the collaboration of anthropologists, historians, geographers and linguists is indispensable.[23] There is no paradox in our conclusion that the well-known work of Paul Bois, *Paysans de l'Ouest*, which examines the region of Sarthe during the French Revolution, is an excellent methodological introduction to the study of Africa![24] This in turn will be dependent upon historical sociology, which alone is capable of filling the gap of our extraordinary ignorance of Africa's social formations. This recognition of the historicity of *terroirs* upon which the State rests is the final nail in the coffin of the received wisdom concerning the inherent extraneity of the postcolonial State. It is quite true that the national government is freely identified with an exogeneous sovereignty. In Ahafo, the Accra government is considered as *aban* (exterior, imposed) and not as *oman* (indigenous, autochthonous).[25] When the Maka of Cameroon go to the *sous-préfecture*, they say that they are going to 'the land of the white man' to indicate in an amusing way that they are entering a universe which is quite foreign to their world of village and lineage.[26] These representations are the norm in situations of authoritarianism or extreme centralisation.[27] They became inevitable in Africa as soon as its leaders defined the 'well-policed' State against society in direct line with the colonial model. None the less, they should not be taken as common currency. They are not peculiar to contexts of extraversion and nor are they proof of the structural extraneity of power; they are simple facts of consciousness. The majority of phenomena – such as 'tribalism' or 'instability' – seen as indicative of the exogeneous nature of the postcolonial State, are indicative, on the contrary, of the reappropriation of institutions of foreign origin by indigenous societies. Far from betraying a lack of historicity or cultural alienation, they attest to the vitality of the colonial graft and the political action which it unleashed. They reveal the density of the social foundations of power rather than their absence. Such observations are not, of course, enough to dignify postcolonial systems with Weberian hallmarks. They do, however, at least allow us legitimately to talk about such structures in terms of the concept of the State, and to a certain extent grant them the benefit of the doubt.

Objections to counter this semantic usage are found wanting whether one makes the differentiation of power in relationship to social stratification, to a dominant political force or to communitarian cleavages the decisive indication of the presence of the State.[28] We have seen this in the course of this work: the generality of factional struggles and the important role of political entrepreneurs give us cause to doubt the absolute preeminence of communitarian organisation over individualised social relationships; economic and religious forces tend to set themselves up as civil society, distinct from the sphere of the government in the strict sense of the term; the sphere of government also gains autonomy *vis-à-vis* ethnic identification, cases of personal charisma or political movements, and has experienced substantial institutionalisation; the adherence to indigenous conceptualisations of politics, which are to a certain extent indifferent to bureaucratic ideas of the *res publica*, is tinged with the simultaneous belief in other repertoires of exterior origin and statist inclinations. Finally, one cannot discount the importance of the eye of the foreign diplomat in contributing to the formation of an African culture of the State. This is not a facetious argument, and serves as an opportune reminder that the production of 'internal dynamics' is indissoluble from the interference of 'outside dynamics'.

The reservations which one must continue to feel about the statist qualifications of postcolonial powers south of the Sahara derive from other processes of 'de-differentiation'. Amongst the most important of these is the irritation of individual strategies which attack institutions from within. Contrary to widely held opinion, African societies are not 'holistic' and nor are they societies in which individualism is particularly 'underdeveloped'.[29] The importance of individuals, even if they have 'neither hearth nor home', seems to be one of the constants in the social life of the continent. In former times, land tenure, the art of war and the mastery of the invisible were its favourite locations, which formed many 'indeterminate areas within the lineage'. The conquest of power, whether segmentary or centralised, did not escape the pernicious influence of such competition. Opportunities of school, salaried work, commerce, agriculture or politics have all, then, focused personal ambitions.[30] In short, one can argue that rather than providing evidence of a communitarian concept of existence, the very compelling restraints in education, in the world of the invisible and in daily social activities simply curb what for want of a better word we continue to call 'individualism', penalising its impetuosity and thereby preserving society from its centrifugal strength.[31] Without doubt this 'individualism' has little in common with the western 'individualism', if indeed this notion has retained its coherence across the centuries.[32] It is none the less true that far from representing the havens of harmony and solidarity so dear to the fantasies of ideologues, African societies have been haunted throughout their history by the spectre of individual violence: that of witchcraft and symbolic manducation.[33] The contemporary civic arena is affected through factional struggles, the rhizomatic functioning of the State and the 'politics of the belly'. One could add that recourse to talk of ethnicity or the exercise of universal suffrage conform to communitarian logic much less frequently than is supposed.[34]

Belief in the holistic character of African societies has been one of the mistakes of interpretation which has had the most serious effect on the comprehension of these societies.[35] This is not to conclude, in the manner of C.G. Rosberg or R.H. Jackson, that the rehabilitiation of the discredited notion of 'personal power' is desirable, nor that postcolonial regimes are structured solely by the action of political entrepreneurs.[36] On the one hand, the expression of personal strategies is not incompatible with the creation of a system of social stratification. The two are linked and ought to be thought of together, including from a Marxian perspective.[37] Inasmuch as it is an historical fact, the definition of a person has a bearing upon the production of inequality. Polygamy, for example, makes the inheritance of patrimony uncertain by encouraging dispersal and social redistribution and by denying some children in a family the possibility of obtaining educational certificates.[38] Reciprocally, one of the major debates in the new problematisation of politics, of which the postcolonial State is the vector, has similarities with relations between the self and the self and between the self and others.[39] The tenor of the city-state, the ethos in which it recognised itself and through which it was to be distinguished from western modernity, the possible invention of a democratic culture will be born *in fine* from this transformation.

On the other hand, actors perform in a context of which they are tributaries. To this extent their progression is not unpredictable. Nor is it predetermined. The structure of inequality, the quest for hegemony, the legitimate problematic of politics are only worth as much as their enunciation to which they are subjected on behalf of the actors. Thus, Michel Foucault defined power as 'an action over actions':

> It is a total structure of actions brought to bear upon possible actions; it incites, it induces, it seduces, it makes easier or more difficult; in the extreme it constrains or forbids absolutely; it is nevertheless always a way of acting upon an acting subject or acting subjects by virtue of their acting or being capable of action.

The analysis must then move towards the intelligence of this mode of 'government', in the sense that the word was understood in the six-teenth century, that is, the 'way in which the conduct of individuals or of groups might be directed'. 'To govern [...] is to structure the possible field of action of others.'[40] In order to designate this mode of 'govern-ment' – or, as Foucault would say, 'governmentality' – we have made use of the Cameroonian expression 'politics of the belly'. Since we began the book with a description of a cartoon by Plantu, let us finish it in a similar way: the caricaturist of the *Cameroon Tribune* whose cartoon of the infamous goat saying, 'I graze, therefore I am', suggests very precisely the contours of what is politically thinkable in postcolonial African societies.[41] This is not to say that this form of 'governmentality' belongs to a traditional culture whose contours cannot possibly be avoided, nor that it avoids the critique of a growing number of African citizens, and nor finally that it covers the totality of the continent's political 'ideo-logic'. But it has crushed most of the strategies and institutions, in particular the Christian churches, the nationalist parties and the civil services, which have worked for the advent of a modern Africa. The experiences of governments which attempted to break free from their grip have either not lasted a long time or have in their turn been absorbed by its practices.

Africa does not, however, 'eat' in a uniform way. The regimes of political manducation vary from the Nigerian or Zaïrois *bulimina* to the Tanzanian or Nigerien slimmers' diet, from the prophetic appetite of an Ahmed Sékou Touré or a Macias Nguema to the schizophrenic greed of Marxist-Leninist leaders, or from the redeeming austerity of a Jerry Rawlings or a Murtala Mohammed to the voluptuous appetite of a Félix Houphouët-Boigny or a Jomo Kenyatta. One must be aware of these variations rather than pontificate upon an eternal Africa. The study of sequences of events, ideological sedimentations, judicial codifications, institutional formalisations, structures for creating or redistributing wealth, political alliances and social exclusions and of the geographic and demographic morphology of each country should enable us to differentiate the national trajectories of politics, pursue comparisons and – perhaps – draw up a typology of the State south of the Sahara.[42]

Africa, furthermore, holds no monopoly in matters of the belly, nor of escape. For proof we need look no further than the increase in academic works dedicated to the description of 'corruption', 'clien-telism' and 'migrations'. Assuming that such commonly found phe-nomena should not be taken as simply morbid, we are forced to admit that the analysis of politics in Africa opens the door to a wider reflection on the nature of politics. Yes, banal Africa – exoticism be damned! –

leads us to some general lessons of methodology. If the majority of phenomena which it has allowed us to see and which taken together serve to typify it, are also found under other skies without none the less being seen as distinctive characteristics of systems of power in Asia, America or Europe, it is perhaps more a matter of degree or proportion. Let us first of all establish whether strategies of 'straddling', for example, are more or less decisive in Abidjan or Lagos than in Moscow, Beijing, Singapore, Washington or Paris! As Max Weber showed in his classic account of magic, in truth intellectual dispositions intervene in this uneven treatment of facts. The condescending perplexity of the observer faced with the political practices south of the Sahara derives less from the fact that these are in themselves astonishing than that such an observer is unable (or unwilling) to reconstruct the subjectivity of the African actors and remains instead a complacent hostage to the paradigm of the yoke.[43] In many respects Africa is a mirror. However distorting it may be, it reflects our own political image and has a lot to teach us about the springs of our western modernity.[44]

But it is no less true that political action in Africa can rightly be perceived as singular as a result of 'the essential historicity of meanings': '"Institutions" which are apparently similar may be radically different because when plunged into another society they are understood with different meanings'.[45] From this point of view the grand concepts of political science are as misleading as those, for example, of the type of anthropology denounced by R. Needham.[46] The munificence of a Houphouët-Boigny towards his community doubtless has little in common with that of Augustus, nor has the 'corruption' of an African civil servant with that of his Soviet, Asian or American equivalent because the symbolisation inherent in these practices, and the material stakes which they carry, are not the same from one culture or historical situation to another. This is clearly evident if one remembers that the theme of the 'belly' south of the Sahara carries several meanings. 'To eat,' is to nourish oneself – 'The glorification of wealth in its most tangible form: the stomach,' observed Michel Leiris when describing 'the impressive hemisphere of black wood [...] , piled high with maize cakes' and 'calabashes of meat' whose presentation marked the high point of a party given by the sovereign of Rey Bouba.[47] It is also to accumulate, exploit, defeat, attack or kill with witchcraft.[48]

Africa, understood in its banality, thus invites comparative study but a comparativism which is far removed from the soft comparativism of the 1960s. Our purpose ought not to be to smooth over the irregularities of historical singularity, but on the contrary to foreground them in order to confront the 'thick descriptions'[49] which we make as research-ers in the field or as users of theory or methodology. It is on this level of work that the notion of 'political trajectory' has some usefulness. It is necessary within the *longue durée* to untangle the lines of historical concatenation, and the schemes of cultural invention underlying con-temporary societies – and to do so in a teleonomic rather than a teleological way, 'not as the effect of a wish, of a plan or a design, but as the unwished result of mechanisms which can be analysed in a purely causal way'.[50] It is possible that in the end these political trajectories will resolve themselves in a universal model of power. None the less, such an idea is methodologically suspect.[51] Symbolic activity has cultural connotations, and political activity is an eminently symbolic activity. In short, the art of power has much in common with the art of love or eating: even if the positions of servitude and domination are limited in number – as in love or alimentation – it would hardly advance our analysis to subsume them all within a single genre of human nature even if we could determine what this was. Despite similar biological beha-viour, the ethic of pleasure amongst the Greeks, Romans, Chinese, the Udritic nomads of Saudi Arabia or western troubadours was not, thanks be to God, uniform, and this naturally is what matters, even if the relative character of facts does not necessarily lead to a relativism of values.[52] In a similar way, the study of politics should be devoted to the understanding of what R. Boudon calls the 'situated rationalities', that is to say, the comprehension of the 'good reasons' which lead to such and such a practice.[53] At the risk of sinking in western provincialism and thereby renouncing the claims of science, this understanding should seek to comprehend the outer limits and the reverse side of what is wrongly thought to be the universal norm.

Such noble intentions, however, come up against one doubt which our survey should have made tangible. We have seen how *homo mandu-cans*, this man who eats , is also a man who flees, a *homo fugens*. In Africa, the share of social defection, the capacity of actors to place themselves outside the political obligations stipulated by the State and the role of escape remain, if not intact, at least real, in anticipation of a hypothetical monopoly of central legitimacy which in Europe was only achieved by the absolutist regimes.[54] But we have also demonstrated that sub-Saharan Africa is no more conspicuously original in their incomplete-ness, whatever may have been the determining role of the specific representations of the invisible. Heterogeneity and incompleteness are essential features of any society. Only the growth of the State or totalitarianism and the efficiency of technology obscure this essential characteristic in the industrialised world. The interest of the African trajectory lies in the fact that it reminds us of this general, even essential, fact. Western thought is, however, incapable of conceptualising such a propriety and of recognising the respective parts of what we have called the 'Full' and the 'Vacuum': 'We can only collect it because it is collectable; we can only categorise it because it is categorisable. But all collection, all categorisation, all organisation which we institute or discover sooner or later reveals itself to be partial, incomplete, fragmentary, insufficent – and even, what is most important, intrinsically deficient, problematic and in the end incoherent,' writes C. Castoriadis.[55]

If we accept Castoriadis' proposition that 'what holds a society together is the overall hold of its world of meanings',[56] we can only progress by furthering the analysis of the 'imaginary social meanings' which predominate south of the Sahara; no longer taking into consideration the actors and their strategies, as – conforming to methodological individualism – we have done in this work, but on the contrary examining the regimes of statements in the specific contexts of their enunciation. Rather than the overly equivocal concepts of culture, ideo-logic, legitimate problematic and hegemony which we have occasionally used in our argument, the concept of 'governmentality' is more likely to avoid the trap of unwarranted totalisation. There is indeed no conceivable 'governmentality' which does not refer to the enunciation of power, at least if one considers the work of Michel Foucault subsequent to *Discipline and Punish*. It remains the case, however, that the premature death of the philosopher prevented him from pursuing this reflection to its conclusion. It also remains the case that the applicability of this concept to historical situations other than the one Foucault labelled as the 'great closing' in his *Madness and Civilisation* is debatable. Finally, it remains the case that Foucault himself was reproached precisely for being guilty of excessive monism, obliterating what Michel de Certeau describes as 'the polytheism of disseminated practices, dominated but not erased' which subsist within 'the privilege of the panoptic mechanism'.[57]

The study of 'governmentalities', historically situated on long-run trajectories, henceforward passes through a narrow door; that which consists of identifying, in any given society, the principal discursive genres of politics, which are necessarily disparate and fragmentary, of restoring their dialogue with the past and in referencing the actual procedures of their interweaving, which are constituent parts of the 'imaginary social meanings' of which C. Castoriadis speaks. Thus will emerge the cultural tenor of politics in the given society. Thus will become clear the dimension of the 'Vacuum' which structures political usage in as much as it can be understood as 'ways of talking': the role of all these effects of *enchâssement* which intercut the enunciation of politics, and which in the end prevent us from reducing social interaction to a dyadic model of the emission and reception of a discourse, or indeed to the dichotomy of dominators and dominated.[58] The invention of politics in contemporary Africa will then appear in the vibrant complexity of which the rope bridge, stretched across this century, offers us a powerful image.

Notes

PREFACE TO ENGLISH EDITION

1. N. Elias *What is Sociology?* New York, Columbia University Press, 1978. p.130.
2. J. Ferguson *The Anti-Politics Machine. 'Development', Depoliticization and Bureaucratic Power in Lesotho,* Cambridge, Cambridge University Press, 1990.
3. A. Giddens *The Nation-State and Violence,* Berkeley, University of California Press, 1987.

PREFACE

1. *Cameroon Tribune* (Yaoundé), 9th Feb. 1985.
2. *La Gazette* (Douala), 515, 6th Dec. 1984, pp. 3 and 14. For a similar case, see also 4th Sept., ibid., 565, 1986, pp. 2 and 6.
3. M. de Certeau, 'Une pratique sociale de la différence: croire' in Ecole Française de Rome, *Faire croire. Modalités de la diffusion et de la réception des messages religieux du xiie au xve siècle,* Rome, Ecole française de Rome, 1979, pp. 363-383.
4. 'President's name used in fraud bid – Prosecution', *Daily Nation* (Nairobi), 6th Oct. 1984.
5. *Cameroon Tribune* (Yaoundé), 6th April 1988.
6. *La Gazette* (Douala), 604, 1988, p. 13.
7. M. Magassouba, 'Guinée: les militaires s'empiffrent!', *Africa international* (Dakar), 204, 1988, p. 26.
8. 'Report of the Constitution Drafting Committee', Lagos, 1976, 1: V, cited and commented on by G. Williams, T. Turner, 'Nigeria' in J. Dunn, ed., *West African States: Failure and Promise. A Study in Comparative Politics,* Cambridge, Cambridge University Press, 1978, p. 133.
9. Cited in A. Sissoko, 'Aspects sociologiques de l'intégration nationale en Afrique noire occidentale: espace politico-administratif et intégration à l'Etat: le cas de la Côte d'Ivoire', Nice, Faculté des lettres et sciences humaines, 1982, pp. 463-464. See also speech of Houphouët-Boigny to a Sanwi delegation *Fraternité-Hebdo* (Abidjan), 2nd Oct. 1981: 'Vous avez demandé des sous-préfectures, c'est ce qu'on nous demande partout où nous passons.'
10. J.-A. Mbembé, *Les Jeunes et l'ordre politique en Afrique noire,* Paris, L'Harmattan, 1985, pp. 122 and passim.
11. P. Laburthe-Tolra, *Les Seigneurs de la forêt. Essai sur le passé historique, l'organisation sociale et les sources ethniques des anciens Bëti du Cameroun,* Paris, Publications de la Sorbonne, 1981, p. 233.

12. J.-F. Bayart, 'Le politique par le bas en Afrique noire. Questions de méthode', *Politique africaine*, 1, Jan. 1981, pp. 53-82; 'La revanche des sociétés africaines', *ibid.*, 11, Sept. 1983, pp. 95-127; 'Les sociétés africaines face à l'Etat', *Pouvoirs*, 25, 1983, pp. 23-39.

13. G. Deleuze, *Foucault*, Paris, Éd. de Minuit, 1986, pp. 23 and 62; H. Sluga, 'Foucault à Berkeley. L'auteur et le discours', *Critique*, 471-472, Aug-Sept. 1986, pp. 840-856.

14. P. Birnbaum, J. Leca, eds., *Sur l'individualisme*, Paris, Presses de la Fondation nationale des sciences politiques, 1986.

15. J.-F. Bayart, 'L'énonciation du politique', *Revue française de science politique*, 35 (3), June 1985, pp. 343-373.

INTRODUCTION: THE HISTORICITY OF AFRICAN SOCIETIES

1. M. Rodinson, *La Fascination de l'islam*, Paris, Maspero, 1980; E.W. Saïd, *Orientalism*, London, Routledge & Kegan Paul, 1978.

2. R. Dumont, *L'Afrique noire est mal partie*, Paris, Le Seuil, 1962, and, with M.-F. Mottin, *L'Afrique étranglée*, Paris, Le Seuil, 1980; C. Turnbull, J.-C. Pomonti, *L'Afrique trahie*, Paris, Hachette, 1979; G. Chaliand, *L'Enjeu africain, Stratégie des puissances*, Paris, Le Seuil, 1980; E. M'Bokolo, *Le Continent convoité*, Paris, Montréal, Études vivantes, 1980; G. Gosselin, *L'Afrique désenchantée*, Paris, Anthropos, 1978; C. Casteran, J.-P. Langellier, *L'Afrique déboussolée*, Paris, Plon, 1978; R. Dumont, *Pour l'Afrique, j'accuse*, Paris, Plon, 1986.

3. Sir Harry H. Johnstone, *History of the Colonization of Africa by Alien Races*, Cambridge, Cambridge University Press, 1899.

4. J. Vansina, 'Knowledge and perceptions of the African past' in B. Jewsiewicki, D. Newbury, eds., *African Historiographies. What History for Which Africa?* Beverly Hills, Sage Publications, 1986, pp. 28-41.

5. A. Grosrichard, *Structures du sérail. La Fiction du despotisme asiatique dans l'Occident classique*, Paris, Le Seuil, 1979. See also C. Guinzburg, *Enquête sur Piero della Francesca*, Paris, Flammarion, 1983; L. Valensi, *Venise et la Sublime Porte. La Naissance du despote*, Paris, Hachette, 1987.

6. F. de Medeiros, *L'Occident et l'Afrique (xiiie - xve siècle)*, Paris, Karthala, 1985.

7. Montesquieu, *De l'esprit des lois*, XXI, 2 in *Œuvres complètes*, Paris, Gallimard, 1951, vol. II, pp. 602-603.

8. Voltaire, *Essai sur les mœurs*, Paris, Garnier, 1963, vol. II, p. 306.

9. *Ibid*, vol. II, p. 305 et vol. I, p. 23.

10. G.W.F. Hegel, *La Raison dans l'histoire. Introduction à la philosophie de l'Histoire*, Paris, U.G.E., 1965, p. 247.

11. Montesquieu, *De l'Esprit des lois*, p. 602.

12. Capitaine Vallier, cited by P.-P. Rey, *Colonialisme, néo-colonialisme et transition au capitalisme. Exemple de la 'COMILOG' au Congo-Brazzaville*, Paris, Maspero, 1971, p. 363 and H. Deschamps, 'Préface' in J. Binet,

Budgets familiaux des planteurs de cacao au Cameroun, Paris, ORSTOM, 1956, p. 5. For an attempt to evaluate the social effects of the forest ecology scientifically, see G. Sautter, *De l'Atlantique au fleuve Congo. Une géographie du sous-peuplement. République du Congo, République gabonaise*, Paris, La Haye, Mouton, 1966 (especially pp. 996-999).

13. L.H. Gann, P. Duignan, eds. *Colonialism in Africa. 1870-1960.* Volume I: *The History and Politics of Colonialism. 1870-1914.*, Cambridge, Cambridge University Press, 1969, p. 10.

14. J.F.A. Ajayi, 'Colonialism: an episode in African history' in L.H. Gann, P. Duignan, eds., *Colonialism*, pp. 497-509.

15. J.-P. Sartre, 'Préface' in F. Fanon, *Les Damnés de la terre*, Paris, Maspero, 1961, pp. 9 and 20.

16. M. Augé, *Pouvoirs de vie, pouvoirs de mort*, Paris, Flammarion, 1977, pp. 21 ff.

17. J.-L. Amselle, ed., *Le Sauvage à la mode*, Paris, Le Sycomore, 1979, p. 15. *Cf.* M. Augé, *Pouvoirs* and *Symbole, fonction, histoire. Les Interrogations de l'anthropologie*, Paris, Hachette, 1979.

18. A. Adler, *La Mort est le masque du roi. La Royauté sacrée des Moundang du Tchad*, Paris, Payot, 1982 and M. Izard, *Gens du pouvoir, gens de la terre. Les Institutions politiques de l'ancien royaume du Yatênga (Bassin de la Volta Blanche)*, Cambridge, Cambridge University Press, Paris, Éditions de la Maison des sciences de l'Homme, 1985 – in contrast with, for example, J. Dunn, A.F. Robertson, *Dependence and Opportunity: Political Change in Ahafo*, Cambridge, Cambridge University Press, 1973; J.D.Y. Peel, *Ijeshas and Nigerians. The Incorporation of a Yoruba Kingdom, 1890s-1970s*, Cambridge, Cambridge University Press, 1983; M. Staniland, *The Lions of Dagbon: Political Change in Northern Ghana*, Cambridge, Cambridge University Press, 1975.

19. G.A. Almond, J.S. Coleman, eds., *The Politics of the Developing Areas*, Princeton, Princeton University Press, 1960, pp. 3-64 and p. 576; G.A. Almond, G.B. Powell Jr, *Comparative Politics. A Developmental Apoproach*, Boston, Little Brown, 1966, p. 2.

20. From *The Gold Coast in Transition* (Princeton, Princeton University Press, 1955) to *The Politics of Modernization* (Chicago, Chicago University Press, 1965), the itinerary of a David Apter is exemplary in this respect.

21. Its star performers – B. Moore, R. Bendix, P. Anderson, T. Skocpol – have nothing to say on the question. S.N. Eisenstadt makes use of the findings of Africanist anthropology but cannot resist the charms of the formalism of models. I. Wallerstein has moved on from postcolonial regimes to 'world systems' and has inclined towards the methodological positions of the dependency school since the publication of *Africa: The Politics of Unity. An Analysis of a Contemporary Social Movement* (New York, Random House, 1967). A.R. Zolberg's pathway is the sole exception, even though he in his turn has moved a long way from his initial preoccupations in sub-Saharian Africa.

22. J.F.A. Ajayi, 'Colonialism: an episode in African history' in L.H. Gann, P. Duignan, eds., *Colonialism*, pp. 497-509; J.-L. Amselle, 'Sur l'objet de l'anthropologie', *Cahiers internationaux de sociologie*, 56, Jan.-Jul. 1974, pp. 98 ff.

23. T Smith, 'The underdevelopment of development literature: the case of dependency theory', *World politics*, XXXI (2), Jan. 1979, pp. 247-288.

24. F.H. Cardoso, 'Les États-Unis et la théorie de la dépendance', *Tiers monde*, XVII (68), Oct.-Dec. 1976, pp. 805-825.

25. B. Barry, *Le Royaume du Waalo. Le Sénégal avant la conquête*, Paris, Karthala, 1985, p. 34 (First edition 1972).

26. See in particular P.-P. Rey, *Colonialismes*. and *Les Alliances de classes*, Paris, Maspero, 1976; C. Meillassoux, *Femmes, greniers et capitaux*, Paris, Maspero, 1975. For a critical presentation of this school, *cf.* F. Pouillon, (ed.), *L'Anthropologie économique. Courants et problèmes*, Paris, Maspero, 1976; H. Moniot, 'L'anthropologie économique de langue française' in Y. Roux, (ed.), *Questions à la sociologie française*, Paris, PUF, 1976, pp. 85-124; W. van Binsbergen, P. Geschiere, eds., *Old Modes of Production and Capitalist Encroachment. Anthropological Explorations in Africa*, London, KPI, 1985; F. Cooper, 'Africa and the world economy', *The African Studies Review*, 24 (2-3), Jun.-Sept. 1981, pp. 13-15; B. Jewsiewicki, J. Letourneau, ed., *Mode of Production: the Challenge of Africa*, Sainte-Foy, SAFI Press, 1985.

27. B. Badie, *Le Développement politique*, Paris, Economica, 1980, pp. 50 ff.; A.R. Zolberg, 'L'influence des facteurs "externes" sur l'ordre politique interne' in M. Grawitz, J. Leca, ed., *Traité de science politique*, Paris, PUF, 1985, vol. I, p. 575.

28. G.A. Almond, G. Bingham Powell Jr., *Comparative Politics*, p. 285.

29. D. Apter, *The Politics of Modernization*, p. 42.

30. S. Amin, *Le développement du capitalisme en Côte d'Ivoire*, Paris, Ed. de Minuit, 1967, pp. 265 and 279-280.

31. See – apart from the collection of the *Review of African Political Economy* – G. Arrighi, J.S. Saul, *Essays on the Political Economy of Africa*, New York, Monthly Review Press, 1973; I.G. Shivji et al., *The Silent Class Struggle*, Dar es Salaam, Tanzania Publishing House, 1974; I.G. Shivji, *Class Struggles in Tanzania*, New York, Monthly Review Press, 1976; M. Mamdani, *Politics and Class Formation in Uganda*, London, Heinemann, 1976; C. Leys, *Underdevelopment in Kenya. The Political Economy of Neo-Colonialism, 1964-1971*, London, Heinemann, 1975; J.S. Saul, *The State and Revolution in Eastern Africa*, London, Heinemann, 1979; Y. Tandon, A.M. Babu, *Debate on Class, State and Imperialism*, Dar es Salaam, Tanzania Publishing House, 1982.

32. *Cf.*, apart from the works already quoted of P.-P. Rey, H. Bertrand, *Le Congo. Formation sociale et mode de développement économique*, Paris, Maspero, 1975.

33. I. Wallerstein, *The Modern World System. Capitalist Agriculture and the Origins of the European World Economy in the Sixteenth Century*, New York, Academic Press, 1974, p. 351.

34. B. Badie, P. Birnbaum, *Sociologie de l'État*, Paris, Grasset, 1979, pp. 178 and 181.

35. G.P. Murdock, *Africa. Its Peoples and their Culture History*, New York, MacGraw Hill, 1959.

36. E. Shils, *Political Development in the New States*, Gravenhage, Mouton, 1962, pp. 30-31.

37. *Cf.* G. Hyden, 'Political science in post-independence Africa' in Organization for Social Science Research in Eastern Africa, *Political Science Workshop*, Nairobi, 15-19 Apr. 1985, (unpublished paper), who emphasises the importance of the studies of F.W. Riggs and S.P. Huntington. At the same time, I. Wallerstein was describing the decline of the great nationalist parties ('The decline of the party in single-party African states' in G. La Palombara, M. Weiner, eds., *Political Parties and Political Development*, Princeton, Princeton University Press, 1966, pp. 201-214).

38. L. Kuper, M.G. Smith, eds., *Pluralism in Africa*, Berkeley, University of California Press, 1969.

39. A.R. Zolberg, 'The structure of political conflict in the new states of tropical Africa', *The American Political Science Review*, LXII (1), March 1968, pp. 70-87 and *Creating Political Order. The Party-States of West Africa*, Chicago, Rand MacNally, 1966.

40. C. Coulon, 'Système politique et société dans les États d'Afrique noire. A la recherche d'un système conceptuel nouveau', *Revue française de science politique*, 22 (5), Oct. 1972, pp. 1050-1051.

41. E. Shils, *Political Development*, p. 30.

42. G. Kitching, 'Politics, method and evidence in the "Kenya debate"' in H. Bernstein, B.K. Campbell, eds., *Contradictions of Accumulation in Africa*, Beverly Hills, Sage Publications, 1985, p. 121 and F. Cooper, 'Africa and the world economy', pp. 1-2 and 9.

43. See in particular G. Althabe, *Oppression et libération dans l'imaginaire. Les communautés villageoises de la côte orientale de Madagascar*, Paris, Maspero, 1969; M. Augé, *Théorie des pouvoirs et idéologie. Étude de cas en Côte d'Ivoire*, Paris, Hermann, 1975; M. Augé, ed., *La Construction du monde. Religion, représentations, idéologie*, Paris, Maspero, 1974. P. Bonnafé, a sympathiser to this approach, nonetheless concluded: 'The dominated have their own way of thinking. Even in relation to the dominant ideology their point of view is different. Some of their ideological elements are irreducible.' (*Nzo lipfu, le lignage de la mort. La sorcellerie, idéologie de la lutte sociale sur le plateau kukuya*, Nanterre, Labethno, 1978, p. 330.) For a sociology of cultural alienation in other respects A. Touré, *La civilisation quotidienne en Côte d'Ivoire. Procès d'occidentalisation*, Paris, Karthala, 1981 and J.-P. Lycops, *L'Agression silencieuse ou le génocide culturel en Afrique*, Paris, Anthropos, 1975.

44. Cited by R. Girardet, *L'Idée coloniale en France de 1871 à 1962*, Paris, La Table Ronde, 1972, p. 54.

45. H. Deschamps, 'Comment incorporer l'Union française aux programmes d'histoire de l'enseignement du second degré', *L'Information historique*, Nov.-Dec. 1954, pp. 20-21, cited in M.Semidei, 'De l'Empire à la décolonisation. A travers les manuels scolaires français', *Revue française de science politique*, XV (1), Feb. 1966, p. 730.

46. F. Eboussi Boulaga, *La Crise du Muntu. Authenticité africaine et philosophie*, Paris, Présence africaine, 1977, pp. 15-16.

47. *Cf.*, for example, G.A. Almond, G.B. Powell, *Comparative Politics*, pp. 325 ff. and J.S. Coleman, 'Conclusion: the political systems of the developing areas' in G.A. Almond, J.S. Coleman, eds., *The Politics of the Developing Areas*, p. 533. Amongst the many critiques of the developmentalist norm, see above all D. Cruise O'Brien, 'Modernization,

order, and the erosion of a democratic ideal: American political science, 1960-1970', *Journal of Development Studies*, IX (4), Jul. 1972, pp. 351-378.

48. G.A. Almond, G.B. Powell, *Comparative Politics*, p. 2.

49. T. Ranger, 'The invention of tradition in colonial Africa' in E. Hobsbawm, T. Ranger, eds., *The Invention of Tradition*, Cambridge, Cambridge University Press, 1983, pp. 211-262; L. de Heusch, 'Tradition et modernité politiques en Afrique noire', *Cahiers internationaux de sociologie*, XLIV, Jan.-Jun. 1968, pp. 63-78; M. Staniland, *The Lions of Dagbon*; L. Ndoricimpa, C. Guillet, ed., *L'Arbre mémoire. Traditions orales du Burundi*, Paris, Karthala, 1984; and, for a more general critique of the idea of tradition, R. Bendix, 'Tradition and modernity reconsidered', *Comparative Studies in Society and History*, IX (3), Apr. 1967, pp. 292-346.

50. F. Eboussi Boulaga, *La Crise du Muntu*, pp. 152 ff. See also J.-P. Hountondji, *Sur la 'philosophie africaine'. Critique de l'ethnophilosophie*, Paris, Maspero, 1977.

51. J. Goody, *La Raison graphique, La domestication de la pensée sauvage*, Paris, Minuit, 1979, p. 95.

52. J. Champaud, *Villes et campagnes du Cameroun de l'Ouest*, Paris, ORSTOM, 1983, pp. 205 ff. and 306 ff.; A. Franqueville, 'La population rurale africaine face à la pénétration de l'économie moderne: le cas du Sud-Cameroun', in C. Blanc-Pamard et al., *Le développement rural en question*, Paris, ORSTOM, 1984, pp. 433-445; S.S. Berry, *Fathers Work for their Sons*, Berkeley, University of California Press, 1985, chap. 2 ; J.-M. Gibbal, *Citadins et villageois dans la ville africaine; l'exemple d'Abidjan*, Paris, Maspero, Grenoble, Presses Universitaires de Grenoble, 1974; 'Villes africaines au microscope', *Cahiers d'études africaines*, 81-83, XXI (I-3), 1981, pp. 7-403; G. Hyden, 'La crise africaine et la paysannerie non capturée', *Politique africaine*, 18 Jun. 1985, p. 105; R.E. Stren, 'The ruralization of African cities: learning to live with poverty', *African Studies Association Annual Meeting*, New Orleans, Nov. 1985, (unpublished paper); J. Havet, ed., *Le Village et le bidonville. Rétention et migrations des populations rurales d'Afrique*, Ottawa, Editions de l'Université d'Ottawa, IDIC, 1986.

53. D.A. Low, J. Lonsdale, 'Introduction: towards the new order, 1945-1963' in D.A. Low, A. Smith, eds., *History of East Africa*, Oxford, Clarendon Press, 1976, vol. III, p. 12.

54. *Marchés coloniaux*, 23rd Nov. 1946, quoted by J.-R. de Benoist, *L'Afrique occidentale française de 1944 à 1960*, Dakar, NEA, 1982, p. 71.

55. J. Marseille, *Empire colonial et capitalisme français. Histoire d'un divorce*, Paris, Albin Michel, 1984; B. Reysset, 'Commerce extérieur et décolonisation', *Marchés tropicaux et méditerranéens*, 21st Dec. 1984, pp. 3129-3165. For a study of the 'adaptive behaviour' of French capitalism confronted by economic nationalism, see G. Rocheteau, J. Roch, *Pouvoir financier et indépendance économique en Afrique. Le cas du Sénégal*, Paris, ORSTOM, Karthala, 1982.

56. J. Marseille, *Empire colonial*, pp. 368-370 and C.-R. Ageron, *France coloniale ou parti colonial?* Paris, PUF, 1978, pp. 297-298. *Cf.* also J.

Lonsdale, 'States and social processes in Africa: a histographical survey', *African studies review*, XXIV (2-3), Jun.-Sept. 1981, pp. 193-194. By way of contrast, in the very different context of the Belgian Congo, J.-L. Vellut can speak of the 'colonial bloc' and 'the incestuous mix' between the business world and the Colonial Ministry, without lapsing into a simplistic and mechanistic explanation of decolonisation. ('Articulations entre entreprises et Etat: pouvoirs hégémoniques dans le bloc colonial belge (1908-1960)' in Laboratoire Connaissance du Tiers-Monde, *Actes du colloque Entreprises et entrepreneurs en Afrique (xixe et xxe siècles)*, Paris, l'Harmattan, 1983, vol. II, pp. 49-79.

57. G. Clarence -Smith, *The Third Portuguese Empire (1825-1975). A Study in Economic Imperialism*, Manchester, Manchester University Press, 1985.

58. N. Swainson, *The Development of Corporate Capitalism in Kenya (1918-1977)*, London, Heinemann, 1980, pp. 5 ff.; J. Spencer, *KAU. The Kenya African Union*, London, KPI, 1985, pp. 10-11 and 78; M. Blundell, *So Rough a Wind*, London, Weidenfeld and Nicolson, 1964; G. Wasserman, 'The independence bargain: Kenya Europeans and the land issue, 1960-1962', *Journal of Commonwealth Political Studies*, IX (2), July 1973, pp. 99-120: D.W. Throup, *Economic and Social Origins of Mau Mau, 1945-1953*, London, James Currey, 1987. For an analysis of comparable cleavages in Tanganyika at the time of German colonisation, see J. Iliffe, *A Modern History of Tanganyika*, Cambridge, Cambridge University Press, 1979, pp. 148 ff., and for a subjective account in the context of French colonisation – in the Ivory Coast in the aftermath of the Second World War – see R. Gautherau, *Journal d'un colonialiste*, Paris, Seuil, 1986.

59. See, for example, C. Messiant, 1961, *L'Angola colonial. Histoire et société. Les prémisses du mouvement nationaliste*, Paris, EHESS, 1983, (unpublished paper); R. Pelissier, *La Colonie du minotaure. Nationalismes et révoltes en Angola (1926-1961)*, Orgeval, Pelissier, 1978, chap. 1.

60. F. Gaulme, 'La fin des pionniers', *Marchés tropicaux et méditerranéens*, 9th August 1985, pp. 1975-1977. On the limits of Portuguese colonisation in Angola, see R. Pélissier, *Les Guerres grises. Résistance et révoltes en Angola (1845-1941)*, Orgeval, 1977, pp. 25 ff.

61. R.A. Joseph, *Radical Nationalism in Cameroun. Social Origins of the UPC Rebellion*, Oxford, Oxford University Press, 1977.

62. A. Giddens, *Central Problems in Social Theory. Action, Structure and Contradictions in Social Analysis*, London, Macmillan, 1979.

63. G. Balandier, *Anthropo-logiques*, Paris, PUF, 1974, p. 189.

64. E. Terray, 'Le débat politique dans les royaumes de l'Afrique de l'Ouest. Enjeux et formes', *Revue française de science politique*, 38 (5), Oct. 1988, pp. 720-730.

65. M. Izard, *Gens du pouvoir, gens de la terre*, pp. 481-482. Cf. also J.H.M. Beattie, 'Checks on the abuse of political power in some African states: a preliminary framework for analysis', *Sociologus*, 9 (1), 1959, pp. 97-114.

66. A. Adler, *La Mort est le masque du roi*, pp. 269 ff., 297 and 154.

67. C. Tardits, *Le Royaume bamoum*, Paris, A. Colin, 1980; J.-C. Barbier, *L'Histoire présente, exemple du royaume kotokoli au Togo*, Bordeaux, Centre d'etude d'Afrique noire, 1983; S.N. Eisenstadt, M. Abitbol, N.

Chazan, 'Les origines de l'État: une nouvelle approche', *Annales E.S.C.*, 6, Nov.-Dec. 1983, p. 1234. See also A. Adler, *La Mort.*.

68. F. Cooper, 'Africa and the world economy', p. 14; J. Guyer, 'Household and community', *African Studies Review*, 24 (2-3), 1981, pp. 87-137; J.-P. Dozon, *La Société bété, Côte d'Ivoire*, Paris, Karthala, 1985, pp. 65 ff.; G. Dupré *Les Naissances d'une société. Espace et historicité chez les Beembé du Congo*, Paris, ORSTOM, 1985, pp. 259 ff. and 'Une mise en perspective' in B. Jewsiewicki, J. Letourneau, eds., *Mode of Production*, pp. 47-48.

69. I. Wilks *Asante in the Nineteenth Century. The Structure and Evolution of a Political Order*, Cambridge, Cambridge University Press, 1975.

70. On these attempts at 'authoritarian modernisation' *cf.*, for example C. Tardits, *Le Royaume bamoum*; I. Wilks *Asante*; and J.D.Y. Peel, *Ijeshas and Nigerians* and 'Conversion and tradition in two African societies: Ijebu and Buganda', *Past and Present*, 77, Nov. 1977, pp. 108-141; A. Pallinder -Law, 'Aborted modernization in West Africa? The case of Abeokuta', *Journal of African History*, XV (1), 1974, pp. 65-82; F. Raison -Jourde, ed., *Les Souverains de Madagascar. L'Histoire royale et ses résurgences contemporaines*, Paris, Karthala, 1983 and S. Ellis, *The Rising of the Red Shawls. A Revolt in Madagascar (1895-1899)*, Cambridge, Cambridge University Press, 1985; J. Bureau, *Éthiopie, un drame impérial et rouge*, Paris, Ramsay, 1987; J. Vansina, *Les Anciens Royaumes de la savane*, Léopoldville, IRES, 1965.

71. G. Dupré, *Les Naissances d'une société*, chap. 3 and 4.

72. P. Mercier, *Tradition, changement, histoire. Les 'Somba' du Dahomey septentrional*, Paris, Anthropos, 1968. *Cf.* also M. Fortes, *The Dynamics of Clanship among the Tallensi*, London, Oxford University Press, 1945 and R. Verdier, *Le pays kabiye, cité des dieux, cité des hommes*, Paris, Karthala, 1982.

73. For concrete examples, see R. Horton, 'Stateless societies in the history of West Africa', in J.F.A. Ajayi, M. Crowder, eds., *History of West Africa*, New York, Columbia University Press, 1976, vol. I, pp. 72-113 and M. Dent 'A minority party: the United Middle Belt Congress', in J.P. Mackintosh, ed., *Nigerian Government and Politics*, London, George Allen and Unwin, 1966, pp. 461-507 (on the Igbo and Tiv of Nigeria); J.-M. Gastellu, *L'Égalitarisme économique des Serer du Sénégal*, Paris, ORSTOM, 1981.

74. I. Wilks, 'The state of the Akan and the Akan states; a discursion', *Cahiers d'études africaines*, 87-88, XXII (3-4), 1982, pp. 231-249.

75. See especially K.O. Dike, *Trade and Politics in the Niger Delta*, Oxford, Oxford University Press, 1956; G.I. Jones , *Trading States of the Oil Rivers: a Study of Political Development in Eastern Nigeria*, London, Oxford University Press, 1963; B. Müller, 'Commodities as currencies: the integration of overseas trade into the internal trading structure of the Igbo of South East Nigeria', *Cahiers d'études africaines*, 97, XXV (1), 1985, pp. 57-77; P.E. Lovejoy, *Salt of the Desert Sun. A History of Salt Production and Trade in the Central Sudan*, Cambridge, Cambridge University Press, 1986, pp. 258-259; J.F.A. Ajayi, R.A. Austen, 'Hopkins on economic imperialism in West Africa', *Economic History Review*, 25, 1972, pp. 303-306; F. Gaulme, *Le Pays de Cama. Un ancien État côtier du*

Gabon et ses origines, Paris, Karthala, Centre de recherches africaines, 1981; B. Freund, *The Making of Contemporary Africa. The Development of African Society Since 1800*, Bloomington, Indiana University Press, 1984, chap. 2; Y. Person, 'Samori' in C.-A. Julien et al., *Les Africains*, Paris, Editions Jeune Afrique, 1977-1978, vol. I, p. 265.

76. E. Leach, *Political Systems of Highland Burma*, London, Bell, 1954; G. Balandier, *Anthropologie politique*, Paris, PUF, 1967 and *Sens et puissance. Les dynamiques sociales*, Paris, PUF, 1971. See, for example, M. Dupire, *Organisation sociale des Peuls. Études d'ethnographie comparée*, Paris, Plon, 1970; J.-P. Warnier, *Échanges, développement et hiérarchies dans le Bamenda pré-colonial (Cameroun)*, Stuttgart, Franz Steiner Verlag Wiesbaden GMBH, 1985; M. Izard, 'La politique extérieure d'un royaume africain: le Yatênge au xixᵉ siècle', *Cahiers d'études africaines*, 87-88, XXII (3-4), pp. 363-385.

77. J. Strandes, *The Portuguese Period in East Africa*, Nairobi, East African Literature Bureau, 1961; H.S. Morris, *The Indians in Uganda*, London, Weidenfeld and Nicolson, 1968; J.-C. Penrad, 'La présence isma'ilienne en Afrique de l'Est. Note sur l'histoire commerciale et l'organisation communautaire', in *Marchands et hommes d'affaires asiatiques*, Paris, EHESS, 1988, pp. 221-236.

78. J.S. Coleman, 'The politics of sub-saharan Africa' in G.A. Almond, J.S. Coleman, *Politics in Developing Countries*, pp. 247-249.

79. C. Messiant, *1961. L'Angola colonial*'; R. Pélissier, *Les guerres grises*; W.G. Clarence-Smith, 'Les investissements belges en Angola, 1912-1961' in Laboratoire Connaissance du Tiers-Monde, *Actes du colloque Entreprises et entrepreneurs*, vol. I, pp. 423-441.

80. C.W. Newbury, 'Trade and authority in West Africa from 1850 to 1880' in L.H. Gann, P. Duignan, eds., *Colonialism in Africa*, pp. 66-99; J.-P. Warnier, *Échanges, développement et hiérarchies*; P.E. Lovejoy, *Salt of the Desert Sun*, chaps 8 - 10; J. Hogendorn, M. Johnson, *The Shell Money of the Slave trade*, Cambridge, Cambridge University Press, 1986.

81. I. Wilks, *Asante*, chap. 1.

82. P. Laburthe -Tolra, *Les Seigneurs de la forêt. Essai sur le passé historique, l'organisation sociale et les normes éthiques des anciens Beti du Cameroun*, Paris, Publications de la Sorbonne, 1981, pp. 210-211 and *Le Tombeau du soleil*, Paris, Le Seuil, Odile Jacob, 1986; G. Donnat, *Afin que nul n'oublie. L'itinéraire d'un anti-colonialiste. Algérie, Cameroun, Afrique*, Paris, L'Harmattan, 1986.

83. P. Laburthe -Tolra, *Les Seigneurs de la forêt*, p. 211.

84. *Cf.*, respectively, J. Copans, 'Ethnies et régions dans une formation sociale dominée. Hypothèses à propos du cas sénégalais', *Anthropologie et société*, II (1), 1978, p. 97; J.-L. Amselle, *Les Négociants de la savane*, Paris, Anthropos, 1977, p. 275; C. Meillassoux, 'Rôle de l'esclavage dans l'histoire de l'Afrique occidentale', *Anthropologie et sociétés*, II (1), 1978, p. 132.

85. J.-P. Warnier, *Echanges, développement et hiérarchies*, p. 3. See also G. Balandier, *Anthropo-logiques*, pp. 184 ff. and J.-L. Amselle, 'Ethnies et espaces: pour une anthropologie topologique' in J.-L. Amselle, E. M'Bokolo, ed., *Au cœur de l'ethnie. Ethnies, tribalisme et État en Afrique*, Paris, La Découverte, 1985, pp. 23-34.

86. G. Balandier, *Sociologie actuelle de l'Afrique noire*.
87. G. Dupré, *Les Naissances d'une société*, and *Un ordre et sa destruction*, Paris, Editions de l'ORSTOM, 1982.
88. See, in particular J. Dunn, A.F. Robertson, *Dependence and Opportunity*: M. Staniland, *The Lions of Dagbon*; J.D.Y. Peel, *Ijeshas and Nigerians*. D.B. Cruise O'Brien, *Saints and Politicians*, Cambridge, Cambridge University Press, 1975; C. van Onselen, *Chibaro. African Mine Labour in Southern Rhodesia. 1900-1933*, London, Pluto Press, 1976; T. Ranger, *Peasant Consciousness and Guerilla War in Zimbabwe. A Comparative Study*, London, James Currey, Berkeley, University of California Press, 1985; R. Palmer, N. Parsons, eds., *The Roots of Rural Poverty in Central and Southern Africa*, London, Heinemann, 1977; L. Vail, L. White, *Capitalism and Colonialism in Mozambique: a Study of Quelimane District*, London, Heinemann, 1980; R. Palmer, 'The Zambian peasantry under colonialism: 1900-1930, in Center of African Studies, *The Evolving Structure of Zambian Society*, Edinburgh, University of Edinburgh, 1980, pp. 1-20; W. Beinart, C. Bundy, *Hidden Struggles in Rural South Africa*, London, James Currey, Berkeley, University of California Press, Johannesburg, Ravan Press, 1987.
89. J. Lonsdale, 'States and Social processes in Africa', pp. 189 ff.
90. F. Cooper, 'Africa and the world economy', and *From Slaves to Squatters. Plantation Labour and Agriculture in Zanzibar and Coastal Kenya. 1890-1925*, Nairobi, Kenya Literature Bureau, 1981, p. 18; G. Hyden, *Beyond Ujamaa in Tanzania. Underdevelopment and an Uncaptured Peasantry*, London, Heinemann, 1980, pp. 38-39.
91. J.-P. Chauveau, J.-P. Dozon, 'Colonisation, économie de plantation et société civile en Côte d'Ivoire', *Cahiers ORSTOM, série sciences humaines*, XXI (1), 1985, pp. 63-80 and J.-P. Chauveau, J. Richard, *Bodiba en Côte d'Ivoire. Du terroir à l'Etat: petite production paysanne et salariat agricole dans un village gban*, Abidjan, Centre ORSTOM de Petit Bassam, 1977. For a more sophisticated analysis, see F. Ruf, 'Différenciations sociales et encadrement agricole: l'exemple du Centre-Ouest ivoirien' in P. Geschiere, B. Schlemmer, ed., *Terrains et perspectives*, Paris, ORSTOM, Leiden, Africa-Studiecentrum, 1987, pp. 77-92. See also, on Nigeria J.D.Y. Peel, *Ijeshas and Nigerians*, pp. 115 ff. and S.S. Berry, *Cocoa, Custom and Socio-Economic Change in Rural Western Nigeria*, Oxford, Clarendon Press, 1975.
92. M.P. Cowen, *Wattle Production in the Central Province: Capital and House-hold Commodity Production, 1903-1964*, Nairobi, 1976, and *Patterns of Cattle Ownership and Dairy Production, 1900-1965*, Nairobi, 1974, and 'Commodity production in Kenya's central province' in J. Heyer, P. Roberts, G. Williams, eds., *Rural Development in Tropical Africa*, London, Macmillan, 1981, pp. 121-142.
93. G. Kitching, *Class and Economic Change in Kenya. The Making of an African Petite-Bourgeoisie*, New Haven, Yale University Press, 1980, chap. iv, v and xi ; T. Ranger, *Peasant Consciousness*; J.-P. Chauveau, J.-P. Dozon, 'Colonisation, économie de plantation et société civile'.
94. D.A. Low, J. Lonsdale, 'Introduction' in D.A. Low, A. Smith, eds., *History of East Africa*, p. 12.
95. G. Hyden, *Beyond Ujamaa*; F. Cooper, 'Africa and the world economy',

pp. 51-52.

96. F. Cooper, *ibid*, pp. 51-52. This theory was much debated in the eight-
ies, particularly in the columns of the *Journal of African History*.

97. A.O. Hirschmann, 'Exit, voice and the state', *World Politics*, XXXI (1),
Oct. 1978, p. 94.

98. Quoted in C. Tardits, *Le Royaume bamoum*, p. 558.

99. R.H. Bates, *Essays on the Political Economy of Rural Africa*, Cambridge,
Cambridge University Press, 1983, pp. 41-42.

100. M. Izard, *Gens du pouvoir, gens de la terre*, pp. 479-480.

101. M. Gluckman, *Order and Rebellion in Tribal Africa*, London, Cohen and
West, 1963.

102. I. Wilks, *Asante*, pp. 534 ff.

103. V. Lanternari, *Les mouvements religieux des peuples opprimés*, Paris, Maspero, 1962 and M. A as, *Prophets of Rebellion. Millenarian Protest Movements against the European Colonial Order*, Chapel Hill, University of
North Carolina Press, 1979, pp. 184-185.

104. W.G. Clarence-Smith, *Slaves, Peasants and Capitalists in Southern Angola,
1840-1926*, Cambridge, Cambridge University Press, 1979, pp. 76-77.

105. J. Bazin, 'Guerre et servitude à Ségou', in C. Meillassoux, ed., *L'Esclavage en période précoloniale*, Paris, Maspero, 1975, pp. 135-181; L. de
Heusch, *Le Roi ivre ou l'origine de l'État*, Paris, Gallimard, 1972.

106. F. Raison-Jourde, 'Introduction', in F. Raison-Jourde, ed., *Les Souverains de Madagascar*, pp. 7-68.

107. J.D.Y. Peel, 'Olaju: a yoruba concept of development', *Journal of Development Studies*, 14 (2), Jan. 1978, pp. 139-165.

108. D.C. Dorward, 'Ethnography and administration. A study of Anglo-
Tiv "working-misunderstanding"', *Journal of African History*, XV (3),
1974, pp. 457-477 and F.A. Salamone, 'The social construction of colonial reality: yauri emirate', *Cahiers d'études africaines*, 98, XXV (2), 1985,
pp. 139-159.

109. E. M Bokolo 'Le Roi Denis. Grandeur et déclin d'un souverain gabonais' in C.A. Julien et al., ed., *Les Africains*, vol. VI, pp. 71-95; P.
Laburthe-Tolra, 'Martin Paul Samba, du service à la rébellion au Kamerun', *ibid.*, vol. XII, pp. 296-327; T.O. Ranger, 'African reactions to the
imposition of colonial rule in East and Central Africa' in L.H. Gann, P.
Duigan, eds., *Colonialism in Africa*, pp. 304 ff.

110. J. Lonsdale 'States and social processes in Africa', pp. 190-191.

111. J.-L. Amselle, E. Grégoire, 'Complicités et conflits entre bourgeoisies
d'État et bourgeoisies d'affaires au Mali et au Niger' in E. Terray, ed.,
L'État contemporain en Afrique, Paris, L'Harmattan, 1987, p. 37. On
Angola, see W.G. Clarence-Smith, 'Class structure and class struggles
in Angola in the 1970s', *Journal of Southern African Studies*, VII (1), Oct.
1980, pp. 116 ff; C. Gabriel, *Angola, le tournant africain?* Paris, Ed. La
Brèche, 1978.

112. M. Delauney, *De la casquette à la jaquette ou de l'administration coloniale à la
diplomatie africaine*, Paris, La Pensée universelle, 1982, pp. 159 ff.

113. R. Jeffries, 'Rawlings and the political economy of underdevelopment in
Ghana', *African Affairs*, 81 (324), Jul. 1982, pp. 307-317; E.J. Berg
'Structural transformation versus gradualism: recent economic devel-
opment in Ghana and the Ivory Coast' in P. Foster, A.R. Zolberg, eds.

Ghana and the Ivory Coast. Perspectives on modernization, Chicago, The University of Chicago Press, 1971, pp. 187-230.

114. Z. Laïdi, *Les contraintes d'une rivalité. Les superpuissances et l'Afrique (1960-1985)*, Paris, La Découverte, 1986, chap. v.

115. G. Dauch, D. Martin, *L'Héritage de Kenyatta. La transition politique au Kenya. 1975-1982*, Paris, L'Harmattan, Aix-en-Provence, Presses Universitaires d'Aix-Marseille, 1985, p. 178.

116. D. Bach, 'L'insertion ivoirienne dans les rapports internationaux' in Y.-A. Fauré, J.-F. Médard, ed., *État et bourgeoisie en Côte d'Ivoire*, Paris, Karthala, 1982, pp. 113 ff.; J. Baulin, *La politique africaine d'Houphouët-Boigny*, Paris, Ed. Eurafor-Press, 1980; R. Higgott, 'Structural dependence and decolonisation in a West African land-locked state: Niger', *Review of African Political Economy*, 17, Jan.-April 1980, pp. 48 ff.; J.-F.Bayart, 'La politique extérieure du Cameroun (1960-1971)', *Revue française d'études politiques africaines*, 75, March 1972, pp. 47-64 and *La politique africaine de François Mitterrand*, Paris, Karthala, 1984; D. Bigo, *Forme d'exercice du pouvoir et obéissance en Centrafrique (1966-1979). Élément pour une théorie du pouvoir personnel*, Paris, Université de Paris-I, 1985, pp. 335 ff.; C.M. Toulabor, *Le Togo sous Eyadema*, Paris, Karthala, 1986, pp. 137 ff.

117. J.-C. Willame, 'La politique africaine de la Belgique à l'épreuve: Les relations belgo-zaïroises (1978-1984)', *Les Cahiers du CEDAF*, 5, Aug. 1985, pp. 1-112.

118. Sources: Interviews conducted in Dakar. See also. J. Mac Rae, J.-F. Devret, *Évolutions et perspectives du Kenya*, s.l. (Paris), ECODEV, SEDES, 1983, p. 4.

119. A. Giddens, *Central Problems in Social Theory*, pp. 76 ff. and 93.

120. J.-P. Sartre, 'Préface' in F. Fanon, *Les damnés de la terre*, p. 9.

121. X. Godard, 'Quel modèle de transports collectifs pour les villes africaines? Cas de Brazzaville et Kinshasa', *Politique africaine*, 17, March 1985, p. 42.

122. See, in particular N. Akam, A. Ricard, *Mister Tameklor, suivi de Francis le Parisien par le Happy Star Concert Band de Lomé (Togo)*, Paris, SELAF, ORSTOM, 1981.

123. T.O. Ranger, *Dance and Society in Eastern Africa. 1890-1970. The Beni Ngoma*, London, Heinemann, 1975, p. 76; J. Spencer, *KAU*, pp. 77 and 104-105; R. Buijtenhuijs, *Le Mouvement 'mau-mau': une révolte paysanne et anticoloniale en Afrique noire*, The Hague, Mouton, 1971, pp. 189-190.

124. E.J. Collins, 'Ghanaian highlife', *African Arts*, X. (1), Oct. 1976, pp. 62-67 and *E.T. Mensah, the King of Highlife*, London, Off the Record Press, no date.

125. J.D.Y. Peel, 'Qlaju'; I. Wilks, *Asante*, pp. 590 ff. and 673 ff.; G. Dupré, *Les Naissances d'une société*, pp. 259 ff.

126. Quoted by I. Wilks, *Asante*, pp. 308-309.

127. F. Gaulme, *Le Pays de Cama*, p. 151; Marquis de Compiègne, *Afrique équatoriale. Gabonais-Pahouins-Gallois*, Paris, Plon, 1876, p. 185; reports of 'evolués' to Governor General Félix Eboué cited by J.-R. de Benoist, *L'Afrique occidentale française de 1944 à 1960*, Dakar, NEA, 1982, p. 28.

128. Marquis de Compiègne, pp. 186 ff.

129. T.O. Ranger, *Dance and Society*, p. 127. Imported cloths are still preferred to local cloths. (E. Ayina, 'Pagnes et politique', *Politique africaine*, 27, Sept.–Oct. 1987, pp. 47–54).

130. G. Balandier, *Sociologie des Brazzavilles noires*, Paris, Presses de la Fondation nationale des sciences politiques, 1955, pp. 92-93.

131. *Libération*, 27 Sept. 1985, p. 33. See also declarations of Guinean novelist W. Sassine, *Jeune Afrique*, 2 April 1986, pp. 51-52.

132. A.R. Zolberg, 'L'influence des facteurs "externes" sur l'ordre politique "interne"' in M. Grawitz, J. Leca, eds., *Traité de science politique*, vol. I, pp. 567-598.

133. *Cf.*, apart from E.R. Leach and G. Balandier, R. Bendix, ed., *State and Society*, Boston, Little, Brown, 1968; R. Collins, *Weberian Sociological Theory*, Cambridge, Cambridge University Press, 1986; P. Anderson, *L'État absolutiste*, Paris, Maspero, 1978; T. Skocpol, *États et révolutions sociales. La révolution en France, en Russie et en Chine*, Paris, Fayard, 1985; A. Giddens, *Central Problems in Social Theory*, and *A Contemporary Critique of Historical Materialism. Volume I: Power, Property and the State*, London, Macmillan, 1981; 'Les relations cardinales. Polarisation internationale et changement politique dans les sociétés du Tiers monde', *Revue française de science politique*, 36 (6), Dec. 1986, pp. 733-861.

134. F. Braudel, *La Dynamique du capitalisme*, Paris, Arthaud, 1985, p. 114.

135. P. Veyne, *L'Élégie érotique romaine*, Paris, Le Seuil, 1983, p. 25.

136. 'Nous avons délibérément renoncé à être "habile" pour pouvoir être intégralement honnêtes. Soyez sûrs que c'est là un effort d'assainissement intellectuel très rude pour un "citoyen de pays colonisé", l'acte de colonisation provoquant automatiquement un réflexe mental de clandestinité', *Congrès constitutif du Parti de la Fédération africaine, Commission de politique générale. Rapport de présentation par Doudou Gueye et résolutions de politique générale*, Dakar, 1, 2 and 3 Jan. 1959, pp. 3 and 5.

137. Cheikh Hamidou Kane, *L'Aventure ambiguë*, Paris, UGE, 1979 (2nd ed.), p. 164.

138. V.Y. Mudimbe, *L'Odeur du père. Essai sur les limites de la science et de la vie en Afrique noire*, Paris, Présence africaine, 1982, pp. 12-13.

139. See, in particular, C. Leys "Capital accumulation, class formation and dependency: the significance of the Kenyan case", *Socialist Register 1978*, pp. 241-266; "What does dependency explain?", *Review of African political economy*, 17, 1980, pp. 108-113; "African economic development in theory and practice", *Daedalus*, 111 (2), Spring 1982, pp. 99-124. On the Kenyan and Ivoirian debates, *cf.* respectively G. Kitching, 'Politics, method and evidence in the "Kenya debate" in H. Bernstein, B.K. Campbell, eds., *Contradictions of Accumulation in Africa*, pp. 115-151; 'A livre ouvert', *Politique africaine*, 9, Mar. 1983, pp. 118-143 and L. Gouffern, 'Les limites d'un modèle? A propos d'*État et bourgeoisie en Côte d'Ivoire*', *ibid.*, pp. 19-34.

140. For a critique of dependency, *cf.* for example B. Jewsiewicki, 'L'histoire en Afrique ou le commerce des idées usagées' in A. Schwarz, ed., *Les Faux Prophètes de l'Afrique ou l'Afr(eu)canisme*, Québec, Presses de l'Université de Laval, 1980, pp. 69-87; B. Freund, *The Making of Contemporary Africa.*; F. Cooper, 'Africa and the world economy', G.

Dupré, *Les Naissances d'une société,*; J. Dunn, A.F. Robertson, *Dependence and Opportunity*; A. Adams, *Le Long Voyage des gens du Fleuve*, Paris, Maspero, 1977 and *La Terre et les gens du Fleuve*, Paris, L'Harmattan, 1985; and perhaps above all the wonderful book of J.D.Y. Peel, *Ijeshas and Nigerians*. On the autonomy of the politics of 'national bourgeoisies', see J. Dunn, ed., *West African States. Failure and Promise. A Study in Comparative Politics*, Cambridge, Cambridge University Press, 1978; J.-F. Bayart, *L'État au Cameroun*, Paris, Presses de la Fondation nationale des sciences politiques, 1979; G. Dauch, D. Martin, *L'Héritage de Kenyatta*; J. Hartmann, *Development Policy Making in Tanzania. 1962-1982: A Critique of Sociological Interpretations*, Hull, The University of Hull, 1983; N. Swainson, *The Development of Corporate Capitalism in Kenya*. On 'popular modes of political action', *cf.* J.-F. Bayart, 'Le politique par le bas en Afrique noire. Questions de méthode', *Politique africaine*, 1, Jan. 1981, pp. 53-82; R. Jeffries, *Class, Power and Ideology in Ghana: the Railwaymen of Sekondi*, Cambridge, Cambridge University Press, 1978; R.H. Bates, *Rural Responses to Industrialization. A Study of Village Zambia*, New Haven, Yale University Press, 1976; G. Hyden, *Beyond Ujamaa*; D. Desjeux, *Stratégies paysannes en Afrique noire. Le Congo. Essai sur la gestion de l'incertitude*, Paris, L'Harmattan, 1987; R. Cohen, 'Resistance and hidden forms of consciousness amongst African workers', *Review of African Political Economy*, 19 Sept.-Dec. 1980, pp. 8-22; 'Histoire, histoires... Premiers jalons', *Bulletin de liaison du Département H de l'ORSTOM*, 3, March 1986, pp. 5-124.

141. P.-P. Rey, 'Le marxisme congolais contre l'État' in A. Corten, M. Sadria, M.B. Tahon, eds., *Les Autres Marxismes réels*, Paris, Christian Bourgois, 1985, p. 190.

142. P. Chabal, 'Introduction' in P. Chabal, ed., *Political Domination in Africa. Reflections on the Limits of Power*, Cambridge, Cambridge University Press, 1986, p. 2. This is the analysis of the influential article of G. O'Donnel ('Developpement à la périphérie. Formation historique comparée de l'appareil étatique dans le Tiers monde et changement socio-économique', *Revue internationale de science sociale*, XXXII (4), 1980, p. 770).

143. G. Hyden, *No Shortcuts to Progress. African Development Management in Perspective*, London, Heinemann, 1983, p. 19. See also R. Sandbrook, *The Politics of Africa's Economic Stagnation*, Cambridge, Cambridge University Press, 1985 or 'Personnalisation du pouvoir et stagnation capitaliste. L'État africain en crise', *Politique africaine*, 26, June 1987, pp. 15-40.

144. G. Balandier, 'Le contexte sociologique de la vie politique en Afrique noire', *Revue française de science politique*, IX (3), Sept. 1959, pp. 598-609.

145. F. Fanon, *Les Damnés de la terre*, p. 29.

146. T. Hodgkin, R. Schachter, *French Speaking West Africa in Transition*, New York, Carnegie Endowment for International Peace, 1960; T.O. Ranger, 'Connexion between "primary resistance" movements and modern mass nationalism in East and Central Africa', *Journal of African History*, IX (3), 1968, pp. 437-453 and IX (4), 1968, pp. 631-640; R. Pelissier, *Les Guerres grises*, p. 190.

147. R.A. Joseph, *Democracy and Prebendal Politics in Nigeria. The Rise and Fall of the Second Republic*, Cambridge, Cambridge University Press, 1987,

chap. 8.

148. J.-L. Amselle, Z. Dunbya, A. Kuyate, M. Tabure, 'Littérature orale et idéologie. La geste des Jakite Sabashi du Ganan (Wasolon, Mali)', *Cahiers d'études africaines*, 73-76, XIX (1-4), 1979, p. 383. *Cf.* also M. Izard, *Gens du pouvoir, gens de la terre*, p. 379.

149. See, for example, S. Bagayogo, 'L'État au Mali. Représentation, autonomie et mode de fonctionnement' in E. Terray, ed., *L'État contemporain en Afrique noire*, pp. 91-122.

150. In the mould, for example, R.H. Bates, *Essays on the Political Economy of Rural Africa*; N. Swainson, *The Development of Corporate Capitalism in Kenya*; J.-F. Bayart, *L'État au Cameroun*, and 'La revanche des sociétés africaines', *Politique africaine*, 11, Sept. 1983, pp. 95-127; T.M. Callaghy, *The State-Society Struggle. Zaïre in Comparative Perspective*, New York, Columbia University Press, 1984.

151. R. Hodder -Williams *An Introduction to the Politics of Tropical Africa*, London, George Allen and Unwin, 1984, p. 222.

152. J. Delange, *Arts et peuples de l'Afrique noire. Introduction à une analyse des créations plastiques*, Paris, Gallimard, 1967.

153. C. Coquery -Vidrovitch, 'Recherches sur un mode de production africain', *La Pensée*, 144, 1969, pp. 61-78.

154. S.N. Eisenstadt, M. Abitbol, N. Chazan, 'Les origines de l'État: une nouvelle approche'; C. Vidal, 'L'histoire et la question de l'État. Une lecture de: *Les Anyi-Ndenye et le pouvoir aux xviiie et xixe siècles* de Claude-Hélène Perrot', *Cahiers d'études africaines*, 87-88, XXII-3-4, 1982, pp. 517-524. See, for example, J. Vansina, *Les Anciens Royaumes de la savane*, Léopoldville, IRES, 1965 and A.I. Salim, ed., *State Formation in Eastern Africa*, Nairobi, Heinemann, 1984.

155. G. Nicolas, *Dynamique de l'islam au sud du Sahara*, Paris, Publications orientalistes de France, 1981 et, dans la lignée de C. Geertz (*Islam Observed: Religious Development in Morocco and Indonesia*, New Haven, Yale University Press, 1968), S. Ottenberg, 'Two new religions, one analytic frame', *Cahiers d'études africaines*, 96, XXIV (4), 1984, pp. 445 ff.

156. F. Braudel, *Ecrits sur l'histoire*, Paris, Flammarion, 1969, pp. 288-313.

157. J. Goody, *Technology, Tradition and the State in Africa*, Cambridge, Cambridge University Press, 1971, chap. ii and *Cuisines, cuisine et classes*, Paris, Centre de création industrielle, 1984; L.A. Fallers, 'Are African cultivators to be called "peasants"?', *Current Anthropology*, 2 (3), Apr. 1961, pp. 108-110.

158. J. Lonsdale, 'States and Social Processes in Africa', p. 139. See also I. Kopytoff, ed., *The African Frontier. The Reproduction of Traditional African Societies*, Bloomington, Indiana University Press, 1987.
In order to construct a scientific object, I have had to greatly simplify what very much more complicated than is immediately understood. Obviously, the characteristics of this "African civilisation" are tendential, and each one could be discussed or refined, as shown by the great Africanist studies in history or anthropology. For the moment, the main point is that subsaharan social structures, even when centralised are at least on another scale from the Ottoman, Chinese or Japanese empires, or the West-European absolutist monarchies.

159. B. Badie, 'Formes et transformations des communautés politiques', in

M. Grawitz, J. Leca, eds., *Traité de science politique, op. cit.*, vol. I, pp. 599-663; P. Birnbaum, 'La fin de l'État?', *Revue française de science politique*, 35 (6), Dec. 1985, pp. 981-998. Systemic analysis and structuro-functionalism attempted to substitute the concept of a political system for the concept of a State. Some studies devoted to sub-saharan Africa, joins these positions by a different, and occasionally outrageously normative, route. Yet, some of the better studies published recently themselves speak of the "decline of the State": see, in particular, N. Chazan, *An Anatomy of Ghanaian Politics: Managing Political Recession. 1969-1982*, Boulder, Westview Press, 1983 and C. Young, T. Turner, *The Rise and Decline of the Zairian State*, Madison, The University of Wisconsin Press, 1985, as well as the critiques of the latter work by J.-C.Willame ('Réflexions sur l'État et la société civile au Zaïre', *Les Cahiers du CEDAF*, 2-3-4, July 1986, pp. 287-306) and by T.M. Callaghy, *The State-Society Struggle*.

160. B. Lacroix, 'Ordre politique et ordre social. Objectivismes, objectivation et analyse politique' in M. Grawitz, J. Leca, eds., *Traité de science politique*, vol. I, pp. 469-565.

161. M. Foucault, 'Le pouvoir, comment s'exerce-t-il' in H. Dreyfus, P. Rabinow, *Michel Foucault. Un parcours philosophique*, Paris, Gallimard, 1984, pp. 308-321; C. Gordon, 'Foucault en Angleterre', *Critique*, 47 (472), Aug.-Sept. 1986, pp. 826-839; P. Veyne, *Le Pain et le cirque. Sociologie historique d'un pluralisme politique*, Paris, Seuil, 1976. On the usefulness of the notion of the State in relation to African societies one can provisionally rely upon the exposition of R. Lemarchand ('The state and society in Africa: ethnic stratification and restratification in historical and comparative perspective' in D. Rothchild, V.A. Olorunsola, eds., *State versus Ethnic Claims: African Policy Dilemmas*, Boulder, Westview Press, 1983, pp. 44-66).

162. M. Henry, *Marx*, vol. I: *Une philosophie de la réalité*, Paris, Gallimard, 1976, p. 109. Apart from the works of G. Balandier, see also A. Touraine, *Production de la société*, Paris, Le Seuil, 1973; P. Veyne, *Les Grecs ont-ils cru à leurs mythes?* Paris, Le Seuil, 1983; and, more directly on Africa, J.-F. Bayart, *L'État au Cameroun*; G. Dupré, *Un ordre et sa destruction* and *Les Naissances d'une société*; B. Freund, *The Making of Contemporary Africa*; D.-C. Martin, *Tanzanie: l'invention d'une culture politique*, Paris, Presses de la Fondation nationale des sciences politiques, Karthala, 1988.

163. G. Balandier, *Anthropo-logiques*, p.220.

164. T. Todorov, *Mikhaïl Bakhtine, le principe dialogique* followed by *Écrits du Cercle de Bakhtine*, Paris, Le Seuil, 1981; J.-F. Bayart, 'L'énonciation du politique', *Revue française de science politique*, 35 (3), June 1985, pp. 343-372.

165. G. Balandier, *Sens et puissance*, pp. 58-59.

166. P. Bourdieu, *Ce que parler veut dire. L'économie des échanges linguistiques*, Paris, Fayard, 1982.

167. On the incompleteness of ancient societies, see E. de Latour, 'Maîtres de la terre, maîtres de la guerre', *Cahiers d'études africaines*, 95, XXIV (3), 1984, pp. 273-297; J. Schmitz, 'L'État géomètre: les leydi des Peul du Fuuta Tooro (Sénégal) et du Maasina (Mali)', *ibid.*, 103, XXVI (3),

1986, pp. 349-394; M. Izard, *Gens du pouvoir, gens de la terre*, pp. 558 ff.

168. H.L. Moore, *Space, Text and Gender. An Anthropological Study of the Marakwet of Kenya*, Cambridge, Cambridge University Press, 1986.

169. R. Boudon, *La Place du désordre. Critique des théories du changement social*, Paris, PUF, 1984; C. Castoriadis, *L'Institution imaginaire de la société*, Paris, Seuil, 1975; M. de Certeau, *L'Invention du quotidien*, vol. I: *Arts de faire*, Paris, UGE, 1980.

CHAPTER ONE: THE SHADOW THEATRE OF ETHNICITY

1. M. Fulbrook, T. Skocpol, 'Destined pathways: the historical sociology of Perry Anderson' in T. Skocpol, ed., *Vision and Method in Historical Sociology*, Cambridge, Cambridge University Press, 1984, pp. 170-210.

2. H. Dreyfus, P. Rabinow, *Michel Foucault, un parcours philosophique*, Paris, Gallimard, 1984, pp. 179 ff.

3. W.M.j. van Binsbergen, *Religious Change in Zambia. Exploratory Studies*, London, Kegan Paul International, 1981, pp. 66-67.

4. A. Kourouma, *Les Soleils des indépendances*, Paris, Le Seuil, 1970.

5. Quoted by B. Verhaegen, *Rébellions au Congo*, vol. II: *Maniema*, Bruxelles, CRISP, Kinshasa, IRES, 1969, pp. 158-159.

6. *Les Cahiers de Gamboma, Instructions politiques et militaires des partisans congolais (1964-1965)*, Bruxelles, CRISP, 1965, pp. 51-52.

7. R. Um Nyobé, *Le Problème national kamerunais, présenté par J.A. Mbembé*, Paris, L'Harmattan, 1984, pp. 99 and 325.

8. 'Conversation with Paul Mba-Abessole, president of the Steering Committee of 'MORENA', *Politique africaine*, 11, Sept. 1983, p. 19.

9. J.-F. Bayart, *L'État au Cameroun*, Paris. Presses de la Fondation nationale des sciences politiques, 1979, p. 138. In fact this rumour, which was current in 1975, must be viewed cautiously, and has been denied by at least one reliable informer.

10. Strictly speaking, this interpretation is not necessarily wrong. Various politically opposing conversations and sources confirm it.

11. *Le Monde*, 17 Apr. 1984.

12. Quoted by H. Bandolo, *La Flamme et la fumée*, Yaoundé, SOPECAM, 1985, pp. 130-131.

13. Mono Ndjana, *De l'ethnofascisme dans la littérature politique camerounaise*, Yaoundé, Club UNESCO de l'Université, 11 Mar. 1987, and memorandum *'Un éclairage nouveau'*, signed by "native priests from the Douala archdiocese', 16th March 1987.

14. J-F. Bayart, 'La société politique camerounaise (1982-1986)', *Politique africaine*, 22, Jun. 1986, pp. 11 ff.

15. J.-F. Bayart, *ibid.* and *L'État au Cameroun;* V. Azarya, *Dominance and Change in North Cameroun: the Fulbe Aristocracy*, Beverly Hills, Sage Publications, 1976.

16. See, for example, F. Gaulme, *Le Pays de Cama. Un ancien État côtier du Gabon et ses origines*, Paris, Karthala, Centre de recherches africaines,

1981; P. Bonnafé, *Histoire sociale d'un peuple congolais*, livre I: *La Terre et le ciel*, Paris, ORSTOM, 1987; G. Dupré, *Les Naissances d'une société. Espace et historicité chez les Beembe du Congo*, Paris, ORSTOM, 1985.

17. F. de Polignac, *La Naissance de la cité grecque*, Paris, La Découverte, 1984, p. 16.

18. G. Pontié, 'Les sociétés païennes' and J. Boutrais, 'Les contacts entre sociétés' in J. Boutrais et al., *Le Nord du Cameroun. Des hommes, une région*, Paris, ORSTOM, 1984, pp. 208-209 and p. 264.

19. J.-F. Vincent, 'Élements d'histoire des Mofu, montagnards du Nord Cameroun', in C. Tardits, ed., *Contribution de la recherche ethnologique à l'histoire des civilisations du Cameroun*, Paris, CNRS, 1981, vol. I, p. 273. See also W.E.A. van Beck, 'L'État, ce n'est pas nous! Cultural proletarization in Cameroon', *Cahiers du CEDAF*, July. 1986, pp. 65-85.

20. J.-Y. Martin, 'L'implantation des populations du Nord et du Centre' and 'Discussion relative au rapport de J.-Y. Martin' in C. Tardits, ed., *Contribution de la recherche ethnologique,* vol. I, pp. 309-321.

21. J.-C. Barbier, 'Le peuplement de la partie méridionale du plateau bamiléké', R. Brain, 'The Fontem-Bangwa: a western Bamiléké group', I. Kopytoff, 'Aghem ethnogenesis and the Grassfields ecumene' in C. Tardits, ed., *Contribution de la recherche ethnologique, op. cit.*, vol. II, pp. 331-353, 355-360, 371-381.

22. P. Laburthe-Tolra, *Les Seigneurs de la forêt. Essai sur le passé historique, l'organisation sociale et les normes éthiques des anciens Beti du Cameroun*, Paris, Publications de la Sorbonne, 1981, pp. 43-126, 192-194, 199.

23. E. Mohammadou, *Ray ou Rey-Bouba. Traditions historiques des Foulbé de l'Adamâwa*, Garoua, ONAREST, Paris, CNRS, 1979.

24. Sources: archives of the diocese of Garoua, 1984.

25. C. Tardits, *Le Royaume bamoum*, Paris, Edisem, Publications de la Sorbonne et Armand Colin, 1980, pp. 880 ff.

26. C.S. Whitaker Jr., *The Politics of Tradition. Continuity and Change in Northern Nigeria. 1946-1966*, Princeton, Princeton University Press, 1970; R. Lemarchand, *Rwanda and Burundi*, London, Pall Mall Press, 1970.

27. P.-J. Hountondji, *Sur la 'philosophie africaine'*, Paris, Maspero, 1977; F. Eboussi Boulaga, *La Crise du Muntu. Authenticité africaine et philosophie*, Paris, Présence africaine, 1977.

28. S.F. Nadel, *Byzance noire. Le royaume des Nupe du Nigeria*, Paris, Maspero, 1971, pp. 45-46 and 125-126.

29. P. Bonte, N. Echard, 'Histoire et histoires. Conception du passé chez les Hausa et les Twareg Kel Gress de l'Ader (République du Niger)', *Cahiers d'études africaines*, 61-62, XVI (1-2), 1976, pp. 237-296; J.-F. Vincent, *Traditions et transition. Entretiens avec des femmes beti du Sud-Cameroun.* Paris, ORSTOM, Berger-Levrault, 1976; H.L. Moore, *Space, Text and Gender. An Anthropological Study of the Marakwet of Kenya*, Cambridge, Cambridge University Press, 1986.

30. M. Augé, *Pouvoirs de vie, pouvoirs de mort*, Paris, Flammarion, 1977, p. 74 and *Théorie des pouvoirs et idéologie. Étude de cas en Côte d'Ivoire*, Paris, Hermann, 1975.

31. A. Adler, *La mort est le masque du roi. La royauté sacrée des Moundang du Tchad*, Paris, Payot, 1982, pp. 83-84, 88-89, 139, 145.

32. See, for example, in addition to M. Gluckman, J.C. Mitchell, *The Kalela Dance. Aspects of Social Relationships among Urban Africans in Northern Rhodesia*, Manchester, Manchester University Press, 1956; A.L. Epstein, *Politics in an Urban African Community*, Manchester, Manchester University Press, 1958; A. Cohen, *Custom and Politics in Urban Africa. A Study of Hausa Migrants in Yoruba Towns*, Berkeley, University of California Press, 1969.

33. F. Le Guennec Coppens, *Femmes voilées de Lamu (Kenya). Variations culturelles et dynamiques sociales*, Paris, Ed. Recherche sur les civilisations, 1983, pp. 35-36. See also F. Cooper, *From Slaves To Squatters. Plantation, Labour and Agriculture in Zanzibar and Coastal Kenya. 1890-1925*, New Haven, Yale University Press, 1980, pp. 158 ff.

34. P. Geschiere, *Village Communities and the State. Changing Relations among the Maka of Southeastern Cameroun since the Colonial Conquest*, London, Kegan Paul International, 1982, chap. ii; P.H. Gulliver, *Neighbours and Networks. The Idiom of Kinship in Social Action among the Ndendeuli of Tanzania*, Berkeley, University of California Press, 1971; C. Young, *The Politics of Cultural Pluralism*, Madison, University of Wisconsin Press, 1976.

35. W. Watson, *Tribal Cohesion in a Money Economy: a Study of the Mambwe People of Northern Rhodesia*, Manchester, Manchester University Press, 1958; E. Schildkrout, *People of the Zongo. The Transformation of Ethnic Identities in Ghana*, Cambridge, Cambridge University Press, 1978; A.L. Epstein, *Politics in an Urban African Community;* A. Cohen, *Custom and Politics.*

36. E. Colson, 'African society at the time of the scramble' in L.H. Gann, P. Duignan, eds., *Colonialism in Africa. 1870-1960*, vol. I: *The History and Politics of Colonialism. 1870-1914*, Cambridge, Cambridge University Press, 1969, p.31; T. Ranger, 'The invention of tradition in colonial Africa' in E. Hobsbawm, T. Ranger, eds., *The Invention of Tradition*, Cambridge, Cambridge University Press, 1983, p. 248; J.L. Amselle, E. M'bokolo, ed., *Au cœur de l'ethnie. Ethnies, tribalisme et État en Afrique*, Paris, La Découverte, 1985; J. Iliffe, *A Modern History of Tanganyika*, Cambridge, Cambridge University Press, 1979, p. 9.

37. J.-P. Dozon, *La société bété, Côte d'Ivoire*, Paris, Karthala, ORSTOM, 1985; A.T. Matson, 'Reflections on the growth of political consciousness in Nandi' in B.A. Ogot, ed., *Politics and Nationalism in Colonial Kenya*, Nairobi, East African Publishing House, 1972, p. 44 and J.E.G. Sutton, 'The Kalenjin' in B.A. Ogot, ed., *Kenya before 1900. Eight Regional Studies*, Nairobi, East African Publishing House, 1976, pp. 22-24; F. Cooper, *From Slaves to Squatters*, pp. 158 ff; P. Bohannan, P. Curtin, *Africa and Africans*, Garden City, Natural History Press, 1971, p. 348; R. Lemarchand, *Rwanda and Burundi*, J.-P. Chrétien, 'Hutu et Tutsi au Rwanda et au Burundi and C. Vidal, 'Situation ethnique au Rwanda' in J.-L. Amselle, E. M'bokolo, eds., *Au cœur de l'ethnie*, pp. 129-165 and 167-184; C. Young, T. Turner, *The Rise and Decline of the Zairian State*, Madison, The University of Wisconsin Press, 1985, chap. 5; C.W. Anderson, F. von der Mehden, C. Young, *Issues of Political Development*, Englewood Cliffs, Prentice Hall, 1967, pp. 31-33.

38. N. Kasfir, *The Shrinking Political Arena. Participation and Ethnicity in*

African Politics with a Case Study of Uganda, Berkeley, University of California Press, 1976, p. 62 (a critique of E. Colson, 'Contemporary tribes and the development of nationalism' in J. Helm, ed., *Essays on the Problem of Tribe*, Seattle, University of Washington Press, 1968, pp. 201-202).

39. M. Mauss, *Œuvres*, Paris, Éd. de Minuit, 1968, I. p. 358.

40. B. Abemba, *Pouvoir et conflit dans la collectivité du Maniema. Essai de description et d'interprétation des phénomènes politiques conflictuels locaux à partir de trois cas concrets*, Brussels, Université libre, 1974, vol. II, pp. 453 ff; C. Coquery-Vidrovitch, *Afrique noire. Permanences et ruptures*, Paris, Payot, 1985, pp. 121-123.

41 N. Kasfir, *The Shrinking Political Arena*, chap. 4.

42. J.D.Y. Peel, *Ijeshas and Nigerians. The Incorporation of a Yoruba Kingdom. 1890's-1970's*, Cambridge, Cambridge University Press, 1983, pp. 223-224. On Tanganyika, see also J. Iliffe, *A Modern History of Tanganyika,* chap. 10.

43. F. Verdeaux, 'L'Aïzi pluriel. Chronique d'une ethnie lagunaire de Côte d'Ivoire' Paris, Ecole des hautes études en sciences sociales, 1981, chap. ii (particularly pp. 63 et 85). *Cf.* also G. Dupré, *Les naissances d'une société*, pp. 26 ff.

44. J.D.Y. Peel, *Ijeshas and Nigerians*, pp. 162 ff; C. Coquery-Vidrovitch, *Afrique noire*, pp. 128 ff.

45. W. van Binsbergen, 'From tribe to ethnicity in western Zambia: the unit of study as ideological problem' *in* W. Van Binsbergen, P. Geschiere, eds., *Old Modes of Production and Capitalist encroachment. Anthropological Explorations in Africa*, London, KPI, 1985, pp. 209 ff.

46. Interview with President Biya, *Cameroon Tribune* (Yaoundé), 20 Feb. 1987, *cf.* A.R. Zolberg, *One Party Government in the Ivory Coast*, Princeton, Princeton University Press, 1964, p. 11 for a similar statement by Houphouët-Boigny.

47. A.R. Zolberg, 'L'influence des facteurs "externes" sur l'ordre politique interne' *in* M. Grawitz, J. Leca, eds., *Traité de science politique*, Paris, PUF, 1985, vol. I, pp. 567-598.

48. J.D.Y. Peel, *Ijeshas and Nigerians*, pp. 220 ff.

49. A. Cohen, 'The social organization of credit in a West African cattle market', *Africa*, 35, 1965, pp. 8-20 and *Custom and Politics*, pp. 144 ff. By contrast, Kola traders voted for the NPC to demonstrate their Hausa identity in their region of origin on which they were commercially dependent.

50. R. Joseph, 'Le piège ethnique. Notes sur les élections au Nigeria (1978-1979)', *Politique africaine*, 3 Sept. 1981, pp. 37 and 39.

51. J. Spencer, *KAU. The Kenya African Union*, London, KPI, 1985, pp. 17-18; J.L. Lonsdale, 'La pensée politique kikuyu et les idéologies du mouvement mau-mau', *Cahiers d'études africaines*, 107-108, XXVII (3-4), 1987, pp. 329-357.

52. See J.R. Nellis, *The Ethnic Composition of Leading Kenyan Government Positions*, Uppsala, Scandinavian Institute of African Studies, 1974 and A. Bigsten, *Regional Inequality and Development. A Case Study of Kenya*, Aldershot, Gower Publishing, 1980.

53. C. Legum, J. Drysdale, *Africa Contemporary Record 1969-1970*, London,

Rex Collings, 1970, B–122/B 124; J. Karimi, P. Ochieng, *The Kenyatta Succession*, Nairobi, Transafrica, 1980; G. Dauch, D. Martin, *L'Héritage de Kenyatta. La transition politique au Kenya. 1975-1982*, Paris, L'Harmattan, 1985; D. Bourmaud, *Le système politique du Kenya: centre et périphérie*, Bordeaux, Institut d'études politiques, (1985), 'Charles Njonjo takes the plunge, *Weekly Review* (Nairobi), 25 Apr. 1980.

54. 'Not an ethnic affair', *Africa Now*, Sept. 1982, pp. 16-19; M. Warsama, 'The plotters', *The Express*, II (1), 1985, pp. 5-12; G. Dauch, 'Kenya: l'ébranlement', *Annuaire des pays de l'océan Indien*, IX, 1982-1983, pp. 319-334.

55. R.A. Joseph, *Radical Nationalism in Cameroun. Social origins of the UPC Rebellion*, Oxford, Oxford University Press, 1977; W.R. Johnson, 'The Union des populations du Cameroun in rebellion: the integrative backlash of insurgency' in R.I. Rotberg, A.A. Mazrui, eds., *Protest and Power in Black Africa*, New York, Oxford University Press, 1970, pp. 671-692.

56. R.C. Fox, X. de Craemer, J.M. Ribeaucourt, 'The "second independence": a case study of Kwilu rebellion in the Congo', *Comparative Studies in Society and History*, VIII (1), Oct. 1965, pp. 101-102; B. Verhaegen, *Rébellions au Congo*, vol. I, Bruxelles, Centre de recherche et d'information socio-politiques, 1966, pp. 61 and 106, and *Rébellions au Congo*, vol. II: *Maniema*, pp. 659 ff.

57. W.G. Clarence-Smith, 'Class structure and class struggles in Angola in the 1970's', *Journal of Southern African Studies*, VII (1), Oct. 1980, pp. 109-126; C. Coquery-Vidrovitch, *Afrique noire*, p. 128 (as well as R. Pelissier, 'Angola, Mozambique: des guerres interminables et leurs facteurs internes', *Hérodote*, 46, 1987, pp. 83-107, for a different interpretation); R. Buijtenhuijs, *Le Frolinat et les guerres civiles du Tchad (1977-1984). La révolution introuvable*, Paris, Karthala, Leiden, ASC, 1987 and *Le Frolinat et les révoltes populaires du Tchad (1965-1976)*, Paris, The Hague, Mouton, 1978.

58. H. Wolpe, *Urban Politics in Nigeria. A Study of Port Harcourt*, Berkeley, 1974, pp. 232-233; A Cohen, *Custom and Politics*.

59. J.J. Okumu, 'The problem of tribalism in Kenya', in P.L. van den Berghe, ed., *Race and Ethnicity in Africa*, Nairobi, East African Publishing House, 1975, pp. 181-202.

60. N. Kasfir, *The Shrinking Political Arena*, p. 104.

61. F. Cooper, *From Slaves to Squatters*, pp. 287-288.

62. *Le Manifeste du négro-mauritanien opprimé. Février 1966-avril 1986. De la guerre civile à la lutte de libération nationale*, (Nouakchott), 1986, pp. 1, 15 ff.

63. R.H. Bates, 'Modernization, ethnic competition and the rationality of politics in contemporary Africa' in D. Rothchild, V.A. Olorunsola, eds., *State versus Ethnic Claims: African Policy Dilemmas*, Boulder, Westview Press, 1983, pp. 152 and 164-165. See also J. Lonsdale, 'States and social processes in Africa: a historiographical survey', *African Studies Review*, XXIV (2-3) Jun.-Sept. 1981, pp. 170 and 201 and, for a precise demonstration, R. Molteno, 'Cleavage and conflict in Zambian politics: a study in sectionalism' in W. Tordoff, ed., *Politics in Zambia*, Manchester, Manchester University Press, 1974, pp. 62-106.

64. J.-P. Dozon, *La société bété*, p. 355.

65. I. Wallerstein, 'Ethnicity and national integration in West Africa',

Cahiers d'études africaines, (3), 1960, pp. 129-139.

66. R.L. Sklar, 'Political science and national integration – a radical approach', *Journal of Modern African Studies*, 5 (1), 1967, p. 6. See also A. Mafeje, 'The ideology of "tribalism"', *The Journal of Modern African Studies*, 9 (2), Aug. 1971, p.259.

67. J.-F. Bayart, 'Clientelism elections and systems of inequality and domination in Cameroun' in G. Hermet, R. Rose, A. Rouquié, eds., *Elections without Choice*. London, Macmillan, 1978, pp. 66-67; G. Hyden, *Beyond Ujamaa in Tanzania. Underdevelopment and an Uncaptured Peasantry*, Heinemann, 1980; J. Lonsdale, 'Political Accountability in African History' in P. Chabal, ed., *Political Domination in Africa. Reflections on the Limits of Power*, Cambridge, Cambridge University Press, 1986, pp. 143-144 and 'States and social processes in Africa', p. 201.

68. *Cameroon Tribune* (Yaoundé), 31 Dec. 1986.

69. H. Bandolo, 'La voie royale', *ibid.*, 8-9 Sept. 1985.

70. J.-Y. Martin, 'Sociologie de l'enseignement en Afrique noire' and R. Mbala Owono, 'École, ethnicité et classes sociales' in R. Santerre, C. Mercier-Tremblay, ed., *La quête du savoir. Essais pour une anthropologie de l'éducation camerounaise*, Montréal, Les Presses de l'Université de Montréal, 1982, pp. 567 ff. and 580 ff. On le crédit mutuel du Cameroun, cf. État nominatif des actionnaires, Douala, unpublished 1987.

71. J.D.Y. Peel, *Ijeshas and Nigerians*, see also N. Kasfir, *The Shrinking Political Arena*, pp. 66 ff. D.B. Cruise O'Brien, *Saints and Politicians. Essays on the Organisation of a Senegalese Peasant Society*, Cambridge, Cambridge University Press, 1975, chap. 5; P.M. Lubeck, *Islam and Urban Labour in Northern Nigeria. The Making of a Muslim Working Class*, Cambridge, Cambridge University Press, 1986; R. Luckham, *The Nigerian Military. A Sociological Analysis of Authority and Revolt, 1960-1967*, Cambridge, Cambridge University Press, 1971, Chap. 8; S.T. Barnes, *Patrons and Power. Creating a Political Community in Metropolitan Lagos*, Manchester, Manchester University Press, 1986.

CHAPTER 2: THE UNEQUAL STATE: 'LITTLE MEN' AND 'BIG MEN'

1. Student's essay collected in Baikwa (North Cameroon) in an agricultural college, Dec. 1984.

2. See K. Marx, *Capital*, New York, The Modern Library, 1936, pp. 12-13 and the commentary by R. Bendix, 'Tradition and modernity reconsidered', *Comparative Studies in Society and History*, IX, (3), Apr. 1967, pp. 308-309 and pp. 334-335. See also the problematics of the 'well-policed state' in M. Raeff, *Comprendre l'ancien régime russe. État et société en Russie impériale*, Paris, Le Seuil, 1982.

3. P. Geschiere, 'Imposing capitalist dominance through the state: the multifarious role of the colonial state in Africa' in W. van Binsbergen, P. Geschiere, eds., *Old Modes of Production and Capitalist Encroachement. Anthropological Explorations in Africa*, London, KPI, 1985, pp. 101 ff. and

P. Geschiere, *Village Communities and the State. Changing Relations among the Maka of Southeastern Cameroon since the Colonial Conquest*, London, Kegan Paul International, 1982, pp. 156 ff.; Note of sous préfet of Loum, 25 Oct. 1968, typescript.

4. 'Plan de campagne pour l'année 1921' and letter from Briaud, regional chief, to the Commissioner for the Republic of Donnala, Abong-Mbang, 14th Dec. 1920, quoted in P. Geschiere, *Village Communities*, p. 104; letter from R. Boussac to the Governor-general of the AOF, 8th March 1928, quoted in République Française, ministère de la Coopération, *Un bilan de l'aide au développement*, Paris, 1985, p. 59; L. Verlaine, *A la recherche de la méthode de colonisation*, cited by L. Zoumenou, *Un précurseur du mouvement démocratique et panafricain en Afrique noire française: Kojo Tovalou Houenou (1887-1936)*, Paris, Institut d'études politiques, 1985, p. 265.

5. D. Bigo, *Forme d'exercice du pouvoir et obéissance en Centrafrique (1966-1979)*, Paris, Université de Paris-I, 1985, pp. 174 and 471; Y. Zoctizoum, *Histoire de la Centrafrique*, vol. II: *1959-1979. Violence du développement, domination et inégalités*, Paris, L'Harmattan, 1984; République Française, Ministère des Relations extérieures, Coopération et Developpement, *Déséquilibres structurels et programmes d'ajustement en République centrafricaine*, Paris, 1985.

6. M. von Freyhold, *Ujamaa Villages in Tanzania, Analysis of a Social Experiment*, London, Heinemann, 1979, p. 36.

7. J.P. Langellier, 'L'échec des doctrinaires de Maputo', *Le Monde*, 25th May 1983.

8. N. Casswell, 'Autopsie de l'ONCAD: la politique arachidière au Sénégal. 1966-1980', *Politique africaine*, 14, June 1984, p. 47.

9. *Marchés tropicaux et méditerranéens*, 1st Feb. 1985, p. 269.

10. H. Lefebvre, *De l'État*, Paris, Union générale d'éditions, 1976, vol. II, pp. 42 ff. See in particular F. Cooper, *From Slaves to Squatters. Plantation Labour and Agriculture in Zanzibar and Coastal Kenya. 1890-1925*, New Haven, Yale University Press, 1980.

11. A. Kourouma, *Les Soleils des indépendances*, Paris, Le Seuil, 1976, pp. 22-23.

12. M. Weber, *L'Éthique protestante et l'esprit du capitalisme*, Paris, Plon, 1985, pp. 57 ff. See for example, M. Augé, *Théorie des pouvoirs et idéologie. Étude de cas en Côte d'Ivoire*, Paris, Hermann, 1975, p. 7; P. Laburthe-Tolra, *Les Seigneurs de la forêt. Essai sur le passé historique, l'organisation sociale et les normes éthiques des anciens Beti du Cameroun*, Paris, Publications de la Sorbonne, 1981, pp. 233 ff. G. Dupré, *Les Naissances d'une société. Espace et historicité chez les Beembé du Congo*, Paris, ORSTOM, 1985, pp. 82 ff., 93 ff., 259 ff.; S.F. Nadel, *Byzance noire. Le royaume des Nupe du Nigeria*, Paris, Maspero, 1971.

13. L. Dumont, *Homo aequalis. Genèse et épanouissement de l'idéologie économique*, Paris, Gallimard, 1976, p. 14.

14. I borrow here the distinction drawn by G. Kitching, *Class and Economic Change in Kenya. The Making of an African Petite-Bourgeoisie*, New-Haven, Yale University Press, 1980, p.455. For simplicity, I retain the notion of 'social stratification' although I accept several critiques by L.A. Fallers *(Inequality. Social Stratification Reconsidered*, Chicago, The

University of Chicago Press, 1973) and although I prefer the 'system of inequality and domination' put forward by G. Balandier *(Anthropologiques*, Paris, PUF, 1974, chap. III).

15. R.H. Bates, *Markets and States in Tropical Africa. The Political Basis of Agricultural Policies*, Berkeley, University of California Press, 1981; 'Les paysans et le pouvoir en Afrique noire', *Politique africaine*, 14, Jun. 1984, pp. 3-91.

16. T. Ranger, *Peasant Consciousness and Guerilla War in Zimbabwe. A Comparative Study*, London, James Currey, Berkeley, University of California Press, 1985; M. Bratton, 'The comrades and the countryside: the politics of agricultural policy in Zimbabwe', *World Politics*, XXXIX (2), Jan. 1987, pp. 174-202; P. Labazée, 'Réorganisation économique et résistances sociales. La question des alliances au Burkina', *Politique africaine*, 20, Dec. 1985, pp. 10-28; J.L. Amselle, E. Grégoire, 'Complicités et conflits entre bourgeoisies d'État et bourgeoisies d'affaires: au Mali et au Niger' in E. Terray, ed., *L'État contemporain en Afrique*, Paris, L'Harmattan, 1987, p. 37.

17. Source: République Française, ministère des Relations extérieures, Coopération et Développement, *Déséquilibres structurels et programmes d'ajustement au Sénégal*, Paris 1985, (particularly pp. 58 and 60). See also N. Casswell, 'Autopsie de l'ONCAD', and D.B. Cruise O'Brien, *Saints and Politicians. Essays in the Organisation of a Senegalese peasant Society*, Cambridge, Cambridge University Press, 1975.

18. See J. Henn, *Peasants, Workers and Capital. The Political Economy of Labor and Incomes in Cameroun*, Cambridge, Harvard University, 1978; P. Demunter, *Masses rurales et luttes politiques au Zaïre. Le processus de politisation des masses rurales du Bas-Zaïre*, Paris, Anthropos, 1975; C. Young, T. Turner, *The Rise and Decline of the Zairian State*, Madison, The University of Wisconsin Press, 1985, pp. 94-95; M.G. Schatzberg, *Politics and Class in Zaïre. Bureaucracy, Business and Beer in Lisala*, New York, Africana Publishing Company, 1980, chap. iv; S. Berry, *Fathers Work for their Sons. Accumulation Mobility and Class Formation in an Extended Yoruba Community*, Berkeley, University of California Press, 1985; B. Beckman, 'Ghana, 1951-78: the agrarian basis of the postcolonial state' in J. Heyer, P. Roberts, G. Williams, eds., *Rural Development in Tropical Africa*, London, Macmillan, 1981, pp. 143-167; P. Konings, *The State and Rural Class Formation in Ghana: a Comparative Analysis*, London, KPI, 1986.

19. République populaire du Congo, présidence de la République, cabinet du chef de l'État, dossier OCV [Office des cultures vivrières], Brazzaville, March 1984, p. 2; G. Courade, 'Des complexes qui coûtent cher. La priorité agro-industrielle dans l'agriculture camerounaise', *Politique africaine*, 14, June 1984, pp. 75-91; C. Arditi et al., *Évaluation socioéconomique du projet SEMRY au Cameroun*, Paris, SEDES, 1983.

20. C. Young, T. Turner, *The Rise and Decline of the Zairian State*, p. 311.

21. W.G. Clarence-Smith, 'Class structure and class struggles in Angola in the 1970s', *Journal of Southern African Studies*, 7(1), Oct. 1980, pp. 116 ff. 'Le MPLA et la paysannerie angolaise: un exemple pour le Zaïre?' in C. Coquery-Vidrovitch, A. Forest, H. Weiss, ed., *Rébellions-révolution au Zaïre. 1963-1965*, Paris, L'Harmattan, 1987, vol. II, pp. 106-114; C.

Meillassoux, C. Verschuur, 'Les paysans ignorés du Mozambique', *Le Monde diplomatique*, Oct. 1985, pp. 14-15; M. Cahen, *Mozambique. La révolution implosée*, Paris, L'Harmattan, 1987, pp. 47-70; P. Chabal, 'Revolutionary democracy in Africa: the case of Guinea-Bissau' in P. Chabal, ed., *Political Domination in Africa. Reflections on the Limits of Power*, Cambridge, Cambridge University Press, 1986, pp. 90 ff.; P. Chabal, *Amilcar Cabral. Revolutionary Leadership and People's War*, Cambridge, Cambridge University Press, 1983; C.G. Rosberg, T.M. Callaghy, eds., *Socialism in Subsaharan Africa. A New Assessment*, Berkeley Institute of International Studies, 1979.

22. M. von Freyhold, *Ujamaa Villages in Tanzania*; A. Coulson, ed., *African Socialism in Practice. The Tanzanian Experience*, Nottingham, Spokesman, 1979; D.F. Bryceson, 'Peasant commodity production in post-colonial Tanzania', *African Affairs*, 81 (325), Oct. 1982, p. 567; P. Raikes, *The Development of Commodity-Producing Peasantry in Tanzania*, Copenhagen, Centre for Development Research, 1978; A. Coulson, 'Agricultural policies in mainland Tanzania, 1946-1976' in J. Heyer, P. Roberts, G. Williams, eds., *Rural development in Tropical Africa*, pp. 52-58; J. Wagao, *State Control of Agricultural Marketing in Tanzania, 1961-1976*, Dar es Salaam, University of Dar es Salaam, Economic Research Bureau, 1982; G. Hyden, *Beyond Ujamaa in Tanzania, Underdevelopment and an Uncaptured Peasantry*, London, Heinemann, 1980; J. Boesen, *Tanzania: from Ujamaa to Villagization*, Copenhagen, Institute for Development Research, 1976; D.C. Martin, *Tanzanie: l'invention d'une culture politique*, Paris, Presses de la Fondation nationale des sciences politiques, Karthala, 1988, chap. vii and xii. Danish researchers have entered into bitter arguments on this point (see J. Boesen, P. Raikes, *Political economy and Planning in Tanzania*, Copenhagen, IDR, 1976 and K.E. Svendsen, *Problems in the Analysis of Developments in Tanzania*, Copenhagen, Centre for Development Research, 1977).

23. J. Mac Rae, J.-F. Drevet, *Évolution et perspectives du Kenya*, s.l. (Paris), ECODEV, SEDES, 1983, pp. 48-49, 77-78, 93 ff.; S.E. Migot-Adholla, 'Rural development policy and equality' in J.D. Barkan, J.J. Okumu, eds., *Politics and Public Policy in Kenya and Tanzania*, New York, Praeger Publishers, 1979, p. 161: R.H. Bates, *Markets and States in Tropical Africa*, pp. 92 ff.; 'Kenya: the agrarian question', *Review of African Political Economy*, 20, Jan.-Apr. 1981, pp. 1-124.

24. A. Touré, 'Paysans et fonctionnaires devant la culture et l'État' in Y.-A. Fauré, J.-F. Médard, eds., *État et bourgeoisie en Côte d'Ivoire*, Paris, Karthala, 1982, pp. 231-251 and 'La petite histoire de Nalewe Kpingbin Tiecoroba. Une émission de la radiodiffusion nationale ivoirienne', *Politique africaine*, 3, Sept. 1981, pp. 44-54.

25. Source: République Française, Ministère de la Coopération, *Déséquilibres structurels et programmes d'ajustement en Côte d'Ivoire*, Paris, 1986. The farmers of the savanna have been more severely affected than the coffee or, particularly, the cocoa growers, who are the political clientele of the régime. See also F. Ruf, 'Structures paysannes hétérogènes: réponses aux prix diversifiés. Cas du riz et du cacao en Côte-d'Ivoire', *Les Cahiers de la recherche-développement*, 8, 1985, pp. 6-9 et Société d'étude pour le développement économique et social, *Evolution et répartition des revenus*

en Côte-d'Ivoire, Paris, 1984.
26. Y.-A. Fauré, J.F. Médard, 'Classe dominante ou classe dirigeante?' and
J.-M. Gastellu, S. Affou Yapi, 'Un mythe à décomposer: la bourgeoisie
de planteurs' in Y.-A. Fauré, J.-F. Médard, eds., *État et bourgeoisie en
Côte d'Ivoire, op. cit.,* Chapter iv and v. See also F. Ruf, 'Les règles du
jeu sur le foncier et la force de travail dans l'ascension économique et la
stratification sociale des planteurs de Côte d'Ivoire. Quelques éléments
d'analyse et signes d'évolution technique', *Économie rurale*, 147-148,
Jan.-Mar. 1982, pp. 111-119.
The idea of a "planters' bourgeoisie" was put forward by S. Amin, *Le
Développement du capitalisme en Côte d'Ivoire*, Paris, Ed. de Minuit, 1967
and by B. Campbell, 'The Ivory Coast' in J. Dunn, ed., *West African
States. Failure and Promise*, Cambridge, Cambridge University Press,
1978, pp. 66-116; it was taken up by L. Gbagbo, *Côte d'Ivoire. Économie
et société à la veille de l'indépendance (1940-1960)*, Paris, L'Harmattan,
1982 and by P. Anyang' Nyong'o, 'The development of agrarian capitalist classes in the Ivory Coast, 1945-1975', *Conference 'The African
Bourgeoisie: the Development of Capitalism in Nigeria, Kenya and Ivory
Coast'*, Dakar, 1980.
27. F. Fanon, *Les Damnés de la terre*, Paris, Maspero, 1961; G. Arrighi, J.S.
Saul, *Essays on the Political Economy of Africa*, New York, Monthly Review Press, 1973.
28. F. Cooper, *From Slaves to Squatters*, pp. 174, 230 ff. 278-279.
29. K. Post, '"Peasantization" and rural political movements in western
Africa', *Archives européennes de sociologie*, 13 (2), 1972, pp. 223-254; G.
Hyden, *Beyond Ujamaa in Tanzania*, pp. 9 ff. See also F. Cooper, *From
Slaves to Squatters*, pp. 269 ff.; L.A. Fallers, 'Are African cultivators to
be called "peasants"?', *Current Anthropology*, 2(2), Apr. 1961, pp. 108-
110; J. Iliffe, *A Modern History of Tankanyika*, Cambridge, Cambridge
University Press, 1979, chap. ix; T. Ranger, *Peasant Consciousness and
Guerilla War in Zimbabwe*.
30. J. Copans, 'From Senegambia to Senegal: the evolution of peasantries'
in M.A. Klein, ed., *Peasants in Africa. Historical and Contemporary Perspectives*, Beverly Hills, Sage Publications, 1980, pp. 77-103.
31. S. Berry, *Fathers Work for their Sons;* J.D.Y. Peel, *Ijeshas and Nigerians.
The Incorporation of a Yoruba Kingdom. 1890s-1970s*, Cambridge, Cambridge University Press, 1983, pp. 127 ff. See also, on Cameroon, A
Franqueville, 'La population rurale africaine face à la pénétration de
l'économie moderne: le cas du Sud-Cameroun' in C. Blanc-Pamard et
al., *Le développement rural en questions*, Paris, ORSTOM, 1984 pp.
433-445.
32. See in particular the critique of G. Arrighi and J.S. Saul by R. Jeffries,
Class, Power and Ideology in Ghana: the Railwaymen of Sekondi, Cam-
bridge, Cambridge University Press, 1978, pp. 169-185. See also R.
Sandbrook, R. Cohen, eds., *The Development of an African Working
Class. Studies in Class Formation and Action*, Toronto, University of
Toronto Press, 1975; R. Sandbrook, *The Politics of Basic needs. Urban
Aspects of Assaulting Poverty in Africa*, London, Heinemann, 1982; J.
Iliffe, 'The poor in the modern history of Malawi' in Centre of African

Studies, *Malawi, an Alternative Pattern of Development*, Edinburgh, Edinburgh University, 1985, pp. 245-292 and *The African Poor. A History*, Cambridge, Cambridge University Press, 1987; P.M. Lubeck, *Islam and Urban Labor in Northern Nigeria. The Making of a Muslim Working Class*, Cambridge, Cambridge University Press, 1986; I. Deblé, P. Hugon et al., *Vivre et survivre dans les villes africaines*, Paris, PUF, 1982.

33. M. Agier, J. Copans, A. Morice, eds., *Classes ouvrières d'Afrique noire*, Paris, Karthala, ORSTOM, 1987.

34. S. Berry, *Fathers Work for their Sons.*

35. A. Peace, 'Prestige Power and Legitimacy in a Modern Nigerian Town', *Canadian Journal of African Studies*, 13 (1-2), 1979, pp. 26-51; P.W. Gutkind, 'The view from below: political consciousness of the urban poor in Ibadan', *Cahiers d'études africaines*, 57, XV-1, 1975, pp. 5-35.

36. R. Price, 'Politics and culture in contemporary Ghana: the big-man small-boy syndrome', *Journal of African Studies*, I (2), summer 1974, pp. 173-204. See also R. Jeffries, *Class, Power and Ideology in Ghana.*

37. M.G. Schatzberg, *Politics and Class in Zaïre*, pp. 53-58; R. Jeffries, *Class, Power and Ideology in Ghana*, chap. 8 and N. Chazan, *An Anatomy of Ghanaian Politics, Managing Political Recession, 1969-1983*, Boulder, Westview Press, 1983, pp. 38-39. Other studies, however, qualify these claims. S. Berry, for example, insists on the fluidity of the lines of social stratification in the context of the Yoruba country (*Fathers Work for their Sons*,) and P. Geschiere demonstrates that access to secondary education is no longer monopolised by the elite in the Maka country (*Village Communities and the State*, p. 333 ff.)

38. République Française, *Déséquilibres structurels et programmes d'ajustement*, *op. cit.* See also C. Vidal, M. Le Pape, *Pratiques de crise et conditions sociales à Abidjan, 1979-1985*, Abidjan, Centre ORS-TOM de Petit Bassam, 1986.

39. G. Kitching, *Class and Economic Change in Kenya*, chap. xii; C. de Miras, 'L'entrepreneur ivoirien ou une bourgeoisie privée de son état' in Y.-A. Fauré, J.-F. Médard, eds., *État et bourgeoisie en Côte d'Ivoire*, pp. 181-229; S. Berry, *Fathers Work for their Sons*, chap. vi; N. Kasfir, 'State, *Magendo* and class formation in Uganda', *Journal of Commonwealth and Comparative Politics*, XXI (3), Nov. 1983, pp. 84-103; A. Morice, 'Commerce parallèle et troc à Luanda', *Politique africaine*, 17, March 1985, pp. 105-120; J. MacGaffey, 'How to survive and become rich amidst devastation: the second economy in Zaïre', *African Affairs*, 82 (328), July, 1983, pp. 351-366 and *Entrepreneurs and Parasites; the Struggle for Indigenous Capitalism in Zaïre*, Cambridge, Cambridge University Press, 1987.

40. G. Kitching, *Class and Economic Change in Kenya.*

41. S. Berry, *Fathers Work for their Sons* and *Cocoa, Custom and Socio-Economic Change in Rural Western Nigeria*, Oxford, Clarendon Press, 1975.

42. J.-M. Gastellu, S. Affou Yapi, 'Un mythe à décomposer: la "bourgeoisie de planteurs"', in Y.-A. Fauré, J.-F. Médard, eds., *État et bourgeoisie en Côte d'Ivoire*, pp. 168 ff.

43. S.D. Mueller, 'The historical origins of Tanzania's ruling class', *Revue canadienne des études africaines*, 15 (3), 1981, pp. 459-497; J. Boesen, B. Storgard Madsen, T. Moody, *Ujamaa. Socialism from Above*, Uppsala,

Scandinavian Institute of African Studies, 1977; M. von Freyhold, *Ujamaa Villages in Tanzania*, pp. 63 ff.; M. Gottlieb, 'The extent and character of differenciation in Tanzanian agricultural and rural society', *The African Review*, 3 (2), June 1973, pp. 241-261; D.-C. Martin, *Tanzanie*, chap. xii.

44. T. Ranger, *Peasant Consciousness and Guerilla War in Zimbabwe, op. cit.* For a different view, see, on Zaïre, *cf.* J. MacGaffey, *Entrepreneurs and Parasites*, pp. 100 ff.

45. G. Balandier, *Anthropologie politique*, Paris, PUF, 1969 (2nd. ed.), pp. 197-198. In the field of political science, the main work of reference appears to be R.L. Sklar ('The nature of class domination in Africa', *Journal of Modern African Studies*, 17 (4), 1979, pp. 531-552 and *Nigerian Political Parties. Power in an Emergent African Nation*, Princeton, Princeton University Press, 1963).

46. A considerable amount has been written on this subject. Only a few references are given here. Those referring to a "political class" are, R. Murray ('Second thoughts on Ghana', *New Left Review*, 42, March-April 1967, pp. 25-39), R. Cohen ('Class in Africa: analytical problems and perspectives', *The Socialist Register 1972*, pp. 231-255), R. Sandbrook (*Proletarians and African Capitalism: the Kenyan Case. 1960-1972*, Cambridge, Cambridge University Press, 1975), and to 'political-administrative class' M.A. Cohen (*Urban Policy and Political Conflict in Africa. A Study of the Ivory Coast*, Chicago, The University of Chicago Press, 1974). T.M. Callaghy retains the notion of a 'political aristocracy' (*The State-Society Struggle. Zaïre in Comparative Perspective*, New York, Columbia University Press, 1984). I.L. Markowitz advances the concept of 'organizational bourgeoisie' (*Power and Class in Africa. An Introduction to Change and Conflict in African Politics*, Englewood Cliffs, Prentice Hall Inc., 1977), R.L. Sklar that of 'managerial bourgeoisie' (*Corporate Power in an African State: the Political Impact of Multinational Mining Companies in Zambia*, Berkeley, University of California Press, 1975). C. Leys adopts the notion of 'bureaucratic bourgeoises' ('The "overdeveloped" postcolonial state: a re-evaluation', *Review of African Political Economy*, 5, 1976, pp. 39-48), after Issa Shivji had introduced it into the 'Tanzanian debate' (see in particular his *Class Struggles in Tanzania*, New York, Monthly Review Press, 1976, more accessible than his earlier works. E. Hutchful uses the notion 'State bourgeoisie' ('A tale of two regimes: imperialism, the military and class in Ghana', *Review of African Political Economy*, 14, 1979, pp. 36-55) as do Y.-A. Fauré and J.-F. Médard (*État et bourgeoisie en Côte d'Ivoire*), J.-L. Amselle compares the Malian 'nomenklatura' to that in the Soviet bloc ('Socialisme, capitalisme et précapitalisme au Mali. 1960-1982' in H. Bernstein, B.K. Campbell, eds., *Contradictions of Accumulation in Africa. Studies in Economy and State*, Beverly Hills, Sage Publications, 1985, pp. 249-266.)

47. J.-L. Vellut, 'Articulations entre entreprises et État: pouvoirs hégémoniques dans le bloc colonial belge (1908-1960)' in Laboratoire 'Connaissance du Tiers-Monde', *Entreprises et entrepreneurs en Afrique. xixe et xxe siècles*, Paris, L'Harmattan, 1983, vol. II, pp. 49-100.

48. J. Vansina, *Les Anciens Royaumes de la savane*, Léopoldville, IRES, 1965; R. Pélissier, *Les Guerres grises. Résistance et révolte en Angola (1845-1941)*,

Orgeval Pélissier, 1977 and *La Colonie du minotaure. Nationalismes et révoltes en Angola (1926-1961)*, Orgeval, Pélissier, 1978, pp. 127-128 and 462-463; M. Cowen, K. Kinyanjui, 'Some Problems of Capital and Class in Kenya' Nairobi, Institute for Development Studies, 1977, pp. 15 ff.

49. R.W. Shenton, *The Development of Capitalism in Northern Nigeria*, London, James Currey, 1986, pp. 122 ff.

50. Account of Mme Dugast in 1942, Archives nationales du Cameroun, Yaoundé, cited by J.-L. Dongmo, *Le Dynamisme bamiléké (Cameroun)*, vol. I: *La Maîtrise de l'espace agraire*, Yaoundé, Centre d'édition et de production pour l'enseignement et la recherche, 1981, pp. 122-124. See also J.-P. Olivier de Sardan, *Les Sociétés songhay-zarma (Niger-Mali). Chefs, guerriers, esclaves, paysans…*, Paris, Karthala, 1984, chap. 11; M. Kilson, *Political Change in a West African State. A Study of the Modernization Process in Sierra Leone*, Harvard, Harvard University Press, 1966.

51. M. Delauney, *Kala-Kala. De la grande à la petite histoire, un ambassadeur raconte*, Paris, Robert Laffont, 1986, p. 88; interviews.

52. D. Rimmer, 'Elements of the political economy' in K. Panter-Brick, ed., *Soldiers and Oil. The Political Transformation of Nigeria*, London, Frank Cass, 1978, pp. 146 ff.; R.L. Sklar, *Nigerian Political Parties* (especially pp. 446-460).

53. G. Kitching, *Class and Economic Change in Kenya*, chap. vii. For similar facts regarding Sierra Leone, *cf.* M. Kilson, *Political change in a West African State*, chap. xiii, and on the Four Communes of Senegal H.-J. Légier, 'Institutions municipales et politique coloniale: les communes du Sénégal', *Revue française d'histoire d'outre-mer*, 55 (201), 1968, pp. 414-465.

54. J. Spencer, *KAU. The Kenya African Union*, London, KPI, 1985, pp. 63 ff.; A.R. Zolberg, *One-Party Government in the Ivory Coast*, Princeton, Princeton University Press, 1964, pp. 192 ff.; R.A. Joseph, *Radical nationalism in Cameroun. Social Origins of the UPC Rebellion*, Oxford, Oxford University Press, 1977, p. 155; R. Rathbone, 'Businessmen in Politics: Party Struggle in Ghana, 1949-1957', *Journal of Development Studies*, 9 (3), April 1973, pp. 391-401.

55. R. Um Nyobé, *Le Problème national kamerunais, présenté par J. A. Mbembé*, Paris, L'Harmattan, 1984, p. 158. See also for examples of corruption in Mungo, *La Voix du Cameroun*, 15, May-July 1954, cited by R. Joseph, *Radical Nationalism in Cameroun*, p. 230.

56. UPS, 'Troisième congrès de l'UPS, 4, 5, 6 février 1962. Rapport sur la vie du parti par Ousmane Ngom, secrétaire politique' pp. 6-7.

57. Documents cited by B. Verhaegen, *Rébellions au Congo*. vol. II: *Maniema*, Brussells, CRISP, Kinshasa, IRES, 1969, p. 263. *cf.* also pp. 267 ff., 436 ff., 632 ff., 637 ff.

58. See for example, on Kenya, G. Kitching, *Class and Economic change in Kenya*, p. 309 and G.C. Mutiso, *Kenya, Politics, Policy and Society*, Nairobi, East African Literature Bureau, 1975, chap. i; on Cameroun, J.-Y. Martin, 'Appareil scolaire et reproduction des milieux ruraux on in ORSTOM, *Essais sur la reproduction de formations sociales dominées*, Paris, ORSTOM, 1977, pp. 55-67; P. Geschiere, *Village Communities and the State*, pp. 275-276; R. Santerre, C. Mercier-Tremblay, ed., *La Quête du*

savoir. Essais pour une anthropologie de l'éducation camerounaise, Montréal, Presses de l'Université de Montréal, 1982; on Tanzania J. Samoff, 'Education in Tanzania: class formation and reproduction', *Journal of Modern African Studies,* 17 (1), 1979, pp. 47-69; on Zaïre, M.G. Schatzberg, *Politics and Class in Zaïre,* pp. 56 ff. We should qualify this; agriculture enabled illiterate farmers to rise socially within the villages leading to a degree of limited accumulation. But it was education which distinguished true 'entrepreneurial planters' from 'village planters'. (J.-M. Gastellu, S. Affou Yapi, 'Un mythe à décomposer: la "bourgeoisie de planteurs" *in* Y.-A. Fauré, J.-F. Médard, eds., *État et bourgeoisie en Côte d'Ivoire,* pp. 159-160 and p. 178.

59. R.A. Joseph, *Democracy and Prebendal Politics in Nigeria. The Rise and Fall of the Second Republic,* Cambridge, Cambridge University Press, 1987, chap. 8 and S. Berry, *Fathers Work for their Sons,* chap. 5.

60. E. Abreu, *The Role of Self-Help in the Development of Education in Kenya (1900-1973),* Nairobi, Kenya Literature Bureau, 1982; F. Holmquist, 'State, Class, Peasants and the Initiative of Kenya Self-Help,'Hampshire College, 1982, J.-P. Dozon, *La Société bété. Côte d'Ivoire,* Paris, Karthala, ORSTOM, 1985, pp. 329 ff.; S. Berry, *Fathers Work for their Sons,* chap. 5.

61. *Le Messager* (Douala), 25 Jan. 1985, p. 10. For similar cases from Zaïre, *cf. Marchés tropicaux et méditerranéens,* 20 Sept. 1985, p. 2332.

62. See, for example, K. Kinyanjuli, 'The Distribution of Educational Resources and Opportunities in Kenya,' Nairobi, Institute of Development Studies, 1974, p. 39; P. Geschiere, *Village Communities and the State,* pp. 329 ff.; J.-Y. Martin, 'Appareil scolaire et reproduction des milieux ruraux' in ORSTOM, *Essais sur la reproduction de formations sociales dominées,* pp. 55-67; M. Mbilinyi, 'Contradictions in Tanzanian education', in A. Coulson, ed., *African Socialism in Practice,* pp. 217-227 and J. Samoff, 'Education in Tanzania'; I. Jacquet, 'Viens, je t'emmène de l'autre côté des nuages... Aspects de la vie quotidienne au Zaïre', *Politique africaine,* 27, Sept.-Oct. 1987, p. 106.

63. M.P. Cowen, 'The British state, State enterprise and an indigenous bourgeoisie in Kenya after 1945', Paper presented to the Conference on the African Bourgeoisie, Dakar, 1980, p. 32.

64. C. Young, T. Turner, *The Rise and Decline of the Zaïrian State,* p. 118; M.G. Schatzberg, *Politics and Class in Zaïre,* pp. 49-50.

65. For the perks enjoyed by Ivoirian civil servants, *cf.* République Française, ministère de la Coopération, *Déséquilibres structurels et programmes d'ajustement en Côte d'Ivoire*; P. Antoine, A. Dubresson, A. Manou-Savina, *Abidjan "côté cours". Pour comprendre la question de l'habitat,* Paris, Karthala, ORSTOM, 1987, chap. vi and for the 1950s, A.R. Zolberg, *One-Party Government in the Ivory Coast,* pp. 192 ff.

66. Speech of M. Houphouët-Boigny, *Fraternité-Matin* (Abidjan), 29 April 1983, p. 17.

67. 'Le Manifeste du nègro-mauritanien opprimé. Février 1966-avril 1986. De la guerre civile à la lutte de libération nationale,' Nouakchott, 1986, p. 15.

68. Accounts cited by A. Sissoko, 'Aspects sociologiques de l'intégration nationale en Afrique noire occidentale: espace politico-administratif et

intégration à l'État: le cas de la Côte d'Ivoire', Nice, Faculté des lettres et sciences humaines, 1982, pp. 536 and 545.

69. Sources 'La justice telle qu'elle est vécue en Alantika-Faro', Archives du diocèse de Garoua, Oct. 1984, see also, N. Barley, *The Innocent Anthropologist. Notes from a Mud Hut*, Harmondsworth, Penguin Books, 1986, p.96.
70. Sources: 'Dossier concernant les souffrances des gens de l'arrondissement de Koza', Diocesan archives of Maroua- Mokolo, Nov. 1984. On the complicity of the chiefs with the 'coupeurs de route' see, *Cameroon Tribune* (Yaoundé), 29-30 March 1987, p.9.
71. 'Zambie: L'elite du pays impliquée dans un trafic de drogue', *Marchés tropicaux et méditerranéens*, 18 Oct. 1985, p. 2591; *ibid.*, 15 Nov. 1985, p. 2830; M. Warsama, 'The plotters', *The Express* (Nairobi), II (2), 1985, pp. 10-14; *Cameroon Tribune* (Yaoundé), 7 April. 1987, p. 10; *ibid.*, 7 July 1987, p. 11; *La Gazette* (Douala), 515, 6 Dec. 1984, pp. 3 and 14.
72. D.J. Gould, *Bureaucratic Corruption and Underdevelopment in the Third World. The Case of Zaïre*, New York, Pergamon Press, 1980, pp. 123-149. See also R.M. Price, *Society and Bureaucracy in Contemporary Ghana*, Berkeley, University of California Press, 1975; R.A. Joseph, *Democracy and Prebendal Politics in Nigeria;* R, Tangri, *Politics in Sub-Saharan Africa*, London, James Currey, Portsmouth, Heinemann, 1985, chap. ii; J.D Greenstone, 'Corruption and self-interest in Kampala and Nairobi: a comment on local politics in East Africa', *Comparative Studies in Society and History*, VIII (2), Jan. 1966, pp. 199-210; M. Szeftel, 'The political process in postcolonial Zambia: the structural bases of factional conflict' in Centre of African Studies, University of Edinburgh, *The Evolving Structure of Zambian Society*, 1980, pp. 76; J.-F. Médard, 'One year of corruption in the political life of Kenya', ECPR Workshop 'Political Corruption in Comparative Perspective', Freiburg-im-Brisgau, 20-25 March 1983,; Republic of Zambia, *Report of the Commission of Inquiry into the Salaries, Salary Structures and Conditions of Service of the Zambia Public and Teaching Services, etc. vol. I: The Public Service*, Lusaka, Government Printer, 1975; Republic of Zambia, *Report of the Commission of Inquiry into the Affairs of the Lusaka City Council*, Nov. 1968, Lusaka, Office of the President, 1969.
73. 'Lettre ouverte au citoyen président-fondateur du Mouvement populaire de la révolution, président de la République, par un groupe de parlementaires', *Politique africaine*, 3, Sept. 1981, pp. 122 and 126-128.
74. Figures given by D.J. Gould in G. Gran, ed., *Zaïre: the Political Economy of Underdevelopment*, New York, Praeger, 1979, p.102 and cited by C. Young, T. Turner, *The Rise and Decline of the Zaïrian State*, p. 245.
75. N. Casswell, 'Autopsie de l'ONCAD', pp. 58 and 69; R.H. Bates, *Markets and States in Tropical Africa*, pp. 26 ff.
76. République Française, ministère de la Coopération, *Déséquilibres structurels et programmes d'ajustement en Côte d'Ivoire*
77. *Marchés tropicaux et méditerranéens*, 22 May 1987, p. 1272; *Africa Confidential*, 13 May 1987.
78. S. Othman, 'Classes, crises and coup: the demise of Shagari's regime', *African Affairs*, 83 (333), Oct. 1984, pp. 450-451.
79. Spartacus, *Opération Manta, Tchad. 1983-1984. Les documents secrets,*

Paris, Plon, 1985, p. 63; *Financial Gazette* (Harare), cited by *Marchés tropicaux et méditerranéens*, 20 March 1987, p.717. See, for example D.S. MacRae, 'The import licensing system in Kenya', *Journal of Modern African Studies*, 17 (1), 1979, pp. 29-46.

80. See S. Othman, 'Classes, crises and coup', pp. 449-450; L. Gouffern, 'Les limites d'un modèle? A propos d'*Etat et bourgeoisie en Côte d'Ivoire*', *Politique Africaine*, 6 May 1982, pp. 19-34; L. Durand-Reville, 'La fin de l'industrie en Afrique?', *Marchés tropicaux et méditerranéens*, 16 Oct. 1987, pp. 2729-2730; E. Grégoire, *Les Alhazai de Maradi (Niger). Histoire d'un groupe de riches marchands sahéliens*, Paris, ORSTOM, 1986, pp. 132 and 180; J. MacGaffey, *Entrepreneurs and Parasites*, chap, 6; D. Newbury, 'From "frontier" to "boundary": some historical roots of peasant strategies of survival in Zaïre' in Nzongola-Ntajala, ed., *The Crisis in Zaïre. Myths and Realities*, Trenton, Africa World Press, 1986, pp. 87-97.

81. 'Gaspillages technologiques', *Politique africaine*, 18, June 1985, pp. 3-87; J.-C. Willame, *Zaïre, l'épopée d'Inga. Chronique d'une prédation industrielle*, Paris, L'Harmattan, 1986; A. Postel-Vinay, 'Réflexions hétérodoxes sur les drames du Tiers monde', *Marchés tropicaux et méditerranéens*, 10 July 1987, pp. 1881-1882.

82. G. Williams, T. Turner, 'Nigeria' in J. Dunn, ed., *West African States. Failure and Promise. A Study in Comparative Politics*, Cambridge, Cambridge University Press, 1978, p. 156 and T. Turner, 'Commercial capitalism and the 1975 coup' in K. Panter-Brick, ed., *Soldiers and Oil. The Political Transformation of Nigeria*, pp. 166-197.

83. S. Othman, 'Classes, crises and coup' p. 452.

84. A. Dahmani, 'Un grand scandale en perspective', *Jeune Afrique*, 27 May 1987; J.-L. Amselle, 'Socialisme, capitalisme et précapitalisme au Mali (1960-1982) 'in H. Bernstein, B.K. Campbell, eds., *Contradictions of Accumulation in Africa*, pp. 257-259 and 'Famine, prolétarisation et création de nouveaux liens de dépendance au Sahel. Les réfugiés de Mopti et de Léré au Mali' *Politique africaine*, 1, Jan. 1981, pp, 5-22.

85. R. Joseph, *Democracy and Prebendal Politics in Nigeria*, On the distinction between prebends and the patrimonial domain E. Wolf, *Peasents*, New York, Prentice Hall, 1966, pp. 51-56.

86. C. Leys, *Underdevelopment in Kenya. The Political Economy of Neo-Colonialism 1964-1971*, London Heinemann, 1975, pp. 193 ff. and 249-250; N. Swainson, *The Development of Corporate Capitalism in Kenya, 1918-1977* London, Heinemann, 1980, p. 191; M. Cowen, K. Kinyanjui, *Some Problems of Capital and Class in Kenya*, pp. 3-32; *Weekly Review* (Nairobi), 6 April. 1984.

87. D.-C. Martin, *Tanzanie*, pp. 193-202; B. Joinet, *A Letter to my Superiors* (Dar es Salaam), 1985-1986; 'Nyerere catches tiddlers but big fish still swim', *New African*, March 1982, pp. 23-24.

88. *Fraternité* (Abidjan), 4 Oct. 1963.

89. C. de Miras, 'L'entrepreneur ivoirien ou une bourgeoisie privée de son état' in Y.-A. Fauré, J.-F. Médard, Ed., *État et bourgeoisie en Côte d'Ivoire*, pp. 212-229; République Française, ministére de la Coopération, *Déséquilibres structurels et programmes d'ajustement en Côti d'Ivoire*, and *Analyse 'ex post' de la promotion des PME et de l'artisanat en Côte d'Ivoire*, Paris, 1986.

90. Y. Lacoste, *Contre les anti-tiers mondistes et contre certains tiers mondistes*, Paris, La Découverte, 1985, pp. 107-109.
91. J.-L, Piermay, 'Le détournement d'espace, Corruption et stratégies de détournement dans les pratiques fonciéres urbaines en Afrique centrale', *Politique africaine*, 21, March 1986, pp. 25-28. See also C. Leys, *Underdevelopment in Kenya*, p. 194 ff. M.A. Cohen, *Urban Policy and Political Conflict in Africa*, pp. 42 ff.
92. *Le Manifeste du négro-mauritanien*, pp. 18 ff., J.-L. Amselle, 'Socialisme, capitalisme et précapitalisme au Mali (1960-1982)' 'in H. Bernstein, B.K. Campbell, eds., *Contradictions of Accumulation in Africa*, p. 253.
93. C. Leys, *Underdevelopment in Kenya*, chap. iii; Y.-A. Fauré, J.-F. Médard, 'Classe dominante ou classe dirigeante' in Y.-A. Fauré, Médard. ed., *État et bourgeoisie en Côte d'Ivoire*, ed., pp. 145-146 and J.-M. Gastellu, S. Affou Yapi, 'Un mythe a décomposer: la bourgeoisie de planteurs', pp. 177-179.
94. C. Young, T. Turner, *The Rise and Decline of the Zaïrian State*, p. 337. M.G. Schatzberg, *Politics and Class in Zaïre*, chap. 7.
95. M.G. Schatzberg, *ibid.*
96. D.J Gould, 'Underdevelopment, administration and disorganisation theory: systematic corruption in the public bureaucracy of Mobutu's Zaïre', Paper presented to *Conference on Political Clientelism, Patronage and Development*, Bellagio, Aug, 1978, p. 56.
97. M.G. Schatzberg, *Politics and Class in Zaïre*, pp. 130 ff. There too the conclusions of J. MacGaffey differ, *(Enterpreneurs and Parasites*, pp. 96 ff.).
98. J. Lonsdale, 'States and social processes in Africa: a historiographical survey', *African Studies Review*, XXIV (2-3), June-Sept, 1981, p. 193.
99. M. von Freyhold turned this expression into a concept, (*'The Workers and the Nizers'*, Dar es Salaam, University of Dar es Salaam, 1973).

CHAPTER 3: THE BOURGEOIS ILLUSION

1. P. Geschiere, *Village Communities and the State. Changing Relations among the Maka of Southeastern Cameroon since the Colonial Conquest*, London, Kegan Paul International, 1982.
2. S.S. Berry, *Fathers Work for their Sons. Accumulation, Mobility and Class Formation in an Extended Yoruba Community*, Berkeley, University of California Press, 1985; R.A. Joseph, 'Affluence and underdevelopment: the nigerian experience', *Journal of Modern African Studies*, 16 (2), 1978, pp. 221-239 and *Democracy and Prebendal Politics in Nigeria. The Rise and Fall of the Second Republic*, Cambridge, Cambridge University Press, 1987, pp. 10 and 83-87; D. Rimmer, 'Elements of the political economy' and T. Turner, 'Commercial capitalism and the 1975 coup' in K. Panter-Brick, ed., *Soldiers and Oil. The Political Transformation of Nigeria*, London, Frank Cass, 1978, pp. 141-197; T. Forrest, 'State capital in Nigeria'. Paper presented to Conference on the African Bourgeoisie, Dakar, 1980.

3. C. Young, T. Turner, *The Rise and Decline of the Zairian State*, Madison, The University of Wisconsin Press, 1985, pp. 178 ff.; T.M. Callaghy, *The State-Society Struggle, Zaïre in Comparative Perspective*, New York, Columbia University Press, 1984, p. 179; M.G. Schatzberg, *Politics and Class in Zaïre. Bureaucracy, Business and Beer in Lisala*, New York, Africana Publishing Company, 1980, pp. 136 ff.; 'Political and economic situation in Zaïre. Fall 1981', Hearing before the Sub-Committee on Africa of the Committee on Foreign Affairs, House of Representatives, Ninety-Seventh Congress, First Session, September 15, 1981, Washington, U.S. Government Printing Office, 1982, pp. 33-36.
4. E. Blumenthal, 'Zaïre: rapport sur sa crédibilité financière internationale, cited in *Jeune Afrique*, 3 Nov. 1982, p. 32.
5. S. Andreski, *The African Predicament*, London, Michael Joseph, 1968, p. 92; J.L., 'La reconduction de M. Ahmed Abdallah à la présidence des Comores', *Marchés tropicaux et méditerranéens*, 23 Nov. 1984, p. 2856; R. Jeffries, 'Rawlings and the political economy of underdevelopment in Ghana', *African Affairs*, 81 (324), July 1982, pp. 314-315; S. Othman, 'Classes, crises and coup: the demise of Shagari's regime', *African Affairs*, 83 (333), Oct. 1984, pp. 451-452; D. Bigo, 'Forme d'exercice du pouvoir et obéissance en Centrafrique, (1966-1979)', Paris, Université de Paris-I, 1985, p. 247; C. Toulabor, *Le Togo sous Eyadema*, Paris, Karthala, 1986, pp. 250 ff.; M. Selhami, 'Un seul gouvernement: la famille', *Jeune Afrique plus*, 8 June 1984, pp. 18-21; J.-L. Amselle, 'Socialisme, capitalisme et précapitalisme au Mali (1960-1982)' in H. Bernstein, B.K. Campbell, eds., *Contradictions of Accumulation in Africa. Studies in Economy and State*, Beverly Hills, Sage Publications, 1985, pp. 249-266; G. Gillard, 'Le Règne de Francisco Macias Nguema sur la Guinée équatoriale: un népotisme méconnu', Bordeaux, Institut d'études politiques, 1980; M. Liniger-Goumaz, *Guinée équatoriale, un pays méconnu*, Paris, L'Harmattan, 1979; J. Oto, *Le Drame d'un pays, la Guinée équatoriale*, Yaoundé, Ed. C.L.E., 1979.
6. J. Barry, *The Sunday Times* (London), 17 Aug. 1975, cited by G. Dauch, D. Martin, *L'Héritage de Kenyatta. La Transition politique au Kenya, 1975-1982*, Aix-Marseille, Presses Universitaires d'Aix-Marseille, Paris, L'Harmattan, 1985, pp. 37-38.
7. *Africa Confidential*, 14 April 1986; interviews.
8. J.-L. Piermay, 'Le détournement d'espace', *Politique africaine*, 21 March 1986, p. 27; P. Péan, *Affaires africaines*, Paris, Fayard, 1983, pp. 102 ff.; A. Assam, *Omar Bongo ou la raison du mal gabonais*, Paris, La Pensée universelle, 1985, chap. iv.
9. Speech of M. Houphouët-Boigny, *Fraternité-Matin* (Abidjan), 29 April 1983, p. 17. M. Houphouët-Boigny is expressing himself in CFA francs. See also the communiqué of the political bureau of PDCI-RDA announcing the banning of any publications of the *Jeune Afrique* group in the Ivory Coast. ('Certes, grâce à Dieu, le président Houphouët-Boigny ne manque pas d'argent. Mais ne vaut-il pas mieux faire envie que pitié?', cited in *Jeune Afrique*, 18 Nov. 1987, p. 70) and J. Baulin, *La Politique intérieure d'Houphouët-Boigny*, Paris, Eurafor-Press, 1982.
10. *Africa Confidential*, 18 Feb. 1987, p. 5. On president Abdou Diouf, see G. Fouger, 'Les fossoyeurs du Sénégal', *Taxi ville*, 5 Feb-March 1988,

pp. 14-16.

11. Interview of Dr Idoko Obe, cited in R.A. Joseph, *Democracy and Prebendal Politics in Nigeria*, p. 150.

12. On this concept and its application to sub-Saharan societies, see J.L. Linz, 'Totalitarian and authoritarian regimes' in F.I. Greenstein, N. Polsby, eds., *Handbook of Political Science*, Reading, Addison Wesley Co, 1975, vol. III, p. 240; J.-C. Willame, *Patrimonialism and Political Change in the Congo*, Stanford, Stanford University Press, 1972; J.-F. Medard, 'La spécificité des pouvoirs africains', *Pouvoirs*, 25, 1983, pp. 15 ff.; R. Sandbrook, J. Barker, *The Politics of Africa's Economic Stagnation*, Cambridge, Cambridge University Press, 1985 and 'Personnalisation du pouvoir et stagnation capitaliste. L'État africain en crise', *Politique africaine*, 26 June 1987, pp. 23 ff.; C. Clapham, ed., *Private Patronage and Public Power: Political Clientelism in the Modern State*, London, Frances Pinter Ltd, 1982; T.M. Callaghy, *The State-Society Struggle*.

13. I. Wilks, *Asante in the Nineteenth Century. The structure and Evolution of a Political Order*, Cambridge, Cambridge University Press, 1975, pp. 195-196, 267 ff., 689 ff.; E. Terray, 'L'économie politique du royaume abron du Gyaman', *Cahiers d'études africaines*, 87-88, XXII-3-4, 1982, pp. 261-262; P.E. Lovejoy, *Salt of the Desert Sun. A History of Salt Production and Trade in the Central Sudan*, Cambridge, Cambridge University Press, 1986, pp. 177 ff.

14. I. Wilks, *Asante in the Nineteenth Century*, pp. 720 ff.

15. C. de Miras, 'L'entrepreneur ivoirien ou une bourgeoisie privée de son état' in Y.-A. Fauré, J.-F. Médard, eds., *Etat et bourgeoisie en Côte d'Ivoire*, Paris, Karthala, 1982, pp. 181-229.

16. A. Cournanel, 'Economie politique de la Guinée (1958-1981)' in H. Bernstein, B.K. Campbell, eds., *Contradictions of Accumulation in Africa*, pp. 207-247.

17. N. Swainson, *The Development of Corporate Capitalism in Kenya, 1918-1977*, London, Heinemann, 1980.

18. J. MacGaffey, *Entrepreneurs and Parasites. The Struggle for Indigenous Capitalism in Zaïre*, Cambridge, Cambridge University Press, 1987. MacGaffey's conclusions are confirmed in the thesis of V. Mukohya, 'African Traders in Butembo, Eastern Zaïre (1960-1980). A Case Study of Informal Entrepreneurship in a Cultural Context of Central Africa, Madison, University of Wisconsin, 1982.

19. République Française, ministère de la Coopération, *Déséquilibres structurels et programmes d'ajustement en Côte d'Ivoire*, Paris, 1986, pp. 99 and République Française, ministère des Relations extérieures, Coopération et Développement, Analyse "ex post" de la promotion des PME et de l'artisanat en Côte d'Ivoire, Paris, 1986.

20. *Marchés tropicaux et méditerranéens*, 31 Oct. 1986, p. 2719.

21. J. Goody, *Technology, Tradition and the State in Africa*, Cambridge, Cambridge University Press, 1980, pp. 51-52. See, for example A. Cohen, *Custom and Politics in Urban Africa. A Study of Hausa Migrants in Yoruba Towns*, Berkeley, University of California Press, 1969; J.-L. Amselle, *Les Négociants de la savane*, Paris, Anthropos, 1977; E. Grégoire, *Les Alhazai de Maradi (Niger). Histoire d'un groupe de riches marchands sahéliens*, Paris, ORSTOM, 1986.

22. J.-P. Warnier, *Echanges développement et hiérarchies dans le Bamenda précolonial (Cameroun)*, Stuttgart, Franz Steiner Verlag Wiesbaden, 1985; J. Champaud, *Villes et campagnes du Cameroun de l'ouest*, Paris, ORSTOM, 1983, pp. 267 ff.

23. M. A. Aduayom, A. Kponton, 'Place des revendeuses de tissus dans l'économie togolaise', in Laboratoire Connaissance du Tiers-Monde, *Entreprises et entrepreneurs en Afrique (xix^{e}e et xxe siècles)*, Paris, L'Harmattan, 1983, vol. II, pp. 385-400; J.-Y. Weigel, *'Nana* et pêcheurs du port de Lomé', *Politique africaine*, 27, Sept.-Oct. 1987, pp. 37-46; E. Ayini, 'Pagnes et politique', pp. 47-54; M.C. Diop, 'Les affaires mourides à Dakar', *Politique africaine*, 4, Nov. 1981, pp. 90-100; D. Fassin, 'Du clandestin à l'officieux. Les réseaux de vente illicite des médicaments au Sénégal', *Cahiers d'études africaines*, 98, XXV-2, 1985, pp. 161-177.

24. K. Polanyi, *La Grande Transformation. Aux origines politiques et économiques de notre temps*, Paris, Gallimard, 1983; K. Marx, F. Engels, *L'Idéologie allemande*, Paris, Éditions Sociales, 1974.

25. M. Mamdani, *Politics and Class Formation in Uganda*, London, Heinemann, 1976.

26. J.-L. Amselle, 'Socialisme, capitalisme et précapitalisme au Mali (1960-1982)' in H. Bernstein, B.K. Campbell, eds., *Contradictions of Accumulation in Africa*, pp. 249-252 and 260-265. See also J.-L. Amselle, E. Grégoire, 'Complicités et conflits entre bourgeoisies d'Etat et bourgeoisies d'affaires au Mali et au Niger' in E. Terray, ed., *L'Etat contemporain en Afrique*, Paris, L'Harmattan, 1987, pp. 23-47; J.-L. Amselle, 'La politique de la Banque mondiale en Afrique au sud du Sahara', *Politique africaine*, 10, June 1983, pp. 113-118; C. Meillassoux, 'A class analysis of the bureaucratic process in Mali', *Journal of Development Studies*, VI (2), Jan. 1970, pp. 97-110.

27. G. Dauch, D. Martin, *L'Héritage de Kenyatta*, pp. 58, 73 ff., 137-139 and G. Dauch, 'Kenya: la chute de la maison Njonjo (1983)', *Annuaire des pays de l'océan Indien*, IX, 1982-1983, pp. 349-350. Elsewhere, G. Dauch writes: 'L'affrontement n'est donc pas classe contre classe, ou nationalistes contre "multinationalistes" comme on l'a quelquefois écrit; mais entre deux coalitions de groupes rivaux au sein de la même classe, en alliances où les mêmes intérêts peuvent se trouver d'un bord *et* de l'autre' ('Kenya: J.M. Kariuki ou l'éthique nationale du capitalisme', *Politique africaine*, 8, Dec. 1982, p. 40).

28. J. Champaud, *Villes et campagnes du Cameroun de l'ouest*, p. 286.

29. 'Muyenga et Takala sur le trottoir', *Le Messager* (Douala), 106, 18 March 1987. In another chronical, Takala explains: 'Je crois, moi qui suis dans les affaires, qu'il est facile aux hauts fonctionnaires de s'enrichir très vite en nous faisant de la concurrence déloyale [...]. Ces messieurs créent partout dans les quartiers, sous les noms de leurs épouses, maitresses ou d'autres hommes de paille, des sociétés fictives qui nous disputent tous les marchés de fourniture à l'Etat en mettant dans leur jeu les gestionnaires des crédits. L'argent de l'Etat passe ainsi du Trésor à leurs comptes bancaires privés, contre factures gonflées ou fausses. Je crois enfin que grâce aux centaines de millions ainsi gagnés en marge de son salaire et des avantages dus à ses fonctions chaque fonctionnaire haut

placé peut aisément entretenir son "réseau" des racines au sommet et jouir d'une assurance d'impunité – tous risques' (*ibid*, 114, 4 August 1987, p. 2). See also P. Ebollo, 'Des larmes pour le malheureux Moussa Yaya?', *La Gazette* (Douala), 23 August 1984, p. 8; 'Fraude douanière: rebondissement d'une vieille affaire', *ibid*, 27 June 1982; 'La fraude douanière: un mal qui répand la terreur', *Cameroon Tribune* (Yaoundé), from 4 to 8 Sept. 1983.

30. J.-L. Amselle, 'Le wahabisme à Bamako (1945-1983)', paper presented to 'Table ronde internationale: les agents religieux islamiques en Afrique tropicale', Paris, Maison des sciences de l'Homme, 1983; J. Copans, *Les Marabouts de l'arachide*, Paris, Le Sycomore, 1980; M.C. Diop, 'Les affaires mourides à Dakar'; D.B. Cruise O'Brien, *Saints and Politicians. Essays on the Organisation of a Senegalese Peasant Society*, Cambridge, Cambridge University Press, 1975.

31. M.P. Cowen, K. Kinyanjui, 'Some Problems of Capital and Class in Kenya', Nairobi, Institute for Development Studies, 1977. pp. 3-30.

32. N. Swainson, *The Development of Corporate Capitalism in Kenya*, pp. 200 ff.; National Christian Council, *Who Controls Industry in Kenya? Report of a Working Party*, Nairobi, East African Publishing House, 1968.

33. J. Iliffe, *The Emergence of African Capitalism*, London, Macmillan, 1983, pp. 30-31 and 65 ff.

34. J.D.Y. Peel, *Ijeshas and Nigerians. The Incorporation of a Yoruba Kingdom. 1890s-1970s*, Cambridge, Cambridge University Press, 1983, p. 164; R.L. Sklar, *Nigerian Political Parties*, Princeton, Princeton University Press, 1963, pp. 446-460.

35. J. Champaud, *Villes et campagnes du Cameroun de l'ouest*, p. 271. *Cf.* also J.-P. Warnier, *Echanges, développement et hiérarchies dans le Bamenda précolonial*, pp. 82 ff.; J.-L. Dongmo, *Le Dynamisme bamiléké (Cameroun)*, vol. II: *La Maîtrise de l'espace urbain*, Yaoundé, Centre d'édition et de production pour l'enseignement et la recherche, 1981, pp. 173 ff.

36. J.-J. Beaussou, 'Genèse d'une classe marchande au Niger: continuité ou rupture dans l'organisation sociale?' in Laboratoire 'Connaissance du Tiers-Monde' *Entreprises et entrepreneurs en Afrique*, vol. I, pp. 205-220; M.A. Aduayom, A. Kponton, 'Place des revendeuses de tissus dans l'économie togolaise', *ibid.*, vol. II, pp. 398-400; M.C. Diop, 'Les affaires mourides à Dakar', pp. 90-100; E. Grégoire, *Les Alhazaï de Maradi (Niger)*; P. Labazée, *Entreprises et entrepreneurs du Burkina Faso*, Paris, Karthala, 1988.

37. D.B. Cruise O'Brien, *Saints and Politicians*, République Française, ministère des Relations extérieures, Coopération et Développement, *Déséquilibres structurels et programmes d'ajustement au Sénégal*, Paris, 1985, pp. 76-77; N. Casswell, 'Autopsie de l'ONCAD: la politique arachidière au Sénégal. 1966-1980', *Politique africaine*, 14 June 1984, pp. 66 ff.

38. A. Morice, 'Commerce parallèle et troc à Launda', *Politique africaine*, 17 March 1985, p. 118.

39. J.-L. Amselle, 'Socialisme, capitalisme et précapitalisme au Mali (1960-1982) in H. Bernstein, B.K. Campbell, eds., *Contradictions of Accumulation in Africa*, pp. 257-258.

40. J.S. Saul, 'The unsteady state: Uganda, Obote and general Amin', *Review of African Political Economy*, 5 Jan.-April 1976, p. 17.

41. A. Cournanel, 'Economie politique de la Guinée (1958-1981)' in H. Bernstein, B.K. Campbell, eds., *Contradictions of Accumulation in Africa*, p. 230.

42. M.P. Cowen, 'The British state, state enterprise and an indigenous bourgeoisie in Kenya after 1945'. Paper presented to Conference on the African Bourgeoisie, Dakar, 1980, p. 34.

43. M.C. Newbury, 'Dead and buried or just underground? The privatization of the state in Zaïre', *Canadian Journal of African Studies*, XVIII (1), 1984, pp. 112-114.

44. T. Forrest, 'State capital in Nigeria', pp. 29-33; T. Turner, 'Commercial capitalism and the 1975 coup' in K. Panter-Brick, ed. *Soldiers and Oil*.

45. C. de Miras, 'L'entrepreneur ivoirien ou une bourgeoisie privée de son état' in Y.-A. Fauré, J.-F. Medard, eds., *État et bourgeoisie en Côte d'Ivoire*, p. 222.

46. J.-J. Beaussou, 'Genèse d'une classe marchande au Niger' in Laboratoire Connaissance du Tiers-Monde, *Entreprises et entrepreneurs en Afrique*; E. Grégoire, *Les Alhazaï de Maradi*.

47. G. Kitching, *Class and Economic Change in Kenya. The Making of an African Petite-Bourgeoisie*, New Haven, Yale University Press, 1980, pp. 451-452.

48. Y.-A. Fauré and B. Contamin *La bataille des entreprises publiques en Côte d'Ivoire,* Paris, Karthala, 1990.

49. T. Forrest, 'State capital in Nigeria', pp. 8 ff and 30; République Française, Ministère de la Coopération, *Déséquilibres structurels et programmes d'ajustement en Côte d'Ivoire*, pp. 22, 45, 131 ff. See also République Française, Ministère des Relations extérieures, Coopération et Développement, *Déséquilibres structurels et programmes d'ajustement au Sénégal*; G. Rocheteau, J. Roch, *Pouvoir financier et indépendance économique en Afrique. Le cas du Sénégal*, Paris, ORSTOM, Karthala, 1982; J.-C. Willame, 'Cameroun: les avatars d'un libéralisme planifié', *Politique africaine*, 18 June 1985, pp. 44-70. Finally, we should mention some exceptions: for example, the Central African Republic, where public expenditure fell from 20% of GDP in the early 60s to 11% in 1984 (République Française, ministère des Relations extérieures, Coopération et Développement, 'Déséquilibres structurels et programmes d'ajustement en République centraficaine, Paris, 1985, p. 10).

50. N. Kasfir, 'State, *magendo* and class formation in Uganda', *Journal of Commonwealth and Comparative Politics*, XXI (3), Nov. 1983, pp. 84-103; A. Morice, 'Commerce parallèle et troc à Luanda'; N. Chazan, *An Anatomy of Ghanaian Politics, Managing Political Recession, 1969-1982*, Boulder, Westview Press, 1983, p. 196; D. Fassin, 'Du clandestin à l'officieux' and 'La vente illicite des médicaments au Sénégal. Economies "parellèles", Etat et société', *Politique africaine*, 23 Sept. 1986, pp. 123-130; J. MacGaffey, 'How to survive and become rich amidst devastation: the second economy in Zaïre', *African Affairs*, 82 (328), July 1983, pp. 351-366; J.-L. Amselle, E. Le Bris, 'De la "pettite production marchande" à l'économie mercantile' in I. Deblé, P. Hugon et al., *Vivre et survivre dans les villes africaines*, Paris, PUF, 1982, p. 173.

51. In an important review article introducing the French public to the 'Kenyan debate' J. Copans translated Cowen's 'Straddling class' by

'bourgeoisie mixte' (J. Copans, 'Le débat sur l'expérience kenyane', *Le Monde diplomatique*, Nov. 1981, pp. 19-20).

52. C. Young, T. Turner, *The Rise and Decline of the Zairian State*, pp. 110 ff.; M.G. Schatzberg, *Politics and Class in Zaïre*, M.C. Newbury ('Dead and buried or just underground?', p. 113) remarks nonetheless that the divide between the 'commercial class' and the 'bureaucratic class' which had almost disappeared at the top was nonetheless evident in the regional councils elected in June 1982.

53. R.A. Joseph, 'Theories of the African bourgeoisie: an exploration'. Paper presented to the Conference on the African Bourgeoisie, Dakar, 1980, pp. 17 ff.; M.G. Schatzberg, *Politics and Class in Zaïre*.

54. B. Freund, *The Making of Contemporary Africa. The Development of African Society since 1800*, Bloomington, Indiana University Press, 1984, pp. 90-91 and p. 140; S.B. Kaplow, 'The mudfish and the crocodile: underdevelopment of a West African bourgeoisie', *Science and Society*, XII (3), Fall 1977, pp. 317-333.

55. R.W. Shenton, *The Development of Capitalism in Northern Nigeria*, London, James Currey, 1986, pp. 125-126. For a similar example from Niger, see also E. Grégoire, *Les Alhazaï de Maradi*, pp. 68 ff. and 81 ff.

56. N. Swainson, *The Development of Corporate Capitalism in Kenya*, pp. 180 ff.

57. S. Cronje, *Lonrho*, Harmondsworth, Penguin Books, 1976.

58. N. Swainson, *The Development of Corporate Capitalism in Kenya*, chap. vii. On the economic collaboration between heads of state and foreign businessmen, see, for example, *Africa Confidential*, 24 June 1987 (on Kenya); *ibid.*, 17 Sept. 1986, 7 Jan. 1987 and 24 June 1987 (on Sierra Leone); C. Young, T. Turner, *The Rise and Decline of the Zaïrian State*, pp. 302-303; and J.-C. Willame, *Zaïre. L'Épopée d'Inga. Chronique d'une prédation industrielle*, Paris, L'Harmattan, 1986.

59. G. Kitching, 'Politics, method and evidence in the "Kenya debate"' in H. Bernstein, B.K. Campbell, eds., *Contradictions of Accumulation in Africa*, p. 131.

60. See especially 'L'Afrique sans frontière', *Politique africaine*, 9, March 1983, pp. 3-83.

61. Sources: République Française, ministère des Relations extérieures, Coopération et Développement *'Déséquilibres structurels et programmes d'ajustement en République centrafricaine'* Paris, 1985 p. 20; *Marchés tropicaux et méditerranéens*, 24 May 1985, p. 1297. See also *ibid*, 10 April 1987, pp. 849-850; O.J. Igue, 'Le Commerce de contrebande et les problèmes monétaires en Afrique occidentale', Cotonou, CEFAP, Université nationale du Bénin, 1977, and Association des Banques centrales africaines, Centre africain d'études monétaires. 'Le Commerce frontalier en Afrique', Dakar, 1984.

62. *Fraternité Matin* (Abidjan), 29 April 1983, p. 16.

63. République Française, *Déséquilibres structurels et programmes d'ajustement en Côte d'Ivoire*, pp. 11-13.

64. Sources: IMF. *International Financial Statistics, 1981-87.*

65. A. Postel-Vinay, 'Refléxions hétérodoxes sur les drames du Tiers monde. L'aggravation de ces drames est-elle fatale?', *Marchés tropicaux et méditerranéens*, 10 July 1987, p. 1882.

66. S. Langdon, 'The state and capitalism in Kenya', *Review of African Political Economy*, 8, 1977, pp. 90-98; S. Amin, *Le Développement du capitalisme en Côte d'Ivoire*, Paris, Ed. de Minuit, 1967.
67. 'Les relations cardinales. Polarisation internationale et changement politique dans les sociétés du Tiers monde', *Revue française de science politique*, 36 (6), Dec. 1986, pp. 733-861.
68. See especially G. Salem, 'De la brousse sénégalaise au Boul'Mich; le système commercial mouride en France', *Cahiers d'études africaines*, 81-83, XXI (1-3), 1981, pp. 267-288.
69. G. Kitching, *Class and Economic Change in Kenya*, pp. 444 ff.; S. Berry, *Fathers Work for their Sons*, pp. 193-194.
70. République Française, *Déséquilibres structurels et programmes d'ajustement au Sénégal,* and *Déséquilibres structurels et programmes d'ajustement en Côte d'Ivoire.*
71. L. Gouffern, 'Les limites d'un modèle? A propos d'*Etat et bourgeoisie en Côte d'Ivoire', Politique africaine*, 6 May 1982, pp. 19-34; 'Gaspillages technologiques', *ibid.*, 18 June 1985, pp. 3-92; J.-C. Willame, *Zaïre: l'épopée d'Inga,*
72. M Weber, *L'Ethique protestante et l'esprit du capitalisme*, Paris, Plon, 1985, p. 71 and R. Collins, 'Weber's last theory of capitalism: a systematisation', *American Sociological Review*, 45 (6), Dec. 1980, pp. 931-932. On this point see the nuanced 'readings' of J. Iliffe, *The Emergence of African Capitalism* and the comments of D.B. Cruise O'Brien, *Saints and Politicians*, pp. 79-81 and T.M. Callaghy, 'The state and the development of capitalism in Africa: theoretical, historical and comparative reflections' in D. Rothchild, N. Chazan, eds., *The Precarious Balance, State and Society in Africa*, Boulder, Westview Press, 1988, pp. 67-99. P. Kennedy, *African Capitalism. The Struggle for Ascendancy*, Cambridge, Cambridge University Press, 1988 is an excellent synthesis.

CHAPTER 4: THE OPPORTUNITY STATE

1. P. Anderson, *L'État absolutiste,* vol. II: *L'Europe de l'Est*, Paris, Maspero, 1978, p. 247. See also L.A. Fallers, *Inequality. Social Stratification Reconsidered*, Chicago, The University of Chicago Press, 1973.
2. Here we take up the critique of F. Cooper, 'Africa and the world economy', *African Studies Review*, 24 (2-3), June-Sept. 1981, pp. 14-15. See also E.P. Thompson, *The Poverty of Theory and Other Essays*, Monthly Review Press, 1978.
3. On the irrelevance of the concepts of feudality and aristocracy to the African societies see, apart from P. Anderson *l'Europe de 'Est* , pp. 227 ff., G. Balandier, *Anthropologie politique*, Paris, PUF, 1969 (2ᵉe éd.), pp. 113-116 and J. Goody, *Technology, Tradition and the State in Africa*, Cambridge, Cambridge University Press, 1971, pp. 13-14, and 76, I. Wilks, 'The state of the Akan and the Akan state: a discursion', *Cahiers d'études africaines*, 87-88, XXII (3-4), 1982, pp. 231-249 and J.D.Y. Peel, *Ijeshas*

and Nigerians. The Incorporation of a Yoruba Kingdom. 1890s-1970s, Cambridge, Cambridge University Press, 1983, pp. 45-46 for some suggestive case studies.

On the concepts of social elders and juniors, see J.-C. Barbier, 'Alliance ou conflit entre le haut et le bas?', *Politique africaine*, 1, Jan. 1981, pp. 130-137 and R.A. Joseph's reply in *Cahiers d'études africaines*, 71, XVIII (3), 1978, pp. 455-457, as well as P. Geschiere, *Village Communities and the State. Changing Relations among the Maka of Southern Cameroon since the Colonial Conquest*, London, KPI, 1982, pp. 10 ff.

4. F. Braudel, *L'Identité de la France. Espace et histoire*, Paris Arthaud, Flammarion, 1986, pp. 61-62.

5. A.B. Diop, *La Société wolof. Tradition et changement*, vol. I: *Les Systèmes d'inégalité et de domination*, Paris, Karthala, 1981, p. 36. On the similar case (in this instance) of Futa Tooro, see also J. Schmitz, 'L'État géomètre: les leydi des Peul Fuuta Tooro (Sénégal) et du Maasina (Mali)', *Cahiers d'études africaines*, 103, XXVI (3), 1986, pp. 349-394.

6. J.-P. Olivier de Sardan, *Les Sociétés songhay-zarma (Niger-Mali). Chefs, guerriers, esclaves, paysans...*, Paris, Karthala, 1984, pp. 58-60 and 128.

7. *Ibid.*, pp. 34-35, and 201 ff.

8. Nobleman's opinion cited by E. Pollet, G. Winter, *Les Sociétés soninké*, Brussels, Ed. de l'Université de Bruxelles, 1972, p. 259.

9. R. Santerre, 'Maîtres coraniques de Maroua' in R. Santerre, C. Mercier-Tremblay, eds., *La Quête du savoir. Essais pour une anthropologie de l'éducation*, Montréal, Presses de l'Université de Montréal, 1982, pp. 364-365.

10. A.B. Diop, *La Société wolof*, pp. 98 ff.; J.-M. Gastellu, *L'Égalitarisme économique des Serer du Sénégal*, Paris, ORSTOM, 1981, pp. 668 ff, 681 ff., 750 ff.

11. See also, for example, J. Weber, 'Types de surproduit et formes d'accumulation. La province cacaoyère du centre-sud Cameroun' in *Essais sur la reproduction de formations sociales dominées (Cameroun, Côte d'Ivoire, Haute-Volta, Sénégal, Madagascar, Polynésie)*, Paris, ORSTOM, 1977, pp. 76-77; J.M. Gastellu, S. Affou Yapi, 'Un mythe à décomposer: la "bourgeoisie de planteurs"' in Y.A. Fauré, J.-F. Médard, eds., *État et bourgeoisie en Côte d'Ivoire*, Paris, Karthala, 1982, pp. 156-157. Moreover, we should keep in mind the fluidity of historical systems of inequality: 'Malgré l'apparente rigidité d'une société que certains auteurs ont qualifiée de "société de castes", on s'aperçoit qu'il n'y a pas d'endogamie stricte de chaque groupe statutaire envisagée du point de vue de la longue durée: au contraire, chaque lignage noble ou ingénu se situe sur un vecteur de changement de condition – et donc, à terme, d'identité', (J. Schmitz 'L'État géomètre' p. 354).

12. See, for example, C. Meillassoux, *Femmes, greniers et capitaux*, Paris, Maspero, 1975; J.-P. Dozon, *La Société bété, Côte d'Ivoire*, Paris, ORSTOM, Karthala, 1985, pp. 318-319; J.-P. Olivier de Sardan, *Les Sociétés songhaï-zarma*, pp. 247 ff.: M. Samuel, *Le Prolétariat africain noir en France*, Paris, Maspero, 1978; F.G. Snyder, *Capitalism and Legal Change. An African Transformation*, New York, Academic Press, 1981; G. Kitching, *Class and Economic Change in Kenya*, pp. 210-211; P. Devauges, *L'Oncle, le ndoki et l'entrepreneur. La petite entreprise congolaise*

à Brazzaville, Paris, ORSTOM, 1977; P.M. Lubeck, *Islam and Urban Labor in Northern Nigeria: the Making of a Muslim Working Class*, Cambridge, Cambridge University Press, 1986.

13. R.W. Shenton, *The Development of Capitalism in Northern Nigeria*, London, James Currey, 1986, p. 120.

14. G. and M. Wilson, *The Analysis of Social Change Based on Observations in Central Africa*, Cambridge, Cambridge University Press, 1954. See, for example, J.D.Y. Peel, *Ijeshas and Nigerians*.

15. G. Kitching, *Class and Economic Change in Kenya*, pp. 282 ff.

16. Opinions quoted respectively in S. Berry, *Fathers Work for their Sons*, p. 193; A. Bonnassieux, 'Der Dendraka à Vridi-Canal. Chronique de la précarité à Abidjan', Paris, EHESS, 1982, p. 158; J.-P. Olivier de Sardan, *Les Sociétés songhaï-zarma*, p. 109.

17. F. Cooper, *From Slaves to Squatters. Plantation Labour and Agriculture in Zanzibar and Coastal Kenya. 1890-1925*, New Haven, Yale University Press, 1980; R.W. Shenton, *The Development of Capitalism, in Northern Nigeria*; L.A. Fallers, ed., *The King's Men: Leadership and Status in Buganda on the Eve of Independence*, London, Oxford University Press, 1964.

18. *Cf.* for example, G. Balandier, *Sociologie actuelle de l'Afrique noire. Dynamique sociale en Afrique centrale*, Paris, PUF, 1971 (3ᵉ ed.); G. Dupré, *Les Naissances d'une société. Espace et historicité chez les Beembé du Congo*, Paris, ORSTOM, 1985 and *Un ordre et sa destruction*, Paris, ORSTOM, 1982; J.-P. Olivier de Sardan *Les Sociétés songhaï-zarma*, Part II; J.D.Y. Peel, *Ijeshas and Nigerians*; P. Geschiere, *Village Communities and the State*: M. Staniland, *The lions of Dagbon: Political Change in Northern Ghana*, Cambridge, Cambridge University Press, 1975; J. Dunn, A.F. Robertson, *Dependence and Opportunity: Political Change in Ahafo*, Cambridge, Cambridge University Press, 1973. On the effects of Arab expansion into Central Africa in the 19th century, see also, B. Abemba, 'Pouvoir et conflit dans la collectivité du Maniema. Essai de description et d'interprétation des phénomènes politiques conflictuels locaux à partir de trois cas concrets', Brussels, Université libre, 1974; J. Vansina, *Les Anciens Royaumes de la savane*, Léopoldville, IRES, 1965, chap. 9.

19. J.-F. Bayart, *L'État au Cameroun*, Paris, Presses de la Fondation nationale des sciences politiques, 1979. For a comment on this, see P. Geschiere, 'Hegemonic regimes and popular protest – Bayart, Gramsci and the State in Cameroon', *Les Cahiers de CEDAF*, July 1986, pp. 309-347.

20. For a remarkable methodology on the crisis, see G. Bois, *Crise du féodalisme*, Paris, Presses de la Fondation nationale des sciences politiques, EHESS, 1976.

21. R. Lemarchand, *Rwanda and Burundi*, London, Pall Mall Press, 1970, pp. 472 ff.; J.D.Y. Peel, *Ijeshas and Nigerians*, pp. 45-46. See also J. Schmitz' comment on the Fouta Toro quoted in Note 11 above.

22. A. Gramsci, *Passato e presente*, Turin, Einaudi, 1966, p. 38.

23. I. Wilks, *Asante in the Nineteenth Century. The Structure and Evolution of a Political Order*, Cambridge, Cambridge University Press, 1975, pp. 699-720.

24. J. Lonsdale, 'States and social processes in Africa: a historiographical survey', *African Studies Review*, XXIV (2-3), June-Sept. 1981, p. 180.

25. F. Braudel, *Écrits sur l'histoire*, Paris, Flammarion, 1969, p. 313.
26. J.-F. Bayart, *L'État au Cameroun*, p. 19. *Cf.* also P. Geschiere, 'Hegemonic regimes and popular protest'.
27. L. Cambrezy, P. Couty, A. Lericollais, J.-Y. Marchal, C. Raynaut, 'La région, territoire de recherche' in C. Blanc-Pamard et al'. *Le développement rural en questions*, Paris, ORSTOM, 1984, pp. 132; J.-P. Olivier de Sardan, *Les Sociétés songhaï-zarma*, pp. 232 ff.
28. F. Cooper, 'Africa and the world economy', p. 18.
29. For a rare analysis of the role of armaments in postcolonial political and social structuration, see R. Luckham, 'Armaments, underdevelopment and demilitarization in Africa', *Alternatives* VI, 1980, pp. 179-245.
30. P. Laburthe-Tolra, *Les Seigneurs de la forêt. Essai sur le passé historique, l'organisation sociale et les normes éthiques des anciens Beti du Cameroun*, Paris, Publications de la Sorbonne, 1981, pp. 369 ff.
31. R.A. Joseph, *Radical Nationalism in Cameroun. Social Origins of the UPC Rebellion*, Oxford, Oxford University Press, 1977.
32. P. Laburthe-Tolra, 'Minlaaba. Histoire et société traditionnelle chez les Beïti du Sud-Cameroun', Paris, Université René-Descartes, 1974; C. von Morgen, *A travers le Cameroun du sud au nord*, Paris, Serge Fleury, Publications de la Sorbonne, 1982; P. Laburthe-Tolra, *Yaoundé d'après Zenker (1895)*, Yaoundé, Université fédérale du Cameroun, 1970; F. Quinn, 'Charles Atangana of Yaoundé', *Journal of African History*, 21, 1980, pp. 485-495.
33. A. Wirz, 'La rivière du Cameroun: commerce précolonial et contrôle du pouvoir en société lignagère', *Revue française d'histoire d'outre-mer*, 60 (219), 1973; R. Gouellain, *Douala. ville et histoire*, Paris, Institut d'ethnologie, 1975.
34. J.D.Y. Peel, *Ijeshas and Nigerians*, chap. v; V. Azarya, *Aristocrats Facing Change. The Fulbe in Guinea, Nigeria and Cameroun*, Chicago, University of Chicago Press, 1978.
35. F. Braudel, *L'Identité de la France. Espace et histoire*, p. 156.
36. G. Balandier, *Anthropo-logiques*, Paris, PUF, 1974, pp. 46-47.
37. Parti socialiste, Circulaire n° 013/86/PS/SG, du 13 mai 1986, signée de M. Abdou Diouf.
38. G. Balandier, *Anthropo-logiques*, chap. 2; M. Abeles, C. Collard, eds., *Age, pouvoir et société en Afrique noire*, Paris, Karthala, Presses de l'Université de Montréal, 1985; J.-P. Dozon, *La Société bété*, pp. 223; P. Geschiere, *Village Communities and the State*; D. Desjeux, *Stratégies paysannes en Afrique noire. Le Congo (Essai sur la gestion de l'incertitude)*, Paris, L'Harmattan, 1987, pp. 54 ff.; J.-P. Olivier de Sardan, *La Société songhaï-zarma*, pp. 113 ff.
39. See, for example, J.-C. Barbier, ed., *Femmes du Cameroun. Mères pacifiques, femmes rebelles*, Paris, Karthala, 1985 or M. Abeles, C. Collard, eds., *Age, pouvoir et société*.
40. See, for example, J.-F. Vincent, *Traditions et transition. Entretiens avec des femmes beti du Sud Cameroun*, Paris, ORSTOM, Berger-Levrault, 1976; D. Paulme, ed., *Femmes d'Afrique noire*, Paris, La Haye, Mouton, 1960.
41. G. Balandier, *Sociologie actuelle de l'Afrique noire*, p. 155; J.-P. Dozon, *La Société bété*, p. 171.

42. J.-P. Dozon, *La Société bété*, pp. 228-229; D. Desjeux, *Stratégies paysannes en Afrique noire*, chap. 6; P. Geschiere, *Village Communities and the State, passim*.

43. J.-F. Bayart, 'L'énonciation du politique', *Revue française de science politique*, 35 (3), June 1985, pp. 346-347.

44. 'Des femmes sur l'Afrique des femmes', *Cahiers d'études africaines*, 65, XVII (1), 1977, pp. 5-199 and 'Gens et paroles d'Afrique, *ibid*., 73-76, XIX (1-4), 1979, pp. 219-327; C. Robertson, I. Berger, eds., *Women and Class in Africa*, New York, Africana Publishing Company, 1986; F. Le Guennec-Coppens, *Femmes voilées de Lamu (Kenya). Variations culturelles et dynamiques sociales*, Paris, Editions Recherche sur les civilisations, 1983; J.Y. Weigel, '*Nana* et pêcheurs du port de Lomé: une exploitation de l'homme par la femme?', *Politique africaine*, 27, Sept.-Oct. 1987, pp. 37-46; J. MacGaffey, *Entrepreneurs and Parasites*, chap. 7; S.B. Stichter, J.L. Parpart, eds., *Patriarchy and Class, African Women in the Home and the Workforce*, Boulder, Westview Press, 1988; M. Monsted, *Women's Groups in Rural Kenya and their Role in Development*, Copenhagen, Centre for Development Research, 1978; G. Dupré, *Les Naissances d'une société*, chap. xv; P. L'Hoiry, *Le Malawi*, Paris, Karthala, Nairobi, CREDU, 1988, p. 143; D. Bigo, 'Forme d'exercice du pouvoir et obéissance en Centrafrique (1966-1979). Éléments pour une théorie du pouvoir personnel, Paris, Université de Paris-I, 1985, pp. 231 ff., 330-332.

45. B. Verhaegen, *Rébellions au Congo*, vol. I, Kinshasa, CRISP, INEP, IRES, 1966, p. 109 and vol. II: *Maniema*, Brussels, CRISP, Kinshasa, IRES, 1969, pp. 334-335, 489.

46. W. Soyinka, *Aké, les années d'enfance*, Paris, Belfond, 1984.

47. Opinion of an elder in Abidjan quoted in A. Bonnassieux, *De Dendraka à Vridi-Canal*, p. 215.

48. G. Balandier, *Sociologie actuelle de l'Afrique noire*, pp. 388-389; J.-D. Gandoulou, *Entre Paris et Bacongo*, Paris, Centre Georges-Pompidou, Centre de création industrielle, 1984 et *Jeunes de Bacongo. Dynamique du phénomène sapeur congolais*, Paris, Université René-Descartes, 1988; S. Bemba, *50 ans de musique du Congo-Zaïre*, Paris, Présence africaine, 1984.

49. See for example, J.D.Y. Peel, *Ijeshas and Nigerians*, chap. vi.

50. A.A. Nwafor Orizu, *Without Bitterness, Western Nations in Post-War Africa*, New York, Creative Age Press, 1944, pp. 293 and 297 (in R.L. Sklar, *Nigerian Political Parties*, Princeton University Press, 1963, p. 73).

51. Figures quoted in J.M. Loucou, 'La vie politique en Côte d'Ivoire de 1932 à 1952, Université de Provence, 1976, p. 398.

52. F. Bebey, *Le Roi Albert d'Effidi*, Yaoundé, Ed. C.L.E., 1976.

53. J.D.Y. Peel, *Ijeshas and Nigerians*, p. 211.

54. B. Verhaegen, *Rébellions au Congo*, vol. I, pp. 109-110; R.C. Fox, W. de Craemer, J.M. Ribeaucourt, '"The second independence": a case study of the Kwilu rebellion in the Congo', *Comparative Studies in Society and History*, VIII (1), Oct. 1965, p. 101.

55. P. Bonnafé, 'Une classe d'âge politique. La JMNR de la République du Congo-Brazzaville', *Cahiers d'études africaines* 31, VIII (3), 1968, p. 357.

56. J.-F. Bayart, *L'État au Cameroun*, p. 19.

CHAPTER 5: CONSERVATIVE MODERNISATION OR SOCIAL REVOLUTION.

1. J.-F. Bayart, *L'État au Cameroun*, Paris, Presses de la Fondation nation-ale des sciences politiques, 1979; P. Geschiere, 'Hegemonic regimes and popular protest – Bayart, Gramsci and the state in Cameroon', *Les Cahiers du CEDAF*, July 1986, pp. 322 ff.
2. C. Coulon, 'Pouvoir oligarchique et mutations sociales et politiques au Fouta-Toro' in J.-L. Balans, C. Coulon, J.-M. Gastellu, *Autonomie locale et intégration nationale au Sénégal*, Paris, Pedone, 1975, pp. 23-80; C. Coulon, *Le Marabout et le Prince. Islam et pouvoir au Sénégal*, Paris, Pedone, 1981; D.B. Cruise O'Brien, *Saints and Politicians*, Cambridge, Cambridge University Press, 1975, p. 64.
3. J.-F. Bayart, *L'État au Cameroun*, pp. 23 ff.
4. C.H. Kane, *L'Aventure ambiguë*, Paris, Julliard, 1961, p. 53.
5. R. Lemarchand, 'Introduction: in search of the political kingdom' in R. Lemarchand, ed., *African Kingships in Perspective. Political Change and Modernization in Monarchical Settings*, London, Frank Cass, 1977, pp. 6-7.
6. C.P. Potholm, 'The Ngwenyama of Swaziland: the dynamics of politi-cal adaptation' in R. Lemarchand, ed., *African Kingships in Perspective*, pp. 129-159.
7. R. Lemarchand, *Rwanda and Burundi*, London, Pall Mall Press, 1970 and 'Burundi' in R. Lemarchand, ed., *African Kingships in Perspective*, 93-126; J.-P. Chrétien, 'Hutu et Tutsi au Rwanda et au Burundi' in J.-L. Amselle, E. M'Bokolo, ed., *Au cœur de l'ethnie. Ethnies, tribalisme et État en Afrique*, Paris, La Découverte, 1985, pp. 129-165; F. Gaulme, 'Succès et difficultés des pays des Grands Lacs: le Burundi', *Marchés tropicaux et méditerranéens*, 24 July 1987, p. 2007 and 'Un coup d'État chasse l'autre', *ibid.*, 11 Sept. 1987, p. 2359, and also the polemic between R. Botte, J.-P. Chrétien and G. Le Jeune, in *Politique africaine*, 12 dec. 1983, pp. 99-108.
8. R. lemarchand, *Rwanda and Burundi*, and 'Rwanda' in R. Lemarchand, ed., *African Kingships in Perspective*, pp. 67-92.
9. C. Young, 'Buganda' in R. Lemarchand, ed., *African Kingships in Per-spective*, pp. 193-235; L.A. Fallers, ed., *The King's Men: Leadership and Status in Buganda on the Eve of Independence*, London, Oxford University Press, 1964.
10. G.L. Caplan, 'Barotseland: the secessionist challenge to Zambia', *The Journal of Modern African Studies*, 6 (3), 1968, pp. 343-360; W. Tordoff, ed., *Politics in Zambia*, Manchester, Manchester University Press, 1974; B. Freund, *The Making of Contemporary Africa. The Development of Afri-can Society since 1800*, Bloomington, Indiana University Press, 1984, p. 240.
11. V. Azarya, *Aristocrats Facing Change. The Fulbe in Guinea, Nigeria and Cameroon*, Chicago, University of Chicago Press, 1978; J. Suret-Canale, 'La fin de la chefferie en Guinée', *Journal of African History*, VII (3), pp. 459-493.
12. M. Kilson, *Political Change in a West African State. A Study of the Modern-ization Process in Sierra Leone*, Cambridge, Harvard University Press,

The State in Africa

1966, chap. 9 and 11; R. Tangri, *Politics in Sub-Saharan Africa*, London, James Currey, Portsmouth, Heinemann, 1985, pp. 39 ff.; F.M. Hayward, 'The state in Sierra Leone: consolidation, fragmentation and decay'. Paper presented to Conference on West African States Since 1976, London, Centre for African Studies, School of Oriental and African Studies, 1987.

13. J. Lonsdale, 'States and social processes in Africa: A historiographical survey', *African Studies review*, XXIV (2-3), June–Sept. 1981, p. 203; J. Iliffe, *The Emergence of African Capitalism*, London, Macmillan, 1983; P. Lubeck, *Islam and Urban Labor in Northern Nigeria; the Making of a Muslim Working Class*, Cambridge, Cambridge University Press, 1986; M. Watts, *Silent Violence. Food, Famine and Peasantry in Northern Nigeria*, Berkeley University of California Press, 1983.

14. R.L. Sklar, *Nigerian Political Parties*, Princeton, Princeton University Press, 1963, pp. 88 ff., 321 ff., 365 ff., 442 ff.; C.S. Whitaker Jr., *The Politics of Tradition. Continuity and Change in Northern Nigeria. 1946-1966*, Princeton, Princeton University Press, 1970.

15. J.N. Paden, *Ahmadu Bello, Sardauna of Sokoto. Values and Leadership in Nigeria*, London, Hodder and Stoughton, 1986.

16. Cited by C.S. Whitaker Jr., *The Politics of Tradition*, pp. 353-354.

17. Nepu, *Sawaba Declaration of Principles*, Jos, Baseco Press, 1950, cited by C.S. Whitaker, Jr., *The Politics of Tradition*, pp. 358-359.

18. R.L. Sklar, *Nigerian Political Parties*, pp. 335-337, pp. 371 and following pages; C.S. Whitaker, Jr., *The Politics of Modernization*, pp. 372-373.

19. C.S. Whitaker, Jr., *The Politics of Tradition*, p. 354.

20. On the subject of this coup, see R. Luckham, *The Nigerian Military. A Sociological Analysis of Authority and Revolt. 1960-1967*, Cambridge, Cambridge University Press, 1971, chap. i.

21. J.N. Paden, *Ahmadu Bello*, p. 495.

22. *Ibid.*, pp. 459 ff., and 696 ff.

23. R.A. Joseph, *Democracy and Prebendal Politics in Nigeria. The Rise and Fall of the Second Republic*, Cambridge, Cambridge University Press, 1987, p. 130.

24. J.N. Paden, *Ahmadu Bello*, p. 705.

25. R.A. Joseph, *Democracy and Prebendal Politics in Nigeria*, chap. 9; S. Othman, 'Classes, crises and coup: the demise of Shagari's regime', *African Affairs*, 83 (333), Oct. 1984, pp. 444-450.

26. R.A. Joseph, *Democracy and Prebendal Politics in Nigeria*, pp. 142. ff. and G. Nicolas, 'Contradictions d'un parti révolutionnaire. Le PRP nigérian', *Politique africaine*, 8, Dec. 1982, pp. 74-102.

27. G. Nicolas, 'Guerre sainte à Kano', *Politique africaine*, 4, Nov. 1981, pp. 47-70; P. Lubeck, 'Islamic protest under semi-industrial capital: 'yan Tatsini explained', Urbana, University of Illinois, 1984, and P.M. Lubeck, *Islam and Urban Labor in Northern Nigeria*.

28. R.A. Joseph, *Democracy and Prebendal Politics in Nigeria*, pp. 132, 140-141 and 149.

29. S. Othman, 'Classes, crises and coup', pp. 450-456.

30. R.A Joseph, 'Principles and Practices of Nigerian military government' in J. Harbeson, ed., *The Military in African Politics*, New York, Praeger, 1987, pp. 79-91.

31. See, for example, the argument started by L.A. Fallers, *Bantu Bureaucracy*, Cambridge, Heffer, 1956 or by R. Horton's typology ('Stateless societies in the history of West Africa' in J.F.A. Ajayi, M. Crowder, eds., *History of West Africa*, New York, Columbia University Press, 1976, pp. 72-113).

32. G. Dupré, 'Une mise en perspective' in B. Jewsiewicki, J. Letourneau, eds., *Mode of Production: the Challenge of Africa*, Sainte Foy, Safi Press, 1985, pp. 46-50; J.-P. Dozon, *La Société bété, Côte d'Ivoire*, Paris, Karthala, 1985, pp. 65 ff.; P. Bonte, 'Classes et parenté dans les sociétés segmentaires', *Dialectiques*, 21, 1977, pp. 103-115.

33. For criticisms of *L'État au Cameroun* see P. Geschiere, *Village Communities and the State. Changing Relations among the Maka of Southeastern Cameroon since the Colonial Conquest*, London, 1982, pp. 10-13 and 'Hegemonic regimes and popular protest', article cited pp. 309-347; J.-C. Barbier, 'Alliance ou conflit entre le haut et le bas?', *Politique africaine*, 1, Jan. 1981, pp. 130-137; R.A Joseph, 'Richard Joseph répond', *Cahiers d'études africaines* 71, XVIII (3), 1978, pp. 455-457.

34. P. Laburthe-tolra, *Les Seigneurs de la forêt. Essai sur le passé historique, l'organisation sociale et les normes éthiques des anciens Bëi du Cameroun*, Paris, Publications de la Sorbonne, 1981. P. Bonnafé also speaks of the 'seigneurs' in kukuya land *(cf. infra)*.

35. P. Bonnafé, 'Age et sexe matériels et sociaux. Un exemple congolais' in M. Abeles, C. Collard, ed., *Age, pouvoir et société en Afrique noire*, Paris, Karthala, Montréal, Presses de l'Université de Montréal, 1985, p. 40. Also, by the same author, *Nzo Lipfu, le lignage de la mort. La sorcellerie, idéologie de la lutte sociale sur le plateau kukuya*, Nanterre, Labethno, 1978 et *Histoire sociale d'un peuple congolais*, Livre I: *La Terre et le ciel*, Paris ORSTOM, 1987.

36. G. Dupré, *Les Naissances d'une société. Espace et historicité chez les Beembé du Congo*, Paris, ORSTOM, 1985, pp. 164 ff.

37. E.E. Evans-Pritchard, *Les Nuer*, Paris, Gallimard, 1968.

38. J.-C. Barbier, 'Alliance ou conflit entre le haut et le bas?', p. 132. On this subject, also see P. Titi Nwel, 'Mbombok à la tête du lignage basaa' and Débat in ORSTOM, *Nature et formes de pouvoir dans les sociétés dites acéphales. Exemples camerounais*, Paris, ORSTOM, 1982, pp. 99, 107, 109; C. Dikoumé, 'Étude concrète d'une société traditionnelle: les Elog-Mpoo', Lille, Université de Lille II, n.d. pp. 210-211.

39. J.-C. Barbier, 'Alliance ou conflit entre le haut et le bas?', especially P. Geschiere, *Village Communities and the State*, pp. 50 ff.; G. Dupré, *Les Naissances d'une société*, pp. 259 ff.

40. J.-P. Dozon, *La Société bété*, pp. 223-240 (especially pp. 236-237). The author provides a critique of one of the major works of French marxist economic anthropology.

41. P. Geschiere, *Village Communities and the State, passim* (especially pp. 45-54, 147-152, 169-181, 194-202, 256-262, 277-280, 313-335).

42. J.-P. Dozon, *La Société bété*, pp. 311-312.

43. Apart from the numerous case studies, see R. Horton, 'Stateless societies in the history of West Africa' in J.F.A. Ajayi, M. Crowder, eds., *History of West Africa*, pp. 72-113.

44. F. de Chassey, 'L'évolution des structures sociales en Mauritanie de la

colonisation à nos jours' and J.-L. Balans, 'Le système politique mauritanien' in CRESM, CEAN, *Introduction à la Mauritanie*, Paris, CNRS,
1979, pp. 235-319.

45. See *Le Manifeste du nègro-mauritanien opprimé – Février 1966-avril 1986.
De la guerre civile à la lutte de libération nationale*, Nouakchott, 1986.

46. P. Geschiere, 'Hegemonic regimes and popular protest', p. 339.

47. We are following the work of G. Dupré, *Les Naissances d'une société,
passim* (especially pp. 121-122, 139, 142, 144-145, 194-195).

48. *Ibid.*, p. 211.

49. H. Bertrand, *Le Congo. Formation sociale et mode de développement économique*, Paris, Maspero, 1975, p. 98.

50. *Ibid.*, pp. 103-104 and 177; P.-P. Rey, *Colonialisme, néo-colonialisme et
transition au capitalisme. Exemple de la 'COMILOG' au Congo-Brazzaville*,
Paris, Maspero, 1971.

51. Sources: interviews.

52. P. Bonnafé, *Histoire sociale d'un peuple congolais. Livre I. La Terre et le
ciel*, pp. 70 and 83.

53. P.-P. Rey, 'Le marxisme congolais contre l'État' in A. Corten, M.
Sadria, M.B. Tahon, eds., *Les Autres Marxismes réels*, Paris, C. Bourgois, 1985, pp. 178-179. Also see D. Desjeux, *Stratégies paysannes en
Afrique noire. Le Congo (Essai sur la gestion de l'incertitude)*, Paris, L'Harmattan, 1987.

54. P.-P. Rey, *Colonialisme, néo-colonialisme et transition au capitalisme*, pp.
456.

55. E. Terray, 'Le climatiseur et la véranda', *in Afrique plurielle, Afrique
actuelle. Hommage à Georges Balandier*, Paris, Karthala, 1986, pp. 37-44.

56. See, for example, G. Balandier, *Sociologie actuelle de l'Afrique noire*, pp.
63-64; P. Geschiere, *Village Communities and the State*, pp. 49-50.

57. F.Cooper, *From Slaves to Squatters. Plantation Labour and Agriculture in
Zanzibar and Coastal Kenya. 1890-1925*, New Haven, Yale University
Press, 1980, p. 72.

58. M.F. Lofchie, *Zanzibar: Background to Revolution*, Princeton, Princeton
University Press, 1965; J. Okello, *Revolution in Zanzibar*, Nairobi, East
African Publishing House, 1967.

59. F. Cooper, *Slaves to Squatters*, H. Kindy, *Life and Politics in Mombasa*,
Nairobi, East African Publishing House, 1972.

60. C. Clapham, *Liberia and Sierra Leone. An Essay in Comparative Politics*,
Cambridge, Cambridge University Press, 1976; A Cohen, *The Politics of
Elite Culture*, Los Angeles, University of California at Los Angeles
Press, 1981; T.P. Wrubel, 'Liberia: the Dynamics of Continuity', *Journal
of Modern African Studies*, 9 (2), August 1971, pp. 189-204.

61. See the hagiographic interpretation by A. Sesay, 'Le coup d'Etat du
Liberia. Facteurs internes et effets régionaux', *Politique africaine*, 7, Sept.
1982, pp. 91-106. For a different point of view, see A. Sawyer, *Effective
Immediately. Dictatorship in Liberia, 1980-1986: a Personal Perspective*,
Brême, Liberia Working Group, 1987.

62. M. Lowenkopf, 'Political modernization in Liberia: a conservative model', *Western Political Quarterly*, XXV (1), March 1972, p. 99; C. Clapham, 'Liberia' in J. Dunn, ed., *West African States. Failure and Promise*,
Cambridge, Cambridge University Press, 1978, p. 122.

63. C. Clapham, 'Liberia'. Paper presented to *Conference on West African States since 1976*, London, Center for African Studies, School of Oriental and African Studies, 1987.
64. *Muntu Dimanche* (Dakar), 19, Dec. 1986. p. 3. On the Afro-Brazilian elite see C.M. Toulabour, *Le Togo sous Eyadema*, Paris, Karthala, 1986, pp. 232-235 and *Peuples du golfe du Bénin*, Paris, Karthala, 1984, pp. 143 ff.
65. H.S. Morris, *The Indians in Uganda*, London, Weidenfeld and Nicolson, 1968, pp. 8-9, 17-18, 144. Also see F. Constantin, 'Sur les modes populaires d'action diplomatique. Affaires de famille et affaires d'État en Afrique orientale', *Revue française de science politique*, 36 (5), Oct. 1986, pp. 672-694; J.-C. Penrad, 'La présence isma'ilenne en Afrique de l'Est. Note sur l'histoire commerciale et l'organisation communautaire' in *Marchands et hommes d'affaires asiatiques*, Paris, EHESS, 1988, pp. 221-236.
66. J. Iliffe, *A Modern History of Tanganyika*, Cambridge, Cambridge University Press, 1979, pp. 264, 375, 521, 555, 562-563.
67. J. Hartmann, 'Development Policy-Making in Tanzania. 1962-1982: A Critique of Sociological Interpretations', Hull, The University of Hull, 1983, pp. 109 ff.
68. Figure cited by D.-C. Martin, *Tanzanie: l'invention d'une culture politique*, Paris, Presses de la Fondation nationale des sciences politiques, Karthala, 1988, pp. 123-124.
69. Interview with Gervaise Clarence-Smith, London, SOAS, 1987; C. Young, T. Turner, *The Rise and Decline of the Zaïrian State*, Madison, The University of Wisconsin Press, 1985, p. 108; M. Mamdani, *Imperialism and Fascism in Uganda*, Nairobi, Heinemann, 1983, pp. 38 ff. N. Kasfir, 'State, *magendo* and class formation in Uganda', *Journal of Commonwealth and comparative politics*, XXI (3), Nov. 1983, pp. 84-103; *Africa Confidential* 28 (13), 24 June 1987.
The problem of the 'Lebanese' in West Africa did not directly affect the social foundations of the state, except perhaps in Sierra Leone and the Ivory Coast. Although colonial writers sometimes worried about this 'terrible Syrian invasion', and saw the time approaching when 'the French element, be they white or coloured, will be submerged by our hosts from Asia minor' (*L'Acajou*, 7, 2 Oct. 1936), the number of these people (21,000 in 1953) was never comparable to that of the 'Asians' in East Africa. Due to the absence of a colony heavily populated by Europeans, the progression of West African countries towards independence was never hampered by the obstacle of multi-racialism. From 1951 onwards, Senegal, which had been the platform for Lebanese politics in the region, turned its back on creole politics. At the same time, the commercialisation of cocoa and coffee by the marketing boards in Ghana and Nigeria deprived Lebanese traders of one of their most lucrative economic resources. Independence led to the generalisation of the limitations on trade, as either preference or monopoly was granted to national merchants or, more commonly, to state-owned companies (especially in Guinea, Mali and Senegal).

However, in Sierra Leone, the connection between Siaka Stevens' regime and Lebanese resources, which was mediated by the powerful businessman, Jamil Said Mohammed, was deeply ingrained in the state and became one of the main points of disagreement between Siaka Stevens and his successor, Momoh, in 1986-1987. More discretely, the association within the Chamber of Commerce and Industry between Lebanese entrepreneurs, the henchmen of the Ivorien political class, and the French business world was one of Houphouët-Boigney's financial and economic resources. The harsh crisis of the 1980s seems to have worked to the interests of the Lebanese in the sense that it brought about the decline of French business interests. At the same time as it suggests the profoundly extraverted and 'compradore' nature of a society which is, in conclusion, closer to Liberia or Sierra Leone than the 'Houphouetist' mythology would lead one to believe, the position of this foreign community in the Ivory Coast's economy appears to be playing a major role in the question of presidential succession. (R. Charbonneau, 'Les Libano-Syriens en Afrique noire', *Revue française d'études politiques africaines*, 26, Feb. 1968, pp. 56-71; S. Ellis, 'Les prolongements du conflit israélo-arabe', *Politique africaine*, 30, June 1988, pp. 69-75; *Africa Confidential*, 1986-1988).

70. R. Pélissier, *Le Naufrage des Caravelles. Études sur la fin de l'Empire portugais (1961-1975)*, Orgeval, Pelissier, 1979.

71. W.G. Clarence-Smith, 'Class structure and class struggle in Angola in the 1970s', *Journal of Southern Africa Studies*, 7 (1), Oct. 1980, pp. 109-126.

In Mozambique, independence mainly benefited the intellectuals from Maputo and Gaza provinces, from where both Eduardo Mondlane and Samora Michel originated. Michel's successor, Joaquim Chissamo, also came from this area. The influence of the 20,000 Luso-Mozambicans was somewhat limited by the Soviet presence, by the existence of the Asian community who were relatively prosperous despite the fact that they were not well-represented in the state apparatus, and, increasingly, by the arrival of foreign experts. The main 'losers' of the past decade appear to have been the 'negro-African' cadres from the northern regions who have been relegated to a secondary position today despite the fact that they provided most of the men for the national liberation struggle; within FRELIMO, they incarnated the orthodoxy of the alliance with the Soviet Union, according to Mariano Matsinhe and Armando Guebuza. (*Africa Confidential*, 28 (17), 19 Aug. 1987).

72. P. Geschiere, *Village Communities and the State*, pp. 201-202.

73. H.S. Morris, *The Indians in Uganda*, pp. 144-145.

74. *Marchés tropicaux et méditerranéens*, 14 August 1987, pp. 2179.

75. M. Kilson, *Political Change in a West African State*, pp. 71 ff. and 157 ff.

76. C. Coulon, 'Pouvoir oligarchique et mutations sociales et politiques au fouta-Toro', in J.-L. Balans, C. Coulon, J.-M. Gastellu, *Autonomie locale et intégration nationale au Sénégal*, p. 53.

77. C.S. Whitaker Jr., *The Politics of Tradition*, pp. 466-467; R.L. Sklar, *Nigerian Political Parties*, pp. 327 ff.; J.N. Paden, *Ahmadu Bello*, pp. 145 ff., 172 ff., 465 ff.; P. Lubeck, *Islam and Urban Labor*, pp. 35 ff.

78. A. Gramsci, *Note sul Maschiavelli, sulla politica e sullo Stato moderno*, Turin, Einaudi, 1966, p. 60 and *Cahiers de prison*, Paris, Gallimard, 1983, vol. II, p. 503 ('In the case of Caesar and Napoleon I, it could be

said that A and B, whilst being distinct and opposed entities, could after a molecular process, still end up in an "absolute" fusion and reciprocal assimilation').

CHAPTER 6: THE RECIPROCAL ASSIMILATION OF ELITES

1. J.-F. Bayart, *L'État au Cameroun*, Paris, Presses de la Fondation nationale des sciences politiques, 1979, pp. 137-138 and 228 ff.
2. *Ibid.*, p. 138.
3. J.-F. Bayart, 'La société politique camerounaise (1982-1986)', *Politique africaine*, 22, June 1986, pp. 5-35.
4. *Le Messager* (Douala), 47, 27 Sept. 1984, p. 3.
5. R.L. Sklar, *Nigerian Political Parties*, Princeton, Princeton University Press, 1963, pp. 480 ff., and 'The nature of class domination in Africa', *Journal of Modern African Studies*, 17 (4), 1979, p. 534.
6. Cited by R.A. Joseph, *Democracy and Prebendal Politics in Nigeria. The Rise and Fall of the Second Republic*, Cambridge, Cambridge University Press, 1987, p. 140.
7. R.L. Sklar, 'The nature of class domination in Africa', pp. 531-552; J.-F. Bayart, 'Les sociétés africaines face à l'État', *Pouvoirs*, 25, 1983, pp. 23-39.
8. A.R. Zolberg, *One-Party Government in the Ivory Coast*, Princeton, Princeton University Press, 1964 (especially Table 20, p. 275) and Y.-A. Fauré, J.-F. Médard, eds., *État et bourgeoisie en Côte d'Ivoire*, Paris, Karthala, 1982; D.B. Cruise O'Brien, *Saints and Politicians*, Cambridge, Cambridge University Press, 1975; J.-L. Balans, C. Coulon, J.-M. Gastellu, *Autonomie locale et intégration nationale au Sénégal*, Paris, Pedone, 1975; J.-P. Olivier de Sardan, *Les sociétés songhay-zarma (Niger-Mali). Chefs guerriers, esclaves, paysans...*, Paris, Karthala, 1984; D.-C. Martin, *Tanzanie. L'invention d'une culture politique*, Paris, Presses de la Fondation nationale des sciences politiques, Karthala, 1988 and G. Dauch, D. Martin, *L'Héritage de Kenyatta. La transition politique au Kenya. 1975-1982*, Paris, L'Harmattan, 1985 (it should be added that these writers doubt the validity of such a hypothesis); G. Kitching, *Class and Economic Change in Kenya. The Making of an African Petite-Bourgeoisie*, New Haven, Yale University Press, 1980; C. Gertzel, *The Politics of Independent Kenya*, Nairobi, East African Publishing House, London, Heinemann, 1970.
9. See, for example, J. Benjamin, *Les Camerounais occidentaux. La minorité dans un État bicommunautaire*, Montreal, Les Presses de l'Université de Montréal, 1972 and D. Darbon, *L'Administration et le paysan en Casamance (Essai d'anthropologie administrative)*, Paris, Pedone, 1988.
10. M.G. Schatzberg, *Politics and Class in Zaïre*, New York, Africana Publishing Company, 1980, pp. 53-55 and pp. 115 ff.
11. D. Desjeux, *Stratégies paysannes en Afrique noire. Le Congo (Essai sur la gestion de l'incertitude)*, Paris, L'Harmattan, 1987 and 'Le Congo est-il

situationniste? 20 ans d'histoire politique de la classe dirigeante congolaise', *Revue française d'études politiques africaines*, 178-179, Oct.-Nov. 1980, pp. 16-40.

12. N. Chazan, 'Politics and the State in Ghana: a third decade reassessment', Paper presented to Conference on West African States since 1976, London, Centre for African Studies, School of Oriental and African Studies, 1987.

13. R. Buijtenhuijs, *Le Frolinat et les révoltes populaires du Tchad, 1965-1976*, La Haye, Paris, New York, Mouton, 1978 and *Le Frolinat et les guerres civiles du Tchad (1977-1984)*, Paris, Karthala, Leiden, Afrika-Studiecentrum, 1987, pp. 92 ff.

14. N. Kasfir, 'State, *magendo* and class formation in Uganda', *Journal of Commonwealth and Comparative Politics*, XXI (3), Nov. 1983, pp. 84-103 and G. Salonges, 'En Ouganda comme ailleurs, un mythe peut en cacher un autre', *Politique africaine*, 11, Sept. 1983, pp. 41-44.

15. K. Marx, F. Engels, *L'Idéologie allemande*, Paris, Éditions Sociales, 1974, p. 71. Also see Z.A. Pelczynski, 'Nation, civil society, state: Hegelian sources of the Marxian non theory of nationality', in Z.A. Pelczynski, ed., *The State and Civil Society. Studies in Hegel's Political Philosophy*, Cambridge, Cambridge University Press, 1984, pp. 275-276.

16. P.-F. Ngayap, *Cameroun. Qui gouverne?*, Paris, L'Harmattan, 1983, p. 14.

17. M.A. Cohen, *Urban Policy and Political Conflict in Africa. A Study of the Ivory Coast*, Chicago, The University of Chicago Press, 1974, p. 196.

18. R. Luckham, *The Nigerian Military. A Sociological Analysis of Authority and Revolt. 1960-1967*, Cambridge, Cambridge University Press, 1971, p. 90.

19. J. Spencer, *The Kenya African Union*, London, KPI, 1985, p. 19.

20. A.R. Zolberg, *One-Party Government in the Ivory Coast*, p. 67.

21. R.L. Sklar, 'The nature of class domination', p. 535.

22. C. Vidal, 'Funérailles et conflit social en Côte-d'Ivoire', *Politique africaine*, 24, Dec. 1986, pp. 13-14.

23. A.R. Zolberg *One-Party Government in the Ivory Coast*, p. 73.

24. J.-P. Chauveau, J.-P. Dozon, 'Au cœur des ethnies ivoiriennes...l'État' in E. Terray, ed., *L'État contemporain en Afrique*, Paris, L'Harmattan, 1987, p. 270.

25. *Fraternité-Matin* (Abidjan), 29 April 1983.

26. *Ibid.*, 13 Jan. 1986.

27. J.N. Paden, *Ahmadu Bello, Sardauna of Sokoto. Values and Leadership in Nigeria*, London, Hodder and Stoughton, 1986, p. 314.

28. *Africa Confidential*, 17 Oct. 1984, p. 2.

29. F.M. Hayward, J.D. Kandeh, 'Perspectives on twenty-five years of elections in Sierra Leone' in F.M. Hayward, ed., *Elections in independent Africa*, Boulder, Westview Press, 1987, p. 43.

30. Information given by G. Balandier, *Afrique ambiguë*, Paris, Union générale d'éditions, 1962, p. 272.

31. For the expansion of sects in Africa, see the article published in *Pirogue*, 40, Jan.-March 1981; *Marchés tropicaux et méditerranéens*, 27 Feb. 1987, p. 474.

32. *Africa Confidential*, 27 May 1987; P. Péan, *Affaires africaines*, Paris,

Fayard, 1983, pp. 34-36; M. Magassouba, *L'Islam au Sénégal. Demain les mollahs?* Paris, Karthala, 1985, pp. 186 ff.; A. Cohen, *The Politics of Elite Culture*, Los Angeles, University of California at Los Angeles Press, 1981, pp. 95 ff.; C.M. Toulabor, *Le Togo sous Eyadema*, Paris, Karthala, 1986, pp. 211-212 and 248 ff. On the njobi rite, see G. Dupré, *Un ordre et sa destruction*, Paris ORSTOM, 1982, chap. XVI.

33. M. Guery, 'Christianisme céleste. Notes de travail. L'Église, la vie spirituelle' Abidjan, 1973, pp. 31-33; *Marchés tropicaux et méditerranéens*, 27 Feb. 1987, p. 474; F. Gaulme, *Le Gabon et son ombre*, Paris, Karthala, 1988, pp. 149-150.

34. Sources: interviews.

35. J. Dehasse, 'Le rôle politique des associations de ressortissants à Léopoldville', Louvain, Institut de sciences politiques et sociales, 1965, pp. 32-34 and 98 ff.

36. E. Goffman, *La mise en scène de la vie quotidienne*, Paris, Éd. de Minuit, 1973 and *Les rites d'interaction*, Paris, Ed. de Minuit, 1974.

37. A. Cohen, *The Politics of Elite Culture*, (especially chap. viii) and J. Vansina, 'Mwasi's trials', *Daedalus*, CXI (2), 1982, p. 60.

38. K. Marx, F. Engels, *L'Idéologie allemande*, p. 128.

39. J.-P. Warnier, *Échanges, développement et hiérarchies dans le Bamenda précolonial (Cameroun)*, Stuttgart, Franz Steiner Verlag Wiesbaden, 1985, pp. 82 ff. and 116 ff.

40. See chap. I as well as J. Champaud, *Villes et campagnes du Cameroun de l'Ouest*, Paris, ORSTOM, 1983, pp. 263 ff. and J.-L. Dongmo, *Le Dynamisme bamiléké (Cameroun). Volume II. La maîtrise de l'espace urbain*, Yaoundé, Centre d'édition et de production pour l'enseignement et la recherche, 1981, pp. 247 ff.

41. S. Othman, 'Classes, crises and coup: the demise of Shagari's regime', *African Affairs*, 83 (333), Oct. 1984, pp. 448 and 454.

42. P. Anyang' Nyong'o, 'Succession et héritage politiques. Le président, l'État et le capital après la mort de Jomo Kenyatta', *Politique africaine*, 3, Sept. 1981, pp. 19-20.

43. K. Marx, F. Engels, *L'Idéologie allemande*, p. 128.

44. See M.A. Cohen, *Urban Policy and Political Conflict*.

45. G. Dupré, *Les Naissances d'une société. Espace et historicité chez les Beembé du Congo*, Paris, ORSTOM, 1985, pp. 297 ff.

46. A. Gramsci, *Note sul Machiavelli, sulla politica e sullo Stato moderno*, Turin, Einaudi, 1966, p. 68.

47. For a comparison between Marx's and Gramsci's conception of "civil society", *cf.* N. Bobbio, 'Gramsci and the conception of civil society' in C. Mouffe, ed., *Gramsci and Marxist Theory*, London, Routledge and Kegan Paul, 1979, pp. 29-31.

48. See N. Chazan, *An Anatomy of Ghanaian Politics. Managing Political Recession, 1969-1982*, Boulder, Westview Press, 1983, chap. 2. On the existence of the associative phenomenom in 'traditional' Africa, *cf.* P. Alexandre, *Les Africains*, Paris, Ed. Lidis, 1981, p. 165.

49. On this idea of the "well-policed" state, *cf.* M. Raeff, *Comprendre l'ancien régime russe. État et société en Russie impériale*, Paris, Le Seuil, 1982.

50. J.-F. Bayart, 'La revanche des sociétés africaines', *Politique africaine*, 11

Sept. 1983, pp. 99 ff.; G. Hyden, *Beyond Ujamaa in Tanzania. Underdevelopment and an Uncaptured Peasantry*, London, Heinemann, 1980.

51. *Marchés tropicaux et méditerranéens*, 17 May 1985, p. 1233.
52. G. Lavau, 'A propos de trois livres sur l'État', *Revue française de science politique*, 30 (2), April 1980, pp. 396-412; B. Lacroix, 'Ordre politique et ordre social. Objectivismes, objectivation et analyse politique', in M. Grawitz, J. Leca, eds., *Traité de science politique*, Paris, PUF, 1985, vol. I, p. 471; Y. Chevrier, 'Une société infirme: la société chinoise dans la transition "modernisatrice"' in C. Aubert, Y. Chevrier, J.-L. Domenach et al., *La Société chinoise après Mao. Entre autorité et modernité*, Paris, Fayard, 1986, pp. 229-315.
53. R. Fossaert, *La Société*, vol. V. *Les États*, Paris, Le Seuil, 1981, p. 174.
54. T.S. Cox, *Civil-Military Relations in Sierra Leone*, Cambridge, Harvard University Press, 1976; F. de Medeiros, 'Armée et instabilité: les partis militaires au Bénin' in A. Rouquié, ed., *La Politique de Mars. Les processus politiques dans les partis militaires contemporains*, Paris, Le Sycomore, 1981, pp. 123-149; R.A. Joseph, *Democracy and Prebendal Politics in Nigeria*.
55. R.L. Sklar, *Nigerian Political Parties*, chap. 6. Also see J.D.Y. Peel, *Ijeshas and Nigerians. The Incorporation of a Yoruba Kingdom. 1890s-1970s*, Cambridge, Cambridge University Press, 1983, pp. 233-235 for a critique of some points in R.L. Sklar's argument.
56. J.-P. Olivier de Sardan, *Les Sociétés songhay-zarma*, pp. 202-203.
57. A.R. Zolberg, *One Party Government in the Ivory Coast*, p. 275.
58. G. Balandier, *Sociologie actuelle de l'Afrique noire*, Paris, PUF, 1971 (new edition), p. 262 and *Afrique ambiguë*, pp. 269-272.
59. See, for example J.-F. Bayart, *L'État au Cameroun*, p. 189.
60. See, for example J. Spencer, *The Kenya African Union*.
61. J.-F. Bayart, *L'État au Cameroun*.
62. *Cf.* for example D. Bourmaud, 'Le Système politique du Kenya: centre et périphérie', Bordeaux, Institut d'études politiques, n.d., pp. 218 ff.
63. J.-F. Bayart, *L'État au Cameroun*.
64. The speeches of Ivoiriens leaders are cited in A.R. Zolberg, *One-Party Government in the Ivory Coast*, p. 326. On the theoreticians of a militant leninist party in Ghana and Tanzania, see Y. Benot, *Idéologies des indépendances africaines*, Paris, Maspero, 1972 (new edition), pp. 333-334 and II. Bienen, *Tanzania: Party, Transformation and Economic Development*, Princeton, Princeton University Press, 1970.
65. J.-F. Bayart, *L'État au Cameroun*, pp. 126-127; G. Dauch, 'Kenya: l'ébranlement', *Annuaire des pays de l'océan Indien*, IX, 1982-1983, p. 323.
66. J.-F. Bayart, *L'État au Cameroun*, pp. 53 and 233.
67. R.L. Sklar, *Nigerian Political Parties*, p. 481.
68. R. Michels, *Les Partis politiques. Essai sur les tendances oligarchiques des démocraties*, Paris, Flammarion, 1971, p. 131.
69. I. Wallerstein, 'The decline of the party in single-party African states' in G. La Palombara, M. Weiner, eds., *Political Parties and Political Development*, Princeton, Princeton University Press, 1966, pp. 201-214. Also see A.R. Zolberg, *One Party Government in the Ivory Coast*, pp. 185 ff., and *Creating Political Order. The Party States of West Africa*, Chicago,

Rand MacNally, 1966, pp. 21-34; R.S. Morgenthau, 'Single-party systems in West Africa', *The American Political Science Review*, LV (2), June 1961.

70. Centre d'étude d'Afrique noire, Centre d'études et de recherches internationales, *Aux urnes l'Afrique!* *Elections et pouvoirs en Afrique noire*, Paris, Pedone, 1978; F.M. Hayward, ed., *Elections in Independent Africa*.
71. M.G. Schatzberg, *Politics and Class in Zaïre*, pp. 117-119; C. Newbury, 'Dead and buried, or just underground? The privatization of the State in Zaïre', *Canadian Journal of African Studies*, 18 (1), 1984, p. 113.
72. Sources: personal observations and *Fraternité-Matin* (Abidjan).
73. J.-F. Bayart, 'La société politique camerounaise (1982-1986), pp. 26-28.
74. *Le Messager* (Douala), 84, 31 March 1986, p. 6.
75. RDPC, Comité central, 'Rapport de la sous-commission de supervision du renouvellement des organes de base du RDPC de l'Extrême-Nord' Yaoundé, 12 March 1986 and 'Rapport de mission sur le renouvellement des bureaux des organes du RDPC et de ses organisations annexes (dans le Centre)', Yaoundé, 25 March 1986.
76. F.M. Hayward, ed., *Elections in Independent Africa*; CEAN, CERI, *Aux urnes l'Afrique!*; J.-F. Bayart, *L'État au Cameroun*.
77. J. Samoff, 'Single party competitive elections in Tanzania' in F.M. Hayward, ed., p. 181.
78. J.D. Barkan, 'The electoral process and peasant-state relations in Kenya' in F.M. Hayward, ed., pp. 228 and 234-235.
79. F.M. Hayward, S.N. Grovogui, 'Persistence and change in Senegalese electoral processes' in F.M. Hayward, ed., p. 240 and D.B. Cruise O'Brien, 'Senegal' in J. Dunn, ed., *West African States. Failure and Promise. A Study in Comparative Politics*, Cambridge, Cambridge University Press, 1978, pp. 187-188.
80. See R. Luckham, *The Nigerian Military*, chap. v; A. Cohen, *The Politics of Elite Culture*.
81. C.M. Toulabor, *Le Togo sous Eyadema*; D. Desjeux, 'Le Congo est-il situationniste?'; F. de Medeiros, 'Armée et instabilité: les partis militaires au Bénin' in A. Rouquié ed., *La Politique de Mars*, pp. 123-149.
82. See, for example, E. Feit, 'Military coups and political development: some lessons from Ghana and Nigeria', *World Politics*, 20 (2), Jan. 1968, pp. 179-193; R.A. Joseph, *Democracy and Prebendal Politics*, and 'Principles and practices of Nigerian military government' in J. Harbeson, ed., *The Military in African Politics*, New York, Praeger, 1987, pp. 79-91.
83. J.N. Paden, *Ahmadu Bello*, chap. 14.
84. R. Luckham, *The Nigerian Military*, p. 112.
85. J.-F. Bayart, *L'État au Cameroun*, chap. vi; D.C. Martin, *Tanzanie: l'Invention d'une culture politique*, chap. V and VI and J. Hartmann, 'Development Policy-Making in Tanzania, 1962-1982: A Critique of Sociological Interpretations', Hull, The University of Hull, 1983; A.R. Zolberg, *Creating Political Order*.
86. J. Champaud, *Villes et campagnes du Cameroun de l'Ouest*, pp. 206-207.
87. J.H. B. den Ouden, 'In Search of personal mobility: changing interpersonal relations in two Bamileke chiefdoms, Cameroon', *Africa*, 57 (1), 1987, pp. 3-27.
88. *La Gazette* [Douala], 510, 27 Sept. 1984, pp. 3, 6 and 9; *ibid.*, 515, 6

Dec. 1984, p. 10.
89. *Cameroon Tribune*, 1-2 Dec. 1985; *ibid.*, 24 May 1986; *ibid.*, 15 April 1983.
90. *Ibid.*, 17 Dec. 1985.
91. J.D.Y. Peel *Ijeshas and Nigerians*, pp. 137-145; P.C. Lloyd, 'Ijebu' in R. Lemarchand, ed., *African Kingships in Perspective*. *Political Change and Modernization in Monarchical Settings*, London, Frank Cass, 1977, pp. 260-283; S.T. Barnes, *Patrons and Power*. *Creating a Political Community in Metropolitan Lagos*, Manchester, Manchester University Press, 1986, chap. 5.
92. R.L. Sklar, *Nigerian Political Parties*, pp. 480-481, criticised by J.D.Y. Peel, *Ijeshas and Nigerians*, pp. 201 ff.
93. Y.-A. Fauré, J.-F. Médard, 'Classe dominante ou classe dirigeante?' in Y.-A. Fauré, J.-F. Médard, eds., *État et bourgeoisie en Côte d'Ivoire*, p. 134.
94. J.-F. Bayart, *L'État au Cameroun*, pp. 188 ff.
95. Press conference given by M. Ayissi Mvodo, Minister of territorial administration, *L'Unité* (Yaoundé), 562, 31 July 1973, p. 6.
96. J.-F. Bayart, 'La société politique camerounaise', p. 32.
97. T.M. Callaghy, *The State-Society Struggle*. *Zaïre in Comparative Perspective*, New York, Columbia University Press, 1984, chap. 7.
98. E. Vernon, 'Semiosis de l'idéologique et du pouvoir', *Communications*, 28, 1978, p. 15.
99. S. Decalo, 'Ideological rethoric and scientific socialism in Benin and Congo-Brazzaville' and K. Jowitt, 'Scientific socialist regimes in Africa: political differentiation, avoidance and unawareness' in C.G. Roseberg, T.M. Callaghy, eds., *Socialism in Subsaharan Africa. A New Assessment*, Berkeley, Institute of International Studies, University of California, 1979, pp. 231-264 and 133-173; Z. Laïdi, *Les Contraintes d'une rivalité. Les Superpuissances et l'Afrique (1960-1985)*, Paris, La Découverte, 1986; A. Corten, M. Sadria, M.B. Tahon, eds., *Les Autres Marxismes réels*, Paris, C. Bourgois, 1985, p. 15.
100. Cited by P.-H. Siriex, *Houphouët-Boigny, ou la sagesse africaine*, Paris, Nathan, Abidjan, Les Nouvelles Editions Africaines, 1986, p. 122; *Fraternité-Hebdo* (Abidjan), 2 Oct. 1981. On the thoughts of J.K. Nyerere, *Cf.* H. Goulbourne, 'Some aspects of ideological functions in the development of the post-colonial state in Tanzania', *Utafiti*, III (2), 1978, pp. 377-396.
101. D. Bigo, 'Formes d'exercice du pouvoir et obéissance en Centrafrique (1966-1979). Eléments pour une théorie du pouvoir personnel', Paris, Université de Paris-I, 1985.
102. *Cameroon Tribune* (Yaoundé), 20 Feb. 1987. For the Zaïrian case, see M.G. Schatzberg, *The Dialectics of Oppression in Zaïre*, Bloomington, Indiana University Press, 1988, chap. 5.
103. Speech made at Seguéla in 1978, cited by P.-H. Siriex, *Houphouët-Boigny*, pp. 379-380.
104. G.N. Anyou Mbida, 'Longévité à notre cher président El Hadj Ahmadou Ahidjo à ce dixième anniversaire de notre indépendance', *La Presse du Cameroun* [Yaoundé], 31 Dec. 1969 and 1 Jan. 1970. The beginning of the poem, which was apparently written by an "intellectual" hoping to

rise socially or economically, compares Ahidjo to Moses when he led the Jews out of Israel in spite of their discouragements and their errors. The Christian inspiration is just as apparent as familial references.

105. P. Anderson, *Imagined Communities. Reflections on the Origin and Spread of Nationalism*, London, Verso, 1983, p. 122.
106. J. Iliffe, *A Modern History of Tanganyika*, Cambridge, Cambridge University Press, 1979, pp. 208-210 and 530.
107. On the role of lingala in the Second Republic of Zaïre, see C. Young, T. Turner, *The Rise and Decline of the Zaïran State*, pp. 152-157 and N.M. Ngalasso, 'État des langues et langues de l'État au Zaïre', *Politique africaine*, 23, Sept. 1986, pp. 7-27; for a less negative analysis of the politics of the national language in Somalia, see D. Morin, 'Le parcours solitaire de la Somalie', *ibid.*, pp. 57-66.
108. G. Balandier, 'Problématique des classes sociales en Afrique noire', *Cahiers internationaux de sociologie*, XII (38), 1965, p. 139.
109. An argument I tried to develop in *L'État au Cameroun*; 'Permanence des élites traditionnelles et nouvelles formes de pouvoir', *Le Monde diplomatique*, Nov. 1981, pp. 17-18; 'Les sociétés africaines face à l'État', *Pouvoirs*; 'État et société civile en Afrique de l'Ouest. Note bibliographique', *Revue française de science politique*, XXXIII (4), August 1983, pp. 747-753 – in opposition to the "radical" argument developed, in particular, by the *Review of African Political Economy* and also the thesis of J.-F. Médard and Y.-A. Fauré in *État et bourgeoisie en Côte d'Ivoire, op. cit.*, On the "reciprocity model", see M. Kilson, *Political Change in a West African State. A Study of the Modernization Process in Sierra Leone*, Cambridge, Harvard University Press, 1966, pp. 259 ff., D.B. Cruise O'Brien, *Saints and Politicians*.
110. M.G. Schatzberg, *Politics and Class in Zaïre*, pp. 166-169.
111. J.D.Y. Peel, *Ijeshas and Nigerians*, pp. 163-164.
112. S.F. Nadel, *Byzance noire. Le royaume des Nupe du Nigeria*, Paris, Maspero, 1971, p. 224.
113. P.E. Lovejoy, *Salt of the Desert Sun. A History of Salt Production and Trade in the Central Sudan*, Cambridge, Cambridge University Press, 1986, pp. 255 ff.
114. J.S. Saul, *The State and Revolution in Eastern Africa*, London, Heinemann, 1979, pp. 178, 182, 194.
115. E.P. Thompson, *The Making of the English Working Class*, New York, Vintage Books, 1963; E.K. Trimberger, 'E.P. Thompson: understanding the process of history' in T. Skocpol, ed., *Vision and Method in Historical Sociology*, Cambridge, Cambridge University Press, 1984, pp. 211-243.
116. M. Henry, *Marx*, vol. I: *Une Philosophie de la réalité*, Paris, Gallimard, 1976, pp. 235-236.
117. M. Weber, *Economy and Society*, Berkeley, University of California Press, 1978, vol. II, pp. 927 ff.
118. G. Balandier, *Anthropo-logiques*, Paris, PUF, 1974, pp. 152-162; P. Bourdieu, *Ce que parler veut dire. L'économie des échanges linguistiques*, Paris, Fayard, 1982, pp. 157-158; F. Cooper, 'Africa and the world economy', *African Studies Review*, 24 (2-3) June-Sept. 1981, p. 19.
119. Taken up by G. Balandier, 'Problématique des classes sociales en

Afrique noire', pp. 140-141 and *Sens et puissance*, Paris, PUF, 1971, pp. 279-280.

120. See, for example, R. Sandbrook, R. Cohen, eds., *The Development of an African Working Class*. *Studies in Class Formation and Action*, Toronto, University of Toronto Press, 1975; M. Agier, J. Copans, A. Morice, eds., *Classes ouvrières d'Afrique noire*, Paris, Karthala, ORSTOM, 1987; C. van Onselen, *Chibaro*. *African Mine Labour in Southern Rhodesia, 1900-1933*, London, Pluto Press, 1976; P.M. Lubeck, *Islam and Urban Labor in Northern Nigeria*. *The Making of a Muslim Working Class*, Cambridge, Cambridge University Press, 1986; R. Jeffries, *Class, Power and Ideology in Ghana*. *The Railwaymen of Sekondi*, Cambridge, Cambridge University Press, 1978; B. Freund, *The African Worker*, Cambridge, Cambridge University Press, 1988.

121. A. Morice, 'Commerce parallèle et troc à Luanda', *Politique africaine*, 17, March 1985, p. 119.

122. D.-C. Martin, *Tanzanie*, p. 204. Also see J.-F. Bayart, *L'État au Cameroun*, on the concept of "hegemonic alliance".

123. Y.-A. Fauré, J.-F. Médard, 'Classe dominante ou classe dirigeante?' in Y.-A. Fauré, J.-F. Médard, eds., *État et bourgeoisie en Côte d'Ivoire*, p. 146.

124. M.G. Schatzberg, *Politics and Class in Zaïre*; R. Price, 'Politics and culture in contemporary Ghana: the big-man small-boy syndrome', *Journal of African Studies*, I (2), summer 1974, p. 176; A. Giddens, *The Class Structure of the Advanced Societies*, London, Hutchinson University Library, 1973.

125. J.-F. Bayart, *L'État au Cameroun*, pp. 183-185 and pp. 224-232 and 'Les sociétés africaines face à l'État'.

CHAPTER 7: THE FORMATION OF A POST-COLONIAL HISTORICAL BLOC

1. C. Buci-Glucksmann, *Gramsci et l'Etat*. *Pour une théorie matérialiste de la philosophie*, Paris, Fayard, 1975, pp. 360 ff.

2. P. Ginsborg, 'Gramsci and the era of bourgeois Revolution' in J.A. Davis, ed., *Gramsci and Italy's Passive Revolution*, London, Croom Helm, New York, Barnes and Noble Books, 1979, p. 48.

3. J. Lonsdale, 'States and social processes in Africa: a historiographical survey', *African Studies Review*, XXIV (2-3), June-Sept. 1981, p. 201.

4. B. Moore, Jr., *The Social Origins of Dictatorship and Democracy*; A.F.K. Organski, *The Stages of Political Development*, New York, A.A. Knopf, 1965.

5. P. Ginsborg, 'Gramsci and the era of bourgeois revolution', in J.A. Davis, ed., *Gramsci and Italy's Passive Revolution*, p. 47.

6. A. Gramsci, *Note sul Machiavelli, sulla politica e sullo Stato moderno*, Turin, Einaudi, 1966, p. 60.

7. A Cabral, *Unité et lutte*, Paris, Maspero, 1980 (new edition); P. Chabal, *Amilcar Cabral*. *Revolutionary Leadership and People's War*, Cambridge,

Cambridge University Press, 1983.

8. R. Michels, *Les Partis politiques. Essai sur les tendances oligarchiques des démocraties*, Paris, Flammarion, 1971, pp. 135 and 197.

9. Cited by Y.-A. Fauré, J.-F. Médard, 'Classe dominante ou classe dirigeante?', in Y.-A. Fauré, J.-F. Médard, ed., *Etat et bourgeoisie en Côte d'Ivoire*, Paris, Karthala, 1982, p. 129. Houphouët-Boigny's 21 October 1945 electoral programme is reproduced in J. Baulin, *La Politique intérieure d'Houphouët-Boigny*, Paris, Eurafor Press, 1982, annexe IV.

10. R.W. Johnson, 'The Parti démocratique de Guinée and the Mamou "deviation"', in C. Allen, R.W. Johnson, eds., *African Perspectives*, Cambridge, Cambridge University Press, 1970, pp. 347-369; J.-P. Alata, *Prison d'Afrique. 5 ans dans les geôles de Guinée*, Paris, Le Seuil, 1976, pp. 70-75; I. Baba Kaké, *Sékou Touré, le héros et le tyran*, Paris, Ed. Jeune Afrique, 1987.

11. A.R. Zolberg, *One-Party Government in the Ivory Coast*, Princeton, Princeton University Press, 1964, pp. 152 ff., 188 ff., 208 ff., 250, 278.

12. Speech by Houphouët-Boigny, Abidjan, 7 Sept. 1958, cited by J. Baulin, *La Politique intérieure*, p. 100.

13. L. Ggagbo, *Côte d'Ivoire. Economie et société à la veille de l'indépendance (1940-1960)*, Paris, L'Harmattan, 1982 and *Côte d'Ivoire. Pour une alternative démocratique*, Paris, L'Harmattan, 1983; M. Amondji, *Félix Houphouët-Boigny et la Côte d'Ivoire. L'envers d'une légende*, Paris, Karthala, 1984.

14. A.R. Zolberg, *One-Party Government*.

15. J. Braulin, *La Politique africaine d'Houphouët-Boigny*, Paris, Eurafor Press, 1980.

16. J. Baulin, *La Politique intérieure ...*, pp. 128.

17. *Ibid.*, pp. 153 ff.; M.A. Cohen, *Urban Policy and Political Conflict in Africa. A Study of the Ivory Coast*, Chicago, The University of Chicago Press, 1974, pp. 174 ff., 196 ff.

18. *Fraternité-Matin* (Abidjan), 3 Oct. 1980; J.-F. Médard, 'Jeunes et aînés en Côte d'Ivoire. Le VIIe Congrès du PDCI-RDA', *Politique africaine*, 1 Jan. 1981, pp. 102-113.

19. J.-F. Bayart, *L'État au Cameroun*, Paris, Presses de la Fondation nationale des sciences politiques, 1979.

20. C. Coulon, 'Elections, factions et idéologies au Sénégal', in CEAN–CERI, *Aux urnes l'Afrique! Élections et pouvoirs en Afrique noire*, Paris, Pedone, 1978, p. 172. Also see F.M. Hayward, S.N. Grovogui, 'Persistence and change in Senegalese electoral processes', in F.M. Hayward, ed., *Elections in independent Africa*, Boulder, Westview Press, 1978, pp. 248 and 254.

21. D.B. Cruise O'Brien, 'Les élections sénégalaises du 27 février 1983', *Politique africaine*, 11 Sept. 1983, p. 8. R. Fatton uses Gramsci's theories of the 'organic crisis' and the 'passive revolution' in a theoretically dubious way to describe Senghor's and Abdou Diouf's politics of liberalisation. 'The democratization of Senegal (1976-1983): "passive revolution" and the democratic limits of liberal democracy'. Paper presented at Los Angeles, XXVIIe Congress of the African Studies Association, 1984, and 'Organic crisis, organic intellectuals and the Senegalese passive revolution', Paper presented at New Orleans, XXVIIe Congress of

the African Studies Association, 1985.

22. A. Sylla, 'De la grève à la réforme. Luttes enseignantes et crise sociale au Sénégal', *Politique africaine*, 8 Dec. 1982, pp. 61-73.

23. *Independent Kenya*, London, Zed Press, 1982, *passim*.

24. J.D. Barkan, J.J. Okumu, 'Patrons, machines et élections au Kenya', in CEAN-CERI, *Aux urnes l'Afrique!* pp. 132-134.

25. Sources: interviews. See J.-C. Willame, 'Chronique d'une opposition politique: l'UDPS (1978-1987)', *Les Cahiers du CEDAF*, 7-8 Dec. 1987, pp. 1-118 and N. Karl I Bond, *Mobuto ou l'incarnation du mal zaïrois*, London, Rex Collings, 1982.

26. Cited in R. Dumont, *Pour l'Afrique, j'accuse*, Paris, Plon, 1986, p. 44.

27. A. Adams, *La terre et les gens du Fleuve*, Paris, L'Harmattan, 1985, chap. viii, G. Hesseling, *Histoire politique du Sénégal. Institutions, droit et société*, Paris, Karthala, Leiden, Afrika-Studiecentrum, 1985, pp. 260-261 and 316-320; J. Copans, 'From Senegambia to Senegal: the evolution of peasantries', in M.A. Klein, ed., *Peasants in Africa: Historical and Contemporary Perspectives*, Beverly Hills, Sage Publications, 1980, pp. 77-103.

28. See, for example J. Champaud, *Villes et campagnes du Cameroun de l'Ouest*, Paris, ORSTOM, 1983, pp. 235-259; D. Desjeux, *Stratégies paysannes en Afrique noire. Le Congo (Essai sur la gestion de l'incertitude)*, Paris, L'Harmattan, 1987.

29. M. von Freyhold, *Ujamaa villages in Tanzania. Analysis of a Social Experiment*, London, Heinemann, 1979, pp. 72-77; G. Hyden, *Beyond Ujamaa in Tanzania. Underdevelopment and an Uncaptured Peasantry*, London, Heinemann, 1980, p. 106; D.-C. Martin, *Tanzanie. L'invention d'une culture politique*, Paris, Presses de la Fondation nationale des sciences politiques, Karthala, 1988, chap. 7 and 14.

30. To use G. Hyden's famous expression, *Beyond Ujamaa in Tanzania*.

31. R. Jeffries, *Class, Power and Ideology in Ghana. The Railwaymen of Sekondi*, Cambridge, Cambridge University Press, 1978; R. Sandbrook, R. Cohen, eds., *The Development of an African Working Class. Studies in Class Formation and Action*, Toronto, University of Toronto Press, 1975; I. Touré, 'Le Travail en Côte d'Ivoire: du collectivisme de fait à la participation provoquée', Abidjan, Faculté des lettres et sciences humaines, 1978, and 'L'UGTCI et le "développement harmonieux". Un syndicalisme anticonflits?', *Politique africaine*, 24, Dec. 1986, pp. 79-90; D.-C. Martin, *Tanzanie*, pp. 100 ff.; P. Mihyo, 'Expériences autogestionnaires dans l'industrie tanzanienne', *Politique africaine*, 8, Dec. 1982, pp. 44-60.

32. M. Cahen, *Mozambique. La Révolution implosée*, Paris, L'Harmattan, 1987, p. 28. Cf., by the same author, 'Etat et pouvoir populaire dans le Mozambique indépendant', *Politique africaine*, 19, Sept. 1985, pp. 52 ff. and 'Corporatisme et colonialisme: approche du cas mozambicain, 1933-1979. II. Crise et survivance du corporatisme colonial, 1960-1979', *Cahiers d'études africaines*, 93, XXIV (1), 1984, pp. 5-24.

33. W.G. Clarence-Smith, 'Class structure and class struggle in Angola in the 1970s', *Journal of Southern African Studies*, VII (1), Oct. 1980, pp. 109-126; M. Cahen, 'Syndicalisme urbain, luttes ouvrières et questions ethniques: Luanda (Angola): 1974-1977/1981. Notes sur une recherche', Paris, L.A. Tiers-Monde, Afrique, 1985.

34. M. Cahen, 'Etat et pouvoir populaire dans le Mozambique indépendant'; N. Chazan, 'Politics and the State in Ghana: a third decade reassessment', Paper presented to Conference on West African States since 1976, London, Centre for African Studies, School of Oriental and African Studies, 1987; P. Labazée, 'Réorganisation économique et résistances sociales. La question des alliances au Burkina', *Politique africaine*, 20, Dec. 1985, pp. 10-28; R. Otayek, 'Burkina Faso: quand le tambour chance de rythme, il est indispensable que les danseurs changent de pas', *Politique africaine*, 29, Dec. 1987, pp. 116-123; 'Discours populistes, mouvements populaires', *Politique africaine*, 8, Dec. 1982, pp. 3-102.

35. M. Chege, 'A tale of two slums: electoral politics in Mathare and Dagoretti', *Review of African Political Economy*, 20 Jan.-April 1981, pp. 74-88; G. Mainet, *Douala. Croissance et servitudes*, Paris, L'Harmattan, 1985, pp. 474 and following pages; L. Bret, 'La zone Nylon à Douala', *Projet*, 162, 1982, pp. 163-174; M. Roumy, 'L'animation, sa place, son rôle dans les problèmes actuels d'intégration et de cohésion sociales au quartier Nylon' and L. Barbedette, 'Formation non conventionnelle au service de l'animation urbain (quartier Nylon – Douala)', Session de formation sur l'environnement urbaine en Afrique intertropicale de l'IDEP, Douala, 1973; D. Fassin, E. Jeannée, G. Salem, M. Revillon, 'Les enjeux sociaux de la participation communautaire. Les comités de santé à Pikine (Sénégal)', *Sciences sociales et santé*, IV (3-4), Nov. 1986, pp. 205-221.

36. See, for example, S. Bagayogo, 'L'État au Mali. Représentation, autonomie et mode de fonctionnement', in E. Terray, ed., *L'État contemporain en Afrique*, Paris, L'Harmattan, 1987, pp. 107-110; J. Fame Ndongo, *Le Prince et le scribe. Lecture politique et esthétique du roman négro-africain postcolonial*, Paris, Berger-Levrault, 1988.

37. J. Goody, *La raison graphique. La domestication de la pensée sauvage*, Paris, Editions de Minuit, 1979, chap. 2.

38. T.O. Ranger, 'Religious movements and politics in sub-saharan Africa', Paper presented at New Orleans, XXVIIe Congress of the African Studies Association, 1985.

39. W.M.J. van Binsbergen, *Religious Change in Zambia. Exploratory Studies*, London, KPI, 1981; M. Schoffeleers, 'Economic change and religious polarization in an african rural district', in Centre of African Studies, *Malawi, an Alternative Pattern of Development*, Edinburgh, University of Edinburgh, 1985, pp. 189-242. Also see G.C. Mutiso's bizarre essay, *Kenya. Politics and Society*, Nairobi, East African Literature Bureau, 1975, chap. 1.

40. *Marchés tropicaux et méditerranéens*, 10 Jan. 1986, p. 85.

41. G. Dauch, D. Martin, *L'héritage de Kenyatta. La transition politique au Kenya. 1975-1982*, Paris, L'Harmattan, Presses Universitaires d'Aix-Marseille, 1985, p. 128.

42. Dossier 381, 'Église chrétienne', Brussels, CEDAF (on the conflict between M. Mobutu and cardinal Malula); P. Chamay, 'L'Église au Burundi. Un conflit peut en cacher un autre', *Etudes*, Feb. 1987, pp. 158-170; J.-P. Chrétien, A. Quichaoua, 'Burundi, d'une République à l'autre', *Politique africaine*, 29, March 1988, pp. 87-94; J.-F. Bayart, *L'État au Cameroun, passim* and 'Les rapports entre les Eglises et l'État du

Cameroun de 1958 à 1971', *Revue française d'études politiques africaines*, 80, August 1972, pp. 79-104.

43. M.G. Schatzberg, *Politics and Class in Zaïre*, New York, Africana Publishing Company, 1980, p. 50. See also 'Essai de profil des prêtres de l'an 2000 au Zaïre. Message du cardinal Malula', *La Documentation catholique*, 1 May 1988, pp. 463-469.

44. See, in particular, D.B. Cruise O'Brien, *The Mourides of Senegal*, Oxford, Clarendon Press, 1971; J. Copans, *Les Marabouts de l'arachide*, Paris, Le Sycomore, 1980; C. Coulon, *Le Marabout et le prince. Islam et pouvoir au Sénégal*, Paris, Pedone, 1981.

45. C.S. Whitaker, Jr., *The Politics of Tradition. Continuity and Change in Northern Nigeria. 1946-1966*, Princeton, Princeton University Press, 1970, p. 315; P.M. Lubeck, *Islam and Urban Labor in Northern Nigeria: the Making of a Muslim Working Class*, Cambridge, Cambridge University Press, 1986, pp. 35-36.

46. R. Delval, *Les Musulmans du Togo*, Paris, Publications orientalistes de France, 1980; J.-L. Triaud, 'L'islam et l'État en République du Niger (1974-1981)', in O. Carré, ed., *'L'Islam et l'État dans le monde d'aujourd'hui*, Paris, PUF, 1982, pp. 246-257; F. Constantin, 'Minorité religieuse et luttes politiques dans l'espace ougandais', *Politique africaine*, 4, Nov. 1981, pp. 71-89; C. Coulon, *Les Musulmans et le pouvoir en Afrique noire*, Paris, Karthala, 1983, chap. 4; M. Lobe Ewane, 'Des intégristes entre le marabout et le prince. La montée du discours fondamentaliste musulman au Sénégal', *Le Monde diplomatique*, April 1985, p. 15. For a different example, see R. Otayek, 'La crise de la communauté musulmane de Haute-Volta. L'islam voltaïque entre réformisme et tradition, autonomie et subordination', *Cahiers d'études africaines*, 95, XXVIV-3, 1984, pp. 299-320.

47. J. MacCracken, *Politics and Christianity in Malawi. 1875-1940. The Impact of the Livingstonia Mission in the Northern Province*, Cambridge, Cambridge University Press, 1977, chap. 8.

48. S. Asch, *L'Église du prophète Kimbangu. De ses origines à son rôle actuel au Zaïre*, Paris, Karthala, 1983; W. MacGaffey, *Modern Kongo Prophets*.

49. Speech by Augustin Denise, 1 November 1968, cited in C. Piault, ed., *Prophétisme et thérapeutique. Albert Atcho et la communauté de Bregbo*, Paris, Hermann, 1975, pp. 70-72.

50. A. Zempleni, 'De la persécution à la culpabilité' and M. Augé, 'Logique lignagère et logique de Bregbo', pp. 153-236.

51. Following the example of other authors, G. Hyden, *No Shortcuts to Progress. African Development Management in Perspective*, London, Heinemann, 1983, p. 19.

52. J. MacCracken, *Politics and Christianity in Malawi*, chap. 8; W. MacGaffey, *Modern Kongo Prophets*, chap. 3 and 4.

53. *Africa Confidential*, 25 (21), 17 Oct. 1984; *Marchés tropicaux et méditerranéens*, 27 Feb. 1987, p. 474 and 12 Feb. 1988, p. 375. See also, on the Congo, M.-E. Gruenais, D. Mayala, 'Comment se débarrasser de l' "inefficacité symbolique" de la médecine traditionnelle?', *Politique africaine*, 31, Oct. 1988, pp. 51-61; A. Kouvouama, 'A chacun son prohète!', *ibid.*, pp. 62-65; J. Tonda, 'Marx et l'ombre des fétiches. Pouvoir local contre *ndjobi* dans le Nord-Congo', *ibid.*, pp. 73-83.

54. Dossier 404/3, 'religion'. CREDU, Nairobi (especially *The Standard* (Nairobi), 23 April 1984, 30 May 1984, 12 July 1984, 17 July 1984; *Daily Nation* (Nairobi), 9 Dec. 1982, 13 August 1985; *Nairobi Times* (Nairobi), 9 Dec. 1982); W.M.J. van Binsbergen, *Religious Change in Zambia*; W.M.J. van Binsbergen, M. Schoffeleers, eds., *Theoretical Explorations in African Religion*, London, KPI, 1985; A. Wipper, *Rural Rebels. A Study of two Protest Movements in Kenya*, Nairobi, Oxford University Press, 1977; G.S. Were, 'Politics, religion and nationalism in Western Kenya, 1942-1962: Dini ya Msambwa revisited', in B.A. Ogot, ed., *Politics and Nationalism in Colonial Kenya*, Nairobi, East African Publishing House, 1972, pp. 85-104.
55. E. de Rosny, *Les Yeux de ma chèvre*, Paris, Plon, 1981; J.-M. Gibbal, *Tambours d'eau*, Paris, Le Sycomore, 1982.
56. See the commentaries of H. Portelli, *Gramsci et le bloc historique*, Paris, PUF, 1972; and C. Buci-Glucksmann, *Gramsci et l'État*, p. 75; and M.-A. Macciochi, *Pour Gramsci*, Paris, Le Seuil, 1974; and C. Mouffe, 'Hegemony and ideology in Gramsci', in C. Mouffe, ed., *Gramsci and Marxist Theory*, London, Routledge and Kegan Paul, 1979, p. 201.
57. On this point, *cf.* H. Portelli, *Gramsci et le bloc historique*, pp. 86-89.
58. A. Giddens, *Central Problems in Social Theory. Action, Structure and Contradiction in Social Analysis*, London, Macmillan, 1979, p. 206.
59. F. Braudel, *L'Identité de la France. Espace et histoire*, Paris, Arthaud, Flammarion, 1986, p. 278.
60. For these different examples, see C. Young, T. Turner, *The Rise and Decline of the Zaïrian State*, Madison, The University of Wisconsin Press, 1985, pp. 152 ff.; E. M'Bokolo, 'La triple stratification zaïroise', *Le Monde diplomatique*, Nov. 1981, p. 21; M.G. Schatzberg, *Politics and Class in Zaïre*, p. 91; F. Gaulme, 'Succès et difficultés des pays des Grands Lacs: le Burundi', *Marchés tropicaux et méditerranéens*, 24 July 1987, p. 2007; R.A. Joseph, *Democracy and Prebendal Politics in Nigeria. The Rise and Fall of the Second Republic*, Cambridge, Cambridge University Press, 1987; *Africa Confidential*, 28 (22), 4 Nov. 1987; *ibid.*, 28 (5), 4 March 1987.
61. *Cf.* especially J.-P. Chauveau and J.-P. Dozon, 'Colonisation, économie de plantation et société civile en Côte d'Ivoire', *Cahiers ORSTOM, série Sciences humaines*, XXI (1), 1985, pp. 63-80 and 'Au cœur des ethnies ivoiriennes... l'État', in E. Terray, ed., *L'État contemporain en Afrique*, Paris, L'Harmattan, 1987, pp. 221-296.
62. See, for example, C.M. Toulabor, *Le Togo sous Eyadema*, Paris, Karthala, 1986; H. Ossebi, 'Affirmation ethnique et discours idéologique au Congo. Essai d'interprétation', Paris, Université René-Descartes, 1982.
63. J.-P. Chauveau, J.-P. Dozon, 'Au cœur des ethnies ivoiriennes... l'État', in E. Terray, ed., *L'État contemporain en Afrique*, p. 269.
64. J.-F. Bayart, *La Politique africaine de François Mitterrand*, Paris, Karthala, 1984, pp. 140 ff.
65. See especially N. Swainson, *The Development of Corporate Capitalism in Kenya. 1918-1977*, London, Heinemann, 1980.
66. C. Buci-Glucksmann, *Gramsci et l'État*, p. 75.
67. *Cahiers de prison*, VII, paragr. 28, in A. Gramsci, *Cahiers de prison*, vol. ii: *Cahiers 6, 7, 8, 9*, Paris, Gallimard, 1983.

68. A. Gramsci, *Il Risorgimento*, Turin, Einaudi, 1966, p. 191.
69. Manifesto of the Parti de la solidarité sénégalaise, *Dakar-Matin*, 2 Feb. 1959 and *Solidarité* (Dakar), 6, 29 August, 1959, cited in C. Coulon, *Le Marabout et le Prince*, pp. 216-217.
70. Speeches cited by P.-H. Siriex, *Houphouët-Boigny ou la sagesse africaine*, Paris, Nathan, Abidjan, Les Nouvelles Editions africaines, 1986, pp. 185 and 193. Also see A.R. Zolberg, *One-Party Government in the Ivory Coast*, pp. 234 and following pages, and, for the case of Léon Mba, F. Gaulme, *Le Gabon et son ombre*, Paris, Karthala, 1988, pp. 133-134.
71. Speeches cited by J.-F. Bayart, *La Politique africaine de François Mitterrand*, p. 140.
72. J.-M. Kalflèche, 'Comment Cheysson est devenu "la bête noire" des Africains', *Le Quotidien de Paris*, 17 August 1983 and 'Mitterrand l'Africain: le risque de l'incohérence', *ibid.*, 3 Nov. 1981.
73. P.-H. Sirieux, *Houphouët-Boigny*, p. 88.
74. C. and A. Darlington, *African Betrayal*, New York, David McKay, 1968, p. 115-121.
75. J.-F. Bayart, *La Politique africaine de François Mitterrand*.
76. G. Duruflé, *L'Ajustement structurel en Afrique (Sénégal, Côte d'Ivoire, Madagascar)*, Paris, Karthala, 1988 and C. Freud, *Quelle coopération? Un bilan de l'aide au développement*, Paris, Karthala, 1988.
77. J.-P. Chauveau, J.-P. Dozon, 'Au cœur des ethnies ivoiriennes... l'État', in E. Terray, ed., *L'État contemporain en Afrique*, p. 221-296.
78. J. Baulin, *La politique africaine d'Houiphouët-Boigny*.
79. Mouvement de redressement national, 'Gabon: livre blanc. 1981', n.d., p. 29 (underlining by J.F. Bayart).
80. J.-F. Médard, 'Charles Njonjo: portrait d'un "big man" au Kenya'. in E. Terray, ed., *L'État contemporain en Afrique*, p. 55.
81. See J. Iliffe, *The Emergence of African Capitalism*, London, Macmillan, 1983 and P.M. Lubeck, *Islam and Urban Labor in Northern Nigeria*.
82. N. Chazan, *An Anatomy of Ghanaian Politics: Managing Political Recession. 1969-1982*, Boulder, Westview Press, 1982; H.B. Hansen, M. Twaddle, eds., *Uganda now. Between Decay and Development*, London, James Currey, Athan, Ohio University Press, Nairobi, Heinemann, 1988.
83. M. Cahen, *Mozambique*.
84. *Africa Confidential*, 29 (3), 5 Feb. 1988; J.-C. Willame, 'Zaïre: système de survic et fiction d'État', *Canadian Journal of African Studies*, 18 (1), 1984, pp. 83-88; J. MacGaffey, *Entrepreneurs and Parasites; the Struggle for Indigenous Capitalism in Zaïre*, Cambridge, Cambridge University Press, 1987, chap. vi.
85. 'Les puissances moyennes et l'Afrique', *Politique africaine*, 10, June 1983, pp. 3-74.
86. J. Okello, *Revolution in Zanzibar*, Nairobi, East African Publishing House, 1967; A. Sesay, 'Le coup d'État au Liberia. Facteurs internes et effets régionaux', *Politique africaine*, 7, Sept. 1982, pp. 91-106; Y.-A. Fauré, 'Ouaga et Abidjan: divorce à l'africaine? Les raisons contre la raison', *Politique africaine*, 20, Dec. 1985, pp. 78-86.
87. *Africa Confidential*, 28 (4), 2 Dec. 1987.
88. *Ibid*; C. Coulon, *Le Marabout et le prince*, pp. 259 and following pages, and *Les Musulmans et le pouvoir en Afrique noire*, chap. 5; J.H. Paden,

Religion and Political Culture in Kano, Los Angeles, University of California Press, 1973.
89. Sources: interviews and personal observations.
90. M. Kilson, *Political Change in a West African State. A Study of the Modernization Process in Sierra Leone*, Cambridge, Harvard University Press, 1966.
91. G. Dauch, D. Martin, *L'Héritage de Kenyatta*, chap. 7 and 8.
92. M. Vovelle, *Idéologies et Mentalités*, Paris, Maspero, 1982, pp. 321.
93. G. Dupré, *Un ordre et sa destruction*, Paris, ORSTOM, 1982, pp. 366 and following pages.
94. E. de Rosny, *Les Yeux de ma chèvre*, p. 93. For similar representations, see W. MacGaffey, *Modern Kongo Prophets*, pp. 130-140.
95. For example, the idea of *sama* ("with the whites"), which is used in Togo to represent the developed southern region and people who work; (C.M. Toulabor, *Le Togo*, p. 37); "of white man's country" which is used in Maka country to refer to the town (P. Geschiere, *Village communities and the State. Changing Relations among the Maka of Southeastern Cameroon since the Colonial Conquest*, London, KPI, 1982, p. 206); of *Kôgo mindélé* ("those who see themselves as the white men of Congo") used in Upper-Congo to represent the Bakongo (G. Balandier, *Sociologie actuelle de l'Afrique noire*, Paris, PUF, 1971, new edition, p. 293); of *Kimundele* (European, as opposed to *Kindombe*, black) and of *Mputu* (Europe) used by the Bakongo from Matadi in Zaïre (W. MacGaffey, *Modern Kongo Prophets*, pp. 97 and 130-140).

CHAPTER 8: ENTREPRENEURS, FACTIONS AND POLITICAL NETWORKS

1. C. Mouffe, ed., *Gramsci and Marxist Theory*, London, Routledge and Kegan Paul, 1979.
2. E.P. Thompson, *The Making of the English Working Class*, London, Victor Gollancz, 1963.
3. *L'Invention du quotidien*, M. de Certeau, vol. I: *Arts de faire* and L. Giard, P. Mayol, vol. II: *Habiter, cuisiner*, Paris, Union générale d'éditions, 1980. See for example R. de Maximy, *Kinshasa, ville en suspens. Dynamique de la croissance et problèmes d'urbanisme. Approche sociopolitique*, Paris, ORSTOM, 1984; A. Bonnassieux, *L'Autre Abidjan. Chronique d'un quartier oublié*, Abidjan, INADES, Paris, Karthala, 1987; P. Antoine, A. Dubresson, A. Manou-Savina, *Abidjan 'côté cours'*, Paris, ORSTOM, Karthala, 1987.
4. J.-F. Bayart, 'Le politique par le bas en Afrique noire. Questions de méthode', *Politique africaine*, 1, Jan. 1981, pp. 53-82.
5. J.-F. Bayart, *L'État au Cameroun*, Paris, Presses de la Fondation nationale des sciences politiques, 1979, pp. 256 ff. and 'La revanche des sociétés africaines', *Politique africaine*, 11, Sept. 1983, pp. 95-127; R. Cohen, 'Resistance and Hidden Forms of Consciousness amongst African Workers', *Review of African Political Economy*, 19, Sept.-Dec. 1980, pp.

8-22.
6. M. de Certeau, *L'Invention du quotidien*, vol. I, *Arts de faire*.
7. B. Verhaegen, *Rébellions au Congo*, Bruxelles, Kinshasa, CRISP, INEP, IRES, 1966 and 1969.
8. R. Buijtenhuijs, *Le Frolinat et les guerres civiles du Tchad (1977-1984)*, Paris, Karthala, Leiden, Afrika-Studiecentrum, 1987. On the Museveni regime, *cf.* G. Prunier, 'Le phénomène NRM en Ouganda. Une expérience révolutionnaire originale', *Politique africaine*, 23, Sept. 1986, pp. 102-114 and 'La réforme économique ougandaise de mai 1987', *ibid.*, 28, Dec. 1987, pp. 129-134.
9. A. Peace, 'Prestige power and legitimacy in a modern Nigerian town', *Canadian Journal of African Studies*, 13 (1-2), 1979, pp. 26-51; P.W.C. Gutkind, 'The view from below: political consciousness of the urban poor in Ibadan', *Cahiers d'études africaines*, 57, XV (1), 1975, pp. 5-35; M. Peil, *Nigerian Politics. The People's View*, London, Cassell, 1976; C.M. Toulabor, 'L'énonciation du pouvoir et de la richesse chez les jeunes "conjoncturés" de Lomé (Togo)', *Revue française de science politique* 35 (3), June 1985, pp. 446-458.
10. J.-F. Bayart, 'Les sociétés africaines face à l'État', *Pouvoirs*, 25, Apr. 1983, pp. 23-39; C. Coulon, *Les Musulmans et le pouvoir en Afrique noire*, Paris, Karthala, 1983 – also, for examples outside Africa – M. Chaui, 'Le Brésil et ses phantasmes', *Esprit*, Oct. 1983, pp. 200 ff.; H. Béji, *Le Désenchantement national*, Paris, Maspero, 1982; J.-L. Domenach, 'Chine: la victoire ambiguë du vieil homme', *Revue française de science politique*, 35 (3), June 1985, pp. 374-400; B. Jobert, 'La crise de l'État indien', *Économie et humanisme*, 266, Jul.-Aug. 1982, pp. 17-27; S. Uwais, 'Sur quelques modes égyptiens de résistance à l'oppression et aux épreuves', *Modes populaires d'action politique*, 2, 1984, pp. 3-11; M.P. Martin, 'Égypte: les modes informels du changement', *Études*, Apr. 1980, pp. 435-452.
11. C. van Onselen, *Chibaro. African Mine Labour in Southern Rhodesia. 1900-1933*, London, Pluto Press, 1976; F. Cooper, *On the African Waterfront. Urban Disorder and the Transformation of Work in Colonial Mombasa*, New-Haven, Yale University Press, 1987; P.M. Lubeck, *Islam and Urban Labor in Northern Nigeria. The Making of a Muslim Working Class*, Cambridge, Cambridge University Press, 1986; A. Peace, *Choice, Class and Conflict. A Study of Southern Nigerian Factory Workers*, London, Harvester Press, 1979; M. Peil, *The Ghanaian Factory Worker*, Cambridge, Cambridge University Press, 1970; R. Jeffries, *Class, Ideology and Power in Africa: the Railwaymen of Sekondi*, Cambridge, Cambridge University Press, 1978; B. Freund, *The African Worker*, Cambridge, Cambridge University Press, 1988; R. Sandbrook, R. Cohen, eds., *The Development of an African Working Class*, London, Longman, 1975; M. Agier, J. Copans, A. Morice, eds., *Classes ouvrières d'Afrique noire*, Paris, Karthala, 1987.
12. T. Ranger, *Peasant Consciousness and Guerilla War in Zimbabwe. A Comparative Study*, London, James Currey, Berkeley, University of California Press, 1985.
13. A. Giddens, *The Class Structure of the Advanced Societies*, London, Hutchinson University Library, 1973, p. 132.

14. D. Austin, 'Introduction' in D. Austin, R. Luckham, eds., *Politicians and Soldiers in Ghana. 1966-1972*, London, Frank Cass, 1975, pp. 7-12.
15. See, for example, the itinerary of R. Sandbrook, from *The Development of an African Working Class* (with R. Cohen, *op. cit.*) and from *The Politics of Basic Needs. Urban Aspects of Assaulting Poverty in Africa* (Toronto, University of Toronto Press, 1982) to *The Politics of Africa's Economic Stagnation* (Cambridge, Cambridge University Press, 1985), by way of 'Patrons, clients and factions: new dimensions of conflict analysis in Africa', *Canadian Journal of Political Science*, 5 (1), March 1972, pp. 104-119. R. Lemarchand is without doubt the person who has analysed this factional dimension of political life with the most thoroughness and rigour (see especially 'Political clientelism and ethnicity in tropical Africa: competing solidarities in nation-building', *American Political Science Review*, LXVI (1), Mar. 1972, pp. 68-90; S.N. Eisenstadt, R. Lemarchand, eds., *Political Clientelism, Patronage and Development*, Beverly Hills, Sage Publications, 1981; 'Bringing factions back into the state' in Nzongola-Ntalaja, ed., *The Crisis in Zaïre: Myth and Realities*, Trenton, Africa World Press, 1982, pp. 51-66).
16. A. Przeworsky, 'Proletariat into a class: the process of class formation from Karl Kautsky's *The Class Struggle* to recent controversies', *Politics and Society*, 7, 1977, pp. 343-401 (often quoted by certain Africanist writers, in particular the historian F. Cooper).
17. D.B. Cruise O'Brien, *Saints and Politicians. Essays in the Organization of a Senegalese Peasant Society*, Cambridge, Cambridge University Press, 1975, chap v. See also C. Coulon, *Le Marabout et le Prince. Islam et pouvoir au Sénégal*, Paris, Pedone, 1981 and 'Elections, factions et idéologies au Sénégal' in CEAN, CERI, *Aux urnes l'Afrique! Elections et pouvoirs en Afrique noire*, Paris, Pedone, 1978, pp. 149-186; W.G. Foltz, 'Social structure and political behavior of Senegalese elites', *Behavior Science Notes*, 4 (2), 1969, pp. 145-163; O.B. Diop, *Les héritiers d'une indépendance*, Dakar, Nouvelles Éditions africaines, 1982, p. 95.
18. Parti socialiste du Sénégal, Groupe d'études et de recherches, *Séminaire sur le thème: les tendances et les clans*, Dakar, 1 Dec. 1984, p. 7; *Le Soleil* (Dakar), 3 Dec. 1984 and *Muntu-Dimanche* (Dakar), 19, Dec. 1986, p. 2. See also the rules drawn up by the Secretary General of the Party for the sale of cards, Parti socialiste du Sénégal, circulaire sur la vente des cartes, Dakar, 28 March 1984, n° 001/84/SG/PS, multigr., and the circulars of 4 May 1984, n° 02/84/PS et du 3 Feb. 1986 n° 011/85/SG/PS.
19. A. Diouf, Secretary General, *Rapport de politique général. Le PS, parti de développement*, Dakar, congrès ordinaire du Parti socialiste du Sénégal, 20-21 Dec. 1986, multigr., pp. 56-58.
20. D.B. Cruise O'Brien, 'Senegal' in J. Dunn, ed., *West African States. Failure and Promise. A Study in Comparative Politics*, Cambridge, Cambridge University Press, 1978, pp. 187-188.
21. Parti socialiste du Sénégal, Groupe d'études et de recherche, *Séminaire sur le thème: les tendances et les clans*, pp. 5-6.
22. *Ibid.*, p. 4.
23. J. Schmitz, 'Un politologue chez les marabouts' *Cahiers d'études africaines*, 91, XXIII (3), 1983, pp. 332 and 335.
24. See in particular E.S. Ndione, *Dynamique urbaine d'une société en grappe:*

un cas, Dakar, Dakar, ENDA, 1987 and D. Fassin, E. Jeannée, G. Salem, M. Réveillon, 'Les enjeux sociaux de la participation communautaire. Les comités de santé à Pikine (Sénégal)', *Sciences sociales et santé,* IV (3-4), Nov. 1986, pp. 205-221. On factional struggles within Islamic brotherhoods, *cf.* C. Coulon, *Le Marabout et le Prince,* pp. 244 ff.

25. J. Schmitz, 'Un politologue chez les marabouts', pp. 334-335. For a more subtle analysis which refuses to reduce the political conflicts of the Nigerian kingdom of Oyo to inter-lineage conflicts, *cf.* R. Law, 'Making sense of a traditional narrative: political disintegration in the kingdom of Oyo', *Cahiers d'études africaines,* 87-88, XXII (3-4), 1982, p. 396.

26. D. Martin, G. Dauch, *L'Héritage de Kenyatta. La transition politique au Kenya. 1975-1982,* Aix, Presses universitaires d'Aix-Marseille, Paris, L'Harmattan, 1985, p. 101.

27. *Ibid., passim; Weekly Review* (Nairobi), 1978-1986; Dossiers 140/221 'Elites politiques: Charles Njonjo', et 404/3 'Religion', Nairobi, CREDU, 1980-1984; R. Sandbrook, 'Patrons, clients and factions', art. cit.; J.D. Barkan, J.J. Okumu, 'Patrons, machines et élections au Kenya' in CEAN, CERI, *Aux urnes l'Afrique!, op. cit.,* pp. 119-147; G. Hyden, C. Leys, 'Elections and politics in single party systems: the case of Kenya and Tanzania', *British Journal of Political Science,* 2 (4), Oct. 1972, pp. 389-420; D. Bourmaud, *Le Système politique du Kenya: centre et périphérie,* Bordeaux, Institut d'études politiques, s.d. (1985), multigr., pp. 261 ff.

28. M. Szeftel, 'The political process in post-colonial Zambia: the structural bases of factional conflict' in Centre of African Studies, *The Evolving Structure of Zambia Society,* Edinburgh, University of Edinburgh, 1980, multigr., pp. 64-95; R Tangri, *Politics in sub-saharan Africa,* London, James Currey, Portsmouth, Heinemann, 1985, chap. ii; N. Chazan, *An Anatomy of Ghanaian Politics. Managing Political Recession. 1969-1982,* Boulder, Westview Press, 1983, pp. 95 ff.; and on Somalia *Africa Confidential,* 27 (12), 4 Jun. 1986 and 27 (22), 29 Oct. 1986.

29. D.-C. Martin, *Tanzanie: l'invention d'une culture politique,* Paris, Presses de la Fondation nationale des sciences politiques, Karthala, 1988, chap. xiv; J.-F. Bayart, *L'État au Cameroun,* Paris, Presses de la Fondation nationale des sciences politiques, 1979, *passim.*

30. PDCI, 'Séminaires d'information et de formation des secrétaires généraux. Yamoussoukro: 3-7 mai 1982. Abidjan: 10-11 décembre 1982. Yamoussoukro: 27-29 décembre 1983' Abidjan, Fraternité-Hebdo, 1985, pp. 8-10 and 11-14. See also A. Bonnal, 'L'administration et le parti face aux tensions', *Politique africaine,* 24, Dec. 1986, pp. 20-28.

31. F. Amani Goly, Party inspector for the Centre West area, 'Entraves internes et externes à la bonne marche des sections' in PDCI, *Le Quatrième Séminaire des secrétaires généraux, Yamoussoukro: 7, 8 et 9 mars 1985,* Abidjan, Fraternité-Hebdo, 1985, p. 17.

32. Declaration of Ansoumane Magassouba, quoted in I. Baba Kaké, *Sékou Touré, le héros et le tyran,* Paris, Jeune Afrique, 1987, p. 60.

33. J. Spencer, *KAU. The Kenya African Union,* London, KPI, 1985; R. Um Nyobé, *Le Problème national kamerunais. Présenté par J.A. Mbembé,* Paris, L'Harmattan, 1984; N. Chazan, *An Anatomy of Ghanaian Politics,* pp. 95 ff.; R. Rathbone, 'Businessmen in politics: party struggle in Ghana, 1949-1957', *Journal of Development Studies,* 9 (3) April 1973, pp. 391-401;

D.E. Apter, *Ghana in Transition*, Princeton, Princeton University Press, 1972.

34. See for example J.-C. Willame, 'Chronique d'une opposition politique: l'UDPS (1978-1987)' *Les Cahiers du CEDAF*, 7-8 Dec. 1987, pp. 1-118; R. Buijtenhuijs, *Le Frolinat et les guerres civiles du Tchad;* R.M. Price, *Society and Bureaucracy in Contemporary Ghana*, Berkeley, University of California Press, 1975.

35. See, for example, F. de Medeiros, 'Armée et instabilité: les partis militaires au Bénin' in A. Rouquié, ed., *La Politique de Mars. Les processus politiques dans les partis militaires contemporains*, Paris, Le Sycomore, 1981, pp. 123-149; A. Morice, 'Commerce parallèle et troc à Luanda', *Politique africaine*, 17, March 1985, pp. 105-120; or the documents produced by a small Zaïrian grouping, the Etudiants congolais progressistes (ECP) – especially tracts published in Autumn 1982 along the lines of 'J.B. Mulemba and A. Kalabela: two political crooks, two anti-democrats, two agitators.'

36. P. Péan, *Affaires africaines*, Paris, Fayard, 1983,

37. M. Mamdani, *Imperialism and Fascism in Uganda*, Nairobi, Heinemann, 1983, pp. 98-99; J.-C. Willame, *Zaïre. L'épopée d'Inga. Chronique d'une prédation industrielle*, Paris, L'Harmattan, 1986, pp. 137-138; N. Swainson, *The Development of Corporate Capitalism in Kenya. 1918-1977*, London, Heinemann, 1980, pp. 274-276; C. Young, T. Turner, *The Rise and Decline of the Zaïrian State*, Madison, The University of Wisconsin Press, 1985, pp. 171 and 176; *Africa Confidential*, 1984-1988.

38. Dossier 140/221, 'Élites politiques: Charles Njonjo', Nairobi, CREDU, 1983-1984; *Weekly Review* (Nairobi), 1983-1984; Republic of Kenya, *Report of Judicial Commission Appointed to Inquire into Allegations Involving Charles Mugane Njonjo (Former Minister for Constitutional Affairs and Member of Parliament for Kikuyu Constituency)*, Nairobi, The Commissions of Inquiry Act, 1984. Another interesting case would be that of the powerful businessman Shariff Nassir, the so-called 'king of the coast', who controls the Mombasa section of Kanu.

39. *Africa Confidential*, 28 (13), 24 Jun. 1987.

40. M. Crozier, *Le phénomène bureaucratique*, Paris, Le Seuil, 1963; J.-C. Thoenig, F. Dupuy, *L'Administration en miettes*, Paris, Fayard, 1985; T. Lupton, C.S. Wilson, 'The social background and connections of "top decision-makers"', *Manchester School of Economics and Social Studies*, 27 (1), 1959, pp. 30-51.

41. See, for example, A.J. Nathan, 'A factionalism model for CCP politics', *The China Quarterly*, Jan.-March 1973, pp. 34-66; W. Cornelius, 'Leaders, followers and official patrons in urban Mexico' in S.W. Schmidt, L. Guasti, J.C. Scott, eds., *Friends, Followers and Factions*, Berkeley, University of California Press, 1977, pp. 337-353; M.D. Sahlins, 'Poor man, rich man, Big-man, chief: political types in Melanesia and Polynesia', *Comparative Studies in Society and History*, V (3), April 1963, pp. 285-303; J.C. Scott, 'Patron-client politics and political change in South-East Asia', *American Political Science Review*, LXVI, March 1972, pp. 91-113; J. Duncan Powell, 'Peasant society and clientelist politics', *ibid.*, LXIV (2) June 1970, pp. 411-425; C.A.O. van Nieuwenhuijze, *Sociology of the Middle East. A Stock-Taking and Interpretation*, Leiden, Brill, 1971,

pp. 668 ff.; J.-M. Bouissou, 'Le Parti libéral-démocrate existe-t-il?',
Pouvoirs, 35, 1985, pp. 71-84 et 'Les factions dans le système politique
japonais: le cas du Parti libéral-démocrate', *Revue du droit public et de la
science politique en France et à l'etranger*, Winter 1981, pp. 1271-1345.
42. J.-P. Dozon, *La Société bété. Histoire d'une 'ethnie' de Côte d'Ivoire*, Paris,
Karthala, ORSTOM, 1985, p. 84. See also J. Vansina, *Les Anciens
Royaumes de la savane*, Léopoldville, Institut de recherches économiques
et sociales, (1965); J.-P. Warnier, *Échanges, développement et hiérarchies
dans le Bamenda précolonial*, Stuttgart, Franz Steiner Verlag Wiesbaden,
1985.
43. J. van Velsen, *The Politics of Kinship: a Study in Social Manipulation
among the Lakeside Tonga of Nyasaland*, Manchester, Manchester University Press, 1964; P.H. Gulliver, *Neighbours and Networks. The Idiom of
Kinship in Social Action among the Ndendeuli of Tanzania*, Berkeley, University of California Press, 1971; P. Geschiere, *Village Communities and
the State. Changing Relations among the Maka of Southeastern Cameroon
since the Colonial Conquest*, London, KPI, 1982.
44. D. Fassin et al., 'Les enjeux sociaux de la participation communautaire',
pp. 217-218.
45. S.T. Barnes, *Patrons and Power, Creating a Political Community in Metropolitan Lagos*, Manchester, Manchester University Press, 1986; A. Peace,
'Prestige power and legitimacy in a modern Nigerian town', A. Cohen,
*Custom and Politics in urban Africa. A Study of Hausa Migrants in Yoruba
Towns*, Berkeley, University of California Press, 1969, pp. 96-97; R.
Price, 'Politics and culture in contemporary Ghana: the big-man small-
boy syndrome', *Journal of African Studies*, I (2), summer 1974, pp.
173-204.
46. B. Joinet, *Tanzanie, manger d'abord*, Paris, Karthala, 1981, pp. 189-191.
See also, on the subject of Angola, L. Monnier, 'L'écrivain, le chien et la
poétique de l'informel à Luanda (Angola)', *Revue européenne des sciences
sociales*, XXVI (81), 1988, pp. 101-119.
47. S.T. Barnes, *Patrons and Power;* E.S. Ndione, *Dynamique urbaine d'une
société en grappe.*
48. R. Price, *Society and Bureaucracy in Contemporary Ghana.*
49. *Cf.*, for example, J.D. Barkan, J.J. Okumu, 'Patrons, machines et élections au Kenya' in CEAN, CERI, *Aux urnes l'Afrique!* p. 142; G. Dauch,
D. Martin, *L'Héritage de Kenyatta*, pp. 66 ff. and p. 75 ff.
50. E. Terray, 'Le climatiseur et la véranda' in *Afrique plurielle, Afrique
actuelle. Hommage à Georges Balandier*, Paris, Karthala, 1986, pp. 37-44.
51. A. Cohen, *The Politics of Elite Culture*, Los Angeles, University of California at Los Angeles Press, 1981.
52. D.-C. Martin, *Tanzanie;* D. Martin, G. Dauch, *L'Héritage de Kenyatta;*
J.-D. Barkan, 'The electoral process and peasant-state relations in
Kenya' in F.M. Hayward, ed., *Elections in Independent Africa*, pp. 213-
237; D. Bourmaud, 'Les élections au Kenya: tous derrière et Moi
devant...' and B. Smith, 'Les élections au Kenya: du passé faisons table
rase!', *Politique africaine*, 31, Oct. 1988, pp. 85-92; D.B. Cruise O'Brien,
Saints and Politicians.
53. J. Bazin, 'Guerre et servitude à Ségou' in C. Meillassoux, ed., *L'Esclavage en période précoloniale*, Paris, Maspero, 1975, pp. 135-181.

54. J. Vansina, *Les Anciens Royaumes de la savane*, p. 149.

55. J.N. Paden, *Ahmadu Bello, Sardauna of Sokoto. Values and Leadership in Nigeria*, London, Hodder and Stoughton, 1986, pp. 202 ff. and p. 313 ff.

56. See in particular N. Chazan, *And Anatomy of Ghanaian politics*, pp. 95 ff.; J.-F. Bayart, *L'État au Cameroun;* C. Young, T. Turner, *The Rise and Decline of the Zaïrian State*, Madison, University of Wisconsin Press, 1985, pp. 153-154.

57. *Africa Confidential*, 17 Oct. 1984.

58. G. Deleuze, F. Guattari, *Rhizome. Introduction*, Paris, Éd. de Minuit, 1976 (in particular pp. 45-46 and pp. 60-63).

59. D. Easton, *Analyse du système politique*, Paris, A. Colin, 1974 and R. Kothari, 'Implications of nation-building for the typology of political systems', *VIIe Congrès de l'AISP*, Bruxelles, 1967.

60. R. Tangri, *Politics in Sub-Saharan Africa*.

61. I. Baba Kaké, *Sékou Touré*, pp. 168 ff.

62. *Ibid.*, pp. 171-172 and 179.

63. A. Diallo, *La Mort de Diallo Telli, premier secrétaire général de l'OUA*, Paris, Karthala, 1983, p. 19. *Cf.* also M. Selhami, 'Un seul gouvernement: la famille', *Jeune Afrique plus*, 8, June 1984, pp. 18-21.

64. On the subject of the LBZ (i.e. Louis Behanzin) dossier, through whom the Touré and Keita clans clashed severely in 1971, see the accounts of two Boiro prisoners: J.-P. Alata, *Prison d'Afrique. Cinq ans dans les geôles de Guinée*, Paris, Le Seuil, 1976, pp. 196-197, 204 ff., 211-213, 237-238 and A.A. Diallo, *La Vérité du ministre. Dix ans dans les geôles de Sékou Touré*, Paris, Calmann-Lévy, 1985, pp. 114 ff.

65. C. Gillard, *Le Règne de Francisco Macias Nguema sur la Guinée équatoriale: un népotisme méconnu*, Bordeaux, Institut d'études politiques, 1980, multigr.; M. Liniger-Goumaz, *Guinée équatoriale, un pays méconnu*, Paris, L'Harmattan, 1979.

66. Quoted in *Marchés tropicaux et méditerranéens*, 7, Feb. 1986, p. 322. *Cf. ibid.*, 29 Aug. 1986, pp. 2203 on the suppression of the 17 July 1986 coup attempt by members of the 'Mongomoclan'.

67. J. Oto, *Le Drame d'un pays. La Guinée équatoriale*, Yaoundé, Éd. C.L.E., 1979, p. 124.

68. A.R. Zolberg, *Creating Political Order. The Party-States of West Africa*, Chicago, Rand Mac Nally, 1966, pp. 33 ff.

69. A.R. Zolberg, *One-Party Government in the Ivory Coast*, Princeton, Princeton University Press, 1964.

70. *Fraternité* (Abidjan), 4 Oct. 1963.

71. M. Warsama, 'The plotters', *The Express* (Nairobi), II (1), 1985, pp. 5-12; D. Goldsworthy, *Tom Mboya. The Man Kenya Wanted to Forget*, Nairobi, Heinemann, New York, Africana Publishing Company, 1982.

72. H. Bienen, *Kenya: the Politics of Participation and Control*, Princeton, Princeton University Press, 1974, p. 75.

73. *Cf.* particularly J. Karimi, P. Ochieng, *The Kenyatta Succession*, Nairobi, Transafrica, 1980; D. Goldsworthy, 'Kenyan politics since Kenyatta', *Australian Outlook* 36 (1) Apr. 1982, pp. 27-31 and 'Kenya: la chute de la maison Njonjo'; G. Dauch, D. Martin, *L'Héritage de Kenyatta.;* J.-F. Medard, 'Jeunes et anés en Côte d'Ivoire. Le VIIe Congrès du

PDCI-RDA', *Politique africaine*, 1 Jan. 1981, pp. 102-113 and Y.-A. Fauré, 'Nouvelle donne en Côte d'Ivoire. Le VIIIᵉ Congrès du PDCI-RDA (9-12 October 1985)', *ibid.*, 20, Dec. 1985, pp. 96-109; C. Wauthier, 'Grandes manœuvres en Côte d'Ivoire pour la succession de M. Houphouët-Boigny', *Le Monde diplomatique*, July. 1985, pp. 1 and 20-21; J.-M. Kalflèche, 'Le congrés de la consolidation', *Géopolitique africaine*, March 1986, pp.113-119; J.-F. Bayart, 'La société politoque camerouaise (1982-1986)', *Politique africaine*, 22, June 1986, pp. 5-35; H. Bandolo, *La flamme et la fumée*, Yaoundé, SOPECAM, 1985; *Africa Confidential*, 27 (19), 17 Sept. 1986; *ibid.*, 28 (1), 7 Jan. 1987; *ibid.*, 28 (13), 24 June 1987; *ibid.*, 28 (21), 21 Oct. 1987 (on Sierra Leone); *Africa Confidential*, 28 (22), 4 Nov. 1987 (on Tanzania); and, for a more general view, L. Sylla, 'Succession of the charismatic leader: the gordian knot of African politics', *Daedalus* III (2), Spring 1982, pp. 11-28.

74. *Cf.* particularly J.-F. Médard, 'Charles Njonjo: portrait d'un "big man" au Kenya in E. Terray, ed., *L'État contemporain en Afrique*, Paris, L'Hartmattan, 1987, pp. 49-87; D. Bigo, 'Forme d'exercice du pouvoir et obéssance en Centrafrique (1966-1979)', Paris, Université de Paris-I, 1985, unpublished thesis., P. L'Hoiry, *Le Malaŵi*, Paris, Karthala, Nairobi, CREDU, 1988, pp. 128-129; J.-F. Bayart, *L'État au Cameroun*, and 'La société politique camerounaise (1982-1986)', as well as the account of; Nguza Karl I Bond, *Mobutu ou l'incarnation du mal zaïrois*, London, Rex Collings, 1982.

75. J. Hartmann, 'Development Policy-Making in Tanzania, 1962-1982: a Critique of Socioligical Interpretations', Hull, The University of Hull, 1983.; J.-F. Bayart, *L'État au Cameroun*, and 'La société politique camerounaise'; F. de Medeiros, 'Armée et instabilité: les partis militaires au Benin' in A. Rouquié, *La Politique de Mars*, pp 141 ff.

76. D. Bourmaud, 'Élections et autoritarisme. La crise de la régulation politique au Kenya', *Revue française de science politique*, 35 (2), April 1985, pp. 206-234; J.F. Bayart, *L'État au Cameroun*, and 'La société politique camerounaise'; J.-M. Kalflèche, 'Le congrés de la consolidation', Y.-A. Fauré, 'Nouvelle donne en Côte d'Ivoire'.

77. *Africa Confidential*, 28 (10), 13 May 1987; *Marchés tropicaux et méditerranéens*, 7 March 1986, pp. 577-580; *ibid.*, 28 March 1986, pp. 857-858; *ibid.*, 19 Sept. 1986, pp. 2375 2376; *ibid* 31 Oct. 1986. p. 2750; N. Casswell, 'Autopsie de l'ONCAD. La politique arachidière au Sénégal, 1966-1980', *Politique africaine,* 14, June 1984, pp. 66 ff.

78. Kamitatu Massamba, *Problématique et rationalité dans le processus de nationalisation du cuivre en Afrique centrale: Zaïre (1967) and Zambie (1969)*, Paris, Institut d'études politiques, 1976, p. 181; D.C. Martin, *Tanzanie*, p. 123.

79. F. Bekalé, 'Le "Makaya" gabonais', *Politique africaine*, 26, June 1987, pp. 112-114; L. Greilsamer, 'La télévision tire à vue', *Le Monde*, 10-11 Nov. 1985; A. Touré, 'La petite histoire de Nalewe Kpingbin Tiecoroba. Une émission de la radiodiffusion nationale ivoirienne', *Politique africaine*, 3, Sept. 1981, pp. 44-54; F. Constantin, 'Dr. Folhumour, I presume' *ibid*, pp. 72-74; *The Best of Kapelwa Musonda*, Lusaka, Neezam, 1979.

80. S. Ellis, 'Les prolongements du conflit israélo-arabe: le cas du Sierra Leone', *Politique africaine*, 30, June 1988, pp. 69-75; *Africa Confidentinal*,

1986-1988.
81. C. Leys, *Underdevelopment in Kenya. The Political Economy of Neo-Colonialism*, London, Heinemann, 1975, chap. vii; Bayart, 'Régime de parti unique et systèmes d'inégalité et de domination au Cameroun: esquisse', *Cahiers d'études africaines*, 69-70, xvii (1-2), 1978, pp. 5-35.
82. K. Marx, *Le 18 Brumaire de Louis Bonaparte*, Paris, Éditions Sociales,1969, p. 92. Regarding the very Sartrian figure of 'the bastard', see, apart from J. Bazin (note 53), the autobiography of J. Okello *Revolution in Zanzibar*, Nairobi, East African Publishing House, 1967 or H. Banholo's account *(La flamme et la fuméw)* of M. Ahidfo's personality. Condottori such as Yoweri Museveni in Uganda or John Karang in Sudan fit this model well.

CHAPTER 9: THE POLITICS OF THE BELLY

1. C. Coulon, 'Élections, factions et idéologies au Sénégal' in CEAN, CERI, *Aux urnes l'Afrique! Élections et pouvoirs en Afrique noire*, Paris, Pedone, 1978, pp. 174 ff.; J.D. Barkan, 'The electoral process and peasant-state relations in Kenya' in F.M. Hayward, ed., *Elections in independent Africa*, Boulder, Westview Press, 1987, p. 228.
2. See, for example, K. Currie, L. Ray, 'State and class in Kenya. Notes on the cohesion of the ruling class', *Journal of Modern African Studies*, 22 (4), 1984, pp. 559-593 (on the Njonjo affair).
3. G. Balandier, *Anthropologie politique*, Paris, PUF, 1969, (2nd ed.) pp. 82-83.
4. *Ibid.*, p. 83.
5. *Jeune Afrique*, 17 Feb., p. 30.
6. D. Fassin et al., 'Les enjeux sociaux de la participation communautaire. Les comités de santé à Pikine (Sénégal)', *Sciences sociales et santé*, IV (3-4), Nov. 1986, pp. 209-217 (particularly pp. 215-216).
7. Parti socialiste du Sénégal, 'Rapport introductif par Monsieur Abdou Diouf, Secrétaire général, Dakar', Conseil national du 31 juillet 1982, p. 14.
8. C. Coulon, *Le Marabout et le Prince. Islam et pouvoir au Sénégal*, Paris, Pedone, 1981, p. 245.
9. Handwritten letter of 22nd April 1963 of UPS party activists in the *secco* at Bossolel, Dakar in UPS archives carton Sine Saloum, 1963.
10. Yoro Kandé, 'Rapport sur les opérations de vente des cartes du parti et les formations des cellules de base', Kolda, 9 April 1963, Dakar, archives de l'UPS, Carton Casamance, cercle de Kolda, 1963. For similar examples of this practice in the Ivory Coast, *cf.* PDCI, *Le quatrième séminaire des secrétaires généraux, Yamoussoukro: 7, 8 et 9 mars 1985*, Abidjan, Ed. Fraternité-hebdo, 1985, *passim*.
11. Sources: interviews.
12. *Les Cahiers de Gamboma. Instructions politiques et militaires des partisans congolais (1964-1965)*, Brussels, CRISP, 1965, p. 57.
13. See, for example, C. Raynaut, 'Disparités économiques et inégalités

devant la santé à Maradi (Niger)', Dakar-Pikine, *Colloque santé et urbanisation*, 2–6 Dec. 1986.

14. B. Malinowski, *Freedom and Civilization*, London, Allen and Unwin, 1947, pp. 266 and 253.
15. See, for example, E. Terray, 'Le climatiseur et la véranda', in *Afrique plurielle, Afrique actuelle. Hommage à Georges Balandier*, Paris, Karthala, 1986, pp. 37–44 and J. Vansina, 'Mwasi's trials', *Daedalus*, CIII (2), Spring 1982, pp. 49–70.
16. J.-P. Alata, *Prison d'Afrique. Cinq ans dans les geôles de Guinée*, Paris, Le Seuil, 1976, pp. 140–141. See also *ibid.*, pp. 193–194 and A. Diallo, *La Mort de Diallo Telli, premier secrétaire général de l'OUA*, Paris, Karthala, 1983, pp. 24–25.
17. C. and A. Darlington, *African Betrayal*, New York, David McKay, 1968, p. 121.
18. A. Diallo, *La Mort de Diallo Telli*, pp. 18, 106 and 118.
19. *Cf.*, for example, A. Peace, 'Prestige power and legitimacy in a modern Nigerian town', *Canadian Journal of African Studies*, XIII (1-2), 1979, pp. 26–51; C. Coulon, 'Elections, factions et idéologies au Sénégal' in CEAN, CERI, *Aux urnes l'Afrique!*, p. 160; P. Laburthe-Tolra, *Les Seigneurs de la forêt. Essai sur le passé historique, l'organisation sociale et les normes éthiques des anciens Beti du Cameroun*, Paris, Publications de la Sorbonne, 1981, pp. 353–375.
20. R. Price, 'Politics and culture and contemporary Ghana: the Big-man Small-boy syndrome', *Journal of African Studies*, I (2), 1974, pp. 173–204.
21. R. Jeffries, *Class, Power and Ideology in Ghana: the Railwaymen of Sekondi*, Cambridge, Cambridge University Press, 1978, p. 182.
22. F. Cooper, 'Africa and the world economy', *The African Studies Review*, 24 (2-3), Jun.-Sept. 1981, p. 18.
23. C. Ake, 'Presidential address to the annual conference of the Nigerian Political Science Association, 1981', *West Africa*, 25 May 1981, pp. 1162–1163; R.A. Joseph, *Democracy and Prebendal Politics in Nigeria. The Rise and Fall of the Second Republic*, Cambridge, Cambridge University Press, 1987, p. 75.
24. G. Dauch, 'Kenya: J.M. Kariuki ou l'éthique nationale du capitalisme', *Politique africaine*, 8, Dec. 1982, pp. 21–43.
25. F. de Medeiros, 'Armée et instabilité: les partis militaires au Bénin' in A. Rouquié, ed., *La Politique de Mars. Les processus politiques dans les partis militaires contemporains*, Paris, Le Sycomore, 1981, pp. 141 ff.
26. A.A. Diallo, *La Vérité du ministre. Dix ans dans les geôles de Sékou Touré*, Paris, Calmann-Lévy, 1985, pp. 68–69. See also the description of the Touré and Keïta clans in I. Baba Kaké, *Sékou Touré. Le héros et le tyran*, Paris, Jeune Afrique, 1987, pp. 168 ff.
27. S. Andreski, *The African Predicament*, London, Michael Joseph, 1968, p. 92; R. Jeffries, 'Rawlings and the political economy of under-development in Ghana', *African Affairs*, 81 (324), July 1982, p. 314.
28. A. Kourouma, *Les Soleils des indépendances*, Paris, Seuil, 1970.
29. Anon., 'La Vie dans les forces aériennes zaïroises', n.d.
30. A. Morice, 'Guinée 1985: État, corruption et trafics', *Les Temps modernes*, 487, Feb. 1987, pp. 112–115.
31. *Horoya* (Conakry), 28 Mar. 1985.

32. A. Morice, 'Guinée 1985', pp. 108-136; F. Gaulme, 'La Guinée à l'heure des réformes', *Marchés tropicaux et méditerranéens*, 13 Jun. 1986, pp. 1565 ff.; *ibid.*, 2 Aug. 1985, pp. 1939-1940.
33. On the diversion of food aid, see J.-L. Amselle, 'Famine, prolétarisation et création de nouveaux liens de dépendance au Sahel. Les réfugiés de Mopti et de Léré au Mali', *Politique africaine*, 1, Jan. 1981, pp. 5-22.
34. J.-C. Willame, *Zaïre: l'épopée d'Inga. Chronique d'une prédation industrielle*, Paris, L'Harmattan, 1986, p. 128.
35. 'Les massacres de Katekelayi et de Luamuela (Kasaï oriental)', *Politique africaine*, 6, May 1982, pp. 82-83.
36. C. Young, T. Turner, *The Rise and Decline of the Zaïrian State*, Madison, University of Wisconsin Press, 1985, pp. 181 and pp. 452-453, note 27; 'Les massacres de Katekelayi et de Luamuela (Kasaï oriental)', p. 87 ('Vous cherchez à toucher le commissaire sous-régional, nous ont-ils demandé. C'est imprudent. Bien qu'il soit lui aussi trafiquant comme tous les hauts cadres du MPR qui se respectent (y compris le président fondateur et son fils âiné que nous avons tous vu acheter du diamant surtout après l'opération de démonétisation), etc.').
37. *Marchés tropicaus et méditerranéens*, 12 Feb. 1988, p. 378.
38. *La Gazette de la nation* (Douala), 2 Aug. 1984. The psychic disequilibria covered by the seizure of the women's market by the powerful are not peculiar to Africa; *cf*, for example, J.-L. Domenach, Hua Chang-Ming, *Le Mariage en Chine*, Paris, Presses de la Fondation nationale des sciences politiques, 1987, pp. 86 and 114.
39. Debate following report of the political secretary in Union nationale camerounaise, 'Procès-verbal des travaux du Premier Congrès extraordinaire de l'Union nationale camerounaise tenu à Yaoundé les 2 et 3 juin 1972', Yaoundé 1972, p. 85. See, in the same vein, *Fraternité-Hebdo* (Abidjan), 15 Sept. 1983: 'Une certaine forme de banditisme est un véritable manifeste politique qui vise autant à dépouiller autrui, à tuer, qu'à créer des désordres politiquement déstabilisateurs.' A banner displayed in Korhogo proclaimed 'La subversion ne passera pas par le Nord.'
40. R.A. Joseph, *Radical Nationalism in Cameroun. Social Origins of the UPC Rebellion*, Oxford, Oxford University Press, 1977, p. 163, note 3.
41. F. Cooper, *On the African Waterfront. Urban Disorder and the Transformation of Work in Colonial Mombasa*, New Haven, Yale University Press, 1987.
42. P.M. Lubeck, *Islamic Protest under Semi-Industrial Capital: 'yan Tatsini Explained*, Urbana, University of Illinois, 2-3 Apr. 1984, roneo.
43. Tibamanya mwene Mushanga, *Criminal Homicide in Uganda*, Kampala, East African Literature Bureau, 1974, p. 106. On crowd lynchings of thieves, see, for example, Nairobi's *Sunday Nation*, 1 Feb. 1981; *Standard*, 21 Jan. 1980; *Daily Nation*, 20 Dec. 1979 and, in Nigeria, G. Nicolas, 'Cette loi qu'on prend entre ses mains. La pratique de l'*instant justice* au Nigeria sous la Seconde République nigériane (1979-1983)', *Droit et cultures*, 7, 1984, pp. 5-29.
44. Union nationale camerounaise, 'Procès-verbal des travaux du II⁰ Conseil national de l'Union Nationale camerounaise tenu à Yaoundé du 21 au 23 janvier 1971, Yaoundé 1971, roneo, p. 65.

45. D. Poitou, 'La Délinquance juvénile au Niger. Approche sociologique', Paris, EHESS, 1975.
46. D. Crummey, ed., *Banditry, Rebellion and Social Protest in Africa*, London, James Currey, 1986; W.G. Clarence-Smith, *Slaves, Peasants and Capitalists in Southern Angola. 1840-1926*, Cambridge, Cambridge University Press, 1979, pp. 37 ff.; C. Coquery-Vidrovitch, *Afrique noire. Permanences et ruptures*, Paris, Payot, 1985, pp. 230 ff.
47. C. Vidal, 'Guerre des sexes à; Abidjan. Masculin, féminin, CFA' in 'Des femmes sur l'Afrique des femmes', *Cahiers d'études africaines*, 65, XVII-1, 1977, pp. 121-153. See also C. Robertson, I. Berger, eds., *Women and Class in Africa*, New York, Africana Publishing Company, 1986 and, for an explicitly political example, at the heart of the Zaïrian apparatus of power, N. Karl I Bond, *Mobutu ou l'incarnation du mal zaïrois*, London, Rex Collings, 1982, p. 29.
48. See in particular J. MacGaffey, *Entrepeneurs and Parasites. The Struggle for Indigenous Capitalism in Zaïre*, Cambridge, Cambridge University Press, 1987, chap. 7; J.M. Bujra, 'Production, Property, Prostitution. "Sexual politics" in Atu', *Cahiers d'études africaines*, 65, XVII (1), 1977, pp. 13-39; M. Vandersypen, 'Femmes libres de Kigali', *ibid.*, pp. 95-120.
49. C. Coulon, 'Elections, factions et idéologies au Sénégal' in CEAN, CERI, *Aux urnes l'Afrique!*, p. 160. See also J.-P. Olivier de Sardan, 'Captifs ruraux et esclaves impériaux du Songhay' in C. Meillassoux, ed., *L'Esclavage en Afrique précoloniale*, Paris, Maspero, 1975, p. 116 who reminds us that 'liberalité est le signe de la noblesse, et plus les dons sont élevés, plus leur auteur se situe haut dans l'échelle sociale") and C.M. Toulabor, 'L'énonciation du pouvoir et de la richesse chez les jeunes "conjoncturés" de Lomé (Togo)', *Revue française de science politique*, 35 (3), June 1985, pp. 455 ff.
50. L. Gbagbo, *Côte-d'Ivoire. Pour une alternative démocratique*, Paris, L'Harmattan, 1983, p. 80.
51. *Fraternité-Matin* (Abidjan), 29 April 1983, p. 16.
52. *Weekly Review* (Nairobi), 30 March 1984.
53. G. Dauch, 'Kenya: J.M. Kariuki ou l'éthique nationale du capitalisme' pp. 30 and 37; J. Spencer, *KAU. The Kenya African Union*, London, KPI, 1985, pp. 66-67. On the role of money in election campaigns, see also the polemic between Mr Kibaki and Mr Shikuku (*Daily Nation* (Nairobi), 12 June 1983) and G. Dauch, D. Martin, *L'Héritage de Kenyatta. La transition politique au Kenya. 1975-1982*, Paris, L'Harmattan, Aix-en-Provence, Presses Universitaires d'Aix-Marseille, 1985, p. 104.
54. Observation recorded at a meeting of the Bannus Bobangis à Léopoldville by J. Dehasse, 'Le Rôle politique des associations de ressortissants à Léopoldville', Louvain, Institut des sciences politiques et sociales, 1965, p. 93. On Nnamdi Azikiwe, see R.L. Sklar, *Nigerian Political Parties*, Princeton, Princeton University Press, 1963, p. 230.
55. P. Alexandre, *Les Africains*, Paris, Lidis, 1981, p. 211; P. Laburthe-Tolra, *Les Seigneurs de la forêt*, pp. 353-375; J.-L. Lonsdale, 'La pensée politique kikuyu et les idéologies du mouvement mau-mau', *Cahiers d'études africaines*, 107-108, XXVII (3-4), 1987, p. 347.
56. T. Todorov, *Mikhaïl Bakhtine, le principe dialogique*, followed by *Écrits du cercle de Bakhtine*, Paris, Seuil, 1981, pp. 123-131.

57. G. Hesseling, *Histoire politiques du Sénégal. Institutions, droit et société*, Paris, Karthala, Leiden, Afrika-Studiecentrum, 1985, pp. 360-361; D. Darbon, *L'Administration et le Paysan en Casamance (Essai d'anthropologie administrative)*, Paris, Pedone, 1988; J.-F. Bayart, *L'État au Cameroun*, Paris, Presses de la Fondation nationale des sciences politiques, 1979, pp. 157-158; R. Luckham, 'The constitutional commission, 1966-1969' in D. Austin, R. Luckham, eds., *Politicians and Soldiers in Ghana, 1966-1972*, London, Frank Cass, 1975, p. 69; K. Panter-Brick, ed., *Soldiers and Oil. The Political Transformation of Nigeria*, London, Frank Cass, 1978, pp. 291-350; D.C. Bach, 'Nigeria et Etats-Unis: convergences d'intérêts et relations de pouvoir', *Politique africaine*, 2, May 1981, pp. 23-24.

58. B.A. Ogot, 'Revolt of the elders: an anatomy of the loyalist crowd in the Mau Mau uprising. 1952-1956' in B.A. Ogot, ed., *Politics and Nationalism in Colonial Kenya*, Nairobi, East African Publishing House, 1972, pp. 134-148; D.L. Barnett, Karari Njama, *Mau Mau from within. Autobiography and Analysis of Kenya's Peasant Revolt*, New York, Modern Reader Paperbacks, 1970.

59. J. Karimi, P. Ochieng, *The Kenyatta Succession*, Nairobi, Transafrica, 1980; D. Goldsworthy, 'Kenyan politics since Kenyatta', *Australian Outlook*, 36 (1), Apr. 1982, pp. 27-31.

60. R.H. Jackson, C.G. Rosberg, *Personal Rule in Black Africa. Prince, Autocrat, Prophet, Tyran*, Berkeley, University of California Press, 1982.

61. K. Deutsch, *Nationalism and Social Communication*, New York, Chapman and Hall, 1953.

62. J.-C. Willame, *Zaïre, l'épopée d'Inga*, pp. 118-119.

63. *Cf.* for example, C.M. Toulabor, *Le Togo sous Eyadema*, Paris, Karthala, 1986; T.M. Callaghy, *The State-Society Struggle. Zaïre in Comparative Perspective*, New York, Columbia University Press, 1984, pp. 284 ff.; M.G. Schatzberg, *The Dialectics of Oppression in Zaïre*, Bloomington, Indiana University Press, 1988; or, for a less dramatic and less well-known example from Tanzania, K. Miti, 'L'opération Nguvu Kazi à Dar es Salaam. Ardeur au travail et contrôle de l'espace urbain', *Politique africaine*, 17, March 1985, pp. 88-104.

64. Cited by P. Geschiere, *Village Communities and the State. Changing Relations among the Maka of Southeastern Cameroon since the Colonial Conquest*, London, KPI, 1982, p. 206.

65. C. Moore, *Fela, Fela, cette putain de vie*, Paris, Karthala, 1982, p. 122.

66. M.G. Schatzberg, *The Dialectics of Oppression in Zaïre*, chap. 3. On the colonial period, see also colonel Vandevalle, J. Brassine, *Les rapports secrets de la Sûreté congolaise*, [Belgium] Lucien de Meyer, 1973.

67. *Jeune Afrique*, 12 Nov. 1986, p. 25.

68. J.-F. Bayart, *L'État au Cameroun*, pp. 206 and 220-221. See A. Mukong, *Prisoner without a Crime*, Alfresco Books, 1985.

69. W. Soyinka, *Cet homme est mort*, Paris, Belfond, 1986.

70. Republic of Kenya, *Report of Judicial Commission Appointed to Inquire into Allegations Involving Charles Mugane Njonjo (Former Minister for Constitutional Affairs and Member of Parliament for Kikuyu Constituency)*, Nairobi, The Commission of Inquiry Act, 1984.

71. D. Bourmaud, 'Le Système politique du Kenya: centre et périphérie',

Bordeaux, Institut d'études politiques, 1985 roneo. T.M. Callaghy, *The State-Society Struggle. Zaïre in Comparative Perspective*, chaps. 5, 6, 7; J.-F. Bayart, *L'État au Cameroun*, chap. vi; C. Coulon, *Le Marabout et le Prince*, pp. 283 ff.; A. Cohen, *The politics of elite culture*, Los Angeles, University of California at Los Angeles Press, 1981.

72. P. Bourdieu, *La Distinction. Critique sociale du jugement*, Paris, Éd. de Minuit, 1979, p. 465.

73. M. Vovelle, *Idéologies et mentalités*, Paris, Maspero, 1982, pp. 319 ff.

74. A.R. Zolberg, *Creating Political Order. The Party-States of West Africa*, Chicago, Rand McNally, 1966, p. 65.

75. J.-A. Mbembe, *Les Jeunes et l'ordre politique en Afrique noire*, Paris, L'Harmattan, 1985, pp. 99 ff.; R. Clignet, M. Stark, 'Modernization and Football in Cameroon', *The Journal of Modern African Studies*, 12 (3), Sept. 1974, pp. 409-421.

76. M. de Certeau, *L'Invention du quotidien, vol. I: Arts de faire*, Paris, U.G.E., 1980, pp. 108 ff.

77. On the importance of representations of the invisible in Congo, see R. Devauges, *L'Oncle, le ndoki et l'entrepreneur. La petite entreprise congolaise à Brazzaville*, Paris, ORSTOM, 1977 Part III; G. Dupré, *Un ordre et sa destruction*, Paris, ORSTOM, 1982, chap. 16; J. Tonda, 'Marx et l'ombre des fétiches. Pouvoir local contre *ndjobi* dans le Nord-Congo', *Politique africaine*, 31, Oct. 1988, pp. 73-83.

78. T. Todorov, *Mikhaïl Bakhtine*, pp. 123 ff.

79. See J.-F. Bayart, 'Quelques livres consacrés à l'étude des représentations et des pratiques thérapeutiques d'origine pré-coloniale', *Revue française d'études politiques africaines*, 133, Jan. 1977, pp. 100-108; J.-P. Dozon, *La Société bété, Côte d'Ivoire*, Paris, Karthala, ORSTOM, 1985, pp. 127 ff.; P. Geschiere, *Village Communities and the State*, (in contrast with M. Augé, *Théorie des pouvoirs et idéologie. Etude de cas en Côte d'Ivoire*, Paris, Hermann, 1975 and P. Bonnafé, *Nzo Lipfu, le lignage de la mort. La sorcellerie, idéologie de la lutte sociale sur le plateau kukuya*, Nanterre, Labethno, 1978).

80. M. Godelier, *L'Idéel et le matériel. Pensée, économies, sociétés*, Paris, Fayard, 1984, pp. 23 ff. and 205 ff.; G. Balandier, *Le Détour. Pouvoir et modernité*, Paris, Fayard, 1985, p. 101. But, with Foucault, we should make clear that 'le pouvoir n'est pas de l'ordre du consentement': 'Il n'est pas en lui-même renonciation à une liberté, transfert de droit, pouvoir de tous et de chacun délégué à quelques-uns (ce qui n'empêche pas que le consentement puisse être une condition pour que la relation de pouvoir existe et se maintienne); la relation de pouvoir peut être l'effet d'un consentement antérieur ou permanent; elle n'est pas dans sa nature propre la manifestation d'un consensus' ('Le pouvoir, comment s'exerce-t-il?' in H. Dreyfus, P. Rabinow, *Michel Foucault, un parcours philosophique*, Paris, Gallimard, 1984, p. 312).

81. N. Kasfir, *The Shrinking Political Arena. Participation and Ethnicity in African Politics with a Case-Study of Uganda*, Berkeley, University of California Press, 1976, p. 227.

82. C. Tardits, *Le Royaume bamoum*, A. Colin, Edisem, Publications de la Sorbonne, 1980, pp. 773-775 and 787-788.

83. From a letter written by Thérèse, a Camerounian woman whose husband, accused of the rape of a minor but more probably a victim of witchcraft, had been sentenced to five years in prison in Douala, 5th April 1980 (cited in *Politique africaine*, 1, Jan. 1981, p. 85).

84. I. Baba Kaké, *Sékou Touré, le héros et le tyran*, Paris, Jeune Afrique, 1987, pp. 180 ff.; A.A. Diallo, *La Vérité du ministre. Dix ans dans les geôles de Sékou Touré*, Paris, Calmann-Lévy, 1985, pp. 168 ff. and 172-173.

85. P. Bourdieu, *La Distinction*, pp. 536 ff.

86. Sources: Diverse archives of UPS and PS in Dakar, of the PDCI in Abidjan and of the UC and UNC in Yaoundé and Douala. See, for example J.-F. Bayart, *L'État au Cameroun*, pp. 272 ff.; P. Geschiere, *Village Communities and the State*, pp. 242 and 249 ff.; D. Desjeux, *Stratégies paysannes en Afrique noire. Le Congo (Essai sur la gestion de l'incertitude)*, Paris, L'Harmattan, 1987, pp. 68 ff.; R.H. Bates, *Rural Responses to Industrialization. A Study of village Zambia*, New Haven, Yale University Press, 1976, p. 209; W. Tordoff, *Government and Politics in Africa*, London Macmillan, 1984, chap. 5; H. Bienen, *Tanzania. Party Transformation and Economic Development*, Princeton, Princeton University Press, 1970; N.N. Miller, 'The rural African party: political participation in Tanzania', *American Political Science Review*, LXIV (2), June 1970, pp. 548-571. According to an opinion poll (whose methodology is admittedly unclear) which showed that Gabonese trust the party more than government *(Marchés tropicaux et méditerranéens*, 26 Sept. 1986, p. 2437).

87. See, for example, on the subject of the Ivory Coast, A. Bonnal, 'L'administration et le parti face aux tensions', *Politique africaine*, 24, Dec. 1986, pp. 20-28; A. Sissoko, 'Aspects sociologiques de l'intégration nationale en Afrique noire occidentale: espace politico-administratif et intégration à l'État: le cas de la Côte d'Ivoire,' Nice, Faculté des lettres et sciences humaines, 1982.

88. On the Organisation des femmes de l'Union nationale camerounaise, see J.-F. Bayart, *L'État au Cameroun, passim*. On the more or less peaceful integration of youth into the party, see, for example, J.-L. Balans, 'Le système politique mauritanien' in CRESM, CEAN, *Introduction à la Mauritanie*, Paris, CNRS, 1979, pp. 299-300; UPS and PS archives in Dakar, J.-F. Médard, 'Jeunes et aînés en Côte d'Ivoire. Le VIIᵉ congrès du PDCI-RDA', *Politique africaine*, 1, Jan. 1981, pp, 102-119; PP. Bonnafé, 'Une classe d'âge politique. La JMNR de la République du Congo-Brazzaville', *Cahiers d'études africaines*, 31, VIII-3, 1968, pp. 327-368. On abuses by militia men, for example, the Kenyan press of March 1981 and the *Weekly Review* (Nairobi), 13 Dec. 1985, pp. 7 ff.; J. Oto, *Le Drame d'un pays, la Guinée équatoriale*, Yaoundé, Ed. C.L.E., pp. 18, 19; D.-C. Martin, *Tanzanie. L'Invention d'une culture politique*, 1979, Paris, Presses de la Fondation nationale des sciences politiques, Karthala, 1988, pp. 113 ff. and K. Miti, 'L'opération Nguvu Kazi à Dar es Salaam'.

89. D. Martin, 'Zizanie en Tanzanie? Les élections tanzaniennes de 1975 ou les petits nons du Mwalimu' in CEAN, CERI, *Aux urnes l'Afrique!*, pp. 79-117 and 'La houe, la maison, l'urne et le maître d'école. Les élections en Tanzanie, 1965-1970', *Revue française de science politique*, XXV (4),

Aug. 1975, pp. 677-716.

90. J.-A. Mbembé, 'Pouvoir des morts et langage des vivants. Les errances de la mémoire nationaliste au Cameroun', *Politique africaine*, 22, June 1986, pp. 37-72.

91. G. Dauch, D. Martin, *L'héritage de Kenyatta*, pp. 35 and ff., 59 ff., 68 ff.; G. Dauch, 'Kenya: J.M. Kariuki ou l'éthique nationale du capitalisme'; D.-C. Martin, *Tanzanie*, pp. 80 ff.; *Marchés tropicaux et méditerranéens*, 6 Mar. 1987, p. 575; J.-C. Willame, 'Chronique d'une opposition politique: l'UDPS (1978-1987)', *Les Cahiers du CEDAF*, 7-8, Dec. 1987, pp. 1-118; J.-F. Bayart, 'La fronde parlementaire au Zaïre (1979-1980)'. *Politique africaine*, 3, Sept. 1981, pp. 90-140.

92. F. Eboussi, *Christianisme sans fétiche. Révélation et domination*, Paris, Présence africaine, 1981, p. 88.

93. *Cf.* for example, unpublished letter Likasi, Nov. 1982 in CEDAF, dossier 'opposition' 016.4.; PDCI, *Le Quatrième Séminaire des secrétaires généraux, passim*; D. Martin, 'Zizanie en Tanzanie?' in CEAN, CERI, *Aux urnes l'Afrique!*, pp. 79-117; J.-F. Bayart, *L'État au Cameroun*, pp. 259-260; *Marchés tropicaux et méditerranéens*, 8 May 1987, pp. 1170 (in UNIP on Lusaka).

94. See particularly, in addition to the collection of *Politique africaine* (1981-1988), R. Jeffries, *Class, Power and Ideology in Ghana*, p.208; R.H. Bates, *Rural Responses to Industrialization*, pp. 256 ff.; and the studies of the Groupe d'analyse des modes populaires d'action politique, Paris, Centre d'études et de recherches internationales, 1980-1985.

95. C.M. Toulabor gives a remarkable illustration of this ('Jeu de mots, jeu de vilains. Lexique de la dérision politique au Togo', *Politique africaine*, 3, Sept. 1981, pp. 55-71).

96. C.M. Toulabor, 'L'énonciation du pouvoir et de la richesse chez les jeunes "conjonctures" de Lomé (Togo)'.

97. S. Bemba, *50 ans de musique du Congo-Zaïre*, Paris, Présence africaine, 1984, p. 158. On the culture of bars, *cf.* R. Jeffries, *Class, Power and Ideology in Ghana*; M.G. Schatzberg, *Politics and Class in Zaïre*, chap. 5; A. Bonnassieux, *L'Autre Abidjan. Chronique d'un quartier oublié*, Paris, Karthala, Abidjan, INADES, 1987, pp. 131 ff.; H. Ossebi, 'Un quotidien en trompe l'œil. Bars et "nganda" à Brazzaville', *Politique africaine*, 31, Oct. 1988, pp. 67-72.

98. M. Bakhtine, *L'œuvre de François Rabelais et la culture populaire au Moyen Age et sous la Renaissance*, Paris, Gallimard, 1970.

99. J.-F. Bayart, *L'État au Cameroun*, p. 257.

100. G. Hyden, *Beyond Ujamaa in Tanzania. Underdevelopment and an Uncaptured Peasantry*, London, Heinemann, 1980 and *No Shortcuts to Progress. African Development Management in Perspective*, London, Heinemann, 1983. For a critique of the concept of an 'uncaptured peasantry', see especially P. Geschiere, 'La paysannerie africaine est-elle captive?', *Politique africaine*, 14, June 1984, pp. 13-33 and the debates in the columns of *Development and Change*, 1986-87, as well as the critique of the 'moral economy' by S.L. Popkin, *The Rational Peasant. The Political Economy of Rural Society in Vietnam*, Berkeley, University of California Press, 1979.

101. P. Gonzales Casanova, *La Démocratie au Mexique*, Paris Anthropos, 1969; F.W. Riggs, *Administration in Developing Countries. The Theory of*

Prismatic Society, Boston, Houghton Mifflin, 1969, Chap. 6.

102. R. Deniel, *Voix de jeunes dans la ville africaine*, Abidjan, INADES, 1979, p. 69.

103. Capitaine Vallier, quoted in P.-P. Rey, *Colonialism, néo-colonialisme et transition au capitalisme, exemple de la 'COMILOG' au Congo-Brazzaville*, Paris, Maspero, 1971, p. 363. See also G. Balandier, *Sociologie actuelle de l'Afrique noire*, Paris, PUF, 19771, (3rd ed.), pp. 171 ff. and M. Michel, *L'Appel à l'Afrique. Contributions et réactions à l'effort de guerre en AOF. 1914-1919*, Paris, Publications de la Sorbonne, 1982, pp. 51 ff and 256.

104. J. Boesen, *Tanzania: from Ujamaa to Villagization*, Copenhagen, Institute of Development Studies, 1976, p. 9; G. Spittler, 'Peasants and the State in Niger (West Africa)', *Peasant Studies*, VIII (1), Nov. 1979, pp. 30-47.

105. J.-P. Olivier de Sardan, *Les Sociétés songhay-zarma (Niger-Mali). Chefs, guerriers, esclaves, paysans...*, Paris, Karthala, 1984, p. 186.

106. M. Izard, *Genns du pouvoir, gens de la terre. Les institutions politiques de l'ancien royaume du Yatenga (Bassin de la Volta blanche)*, Cambridge, Cambridge University Press, Paris, Éditions de la Maison des sciences de l'Homme, 1985, pp. 481-482.

107. J. Boesen, *Tanzania*, p. 7; C. Young, T. Turner, *The Rise and Decline of the Zairian State*, p. 241; J.-L. Dongmo, *Le Dynamisme bamiléké (Cameroun)*, vol. I: *La Mâtrise de l'espace agraire*, Yaoundé, Centre d'édition et de production pour l'enseignement et la recherche, 1981, pp. 155 ff. and A. Beauvilain, J.-L. Dongmo, et al., *Atlas aérien du Cameroun. Campagnes et villes*, Yaoundé, Université de Yaoundé, Département de géographie, 1983, p. 62.

108. C. Young, P. Turner, *The Rise and Decline of the Zairian State*, p. 241.

109. R. van den Bogaerd, 'L'Église zaïroise au service de la nation?', 1978, pp. 29-40 (Brussels, CEDAF, dossier 381.1, 'Eglise chrétienne'). See also 'Construire une Eglise zaïroise authentique', Idiofa, 1974-1977.

110. E.J. Keller Jr., 'A twentieth century model: the mau mau transformation from social banditry to social rebellion', *Kenya Historical Review*, I (1), 1973, pp. 189-205; R. Buijtenhuijs, *Le Mouvement Mau Mau. Une révolte paysanne et anti-coloniale en Afrique noire*, Paris, La Haye, Mouton, 1971; J. Iliffe, 'The organization of the Maji Maji rebellion', *Journal of African history*, VIII (3), 1967, pp. 495-512; D. Lan, *Guns and Rain. Guerrillas and Spirit Mediums in Zimbabwe*, London, James Currey, Berkeley, University of California Press, 1985; P. Doornbos, 'La revolution dérapée. La violence dans l'est du Tchad (1978-1981)', *Politique africaine*, 7, Sept. 1982, pp. 5-13; C. Geffray, M. Pedersen, 'Nampula en guerre', *ibid.*, 29 March 1988, pp. 28-40.

111. M. Augé, *Pouvoirs de vie, pouvoirs de mort*, Paris, Flammarion, 1977; M. Sahlins, *Au cœur des sociétés. Raison utilitaire et raison culturelle*, Paris, Gallimard, 1980.

112. P. Anderson, *Imagined Communities. Reflections on the Origin and Spread of Nationalism*, London, Verso, 1983, p. 122.

113. F. de Polignac, *La Naissance de la cité grecque*, Paris, La Découverte, 1984.

114. *Ivoire-Dimanche* (Abidjan), 769, 3 Nov. 1985, p. 8.

115. *Conférence de presse, 1ᵉʳ déc, 1980* (probably by R. van der Bogaert on

behalf of *Links*, a weekly publication of the Socialistische Partij), Brussels CEDAF, dossier 016.4 'opposition'; D. Jean P. Borel, 'J'ai marché pendant 600 km dans les maquis du Zaïre', *Oxygène* (Brussels), 1981, pp. 4-7; 'Entretiens avec le PRP dans les maquis du Zaïre', *Info-Zaïre* (Brussels), 37, Dec. 1982-Feb. 1983, pp. 2-35; B. Nater, 'Dans les provinces "libérées" avec les guérilleros de la Résistance nationale', *Le Monde*, 2 Jan. 1987, p. 2; C. Geffray, M. Pedersen, 'Nampula en guerre'.

116. *Salongo* (Kinshasa), 8 Dec. 1982, p. 6.

117. S. Asch, *L'Église du prophète Kimbangu. De ses origines à son rôle actuel au Zaïre*, Paris, Karthala, 1983.

118. M.G. Schatzberg, *The Dialectics of Oppression in Zaïre*, pp. 125 ff.

119. W.M.J. van Binbergen, *Religious Change in Zambia. Exploratory Studies*, London, Kegan Paul International, 1981, pp. 288 ff.

120. M.G. Schatzberg, *The Dialectics of Oppression in Zaïre*, pp. 116 ff.

121. Quoted in C. Coulon, *Le Marabout et le prince*, p. 276.

122. *Ibid.*, pp. 277 ff.

123. P.-P. Rey, *Les Alliances de classes*, Paris, Maspero, 1973; P.-P. Rey, ed., *Capitalisme négrier. La marche des paysans vers le prolétariat*, Paris, Maspero, 1976 (particularly p. 66); C. Meillassoux, *Femmes, greniers et capitaux*, Paris, Maspero, 1975; M. Samuel, *Le Prolétariat africain noir en France*, Paris, Maspero, 1978; J.-L. Amselle, ed., *Les Migrations africaines*, Paris, Maspero, 1976. On the complexity of migration J. Boutrais et al., *Le Nord du Cameroun. Des hommes, une région*, Paris, ORSTROM, 1984, Part iv; J. Barou, 'L'émigration dans un village du Niger', *Cahiers d'études africaines*, 63-64, XVI (3-4), 1976, pp. 627-632; J.-P. Olivier de Sardan, *Les Sociétés songhay-zarma*, pp. 255 ff.; A. Adams, *Le long Voyage des gens du Fleuve*, Paris, Maspero, 1977; O. Dia, R. Colin-Nogues, *Yâkâré, L'Autobiographie d'Oumar*, Paris, Maspero, 1982; S. Berry, *Fathers Work for their Sons. Accumulation, Mobility and Class Formation in an Extended Yoruba Community*, Berkeley, University of California Press, 1985, Chap. 2; R.H. Bates, *Rural Responses to Industrialization*, pp. 252 ff.

124. W.G. Clarence-Smith, *Slaves, Peasants and Capitalists in Southern Angola*, pp. 37 ff. and 79-80; M. Michel, *L'Appel à l'Afrique*, pp. 51 ff.; G. Pontié, *Les Guiziga du Cameroun septentrional. L'organisation traditionnelle et sa mise en contestation*, Paris, ORSTOM, 1973, pp. 206 ff.; J.-F. Bayart, *L'État au Cameroun*, pp. 260-261; G. Spittler, 'Peasants and the State in Niger'.

125. *Cameroon Tribune* (Yaoundé), 16 Jul. 1983.

126. N. Chazan, *An Anatomy of Ghanaian Politics. Managing Political Recession, 1969-1982*, Boulder, Westview Press, 1983, pp. 193 ff.

CONCLUSION: OF 'TERROIRS' AND MEN

1. G. Nicolas, 'Les nations à polarisation variable et leur État: le cas nigérian' in E. Terray, ed., *L'État contemporain en Afrique*, Paris, L'Harmattan, 1987, pp. 157-174.

2. *Ibid.*, J.D.Y. Peel, *Ijeshas and Nigerians: the Incorporation of a Yoruba Kingdom, 1890s-1970s*, Cambridge, Cambridge University Press, 1983; R.A. Joseph, *Democracy and Predendal Politics in Nigeria. The Rise and Fall of the Second Republic*, Cambridge, Cambridge University Press, 1988; T.M. Callaghy, *The State-Society Struggle: Zaïre in Comparative Perspective*, New York, Columbia University Press, 1984; M.G. Schatzberg, *Politics and Class in Zaïre*, New York, Africana Publishing Company, 1980 and *The Dialectics of Oppression in Zaïre*, Bloomington, Indiana University Press, 1988.

3. J.N. Paden, *Ahmadu Bello, Sardauna of Sokoto. Values and Leadership in Nigeria*, London, Hodder and Stoughton, 1986.

4. E. Bloch, *La Philosophie de la Renaissance*, Paris, Payot, 1974, pp. 59 ff. On Russia, see also, M. Raeff, *Comprendre l'Ancien régime russe. État et société en Russie imperiale*, Paris, Le Seuil, 1982, chap. I.

5. R. Kothari, 'Démocratie et non-démocratie en Inde', *Esprit*, 107, 1985, p. 21 and *Politics in India*, Boston, Little, Brown, 1970; C. Hurtig, *Les Maharajahs et la politique dans l'Inde contemporaine*, Paris, Presses de la Fondation nationale des sciences politiques, 1988; S. Mardin, *The Genesis of Young Ottoman Thought. A Study in the Modernization of Turkish Political Ideas*, Princeton, Princeton University Press, 1962; B. Lewis, *The Emergence of Modern Turkey*, London, Oxford University Press, 1968 (2nd ed.); A. Kazancigil, E. Özbudun, eds., *Atatürk, Founder of a Modern State*, London, C. Hurst, 1981; O. Roy, *L'Afghanistan. Islam et modernité politique*, Paris, Le Seuil, 1985; L. Binder, *Iran. Political Development in a Changing society*, Berkeley, University of California Press, 1962; J.A. Bill, *The Politics of Iran: Groups, Classes and Modernization*, Columbus, C.E. Merrill, 1972; M. Zonis, *The Political Elite of Iran*, Princeton, Princeton University Press, 1971.

6. C. Coulon, *Le Marabout et le Prince. Islam et Pouvoir au Sénégal*, Paris, Pedone, 1981, pp. 289-290; J. Copans, *Les Marabouts de l'arachide. La confrérie mouride et les paysans du Sénégal*, Paris, Le Sycomore, 1980.

7. E. de Latour, 'Maîtres de la terre, maîtres de la guerre', *Cahiers d'études africaines*, 95, XXIV (3), 1984, pp. 273-297; J. Schmitz, 'L'État geomètre: les leydi des Peul du Fuuta Tooro (Sénégal) et du Maasina (Mali)', *ibid.*, 103, XXVI (3), 1986, pp. 349-394; M. Izard, *Gens du pouvoir, gens de la terre. Les institutions politiques de l'ancien royaume du Yatenga (Bassin de la Volta blanche)*, Cambridge, Cambridge University Press, Paris, Editions de la Maison des sciences de l'Homme, 1985, pp. 558 ff.; H.L. Moore, *Space, Text and Gender. An Anthropological Study of the Marakwet of Kenya*, Cambridge, Cambridge University Press, 1986.

8. C. Tardits, *Le Royaume bamoum*, Paris, A. Colin, 1980.

9. G. Lavau, 'A propos de trois livres sur l'État', *Revue française de science politique*, 30 (2), April 1980, pp. 398-399.

10. E. Weber, *La Fin des terroirs. La modernisation de la France rurale (1870-1914)*, Paris, Fayard, Recherches, 1983; K. Pomian, *L'Ordre du temps*, Paris, Gallimard, 1984.

11. F. de Polignac, *La Naissance de la cité grecque*, Paris, La Découverte, 1984, p. 16.

12. M. Foucault, *History of sexuality*, vol. III: Penguin; Harmondsworth, 1990.

13. M. Weber, *L'Éthique protestante et l'esprit du capitalisme*, Paris, Plon, 1985, p. 11.
14. J.-F. Bayart, 'L'hypothèse totalitaire dans le Tiers monde: le cas de l'Afrique noire', in G. Hermet, ed., *Totalitarismes*, Paris, Economica, 1984, pp. 201-214.
15. G. Hermet, 'L'autoritarisme', in M. Grawitz, J. Leca, eds., *Traité de science politique*, Paris, PUF, 1985, vol. II, p. 271.
16. R. Hodder-Williams, *An Introduction to the Politics of Tropical Africa*, London, George Allen and Unwin, 1984, p. 233.
17. Let us use a partial and one-sided *reductio ad absurdum*. Everybody agrees that the Renaissance was a decisive moment in this process. Yet, who, one hundred years later in the 17th century, would have sworn on the arrival in France of a Weberian state if, by extraordinary foresight, he had conceived of such an model with which to confront the practices of accumulation and 'straddling' of a Mazarin, a Richelieu, a Fouquet or a Colbert? *Cf.* especially, D. Dessert, *Argent, pouvoir et société au Grand Siècle*, Paris, Fayard, 1984.
18. R.F. Stevenson, *Population and Political Systems in Tropical Africa*, New York, Columbia University, 1968.
19. B. Badie, P. Birnbaum, *Sociologie de l'État*, Paris, Grasset, 1979, pp. 135-136.
20. On these gangs of children, see, for example, A. Agbo, H. Ouattara, Y. Kore, 'La Marginalité sociale. La délinquance juvénile: manifestations et perspectives (le cas des gardiens de voitures du Plateau)', Abidjan, Faculté des lettres et sciences humaines, 1985; the novel by M. Sow, *Su suuf seddee. L'échec*, Dakar, ENDA, 1984; D. Poitou, *La délinquance juvénile au Niger. Approche sociologique*, Paris, EHESS, 1975 and, with R. Collignon, 'Délinquance juvénile et marginalité des jeunes en milieu urbain d'Afrique noire. Eléments de bibliographie (1950-1984)', Paris, EHESS, Centre d'études africaines, 1985, and, on the world of urban marginality, the novels of the Kenyan writer Meja Mwangi.
21. G. Dauch, D. Martin, *L'Héritage de Kenyatta. La transition politique au Kenya. 1975-1982*, Paris, L'Harmattan, Aix-en-Provence, Presses Universitaires d'Aix-Marseille, 1985, pp. 203 ff.; J.D. Barkan, 'Comment: further reassessment of conventional wisdom: political knowledge and voting behaviour in rural Kenya', *American Political Science Review*, 70 (2), June 1976, pp. 452-455; D. Berg-Schlosser, 'Modes and meaning of political participation in Kenya', *Comparative Politics*, 14 (4), July 1982, pp. 397-415; D. Bourmaud, 'Elections et autoritarisme: la crise de la régulation politique au Kenya', *Revue française de science politique*, 35 (2), April 1985, pp. 206-235 and 'Les élections au Kenya: tous derrière et Moi devant', *Politique africaine*, 31, Oct. 1988, pp. 85-87.
22. *Cf.*, for example, B. Verhaegen, *Rébellions au Congo.*, vol. II: *Maniema*, Brussels, CRISP, Kinshasa, IRES, 1969, pp. 215 ff., 288 ff., 319 ff.; B. Abemba, 'Pouvoir et conflit dans la collectivité du Maniema. Essai de description et d'interprétation des phénomènes politiques conflictuels locaux à partir de trois cas concrets', Brussels, Université libre, 1974; J. Dunn, A.F. Robertson, *Dependence and Opportunity: Political Change in Ahafo*, Cambridge, Cambridge University Press, 1973, chap. VI; A. Sissoko, 'Aspects sociologiques de l'intégration nationale en Afrique

noire occidentale: espace politico-administratif et intégration à l'État: le cas de la Côte d'Ivoire', Nice, Faculté des lettres et sciences humaines, 1982; J.-P. Chauveau, J. Richard, 'Bodiba en Côte d'Ivoire. Du terroir à l'État: petite production paysanne et salariat agricole dans un village gban', Abidjan, Centre ORSTOM de Petit Bassam, 1977; G. Dupré, *Un ordre et sa destruction*, Paris, ORSTOM, 1982, chap. 14 and *La Naissance d'une société*, Paris, Ed. de l'ORSTOM, 1985, pp. 158 ff.; F. Gaulme, *Le Pays de Cama. Un ancien État côtier du Gabon et ses origines*, Paris, Karthala, Centre de recherches africaines, 1981, pp. 84-85; T.O. Ranger, *Dance and Society in Eastern Africa. 1890-1970. The Beni Ngoma*, London, Heinemann, 1975, p. 112.

23. See, for example, J. Schmitz, 'L'État géomètre: les leydi des Peul du Fouta Toro (Sénégal) et du Maasina (Mali)', *Cahiers d'études africaines* 103, XXVI (3), 1986, pp. 349-394; J. Gallais, *Hommes du Sahel. Espaces-temps et pouvoirs: le delta intérieur du Niger, 1960-1980*, Paris, Flammarion, 1984; J.-P. Warnier, *Echanges, développement et hiérarchies dans le Bamenda pré-colonial (Cameroun)*, Stuttgart, Franz Steiner Verlag, 1985; A. Beauvilain, J.-L. Dongmo et al., *Atlas aérien du Cameroun Campagnes et villes*, Yaoundé, Université de Yaoundé, 1983; J. Boutrais et al., *Le Nord du Cameroun. Des hommes, une région*, Paris, ORSTOM, 1984, Part II; *Atlas linguistique du Cameroun. Inventaire préliminaire*, Paris, ACCT, Yaoundé, CERDOTOLA and DGRST, 1983; P. Laburthe-Tolra, *Les Seigneurs de la forêt. Essai sur le passé historique, l'organisation sociale et les normes éthiques des anciens Beti du Cameroun*, Paris, Publications de la Sorbonne, 1981, pp. 44 ff. and 261 ff.

24. P. Bois, *Paysans de l'ouest. Des structures économiques et sociales aux options politiques depuis l'époque révolutionnaire*, Paris, La Haye, Mouton, 1960.

25. J. Dunn, A.F. Robertson, *Dependence and Opportunity*, pp. 33-37.

26. P. Geschiere, *Village Communities and the State. Changing Relations among the Maka of Southeastern Cameroon since the Colonial Conquest*, London, KPI, 1982, p. 206.

27. J.-F. Bayart, 'L'énonciation du politique', *Revue française de science politique*, 35 (3), Jun. 1985, pp. 947-949.

28. B. Badie, P. Birnbaum, *Sociologie de l'État*; P. Birnbaum, 'La fin de l'État?', *Revue française de science politique*, 35 (6), Dec. 1985, pp. 381-398 and 'L'action de l'État. Différenciation et dédifférenciation' in M. Grawitz, J. Leca, eds., *Traité de science politique*, Paris, PUF, 1985, vol. III, pp. 643-682.

29. E. Shils, *Political Development in the New States*, Gravenhage, Mouton, 1962, pp. 37 ff. On the concept of 'holism', see L. Dumont, *Homo aequalis. Genèse et épanouissement de l'idéologie économique*, Paris, Gallimard, 1977 and, for a critique of this approach, P. Birnbaum, J. Leca, eds., *Sur l'individualisme*, Paris, Presses de la Fondation nationale des sciences politiques, 1986.

30. J.H.B. den Ouden, 'In search of personal mobility: changing interpersonal relations in two Bamileke chiefdoms, Cameroun', *Africa*, 57 (1), 1987, pp. 3-27; G. Le Moal, 'Les activités religieuses des jeunes enfants chez les Bobo', *Journal des africanistes*, 51 (1-2), 1981; J.-P. Dozon. *La Société bété, Côte d'Ivoire*, Paris, Karthala, Ed. de l'ORSTOM, 1985, pp. 229 ff.; G. Kitching, *Class and Economic Change in Kenya. The Making of*

an African Petite-Bourgeoisie, New-Haven, Yale University Press, 1980, pp. 291 and 309–310; P. Geschiere, *Village Communities and the State*, pp. 50 ff. and 238 ff.; L.U. Ejiofor, *Dynamics of Igbo Democracy. A Behavioural Analysis of Igbo Politics in Aguinyi Clan*, Ibadan, University Press Ltd., 1981, chap. 4.

31. See, for example, J. Rabain, *L'Enfant du lignage. Du sevrage à la classe d'âge*, Paris, Payot, 1979; P. Geschiere, *Village Communities and the State*, pp. 321 ff.; G. Balandier, *Sociologie actuelle de l'Afrique noire*, Paris, PUF, 1971 (3rd ed.), pp. 140 ff.; W. MacGaffey, *Modern Kongo Prophets. Religion in a Plural Society*, Bloomington, Indiana University Press, 1983, p. 146.

32. On the limits of individualism, see, M. Foucault, *History of Sexuality*, vol. 3, and, on the conception of the person in Africa, see CNRS, *La Notion de personne en Afrique noire*, Paris, CNRS, 1981 and P. Riesman, 'The person and the life cycle in African social life and thought', *XXVIIIe Congress of the African Studies Association*, New Orleans, 23–26 Nov. 1985.

33. E. de Rosny, *Les Yeux de ma chèvre*, Paris, Plon, 1981.

34. J.D.Y. Peel, *Ijeshas and Nigerians*, pp. 222–226; D.L. Cohen, 'Elections and election studies in Africa' in Y. Barongo, ed., *Political Science in Africa. A Critical Review*, London, Zed Press, 1983, pp. 80 ff.

35. J. Goody, *La Raison graphique. La domestication de la pensée sauvage*, Paris, Ed. de Minuit, 1979, pp. 62 ff.; G. Balandier, *Anthropo-logiques*, Paris, PUF, 1974, pp. 175–176, 183, 212.

36. R.H. Jackson, C.G. Rosberg, *Personal Rule in Black Africa. Prince, Autocrat, Prophet, Tyrant*, Berkeley, University of California Press, 1982.

37. M. Henry, *Marx*, vol. I: *Une philosophie de la réalité*, Paris, Gallimard, 1976, pp. 232 ff.

38. P. Geschiere, *Village Communities and the State*, p. 334.

39. M. Foucault, *History of Sexuality*, vol. 3. See, on the subject of Africa, C. Piault, ed., *Prophétisme et thérapeutique. Albert Atcho et la communauté de Bregbo*, Paris, Hermann, 1975, and M. Augé, *Théorie des pouvoirs et idéologie. Étude de cas en Côte d'Ivoire*, Paris, Hermann, 1975.

40. M. Foucault, 'Le pouvoir, comment s'exerce-t-il?' in H.L. Dreyfus, P. Rabinow, *Michel Foucault, un parcours philosophique*, Paris, Gallimard, 1984, pp. 313–314.

41. *Cameroon Tribune* (Yaoundé), 8–9 May 1988.

42. See particularly T. Ranger, *Peasant Consciousness and Guerilla War in Zimbabwe. A Comparative Study*, London, James Currey, Berkeley, University of California Press, 1985.

43. R. Boudon, *L'Idéologie ou l'origine des idées reçues*, Paris, Fayard, 1986, pp. 109–110.

44. See in particular G. Balandier, *Le Détour. Pouvoir et modernité*, Paris, Fayard, 1985.

45. C. Castoriadis, *L'Institution imaginaire de la société*, Paris, Seuil, 1975, p. 491. See also P. Veyne, *Les Grecs ont-ils cru à leurs mythes?* Paris, Seuil, 1983.

46. R. Needham, ed., *La Parenté en question. Onze contributions à la théorie anthropologique*, Paris, Le Seuil, 1977.

47. M. Leiris, *L'Afrique fantôme*, Paris, Gallimard, 1988, p. 222.

48. See, for example, the autobiography of an mbororo Peul, recorded in fulfulde and translated into French, which uses the action of 'eating' in these different senses (H. Bocquené, *Moi un Mbororo, Ndoumi Oumarou, peul nomade du Cameroun*, Paris, Karthala, 1986, *passim*).
49. C. Geertz, *The Interpretation of Cultures*, New York, Basic Books, 1973, chap. I.
50. R. Boudon, *L'Idéologie*, p. 280.
51. C. Lévi-Strauss, 'Les champignons dans la culture. A propos d'un livre de M.R.G. Wasson', *L'Homme*, X (1), Jan.-March 1970, pp. 5-16; J. Pouillon, 'Une petite différence?' in B. Bettelheim, *Les Blessures symboliques. Essai d'interprétation des rites d'initiation*, Paris, Gallimard, 1977, pp. 235-247.
52. M. Foucault, *History of Sexuality*; K.J. Dover, *Homosexualité grecque*, Grenoble, La Pensée sauvage, 1982; J. Boswell, *Christianity, Social Tolerance and Homosexuality*, Chicago, The University of Chicago Press, 1980; T. Labib Djedidi, *La Poésie amoureuse des Arabes: le cas des 'Udrites*, Alger, SNED, 1974; R. van Gulik, *La Vie sexuelle dans la Chine ancienne*, Paris, Gallimard, 1971.
53. R. Boudon, *L'Idéologie*, pp. 128 and 25.
54. P. Anderson, *L'État absolutiste*, vol. II: *L'Europe de l'Est*, Paris, Maspero, 1978, pp. 21-22; B. Badie, P. Birnbaum, *Sociologie de l'État*, pp. 73-74; S. Finer, 'State building, state boundaries and border control', *Social Sciences Information*, 13 (4-5), pp. 80-82 and 98.
55. C. Castoriadis, *L'Institution imaginaire de la société*, p. 371.
56. *Ibid.*, p. 481.
57. M. de Certeau, *L'Invention du quotidien*, vol. I: *Arts de faire*, Paris, UGE, 1980, pp. 105 ff.
58. E. Goffmann, *Façons de parler*, Paris, Éd. de Minuit, 1987 (especially chap. III).

Index

Abiola, M.K.O., 161
absentee landlords, 67, 68
accumulation and positions of power, 24-5, 70-90, 95, 96-9, 242-3
Acheampong, General, 88
Action Group (Nigeria), 54, 96
Aderemii II, Sir Adesoji, 172
Adingra, Prince Kwame, 172
Adiou-Krou, 52
Afro-Shirazi Union, 143-4
Agni, 195, 198
Agricultural Improvement Funds, 73
agricultural sector, 21, 34, 69
  incomes, 63-4, 67
  inequality and, 63-8
Ahidjo, Ahmadou, 44, 45, 46, 91, 94, 95,150, 173, 174, 185, 194, 220, 227, 245, 247
aid
  food, 79, 80
  public development, 26-7
Aizi, 52, 53
Akan monarchy, 16
Alavi, 7
All People's Congress (Sierra Leone), 126
Alladian, 52
Alliali, M., 213
Almond, G.A., 7
Althusser, Louis, 4
Alves, Nito, 147, 187
Amicale Gilbert Vieillard (AGV), 124
Amin Dada, General, 8, 85, 89, 147
Amin, Samir, 6, 7, 8, 195
Amselle, J.-L., 92, 97-8
Anderson, Perry, 41, 175
Angola, 19, 25, 55, 66, 70, 74, 141, 147, 152, 174, 175, 187, 200, 256

anthropology, 4
Anyang' Nyong'o, P., 161
Apter, David, 7
Arabs in Zanzibar, 142-4
arap Moi, Daniel see Moi, Daniel arap
aristocracy, notion of, 133, 134
Aristotle, 2
army and reciprocal assimilation of elites, 168, 169
Asanti, 16, 17, 20, 109
Asian minority, 146-7, 148
Association confraternance des chef coutumiers, 172-3
Association da la Jeunesse Mauritanienne, 114
Association islamique du Niger, 189
Assogba, Janvier, 227
Assouan, Usher, 183
Atcho, Albert, 190, 191
Auge, Marc, 49, 191
authoritarianism, theory of, 182
autonomy of the State, 7-9
Awolowo, Chief, 54, 75, 96, 161, 172
Azikiwe, Nnamdi, 96, 114, 242

Ba-Kongo, 114
Babangida, General, 133
Badie, Bertrand, 8, 264
Bagaza, Colonel, 122
Bakhtine, Mikhail, 37, 244
Balandier, Georges, 4, 15, 18, 20, 33, 36, 37, 70, 90, 99, 176, 181, 228
Balewa, Abubakar Tafawa, 129, 149
Bamiléké, 48, 112, 170

Bamoum, 16, 48-9
Banda, Hastings, 199
banditry, 240, 241, 264
Banny, Konan, 184
Baoulé, 172, 195
Barbier, J-C., , 133, 134
Barotseland, 123, 170
Barry, Boubacar, 6
Barry, Diawadou, 124
Barry, Ibrahima, 124
Bassa, 111, 134
Bates, Robert, 56
Beavogui, Louis Lansana, 222
Bebey, F., , 114
Bedie, Konan, 158, 185
Beembe, 17, 20, 134, 138
Belgian Congo, 33, 70, 141
Belgium and Zaire, 26
Bello, Ahmadu, 127, 148, 243, 261
Benin, 17, 146, 174, 194, 234
Beresford-Stoocke, Sir George, 125
Berry, S., 69, 103, 107
Beti, 19, 45, 48, 111, 134-5, 137
Biafra, 26, 51
Biney, Pobee, 187
Birnbaum, Pierre, 8, 264
Biya, Paul, 44, 45, 46, 48, 58, 90,
  91, 94, 150, 151, 173, 174, 195,
  227
Bloc africain de Guinée (BAG), 124
Bloc démocratique gabonais, 164
Bloc démocratique sénégalais, 146
Blondy, Alpha, 30
Boganda, Barthélemy, 62
Bois, Paul, 265
Boka, Ernest, 184
Bokassa, Jean-Bedel, 8, 26, 88, 174
Bongo, Omar, 89, 159, 174, 201
Bonkano, Oumaro Amadou, 201
Bonnafe, P., 115
Bornou, 20
Boudon, R., 270
Boulaga, Fabien Eboussi, 10, 188
Bourdieu, Pierre, 58, 248
bourgeoisie, 87-103, 176, 195, 254
Boussac, Robert, 61
Braudel, F., 31, 34, 109, 119, 193
Britain and Kenya, 13
Brou, Therese, 197
Buganda, 17, 170
Buhari, General, 132, 133, 162
Bukulu, Mwa, 17, 138
Bulu, 45
Bunyoro, 17
bureaucracy,
  as means of government, 246

and reciprocal assimilation of
  elites, 163, 168-9
'bureaucratic' bourgeoisie, 90-9, 176
Burkina Faso, 63, 187
Burundi, 49, 51, 121-2, 123, 154,
  170, 175, 189
'business' bourgeoisie, 90-9
business world and reciprocal assimilation of elites, 161
Buyoya, Major, 122

Cabral, Amilcar, 182
Callaghy, T.M., 173
Cameroon, 14, 16, 19, 26, 69, 72,
  111-12, 120, 135-7, 152, 155, 162,
  166-7, 173, 194, 195, 196, 244
  'business' bourgeoisie, 94
  colonialism, 14
  corrupt practices, 73, 77
  education and social stratification,
    75
  ethnicity, 44-9, 55, 57-8
  party system, 165
  police activity, 246
  public expenditure, 64
  reciprocal assimilation of elites,
    150-1, 154, 170-1
  mechanisms of 'straddling', 96-7
  transformism, 185
capital
  accumulation of *see* accumulation
  private transfer of, 101-2
  transnationalisation of, 102
capitalist world system, 12-13
caste identities, 106-7
Castoriadis, C., 271
Central African Republic, 88, 256
centralisation of power, 110, 261-2
*Centre d'études, de recherches et d'éduca-
  tion*, 185
Chad, 25, 50, 55, 152, 153, 209, 256
Chauveau, J.-P., 21
Cheichka, Mohamedou Ould, 201
chiefdoms, 121
chieftaincy and reciprocal assimilation of elites, 163, 169-73
Christianity, 30, 188, 243
Ciroma, Mallam Adamu, 131
Cissé, Mamadou, 201
Cissoko, Baba, 201
city-state, 262
civil service
  accumulation and positions of
    power in, 78, 81-3
  see also bureaucracy

civil society and reciprocal assimilation of elites, 155, 157-63, 176
civil war, 55
'clan' struggles, 211, 213
    see also factional struggles
'clanification', 50
class *see* social stratification
class struggle, 23, 210
Clemenceau, Georges, 10
clothing, Western influences on, 29-30
Club nation et développement, 185
coercion and maintenance of regimes, 221-2, 223, 245-6
Cohen, A., 219
Coleman, James, 18
colonialism, 5, 13, 14, 20-1, 141
    administrative differences, 14
    and ethnic awareness, 51-3
    and social stratification, 70-1, 107, 108
colonisation, 12, 14-15, 20, 21, 33, 154
    cultural influences of, 27-8, 141
    and strategies of extraversion, 24-5
Comité de soutien à l'action du président Abdou Diouf (COSAPAD), 185
Comité militaire du parti (CMP), 152, 169
Committee of Concerned Citizens *see* 'Kaduna mafia'
Communauté économique de l'Afrique de l'Ouest, 75
communications, 19
company rule, 14
'comprador class', 102, 176
concatenation, problematic of, 181
Congo, 55, 139-40, 152, 158, 169, 174, 175, 194, 195
    see also Belgian Congo
Congo-Brazzaville, 8, 64, 115, 138-9
Congo-Léopoldville, 51, 73-4, 114, 209
conservative modernisation, models of, 119, 121-2, 125-6
constitutional revision, 244
Conta, Lansana, 237
Convention People's Party, 73
cooperatives, 186
corruption, 71-2, 73-4, 76-8, 226-7, 235-9, 243, 269
Coulon, Christian, 9, 258
Council for Understanding and Solidarity (CUS), 132
Cowen, M.P., 21, 69, 75, 98

Crédit mutual de Cameroon, 161
Creoles, 144-5, 147, 159
creolisation, 28
criminality
    juvenile, 240-1
    and power, 77-8
Cruise O'Brien, Donal, 97, 168, 212
cultural influences of trade and colonisation, 27-8
cultural pluralism, 243-4
culture of derision, 252-3
Cultures et Elevages du Zaire (CELZA), 88
Cuoco, V., 180
customs duties, 79-80

Dadah, Moktar Ould, 138
Dahomey, 20
Dantata, Alhassan, 149
Daouda, Youssoufa, 44
Daoudou, Sadou, 44
Dauch, G., 93
de Certeau, Michel, 208, 271
decolonisation, 13, 25, 33, 141
Delauney, M., 72
Deleuze, G., 4
delinquency, 239-41, 264
Démocrats sociales de Guinée (DSG), 124-5
Denis, King, 24
Denise, Augustin, 190-1
dependency, 14
    exploitation of, by African governments, 21-32
dependency theory, 5, 6, 7, 8, 11, 12, 195
Der Thiam, Iba, 185
Deschamps, Hubert, 3, 10
desertion, 258
despotism, 2, 8
Deutsch, K., 245
development and inequality, 60-3
developmentalist theory, 6-7, 9, 11
Dia, Mamadou, 211
Diagne, Blaise, 159, 211
Diallo, Alpha-Abdoulaye, 234
Diallo, Yacine, 124
Diouf, Abdou, 162, 185, 186, 211, 225
Diouf, Galandou, 211
Dioulo, Emmanuel, 184
Direction et controle des grands travaux (DCGTX), 79
Doe, Sergeant, 145, 148, 200
Domenach, 102
dominant class

formation of, 126-7, 154-79
see also hegemony
domination
and inequality, 62-3, 110-11
sociology of, 9
Dozon, J.-P., 21
Duala, 111
Dupré, G., 20, 203
Durkheim, Emile, 4

economic austerity programmes, 225-6
economic integration
regional, 101
with western world, 199-200
ECOWAS scandal, 200
education, 29
and reciprocal assimilation of elites, 157, 159
and social stratification, 75
ekong witchcraft, 203
Ekra, René, 158
elections and reciprocal assimilation of elites, 163, 166-8
elites,
reciprocal assimilation of, 150-79
see also dominant class
emigration, 22, 258-9
Engulu, Baanga, 84
entrepreneurs, political, 207-27, 266
Equatorial Guinea, 88, 91, 152
escape, role of, 252-9, 270
Ethiopia, 17
ethnic consciousness, 42-51
and colonial rule, 51-3
and ethnology, 53
ethnicity, 41-59, 110
ethnology and ethnic consciousness, 53
Europeanisation, 28
Evans-Pritchard, E.E., 4, 16
evasion, tactics of, 254
'évolués', 136, 198
Ewuare, Oba, 17
'exit option', 256-9
exploitation, 61-2
of women, 107
externality of the State, 7-8
extraversion
resources of, 74-5
strategies of, 20-32, 196-200
Eyadéma, Gnassingbe, 26, 88, 168

factional struggles, 210-23, 229-30, 232, 233-4, 266, 267
Fadouop, Wabo, 171
family

and factional struggles, 220, 221-2
and reciprocal assimilation of elites, 155, 158
see also kinship relationships
Fanon, F., 4, 33
Faure, Yves, 178
Fédération des associations islamiques du Sénégal, 190
Fédération des etudiants d'Afrique noire en France (FEANF), 159
Finley, Moses, 15
Foccart, Jacques, 25
Folawiyo, Alhaji Yinka, 92
Fonlon, Bernard, 243
food aid, 79, 80
forced labour, 61-2, 72
see also slavery
foreign intervention in internal affairs, 25-6
foreign investment and the business community, 100
Fortes, 16
Foucault, Michel, 267, 271
Fouda, Andra, 95
Foulbé, 47
see also Fulani
founding class, idea of, 192, 195
Fouta Djalon, 170
France
forms of colonial rule, 14
relations with former possessions, 26
Franco-African links, 196-9
Frank, Andre Gunder, 6
freemasonery, 159
FRELIMO (Front for the Liberation of Mozambique), 66
FROLINAT, 153, 209
Fulani/Foulbé, 47, 124, 125, 126, 173, 196
funerals and reciprocal assimilation of elites, 157

Gabon, 25, 89, 159, 164, 195
Garba, Joseph, 130
Gaulme, F., 14
Gelega II, V.S., 171
Geschiere, P., 133, 135, 138
Ghana, 62, 69, 88, 109, 153, 165, 187
factional struggles, 210
freemasonery, 159
graduate emigration, 259
Giddens, Anthony, 27, 179
Gikuyu, Embu, Meru Association (GEMA), 55, 161

Gluckman, M., 4, 23, 210
Goffman, E., 160
Gold Coast, 14
governmentality, 249, 268, 271
Gowon, Yakubu, 129, 130
graduates, emigration of, 259
Gramsci, Antonio, 149, 162, 180-1,
    182, 192, 193, 195, 196
Great Nigerian People's Party, 131,
    132
*Groupe de rencontres et d'échanges pour
    un Sénégal nouveau* (GRESEN),
    185
Guattari, F., 4
Gueye, Lamine, 146, 211
Guinea, 33, 88, 152, 154, 169, 196,
    234, 237-8
    factional struggles, 215, 221-2
    private bourgeoisie, 91
    social revolution, 124-5
Guinea-Bissau, 66, 147
Gulama, Julius, 148, 172

Habré, Hissène, 79, 201
Habyarimana, Major-General, 123
Hady, Thierno, 201
Hegel, G.W.F., 3
hegemonic crisis, 108-9
hegemony
    absence of, 104-9
    pursuit of, 110-15, 119-204, 208
Henry, M., 177
Hirschman, A.O., 22
'historic postcolonial bloc', 192-204,
    208
historicity of African societies, 1-37
Hodder-Williams, Richard, 33
horso, 105
Houphouët-Boigny, Félix, 25, 67,
    76, 79, 89, 91, 101, 158, 172, 173,
    174, 183, 184, 189, 196, 197, 201,
    213, 214, 220, 223, 225, 242
Hutu, 121, 122, 123
Hyden, G., 21, 163, 209, 254

Ibrahim, Waziri, 131
ideology and reciprocal assimilation
    of elites, 163, 173-4
Igbo, 16, 51, 54
Ilesha, 96
Iliffe, John, 96
Imerina, 17
IMF (International Monetary Fund),
    27, 64, 163
imperialism, 3

import income and social polar-
    isation, 87
import tariffs, 79-80
income(s)
    import, 87
    inequality, 64, 67
    rural, 63-4
Indian minority, 146, 147, 148
indirect rule, 52
individualism, 266-7
inequality, 60-86, 153
    and development, 60-3
    and domination, 62-3, 110-11
    of income, 64, 67
informal economy, 68, 69, 99, 237
institutionalisation of the State,
    263-4
intellectuals' absorption into dom-
    inant class, 182-5, 186, 188
intelligence services, 245-6
International Monetary Fund (IMF),
    27, 64, 163
international relations, 26-7
investment, foreign, 100
Islam, 177, 188, 189-90, 249, 257
Islamic brotherhoods, 162, 201
isolation, theme of, 3
Ivory Coast, 25, 69, 82, 83, 89,
    134-5, 137, 152, 154, 155, 162,
    166, 172-3, 189, 190, 194-5, 198,
    223, 247
    agricultural sector, 67-8, 70
    and Biafra, 26
    constitutional revision, 244
    education and social stratification,
        75
    ethnicity, 51, 52-3
    factional struggles, 213-15, 231
    and France, 196-7
    freemasonry, 159
    funerals and fusion of dominant
        elites, 157
    private sector, 91, 98
    private transfer of capital from,
        101-2
    public expenditure, 99
    'transformism' in, 183-5
Izard, M., 15, 254

Jackson, R.H., 244, 267
Japan, 19
Jeffries, Richard, 233
JEUCAFRA, 72
Jeunesse camerounaise française, 114
*Jeunesse du Mouvement national de la
    révolution*, 115

Jeunesse RDA de Côte d'Ivoire
  (JRDACI), 184
Johnson, Rev, 53
Johnston, Sir Harry H., 2, 3
Joinet, B., 218
Joseph, R., 80, 100, 133
Juvento, 114

Ka, Moustapha, 211, 212
'Kaduna mafia', 130, 131, 132, 161
Kagame, Abbé, 53
Kalenjiin, 51, 55
Kamga, Ngrie, 170
Kande, Yoro, 230-1
Kane, Cheikh Hamidou, 31, 120
Kano, Amina, 131
Kano, Aminu, 129, 131, 132
KANU (Kenya African National
  Union), 161, 213
Kariuki, Josiah Mwnagi, 234, 242
Karume, Njenga, 92
Kasfir, Nelson, 52, 249
Kaunda, Kenneth, 174
Kayibanda, Gregoire, 123
Keita, Modibo, 91, 93, 201
Kenya, 69, 88, 141, 152, 153, 154,
  158, 161, 165, 192, 195, 200, 219,
  234
  agricultural sector, 67, 68
  bourgeoisie formation in, 93-4
  'Change the Constitution'
    Campaign, 55, 244
  civil service, 81
  colonialism in, 13, 14
  criminality and power in, 77-8
  ethnicity in, 54-5
  factional struggles, 213
  Local Native Councils, 73
  private sector, 91
  security services, 246
  'straddling' in, 71
Kenya Africa Union, 161
Kenya African Democratic Union,
  165
Kenya African National Union
  (KANU), 161, 213
Kenyatta, Jomo, 54, 88, 155, 158,
  165, 167, 185, 242
Kerekou, Mathieu, 168, 201
Khaldun, Ibn, 219
Khama, Seretse, 121
Kibaki, 55
Kikuyu, 51, 54, 55, 161
Kikuyu Central Association, 73, 155
Kilson, M., 148, 177, 202
Kimbanguism, 190, 257

kingdoms, 121
kinship relationships, 105-6, 107-8
  see also family
Kirdi, 47
Kitching, G., 69, 73, 101, 103, 111
Koffi, Aoussou, 201
Kongo kingdoms, 16
Kothari, R., 221
Kotoko, 47
Kotokoli, 16
Kountché, Moumini, 89
Kountché, Seyni, 25, 89
Kourouma, A., 62, 235
Kukuya, 134, 139
Kuti, Fela Ransome, 245
Kwadwoa, Osei, 16, 17

labour, forced, 61-2, 72
  see also slavery
Lacroix, B., 36
Laidi, 102
land ownership, 82-3
language, 255
  as an instrument of inclusion,
    175-6
  flexibility of, 243
Lanternari, V., 23
Lavau, Georges, 262
Leach, Edmund, 4, 18
Leiris, Michel, 269
Lemarchand, René, 122
Lemke, Ahmed, 143
Lenin, V.I., 3
Lesotho, 121
Liberia, 144, 145, 159
Libock, 57
lineage societies, 16, 17, 133-40, 148,
  155
  see also segmentary societies
Lissouba, 57
Litunga, 123
Local Native Councils
  (LNC)(Kenya), 73
Lonhro, 100
Lonsdale, John, 85, 109
Low, David, 85
Lozi, 123
Lugard, Lord, 52
Lumpa church, 257
Lumumba, P., 42, 255
Luo, 55, 161

Maboti, Litho, 88
McCracken, J., 190
MacGaffey, J., 91

Maigari, Bello Bouba, 44
Maka, 135-7
Malagasy monarchies, 23
Malawi, 79
Mali, 33, 63, 88
  bourgeoisie in, 92-3
  Mandingo Empire, 16
  mechanisms of 'straddling' in,
    97-8
Malinke, 18
Malinowski, B., 231, 232
Mamdani, M., 92
Mandingo Empire, 16
Margai, Milton, 125, 148, 172
Martin, D., 93, 178
Marx, Karl, 61, 104, 155, 161, 227
Marxism-Leninism, 173-4, 243
Matip, Mayi, 171
matrimonial practices and reciprocal
  assimilation of elites, 157-9
Mauritania, 56, 80, 138, 175
Mauss, Marcel, 51
Mba, Léon, 25, 159, 164, 196, 232
M'haye, Djily, 201
Mbida, André-Maria, 43, 45, 134
Mboya, Tom, 55, 223
Medard, Jean-Francois, 178
Mfecane, 18
Michels, R., 165, 166, 182
Micombero, Colonel, 121
military bureaucracy and reciprocal
  assimilation of elites, 168, 169
minorities, non-native, 141-7
Mirambo, 17
missionaries and production of eth-
  nicity, 53
Mitterrand, François, 197
Mobuto, President, 83, 84, 87-8,
  173, 174, 186, 189, 202, 220, 226,
  242, 245
modernisation
  authoritarian, 17
  voluntarist conception of, 61
  see also conservative
    modernisation
modernisation theory, 6-7
modernity and tradition, 9, 11-12,
  172
Mofu, 47
Mohammed, Abdul Rahman, 144
Mohammed, Murtala, 130, 227
Moi, Daniel arap, 51, 54-5, 81, 88,
  94, 165, 167, 188, 189, 216
Momoh, General, 88, 158
Montesquieu, Charles-Louis de
  Secondat, 3

'moralisation' campaigns, 226
Morice, A., 178, 237
Moundang, 15, 50
Mouride brotherhood, 120, 257-8
*Mouvement des étudiants et élèves de
  Côte d'Ivoire* (MEECI), 184
Movement for Justice in Africa
  (MOJA), 145
Mozambique, 62, 66, 74, 147, 152,
  175, 187, 200
  partitioning in, 256
  workers' commissions, 187
MPLA, 25, 66, 147, 187
Mulele, Pierre, 255
Murdock, G.P., 8
Muridiyya brotherhood, 201
music, 28
mutual aid associations, 162
Mvang, 138
Myènè, 29
mystic societies and reciprocal assi-
  milation of elites, 159-60

Nadel, S.F., 4, 49
'national bourgeoisie', 99-103
National Council of Nigeria and the
  Cameroons, 96
National Council of Nigerian Citi-
  zens, 54
National Party of Nigeria (NPN),
  131, 132, 151
National Union for the Total Inde-
  pendence of Angola (UNITA),
  24, 147
Ndongo, Sally, 228-9
Needham, R., 269
Ngouabi, Marien, 168
Nguema, Macias, 88, 222
Nguema, Obiang, 222
Nicolas, Guy, 261
Niger, 25, 26, 63, 89, 152, 164
  private sector, 98
  Songhay-Zarma societies, 105-6
Niger delta, 14, 17-18
Nigeria, 16, 49, 52, 54, 73, 74, 80,
  87, 98, 126-33, 135, 148-9, 151-2,
  154, 162, 163, 189, 200, 220, 251
  corruption, 79
  education and social stratification,
    75
  foreign firms, 100
  public expenditure, 99
  and reciprocal assimilation of
    elites, 151-2, 154
  security services, 246
Nigerian Youth Movement, 114

Njonjo, Charles, 54, 55, 199, 200, 216, 243, 246
Nkoya, 53
Nkrumah, Kwame, 6, 85, 91, 109, 220
Northern Elements Progressive Union (NEPU), 127-8, 131, 251
Northern People's Congress (NPC), 127, 128, 131, 149, 163
Nupe, 49
Nyerere, Julius, 81, 143, 147, 169, 174
Nyoba, Um, 43, 73
Nzabi order, 20
Nzambi-Mpungu sect uprising, 254-5

Obasanjo, Olusegun, 80, 130
Odinga Oginga, 54, 55, 161, 165
Office national de coopération et d'assistance au développement (ONCAD), 78, 97, 99
Okello, John, 144, 200
Oloitipitip, 242
Olympio, Sylvanus, 184
Omani aristocracy, 23-4, 142-3, 144
Operation Maduka, 147
organic crisis, concept of, 108-9, 110
Oyo, 18, 20

Pahouin, 48
Pakistani minority, 147, 148
paradigm of the yoke, 2-10, 195, 208
Pareto, V., 4
Parti congolais du travail, 139
Parti démocratique de Guinée (PDG), 124, 125, 215
Parti démocratique de la Côte d'Ivoire (PDCI), 164, 172, 183-4, 213, 223
Parti démocratique sénégalais (PDS), 251
Parti socialiste (Senegal), 185
Parti soudanais du Progrés (PSP), 92, 93
partitioning, 256
party system
and reciprocal assimilation of elites, 154, 163-6, 182-3
see also single party system
'passive revolution', notion of, 180-92, 207-8
paternalism, 174-5
patrimonialism, 82
patronage, political, 97
'peasantisation', 68
peasantry, 66-8

peasants movements, autonomy of, 186-7
Peel, J.D.Y., 24, 59
People's Redemption Party (PRP), 131, 132, 251
perquisites of public service employment, 75-6, 78
Plantu, 1
police activity, 245-6
political action, 207-59
political entrepreneurs, 207-27, 266
political hierarchy and accumulation of wealth, 87-90
political networks, 217-27
political participation, 249-51
political parties
and reciprocal assimilation of elites, 154, 163-6, 182-3
see also single party system
political patronage, 97
political society and reciprocal assimilation of elites, 162-76
political spaces, formation of, 242-52
political stability and reciprocal assimilation of elites, 153
political trajectory, notion of, 270
politics of the belly, 228-59, 267, 268
Popular Movement for the Liberation of Angola (MPLA), 25, 66, 147, 187
'population removal', 187
Portugal, 13, 18
Postel-Vinay, A., 102
Poulantzas, N., 7
Powell, G. Bingham, 7
power
and accumulation, 24-5, 70-90, 95, 96, 242-3
centralisation of, 110, 261-2
and criminality, 77-8
differentiation of, 265-6
prebendalism, 78
predation, positions of, 76-8
presidential succession, problem of, 223-7
Price, R., 69
prices, producer, 63-4, 67
private sector, 90-9
professional associations, 162
Progressive Alliance of Liberians (PAL), 145
property ownership, 82-3
prostitution, 113, 241
protectionism, 79-80
public expenditure
distribution of, 64-5

in Ivory Coast, 99
in Nigeria, 99
public sector
    corruption in, 76-7, 78-9
    perquisites of employment in,
        75-6
    salaries, 75, 78

Qadiriyya brotherhood, 201

Rabeh, 17
racial segregation in Republic of
    South Africa, 13
radio and the culture of derision,
    252-3
Ramage, R.O., 125
Rancikre, 4
Ranger, T., 210
Raphaello Hassan and Co., 100
Rassemblement démocratique africain
    (RDA), 164, 172, 183
Rawlings, Jerry, 62, 200, 243, 247
rebellion, rural, 55
reciprocal assimilation of elites,
    150-79
regional economic integration, 101
regional factors and structuring of
    the State, 194-5
religion
    and political escape, 256-8
    Western influences on, 30
religious cults, 255
religious elites, 159, 177, 188-92, 201
Rey, P-P., 139-40
Rhodesia, 13, 141
Rimi, Abubakar, 132
Rodinson, Maxime, 1
Rodney, Walter, 6
Rosberg, C., 244, 267
Rostow, W.W., 11
rural incomes, 63-4, 67
rural rebellion, 55
ruralisation, 12
Ruvuma Development Association,
    66, 186
Rwagasore, Prince, 121
Rwanda, 49, 51, 53, 79, 122-3, 142,
    170, 175, 189

Said, Edward, 1
salaries, public sector, 75, 78
Salazar, Antonio de Oliveira, 13
Salek, Ould, 201
Saller, Raphaël, 197
Samba, Martin Paul, 24
Samoff, J., 167
Samori, 17, 18

San Salvador, 220
Sankara, Thomas, 200, 227, 243
Sanusi, Emir, 127
Sardan, J.P. Olivier, 105
Sartre, Jean-Paul, 4, 27
Sassou Nguesso, Denis, 158, 201,
    220, 225
Saul, John, 177, 210
savage, image of, 4
Schatzberg, M.G., 85, 100, 245
secret brotherhoods and reciprocal
    assimilation of elites, 159-60
security services, 245-6
segmentary societies, 16
    see also lineage societies
Sékou Touré, Ahmed, 88, 91, 98,
    124, 125, 169, 183, 221, 233
Sékou Touré, Andree, 222
Selek, Nkal, 138
Senegal, 62, 73, 105, 119-20, 146,
    152, 154, 159, 162, 167, 186, 189,
    194, 219, 251
    agricultural incomes, 63-4
    constitutional revision, 244
    factional struggles, 211-12
    political patronage, 97
    public sector corruption, 78
    structural adjustment plan, 64
    transformism in, 185
Senegambia, 14
Senghor, Leopold, 63, 146, 167,
    185, 211, 257
seniority, antagonism of, 113, 114
Shagari, Alhaji, 131
Shaka, 17
Shirazi, 143
Sierra Leone, 88, 125-6, 144-5, 158,
    159, 163, 227
Sierra Leone Organisation Society,
    125
Sierra Leone People's Party (SLPP),
    125-6, 145, 148, 163
sinecures, 79
single party system, 247, 251-2
Sklar, Richard, 57, 151, 163, 165,
    171, 181
slavery, 17, 18-19, 23, 105-6
Smith, Ian, 141
smuggling industry, 101
Sobhusa II, 121
social identity, 255
social mobility, 69
social revolution, models of, 119,
    122-5
social space, reconstruction of, 107,
    110

social stratification, 62, 63, 68-9,
  104-5
  and colonialism, 70-1, 107, 108
  and education, 75
  and ethnicity, 56-7, 58
  see also bourgeoisie; dominant
    class; peasantry; working
    class
Sokoine, Edward, 147
Sokoto, 17, 20
Somalia, 138, 175
Songhay-Zarma, 105-6
Soppo Priso, Paul, 92, 94
South Africa, Republic of, 13, 14,
  141
Sowemino, S., 161
Soyinka, Wole, 113, 188, 246
Spark, 165
Spencer, J., 155
Stevens, Siaka, 88
'straddling', mechanisms of, 69-70,
  71, 81-2, 96-8, 99, 176, 177, 216,
  269
structural adjustment, politics of,
  225-6
structuration theory, 179
student associations, 159
Swahili, 50
Swainson, N., 100
Syndicat agricole africain, 73, 155

Tanganyika, 33, 62, 146-7
Tanganyika African National Union
  (TANU), 66, 146, 165
Tansi, Sony Labou, 188
Tanzania, 70, 81, 144, 147, 152, 154,
  169, 175, 186, 226, 239
technology, 29
  political use of, 245
Tempelsman, Maurice, 88
territorial unification, 245
terroirs, historicity of, 265
tertiary sector, 69
Thiam family, 158
Thomas, Bode, 172
Thompson, E.P., 208
Tijaniyya brotherhood, 149, 201
Tiv, 135
Tobie, Kuoh, 95
Togo, 16, 88, 146, 189, 194
Tooroodo oligarchy, 119-20
Toulabor, C.M., 253
trade, external, 18-19, 23-4
trade unions, 187
tradition and modernity, 9, 11-12,
  172

'transformism', 182-92, 209
Traoré, Moussa, 88, 93, 201
tribalism, 41, 42-3, 55, 216, 265
True Whig Party, 145, 148
Tshombe, Moise, 226
Tubman, William, 148 145, 186
Tukur, Mahmud, 133
Tutsi, 121, 122

Udoji, J., 161
Uganda, 52, 56, 79, 147, 152, 256
Uganda Muslim Supreme Council,
  190
Union des Populations du Cameroun
  (UPC), 43, 55, 73, 173, 251
Union Musulmane du Togo, 189-90
*Union nationale des étudiants de Côte
  d'Ivoire* (UNECI), 183, 184
*Union pour la démocratie et progrès
  social* (UDPS), 186, 251
*Union pour le développement écono-
  mique de la Côte d'Ivoire* (UDECI),
  183
*Union pour le progrès islamique du
  Sénégal*, 190
Union progressiste guinéene, 125
Union progressiste Sénégalaise (UPS),
  185
*Union soudanaise du Rassemblement
  démocratique africain* (USRDA), 92,
  93
UNITA, 25, 147
United Africa Company, 100
United States, 19
Unity Party of Nigeria, 131, 132,
  161
urbanisation, 264

Vallier, Captain, 3
Vansina, Jan, 4, 220
Veyne,P., 31
'villagisation' policy, 187
Vovelle, M., 202

Wade, Abdoulaye, 211
Wallerstein, Immanuel, 8, 57
wealth, acquisition of *see*
  accumulation
Weber, Max, 4, 31, 103, 178, 216,
  263, 269
Wilks, Ivor, 91
witchcraft, 203, 248-9
Wolof, 105, 120, 194
women
  exploitation of, 107
  social position of, 112, 113, 115

workers' movements, 187
working class, 68
World Bank, 27, 64, 163

Yacé, M., 223
Yacé, Philippe, 81, 158, 184
Yar'Adua, Shehu, 130
Yauri Day Book, 24
Yaya, Moussa, 95
Yoruba, 18, 24, 33, 52, 53, 54, 68-9, 171-2
Youlou, Abbe Fulbert, 184
Young African Union, 114
'youth', social position of, 112-14
youth protest movements, 114-15
Youth Social Circle of Sokoto, 114

Zaïre, 26, 69, 98, 152, 154, 162, 166, 175, 177, 186, 251

Air Force corruption, 235-6
intelligence services, 245-6
Kimbanguism, 190, 257
power and accumulation in, 78, 83-5, 87-8, 99
roads and transport, 65
'Zaïrianisation', 84, 85, 88, 99
Zambia, 123, 157, 192, 257
Zanzibar, 20, 23-4, 51, 56
Zanzibar African Youth Movement, 114
Zanzibar Nationalist Party (ZNP), 144
Zanzibar and Pemba People's Party (ZPPP), 144
Zempleni, A., 191
Zikist movement, 114
Zimbabwe, 33, 63, 70, 141, 200
Zolberg, Aristide, 9, 53, 223, 247